Ancient Greece

Ancient Greece

A POLITICAL, SOCIAL, AND CULTURAL HISTORY

THIRD EDITION

Sarah B. Pomeroy
*Hunter College and the City University of
New York Graduate Center, Emerita*

Stanley M. Burstein
California State University, Los Angeles, Emeritus

Walter Donlan[†]
University of California, Irvine, Emeritus

Jennifer Tolbert Roberts
City College and the City University of New York Graduate Center

David W. Tandy
University of Tennessee, Knoxville

New York   Oxford
OXFORD UNIVERISTY PRESS

Oxford University Press, Inc., publishes works that further Oxford University's
objective of excellence in research, scholarship, and education.

Oxford   New York
Auckland   Cape Town   Dar es Salaam   Hong Kong   Karachi
Kuala Lumpur   Madrid   Melbourne   Mexico City   Nairobi
New Delhi   Shanghai   Taipei   Toronto

With offices in
Argentina   Austria   Brazil   Chile   Czech Republic   France   Greece
Guatemala   Hungary   Italy   Japan   Poland   Portugal   Singapore
South Korea   Switzerland   Thailand   Turkey   Ukraine   Vietnam

For titles covered by Section 112 of the U.S. Higher Education Opportunity
Act, please visit www.oup.com/us/he for the latest information about
pricing and alternate formats.

Published by Oxford University Press, Inc.
198 Madison Avenue, New York, NY 10016
www.oup.com

Library of Congress Cataloging-in-Publication Data
Pomeroy, Sarah B.
Ancient Greece : a political, social, and cultural
history / Sarah B. Pomeroy . . . [et al.].—3rd ed.
    p. cm.
Includes bibliographical references and index.
ISBN 978-0-19-984604-7
1. Greece—Civilization—To 146 B.C.—Textbooks.
I. Pomeroy, Sarah B. II. Title.
DF77.A595 2012
938—dc23 2011031035

Printing number: 9 8 7 6 5 4 3 2 1

Printed in the United States of America
on acid-free paper

For our students

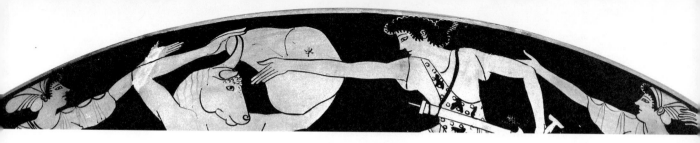

CONTENTS

MAP AND BATTLE PLANS

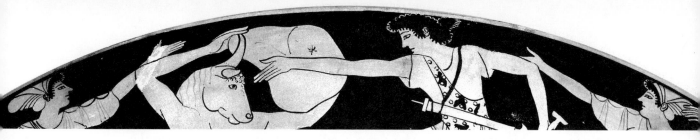

PREFACE

This book is designed to share with readers a rich and complex vision of ancient Greece that has been forged by the collaboration of several scholars with different backgrounds and varying interests. We undertook the writing of the first edition almost two decades ago because of our frustration in the search for a single volume that provided readers with a comprehensive history of Greek civilization from its beginnings in the second millennium BC through the Hellenistic era. At that time it had been more than a quarter of a century since the last attempt to tell the story of Greece in depth from the Bronze Age though the Hellenistic era. We hoped that what we wrote would be useful and give pleasure both to the general reader and to the student who is asked to read it in college. Our intent was to write a book that was long enough to provide depth and detail, and short enough to enable the instructor to assign primary sources that would expand the student's understanding of a world that is both familiar and alien. It would also incorporate the fruits of the most recent scholarship, while providing a balance between political, military, social, cultural, and economic history. The many kind words and reviews our book received indicated that we achieved our goals.

Scholarship does not stand still, however. Even since we began work on the third edition of *Ancient Greece*, exciting discoveries have been made in all areas of Greek history. Incorporating the results of this scholarship in this new edition has been both challenging and pleasurable. In the process we have reviewed every paragraph, revised and expanded the suggested readings, and improved the illustration program. We have paid particular attention to the finds of underwater archaeologists. As before, we have profited enormously from the work of innumerable scholars whose names never appear in our book. We are also greatly indebted to Charles Cavaliere of the Oxford University Press and his excellent staff for their support and help, and to the following readers who took time out from busy schedules to examine our work and make numerous useful criticisms and suggestions: Greg Anderson, The Ohio State University; Charles W. Hedrick, University of California, Santa Cruz; Carol G. Thomas, University of Washington; Teresa Leslie, University of West Georgia; R. Scott Moore, Indiana University of Pennsylvania; Jonathan Scott Perry, University of South Florida Sarasota-Manatee; Kathryn Simonsen, Memorial University of Newfoundland.

We must also thank Robert Lejeune, who offered computer assistance when it was most needed and endured our assorted technoflubs with remarkable patience, and Miriam Burstein, who again handled with grace and firmness the challenging task of reminding us that we were writing for ordinary mortals, not omniscient deities. Finally, we acknowledge with thanks the publishers who have generously granted permission to quote from translations published by them. Walter Blanco was kind enough to give us access to passages that are slated to appear in the second edition of the Norton Critical Edition of Herodotus. All other translations from Herodotus and Thucydides in this book also are by him. Similarly, all translations from Xenophon's *Hellenica* are from John Marincola's version in the *Landmark Xenophon's Hellenika*. All unattributed translations in the text are by the authors..

The authors would also like to call the reader's attention to three features of our book: the timeline at the beginning, which provides a brief but comprehensive overview of Greek history; the extensive glossary at the end, which provides capsule descriptions of many of the terms that occur in the book; and the color plates, which bring our readers closer to the physical reality of the remarkable objects and buildings the Greek created. Abbreviations for standard works follow those used in *The Oxford Classical Dictionary*, 3rd ed. (Oxford: Oxford University Press).

We hope this new edition will, like its predecessor, help teachers, students, and general readers explore and enjoy the fascinating history of ancient Greece. The late Walter Donlan's contributions to the success of the previous two editions were great and will be sorely missed. Fortunately, another distinguished historian of early Greece, David Tandy, has joined our team, and he has thoroughly revised the sections of the book dealing with prehistoric and Archaic Greece in the light of the best contemporary scholarship.

NEW TO THE THIRD EDITION

- Coverage of early Greece has been extensively revised by new co-author David Tandy.
- Extensively revised art program now includes two 8-page color inserts.
- Updated to reflect the most current scholarship.

Jennifer Roberts, New York City   *Sarah Pomeroy, New York City*
Stanley Burstein, Los Alamitos, California   *David W. Tandy, Knoxville, Tennessee*

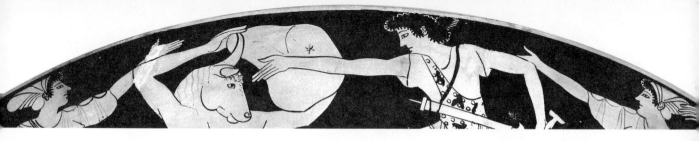

TRANSLATIONS USED
BY PERMISSION

Barker, Ernest. 1973. *The Politics of Aristotle*. Oxford: Oxford University Press.

Benardete, Seth. 1959. *The Persians*, from *The Complete Greek Tragedies*, David Grene and Richmond Lattimore, eds. Chicago: University of Chicago Press.

Blanco, Walter. 1992. *The Histories*, from *Herodotus: The Histories*, Walter Blanco and Jennifer Roberts, eds., New York: W. W. Norton.

———. 1998. *The Peloponnesian War*, from *Thucydides: The Peloponnesian War*, Walter Blanco and Jennifer Tolbert Roberts, eds. New York: W. W. Norton.

Brunt, P. A. 1976. *Arrian: Anabasis of Alexander*. Vol. I. Loeb Classical Library. Cambridge, MA and London: Harvard University Press.

Burstein, Stanley M. 1985. *The Hellenistic Age from the Battle of Ipsos to the Death of Kleopatra VII*. Cambridge: Cambridge University Press.

Chinnock, E. J. 1893. *Arrian's Anabasis of Alexander and Indica*. London and New York: G. Bell & Sons.

Dickinson, Patric. 1970. *Aristophanes, Plays*. Vol. 1. Oxford: Oxford University Press.

Gagarin, Michael, and Paul Woodruff, eds. 1995. "Encomium of Helen," in *Early Greek Political Thought from Homer to the Sophists*. Cambridge: Cambridge University Press.

Green, Peter. 1997. *The Argonautika: The Story of Jason and the Quest for the Golden Fleece*. Berkeley and Los Angeles, University of California Press.

Grene, David, and Richmond Lattimore, eds. 1959. *The Complete Greek Tragedies*. Chicago: University of Chicago Press.

Hanson, Ann. 1975. "Hippocrates: *Diseases of Women 1*," *Signs* 1: 567–584.

Heisserer, A. J. 1980. In *Alexander the Great and the Greeks: The Epigraphic Evidence*. Norman: University of Oklahoma Press.

Jameson, M. 1970. "A Decree of Themistocles from Troizen," *Hesperia* 29 (1960): 200–201, modified by P. Green. 1970. *Xerxes at Salamis*. New York and London: Praeger.

Lattimore, Richmond. 1959. *Agamemnon*, from *The Complete Tragedies*, David Grene and Richmond Lattimore, eds. Chicago: University of Chicago Press.

Lombardo, Stanley. 1997. *Homer, Iliad*. Indianapolis, IN: Hackett Publishing Company.

Lombardo, Stanley. 2000. *Homer, Odyssey*. Indianapolis, IN: Hackett Publishing Company.

Marchant, E. C. 1925. *Xenophon*. Vol. 7, *Scripta Minora*. Loeb Classical Library. Cambridge, MA.

Marincola, John. 2009. *The Hellenika*, from *The Landmark Xenophon's Hellenika*, Robert B. Strassler, ed. New York: Random House.

Nisetich, Frank. 2005. *The New Posidippus: A Hellenistic Poetry Book*, Kathryn Gutzwiller, ed. Oxford: Oxford University Press.

Papillon, Terry L. 2004. *Isocrates II. The Oratory of Classical Greece*. Austin, Texas: University of Texas Press.

Parker, Douglass. 1969. *Lysistrata*, from *Aristophanes: Four Comedies*, William Arrowsmith, ed. Ann Arbor: University of Michigan Press.

Pomeroy, Sarah B. 1994. *Xenophon: Oeconomicus, A Social and Historical Commentary*. Oxford: Clarendon Press.

Pomeroy, Sarah B. 2002. *Spartan Women*. New York: Oxford University Press.

Race, William H. 1997. *Pindar. Olympian Odes, Pythian Odes*. Cambridge, MA: Harvard University Press, Loeb Classical Library.

Saunders, A. N. W. 1975. *Demosthenes and Aeschines*. Harmondsworth, UK: Penguin.

Scott-Kilvert, Ian. 1960. *The Rise and Fall of Athens: Nine Greek Lives by Plutarch*. Harmondsworth, England: Penguin.

Sherman, C. L. 1954. *Diodorus of Sicily, Library of History*. Vol. VI. Loeb Classical Library. Cambridge, MA: Harvard University Press.

Tandy, David W., and Walter C. Neale, trs. and eds. 1996. *Hesiod's* Works and Days*: A Translation and Commentary for the Social Sciences* (© by the Regents of the University of California). Berkeley and Los Angeles: University of California Press.

Todd, O. J. 1968. *Xenophon: Memorabilia and Oeconomicus*. Cambridge, MA: Harvard University Press.

Warner, Rex. 1959. *Medea*, from *The Complete Greek Tragedies*, David Grene and Richmond Lattimore, eds. Chicago: University of Chicago Press.

Waterfield, Robin. 1994. *Plato. Symposium*. Oxford: Oxford University Press.

Waterfield, Robin. 1998. *Plutarch. Greek Lives*. Oxford: Oxford University Press.

Welles, C. B. 1934. *Royal Correspondence in the Hellenistic Period*. London: Yale University Press.

West, M. I. 1991. *Greek Lyric Poetry*. Oxford: Oxford University Press.

———. 2005. "A New Sappho Poem." *Times Literary Supplement*, June 26.

Wyckoff, Elizabeth. 1960. *Antigone*, from *The Complete Greek Tragedies*, David Grene and Richmond Lattimore, eds. Chicago: University of Chicago Press.

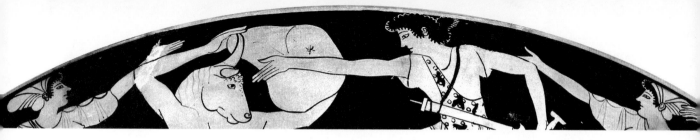

TIMELINE

PERIOD	MILITARY EVENTS	POLITICAL & SOCIAL EVENTS	CULTURAL DEVELOPMENT
7000–3000 Neolithic		Permanent farming villages	Domestication of plants and animals; pottery
3000–2100 Early Bronze Age		Social ranking emerges; villages and districts ruled by hereditary chiefs	2500 Widespread use of bronze and other metals in Aegean
2100–1600 Middle Bronze Age	2250–2100 Lerna and other sites destroyed	2250–2100 Incursions of Indo-European-speakers into Greece	2250–2100 Indo-European gods introduced into Greece 1900 First palaces in Crete 1900 Mainland contacts with Crete and the Near East 1800 Cretans develop Linear A writing
1600–1200 Late Bronze Age		1600 Mycenae and other sites become power centers; small kingdoms emerge	1600 Shaft graves

continued

Period	Military Events	Political & Social Events	Cultural Development
	1490 Mycenaeans take over Crete		1500 Tholos tombs
			1450 Linear B writing
	1375 Knossos destroyed	1400–1200 Height of Mycenaean power and prosperity	1400 New palaces in Greece
	1250–1225 "The Trojan War"		
1200–900 Early Dark Age	1200 Invaders loot and burn the palace centers	1200–1050 Palace system collapses	1200 Cultural decline
		1050 Small chiefdoms established; migrations of mainland Greeks to Ionia	1050 Iron technology
		1000 Dorian Greeks settle in the mainland and the islands	1000 Monumental building at Lefkandi
900–750/00 Late Dark Age		900 Population begins to increase; new settlements established; trade and manufacture expand	
		800 Rapid population growth	800 Greeks develop an alphabet; earliest temples built
			776 Traditional date of first Olympian games
750/700–480 Archaic Period	730–700 First Messenian War; Lelantine War	750–700 City-states emerge	750–720 *Iliad* and *Odyssey* composed
		750 Overseas colonization to the West begins	720 "Orientalizing period" in art begins
	700–650 Evolution of hoplite armor and tactics		700 Hesiod; period of lyric poetry begins
	669 Battle of Hysiae	670–500 Tyrants rule in many city-states	

continued

Period	Military Events	Political & Social Events	Cultural Development
	650 Second Messenian War	650 Colonization of Black Sea area begins; earliest known stone inscription of a law; "Lycurgan Reforms" at Sparta; the "Great Rhetra" (?)	650 Temples built of stone and marble; Corinthian black-figure technique
		632 Cylon fails in attempt at tyranny in Athens	Poetry of Sappho, Alcaeus
		620 Law code of Draco in Athens	
		600 Lydians begin to mint coins	600 Beginnings of science and philosophy (the "Presocratics")
			582–573 Pythian, Isthmian, Nemean games inaugurated
		560–510 Peisistratus and his sons tyrants of Athens	Peisistratus expands religious festivals at Athens
		550 Sparta dominant in the Peloponnesus	
			530 Athenian red-figure technique
		507–501 Cleisthenes institutes political reforms in Athens	
	499 Ionian Greeks rebel from Persian empire	.	Pindar begins to write
	494 Defeat of Argos by Peloponnesian League in Battle of Sepea		Fifth-century rationalists and scientists; Hippocrates; advances in medicine; increase in literacy
	490 Battle of Marathon	489 Trial of Miltiades	
		486 Decision to choose Athenian archons by lot	
		482 Ostracism of Aristides	

continued

Period	Military Events	Political & Social Events	Cultural Development
	480–479 Battles of Thermopylae, Artemisium, Salamis, Plataea, Mycale; Xerxes driven from Greece		
480–323 Classical Period			Classical style in sculpture
		477 Foundation of Delian League	
			470–456 Construction of temple of Zeus at Olympia
		Growth of democracy in Athens; Themistocles driven out of Athens, flees to Persia	
	464 Helot rebellion in Sparta	460s Prominence of Cimon	
		461 Reforms of Ephialtes at Athens; Pericles rises to prominence	
	460–445 "First" Peloponnesian War		
			458 Aeschylus' *Oresteia*
		454 Athenians move treasury from Delos to Athens	
		Flourishing of Greek trade and manufacture	451 Pericles carries law limiting citizenship at Athens
			Herodotus at work on his *Histories*
			447–432 Construction of Parthenon at Athens
			Sophists active in Athens
	431–404 Peloponnesian War		Thucydides begins his *History*

continued

Period	Military Events	Political & Social Events	Cultural Development
		429 Death of Pericles	428 Sophocles' *Oedipus Tyrannus*
			425 Aristophanes' *Acharnians*
		423 Thucydides exiled from Athens	
		422 Deaths of Brasidas, Cleon	
		421 Peace of Nicias	
	415–413 Sicilian campaign		415 Euripides' *Trojan Women*
		411–410 Oligarchic coup in Athens; establishment of Council of 400; regime of the 5000	411 Aristophanes' *Lysistrata*
		407 Ascendance of Dionysus I at Syracuse	
	403–377 Sparta the most powerful state in Greece	404–403 Regime of the Thirty Tyrants in Athens	
		399 Trial and execution of Socrates	399–347 Dialogues of Plato; foundation of the Academy
	395–387 Corinthian War	Fourth century: Rise of class of rhetores at Athens; economic inequalities and social stasis throughout Greece	399–360 Writings of Xenophon
	377 Establishment of Second Athenian Naval Confederacy		
	377–371 Athens the most powerful state in Greece		375–330 Work of Praxiteles
	371 Theban victory over Spartans at Leuctra		
	371–362 Thebes the most powerful state in Greece		368–348 Aristotle studies at Academy

continued

Period	Military Events	Political & Social Events	Cultural Development
		Serious population decline in Sparta; impoverished class of "Inferiors" at Sparta; increasing amount of property in hands of Spartan women	
	359 Defeat of Perdiccas III		359 Accession of Philip II
	357 Siege of Amphipolis	357 Marriage of Philip II to Olympias	
		357–355 Social War	
		356 Birth of Alexander the Great; outbreak of Third Sacred War	356 Philip II's Olympic victory
			355 Demosthenes' first speech
	352 Battle of Crocus Field		
	348 Capture of Olynthus		
			347 Death of Plato
		346 End of Third SacredWar; Peace of Philocrates	346 Isocrates' *Philippus*
	340 Athens and Macedon at war		
	338 Battle of Chaeronea	338 Assassination of Artaxerxes III; foundation of Corinthian League; marriage of Philip II and Cleopatra	338 Death of Isocrates
		338–325 Administration of Lycurgus at Athens	
	336 Invasion of Asia Minor by Philip II	336 Accession of Darius III; assassination of Philip II; accession of Alexander III	
	335 Revolt of Thebes	335 Destruction of Thebes	335 Aristotle returns to Athens; founding of Lyceum

continued

Period	Military Events	Political & Social Events	Cultural Development
	334 Battle of Granicus		
	333 Battle of Issus	333 Alexander at Gordium	
	331 Battle of Gaugamela	331 Foundation of Alexandria	331 Visit to Siwah by Alexander
	330–327 War in Bactria and Sogdiana	330 Destruction of Persepolis; death of Philotas	
		329 Assassination of Darius III	
		328 Murder of Cleitus	
	327–325 Alexander's invasion of India	327 Marriage of Alexander and Roxane	
	326 Battle of the Hydaspes		
		324 Exiles decree	
323–30 Hellenistic Period		323 Death of Alexander III; accession of Philip III and Alexander IV	
	323–322 Lamian War	322 Dissolution of the Corinthian League	322 Deaths of Aristotle and Demosthenes
	321 Invasion of Egypt	321 Death of Perdiccas; Antipater becomes regent	321–292 Career of Menander
	318–316 Revolt against Polyperchon		
		317 Demetrius of Phaleron becomes tyrant of Athens	
	315–311 Four-year war against Antigonus	315 Freedom of Greeks proclaimed by Antigonus the One-Eyed	
		311 Peace between Antigonus and his rivals	

continued

PERIOD	MILITARY EVENTS	POLITICAL & SOCIAL EVENTS	CULTURAL DEVELOPMENT
	307 Demetrius [son of Antigonus] invades Greece	307 End of tyranny of Demetrius of Phalerum at Athens	307–283 Foundation of the Museum and Library
	306 Battle of Salamis	306 Antigonus and Demetrius acclaimed kings	306 Epicurus founds Garden
	305–304 Siege of Rhodes		305 Ptolemy, Seleucus, Lysimachus, and Cassander declare themselves kings
	301 Battle of Ipsus	301 Death of Antigonus; division of his empire	301 Zeno founds Stoa
			300–246 Construction of the Pharos
		283 Death of Ptolemy I; accession of Ptolemy II	283–222 Work of Theocritus, Callimachus, Apollonius of Rhodes
	281 Battle of Corupedium		281 Deaths of Lysimachus and Seleucus
	279 Invasion of Gauls		246 Eratosthenes becomes librarian at Alexandria
		237–222 Reign of Cleomenes III at Sparta	
	222 Battle of Sellasia	222 Exile of Cleomenes III; end of his reforms at Sparta	
	200–197 Second Macedonian War		
		196 Flamininus proclaims freedom of the Greeks at Isthmian games	
	171–168 Third Macedonian War		

continued

Period	Military Events	Political & Social Events	Cultural Development
		167 End of the Macedonian monarchy	167 Polybius comes to Rome
	146 Sack of Corinth	146 Rome annexes Macedon and Greece	
	31 Battle of Actium	30 Suicides of Mark Antony and Cleopatra VII; Rome annexes Egypt	

Ancient Greece

Introduction

One of the greatest of the Greek cultural heroes was Odysseus, a man who "saw the towns of many men and learned their minds, and suffered in his heart many griefs upon the sea..." (*Odyssey* 1.3–4). Like their legendary hero, the Greeks were irresistibly drawn to distant shores. From early in their history and continually throughout antiquity they ventured over the seas to foreign lands seeking their fortunes as traders, colonizers, and mercenary soldiers. Their limited natural resources forced the Greeks to look outward, and they were fortunate in being within easy reach of the Mediterranean shores of Asia, Africa, and Europe. By the fifth century BC, they had planted colonies from Spain to the west coast of Asia and from North Africa to the Black Sea. The philosopher Plato (c. 429–347 BC) likened the hundreds of Greek cities and towns that ringed the coasts of the Mediterranean and Black seas to "frogs around a pond" (*Phaedo* 109b). Those far-flung Greeks left a priceless legacy of achievements in art, literature, politics, philosophy, mathematics, science, and war. Their story is a long and fascinating one.

A BIRD'S-EYE VIEW OF GREEK HISTORY

Greek culture was forged in the crucible of the Bronze Age civilizations that cropped up in worlds as diverse as unified Egypt and fragmented Mesopotamia. Absorbing key skills from these highly developed neighbors—metallurgy, for example, and writing—the Greeks built a distinctive culture marked by astonishing creativity, versatility, and resilience. In the end, this world dissolved, as Greek civilization, having reached from France and Italy in the west to Pakistan in the east, merged with a variety of other cultures—Macedonian, Syrian, Iranian, Egyptian, Roman, and finally Byzantine. Greek became the common language throughout the Near East and was the language in which the texts collected in what we call the New Testament were written. Through its incorporation into the Roman Empire and the fusion of Greek and Italian elements in mythology and architecture, a hybrid culture known as "Classical" came to hold an important place in the traditions of Europe and the Americas.

Between the decline of the Bronze Age and the diffusion of Greek culture throughout the Mediterranean world, Greek civilization attained an extraordinary richness marked by diversity within unity. The world of the Homeric epics, the *Iliad* and the *Odyssey*, was radically different from that of the fifth and fourth centuries. Yet the epics remained the texts most commonly taught in schools, and Alexander was rumored to have carried a copy of Homer's work as he traveled,

Figure I.1 Odysseus and the Sirens (Attic jug c. mid-fifth century BC) illustrating Homer's story (*Odyssey* 12.158–200) of how Odysseus satisfied his desire to hear the Sirens' song while tied to his ship's mast as it sailed past the Sirens' island. Odysseus' ship is depicted as a contemporary Athenian warship with ram and protective eye at the bow. London, British Museum.

lamenting that he had no great poet to immortalize him as Homer had immortalized Achilles. Though religion inspired much of architecture, literature, and even athletic competitions, which were held to honor the gods, Greek government and society often seemed to function in an entirely secular manner. Marriage, for example, was a purely civil affair, and divorce was not believed to distress the gods at all. The gods were nowhere and everywhere. Ideals of equality were preached by men who usually owned slaves and believed in the inferiority of women.

Stolid, warlike Sparta and cultivated, intellectual Athens considered themselves polar opposites. The funeral oration for the war dead Thucydides put in the mouth of the Athenian statesman Pericles encapsulated many of the differences seen from the Athenian point of view. Yet people in both cities lived by agriculture, worshipped Zeus and the other Olympian gods, subjected women to men, believed firmly in slavery (provided they were not slaves themselves!), sacrificed animals, considered war a constant in human life, preached an ethic of equity among male citizens, cherished athletics and delighted in the Olympics and other competitions, enjoyed praising the rule of law, considered Greeks superior to non-Greeks, and accepted as axiomatic the primacy of the state over the individual.

The history of the ancient Greeks is one of the most improbable success stories in all of world history. A small people inhabiting a poor country on the periphery of the civilizations of Egypt and the Near East, the Greeks created one of the world's most remarkable cultures. In almost every area of the arts and sciences they made fundamental contributions, and their legacy is still alive in western and Islamic civilizations. Throughout the Renaissance and the eighteenth century, Sparta was cherished as the model of a mixed and therefore stable constitution. In the nineteenth and twentieth centuries, more attention was focused on Athens, where it is possible to witness the gradual erosion of privilege based on wealth and lineage and the growth of democratic machinery—law codes and courts, procedures for selecting officials and holding them accountable, and public debates and votes on matters of domestic and foreign policy. Athens and Sparta fought ruinous wars with each other, and the propensity of the Greek states for fighting one another shaped much of their history.

The devastating Greek world war of 431–404 known as the Peloponnesian War (because of Sparta's location on the peninsula of the Peloponnesus) placed a damper on the extraordinary burst of creativity that had marked the fifth century—the tragedies of Aeschylus, Sophocles, and Euripides; the comedies of Aristophanes; the building of the Parthenon at Athens and the temple of Zeus at Olympia. Throughout this painful era and the decades that followed, thinkers continued to explore the questions that had intrigued Greek intellectuals at least as far back as the sixth century—the origins of the universe and the mechanisms by which it functioned; the relation between *physis* (nature) and *nomos* (custom, or law); how and what mortals can know about the gods; what these gods might want from people; whether indeed true knowledge was possible for humans; what the best rules might be by which people could live together in society; what the best form of education was—who was most qualified to direct it, and how many could profit from it; under what circumstances the rule of a single wise man might after all be best. New questions were also posed—whether involvement in politics ought really to be the focus of a man's life; whether the individual might find identity separate from the state; whether war was worth the sacrifices it entailed; and even whether slavery and the disfranchisement of women were necessary (though those radical speculations did not result in social change). Inevitably, the conquests of Alexander, the mass marriages he celebrated between Macedonian soldiers and women from Persia and Media in 324 BC, and the hybrid culture that was forged throughout western Asia and Europe challenged conventional Greek assumptions about the clear line that divided Greeks from the non-Greek peoples they called barbarians—people whose language sounded like "bar, bar." In some of the lands incorporated into the new Macedonian empires, women enjoyed higher status than in most of the Greek world, and this sometimes rubbed off on the colonial Macedonian aristocracy, changing long-entrenched mores.

The country that the poet Byron labeled the "land of lost gods" continues to live on in the modern imagination. During the past decades, our understanding of ancient Greece has vastly expanded. Even though the Greeks left us a comparatively rich record, we possess only a tiny fraction of what was originally there. Yet there is good news, too. Every year new discoveries are made that continue to enlarge our fund of information, while, at the same time, new ways of looking at the old sources have broadened our perspectives. Archaeology has revealed the critical importance of the Dark Age, while comparative anthropology has illuminated the nature of Archaic society and made clear the oral character of early Greek culture. At the same time, social historians have veered away from the traditional preoccupation with the elite, who left written records of their doings, and have been tireless in ferreting out evidence that throws light on the lives of those who do not generally speak for themselves—women, for example, and slaves.

SOURCES: HOW WE KNOW ABOUT THE GREEKS

Sources are the raw material of history out of which historians weave their stories. Just about everything preserved from antiquity is a potential source for writing ancient history. Our sources fall into two broad categories: the physical remains, which include anything material, from bones to buildings, and the written remains, which include the words of the Greeks themselves or of others who wrote about them in antiquity. Of course, the line between the material and the written is often blurred, as in the case of words scratched on a piece of pottery, or an inscription carved on a stone pillar.

Historians, using documents, inscriptions, and literary texts, construct an account of past events. They are concerned, however, not only with events but also with the people involved in them: what they did, why they did it, and the changes brought on by their actions. Given that our primary sources are at least two thousand years old, and in many cases much older, it is not surprising that most of them require rehabilitation or reconstruction before they can be of use. But, fortunately, historians do not have to examine such artifacts from scratch. They rely on archaeologists to excavate, classify, and interpret most of the material evidence; paleographers to decipher and elucidate the texts written on papyrus and parchment; epigraphists and numismatists to interpret inscriptions on stones and coins. Without the expertise of specialists who process the raw sources, the work of historians would not be possible.

Retrieving the Past: The Material Record

The material record has expanded enormously during the past two centuries thanks to archaeology. Some of the most remarkable discoveries have been made underwater. Modern scuba gear has allowed archaeologists to explore the remains of cities built on now sunken shorelines such as Phanagoria in the Black Sea and the royal quarter of Alexandria and to recover lost works of art such as the spectacular Riace bronzes. (See Plates XVIIIa and XVIIIb.) Less dramatic but more informative are shipwrecks, virtual time capsules which provide invaluable evidence about ancient ships, their crews and cargoes, and patterns of trade. (See Plate I.) Nevertheless, the reality is that most of Ancient Greece lies underground.

Except for a few stone buildings, mostly temples, which have survived above ground, the vast bulk of the material record of Greek history has been dug up from beneath, very often from dozens of feet below the present surface. Materials decay, and the soil of Greece is not good for preserving things. Accordingly, artifacts made of wood, cloth, and leather are rarely found. Metals fare better: gold and silver last almost forever; bronze is fairly durable, iron more subject to corrosion. Another material, virtually indestructible, is terra-cotta, clay baked at very high temperatures. Clay was used in antiquity for many different objects, including figurines and votive plaques, but most of our clay objects are vessels that archaeologists have found by the thousands in graves and other sites. It is mainly on the basis of pots that they are able to construct a chronology for prehistoric and early historic Greece that can be translated into actual dates.

Clay pots were made wide-bellied or slender-bodied, long-necked or widemouthed, footed or footless, with one, two, three, four, or no handles. Some pots, such as the perfume flasks called *aryballoi*, stood only two or three inches high; others, like the *pithoi* used for storing olive oil, grain, and other things, were often as big as a human being. In the ancient world, clay vessels served virtually every purpose that a container can serve; thus they had to be made in all sizes and shapes. They were our bags, cartons, and shipping crates, our cooking pots, bottles, and glasses, as well as our fine stemware and "good" china bowls. Because they underwent gradual changes in style and decoration while preserving their basic shapes, vases can be placed in relative chronological sequences. Earthenware from one site is cross-dated with examples from other sites, thus confirming that site A is older or younger than sites B and C. But if a datable object from an outside society is found amidst the Greek material, it is often possible to establish "absolute" or calendar dates. Given a scarab inscribed with the name of an Egyptian king, the dates of whose reign are independently known, it follows that the Greek objects found with it in that deposit belonged approximately to the same time. Through the repeated process of establishing key cross-dates, a workable chronology emerges that allows us to place an object or grave or building in real time: "late fourteenth century BC" or "around 720 BC." Today's archaeologists also have at their disposal more scientific techniques for dating objects and sites, such as measuring the radioactive decay of organic materials (carbon-14 dating) and dendrochronology (the counting of tree rings).

Yet, notwithstanding the success that modern archaeology has had in bringing the ancient past to light, wordless objects can tell us only so much about how people lived, what they experienced, or what they thought.

RETRIEVING THE PAST: THE WRITTEN RECORD

Ancient writings were inscribed upon many different materials, including clay, stone, metal, and papyrus (and from the second century BC on, parchment). We also have records written on clay tablets from a very brief time in the late second millennium BC in a syllabic script called Linear B. But most of the written sources that have come down to us were composed in the Greek alphabet, which was adapted to the needs of Greeks from the Phoenician alphabet in the eighth century BC. With the rapid spread of the alphabet came a torrent of written texts that would continue unabated throughout the rest of antiquity.

The most common medium for writing in the ancient Mediterranean was papyrus (the paper of antiquity), which had been used in Egypt since the third millennium. Papyrus sheets were made by bonding together layered strips sliced from the papyrus reed; these were then glued together to form a long roll, 20 or more feet long. Words were written horizontally to form columns, which the reader isolated by scrolling back and forth along the roll. A papyrus roll could hold, on average, a play of about fifteen hundred lines, or two to three "books" of Homer's *Iliad* or *Odyssey*. Every text had to be copied by hand, usually by slaves—a time-consuming and expensive proposition. The ancient Greeks were fairly assiduous in preserving the works of authors from their past. A visitor to the great library at Alexandria during the first century BC would have had access to about 500,000 book-rolls, while the collection at Pergamum is said to have exceeded 200,000 rolls. Unfortunately, most of these materials have been lost.

Already by this time, the process of selection had begun. The Alexandrian scholars themselves appear to have used the term "those included" to denote a list of authors who were deemed most worthy of being studied in schools. Naturally, the "included" writers had the best chances for survival. And as literary tastes continued to change during later antiquity, many manuscripts ceased to be selected for copying and crumbled into dust. Fortunately, papyrus endures well in a hot, dry environment, as in the desert sands of Egypt, where many thousands of Greek papyri, dating from the fourth century BC onward, have been found. Although most of these are contemporary documents, the desert dumps have also preserved major literary works from all periods of Greek antiquity that otherwise would have been lost completely. Moreover, hundreds of inscriptions on stone and metal, including coins, survive, ranging in subject matter from private funerary epitaphs and dedications to public decrees, treaties, and laws. The latter are especially valuable, because they preserve information about public life that is seldom recorded elsewhere.

Our literary sources are a diverse group, written in many different genres, that is, categories of composition defined by form and content. These include not only the prose genres of history, biography, oratory, and philosophy, but also poetic genres that are generally regarded as fictional, such as epic, lyric, tragedy, and comedy. Naturally, modern historians rely especially on the writings of ancient historians and biographers, but poetry is no less useful as a source.

Of course, there is a big difference between mythical and historical narratives of the past. We don't expect historical veracity from Homer's account of the Trojan War. At the same time, not even a historian who strives for veracity can give us a truly objective and unbiased account of the past. The ancient historians, no different from us really, aimed to convey only what they deemed historically significant. Because they selected some facts to the exclusion of others, even two roughly contemporary historians—Herodotus and Thucydides in the fifth century, for example—would necessarily produce different accounts of the same past events. Another limitation of our written sources is that, with very few exceptions, they are all produced by a privileged group: urban males, mostly from the upper class. To illuminate the lives of women, the very poor, and slaves, who do not generally speak for themselves, historians employ a variety of strategies, often drawing upon gender studies, anthropology, cultural studies, and other interdisciplinary approaches.

PERIODIZATION

Periodizing is the grouping together of chronological sequences and assigning each one a label, such as "the Middle Ages" or "the Renaissance." For historians, periodization is a necessary evil. An evil because it distorts, drawing artificial lines through the continuous flow of time and treating each slice as if it were a separate, discrete, bounded, and static block. And yet, this process of chopping history is necessary; it provides a convenient way of understanding history, a way that has been characterized as a shorthand for thinking about the past.

Historians of ancient Greece conventionally divide the Greek experience into the following blocks. The dates given here are rounded out to a high degree, and are meant only as a rough guide. The book's timeline offers a somewhat more refined division and subdivision.

Neolithic/New Stone Age	7000–3000 BC
Bronze Age	
Early Bronze Age	3000–2100
Middle Bronze Age	2100–1600
Late Bronze Age	1600–1200
Dark Age/Iron Age	1200–750/700
Archaic period	750/700–480
Classical period	480–323
Hellenistic period	323–30

FROGS AROUND A POND

In Plato's philosophical dialogue *Phaedo* (109b), Socrates, speaking of the vastness of the earth, remarks that "we," meaning the Greeks, occupy only the small portion of it that extends from the western edge of the Mediterranean Sea to the eastern edge of the Black Sea, "dwelling around the sea like ants or frogs around a pond." Socrates' offhand quip reveals something about how the Greeks experienced their environment. First, the seas were their highways; to travel meant going aboard a ship. Second, as Socrates informs us, to the Greeks home meant not just their original homeland—the Greek mainland and its adjacent islands—but anywhere along the coastal waters from Spain to Ukraine. Greeks, then, not only lived all around the ancient Mediterranean world but were also part of that remarkable mix of disparate peoples and cultures that met and mingled along the maritime trade routes.

As early as the third millennium BC, the people who lived on the Greek mainland and the Aegean islands began to have contacts with the established civilizations of the Near East and Egypt and even far beyond. Relations with those other nations and peoples could be in turn friendly or hostile, depending on how the political winds were blowing at any given time. At certain periods Greeks focused more intently on one or another part of the Mediterranean world, but there was never a time when they were not actively engaged within the whole of that wide orbit, traveling, migrating, exchanging goods, learning new things, disseminating their own ideas and customs.

CITY-STATES

The "ants and frogs" to which Socrates referred in the *Phaedo* were what are now called city-states. Although the ancient Greek city-state is probably the most famous example of this type of political organization, it is only one example out of many. The city-state was a common political form both in ancient times and later. But because the city-state has all but disappeared from the political landscape, it requires some clarification. (A living relic of the once numerous medieval city-states is tiny Monaco, which received independence in AD 1419.)

As the name indicates, the city-state is a state, that is, an independent entity, self-ruling, and not part of a larger state. As for its layout, a city-state comprises a city, the center of government, and its outlying territory. The Greek word *polis* denotes both the central city (or town) and the state itself: the polis-city, its countryside, and its citizens, both those who lived in the city and those who lived in outlying villages.

Quite possibly the city-state represents the earliest form of multifaceted social organization. The first civilization, Sumer in Mesopotamia, emerged in the form of a number of independent city-states toward the end of the fourth millennium. It appears that the rulers of the city-states succeeded in inculcating in the people a sense of loyalty and pride in their own polities.

The desire to remain independent, though it knitted the community together, also fomented bloody interstate rivalry. The Greeks, for example, were constantly declaring war on other *poleis* (plural), often on the flimsiest of grounds. In the same way, the Sumerian city-states had been caught up in a cycle of violence, as the king of this or that state attempted forcibly to dominate the others. Eventually, weakened by their constant squabbles, the Sumerian microstates were conquered by an outsider, Sargon of Akkad (c. 2350 BC), who incorporated them into his growing empire. Over two thousand years later, the Greek poleis would suffer a similar fate at the hands of another outsider: Rome.

GREEK CITY-STATES

Just as all city-states have elements in common, so do they also exhibit unlike features, because of the particular conditions that shape them. So, while the Greek city-states—which emerged in the eighth century—were not quite as unique as some European historians have made them out to be, nevertheless the Greek states can be distinguished from all the others in the ancient Mediterranean world because of the Greeks' philosophical discourse about what a state should be, the range of "constitutions" they experimented with, and the equipoise they attained (or sought to attain) between the good of the individual and the common good.

Other special characteristics of the polis system stand out. Sheer numbers, for one: when Plato wrote the *Phaedo* (c. 360 BC) there might have existed a thousand or more independent poleis. Size is another. City-states, by definition, are small in size, though not necessarily in population, but almost all Greek city-states were very small both in size and population, with "city" centers that often were little more than overgrown villages. The little island of Ceos (50 square miles) provides an example of how small the poleis were and how determined to remain autonomous; it contained four independent poleis, three of which minted their own coins.

City-states understandably hog the spotlight in Greek history. The most famous Greek states—Athens, Sparta, Corinth—were all city-states. Not all Greeks, however, lived in isolated city-states. Throughout central, northern, and western

Greece and much of the northern and central Peloponnesus, city-states partially overcame their particularism, uniting to form federal leagues, which Greeks called *ethnē* ("nations").

Although the heyday of Greek federalism was the Hellenistic period, federal leagues existed as early as the Archaic period. No single form of political organization was characteristic of all Greek leagues. Some, like the Thessalian League, included separate farmsteads, villages, and small city-states united only by a belief in common kinship; others, like the Boeotian and Achaean leagues, were composed entirely of city-states. All leagues, however, were governed by councils of representatives from the member states of the leagues, and by assemblies. Open to all free male league citizens, assemblies usually met a few times a year during festivals held at a common league sanctuary to elect officials, settle disputes between members, and deal with relations with foreign states. In addition, these governing bodies could mobilize pan-league armies to deal with foreign threats.

When all is said and done, what stands out about the Greeks is the great paradox: a single people, yet totally disunited and regularly at war with itself. The Greeks knew themselves by a common name, *Hellēnes* (after *Hellēn*, their mythical ancestor), and *Hellas* ("Greece") meant anywhere Hellenes had put down roots. The historian Herodotus described the Greeks as having "the same blood and a common language, having temples and sacrifices to the gods in common, and having similar customs" (8.144). We shall see as this story unfolds how greatly that conjunction of political particularism and shared sense of nationality (which itself transcended "ethnic" bounds) contributed to the intellectual and artistic achievements for which the ancient Hellenes are acclaimed. Greek history, therefore, is about what kind of life the *politai*—the citizens—made for themselves, whether they lived in city-states or federal leagues.

Suggested Readings

Bodel, John, ed. 2001. *Epigraphic Evidence: Ancient History from Inscriptions*. London: Routledge. Collection of essays concerning the value of epigraphic evidence for reconstructing the history of Greece and Rome.

Boys-Stones, George, Barbara Graziosi, and Phiroze Vasunia, eds. 2009. *The Oxford Handbook of Hellenic Studies*. Oxford: Oxford University Press. Massive collection of articles on all aspects of the historiography and methodology of Greek history.

Easterling, P. E., and E. J. Kenney, eds. 1985. *The Cambridge History of Classical Literature*. Cambridge: Cambridge University Press. Separate chapters on individual authors and genres by distinguished critics cover the entirety of ancient Greek literature, from Homer to the period of the Roman Empire.

Griffith, Robert, and Carol G. Thomas, eds. 1981. *The City-State in Five Cultures*. Santa Barbara and Oxford: Oxford University Press. Description and comparative analysis of city-states in Sumer, Greece, Italy, Germany, and Nigeria, with an eye to defining the city-state form and its preconditions.

Hedrick, Charles W., Jr. 2006. *Ancient History: Monuments and Documents*. Oxford: Blackwell. Lucid introduction to the sources used by ancient historians and the methods of analyzing them.

Luce, T. J. 1997. *The Greek Historians.* London: Routledge. Brief introduction to the major ancient Greek historians and their works.

Morley, Neville. 1999. *Writing Ancient History.* Ithaca, NY: Cornell University Press. Introduction to the methods and goals of contemporary ancient historiography.

———. 2000. *Ancient History: Key Themes and Approaches.* London: Routledge. Useful survey of the principal concepts and theories of contemporary ancient historiography.

Morris, Ian. 2000. *Archaeology as Cultural History: Words and Things in Iron Age Greece.* Oxford: Blackwell. Provocative analysis of the relationship of archaeology and history in the study of early Greek history.

Renfrew, Colin, and Paul Bahn. 1991. *Archaeology: Theories, Methods, and Practice.* New York: Thames & Hudson. Comprehensive introduction to the discipline of archaeology today: what it is, what it does, and how it is done.

CHAPTER ONE

Early Greece and the Bronze Age

Before the late nineteenth century, when archaeologists unearthed three famous cities from the mythical Age of Heroes, no one knew that advanced civilizations had existed in the Aegean during the Bronze Age. First, in 1871, came the excavations of Heinrich Schliemann in Turkey. An eccentric German businessman-turned-archaeologist, Schliemann rejected the view prevalent among scholars of his day, who dismissed the Greeks' war against Troy as just another mythical tale. Convinced that the Trojan War had actually taken place just as it was recounted in the *Iliad* and the *Odyssey*, the early epic poems attributed to Homer, Schliemann followed the advice of Frank Calvert, a British diplomat and experienced amateur archaeologist, who had already conducted trial excavations at a place called Hissarlik on the northwest coast of Anatolia, and began large-scale diggings at the site. In 1872–1873 his labors bore fruit, revealing the massive ruins of a Bronze Age walled citadel, which he identified as the fabled Troy. The news electrified the scholarly world and captured the public's imagination. Schliemann's own imagination led to the adornment of his wife in the earrings and necklaces that were part of "Priam's Treasure." (See Plate IIa.).

Later scholarship proved that "Priam's Treasure" had been buried much earlier than Schliemann believed, but the fact remains: there really had been a Troy just where Homer said it was located!

In 1876, four years after beginning excavations at Troy, Schliemann turned to the site of **Mycenae** in southern Greece, which tradition held to be the city of King Agamemnon, the leader of the Greek invasion of Troy. Because of Mycenae's importance in myth and, as we now know, in history, the Late Bronze Age in Greece (c. 1600–1200 BC) is commonly referred to as the Mycenaean

Figure 1.1a German businessman turned archaeologist Heinrich Schliemann (1822–1890), excavator of Troy and Mycenae.

period. Oddly, although the site of Mycenae had been known since antiquity, and some of its ruins were still above ground, no one had systematically excavated there. Here Schliemann's luck also held: almost immediately he discovered buildings and royal graves rich in gold. He apparently believed that he had found Agamemnon's death mask (although the story that he sent a telegram out to the King of Greece exclaiming "I have gazed upon the face of Agamemnon!" is almost certainly apocryphal). The pioneering Schliemann's finds are not by themselves conclusive evidence of a large-scale war between Troy and Mycenae. Nevertheless, the impressive ruins unearthed at both sites (especially at Troy in the last 20 years), with their immense wealth in gold and other costly things, do prove correct the Greeks' remembrance of their Heroic Age as a time of fabulous wealth and splendor.

No less spectacular was Sir **Arthur Evans'** discovery in 1900 of a huge complex at **Cnossus** on the island of Crete, twenty-four years after Schliemann had begun his excavations at Mycenae. Evans became obsessed with the palace, and he spent much of his personal fortune on restoring significant portions of it. Although some of his restorations have been shown to be inaccurate, the

Figure 1.1b. Gold mask from one of the early shaft graves at Mycenae. Scholars now believe that this is the mask that Schliemann identified with the face of Agamemnon, king of Mycenae.

size and magnificence of the palace gave credence to the legend that in ancient times Cnossus had been the center of a powerful naval state. Evans called this first Aegean civilization Minoan, after Minos, the mythical king of Cnossus, who lived, according to Homer, three generations before the Trojan War. Just as the **Mycenaean civilization** was associated with the pioneering archaeological work of Heinrich Schliemann, the Minoans belonged to Arthur Evans, who built an ample permanent residence for himself in Cnossus. Schliemann and Evans added more than a thousand years to the history of Greece and showed that the ancestors of the historical Greeks lived in a totally different world from that of classical Greece. But that was only the beginning. More than a century of additional work by numerous talented archaeologists—Greek and non-Greek—has extended the history of Greece back thousands of years more and revealed that it was even more remarkable and complex than Schliemann and Evans could have imagined.

When exactly did Greek history begin? In the third century BC, an anonymous Greek historian living on the island of Paros began his history in 1582 BC, when Greek tradition claimed that kings began to rule in Athens.

DOCUMENT 1.1

The Parian Marble (IG I2.5, 444).

Set up publicly in a gymnasium where it could easily be read, the Parian Marble provided the citizens of Paros with a summary of Greek history from the earliest rulers to the author's own lifetime. The selections translated here include the origin of kingship at Athens and the reign of Deucalion, who was believed to have created the ancestors of the Greeks after the flood by throwing stones behind his back. These earliest entries are more myth than history; the flood myth, found all over the Greek world, was borrowed at an early date from the Near East.

From all kinds of records and common histories, I have recorded our times from the beginning, starting with Cecrops, who became the first king of Athens, until [*...]yanax was archon at Paros and Diognotus was archon at Athens. [264/3 BC]

   1. Since Cecrops became king of Athens and the place took the name Cecropia, which was previously called Actica from Actaeus, who was born from the earth, 1,318 years. [1582 BC]

   2. Since Deucalion became king by Mt. Parnassus in Lycoreia, when Cecrops was king of Athens, 1,310 years. [1574]

   4. Since the flood in Deucalion's lifetime happened and Deucalion fled the rains from Lycoreia to Athens to the side of Cranaus and he laid the foundation of the temple of Zeus the Olympian and made sacrifice for safety, 1,265 years, when Cranaus was king of Athens. [1529]

   6. Since Hellen son of Deucalion became king of Phthiotis and the Hellenes took their name who were previously called Graeci and...., when Amphictyon was King of Athens, 1,257 years. [1521]

*Square brackets indicate that the text is missing letters or words.

Until recently, modern historians preferred a more recent date, 776 BC, the year the Olympic games were founded. Despite these differences, however, there had been agreement that Greek history began with the appearance of reliable written records. Today, historians take a more radical view, for the archaeological revolution that Schliemann and Evans began has pushed the beginning of Greek history back to about 40,000 years ago and revealed a history different from anything ancient and modern historians of Greece imagined.

Forty thousand years ago, during the Paleolithic period, or Old Stone Age, small groups of hunter-gatherers biologically identical to modern humans roamed mainland Greece. For millennia they struggled to cope with the harsh environment of the Great Ice Age. Caves provided them with welcome shelter and preserved invaluable evidence of their lives. One such cave in particular, the **Franchthi Cave** in southeastern Greece, which was inhabited almost continuously from c. 20,000 to 3000 BC, has enabled archaeologists to reconstruct life in Greece from the Stone Age to the early **Bronze Age** when the first complex societies in Greece developed (Figure 1.2).

The archaeological record preserved at the Franchthi Cave shows that about 12,000 years ago life in Greece changed dramatically as the ice sheets that had covered northern Eurasia for tens of thousands of years began to melt. The climate of Greece became warmer and wetter, while the large animals the inhabitants of the cave had hunted gradually disappeared. At the same time, rising sea levels in the Mediterranean and Aegean basins flooded low-lying coasts, creating the physical geography of ancient Greece. The hunter-gatherers of the Franchthi Cave adapted

Figure 1.2. The Franchthi Cave has provided invaluable archaeological evidence about life in early Greece.

to the new environment, and by about 8000 BC they were regularly gathering wild oats and wild barley, as well as wild legumes, including lentils, peas, and beans; they were also fond of red deer. That they were in touch with the outside world is reflected in their use of tools made from obsidian obtained from the island of Melos, 80 miles away. Burials within and around the cave reveal that they practiced ritual disposal of their dead. Paleoanthropologists have used forensic techniques to link a high incidence of malaria (indicated by increased skull thickness in many males) to (relatively) high child mortality. One young man, age twenty-five, died from a blow to the side of his head by a blunt object. These details about death can be teased from the skeletal remains. A thousand years later, at the beginning of the Neolithic (New Stone) Age (c. 7000–3000 BC), the lives of the inhabitants of the Franchthi Cave and other sites in Greece would change forever as they made the transition from collecting their food to producing it themselves, thereby making possible the emergence of settled life and ultimately of civilization in Greece and the Aegean basin.

DOMESTICATION

The **domestication** of wild plants and animals was a watershed in human history. This major step is thought to have occurred independently in no more than four to seven places and with absolute certainty only three times, the earliest around 8000 BC, probably in southeast Anatolia (modern Turkey). The other two places were China (rice, millet) around 6800 BC and Mesoamerica (maize, squash) around 4000 BC.

Clearly, the proximity of Greece to the prime source of plant and animal domestication (the "fertile crescent," as it has been called) gave its inhabitants a head start over the other peoples of Europe. Farming and husbandry, for example, did not reach central Europe until around 5400 BC and Britain until around 4000 BC. The earliest Greek agriculturalists grew the same eight "founder crops" that were produced in the Near East: emmer wheat, einkorn wheat, barley, peas, lentils, chickpeas, fava beans, and flax, not all of which have wild forebears in Greece. This was accompanied by the first signs also of domesticated animals. This "package" of plant and animal cultivars most likely reflects the arrival of new populations, whose numbers need not have been large; their mixing with local hunter-gatherer groups was sufficient to generate the demographic expansion that we see at this time of decreased movement and increased permanence of settlement. Significantly, this is one of countless occasions when outsiders came into Greece, settling there and thus adding elements of their own culture to the ways of the existing inhabitants. Throughout antiquity, the cultural exchanges between Greece and the older civilizations of western Asia and northern Africa were close, deep, and continuous.

SOURCES FOR EARLY GREEK HISTORY

True history, in the sense of specific events involving specific persons, would not begin until the eighth century BC, when the reintroduction of writing made it possible for Greeks to record what was happening—and what had happened— in their world. Everything before that is prehistory. Yet thanks to the science of archaeology, we now know infinitely more about the society and culture of prehistoric Greece than did the later Greeks themselves, who knew it only through myths and legends. Aegean archaeologists are fortunate, for they have a wide and varied assortment of material from which to reconstruct the culture: architecture, wall paintings, sculpture, painted pottery, engraved seal stones, and, most important, written records, preserved on clay tablets. Those kinds of evidence have added immeasurably to our understanding of early Greeks. Even so, many questions remain unanswered or only partially answered. Archaeologists can reconstruct with some accuracy the material culture of a society. Inferences about social behavior and ideologies made from archaeological remains, however, are much more problematic.

What we miss the most, especially for the earliest times, is written sources. Whereas the civilizations of the Near East and Egypt had writing by the late Neolithic period, the prehistoric Greeks left no written records except for the Linear B tablets near the end of the Late Bronze Age. The Greeks of the historical period had as their source material a body of orally transmitted myths and legends, some of which probably went back to the second millennium BC; these stories were generally regarded as their ancient history. The central event of their distant past was the Trojan War, which, if it really happened, would have taken place in the thirteenth century BC. The Trojan War and its immediate aftermath are the setting for the earliest texts that we have, Homer's *Iliad* and *Odyssey*, two long epic poems that are believed to be the end product of a tradition of oral poetry going back many centuries. It is currently thought that these two epic poems were committed to writing in the later eighth century or early in the seventh. The use of these poems as historical sources has been debated since the end of antiquity and is still a matter of controversy. This question will be taken up in Chapter 2.

THE LAND OF GREECE

A history of the Greeks begins with the land, for the physical environment of a people—the landscape, the climate, and the natural resources—shapes how they live and develop. Mainland Greece occupies the southern portion of the Balkan peninsula, which juts far into the eastern Mediterranean Sea. The land area of ancient Greece was further extended by the Greek islands to the west and east of the mainland, embracing the large islands of Crete, Rhodes, and Cyprus further to the south. (See the map on the inside front cover.)

Modern Greece is about the size of England or the state of Alabama in the United States. The landscape is very rugged, with mountains covering almost 75 percent of the land. Only about 30 percent of the land can be cultivated at all, and only about 20 percent is classified as good agricultural land. Except in the northern mainland, where there are extensive plains, the mountains and lower hills cut the land into many narrow coastal plains and upland plains and valleys. The mountain ranges, which are not terribly high (3,000–8,000 feet) but quite steep and craggy, made overland travel very difficult in antiquity, and to some extent separated the small valleys and their people from one another.

By far the easiest way to travel was by sea, especially in the islands and the southern mainland, where the coast is never more than 40 miles away. The chains of islands in the Aegean Sea facilitated sea voyages. It is true that the rugged coastlines offer relatively few good harbors—those choice locations were continuously occupied from earliest times—yet sailors were seldom far from land where they could beach their boats safely for the night or find haven from a threatening storm. Throughout antiquity, the narrow Aegean tied the Greeks to the Near East and Egypt, commercially, culturally, politically, and militarily. The commercial contacts were especially vital because except for building stone and clay, a fair amount of iron ore, and pockets of silver, Greece is not well endowed with natural resources. The necessity to trade overseas for raw materials, especially copper and tin for making bronze, disposed the Greeks very early in their history to take to the sea and mingle with people from the other, older civilizations to the east and south.

The **Mediterranean climate** is semiarid, with long, hot, dry summers and short, cool, moist winters, when most of the rain falls. This general pattern varies from region to region in Greece. Northern Greece has a more continental climate, with much colder and wetter winters than the south. More rain falls on the western side of the Greek mainland than on the eastern side, while the Aegean islands receive even less. Water, the most precious of natural resources, is scarce in Greece because there are very few rivers that flow year-round, and few lakes, ponds, and springs. Thus irrigation on a large scale, as in the huge river valleys of Egypt and Mesopotamia, was not possible. Farming depended totally on the limited (and too often unreliable) annual rainfall. The soil in Greece, though rocky, is fairly fertile, the richest plowland being in the small plains where, over the ages, earth washed down from the hills has formed deep deposits. The lower hillsides, which are rockier, can be cultivated through terracing, which prevents the soil from washing further down the slope and captures soil from above. The jagged mountains support only wild vegetation, though some enclose mountain valleys suitable for farming and for grazing animals. Wood, essential for fuel and construction, especially shipbuilding, was originally abundant in the highland areas. Forests became depleted as time went on, however, and by the fifth century BC the more populous regions were forced to import timber.

It should be emphasized that this description of the land and resources of Greece is a generalization. Though Greece is small in area, local landscapes vary in the quantity and quality of farmland, pastureland, and raw materials. There are many microclimates within which production was unpredictable because of the year-to-year variability of rainfall. On the whole, however, the land, which the Greeks called Gaea, allowed the majority of the farmers a decent though modest living. But Gaea, "Mother Earth," offered no guarantees. Drought, especially in the more arid regions, was a constant and dreaded threat. A dry winter meant a lean year, and a prolonged drought meant hunger and poverty for entire villages and districts. Torrential rainstorms, on the other hand, could send water rushing down the hillsides and through the dry gullies, suddenly wiping out the terraces, flooding the fields, and destroying the crops. Life on the sea was equally unpredictable. The Aegean, though often calm with favoring winds, could just as suddenly boil up into ferocious storms that sent ships, cargo, and sailors to the bottom.

Plants and Livestock

In general, the soil and climate amply supported the "**Mediterranean triad**" of grain, grapes, and olives. Bread, wine, and olive oil were the staples of the Greek diet throughout antiquity and for long afterward. Grains—barley, wheat, and oats—grow well in Greek soil. Olive trees and grapevines, which were cultivated by the end of the Neolithic period, also flourished. Legumes (peas and beans) and several kinds of vegetables, fruits (especially figs), and nuts rounded out and varied the basic components of bread, porridges, and olive oil. Cheese, meat, and fish, which are rich in proteins and fat, supplemented the diet. Meat provided a very small part of the average family's daily food intake, however, and because fish are not abundant in the Mediterranean, they were usually eaten as a small "relish" with the meal. The Greeks did not care for butter and drank little milk. Their beverages were water and wine (usually diluted with water). Honey was used for sweetening, and various spices enhanced the flavor of food. Though it might appear monotonous to modern tastes, the Greek diet was healthful and nourishing.

The pasturing of small animals did not interfere with agriculture; flocks of sheep and goats grazed on hilly land that could not be farmed and on the fallow fields, providing manure in return. As suppliers of wool, cheese, meat, and skins, small livestock had great economic importance. The Greeks also kept pigs, particularly prized for their meat, and fowl (guinea hens early, but no chickens until the sixth century BC). The two largest domesticated animals, horses and cattle, occupied a special niche in the economy and culture. Oxen (castrated bulls) or mules and hinnies (hybrids of the horse and donkey) were essential for plowing and for drawing heavy loads. A farmer without ready access to a yoke of oxen or a pair of mules would be classified as poor. Herds of cattle and horses did compete with agriculture, since the stretches of good bottomland they required for grazing were also the best farmland. Practically speaking, there could be large-scale ranching of cattle and horses (except in the vast northern plains) only in times of low population density. Because they were such costly luxuries, cattle and horses were a status symbol for the rich. Cattle were raised mainly for their meat and hides. Horses were the primary markers of high social status: beautiful creatures, very expensive to maintain, and useful only for riding and for pulling light chariots, since the lack of an efficient horse collar prevented them from pulling heavy loads.

This agricultural and pastoral way of life remained essentially unchanged throughout Greek history. The fundamental economic fact that ancient Greece was a land of small-scale farmers (most of whom lived in farming villages and small towns) governed every aspect of Greek society, from politics to war to religion. It has been estimated that even in the fifth to third centuries BC, the peak population period, possibly as many as 80 percent of the male citizens of a **city-state** were engaged in agriculture, while the women worked mostly indoors. One of the major unifying forces within the Greek city-states was the citizen-farmers' devotion to their small agricultural plain and its surrounding hillsides, and their willingness to die defending their "ancestral earth," as the poet Homer called it. And the primary disunifying force throughout Greek history was the perpetual tension between citizens who had much land and those who had little or none.

Life in Late Stone-Age Villages

Adopting agriculture usually requires people to settle down permanently in local groups. Accordingly, just as in the Near East, small farming villages began to dot the Greek landscape in the Late Stone Age, although they were much fewer and more scattered than in the populous east. During the earlier Greek Neolithic period, the main area of habitation was in the north on the well-watered plain of Thessaly, where villages were bigger and architecturally more advanced than those in the less populated south. In 5500 BC, for example, the prosperous farming village of Sesklo may have had over fifteen hundred inhabitants, comparable to larger villages in the contemporary Near East. The later Neolithic Thessalian hilltop village of Dimini even displays impressive signs of incipient urbanization, including a large building with a central hall (*megaron*) atop the hill, surrounded by smaller houses built inside retaining walls on the slopes of the hill. For the most part, however, while villages throughout the Near East tended to expand steadily in size and population, Greek villages generally remained small, seldom exceeding a hundred to three hundred residents, although these small villages must have cooperated to create reproductive populations of up to 1,000 persons.

Life in the early Greek villages remained simple; hunting and foraging continued alongside agriculture and stock raising. Houses were similar to those of the Near East, built of sun-dried mud bricks laid over low stone foundations, with floors of stamped earth and flat or pitched roofs made of thatch or brush. Farmers broke the earth with digging sticks; their hoes, sickles, axes, and knives were of polished stone and flint. Yet the Neolithic villages were also sites of new skills. The arts of weaving and pottery making produced items that were not only utilitarian but aesthetically pleasing as well. Excavations also yield dozens of figurines of clay and marble, depicting humans (mostly females) and animals. Far from

Figure 1.3. Neolithic marble figurine of a standing nude female figure from Sparta (c. 5000–4000 BC). This extraordinarily well-preserved sculpture impressively renders in stone an image frequently executed in clay at this early date.

being drab, their material world was brightly colored; it appears that even their one- or two-room houses were decorated with painted designs.

The uniformity of material culture—house plans, grave types, burial goods—in these villages suggests that social relations would have been egalitarian, with no inequality apart from sex, age, and skill. Families would have cooperated and shared with their neighbors, most of whom were kinfolk.

Much as in the previllage periods, leadership was probably transient, assumed now by one man, now by another, as the need arose for a decisive voice. With the growth of population, however, and the addition of increasingly complex communal projects, permanent leadership roles emerged. Anthropologists use the terms "big man" or "head man" to describe such leaders. A head man was one who was better at getting things done. His wisdom, courage, and skill in resolving disputes propel him to the front and keep him there. In time this position becomes a sort of office, into which a new man steps, having demonstrated that he is better suited than other would-be leaders, or when the old head man retires or dies (or is pushed out). Henceforth, the division into two status groups, the very small group of leaders and the large group of the led, would be a permanent feature of Greek political life.

Greece and the Near East in the "Final Neolithic" Period (c. 4000–3000 bc)

At this point, it is important to note the disparity in the tempo of development between Greece and the societies of western Asia and northern Africa. It appears that during the seventh to fifth millennia, technological and social developments in Greece more or less kept pace with advances in the Near East and Egypt. By the end of the fifth millennium, however, in what is now southern Iraq, changes had occurred that would leave Greece and the rest of Europe far behind. Farmers moving into the alluvial plain that later Greeks named Mesopotamia—"the land between the rivers" Tigris and Euphrates—succeeded in taming the marshes and channeling the rivers' unpredictable annual floods. The fertile soil brought forth a superabundance of food, setting off a cycle of population growth, which stimulated more extensive production, which fed more people. Fourth-millennium Mesopotamia experienced an urban explosion: in 3000 bc, the Sumerian city of Uruk covered 500 acres, with a population of fifty thousand, while other city-state centers were not far behind. Greece would not see urban complexes that large for well over two millennia.

The Sumerian city-states that emerged in the fourth millennium were the archetypes of all the ultracomplex societies that would arise in antiquity. Details would differ, but the model would be the same: atop the social pyramid was a narrow stratum of powerful families or clans, one of which would be (or claim to be) the royal dynasty. Beneath this hierarchy were ranks of officials—military leaders, priests and priestesses, managers, scribes, and so on—beholden to and supported by the king. Finally, making up the wide base of the pyramid, were the mass of free families, whose economic status might have ranged from wealthy or well off—merchants, landowners, skilled craftsmen—down to poor farmers and common laborers. And beneath them all were the slaves, who did not count as persons.

Although at no time did Greek leaders hesitate to use religion to influence their followers, one thing that seems never to have suited the Greeks was to put temples and the priesthoods at the center of political and economic power, as in Mesopotamia and Egypt, where the will of the leader was identified with the will of the gods.

GREECE IN THE EARLY AND MIDDLE BRONZE AGES (C. 3000–1600 BC)

The technology of separating copper from its ores, melting and refining it, and making things out of it goes back to the sixth millennium BC. Unlike gold, silver, and lead, which were used exclusively for making ornaments, molten copper was also used to cast tools in molds. Its disadvantage was that it was soft. Toward the end of the Neolithic, probably in Sumer, smiths discovered that adding 10 percent of tin to the copper produced a much harder metal, bronze. Bronze metallurgy came to Greece and its islands around 3000 BC, and by about 2500 had become widespread throughout much of Europe. To get their tin, Greeks had to have been in contact, however indirectly, with its sources in northern Europe and central Asia.

The social and economic impact of bronze was huge; it made work and war far more efficient. But it also hastened the widening of the gap in wealth and prestige between the higher-ranked families and the rest of the people. Since supplies of copper and tin were located far apart and could be obtained only through long-distance trade, only those with large surpluses of produce had access to both ingredients. For ordinary people, however, the Stone Age lasted well into the Bronze Age.

The site of **Lerna**, on the bay of Argos, provides a picture of the changes that came about after 3000 BC. Founded in the sixth millennium, and unchanged for many centuries, the small village expanded rapidly in the Early Bronze Age, growing into a thriving, populous town. Its houses now became larger and better constructed, and the town itself was surrounded by a thick fortification wall. The largest building (83 feet by 40 feet), known as the House of the Tiles, had two floors, a corridor along one side, a monumental entrance as well as several sections accessible only from the exterior, and a roof made of tiles rather than thatch (see Figure 1.5). The "corridor house" is a distinctive type that has been found also at at least three other sites on the mainland. Archaeologists speculate that it served several functions: as the dwelling of the chief and his family, as a feasting hall, and also as a place for communal storage; the corridor houses are clearly signs of sociopolitical hierarchy, as larger towns came to dominate surrounding villages and hamlets.

Figure 1.4. Cycladic marble figurine of a male figure playing double pipes from Keros (c. 2500–2200 BC). This highly abstracted human image was once enlivened with painted details. Athens, National Archaeological Museum.

Similar sites in southern Greece also indicate both settlement hierarchy and an incipient sociopolitical hierarchy. This system of ranking would likely have consisted of a hereditary chief and a few other prominent men, who administered the affairs of the town and its outlying settlements. Women derived their status from the men to whom they were related. Third-millennium Greece, though on a much smaller scale and with fewer visible signs of wealth, was experiencing the same kinds of demographic, political, and social change that had occurred in Mesopotamia more than a thousand years earlier. Population growth (although episodic, now here, now there), improvements in farming and crafts techniques, monumental architecture, and greater organizational complexity occur in the Aegean islands as well as on the mainland.

Around 2250, and continuing for about a century, there is evidence of severe destruction at almost all the sites throughout Greece and the islands; Crete was

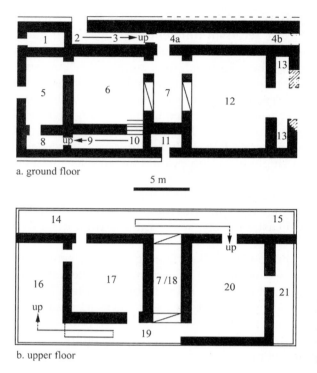

a. ground floor

5 m

Figure 1.5. Plan of the House of the Tiles at Lerna (c. 2200). Note the several access points from the outside. It is uncertain exactly what the building was used for, but there are several examples of this building type to be found at this time on the mainland.

b. upper floor

not spared, but it suffered less. What could have caused these events? Invaders? Internal warfare, perhaps growing out of persistent drought conditions? A combination of both? The answer is still in doubt, but the appearance of new styles of pottery decoration and new types of houses and graves suggests an incursion, if not an invasion, of new people. The distribution of these new elements, however, is not uniform, and the sites, most of which (like Lerna) remained occupied or were soon reoccupied, show an overall continuity of culture. Clearly, though, the disruptions put a halt to the progress and promise of the Early Bronze Age. The Middle Bronze Age (c. 2100–1600) appears to have been much poorer; architecture and grave goods give little indication of social stratification. Greece appears to have taken a step backward to a simple village life. What gives historical significance to this rather drab period is that its end marks the beginning of the first high civilization in Europe; and in the view of many, though by no means all, Greek-speakers first entered Greece at the beginning of the Middle Bronze Age.

The First Greek-Speakers

Despite the ongoing controversy about when the newcomers entered, it is unanimously agreed that they spoke a language that belonged to a language family called **Indo-European**. Early modern linguists, beginning in the eighteenth century, came to recognize that basic terms in different languages bore many similarities to one another, as well as to entire families of spoken languages, such as the Germanic and Slavic families. They observed, for example, a striking similarity in words such as "mother": Sanskrit *mātā* (stem *mātar-*), Greek *mētēr*, Latin *māter*, Anglo-Saxon *mōdor*, Old Irish *māthir*, Russian *mat'* (stem *mater-*). The close likenesses in vocabulary and syntactical structure among ancient languages and their descendants soon led to the insight that they had all sprung from a common linguistic ancestor, which was later termed Proto-Indo-European. It was reasoned that there had once been a single Indo-European homeland, located perhaps in the vast steppes north of the Black and Caspian seas, or possibly further south in eastern Anatolia. Beginning in the fourth or third millennium, as most scholars argue today, the parent language split into separate language families as the people who spoke it spread east and west across Eurasia from Ireland to Chinese Turkestan.

What were these speakers of proto-Greek like? During the nineteenth and early twentieth centuries, there was considerable conjecture about the nature of their social organization and culture. At that time, many favored northern Europe as the Indo-European homeland and envisaged the newcomers as a superior race of horse-riding nomadic "Aryan" warriors, who swept down into southern Europe and used violence to impose their languages and customs on the weaker, unwarlike, agrarian natives. Such suppositions came out of a racially biased Eurocentrism. No scholar today accepts any part of this "Aryan myth," which was among the pretexts for so many crimes against humanity in the nineteenth and twentieth centuries, culminating in the horrors perpetrated by the Nazis and Fascists in the 1930s and 1940s. The residents of Greece when the Greeks arrived were warriors, too, and had essentially the same array of weapons as the intruders, although they lacked, likely to their significant disadvantage, the horse and chariot. The reconstructed lexicon of Proto-Indo-European contains all the vocabulary pertaining to farming, herding, weaving, building, and other technologies—the skill sets that we recognize in the artifacts of the indigenous Greeks. The Indo-European kinship vocabulary shows that the people were organized in families and larger groups (clans and tribes) that were patrilineal (descent was reckoned in the male line) and patriarchal (the father was the supreme authority figure). We have no such direct information about the kinship structure of the earlier inhabitants, but it is more likely than not that their kinship system was also patrilineal.

Pre-Hellenic religion remains a blank; the only evidence is the ubiquitous female figurines found throughout the Cyclades, which used to be called Cycladic idols and were believed to represent fertility goddesses (Figure 1.3). Many male figures have also been discovered, however, so that the original significance and use of these Cycladic figurines are not known (Figure 1.4). About the first Greek speakers, we know one thing for sure: their primary divinity was a powerful male sky/weather god, whom they called Zeus. Greek replaced the earlier language(s) by the beginning of the Late Bronze Age (c. 1600), leaving only place names or borrowed words, such as *hyakinthos* (hyacinth) and *melissa* (bee). Such wholesale linguistic adoption would seem to imply either an overwhelming number of newcomers, which is unlikely, or political and military conquest. This remains a mystery.

We may consider the five hundred years of the Middle Bronze Age—undisturbed by any cultural break—as a long period of adjustment or transition, during which the earlier people and the newcomers gradually fused into a single people speaking a single language and with a culture that blended elements of both. Nor, despite its apparent material decline, was the Middle Bronze Age totally stagnant. Population increased, new settlements grew up, and contacts with the civilizations of Crete and the Near East began. These circumstances would lead, toward the end of the period, to a sudden cultural quickening that ushered in the high Minoan and Mycenaean civilizations of the Late Bronze period.

MINOAN CIVILIZATION

Covering an area of 3,400 square miles, Crete, among the islands of the eastern Mediterranean, is rivaled in size only by Cyprus. It was settled around 7000 BC by Neolithic farmers and stock raisers, possibly from Anatolia. Though the island is mountainous and has few water resources, the fertile plains in the central and eastern parts are able to sustain large populations. Down through the Neolithic period and the Early Bronze Age, the Cretans followed the typical Aegean path of steady growth and expansion. Fragments of large-scale buildings and some relatively rich graves indicate that by the middle of the third millennium certain kinship groups had achieved levels of wealth and rank that placed them in positions of local authority. Around 2200, just as on the mainland, there seems to have occurred a period of considerable instability in Crete, marked at many settlements more by disruption than by destruction. Then, around 2100, Crete began to recover: population boomed, some towns became population centers, and the first huge multiroom complex was completed around 2000 at the town of Cnossus, followed by similar, though smaller, palaces at Phaistos, Mallia, Zakro, and other settlements. Crete had become a land of small city-states, each palace center controlling an area of a few hundred square miles.

The Minoan Palaces: Their Economies

What we call a "palace" was actually a multifunctional maze of rooms—residential quarters, workshops, and storerooms—clustered around a large central courtyard. The complex that we see today at Cnossus was begun around 1700 BC, after it and other early palaces had been destroyed by fire. During its existence, Cnossus underwent numerous restorations and additions until its final destruction around 1375. As in the East, the Minoan palace was the central place of the entire state: the political and administrative center and the focal point of economic activity, state ceremony, and religious ritual. The Minoans eventually adopted the economic model of the "redistributive" system that had been standard in Egypt and the Near East since the third millennium, although in the first centuries of the Middle Bronze Age, the small scale of storage areas, the absence of clay sealings, and the

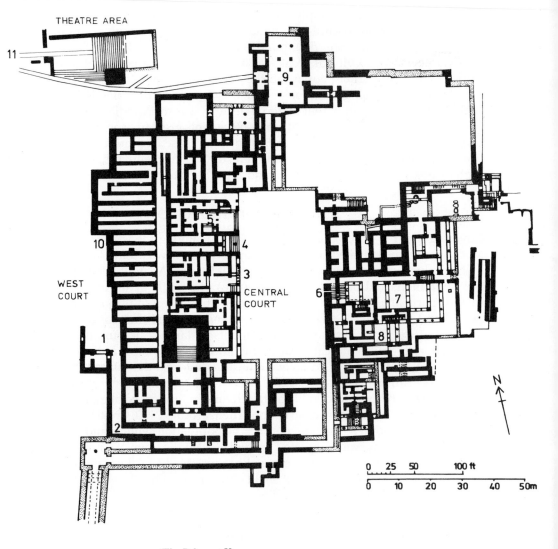

THEATRE AREA

WEST
COURT

CENTRAL
COURT

N

0	25	50		100 ft
0	10	20	30	40	50m

The Palace at Knossos.

1 West Porch
2 Corridor of the Procession
3 Palace Shrine
4 Stepped porch
5 Throne Room
6 Grand Staircase

7 Hall of the Double Axes
8 'Queen's Megaron'
9 Pillar Hall
10 Store-rooms
11 Royal Road, to Little Palace

Figure 1.6a. Plan of the Minoan palace at Cnossus, Crete (c. 1400 BC).

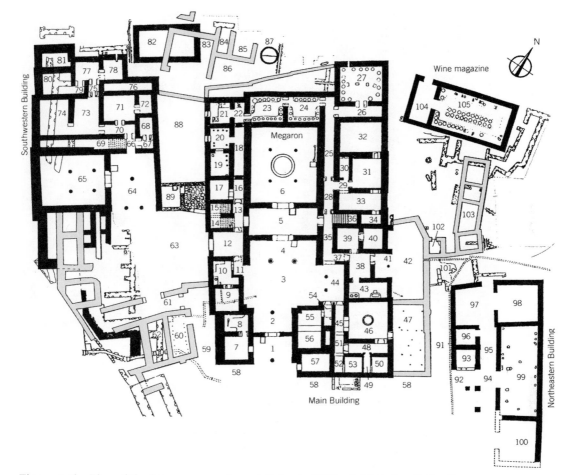

Figure 1.6b. Plan of the Mycenaean palace at Pylos (c. 1200 BC). Note the distinctive megaron in the center of the complex, in contrast to the open central court at Cnossus.

small crafts areas indicate that these earliest palatial centers were more consumption centers than redistributive ones. The central authority wielded considerable control over the allocation and use of the surrounding land, much of which belonged directly to the palace or temple but was allocated to various officials, including priests and priestesses.

Food and animals raised on the palace's lands, along with produce levied from private farms, were funneled into the palace, stored, and distributed back out to

Figure 1.6c. View of the ruins of the Minoan palace at Cnossus, Crete.

the villages as the palace saw fit. The influx of food and raw materials supplied the Minoan palace elite with luxuries and workers (both inside and outside the palace) with necessary tools and materials. In addition, the great quantities of grain and olive oil stored in the palace formed a reserve for distribution to the populace in times of famine or other calamity.

A key factor in the economic growth and the expansion of power at the center was the close association with Egypt and the Levant. In the Early Bronze Age, the Cretans had traded extensively with the Cyclades and also had established contact with the East, but it was only at the beginning of the Middle Bronze Age that its location—equidistant from three continents—made Crete a crossroad for Mediterranean trade. Before that, a long period of political and military disturbances throughout the Near East had essentially shut off the flow of goods in the eastern Mediterranean. The return to stability in the region around 2000 sparked a huge resurgence of maritime trade. It was during this time that Crete became part of the network of international commerce, not only shipping its own products but also acting as a transit point, carrying goods from other countries, as well as establishing its own commercial stations in the Cyclades.

It was also around this time (c. 1900 BC) that Cretans developed pictographic writing, for the purpose of management. In pictographic scripts a picture stands for an object or idea (as in "I ♥ New York"). This early form of writing evolved (perhaps inspired by Egyptian hieroglyphics) into a more advanced linear script made up of specific signs that stood for syllables and were joined together to form the sound of the words themselves. Evans concluded immediately that these writings, preserved on small clay tablets, had been used for keeping the economic records of the palaces. In the destruction level at Cnossus, Evans also found around three thousand clay tablets inscribed with a more elaborate version of the linear script. He named the earlier script **Linear A** and this later one **Linear B**, supposing that the B tablets represented a more advanced form of Linear A and that both scripts recorded the unknown Cretan language. These were sensible assumptions, but, as we will see, they were dead wrong.

The Minoan Palaces: Architecture and Art

Minoan art and architecture owed a large debt to the Near East, to Egypt especially. The Minoans, by virtue of their expanding commercial and diplomatic relations with these older civilizations, adopted both the eastern building techniques and certain elements of design, yet adapted them to suit their own visual style. Indeed, there was nothing in the realm of monumental architecture at that time that looked quite like a Minoan palace. In the East, the predominant function of palace art and architecture was to glorify the royal household. Kings were depicted as mighty conquerors and powerful rulers. In Minoan art, on the other hand, there are no scenes representing kings as heroic warriors and indeed very few, if any, images of royal pomp. The subjects and motifs of the wall paintings are plant and animal life and scenes of human activity, religious processions, or rituals.

The spirit of Minoan palace art is serene and lighthearted, even playful at times. Minoan painters were particularly adept at conveying a sense of movement and life. The frescoes and figurines depict both men and women as youthful, slender, and graceful. The men are smooth-shaven and are usually shown wearing only a short kilt, similar to the Egyptian male dress. The women wear elaborate flounced skirts and a tight, sleeved bodice that exposes their breasts. Both men and women have long hair, stylishly curled, and wear gold bracelets and necklaces.

Visitors to the ruins of the palace at Cnossus would have been dazzled by the intricacy and size of the original, which covered five acres with perhaps three hundred rooms organized around a large rectangular **central court**, the distinctive feature (along with storage rooms) of the Minoan palace as an architectural type. The palace was sturdily constructed of stone and mud brick, reinforced with timbers to help withstand earthquakes; it stood two and three stories high, with basements beneath. Light wells brought daylight and fresh air into the interior of the palace. A system of conduits and drains provided many of the rooms with running water and waste disposal. Porticoes (with columns that were narrower at the bottom than at the top and thus seem upside down to us) and numerous balconies and loggias, all brightly painted, gave the exterior a theatrical look. Minoan art, much admired today for its sophistication, vitality, and exuberance, also found favor in other cultural circles: frescoes with Minoan motifs have been found in royal palaces in Syria-Palestine and Egypt, painted with Minoan and not Egyptian colors.

But the Minoan effect was most prevalent among the Aegean islands, where local artists experimented with Minoan styles. A particularly detailed example of the Cycladic islanders' absorption of Minoan art, architecture, religion, dress, and lifestyles into their own island cultures is Akrotiri on the island of **Thera** (modern Santorini), 80 miles north of Crete. In 1967, the Greek archaeologist Spyridon Marinatos began excavation of a large town, which lay buried deep under layers of volcanic ash. The explosion that tore apart the tiny island—considered the most powerful volcanic eruption in all of history—occurred, according to ice core, dendrochronological, and radiocarbon datings, in 1628 BC. (Archaeologists continue to struggle with this scientific conclusion, as it contradicts the accepted ceramic chronology.) As in the city of Pompeii in Italy, buried by an eruption of Mount Vesuvius in 79 AD, the hardened ash had formed a protective membrane, allowing us today an unparalleled picture of town life at the height of the **Minoan civilization**. Many frescoes feature animals and plants in settings reminiscent of the Nile, and finds of Linear A tablets on Thera and other islands also show that the Cyclades were integrated into the orbit of Cretan trade. It is possible that the islands were part of a Minoan empire; more likely, however, they were independent trading partners.

The Social Classes of Crete

Sharp distinctions in wealth, privilege, and status distinguished a small number of families from the rest of the families in the Minoan city-states. That those who lived in the palaces embodied the top of the social pyramid is clear; it is not clear whether one person stood above them all. Evans believed that Cnossus was ruled by a priest-king and queen and identified one room as the "Queen's Megaron"; Egyptian kings and queens, after all, reigned as gods, and Mesopotamian rulers were seen as representatives of the gods. Additional evidence came from the palaces themselves, which Evans assumed to have been the centers of worship, given the abundance of images of divinities and cultic symbols. The absence of any definitive image of a king in Minoan iconography, however, has given rise to alternative possibilities: for example, that the ruling power was invested in a single lineage, possibly one with priestly jurisdiction. In the towns and in the countryside, we also find numerous spacious houses, two and three stories high and lavishly decorated with frescoes. These "villas," the largest of which resemble small palaces, although they lack the distinctive central court, may indicate the existence of a lower tier of elite families, perhaps part of the administration, or possibly wealthy traders.

The population at Cnossus at its height has been estimated at 17,000 persons, but the many thousands of ordinary farmers and crafts workers, at Cnossus and elsewhere on Crete, have left few traces of their lives. The majority lived and worked in villages or small towns. One such town is Gournia in northeastern Crete, which was excavated in the early twentieth century by an American archaeologist, Harriet Boyd Hawes. The town was built on a rocky hillside, with a small-scale palace perched above it. The flat-roofed houses, packed closely together, vary in size, but almost all were well made; many had two floors. On average, ordinary houses in Crete were much roomier than those in Greece or, for that matter, the Near East. Implements found in the houses show that the occupants fished and farmed and raised stock. Tools and imported raw materials are evidence of a bustling crafts industry. The remains of other settlements also reveal that the families that made up the broad base of the social pyramid lived simply but comfortably. Life expectancy at birth (on Crete as well as the mainland) was approximately thirty-five years for men, under thirty for women; few individuals reached their fifties, much less sixties. Skeletal remains reveal an average height for men of 1.67 meters (5′6″), for women 1.55 meters (5′1″); there is variety in the quality of teeth and a high incidence of malnutrition, presumably resulting from limited access to resources. It has been said that Crete appears to be a class-based society where there was little class inequality. That construct does not include slaves—men, women, and children captured in war or kidnapped, transported, and sold in the markets along with other goods. The slaves have left no evidence whatever of their bitter existence. We have no idea of their numbers relative to the free population. But we can now say with absolute certainty, based on evidence in written records, that slaves toiled in the palaces, villas, towns, and villages of Crete.

Minoan Religion

Throughout history the conviction that powerful supernatural beings and forces exist in another realm and control the natural world has been close to universal. Also ubiquitous are cult and ritual—the acts of devotion to the divine beings—and religious myths, the suppositions about them told in story form as part of ritual activity. Among agrarian peoples, the relationship of mortals to immortals revolves around the continuation of the fertility of the land and animals. To appease the gods, who can bestow or remove the blessings of nature at will, the people make communal displays of respect, including prayers and sacrifices of food, animals, and even, at times, humans. All these acts (including possible human sacrifice) are indicated in Minoan religion, which appears—we can never be certain—to have been focused on fertility. Paintings, vases, figurines, objects, seal rings, all express aspects of nature, both vegetation and animals, particularly bulls and wild goats, but also birds and snakes. Communal rituals took place in deep caves, in shrines at tops of hills ("peak sanctuaries"), and, more privately, in shrines in the palaces, villas, and houses. Possibly the large open courtyards of the palaces were also places of public cult. The dangerous sport of bull leaping, in which male and female athletes vault over a charging bull, also took place in the courtyards, where archaeologists have found postholes for barriers that protected spectators. The principal recipient of worship is a goddess dressed in the Minoan style; most often she is depicted in outdoor settings attended by priests and priestesses, although the women devotees far outnumber males in these scenes. So too, in processions and sacrifices priestesses outrank the priests. The

Figure 1.7a. Engraved gold signet ring from Cnossus showing women worshipping a goddess. These female figures with bare breasts wear the flounced skirts characteristic of Minoan dress. Heraclion, Archaeological Museum.

Figure 1.7b. Bull Leaper Fresco, Cnossus (c. 1450 BC). The different skin colors are believed to indicate gender, dark for male and light for female.

few depicted figures who appear to be male gods have been referred to as the "consorts" of the great goddess. What is most striking about the Minoan "Lady" is her commanding presence; her iconography states that she is in charge of the Minoans' world, and she favors female acolytes over males. In general Minoan

Figure 1.8. A carved stone libation vessel in the form of a bull's head, from Cnossus. This artifact of the Late Bronze Age, called a rhyton, has a rock-crystal eye and an inlaid band of white shell on its muzzle. The original horns of wood covered with gold leaf were lost and have been restored. Heraclion, Archaeological Museum.

women are shown participating in a wide range of social and religious activities (Figure 1.7a).

GREECE AND THE AEGEAN IN THE LATE BRONZE AGE (1600–1200 BC)

The histories of the Cretans and the Greeks are intertwined. The connection between them began around 2000 BC, when Minoans commenced trading relations with southern and central Greece. The Minoans seem to have had a remarkable effect on the developing Mycenaean Greek civilization. In the course of their interchanges, the Greeks did not just borrow single elements from the Minoan cultural repertoire; they adopted wholesale the model of the Minoan state, right down to the writing system. Indeed, the evidence of Minoan influence on Greece was so striking that Arthur Evans, the excavator of Cnossus, was convinced that the mainland Greek palaces of the fourteenth and thirteenth centuries had been occupied by Cretan kings—loyal subjects of the king of Cnossus, whose mighty "sea power" had conquered Greece. Actually, it was the other way around: by 1450, Greek kings were living in the Cretan palaces. And when Mycenaean civilization came crashing down at the end of the thirteenth century, Greeks continued to live in Crete. By 800 BC, or perhaps earlier, the island of Crete was linguistically and culturally Hellenic.

A question that has puzzled archaeologists about the Minoans—how could a society that was apparently not particularly stratified be suddenly transformed into one that was?—may also be asked of Greece at the beginning of the Late Bronze Age. The Mycenaean period too starts off with a bang. The enormous amount of treasure that Schliemann found in the graves at Mycenae has no parallel in the whole of the Aegean area. The seemingly sudden appearance of extremely wealthy families at Mycenae at the end of a period that most archaeologists consider to have been generally poor has not yet been explained. What we can say is that despite the lack of impressive remains, Middle Bronze Age Greece saw an increase in the number of settlements and in the size of existing settlements; that there was close contact with Crete; that grave goods, rare in early Middle Bronze Age burials, became more numerous toward the end; and that the contents of the graves uncovered at Mycenae reveal that the interred men were warriors and well-adorned women, who in life were proud of their status, and in death competed with other warrior families in displaying their riches. The men found in Grave Circle A at Mycenae were buried as warriors, some with breastplates and several with gold death masks; several of the women there were accompanied by elaborate gold jewelry and silver drinking cups.

The Shaft Graves and Tombs

There are two grave circles at Mycenae, an earlier one used from the late seventeenth century BC to about 1500 and a much richer one in use from around 1600 to a little after 1500. Most of these "**shaft graves**"—deep rectangular pits into which the bodies were lowered—contain several burials. The earlier graves contained many bronze weapons (swords, daggers, spearheads, and knives) and quantities of local pottery, but little gold or jewelry. By comparison, a single one of the graves from the later cemetery, containing the bodies of three men and two women, held not only an arsenal of weapons (forty-three swords, for example), but also hundreds of other expensive objects, including gold jewelry adorning the bodies of the women. All the precious materials, such as gold, silver, bronze, ivory, alabaster, faience, and amber, came from elsewhere, reaching Mycenae via the extensive trading networks that linked Crete, Cyprus, Egypt, Mesopotamia, Syria, Anatolia, and western Europe. Many of the items in the graves are imports, and those made locally (some perhaps by foreign craftsmen) present an eclectic mix of traditional Greek and foreign elements. How these warrior chieftains were able to pay for such extravagant burial displays (and still have plenty left over) remains a mystery, especially since there is no indication of an infrastructure that would have enabled them to exploit the production of the surrounding countryside. The great palaces at Mycenae, Tiryns, **Pylos**, and elsewhere would not be built until 1400 BC, and evidence for underlying proto-palaces is scanty in the extreme; the village of Mycenae itself has no discernible structures dating as early as 1600.

All we have are the graves and their contents. What these appear to tell us is that at some point, possibly in the latter part of the seventeenth century, local chiefs successfully augmented their powers: they created ruling dynasties that in the space of four or five generations managed to organize and expand the local economies, taking full advantage of their favorable location in the booming Mediterranean trading economy and of the lessons in statecraft the chiefs had learned from the Minoans and others.

Evidence of the growing power and resources of the Mycenaean elite, and a conspicuous statement of their "arrival" on the international scene, was their adoption in the sixteenth century of a different type of tomb, called a ***tholos*** (Figure 1.9a and 1.9b). Significantly, the tholos was very likely derived from a similar type of tomb common in Minoan Crete, but the Mycenaean form was far more impressive, both in size and construction. The largest are regarded as the highest achievement of Mycenaean engineering. Tholoi (plural) were large stone chambers, shaped somewhat like beehives, which were cut horizontally into a hillside. Their high vaulted burial and ceremonial chambers, which were covered over by earthen mounds, closed by huge bronze doors, and approached through a long stone-lined passageway. Unfortunately, most of the tholoi were pillaged centuries ago, but the few that were not completely plundered have yielded burial gifts almost as costly as those of the shaft graves.

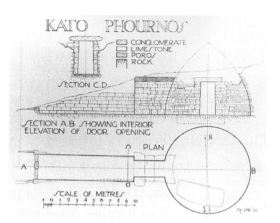

Figure 1.9a. Plan and cross section of a Mycenaean *tholos* tomb.

Figure 1.9b. Interior vault of a *tholos* tomb at Mycenae (the so-called Treasury of Atreus).

Figure 1.9c. A bronze dagger inlaid with a scene of a lion hunt, from a later shaft grave at Mycenae.

Mycenaeans Take Over Crete: The Decipherment of Linear B

When the first shaft graves at Mycenae were being dug, the Minoans had been riding high for almost 400 years. They had established trading outposts throughout the Cyclades; the Mycenaeans were not only among their best customers, trading extensively with Cretan merchants, but also organized their fledgling palace states on the Minoan model. In the fifteenth century BC, the Mycenaeans also expanded their reach by founding settlements along the Anatolian coast. A much bolder adventure was to take control of Crete. Around 1490, almost all the Minoan palaces were burned to the ground. Cnossus, however, suffered little damage to the palace and soon began to thrive again as the center for Greek rule over the island.

We know for sure that it was Mycenaeans who took over Minoan Crete because of the decipherment in the 1950s of Evans' Linear B tablets. All along, Evans had insisted that the Mycenaean palaces were under the control of the older and more advanced Minoan civilization. The discovery in 1939 of six hundred more Linear B tablets at the palace complex of Pylos on the southwestern Greek mainland served to strengthen his theory of Minoan hegemony (Figure 1.6b). With the addition of the new tablets, there was now a sufficient amount of material to allow serious attempts at deciphering the Linear B tablets. Even so, the tablets presented an enormous challenge. The script was totally unlike any of the other writing systems in use among the Late Bronze Age civilizations, and no one knew what the underlying language was. Relatively little progress was made until the early 1950s, when a brilliant British amateur linguist and cryptologist, **Michael Ventris**, broke the code. Building on the work of earlier scholars such as the American Alice Kober, Ventris worked from the hypotheses that the signs stood for whole syllables rather than single letters and that the language might possibly be Greek (and not Minoan, after all). These hypotheses successfully decoded the phonetic values of some of the signs. For example, a combination of three signs—*ti-ri-po*—yielded the syllabic equivalent of the Greek word *tripous* (tripod).

In 1953 Ventris and his collaborator, John Chadwick of Cambridge *University, jointly published their findings in a famous article that completely changed our picture of the Bronze Age Aegean. It is now certain beyond any doubt that (1) Greek was the language of the Mycenaeans, (2) the Mycenaeans had adapted the Cretan Linear A script to their own Greek language for the same purpose as the Minoans had, to keep palace records, and (3) Mycenaeans were ruling in Crete by at least the fifteenth century BC.

Under the rule of the already Minoanized usurpers, however, Cretan society and culture did not change much. For the mass of the people, life went on as before, although they now paid their taxes to kings who spoke Greek. And the new kings ruled and lived much in the manner of Minoan kings, although they did adhere to certain mainland ways (in burial rites, for example). From the fifteenth century onward, we can speak of a Minoan–Mycenaean society, a dynamic fusion of the two cultures, which was further enriched by continuing influences from the Near East and Egypt.

It is possible that under Mycenaean rule Cnossus controlled much of central and western Crete (an area of perhaps 1,500 square miles), having incorporated the territories of the formerly independent or semi-independent palace centers. But this success was relatively short-lived. Around 1375, Cnossus was burned and looted, and although the ruined palace continued to be occupied, the days of Cnossian hegemony of the island were over, and Mycenaean Crete sank in importance while Mycenae and the other mainland centers reached the zenith of their prosperity and influence in the Aegean. It is not known who destroyed Cnossus and set off the irreversible decline of the entire Cretan economy and culture. The most likely suspects are mainland Mycenaeans, tempted by the riches of the Cretan palaces and perhaps eager to get rid of their biggest rival in the Mediterranean trade.

THE YEARS OF GLORY (C. 1400–1200 BC)

Mycenaean civilization reached its peak in the final centuries of the Late Bronze Age. Imposing palaces were built throughout southern and central Greece, reaching as far north as Iolcus in Thessaly. Archaeologists have counted over fifteen; undoubtedly there were more. As in Crete, the palace complexes were the administrative, economic, and religious centers of small principalities. We could call them city-states, except that unlike Crete, where palace and town were integrated into an urban whole, Mycenaean palaces were walled off from the relatively small settlements below. The territories of these mini-states seldom exceeded 400 square miles; the largest—whose center, fortunately, is the best preserved—was Pylos, covering an area of around 1,250 square miles.

The Greeks were living in heady times. From 1500 to 1200, Egypt, the Near East, and the Aegean were integrated in an international nexus of diplomacy, shifting alliances, wars, trade, and cultural transmission. Empires were created, flourished, and fell apart, as new ones took their place. Besides the huge territorial state (New Kingdom Egypt, the ever-expanding empire of the **Hittites** in Anatolia, Babylonia in southern Mesopotamia, and the Assyrians in the north), there were the city-states in Syria and Palestine, which lived as dependencies of one or another of the great powers. The Greeks were players in international politics, but rather minor ones, off on the periphery—which was to their advantage, since they could deal with the East without getting enmeshed in its squabbles. In the eyes of the great powers, Crete, the islands, and Greece were useful, but not worth going after. Aside from the inevitable interstate quarrels, Mycenaean Greece was probably relatively peaceful and prosperous, well populated but not overpopulated (the population of Mycenae itself probably did not exceed 6,400 persons), and better situated than the East to take advantage of the lucrative trade with the growing civilizations of the West. At the end of the thirteenth century, the Greeks, rulers and ruled alike, could look forward to an even rosier future.

Palace Architecture

The decorative features of the Mycenaean palaces closely followed the Minoan styles; architecturally and in other respects, however, they were notably different. For one, the Mycenaean centers were much smaller and less well built, and, unlike the Cretan palaces, were usually located on a commanding hill and fortified by high, thick walls. Even in their ruined state, the encircling walls of Mycenae and Tiryns are an impressive sight still today. Later Greeks called the massive rough stone masonry used in parts of these walls Cyclopean, believing that only the mythical primitive race of giant Cyclopes could have cut and moved these massive blocks. The fortifications were well engineered, taking full advantage of the natural slopes, with refinements that allowed defenders to fire down on two sides at attackers storming the gates (see Figure 1.9c). Such costly defense works were obviously not built just for show, although clearly they also served to awe foe and people alike with the might of the king on the hill. In addition, the Mycenaeans accomplished other impressive feats of engineering, including a complex of roads connecting several of the palatial centers, the draining of the enormous Lake Copais in Boeotia, and an elaborate anti-silting design for the harbor at Pylos.

The Mycenaeans utilized space within their palaces differently from the Minoans. In place of the open paved courtyard of the Cretan complexes, they made the *megaron* the focus of their palaces—a large rectangular hall with a smaller anteroom, and a portico in the front, opening onto a courtyard. The megaron is the distinctive characteristic of many palaces on the mainland. In the middle of the great hall stood a large, raised circular hearth, flanked by four columns that supported a balcony; a kind of chimney was built into the roof above the hearth to draw off the smoke. The megaron was clearly the ceremonial center of the palace, used for feasts, councils, and receptions of visitors. The megaron—without the balcony—hearkens back to Sesklo and Dimini in late Neolithic times. In essence, this central structure, where the king had his throne, was a monumental version of the ordinary house. The great megaron room would survive as the chieftain's house during the long Dark Age that followed, and as the basic plan of the Greek temple, the god's house, from the eighth century onward.

The Mycenaean palaces resembled their Minoan counterparts most in embellishments, such as the use of cut stone, the Minoan column shape, and plastered walls with brightly colored frescoes. It would be an exaggeration, however, to say that the Mycenaean palaces measured up to the Minoan palaces in luxury, refinement, and beauty. Mycenaean painting, moreover, demonstrates a distinctly un-Minoan preference for martial themes, such as personal combat, sieges, and hunting scenes. Also, women and men are usually shown wearing the traditional Minoan attire, but other depictions, as on painted vases, reveal that mainland men normally wore a loose woolen or linen tunic, cinched by a belt, and women wore a longer version of the same tunic.

Relations Among the Palace-States

Were the palace-states ever coerced into forming a single kingdom, subject to a single ruler, presumably the king—called the *wanax* in Linear B—of Mycenae? Most experts today think not. Rather, the strong fortifications and the prominence

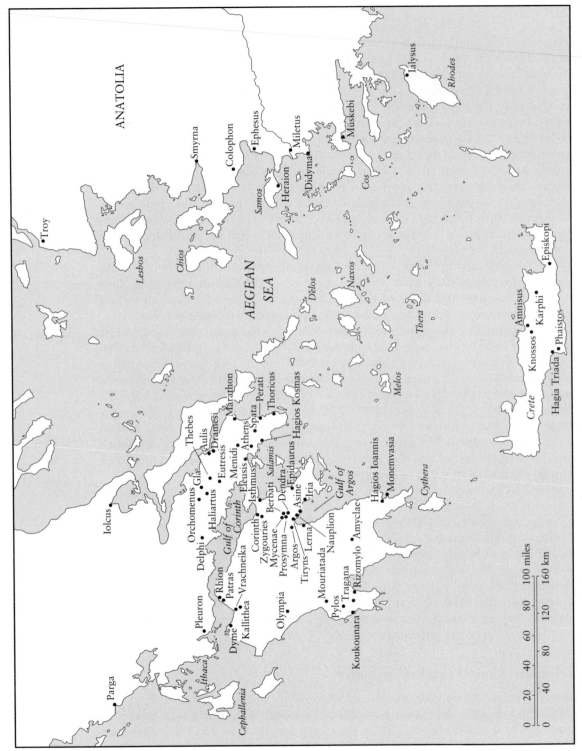

Figure 1.10a. Mycenaean sites in the thirteenth century BC.

Figure 1.10b. View of the ruins of the *megaron* hall of the Mycenaean palace at Pylos, thirteenth century BC.

Figure 1.10c. The "Lion Gate" entrance to the citadel of Mycenae.

of weapons in graves and of military motifs in art make it highly likely that rival states sought dominance and that feuds, fragile alliances, broken truces, and pitched battles were commonplace. Archaeology reveals very few examples, however, of all-out warfare. Particularly ambiguous is the political situation in Argolis on the Peloponnesus. It held ten important towns, including the impregnable fortresses of Mycenae and Tiryns, only a few miles apart. It is possible that the king of Mycenae was the sole ruler of the region, just as the king of Pylos was of Messenia. In that case, we should see the palace at Tiryns as an adjunct of the palace at Mycenae. We must not assume, however, that all Mycenaean kingdoms were structured alike. It is equally possible that Tiryns and the other strongholds were semi-independent polities, whose leaders recognized the ruler of Mycenae as their superior. The palace-towns of Athens and Thebes may have held similar dominant positions in the regions of Attica and Boeotia.

The Mycenaeans in the Wider World

The Mycenaeans' place in the multinational network of exchange has never been in question. In their heyday, around 1300, Mycenaeans were actively trading—and pirating, no doubt—all across the Mediterranean, from Sardinia, southern Italy, and Sicily in the west to Troy down to the Levant and Egypt in the east, and as far as Macedonia in the north. Mycenaean settlements and trading posts were strung along the Asian coastline and throughout the islands, including Rhodes and Cyprus.

For a long time, though, it was uncertain where the Mycenaeans stood in the arena of international politics. This was the time of great empires: a small, close "club" of interacting kingdoms that dominated other kingdoms and ruled them as vassal states. The two greatest of these were Egypt, then at its most expansive, and the Hittite empire, which covered most of Anatolia and Syria. Whether the Greeks were included in the club of great powers has hinged on letters in the Hittite archives referring to a land called **Ahhiyawa**, which phonetically resembles "Achaeans," the most frequent name in the Homeric epics for the Greeks who conquered Troy—an event that, if true, would have occurred in the later thirteenth century.

The Administration of a Mycenaean Kingdom

A memorable figure for readers of the *Iliad* and the *Odyssey* is the aged warrior Nestor, who, Homer tells us, lived in a magnificent many-roomed house in a town called Pylos, from which he ruled over a large area of Messenia. The discovery in 1939 of the "palace of Nestor" by the American archaeologist Carl Blegen further validated Greek folk memory of ancient places and their original names (see Figures 1.6b, 1.10b). As significant as the excavated palace complex itself is the cache of Linear B tablets found in the archive rooms. The sun-dried clay tablets in Pylos, Mycenaean Cnossus, and other centers were not intended to be permanent records. They were preserved only because they were baked hard in the fires that destroyed the palaces. What we have, in fact, are just scribes' short-term notations concerning personnel and production from the final year of a palace's existence. Yet as terse and often puzzling as these documents are, taken all together they reveal much about the administration of the Mycenaean palace centers—which all appear to have operated in much the same manner—during the last two hundred years of the Late Bronze Age.

The large kingdom of Pylos on the western coast of the Peloponnesus was carefully organized. Its territory, containing two hundred or so villages and small towns spread over an area of 1,250 square miles, was divided into two "provinces," each subdivided into several "districts," which were named after each district's principal town. The central authority apparently reached out into each division: the titles *korete* and *prokorete* found on the tablets may have designated the governor of a district and his deputy. A larger group of officials appear on the tablets with the title *qasireu*; these men seem to have been in charge of affairs at the town and village level. Another group has received from modern scholars the name "collectors" or "owners"; these men appear to have been independent to some degree and to have been concerned with acquiring and distributing commodities (flocks, textiles, oils). The correspondence of these titles to specific functions is by no means certain; the duties and rank of other officials named on the tablets are also best guesses, and there are several other titles for members of the palace bureaucracy that defy guessing.

There is more certainty, however, about two figures whose titles are found only in the singular, which indicates that there was only one of each. The **wanax**, who appears in both the Cnossus and Pylos tablets, is, as already mentioned, the king. This title (which is not Indo-European) is used in the Homeric epics as an alternative for the normal word for king (*basileus*). The other sole figure is the *lawagetas*, who occurs second to the wanax in the list of major landholders at Pylos. His title may be translated as "leader of the people," and he may possibly have been the war-leader under the wanax. The numerous guessed-at and unguessable group titles seem to be arranged hierarchically under three headings: administrative officials, military subordinates, and religious administrators, the priests and priestesses.

Figure 1.11a. A Linear B tablet from Mycenaean-ruled Cnossus. In the numbering system it illustrates, circles stand for hundreds, horizontal lines for tens, and vertical lines for units.

Figure 1.11b. Drawing of a chariot tablet from Cnossus recording the assignment of weaponry to a chariot warrior. The tablet, which contains the man's name written in Linear B syllabic signs followed by ideograms for his weapons, may be translated as follows: To Opilimnios 1 corselet 1 wheeled chariot 1 horse.

Social and Economic Relations

The only way to make a centralized production and distribution system work smoothly was to employ very large numbers of persons in specialized administrative tasks. Such a system creates and institutionalizes a sharply defined division between managers and producers; the latter—farmers, herders, artisans, fishermen, laborers—support the former, allowing them more comfortable lives, greater leisure, and higher social status. Exploitation, however, is a matter of perception; in hierarchical societies, inequality is generally normalized. It is impossible for us to know what level of consciousness the exploited masses had of being exploited or (a different story altogether) to what degree they chafed at the inequities of a class society. The best available measurement of actual economic disparity would be the allocation of land, the basic resource. Yet though land tenure figures prominently in the clay tablets, the complex system of "ownership" and distribution is not well understood. It appears that higher officials received land from the wanax in return for their service to the palace; possibly a similar relationship existed between such officials and their subordinates down the line. Tenants would likely have worked those lands. But land tablets also indicate that other non-elite families held plots in their own names. One Pylos tablet reveals that land is owned by the *damos*, the word that in later Greece means "the people," but at this time seems to refer to a village. Apparently then, land may belong to a community.

The markers of class in the Late Bronze Age were highly visible. Interment in tholoi was reserved for the top-ranked, chamber tombs and shaft graves served for the lesser elite, simple cist graves (burials cut out from rock or dug into the earth and lined with rock) for the rest. Houses, furniture, dress, and ornamentation all branded economic and social strata. The highest-ranked officials might have had substantial houses on the citadel itself and lesser officials and ordinary folk in the lower town, but most of the people lived in country villages. On the other hand, there are no Mycenaean equivalents of the comfortable, airy "villas" of late Minoan Crete; Mycenaean upper-class houses were essentially larger, sturdier, and better-furnished versions of the small mud-brick houses of the ordinary villagers. What little the archaeological material tells us about the living standards of the mass of the free population in Greece and Mycenaean Crete—or in the contemporary Near East, for that matter—is that they were much the same as those of their Middle Bronze Age ancestors, who, we observed above, did not enjoy long lives; nor is there any indication in the Linear B tablets that, even though they now lived under the long shadow of the palace, its interference in their lives was all-pervasive.

The truly oppressed probably were the slaves. References to "captives" and "bought" show that the Mycenaean warrior-aristocrats were active in the slavery business. The Pylos tablets record over six hundred slave women, along with their children, who labored as grinders of grain, bath attendants, flax workers, weavers, and so on. The gods and high-ranking individuals also owned slave workers.

The Palace Economy: Manufacture and Trade

The great value of the Linear B tablets is the insight they offer into the actual workings of an ancient redistributive economy whose goal was to keep the kingdom profitable for the palace. What the land furnished—its plants, trees, and animals—had to feed the people, supply infrastructure (roads, bridges, etc.), maintain a military and a fleet, buy raw materials, and cope with nature's vagaries—a delicate balancing act. Hence the need to know, almost daily, what came into the storerooms and workrooms and what was distributed back out as food rations and raw materials to feed and supply palace personnel and workers inside the complex and in villages outside. Oversight was comprehensive. Officials were sent out into the countryside on regular inspections, and the taxes in produce and animals levied on individuals and villages were meticulously recorded. A typical tablet from Cnossus reports: "Men of Lyktos 246.7 units of wheat; men of Tylisos 261 units of wheat; men of Lato 30.5 units of wheat." Similarly, any deficiencies in the assessments were reported. The administrative reach of the palace was truly impressive: one set of Linear B documents at Cnossus, all entered in the handwriting of a single scribe, indicate the monitoring of about 100,000 sheep.

The workshops turned out goods for both domestic consumption and export. A wide array of specialists is listed for the palaces and other locations: carpenters, masons, bronze smiths, goldsmiths, bow makers, armorers, leather workers, perfume makers, and more. Women worked mostly in the textile sector, as carders, spinners, weavers, and embroiderers. The workshop areas of the palace must have been noisy, bustling places with interesting smells. The wanax kept a close eye on the workshops and the storage areas, and his scribes scrupulously wrote down everything that came in and was stored or sent out. Here are representative entries: "one ebony footstool inlaid with figures of men and a lion in ivory"; "to all the gods, one amphora of honey"; "one pair of wheels, bound with bronze, unfit for service."

What was not needed at home was exchanged abroad. The palace exported native products and goods manufactured from them: olive oil (both plain and perfumed), wine, hides, leather and leather products, textiles, fine pottery, and possibly timber. Other exports were luxury items crafted by Mycenaean artists out of imported materials: copper, tin, bronze, gold, silver, ivory, amber, dyes, spices, and exotic woods. Along with the imports of raw materials came foreign manu-factures and products, luxuries to delight the Mycenaean elite. But the most usual way for rulers to acquire prestigious luxury items was gift exchange, a system that both circulated rare goods and fostered mutual respect and brotherhood. Breaches of the customary reciprocity elicited sharp responses. In a message to a king of Ahhiyawa, a Hittite king complains, "But when [my brother's messenger] arrived at my quarters, he brought me no greeting and he brought me no present."

The huge amount of production in certain industries—textiles, bronze work, perfumed oil—attests to the magnitude of palace trade. The existing tablets give no information about who moved the goods, but a merchant ship that may have had a Mycenaean passenger and was wrecked shortly before 1300 off the southern Anatolian coast was carrying ten tons of copper and one ton each of tin (combined with copper to make bronze) and terebinth resin (used in the manufacture of perfumed oil and incense), together with smaller amounts of glass, raw ivory, and various kinds of finished metal tools. It is perhaps more likely that, as in the Near East, they were conveyed by private merchants spon-sored by the palace, rather than in the wanax's own ships. This brings up another question: Were there secondary or parallel economies independent of the palaces (aside from the obligatory payment of certain dues or taxes)? The answer is cer-tainly yes; the world of agrarian villages in the hinterlands, though probably connected to the rarefied world of the palace and subject to its demands, was to some extent insulated.

Mycenaean Religion

Evidence of Mycenaean Greek religion is virtually nonexistent before 1600 BC, at which point we observe the wholesale adoption of the sacred symbols and cult objects of the Minoans, as well as worship of their female deities. Mycenaean frescoes and gold and silver rings faithfully reproduce Minoan scenes of wor-ship. The mainlanders adopted the entire panoply of Minoan religious symbols: snakes, birds, bulls, stylized bull's horns, and axes with double heads. Although we should probably consider these customs to have been just as integral to the Mycenaeans' religious ceremonies as they were to the Minoans', that does not nec-essarily mean that the two peoples' beliefs and rituals were the same. Mycenaeans and Minoans worshipped in different places, for example: the Minoans in caves, sanctuaries on mountain peaks, and palace shrines, the Mycenaeans mostly in cult centers that were not part of the palace complex itself.

From her prominence in Mycenaean imagery, however, it appears that the "Mother Goddess" was the Aegean divinity most thoroughly assimilated into the Greeks' pantheon. This is understandable; as agropastoralists themselves, the first

Greek-speakers would likely have been particularly receptive to an ancient and powerful deity in charge of crops and animals. In fact, the tablets assign the title *potnia* (lady, or mistress) to some of the female deities, a title that would survive in the Homeric epics as an honorific attached to Olympian goddesses like Hera and Athena. Yet according to the tablets, male gods were almost as numerous and just as important as the female gods in Mycenaean worship, even though images representing male gods were very rare in art. There is no explanation for this curious fact.

Testifying to the antiquity of many of the gods and goddesses of Classical Greece is their presence on tablets from Mycenaean Cnossus and Pylos. The names of around thirty Mycenaean gods and goddesses have been firmly or tentatively identified. Not all of these deities were known in later times, but quite a few bear the names of the major gods of Greek religion: Zeus, Hera, Poseidon, Hermes, Athena, Artemis, Dionysus, and possibly Apollo and Ares, as well as some minor divinities. Zeus, the supreme god of the Olympian religion, is plainly the primordial Indo-European "sky-father," brought in by the earliest Greek-speakers. *Zeus patēr* (Zeus the father) is the same deity as Indic *Dyaus pitā,* both formed from the same Indo-European roots, as are also Latin *Iuppiter* and (without the *patēr* element) Old English *Tiw* (who gives us *Tues*-day). The names of Hera, Poseidon, and Ares also come from Indo-European roots. Conspicuously absent, however, is Demeter, whose role as goddess of crops must have been held by Potnia.

What role did the wanax play? As in Crete, the palace controlled the operations of religion; the tablets underscore just how firm that control was. Scribes meticulously itemized the gifts of land, animals, precious objects, and human labor—value extracted from the people by the palace for the gods, to be used for the maintenance of their sanctuaries and of the priests and priestesses who served them. We may assume that the wanax, like his counterparts everywhere else, was buttressing his right to rule by linking himself to the protecting power of the gods. Nothing in the tablets, in the images, or in the myths about the Heroic Age that have come down to us suggests that the wanax was considered divine himself, either in his lifetime or after death, or that he functioned as a priest-king over a theocratic state.

Warfare

There can be no mistake that the Mycenaean wanax was a warrior-king. Even without direct evidence, we may be sure that the wanax and his military commander (lawagetas) were present on the battlefield and fought alongside their other commanders—just as did the warrior-chiefs in the *Iliad* and the political leaders of the Classical city-states, many of whom were killed in battle. Everything about the palaces shouts war: the ferocious battlements, the paintings of land and sea battles and hunts of wild beasts, the bronze weapons in the graves of the elite, and the massive amount of armaments listed on the tablets.

We may assume also that the palace directed all military operations. Troop movements of "rowers" and "[coastal] watchers" and the disbursements of weapons and rations for the soldiers are all recorded on the tablets. But the actual organization of the military is beyond our knowledge, though it is likely that its units were recruited from all over the kingdom. Nor do we know anything about formations and tactics; however, vase paintings, frescoes, seal rings, the tablets, and extant artifacts tell us much about weapons, armor, and ornaments. Mycenaean warriors were heavily armored. The officers, who were more elaborately equipped than the common soldiers, wore helmets of bronze or boars' tusks, corselets made of bronze plates, and bronze greaves (knee and shin protectors) (Figure 1.12a). The soldiers were protected by leather helmets and padded linen chest guards. All the combatants carried large shields made of ox hide stretched over a wooden frame. Weapons were bronze swords and daggers; heavy, bronze-tipped thrusting spears and light throwing spears; bows and arrows; and slings.

The most impressive weapon of all, however, was the battle chariot. Invented in the early second millennium (just where is uncertain), the chariot was a lightweight platform set atop two high, spoked wheels and pulled by two horses; it could carry two passengers for many miles at a pace previously unknown on land. At first the chariot was used by the nobility only for speedy communication, hunting, ceremonies, and racing. By the seventeenth century, it had been adapted for warfare and was deployed in large numbers for massed

Figure 1.12a. Bronze plate armor and boar's-tusk helmet from Dendra in Argolis (c. 1400 BC). Nauplion, Museum.

chariot charges against an enemy's chariots and infantry, one man driving and the other shooting arrows. Chariots had become the main weapon of war among the armies of Egypt and the Near East before appearing in Greece around 1600 BC. From the very first, the Mycenaeans used them in battle as well as for a whole range of peaceful purposes. A question that still puzzles scholars is whether the chariot's deployment was confined to conveying heavily armored elite warriors to and from the fighting—which is almost the sole function ascribed to it in the eighth-century Homeric epics—or whether the chariot corps was the mainstay of Mycenaean warfare, as in Egypt and the kingdoms of the Near East. Some argue

Figure 1.12b. Vase from thirteenth-century Mycenae, showing a line of ordinary soldiers on the march, armed with helmets, shields, and long spears, and a mourning woman who watches their departure. Athens, National Archaeological Museum.

that a mass formation of chariots charging across the broken terrain of Greece is just not feasible, whereas such a tactic was well suited to the vast stretches of flatland in the East. For others, the huge expenditures of labor and material put into making chariots, not to mention raising and feeding horses and training and outfitting charioteers—abundantly recorded in the tablets—would make sense only if the chariot arm was the main fighting force. It is, in fact, conceivable that mini-versions of eastern-style chariot warfare took place on the plains that lay below the Mycenaean fortresses. The wanax of Cnossus had a corps of perhaps two hundred chariots, and Pylos may have had nearly as many. These are few compared with the thirty-five hundred Hittite chariots the pharaoh Rameses II (1298–1232 BC) claimed to have defeated in a single battle, but they fit the small scale of the Mycenaean kingdoms.

THE END OF THE MYCENAEAN CIVILIZATION

At the apparent height of its prosperity, the Mycenaean civilization suffered a fatal blow. Beginning a little before 1200 BC, the palaces, still rich, still functioning normally, were consumed by fire one by one. During the period of initial destruction—less than two generations—many towns and villages were also either razed or abandoned. The devastation began a rapid downward spiral so severe that by the end of the twelfth century the palace system had effectively vanished; the Mycenaean kingdoms no longer existed. Order gave way to turbulence and restless wanderings. Many centers, Pylos among them, were never reoccupied after the initial devastation; others recovered and even enjoyed a brief resurgence, but soon succumbed to further attacks. The ruined citadel of Tiryns was left forever vacant, but the lower town grew considerably in size and population in the twelfth century. Some inhabitants, at least, still lived prosperously, and perhaps even some sort of centralized control was retained. Yet by about 1100, Tiryns, like other mainland sites that had retained or gained some of their old vitality, was beginning to empty out, and like Mycenae, lived on as a small village huddled beneath the ruined fortifications of its once mighty palace. Athens suffered a similar fate. Though it was one of the very few centers that had escaped destruction, it nevertheless was greatly reduced in population. The thousands who abandoned their towns dispersed in all directions, some to other parts of the mainland such as eastern Attica, Messenia, and Achaea; others to the Cycladic islands and the island of Cephallenia in the west; and others in great numbers to far-off Cyprus. In Crete, many moved out of their coastal towns up into the mountains, where they established refugee villages.

The Mycenaean Collapse in Context

The Greeks were not alone in their calamities. In the decades around 1200, the entire eastern Mediterranean region was overwhelmed by turmoil that was felt even in the west, in Italy, Sicily, and the adjacent islands. The vast Hittite empire fell apart; its capital, Hattusas, was destroyed, as well as many of the cities and towns in Anatolia and Syria. The invaders were apparently nomadic tribes from north and east of Anatolia. Bands of marauders also came from all over the Mediterranean; Egyptian inscriptions call them "[men from] the northern lands" and "[peoples of] the countries of the sea." Led by Libyans, these "sea peoples" attacked Egypt in 1208 and three more times in the early twelfth century. They were repelled, though at great cost. The Kingdom of Egypt survived, although it never fully recovered its former power. Inscriptions on Rameses III's mortuary temple boasting of his "victories" over the Sea Peoples record these enemies' names. Unfortunately, after 150 years scholars are still arguing over just who they were. Among those listed are Ekwesh, whom some have identified as Homer's Achaeans, that is, the Mycenaean Greeks. This particular identification may or may not be correct, but it is commonly believed that Mycenaean Greeks were among the Sea Peoples. Another casualty of the times was the city-state of Troy, besieged and burned between about 1250 and 1200. Here too, the Mycenaean Greeks are implicated as the sackers, according to the legend of the Trojan War, although the archaeological record does not allow us to know whether that is true.

The Mycenaean Collapse: Who, What, and Why?

We cannot say with any certainty what or who destroyed the Mycenaean palaces; neither can we know why the Mycenaean civilization itself disappeared after the destructions of the palaces. We can say with some certainty that the destructions and the subsequent collapse of the Greek system of palaces were somehow connected to the catastrophes that plagued the eastern Mediterranean at the same time. Many causes have been proposed. Some hypothesize that the palace centers fell to marauders—the Sea Peoples, perhaps—or to migrating invaders, the Greek-speaking "Dorians" from the northern and western fringes of Greece who, according to legends, had returned to southern Greece to reclaim the lands from which they had been exiled many generations before. Some propose that the destructions resulted from internal causes—natural disasters, such as massive earthquakes or floods—or man-made catastrophes, such as wars among the kingdoms, resulting in mutual annihilation, or else revolts of the Mycenaean peasants and slaves, rising up against their oppressive masters. Others speculate that years of drought or depletion of arable land through overuse or other unwise farming practices eroded the centralized authority, making the palaces vulnerable to attacks from within or without.

Archaeologists have discerned early signs of trouble around 1250: manufacture and exports of luxury goods appear to have tailed off, and the technical and artistic quality of fine pottery diminished. These may be indications of a faltering economy. Some see hints of anxiety concerning the threat of attack. Mycenae and Tiryns, the only two centers that survived as late as 1100, considerably strengthened their circuit walls at this time, and new measures were taken to ensure water supply within the citadels. Of course, the significance of such "signs" may be based on retrospect; strengthening walls and improving infrastructure can also be a sign of power and wealth.

Any of these posited causes is plausible as a factor contributing to the destructions, yet no one of them alone can account for the complete and total dissolution of the Mycenaean palace-states. Since no single cause could have had such widespread and profound effects, many have explained the breakdown in terms of a web of negative socioeconomic agents, which together brought about a disequilibrium that disabled the "subsystems" of the entire palace system (its various spheres of activity, such as trade, agricultural production, metallurgy, and the crafting of artifacts). Marauding bands of "sea peoples" could have provided one catalyst by obstructing sea trade in the eastern Mediterranean, which in turn could have cut off the supply of tin and copper for bronze production. If external trade ceased, not only goods but social contacts too would be lost, preventing the exchange of ideas as well as objects. For example, a natural disaster such as a prolonged drought could have put pressure on the food-distribution subsystem, which may have already been undermined by the inefficiency of the top-heavy palace bureaucracies. Any combination of bad news could have been too much for the ponderous bureaucracies to rectify. And as one area of the governmental system faltered, other areas were affected, until the entire ruling structure broke down and became easy prey for attackers.

><del>≫</del>———<del>≪</del><

From the New Stone Age until the Late Bronze Age, Greece was a stateless society of farmers and shepherds led by local chieftains, while the civilizations of the East emerged and became mighty. Propelled by outside contact, especially with Crete, Greece made a sudden leap into civilization and incipient statehood around 1600 BC. The Mycenaean states reached their height of power and sophistication around 1300. For a brief period, they were an important presence in the eastern Mediterranean and attained a level of economic power approaching that of the older civilizations. Then, around 1200, the Mycenaean civilization began to disintegrate and by 1100 had fallen apart completely.

With the destruction of the palaces, the Near Eastern type of social and economic organization would disappear forever from Greece. In Egypt and the Near East, however, which also suffered severe shocks in the late thirteenth century, the ancient pattern of highly centralized, rigidly hierarchical, monarchical states continued. This is perhaps an indication that underneath the veneer of great wealth and stability, the Mycenaean economy and government were essentially fragile systems.

We will probably never know for certain why the Mycenaean civilization ended so abruptly and with such finality. This we do know: with the end of the first stage of Greek civilization came the beginning of a new era, so different that the Greeks, when they looked back upon their past (that is, the Late Bronze Age), could only imagine it as a kind of mythical dream world, a time when gods and humans mingled together.

KEY TERMS

Ahhiyawa	Indo-European languages	Mycenae
Arthur Evans	Lerna	Mycenaean civilization
Bronze Age	Linear A	Pylos
central court	Linear B	shaft graves
Cnossus	Mediterranean climate	Thera
domestication	Mediterranean triad	tholos
Franchthi Cave	megaron	wanax
Heinrich Schliemann	Michael Ventris	
Hittites	Minoan civilization	

SUGGESTED READINGS

Barber, Elizabeth Wayland. 1994. *Women's Work: The First 20,000 Years. Women, Cloth, and Society in Early Times.* New York and London: W. W. Norton. The history of textile manufacture as women's work and art from the Paleolithic through the Iron Age, including weaving techniques and myths about weaving. A major study of women's principal contribution to the ancient economy.

Chadwick, John. 1967. *The Decipherment of Linear B*. 2nd ed. Cambridge: Cambridge University Press. The story of how the Linear B tablets were deciphered, told by one of the principal investigators.

———. *The Mycenaean World*. 1976. Cambridge: Cambridge University Press. A lavishly illustrated description of the workings of the palace societies of Mycenaean Greece, with emphasis on the Kingdom of Pylos.

Castleden, Rodney. 1993. *Minoans: Life in Bronze Age Crete*. London: Routledge. Written for the non-specialist, the book recreates the society and culture of the Cretan civilization.

Davis, Jack L., ed. 1998. *Sandy Pylos: An Archaeological History from Nestor to Navarino*. Austin: University of Texas Press. Excellent introduction to the history of Pylos and the history of its excavation.

Dickinson, Oliver. 1994. *The Aegean Bronze Age*. Cambridge: Cambridge University Press. A scholarly, but accessible, survey of all aspects of the prehistoric Aegean cultures from the Early Bronze Age to the collapse of Mycenaean civilization.

Drews, Robert. 1993. *The End of the Bronze Age: Changes in Warfare and the Catastrophe ca. 1200 B.C.* Princeton, NJ: Princeton University Press. An overview and detailed analysis of late-twentieth-century theories of the fall of the great civilizations of the Late Bronze Age.

Duhoux, Yves, and Anna Morpurgo Davies, eds. 2008. *A Companion to Linear B: Mycenaean Greek Texts and Their World*. Vol. 1. Louvain-la-Neuve: Peeters. Up-to-date contributions by top-notch scholars on various aspects of the Mycenaean world, using the Linear B tablets as their starting point.

Finkelberg, Margalit. 2005. *Greeks and Pre-Greeks: Aegean Prehistory and Greek Heroic Tradition*. Cambridge: Cambridge University Press. Brilliant analysis of the evidence for Bronze Age society in Greek legends and myths.

Fitton, Lesley J. 1996. *The Discovery of the Greek Bronze Age*. Cambridge, MA: Harvard University Press. A sparkling survey of the pioneering excavators, their excavations, and the controversies that swirled around their discoveries of Bronze Age Aegean cultures.

Friedrich, Walter L. 2000. *Fire in the Sea, the Santorini Volcano: Natural History and the Legend of Atlantis*, translated by Alexander R. McBirney. Cambridge: Cambridge University Press. A lucid, beautifully illustrated account of the geology and archaeology of the island of Santorini.

Preziosi, Donald, and Louise A. Hitchcock. 1999. *Aegean Art and Architecture* (Oxford History of Art). Oxford: Oxford University Press. A comprehensive introduction to the art and architecture of Greece, Crete, and the Cycladic islands from 3300 to 1000 BC.

Shelmerdine, Cynthia W. ed. 2008. *The Cambridge Companion to the Aegean Bronze Age*. Cambridge: Cambridge University. Lucid essays by leading scholars on all aspects of the Aegean Bronze Age.

van Andel, Tjeerd, and Curtis Runnels. 1987. *Beyond the Acropolis: A Rural Greek Past*. Stanford, CA: Stanford University Press. A description of the topography, flora and fauna, and subsistence strategies of ancient Greek farming life.

CHAPTER TWO

The "Dark Age" of Greece and the Eighth-Century "Renaissance" (c. 1200–750/700 BC)

The archaeological remains from the late twelfth century give the impression that a giant hand had suddenly swept away the splendid Mycenaean civilization, leaving in its wake only isolation and poverty. By 1050 BC, the palace centers were in ruins or uninhabited; so were the scores of once bustling towns and villages across the entire Greek world. The cultural losses were catastrophic and long lasting. For the next 400 years, no monumental stone structures would be built in Greece. The art of writing was forgotten and would not return until the eighth century. Supplies of bronze and other metals dwindled to a trickle as vital trade links were broken. It would be 150 years before Greek craftsmen again turned out objects of gold, silver, and ivory. Nor are the luxury goods and weapons buried with the Mycenaean elite found in the graves of the postdestruction period. By contrast to the brilliant age that had gone before, Greece seemed to have truly descended into a dark age. Yet paradoxically, during those same obscure centuries, a new Greece was rising, radically different from both the old Greece and the other societies of the ancient Mediterranean. The patterns of social and political integration that emerged from the shattered palace-states would set Greece on the path to a new kind of state government, the city-state (polis), which arose in the eighth century BC. The roots of the Greek city-state, considered by many to have been the cradle of western democracy and legal equality, were firmly planted in the **Dark Age**.

SOURCES FOR THE DARK AGE

Historians call this period the Dark Age not so much because of its cultural decline as on account of its archaeological obscurity. The rich material record of the Late Bronze Age turns nearly blank in the eleventh and tenth centuries, and though material finds increase after 900 BC, they are relatively meager until about 700. Even so, the archaeology of this period has made significant progress since the 1960s. A number of new settlements have been discovered. A technique called survey archaeology, in which a team of investigators systematically walks large areas of the terrain, is also providing a picture of the sparsely populated Dark Age countryside. Moreover, the increasing use of the comparative methods of anthropology and sociology to analyze the material evidence has furthered our knowledge of how these societies functioned.

DOCUMENT 2.1

The fifth-century BC Athenian historian Thucydides summarizes the history of the period after the Trojan War.

Even after the Trojan War, Greece continued to undergo migration and colonization and thus lacked the tranquility necessary for growth. The return of the Greeks from Troy after such a long absence resulted in political changes. In general, there was civil strife in the cities, thus creating exiles who founded yet other cities. The present day Boeotians, for example, were forced out of Arne by the Thessalians sixty years after the fall of Troy and founded what is now Boeotia in the former Cadmeian territory. . . . Furthermore, the Dorians, along with the Heraclids, captured the Peloponnese eighty years after the war. After a long time, and, with great difficulty, Greece achieved a secure peace and sent forth not forced migrants any longer, but colonists. The Athenians settled Ionia and most of the islands, whereas the Peloponnesians settled most of Italy and Sicily and places here and there in Greece. All of these colonies were founded after the Trojan War.

The Peloponnesian War 1.12

Ancient Greeks, however, knew nothing about a "Dark Age." Instead, Greek writers such as the fifth-century BC historian Thucydides believed that a period of turmoil followed the Trojan War. Otherwise there was no sharp break between the era of the heroic kingdoms and their own times. The collapse of Mycenaean civilization and the end of the Bronze Age left no mark on Greek folk memory. Nevertheless, later literary sources, such as the passage by Thucydides quoted in Document 2.1, preserve stories about the "Dark Age" that were the product of a rich, centuries-long oral tradition. Not only were these ancient stories preserved, but they were also altered as conditions changed and as new motifs—primarily from the Near East—filtered into Dark Age culture.

This vigorous and supple tradition of storytelling comes alive for us in the earliest Greek literature, the *Iliad* and the *Odyssey*, which were set down in writing in the eighth to early seventh centuries BC, and **Hesiod**'s *Theogony* and *Works and Days*, committed to writing a little before or a little after 700 BC. The *Iliad* and *Odyssey* are fictional constructs. They were not produced for historical purposes, nor were they intended to serve as guides for reconstructing any period of Greek history. Understandably, therefore, their value as sources for Greek history is controversial.

The problem is that while the two epics are set during the Trojan War and its aftermath and hence describe events that, if they really happened, took place in the thirteenth century, the poems themselves were first written down more than 500 years later. During their innumerable retellings, both the events and their social contexts underwent radical transformations so that we view the behavior of the larger-than-life heroes of the *Iliad* and *Odyssey* from multiple temporal perspectives, as though they were characters in historical novels. An analogy would be Sir Walter Scott's novel *Ivanhoe,* which is set in twelfth-century England but was composed in England in 1819. Reading it during the twenty-first century, we get a glimpse of a nineteenth-century view of the 1100s, a view that was nostalgic already in its own time.

For this reason, some scholars contend that the **Homeric epics** are historically useless, amalgams of bits of real and imagined material that cannot be separated. Yet the poems seem to presuppose that the customs, institutions, and values depicted in them are familiar to contemporary audiences without anyone's explaining the rules. As will be shown later, this authorial point of view suggests that the social usages Homer describes could not have been merely frozen memories of centuries past, but were rather a simplified representation of a fairly consistent society, namely, that of the late "Dark Age," around the eighth century BC. Even if the men Homer called Achilles and Odysseus never lived, the society in which he placed them was a real one.

Unlike the *Iliad* and the *Odyssey*, Hesiod's *Works and Days* is firmly located in the poet's own time and place, and tells of ordinary people. Hesiod was also the first to have composed under his own name, using the personal voice represented by "I." In *Works and Days*, Hesiod purports to give advice about farming and sailing; he tells of his dispute with his brother, Perses, and of his relations with the inhabitants of the Boeotian towns of Ascra and Thespiae. This poem was traditionally accepted as autobiographical and more viable as a historical source than Homer's narratives, but most scholars now maintain that Hesiod has adopted a literary persona and that the details he provides about his own life are fictitious. But whether "Hesiod" was a real person and was divulging his own biography matters little; no one doubts that *Works and Days* offers a wealth of information about rural life around 700 BC. Hesiod's other long epic, the *Theogony*, narrates the "birth of the gods," just as its title suggests. In it are the genealogies of about three hundred divinities, including personified abstractions, such as Earth, Sea, and Sky. The series of myths that deals with the events leading up to the kingship of

Zeus is closely related to stories preserved in cuneiform tablets dating to the second millennium BC and found at the Hittite capital of Hattusas in central Turkey, clear evidence that mythical traditions and legends originating in the civilizations of the ancient Near East were known in Greece during the Dark Age.

DECLINE AND RECOVERY (C. 1200–900 BC)

The low point of the Dark Age was reached in the two centuries after 1200 BC. Archaeological evidence indicates that all across the Greek world towns and villages were left abandoned, their inhabitants either dead or gone to other places, some as close as Achaea and Arcadia to the north, some as far away as the Cyclades, and others across the sea to Palestine and **Cyprus**. While movements and dislocations of people can create an exaggerated impression of overall depopulation, the evidence suggests that in the two centuries following 1200, mainland Greece emptied out far more than it filled up. By 1050 BC, Greece's population was probably the lowest in a thousand years. Some scholars estimate that by 1050 the population of Greece may have been as little as 30 percent of what it had been in 1200. Even at the nadir of the Dark Age, however, the break between the Bronze and Iron Ages was not as complete as scholars once thought. Despite the disappearance of the palaces and their sophisticated elite culture, continuity with many aspects of the Mycenaean past continued.

Continuity

What survived the transition of the Mycenaean world to the Dark Age and what was lost? For those who remained in Greece, life was simpler than it had been during the palace period, but that does not mean that Greece lapsed into a primitive state. The people primarily affected by the disappearance of the palaces were their staffs and dependents, who relied for their support on the redistributive system with its allotments and exactions, and the craftsmen and other specialists who serviced them. Outside that narrow circle, farmers continued to farm, growing the same crops they had always grown; herders tended their flocks as before; women spun and wove their wool and flax. Potters, metalworkers, and carpenters still practiced their crafts (although at a lower level of skill and refinement), and the people kept worshipping their gods and performing religious rituals. In short, the timeless rhythm and activities of the agricultural year and the daily activities of the farming village remained unchanged, and would remain constant over the following centuries. Most important, people continued to speak Greek and poets continued to tell stories of the Mycenaean past.

Equally important, cultural development was never completely stagnant. At the very time when material culture in Greece appears to have reached its nadir—the late eleventh century BC—Greek smiths mastered the latest techniques for smelting and working **iron**. Iron was far more difficult to process than bronze, requiring furnaces that reached far higher temperatures than those needed to smelt copper and tin ores. The breakdown of the trade networks that had brought copper and especially tin to Greece in the Bronze Age led to the gradual disappearance of bronze and forced Greek craftsmen to master the technology to work the iron ore that was plentiful throughout the eastern Mediterranean.

Although iron artifacts are attested as early as 2000 BC, iron was long regarded as a rare and precious commodity, used only for luxury items, such as rings. Intentional smelting of iron ore appears to have occurred only around 1200–1150, and metalworkers (in Anatolia or the Levant or Cyprus) made the technological improvements required for the multistage process of producing quality iron (hard and unbending) in quantity. Iron weapons and tools were harder and kept their edge better than bronze implements. By 950, almost every weapon or tool found in Greek graves is made of iron, not bronze.

Greece, in fact, was ahead of many areas of the Near East in the adoption of advanced iron technology. In Palestine, for example, iron replaced bronze for utilitarian objects only in the later tenth century; the use of iron did not become common in Mesopotamia until the ninth century and even later in Egypt, and in both areas it was reserved for the palaces. That certain regions of Greece made early use of iron technology also indicates that, although trade in goods declined, the lines of communication never completely closed. However great the disruptions caused by the collapse of the centralized government, they did not eradicate the art of seafaring. At no time did carpenters cease to build seaworthy ships or seamen forget their skills and the accumulated lore of the stars, winds, and currents. Only the odd piece of pottery or metal from the Levant, Crete, or Cyprus is found in Greece—and vice versa—but this is not proof of "isolation."

Around 1050, the combination of several new techniques and small inventions produced a superior pottery that was well proportioned and finely decorated. A faster potter's wheel improved the shape of the vases. For the first time, potters were using a compass, to which several brushes were attached, to draw perfect arcs, half-circles, and concentric circles. Lines were drawn with a ruler instead of freehand. New shapes and designs emerged, enhanced by a more lustrous glaze achieved by firing at a higher temperature. This new style, called **Protogeometric** (c. 1050–900), was far superior both technically and aesthetically to the preceding style (Submycenaean, c. 1125–1050); it seems to have originated in Attica, but spread fairly rapidly though many parts of Greece, each locale experimenting with its own style. Indeed, because of its distinctiveness and its easily recognizable regional variations, "Protogeometric" is also used to refer to a period within the Dark Age (c. 1050–900), as is also its mature form, **Geometric** (c. 900–700).

Bridging the Sea

According to legends, Athens played a key role in what is called the **Ionian migration**, which also began around 1050. There was a segment of the Greek people named Ionians, after their eponymous ancestor, Ion (a grandson of Hellen, the ancestor of all the Hellenes). As the story goes, the Ionians fled to Athens to

Figure 2.1. A Late Protogeometric belly-handled amphora (storage jar) (c. 950–900 BC) from the Ceramicus cemetery in Athens with compass-drawn concentric circles foreshadowing the Geometric style. Athens, Ceramicus, Oberländer Museum.

escape the northern Dorians, who had expelled the descendants of Ion from their homeland in Achaea. Having been received kindly by the Athenian king, who treated them as kin, they settled in Attica for a while, and then, along with other refugees, migrated to a strip of the Anatolian coast, which they called Ionia. These Ionians established a new community at the old settlement of Mycenaean Miletus, which had been destroyed in the twelfth century. In this case, the archaeological evidence appears to validate the ancient legend of migrations from Athens, one of the few centers that survived the catastrophes of the Late Bronze Age. Other major sites on both the Asian mainland (e.g., Ephesus, Colophon) and the offshore islands (Chios, Samos) were founded between 1050 and 950. That in historical times Ionian Greeks on both sides of the Aegean shared the same dialect, the same tribal names, and the same festivals further confirms the veracity of the ancient legends.

At approximately the same time, Aeolians—Greeks who lived in Thessaly in northern Greece and spoke the Aeolic dialect—established settlements north of the Hermus River in Anatolia. Their earliest settlements were few because of resistance by the Mysians, an Anatolian people who controlled the most fertile stretch of the coastal plain. At some point, perhaps around 900, Dorians—Greeks who lived in the Peloponnesus and spoke the Dorian dialect—migrated to the southern region of coastal Anatolia, settling in the islands of Cos and Rhodes and later the promontories of Caria. There had been a fairly significant Mycenaean presence in Anatolia in the Late Bronze Age, but it was really the migrations of the eleventh and tenth centuries that tied north, central, and southern Greece and the Aegean islands directly to that part of Asia. Coastal Anatolia was becoming part of Greece, the Greeks there were becoming part of the Near East, and the Aegean Sea was destined to become the "Greek Sea."

The Near Eastern "Dark Age" (1200–1000)

As we saw in Chapter 1, destruction and upheaval also gripped the Near East in the late thirteenth and twelfth centuries. The result was the unraveling of the integrated system that had worked so well during the Late Bronze Age. What exactly happened there afterward is unclear because the collapse of the great powers brought with it the almost total disappearance of documentary sources. It is clear, however, that the disruptions were accompanied by numerous large movements, both of internal populations and of new peoples from the north and east, who took advantage of the power vacuum. Whereas in the Late Bronze Age the imperial powers—chiefly Egypt, Hatti (the Hittites), and the newest force, Assyria from northern Mesopotamia—had competed for sovereignty over present-day Syria, Lebanon, Israel, and Jordan, the aftermath of the upheavals took on the character of a free-for-all.

Changes were particularly dramatic in the areas with which the Greeks would later have the most contact. By the late tenth century, Anatolia and the Syro-Palestinian region were divided into a number of small states. In Anatolia, Phrygians and Lydians occupied what had been the western provinces of the Hittite empire, while in Syria neo-Hittite kingdoms and Aramaean tribal states jostled for power. Further south, the city-states of Tyre, Sidon, and Byblos occupied the coast of **Phoenicia**. Even more complex was the situation inland in Canaan, where the Hebrew kingdoms of Israel and Judah competed for power in the interior and the city-states of the coast, which were dominated by the Philistines. Archaeological evidence indicates that the Philistines were the Peleset, one of the Sea Peoples who had immigrated from the Aegean. Their pottery is very close in style to that of the twelfth-century Mycenaeans, and in one of their five city-states archaeologists discovered a large megaron hall, with hearth, along with cultic objects of a Mycenaean type. Within a few generations, however, the Philistines became linguistically and culturally Canaanites. The experience of the Mycenaeans who took refuge in Cyprus was different.

Cyprus, Phoenicia, and the Greeks

The third largest island in the eastern Mediterranean, richly endowed with copper, and a short sail from southern Anatolia, the Levant, and Egypt, Cyprus was destined to be a major center of trade and commerce. In the Late Bronze Age, ships from all ports on the eastern Mediterranean visited Cyprus, lured not only by copper ingots but also by expertly crafted luxury items, which exhibit an amalgam of local, Egyptian, Near Eastern, and Aegean styles. The Cypriot–Aegean connection began early, first with the Minoans in the early second millennium and then with the Mycenaean Greeks. The relationship would remain strong and mutually beneficial. When, around 1500, the Cypriots took to writing their language, the script they adopted was a form of Minoan Linear A, which, with modifications, they would use until almost 300 BC. During the fourteenth and thirteenth centuries BC, a great deal of quality Mycenaean ware was deposited in elite graves. Whether this indicates an actual Mycenaean presence on the island or simply a preference for Greek pottery is uncertain. There is no question, however, that during the twelfth century large numbers of Mycenaeans (as well as many from the Levant) found safe haven in Cyprus, which, though it had suffered its share of destruction, remained internally stable.

Around 1050, a number of new settlements in Cyprus appear that show continuities with the Late Bronze Age, including tombs of Mycenaean types. As far as is known, these new foundations were city-kingdoms, likely patterned on the Mycenaean model. Indeed, the kings bear the Mycenaean title wanax. Thus, for the mixed population of the island, whether "old Cypriots," Greeks, remnants of the Sea Peoples, entrepreneurs from the Levant, or restless wanderers, there was no Dark Age.

Among the twelfth-century immigrants to Cyprus were traders and artisans from Phoenicia, taking advantage of opportunities created by the disappearance of cities such as Ugarit in Syria, which had dominated trade with Cyprus in the Bronze Age. But in the ninth century, as the first in a long series of overseas settlements, Phoenicians from Tyre settled at the Greek city of Citium (modern Larnaca). Nevertheless, this important port city, which was originally founded by Mycenaean refugees, apparently remained predominantly Greek and was ruled by Greek kings until the sixth century BC. We can point to no better example of peaceful cohabitation than the erection, in the late ninth century, of a temple to the Phoenician goddess Astarte on the foundation of a temple that the Mycenaeans had abandoned around 1000.

The Mycenaeans who sought refuge in western Anatolia, the southern Levant, Cyprus, and even Crete at the end of the Bronze Age established new communities that would have long and rich histories. Some of those who remained in the Greek homeland or moved to the Cyclades also enjoyed a brief but unsustainable recovery. Yet it was precisely in those areas, not the new and richer immigrant settlements, that the foundations of Archaic and Classical Greek civilization were laid in the eighth century BC.

THE NEW SOCIETY OF THE DARK AGE

The material remains are extremely sparse for the eleventh and most of the tenth centuries. This has greatly frustrated historians, for it is during this period that the last vestiges of the centralized state system disappear and are succeeded by new sociopolitical structures. It is only around 900, as material evidence increases, that the contours of the new social order emerge, but the processes of transition and transformation remain elusive.

Settlements during the early years of the Dark Age were not numerous and generally small, most of them with only several dozen inhabitants. There were a few exceptions, such as Athens, Argos, Cnossus, and Corinth, which at this time had populations probably in the very low thousands. Verification is not possible, however, because the population areas lie deep under later structures. In the excavated sites, the buildings, mainly houses, were cramped and poorly constructed. Frequently, only a graveyard proves that there had been a settlement nearby. The graves themselves contain very little: a few pots and an occasional iron spearhead, sword, or knife. Personal adornments are sparse, a few long pins or arched safety pins of iron or bronze, bronze or iron finger rings. From 1100 to 900, huge areas of what had been Mycenaean Greece appear to conform to the traditional picture of a depopulated landscape, with a scattering of poor hamlets whose inhabitants had little or no contact with the world beyond and whose horizons were regionally bounded. Nevertheless, at the same time that early Iron Age Greek people were transforming the Mycenaean past into a Heroic Age and had completely forgotten what a centralized redistributive system was and how it functioned, one thing remained fixed in their memory: they had always had kings.

Two types of evidence indicate that the new communities were led by a paramount figure; one is linguistic and one archaeological. In Chapter 1, we mentioned a figure in the Linear B tablets called *qasireu*, who seems to have been a minor official, a sort of mayor or head of a town or village within a Mycenaean kingdom. The Mycenaean title survived into later Greek, transformed into **basileus** in the Greek alphabet. The meaning of the term, however, was modified to suit the changed sociopolitical context. From Homer and Hesiod on (and still today), *basileus* is the word for king. It is reasonable to assume, therefore, that when the palaces and their centralized administrations disappeared, the title, rank, and authority of the *qasireu/basileus* survived, together with the local communities these officials administered. Supporting this assumption is the fact that the Mycenaean term for king, *wanax* (in the form *anax*), also appears in the Homeric epics as an equivalent of *basileus*, but it is applied only to male gods (e.g., Zeus, "anax of men and gods") and to Agamemnon ("anax of men"), the leader of the entire Greek force at Troy.

The archaeological indication of the survival of the idea of monarchic rule is the presence in Dark Age settlements of relatively large apsidal (curved at one end) structures, which have been referred to variously as "chieftains' houses" or "houses of the local basileus." The earliest of these—found in the 1970s and 1980s—are dated to the late eleventh and tenth century. The discoveries made archaeologists reconsider the accepted opinion that large buildings, implying some sort of central coordination on the village level, were not possible in the early Dark Age. Examples of such early chieftains' houses are widespread: far to the north in Thessalonica, at Asine in southern Argolis, at Koukounaries on the island of Paros, and most notably at **Nichoria** in western Messenia and **Lefkandi** in Euboea, two sites that reveal much about the nature and extent of "kingly" power in Dark Age Greece.

Nichoria and Lefkandi

Nichoria in southwestern Peloponnesus was excavated in the 1970s. Originally a large subsidiary town of the kingdom of Pylos, Nichoria was abandoned around 1200; it came back to life about 1075 as a much smaller village-cluster, with a peak population of about two hundred in the early ninth century BC. Dark Age Nichoria was fairly prosperous in a humble way. There was an abundance of good farmland and plenty of open pasture for animals, notably cattle, with forty or fifty families dwelling on a ridge overlooking a plain. At the center of the ridge top, excavators uncovered a large tenth-century building, consisting of a spacious megaron and a small porch (room 2), which they identified as the "village chieftain's house" (Figure 2.2a–b).

A remodeling in the ninth century added another room at the rear (room 3) and a bigger courtyard in front, enlarging the house to an impressive size (52 feet by 23 feet). The chieftain's house probably also functioned as the religious center, and perhaps as a communal storehouse. This where the elders gathered to feast and talk about local affairs. Although much better constructed than the surrounding houses, it had the same shape and was made of the same materials: its floor was packed earth and its walls were of mud brick, supporting a steep thatched roof.

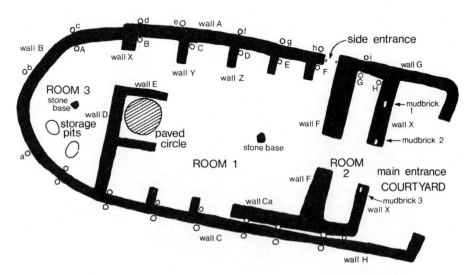

Figure 2.2a. Artist's plan and drawing of the ninth-century "village chieftain's house" at Nichoria.

Clearly, the family that lived there enjoyed very high status in Nichoria itself and in the surrounding countryside. Yet they lived in a style that was not much different from that of their neighbors. In fact, the small, later additions to the front (room 2) and rear (room 3) of the chief's house are the only design differences between it and the other houses in the community (figure 2.2c).

At the opposite end of Greece from Nichoria—at Lefkandi on the island of Euboea—stood a much wealthier settlement that is still yielding up its secrets today. Like Nichoria, Lefkandi had been a bustling Mycenaean town that revived after the collapse of the palace system and prospered during the Dark Age; it was one of the few settlements we know of that maintained nearly continuous contact with the outside world. In 1981, the owner of the highest point

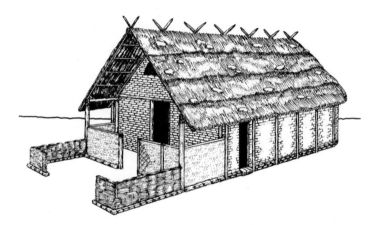

Figure 2.2b. Artist's rendition of Figure 2.2a. Note the small difference between this chief's house and an ordinary house (Figure 2.2c).

Figure 2.2c. Artist's conception of an "ordinary" Dark Age house.

of the Toumba hill applied for a permit to begin to build there. Preliminary emergency excavations indicated an enormous structure; excavators began planning a major discovery. Unfortunately, their plans were not shared with the local bulldozer operator, who on the Feast of Panayia in August cleared nearly the entire building site for the permit-holder. Even this removal of a full third of the structure did not prevent the archaeologists from completing their discovery: the largest Dark Age building yet found (Figure 2.2d). Dated to about 950 BC, the long, narrow structure (160 feet by 30 feet) covered more than twice the area of any contemporary building. Whether this was a chief's house or a communal dwelling akin to the wigwams of the archaic North American native groups is uncertain. But the biggest surprise of all was the discovery of two burial shafts sunk into the building's central room.

In one of the shafts lay two pairs of horses, one on top of the other—reminiscent of the grave offerings given to exceptional warriors during the Late Bronze Age, centuries earlier. The other compartment held the remains of two humans: a cremated man (a warrior) and an inhumed woman, presumably his wife. The man's ashes were well preserved in a large bronze amphora that had been made in Cyprus about a century before the funeral. Next to it lay an iron sword, a spearhead, a razor, and also a whetstone for sharpening the weapons—the toolkit of a fighting man. The horse sacrifices and the costly imports deposited in the couple's grave suggest to some scholars that this man had been a wealthy hereditary chief with Eastern contacts. Others posit that he belonged to an elite "warrior class."

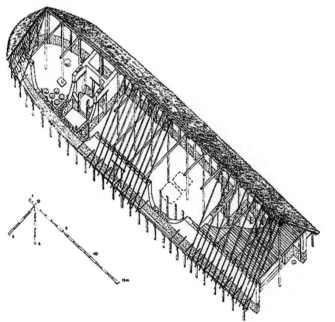

Figure 2.2d. Axiometric reconstruction of the "chief's house" at Lefkandi, showing the grave of the basileus of Lefkandi and his consort (c. 950 BC). This is the largest Dark Age building yet discovered.

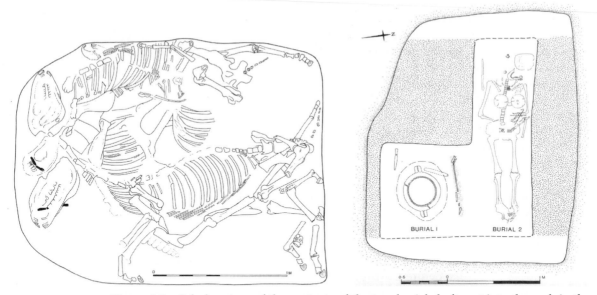

Figure 2.2e. Ink drawings of the contents of the two burial shafts cut into the rock in the center of the "chief's house." On the left, the remains of four horses, some with iron bits in their mouths, sacrificed and thrown headfirst into their pit. On the right, the skeleton of a women elaborately adorned with gilt hair coils, a gold pendant and necklace of gold and faience beads on her neck, gold discs with spiral design on her breasts, an iron knife (suspiciously?) next to her head; to her right are the cremated remains of a warrior in a bronze amphora decorated with hunting scenes.

The woman whose skeleton was found beside the warrior has aroused at least as much curiosity as her spouse. Gold-plated coils flanked her head, broad gold rings decorated her fingers, and her breasts were covered with large disks made of fine gold foil. Around her neck, the excavators found the gold beads and central pendant of an elaborate necklace believed to have been fashioned in the Near East at least 650 years before the time of the burial. This necklace might have been a family heirloom, or it might have been purchased from Near Eastern traders roaming the Aegean Sea. All her adornments reveal that the woman's social status was equal to the man's. But how can we explain the ivory-handled dagger that had been positioned beside her head? Was this woman offered as a sacrifice to the man along with the horses? Or did she die suddenly while attending the funeral rites for her cremated husband? We cannot tell the whole story here; there is no archaeological certainty that she was buried at the same time as the warrior.

Soon after the funeral, the whole building was demolished and covered over with a mound of earth and stones so huge that its construction must have required the labor of the entire community. As soon as the building was filled in, a cemetery sprang up next to the mound, although there were no graves in the immediate vicinity while the building stood. Possibly the burials belonged to kinfolk and followers of the basileus or, as has been suggested, a new ruling nobility that took control of affairs at Lefkandi. In any case, their graves were spectacularly rich, containing an abundance of prestige items such as weapons, jewelry, and bronze vessels imported from all parts of the eastern Mediterranean and beyond, as well as high-quality local and imported pottery, much of it from Athens and northern Greece. Whether the building was the couple's house or the mausoleum of the basileus of Lefkandi, from it and the surrounding cemetery, we see that by the mid-ninth century BC, society at Lefkandi had become stratified, with the basileus and his supporters enjoying access to exotic luxuries and able to mobilize the labor of the community for large-scale projects.

REVIVAL (C. 900–750 BC)

Though social institutions remained constant, the pace of material progress quickened around 900 BC. As usual, vases found in graves provide the main index of change and development. The Protogeometric potters and painters of the tenth century were still very conservative and did not experiment much, but they continued to refine their techniques. However, around 900, as the late Protogeometric style evolves into the **Geometric style**, a new artistic and aesthetic spirit becomes evident. There is no dramatic break with the tradition, and in some regions the old style continues for some time. Nevertheless, a remarkable proliferation of geometric designs marks the Geometric as a distinctly new period.

In the Early Geometric period, the vase makers added new shapes and decorative motifs to their repertoires. The circles and semicircles that had been the staple designs of the Protogeometric vases were largely replaced by more linear and angular motifs, such as the meander pattern (also called the Greek key design), zigzags, triangles, and cross-hatching, set into clearly defined zones and bands. Geometric potters display a growing command of increasingly elaborate linear decoration, gradually filling the entire surface of the vase. The vases become larger and more ambitious, show-off pieces for artists and costly trophies for buyers.

In the early eighth century, the vase painters began to depict living creatures once again, reviving a motif that had virtually disappeared after 1200. At first they drew birds, horses, and other animals, reproducing them cookie-cutter style on the vase. Human figures reappear around 760 to 750, and soon the pictorial elements begin to dominate, until representational drawing takes over most of the surface and geometric design recedes into the background. Late Geometric (c. 750–700) is linked to the past but has unmistakably broken with it. Accordingly, Late Geometric vase painting and other cultural innovations of the "eighth-century renaissance" will be treated later in this chapter.

Other indications of material progress, consistent with the developments in the potter's art, become visible at the beginning of the Geometric period. Ninth-century Greek craftsmen were now producing luxury items like fine gold jewelry and ivory carvings for domestic consumption (see Figure 2.3). This development attests not only to the revival of craft skills and a market for them, but also to a

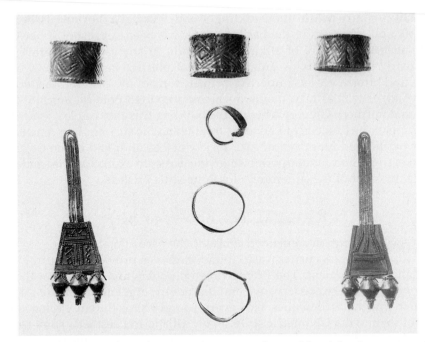

Figure 2.3. Gold jewelry from the cremation grave of a wealthy Athenian woman (c. 850 BC). In addition to the jewelry, she was buried with a number of fine vases, bronze and iron pins, ivory seals, and a faience necklace. (See Plate IIIa.)

renewed availability from abroad of raw materials, including bronze, which begin to appear in larger quantities as a result of increasing trade with the Near East. These domestic luxury items, as well as imported ones, turn up with increasing frequency in ninth- and eighth-century burials. With rare exceptions like Lefkandi, grave goods from before about 900 reveal little disparity in wealth or social status. In the ninth century, it is possible for the first time to speak of "rich" and "ostentatious" graves, although the distinctions of wealth are generally slight until the Late Geometric (c. 750–700).

Houses also were for the most part better built in the ninth century, reflecting the general rise in prosperity. But there were no major changes in building style and materials, and the top families were only a little more comfortably housed than the rest. There are still no certain signs of communal buildings. The earliest of these, the freestanding temple of a god, would not appear until about 800.

HOMER AND ORAL POETRY

The two great epic poems, the *Iliad* and the *Odyssey*, were not produced until the Late Geometric period, but they are introduced here because the texts as we have them are really the culmination of a long oral tradition going back centuries before the eighth century. Epic poems are long narrative tales, told in verse and sung or recited in front of an audience. The Homeric epics are the oldest surviving literature of Europe, though they are quite young compared with the epic poetry of the Near East, which goes back at least to the third millennium BC. Although the later Greeks revered Homer as their first and greatest poet, they knew nothing about him. Tradition had it that he was an Ionian, from Smyrna or Chios; some said that he was blind (Figure 2.4). Widely different dates were given for his lifetime, most of them before 700 BC according to our reckoning of time.

Most scholars of the Homeric poems place their composition between about the later eighth and early seventh century BC. Differences between the two poems have led many to question whether the *Iliad* and the *Odyssey* were the work of a single poet. The method of their composition has also been a matter of controversy. In our own time, as early as the eighteenth century, suspicions had arisen that the poems had been composed orally, and not written down, because so much of the narrative consists of frequently repeated combinations of stock phrases. But the composition of extremely long and complex poems without writing—the *Iliad* is around 16,000 lines and the *Odyssey* 12,000—seemed impossible. A theory thus arose that the poems as we now have them were "stitched" together centuries later, out of short "lays" or "ballads" that told about the deeds of olden heroes. The real authors of the *Iliad* and *Odyssey*, according to this theory, were the generations of

Figure 2.4. Blind Homer. Roman marble copy of the head of a Hellenistic imaginary portrait (c. 200 BC). Boston, Museum of Fine Arts.

anonymous, literate poet-editors who collected, expanded, and elaborated on the traditional oral songs.

A major shift in opinion occurred when it was shown that illiterate poets could in fact compose long poems that had the complexity and stylistic excellence of written poetry. In the early 1930s, a young classical scholar, Milman Parry, and his coworker, Albert Lord, made phonograph records of illiterate Bosnian singer-poets singing a traditional type of south Slavic epic-heroic poetry. Comparing recordings of the same poems—some over ten thousand lines—made at different times, Parry and Lord discovered that no two performances were exactly the same. It turned out that the singer had not learned and memorized his poem, but was rather composing, or, more correctly, "recomposing" it as he went along. This was possible because the story content was traditional and was sung in a highly formalized style.

Parry concluded that the Homeric poems had been created in a similar manner. Homer, he believed, was the greatest in a long succession of singer-poets, who had learned the difficult craft of **oral composition** from the preceding generation of poets, who in turn had learned it from their elders. In retelling the ancient stories, which were familiar to the audiences, Homer drew on an inherited stock of traditional "formulas" (fixed phrases, lines, and blocks of text) and "themes" (typical scenes, story patterns) that he had memorized and could vary as the occasion demanded. Over a lifetime of private recitations, "writing" the poetry in his mind, and public performances and reperformances, Homer crafted and perfected the poems that bore his personal signature. The oral-formulaic theory, as it is called, is now universally accepted and in fact has greatly influenced the worldwide study of other "oral literatures" of the past and present.

On the question of when the Homeric poems were committed to writing, and thus frozen, so to speak, the prevailing view today is that they were written down very near the time of their composition. It was during this time that the art of writing returned to Greece. Lord argued that the illiterate Homer dictated his epics to persons who could write. Other scholars, however, believe that for generations, the poems as we have them were memorized and transmitted orally by professional reciters called "rhapsodes," not to be written down until perhaps as late as the sixth century. Still others maintain that Homer was trained in the oral tradition but had learned to write, and was therefore a writing poet. Whatever the actual role of writing in the final composition of the two great epics, it is agreed that they represent the culmination of a very long oral-epic tradition, which ceased to evolve with the advent of writing.

In the words of one of Parry's Bosnian singers, epic poetry "is the song of the olden time, of the deeds of the great men of old and the heroes over the earth." Such too were the songs that had been sung and resung in Greece continuously since the Bronze Age; in the intervening centuries, stories and themes from the heroic literatures of the ancient Near East also found their way into the slowly evolving Greek oral-epic tradition. For the Greeks of the Dark Age and later, the "olden time" was an age of heroes, a relatively brief period that encompassed a generation or two before, and one generation after, the Trojan War; this, in our dating system, was approximately the thirteenth century BC.

The story of the Trojan War is a classically simple saga. Paris, the son of King Priam of Troy, seduced and brought back to Troy the beautiful Helen, the wife of Menelaus, ruler of the Spartans. To avenge the insult, Menelaus and his brother, Agamemnon, anax (wanax) of Mycenae, gathered a huge army of Achaean warriors, who sailed to Troy and destroyed the city after a ten-year siege. Whether such an expedition actually occurred is unimportant; for the Greeks themselves, the Trojan War was the pivotal event of their early history.

The *Iliad* and the *Odyssey* do not narrate the entire Trojan War. The *Iliad* compresses the action into about forty-five days in the last year of the war, and the *Odyssey* narrates the last forty-two days of the ten-year-long return home of one warrior-chief, Odysseus. The poems assume that the eighth-century audiences knew the rest of the plots and actions. In the seventh and into the sixth century, an "Epic Cycle" of separate, and shorter, poems was constructed around the two great poems, completing the story of Troy. These lesser epics, sometimes attributed to Homer himself, narrated the events leading up to the war, events during the war, including the Sacking of Troy, and the "returns" of other Greek chiefs.

Late Dark Age (Homeric) Society

The nagging question for historians is this: Do the epics tell us anything about actual Greek society, whether of Homer's own day (late eighth or perhaps early seventh century) or of some earlier date? Or are they pure fictions, which have only symbolic meaning? The answer, of course, is somewhere in the middle. The Homeric world was a past world that was in every way bigger, better, and more fantastic than the environment of the poet's contemporary audiences. For instance, Hector, the Trojan leader, picks up a stone to use as a weapon, "which two men, the best in the land, could not easily lift from the ground onto a wagon, men such as mortals are today" (*Iliad* 12.445–449). Such a scene serves the purpose of "epic distancing," which gives the aura of a long-ago heroic society. The poet deliberately leaves out innovations that were known to him, such as the reintroduction of writing. Nevertheless, aspects of that imaginary world—its interests, passions, ideologies, and to some degree its social institutions—must have conformed to audience's real-life experiences. The norms and values of Homeric society are internally consistent and coherent enough to be given a place in the not-so-long-ago past, which we may assign roughly to the end of the Greek Dark Age.

The Homeric Chiefdoms

The geographical and political map of the Homeric world consists of distinct regions and peoples. For example, in the "Catalogue of the Ships" in the *Iliad* (2.484–759), which lists the contingents that made up the Greek army at Troy, the entry for the large region of Aetolia reads:

The Aetolians were led by Andraemon's son,
Thoas. They lived in Pleuron, Olenos, Pylene,

> In seaside Chalcis and rocky Calydon....
> Forty black ships followed Thoas to Troy.
> (*Iliad* 2.638–644; Lombardo)

The official title carried by warrior leaders like Thoas is basileus. As already mentioned, the word survives in the Linear B tablets as the title of a minor local official within a Mycenaean kingdom. Although basileus is routinely translated as "king," in the Homeric society of the *Iliad* and *Odyssey basileis* (plural) clearly are not kings in the sense of monarchs who hold absolute sway over their subjects.

Thoas is the paramount chief in Aetolia, superior in authority to the local chiefs of the villages listed here and the acknowledged leader of all who call themselves Aetolians. Elsewhere in the Iliad he is described as "Thoas, who in the whole of Pleuron and steep Calydon ruled over the Aetolians, and was honored like a god by the people" (*Iliad* 13.216–218). The "people" is the *dēmos* (the root of many English words, such as *demo*-cracy, *demo*-graphics, and epi-*demic*). *Dēmos*, which on the Linear B tablets (in the form *damo*) apparently referred to a village community, signifies, from Homer on, both a territorial unit and the people who live in it. Thus, *dēmos* in this passage indicates both Aetolia, the region, and the Aetolians, the people.

A good-sized demos often contained other chiefs, lower in stature but called by the same title of basileus. These local chiefs, though subordinate to the paramount chief, were essentially independent of him. One indication of the looseness of the power structure is that the paramount chief is called simply basileus, with no other title to distinguish him from the basileis who rank below him. In fact, there are no other official titles of rank in Homer.

Chiefs and Followers

Because epic poetry concentrates almost exclusively on the activities of basileis and their families (largely ignoring the mass of the ordinary people), the *Iliad* and the *Odyssey* provide a fairly detailed description of chieftainship. As is common among **chiefdom** societies everywhere, the office and title of basileus passed from father to son. But inheritance alone was not enough; the young chief also had to be competent to fulfill his role, namely, to lead his people in war and peace. For the successor of the paramount basileus, there is an additional challenge—to secure the compliance of the local chiefs in the demos. A paramount basileus should have the capabilities of a man like Thoas, who was

> by far the best of the Aetolians,
> [And] was not only good with javelin and sword,
> But very few Greeks of his generation
> Could vie with him when the young men debated.
> (*Iliad* 15.282–284; Lombardo)

The two prime requisites of leadership, skill in battle and the ability to persuade, are encapsulated in the advice that the basileus Peleus gives to his young son Achilles as he sends him off to the Trojan War: "Be both a speaker of words and a doer of deeds." Above all, it is the deeds, "the works of war," that make a man the leader. In Homer, as in many chieftain societies worldwide, a chief's status is measured by the number of warriors who follow him. A chief who does not show himself a good warrior will find few who are willing to follow his lead. For example, in the "Catalogue of the Ships," we are told that Nireus, the son of the basileus of the island of Syme, led only three ships to the Trojan War. Although he was the handsomest of the Greeks at Troy (next to Achilles), Nireus was "a weak man, and few people followed him" (*Iliad* 2.671–675). By contrast, Agamemnon was acknowledged as the leader of the entire Greek army at Troy, because, as the commander of one hundred ships from the region around Mycenae, "he led by far the most troops."

All basileis, both local chiefs and the paramount, have their own personal followings. The men who follow a chief are called by him and call each other *hetairoi* ("companions"), a word that conveys a deep feeling of mutual loyalty. Thus the "army" of a demos is composed of several individual bands of hetairoi, each under the command of its own basileus, and all under the command of the paramount. The entire fighting force of the demos, however, is mustered together under the paramount basileus only when there is an all-out war, usually for defense of the demos when an enemy has attacked in force. Otherwise, a local or a paramount chief is free to raise his own following and go on raiding expeditions against villages of another demos, either to even the score in some ongoing quarrel or just to steal or plunder livestock, valuables, and women. Commonly, a chief recruits his followers with a large feast, showing that he is a generous leader and thereby binding his followers to him. For instance, Odysseus (posing as a warrior-leader from Crete) describes how he made a raiding expedition into Egypt. Having fitted out nine ships, he says, he gathered a following:

> I feasted them [*hetairoi*] for six days, giving them
> All the animals they needed for sacrifice—
> Enough for the gods and for their own banquets.
> On the seventh day we set sail for Crete....
> (*Odyssey* 14.248–253; Lombardo)

Heroes express themselves by raiding the livestock of others. Raids not only enrich the raid leader and his men, but also serve as a test of their manliness, skill, and courage, and thus bring honor and glory. Whether on a raid or in a war, the basileus is the one most severely tested, for he is literally the leader, stationing himself "among the front-fighters." The leader is obliged to risk his life fighting at the front of his army (a custom that persisted throughout ancient Greek history). In return for his leadership, the demos is under obligation to provide the basileus with honors and material gifts.

DOCUMENT 2.2

Sarpedon, leader of the Lycian allies of the Trojans, addresses Glaucus, his close hetairos and second in command of the Lycians, on the reciprocal obligations between chiefs and the people.

> Glaucus, you know how you and I
> Have the best of everything in Lycia—
> Seats, cuts of meat, full cups, everybody
> Looking at us like we are gods?
> Not to mention our estates on the Xanthus,
> Fine orchards and riverside wheat fields.
> Well, now we have to take our stand in the front,
> Where all the best men fight, and face the heat of battle,
> So that many an armored Lycian will say,
> "So they're not inglorious after all,
> Our Lycian lords who eat fat sheep
> And drink the sweetest wine. No,
> They're strong, and fight with our best."

Iliad 12.310–321; Lombardo

Reciprocity—mutual and fair exchange—governs all social relationships in the Homeric world and is the core of the leader–people relationship. The giving and the receiving should ideally balance each other. So, too, fairness is the rule in the apportionment of the spoils of war. Following a raid, the booty is gathered together. First the leader takes his share (and something extra as the leader's "prize"), and, under his supervision, special rewards for valor are given out. The rest is then given to the men "to divide up, so that no one may go cheated of an equal share."

A leader who keeps more than he deserves or distributes prizes unfairly risks losing the respect of his followers. To a chief, being called greedy is almost as devastating an insult as being called cowardly. In short, a basileus cannot afford not to appear generous and openhanded. Similarly, Homeric chiefs engage in a constant exchange of gifts and feasts with other chiefs and important men. This is both a way of showing off their wealth and a means to cement friendships, win new friends, and collect obligations through a display of generosity.

Despite the great authority given him by his position, a basileus has limited ability to coerce others to follow his lead. He is only a chief, not a king. Thus, in the *Odyssey*, Odysseus' hetairoi simply refuse to obey him on several occasions. Once, when his followers decide to do exactly the opposite of what he has ordered them to do, Odysseus can only say that as "one man alone" he must abide by the will of the many. Odysseus' helplessness illustrates the fundamental fragility of leadership authority in this type of low-level chieftainship.

Government in the Late Dark Age

Governmental institutions in Homeric society were few and simple. A council, the *boulē*, made up of chiefs and other influential men, met in the great hall (megaron) of the ruling chief to formulate policy for the demos. The leader had the deciding voice in the discussions, but usually he heeded the advice and counsel of the "elders," as the boule members were called (though many were actually younger men). Their deliberations were presented to an assembly of the people, held outdoors in the *agora*, or "place of gathering." Attending were men of fighting age and older; women did not attend. In the Homeric assembly, only men of high rank could bring up a matter for discussion, and although it was within the rules that any member of the demos could speak, rarely did an ordinary man speak out. (See Document 2.3.) The demos made its will known by shouting, muttering, or total silence. The assembly aimed to achieve consensus, both among the leaders and between leaders and people. The council and the assembly would remain the essential organs of government in the later city-states.

DOCUMENT 2.3

By way of illustration of how a basileus was able to coerce his inferiors to be compliant, we offer this passage from the Iliad, *in which Thersites, an ordinary soldier, has spoken out at an assembly. Homer describes him as the "the ugliest soldier at the siege of Troy, bowlegged, walked with a limp, his shoulders slumped over his caved-in chest, and up top scraggly fuzz sprouted on his fuzzy head" (Iliad 2.216–219). His speech in criticism of the paramount Agamemnon is answered by a speech by Odysseus bidding him to keep his words to himself. Then:*

> And with that he whaled the staff down
> On Thersites' back. The man crumpled in pain
> And tears flooded his eyes. A huge bloody welt
> Rose on his back under the gold stave's force.
> And he sat there astounded, drooling with pain
> And wiping away his tears. The troops, forgetting
> Their disappointment, had a good laugh
> At his expense, looking at each other and saying:
> "Oh man! You can't count how many good things
> Odysseus has done for the Greeks, a real leader
> In council and in battle, but this tops them all,
> The way he took that loudmouth out of commission.
> I don't think he'll ever be man enough again
> To rile the commanders with all his insults."

Iliad 2.265–277; Lombardo

Besides being the military and political leader, the leading basileus had a religious and judicial role in the life of the community. His sole, but very important, religious duty was to preside at public sacrifices to the gods. When he prayed to the gods at a sacrifice, he was the spokesman for the people, similar to a father sacrificing on behalf of his family. The basileus was not, however, one of the priests of the gods, nor did he claim to have a special personal relationship with the gods, although Homer firmly emphasizes that Zeus upholds and fosters the ruling authority of the office of basileus.

During the Dark Age, chiefs probably played a lesser role in judicial matters, because the judicial process was in an early stage of development. The only law was custom, that is, the community's traditions regarding right and wrong in particular situations. (A system of formal and written laws would not emerge until the seventh century.) Much of this custom-law involved procedures for settling differences privately. Even the most antisocial act, murder within the demos, was not a crime in the sense that it required arrest and trial of the alleged murderer by the society at large. It was the custom, rather, that the families of the killer and the victim should come to an agreement on a material "penalty" as compensation, thus avoiding a socially destabilizing feud between the families. When the parties could not reach a private agreement, the dispute was brought before a court. Homer describes a dispute over the payment of the murder compensation, which is heard and decided by a group of "elders" (probably chiefs), one of whom will receive a reward of gold for speaking the "straightest judgment." The lawsuit takes place in an assembly, with the people pushing and shoving and shouting encouragement to one party or the other (*Iliad* 18.497–508). The council, assembly, and law court are all there is of government in Homer, but they were sufficient. They would remain the essential organs of government, in a more highly evolved form, in the later city-states.

Foreign Relations

"Diplomatic" relations between one chiefdom and another were conducted by the chiefs themselves or by a trusted companion. As part of his training, Odysseus was sent at a young age to Messenia by his "father and the other elders" on an embassy to collect a "debt" owed to the Ithacans. This was a serious affair, for the Messenians had raided Ithaca and stolen three hundred sheep and their shepherds. If negotiations failed, the Ithacans would stage a revenge raid, and the bad feelings would likely escalate into an all-out war.

While he was in Messenia, young Odysseus stayed at the house of a guest-friend (*xenos;* plural *xenoi*). **Guest-friendship** (*xenia*) was a reciprocal relationship in which xenoi were pledged to offer each other protection, lodging, and assistance whenever one traveled to the other's demos. The relationship was handed down from generation to generation between the families of xenoi. While in Messenia, Odysseus stayed at the house of Ortilochus, an important man in his demos, though not the chief. Many years later, Odysseus' son, Telemachus, would stay overnight with the son of Ortilochus, on his way to visit Menelaus in Sparta and again on his return trip. The hospitality often included a lavish feast and sometimes musical entertainment. At the end of the visit, the host guest-friend gave his xenos a valuable parting gift (e.g., a sword or a gold cup). The gift was the material token of their bond of close friendship, given to ensure that whenever the donor visited the demos of his friend, he would receive in return the same protection, hospitality, and a gift of at least the same worth.

Guest-friendship was an indispensable device for foreign relations in the Dark Age, for a stranger arriving in another demos had no rights and could be mistreated and even killed. The custom was particularly useful in sensitive situations. For example, when Agamemnon and Menelaus made a long visit to Ithaca to persuade Odysseus to join in the expedition against Troy, they did not stay with him but with a guest-friend of Agamemnon's. They used the hospitality of the guest-friend not because they did not have a friendly relationship with Odysseus, but because the delicate task of recruiting foreign allies required a neutral base. As a means of diplomatic relations, the practice of *xenia* persisted, in a somewhat different form, into the second century AD.

Social Values and Ethics

The code of behavior followed by Homeric males is typical of warrior societies. A man is called good (*agathos*) when he exhibits bravery and skill in fighting and athletic contests. He is bad (*kakos*) if he is a coward or useless in battle. A "good man" should honor the gods, keep promises and oaths, and be loyal to friends and fellow warriors. He should exhibit self-control, be hospitable, and respect women and elders. It is proper to show pity even toward captured warriors and to refrain from defiling the corpses of the enemy. These gentler qualities are desirable, but they are not required; a man may be merciless and cruel but still be *agathos*. We will see in the next chapter that by the sixth century the terms *agathos* and *kakos* had taken on political and economic connotations.

Being good at slaughtering and pillaging brings honor and glory, as well as wealth, and so warriors compete with one another in the art of killing. The purpose of this excessive striving is to enhance and preserve one's **timē**, one's value and worth, respect and honor. The spirit of competition permeates every facet of Greek life and is not bounded by class or gender. The highest good is to win and be called the best (*aristos*), whether in spear throwing, running, or chariot racing; in speaking or in displays of cunning; or in weaving or crafting pots. This type of extracompetitive society is called agonistic, from the Greek word *agōn* (contest, struggle). The instinct to compete and win permeates the society. A poor farmer is roused to work hard when he sees his neighbor getting rich, says Hesiod (c. 700); and "potter resents potter and carpenter resents carpenter, and beggar is jealous of beggar and poet of poet" (*Works and Days* 20–26). *Timē* is always public recognition of one's skills and achievements. It always involves some visible mark of respect: the seat of honor and an extra share of meat at a feast, or an additional portion of booty, or valuable prizes and gifts, including land. To modern readers, Homeric warrior-chiefs may appear overly greedy for material things, but their purpose in acquiring and possessing many animals and precious objects was mainly to increase their fame and glory. Not to be honored when honor was due, or, worse, to be dishonored, were unbearable insults. Thus, when Agamemnon in the *Iliad* grievously dishonored Achilles by taking back the captive girl Briseis, a "prize of honor" awarded to Achilles by the army, a great quarrel arose between them that led to disaster for all the Greeks.

Figure 2.5. Bronze statuette of lyre player. A seated bard, or rhapsode, is shown singing while he plays his stringed instrument. For the Greeks, values were reinforced by listening to such singers. Late eighth or early seventh century BC. Heraclion, Archaeological Museum.

Valuations of good and bad in respect to women and the behavior expected of them are determined by the male ethic. Within their communities, women are regarded with great respect by men. There is little trace in epic of the misogyny (from *misogynia*, "hatred of women") that often appears in later Greek literature. In Homer, women are not reviled or treated contemptuously, and also appear to have had more social freedom than those of later periods. Women go freely about the village and countryside and participate in festivals and religious events. And though they have no political voice, women are nevertheless part of "public opinion." The women of high-status households join the company of their husbands and the other men in the great hall after supper and take part in the conversation. The wife of a chief, especially a paramount chief, is held in high esteem and may even partake of her husband's authority, as does Arete, the wife of Alcinous, the basileus of the Phaeacians, in the *Odyssey*. Odysseus, disguised as a wandering beggar, flatters Penelope (who may not recognize him as her husband), saying that her "fame goes up to broad heaven, as of some blameless basileus."

The qualities that define a "good" woman in Homer are narrowly circumscribed by her domestic assignment as housewife and mother. Women are honored for their beauty, skill and diligence in weaving, careful household management, and good practical sense. Like men, women are also compared with one another, though only within the few areas of excellence allowed them; for example, this one or that one "surpassed her age-mates in beauty and work [i.e., weaving] and intelligence." They are expected to act modestly in public and in the company of men, and above all to be chaste. Although men are permitted to have concubines, adulterous women bring great disgrace and dishonor upon themselves and their families.

As in later Greece, women are under the strict control of their male relatives and husbands from birth to death. They are the most valuable prizes of raid and war, not only because of their intrinsic value—as workers or concubines, or as goods to be bartered or given away—but also because capturing an enemy's mother, wife, daughter, or sister is the ultimate insult.

DOCUMENT 2.4

Andromache mourns over the body of her husband Hector, slain by Achilles. Her lament centers on the fate of the helpless women and children.

> White-armed Andromache led the lamentation
> As she cradled the head of her man-slaying Hector:
> "You have died young, husband, and left me
> A widow in the halls. Our son is still an infant,
> Doomed when we bore him. I do not think
> He will ever reach manhood. No, this city
> Will topple and fall first. You were its savior,
> And now you are lost. All the solemn wives
> And children you guarded will go off soon
> In the hollow ships, and I will go with them.
> And you, my son, you will either come with me
> And do menial work for a cruel master,
> Or some Greek will lead you by the hand
> And throw you from a tower, a hideous death,
> Angry because Hector killed his brother,
> Or his father, or son.

Iliad 24.723–737; Lombardo

Slavery

Slavery did not come under the heading of wrong for the Greeks. Enslavement was not even discussed as a moral issue until the late fifth century BC, and even though some expressed repugnance for it, the institution flourished in Greece throughout pagan antiquity and for centuries after the establishment of Christianity. The ancient Greek attitude toward slavery was simple: it was terrible to become a slave but good to own one. Slavery was a by-product of war and raid. One became a slave by being captured or kidnapped—human booty. Greeks did not breed slaves on a large scale, and indeed felt some qualms about enslaving other Greeks (although they did it), preferring to buy and sell non-Greeks. Eumaeus, Odysseus' swineherd, who had been kidnapped as a child by Phoenician traders and sold to Odysseus' father, sums up the degradation of slavery in a sentence: Zeus "takes away half of a man's worth when the day of enslavement comes upon him" (*Odyssey* 17.322–323).

Religion

By the eighth century, Greek religion had attained essentially the form it was to have throughout the rest of pagan antiquity. Yet little else is known about the evolution of religion after the collapse of the Mycenaean society except that some of the gods whose names appear on the Linear B tablets disappeared, and possibly one or two gods were added to the group of major gods. For example, Aphrodite, the Greek goddess of erotic love, may have been a post-Mycenaean import from the Near East, modeled on the Semitic love goddess Astarte/Ishtar, and one of Aphrodite's lovers, Adonis (Semitic *adon*, "lord"), is clearly Near Eastern. In the centuries after 700, the Greeks did adopt or assimilate a few other gods from the Near East and Egypt. There were also important later developments in religious ethics. In all essentials, however, Greek religion would remain for the next thousand years exactly as it was represented in Homer and Hesiod.

The two basic features of Homeric worship go back to the old Mycenaean–Minoan religion. These are **polytheism**, the worship of many gods and goddesses (singular *theos*; plural *theoi*), and the ritual ways of honoring the gods with sacrifices and prayers, processions, music, dancing, and hymn singing. Like the other Mediterranean religions, Greek religion was formal, ritualistic, and communal, not private and meditative. But unlike some, it never developed a uniform set of doctrines or compulsory beliefs. Different and contradictory ideas about the gods coexisted comfortably in Greece, a legacy of the microenvironments that the landscape dictated.

Hesiod's epic poem, the *Theogony* ("the genealogy of the gods"), provided an influential account of the beginnings of the universe and the history of the gods up to the supremacy of Zeus and the other "Olympian" gods. According to Hesiod, the Olympians were a third generation of gods, descended from the primal pair of cosmic divinities Gaea (Earth) and Uranus (Sky). The story closely parallels much older Mesopotamian accounts of the origins of the gods and is clearly influenced by them.

There were violent conflicts between the generations. Uranus would not allow his children to be born, and hid them within their mother, Gaea. Gaea persuaded her imprisoned son Cronus to cut off Uranus' genitals with a sickle, freeing his brothers and sisters, who made up the next generation of gods, the Titans. Cronus, in his turn, tried to eliminate his children by Rhea, his Titan wife, by swallowing them as they were born. But Rhea deceived Cronus into swallowing a stone instead of her last-born, Zeus, and later she used "deep suggestions" to induce Cronus to vomit up the others. Then Zeus, with the help of the mighty thunderbolt and the powerful monster sons of Uranus, led his brothers and sisters in a violent ten-year war against the Titans from their stronghold atop Mount Olympus. Successful in the battle, the Olympians imprisoned the Titans deep in the earth. After overcoming a final challenge by the monster Typhoeus, Olympian Zeus reigned forever over the universe. After their victory, the gods divided up control of the universe. Zeus received command of the heavens and the sky, Poseidon the seas, and Hades the Underworld, where the souls of humans go when they die; all the Olympians shared control of their grandmother Earth and the creatures on Earth, including humans.

The Olympian gods, therefore, were not the creators of the universe, but rather the offspring of three and four generations of sexual unions, beginning with Earth and Sky. As the descendants of the physical universe, the gods embodied the forces of nature; Zeus in effect *was* the sky and all its phenomena. But the Greeks anthropomorphized their deities, portraying them as idealized men and women with special powers to control and direct nature. Thus paintings and statues depict Zeus as a human holding or hurling the thunderbolt. All aspects of nature were endowed with human form; woods, mountains, sea, rivers, and springs were inhabited by countless spirits, imagined as beautiful maidens or youths. Even emotions and behaviors—fear, pity, hate, prayers, rumor, and so on—were all perceived as divinities in human form, who, like the rest of the cosmos, had come into being through procreation.

In their totality, the gods, nature spirits, and abstractions represent the whole of being. The diversity of the supernatural realm offered the Greeks a satisfactory way of ordering and explaining the baffling complexity of human experience, from the vast mysterious universe of stars and planets to the benign and hostile world of nature to the confusing inner world of the human psyche. The divine world mirrors the human condition. So, for example, Ares, the god of war, is the spirit of blood lust that enters a warrior and makes him eager to kill and destroy. Aphrodite, the goddess of love, is the irresistible force of sexual desire. Athena represents the sphere of practical wisdom (weaving, carpentry, metalworking, technology in general), while Apollo's wisdom extends to music, poetry, and philosophy. Artemis, like Athena, is a perpetual virgin, but whereas Athena is a friend and helper of warrior-heroes, Artemis shuns all contact with males and lives in the forests, as both hunter and protector of animals.

In Homer and in Hesiod, these powerful divinities look and think exactly like humans; their actions are just as unpredictable. But they are unbridgeably set apart from mortal beings because of their infinitely superior powers and their immortality and agelessness. Mortals (*hoi thnētoi*, "the ones who die") are playthings of the gods (*hoi athanatoi*, "the deathless ones"), who squabble among themselves over the fate of this or that person or group. The complex intersection of the eternal divine and ephemeral mortality lay at the base of all later Greek philosophical and scientific speculation about the order and structure of the universe and the human condition.

The Greeks worshipped the gods out of awe for their power to do good or harm to people. The gods demanded that their power be acknowledged through gift giving and other marks of respect. Mortals gave these willingly and in abundance because of their fundamental conviction that the gods were disposed to help and protect those who honored them, though realizing at the same time that capricious deities might do just the opposite. Every community had its special protecting god or gods and, in trying to keep their favor, spared no expense or effort in honoring them. After the Dark Age, the Greek city-states would lavish on the gods gifts of public land, huge temples, expensive private dedications, festivals, and thousands of sacrificed animals.

In Homer, the gods insist on their proper honors but not much else. Their concern with morality as we now understand it is limited. Certain acts, such as incest or homicide, were thought to "pollute" the perpetrator, who must be ritually purified before being readmitted into the society. There were also dozens of other minor taboos (such as touching a corpse) that polluted a person for a few hours or days. But most deeds that are condemned by the major modern religions as sins against God, such as stealing, adultery, and rape, were not the concern of the gods. As far as interpersonal behavior is concerned, the gods in Homer primarily condemn only oath breaking and mistreatment of strangers, suppliants, and beggars. Oaths, which were taken in the names of the witnessing gods, were especially important, because they sealed the contracts between individuals and between communities. A few times, however, the gods in Homer do show some concern for fairness and justice within the society. Thus, Zeus is said to send severe wind- and rainstorms against those "who make crooked decrees, using force, in the assembly, and drive out justice, heedless of watchfulness of the gods" (*Iliad* 16.384–388). Beginning with Hesiod, the idea of Zeus as the upholder of justice (*dikē*) would become an increasingly common theme in literature.

In many religions, earthly sorrow and suffering are eased by the promise of a paradise after death for those who have lived righteously. The Greeks did not have this consolation. Their conceptions of a personal afterlife remained vague and undeveloped throughout the Archaic and Classical periods. For most Greeks, existence in any meaningful sense ended when the soul (*psychē*) left the body at the moment of death. There is some punishment of sinners in Hades, but it is reserved for those who have insulted or tried to trick the gods. Later, however, through the influence of mystery cults (such as the worship of Demeter at Eleusis) and of philosophical speculation, ideas of a blissful afterlife for the morally good and eternal torment for the bad would become more highly developed.

Olympian religion was much more concerned with the here and now and propitiation of the gods for special favors through formal rituals. As in the Mycenaean Age, there were special priests and priestesses, who had care of the special prayers and rituals and sacred objects that made up the cult of a god. There was never, however, a professional priestly class or caste, set apart from the rest of the people, as in the Near East and Egypt. Greek priests and seers did not dress or live differently from other citizens; their official duties generally took up very little time and required little in the way of preparation and training. Priests and priestesses came almost exclusively from the upper ranks of society, and a large number of priesthoods were hereditary within a single lineage. Priesthoods increased the prestige of the leading families and thus buttressed their claim to leadership positions, but the office itself held little political authority or opportunity for economic gain.

COMMUNITY, HOUSEHOLD, AND ECONOMY IN THE LATE DARK AGE

In 800 BC, most Greek settlements were still quite small, containing a few dozen families. A handful of major settlements, such as Argos, Athens, Cnossus, Corinth, Lefkandi, and Sparta, probably held several hundred families or more. All the important sites and most of the smaller ones had been continuously occupied since the Bronze Age, for the obvious reason that they were good places for people to live. With their surrounding fields and pastures, they were for the most part economically self-sufficient.

The farmer's life was village life, and so was the herdsman's. The isolated farmstead out in the countryside was rare in early Greece; farmers lived in the villages and walked out each morning to their plots, as they still do today in rural areas of Greece. Greek villages were enduring, close-knit communities. Families lived in them for innumerable generations, intermarrying with other families in the village and in other villages of the demos. The small village may be likened to an extended family, with the village chief as a sort of father. As we have seen, law was customary law; on the whole, concern to avoid public disapproval sufficed to deter antisocial behavior. Difficult disputes were resolved by the chief and the simple court of the village elders. Survival of the village depended upon cooperation among the families, and so they could not afford to let bad feeling between neighbors and relatives destroy the solidarity of the community. Social relationships were somewhat more complex in the larger settlements of several thousand inhabitants, but they were not qualitatively different.

The separate settlements within a territorial demos were likewise linked together by bonds of kinship and interdependence. Villages might quarrel with one another, with the inhabitants even coming to blows, but they were unified against threats from outside. Odysseus describes how he and his men, on their way home from the Trojan War, attacked and pillaged a seacoast town of a people called the Cicones. Instead of sailing off immediately, as Odysseus ordered, the men stayed all night, feasting on the plundered cattle, sheep, and wine. But "in the meantime, the Cicones went and called the other Cicones, who were their neighbors…dwelling inland." The next morning these men from the neighboring villages counterattacked and killed a number of Odysseus' men before they could escape in their ships (*Odyssey* 9.39–61). Inside the boundary formed by the settlements that shared the demos name, a person or family could live and move safely. All the Cicones considered themselves akin to one another, as did Ithacans or Athenians; they all "belonged." Once outside the home territory, one was "in the demos of others," in an alien country, so to speak, where the protection of tribal ties ended and one was a stranger, without rights. The largest social community that a Greek experienced was the demos.

The smallest, and the fundamental, social unit was the household (*oikos*). The oikos, not the individual, was the atom of Greek society. The household was the center of a person's existence; the overriding concern of every member was its preservation, economic independence, and social standing. The primary meaning of *oikos* is house, which to the Greeks signified not only the dwelling itself but also the family, the land, the livestock, and all other property and goods, including slaves.

The ancient Greeks were monogamous, and the core of the oikos was the nuclear family of father, mother, and children. Greek society was patrilineal and patriarchal. The father was supreme in the household by custom and later by law. Descent was through the father, and on his death the property was divided equally among his sons. Although daughters did not inherit directly, they received a share of their parents' wealth as a wedding dowry. A new bride took up residence in the house of her husband; thus their children belonged to the husband's oikos, not to hers.

In Homeric society, the *oikoi* (plural) of the leading families—which are the only ones described—are residentially compact units. The five married sons of Nestor, basileus of the Pylians, continue to reside in the paternal oikos with their wives and children, occupying separate rooms set off from the main dwelling. Moreover, Nestor's married daughters also live in the family compound with their husbands. It is a common practice for a chief or important man to bring his daughter's husband into his household in contradiction of the normal custom. In this way, the daughter's birth family retains her labor, and also gains a man and the children. The clear purpose of these postnuptial residence customs in Dark Age Greece was to maximize the fighting force and the workforce of the oikos. In later times, sons would normally leave the house and set up an oikos of their own after they married, and all daughters would become part of their husband's oikos.

For the elite households of the Dark Age, the aim was to have the largest possible number of members, by birth, marriage, or affiliation. Males of fighting age were especially sought. Telemachus, Odysseus' son, was helpless against his mother's suitors because there were no kinsmen to back him up. As the only son of an only son, he had no brothers, brothers-in-law, uncles, or cousins; in addition, the family's retainers had gone off to war with Odysseus.

All members of an oikos did a share of the work. The sons of basileis tended the flocks and herds, the main wealth of the family, and also did farmwork and other household jobs. Odysseus, Homer tells us, built his and Penelope's bedroom and bed by "himself and no one else." The wives and daughters of basileis worked alongside the women slaves in the tasks of spinning and weaving, the most important domestic activities. The labor input of elite women in cloth production amounted to nearly a full-time occupation. The daughters did other tasks, such as fetching water from the communal fountain or washing clothes by the river. Penelope has a flock of geese that she takes care of personally.

Most of the labor of a wealthy oikos, however, was provided by female and male slaves (either bought or captured), and by hired workers called **thetes** (singular *thēs*), poor free men who did hard work for low pay. Poor free women, usually widows without close kinfolk, also worked for wages, as spinners and weavers or as nursemaids. Homer refers to this category of workers as those who labor "under necessity"; in an important sense poor free persons, male and female, endured a lower standing in society than even slaves, for slaves were considered part of and enjoyed the protection of the oikos, while dependent laborers belonged nowhere and had nowhere to turn for protection. The main economic resource for each of the families in a village or town was its ancestral plot of farmland, called a **klēros** (plural *klēroi*), on which would be located a family's oikos. It is not known how these were originally acquired. Both Homer and early historical sources indicate that in brand-new settlements, such as overseas colonies, the founder basileus distributed the kleroi among the new inhabitants more or less equally. Yet, however fair the original division of land may have been, inequities soon crept in. In Homer some families own "many kleroi," while others in the demos are "lotless men" (*aklēroi*). Although there is no way of determining the percentages of either the land-rich or the landless within the populations, most likely both groups were proportionally small. Before around 750, when land was becoming scarcer, it is highly probable that most families owned a kleros that gave them a sufficient living.

The minority without a kleros had to hire on as thetes, a galling life not only because of the hard work for very little pay (essentially their keep), but also because of the indignity of working for another man's family, a condition that was abhorrent to all Greeks. To express the dismalness of existence in Hades, the ghost of Achilles tells Odysseus, "I would rather work the land as a *thēs*, even for man who had no *klēros*, for a man who had hardly any livelihood, than be ruler over all the corpses that are dead" (*Odyssey* 11.489–491). A lotless man, whatever the reasons for his situation, would eke out a precarious existence on a poor patch of unclaimed marginal land, far from the deep-soiled bottomlands and gentler slopes where the kleroi were located. After the eighth century, the shortage of available land would become widespread and would be a serious point of tension between the wealthy few and a growing mass of poor citizens.

The economies of ordinary and elite households in the Dark Age differed primarily in scale. The prominent oikoi had large workforces, whereas average households had only one or perhaps two slaves or hired hands to share the workload. High-ranking families also farmed proportionately more land, needed to feed their larger households and to supply bread and wine for the feasts they provided to friends, followers, and the community at large. A Homeric chief sometimes received a sizable piece of prime farmland, called a *temenos*, awarded by the people in recognition of his services to the community. The agricultural surpluses of the elite, however, would not have risen much above their own increased consumption needs, since at that time there was little opportunity for trade in foodstuff.

In addition to kleros size and the number of inhabitants, the major economic difference between rich and poor households seems to have been in the number of animals owned. Odysseus' chief swineherd, Eumaeus, gives an account of his master's "unspeakably great" livelihood:

> Twenty men together
> Could not match his wealth. Let me count it for you.
> Twelve herds of cattle over on the mainland,
> And as many flocks of sheep, droves of swine,
> And spreading herds of goats, eleven in all,
> Range our island's coasts. Good men watch them....
> (*Odyssey* 14.98–104; Lombardo)

To these fifty-nine flocks and herds we may add the 960 pigs that Eumaeus and four other swineherds managed on Ithaca. Such large numbers are perhaps epic exaggerations, but the reality need not have been so far off, in view of the very large amount of available grazing land. An ordinary farmer would have had a yoke of oxen for plowing, perhaps a mule; no doubt he pastured some sheep and goats for his family's wool, cheese, and manure. But his oikos, even with a slave or two, was too small to herd large numbers of animals or to build and maintain the many huts and pens required.

Only the elite could command the labor force for large-scale stock raising. As a consequence, their families enjoyed an abundance of the preferred protein from meat, as well as a large surplus of wool, hides, and fertilizer. In fact, it was probably woolen goods and leather, produced within the oikos, that paid for the imported metal goods and ornaments the Dark Age elites valued as "treasure" and used for gift exchanges among themselves. The main value, however, of livestock was as meat for feasts, something only the wealthy few could provide in quantity.

Animal wealth was therefore prestige wealth. The very sight of large herds roving the pastures and hillsides was evidence of the owner's rank and status. It was also proof of his prowess as a warrior, since the most prestigious way of acquiring animals (as well as treasure) was by raiding. There was a certain circularity in this animal economy. Chiefs slaughtered large numbers of their animals in order to recruit warriors for raids that were conducted primarily for the purpose of acquiring animals for slaughter. It was not efficient in purely economic terms, but, as in all archaic rank societies, the aim of acquiring wealth was not to keep it but to exchange it for influence and good reputation.

That cattle measure the worth of objects of other kinds indicates the high value placed on them in Homeric society. For example, the first prize in a wrestling contest is a large bronze tripod, "which the Achaeans valued at twelve cattle's worth" (*Iliad* 23.702–705). This does not mean, of course, that cows, bulls, and oxen were used as actual payment; rather, in an exchange of goods the transacting parties mentally converted the value of the objects involved into cattle as the standard of value, a practice common in premonetary societies. (In Latin, the root of the word for money, *pecunia*, is *pecus*, or livestock.)

Therefore, the archaeologically visible wealth in the tenth and ninth centuries—valuable small objects deposited in graves—does not begin to measure the true extent of elite wealth and its social power. Nevertheless, the economic and social gulf between the top stratum and the mass of small farmers was not nearly as wide in 800 as it had been in the Late Bronze Age. If anything, we would expect Homer to exaggerate the differences in the lifestyles of the chiefs and the ordinary folk, but instead he shows the elite living not much more luxuriously.

Though the elite do have some things the others cannot afford, such as horses and chariots and precious metal items, most of the distinctions are merely relative—more of this, better of that. The daily lives of Homeric chiefs and their families are easier and more pleasant; they have more servants, and, most important, more leisure time. Yet, all in all, their way of life is more like than unlike the kind of life led by those in the average households. The Homeric poems and the material record concur that social class distinctions between the "nobles" and the "commoners" had not progressed very far in the course of the tenth and ninth centuries.

THE END OF THE DARK AGE (C. 750–700 BC)

It was in the eighth century that Greek society underwent rapid changes. Some of these, such as developments in art and culture, were the result of an acceleration of the existing patterns of growth. Other, deeper, changes reflect a radical break with the past, particularly in economic and political relationships. The rapid developments that mark the end of the Dark Age have earned it the title of "the eighth-century renaissance." The last half of the eighth century is also viewed by many as the beginning of the Archaic Age (c. 750–480 BC), the period in which the social and cultural movements that started early in the eighth century would reach maturity.

Population Growth, Land Shortage, and the Rise of a Landowning Aristocracy

A major factor of change was a widespread rise in population in the early eighth century, after centuries of negligible growth. There is some disagreement about the rate of population growth, but most concur that there were considerably more people in Greece in the late eighth century BC than at any time within the preceding four centuries. Population would continue to rise in most regions for the next 200 years. The reason for this increase remains one of many unsolved questions of early Greek history. Certainly the material and social conditions at the end of the ninth century favored population increase.

The presence of many people where there had been but few a generation or two before was bound to have a great impact on Greek society. To feed a growing population, land that had traditionally been pasture had to be converted to the production of grain, a much more effective use of land in terms of sustenance yield per acre. At first, this must have created tension between those seeking to put the fields under grains and those accustomed to having the fields under hooves. By the early seventh century, extension of farmland was accompanied by more intensive methods of farming to increase yield and variety of crops; an agrarian economy was now in place, and it was dominated by an aristocracy of large landowners.

Later written sources do not mention how the class of large proprietors came into being, but it is not difficult to piece together what might have happened. It was most certainly the leading households that were most active in converting pastureland into agricultural land. Although grazing land was nominally open to all to use, in reality the chieftain families had long before appropriated the best for themselves; the moist grassy meadows, where cattle and horses grazed, were potentially the finest grainlands. Generations of use had conferred on these elites what amounted to exclusive grazing rights. No doubt this prior occupancy gave the leading families some legal right to plow and plant the traditional pasture-lands. In any case, as arable land became more precious, the chiefs and other prominent family heads came to own a disproportionate amount of it. In the span of two or three generations they transformed themselves into large-scale farmers, with smaller flocks and herds. The rest of the population continued to live off their small to medium-sized farm plots and a few (perhaps now fewer) sheep and goats.

The growing disparity in land distribution began to have a severe effect as rising populations and the custom of dividing the kleros equally among sons made family plots smaller. One early sign of land hunger was the emigration, starting in the second half of the eighth century, of substantial numbers of people from mainland and island Greece into southern Italy and Sicily, beginning a long wave of colonization that would eventually plant scores of new Greek communities from Spain to the shores of the Black Sea and beyond. Trade and the profits that could be earned attracted some, but for most it was the promise of a good-sized kleros on good soil. Among these no doubt were landless men; more, however, were seeking a better livelihood than their land at home could give them.

Although scarcity of land was certainly the primary motivation for emigration, this scarcity must be put into perspective. Nowhere in eighth-century Greece did the population approach the carrying capacity of the land. In fact, the filling in of the countryside continued through the seventh and into the sixth century. The problem was not that there was no land, but rather that the most productive land was concentrated in the hands of a minority of the families. Sons whose inherited share of their paternal kleros was insufficient for a decent livelihood were forced either to seek marginal land in the demos or to emigrate overseas. Colonization and the tremendous impact it would have on the political, economic, and cultural development of the homeland during the seventh and sixth centuries will be discussed in the next chapter.

Trade and Commerce

Early colonization was connected to widening contacts with the Near East and western Europe. Long-distance seaborne trade, both among Greeks and between Greeks and foreigners, had been increasing slowly in the tenth and ninth centuries, but it expanded considerably in the eighth. The earliest evidence for serious Greek involvement in overseas trade is the presence of Euboean Greeks, around 825, at an international trading post at Al Mina in northern Syria, although whether the Greeks were residents or visitors, whether they were traders or mercenaries, is still the subject of vigorous debate. A Greek trading colony was founded shortly after 800 at Pithecusae (today Ischia) in southern Italy. Working with their more experienced Phoenician partners, the Euboeans soon established a trading circuit that stretched between Al Mina in the east and Pithecusae in the west. By the early seventh century, Greeks had once again become important participants in the Aegean and in the wider Mediterranean trade.

As it had in the Late Bronze Age, the need for raw materials, especially metals, drove long-distance trade. Imports of copper and tin, iron, and gold increased considerably from the later eighth century on, as well as imports of rare and expensive materials such as ivory, amber, and dyes, and objects made of or with these. In return, Greeks were exporting larger quantities of fine pottery and metalwork

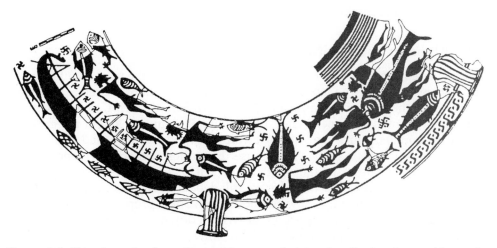

Figure 2.6. Drawing of a Late Geometric crater (mixing bowl) showing a shipwreck (c. 725–700 BC) from Pithecusae (Ischia), Italy. Ischia Museum.

abroad and probably also fine woolen goods, cattle hides, and leather. Production of olive oil and wine for overseas markets would begin in the later seventh century, followed still later by exports of building stone and marble, for which Greece was famous, and silver, which was abundant in regions such as Attica and Thrace.

Trade at the local or regional level within Greece was largely restricted to a few hundred square miles. Crafts goods would have consisted mainly of plain pottery and utilitarian metal manufactures, such as iron axes and spear points, as well as some locally made luxury items for the wealthy. A large variety of local produce would have been exchanged. Besides the staples of grain, wine, and olive oil, producers would have bartered honey, fruit, and cheeses; a cow or goat; a catch of fish; or a load of lumber. As with foreign trade, the primary means of transport was by sea. Hesiod, for example, assumes that a farmer will put part of his surplus production in a boat and sail a fair distance for "profit." Goods were also hauled on land, along rough wagon tracks or by steep mule and footpaths through rugged passes. In this way, local and regional economies were able to produce and to distribute by themselves all that was necessary to satisfy the wants and needs of ordinary people.

Farmers, craftsmen, sailors, shipbuilders and outfitters, and carters were among those who found new economic opportunities in the steady increase of commerce and trade in the eighth and seventh centuries. The main beneficiaries, however, were the big landholders, who could produce large surpluses for the market and could subsidize the costs and bear the losses of long sea voyages. For these wealthy families, costly foreign and domestic manufactures continued to be emblems of status, whose function was almost exclusively to impress others and to be given away, just as in the ninth and earlier centuries. Gold cups and silver plates, bronze tripods, and horses were the ritual coinage of elite social relationships and would remain so even after the introduction of silver coins after 600.

The Alphabet and Writing

The increased contacts with the East were responsible for the most significant cultural achievement of the late Dark Age, the Greek **alphabet**. Greeks borrowed letters from the Phoenician alphabet, a northern Semitic script, to represent the consonant sounds of Greek. They used other Phoenician letters to represent the vowel sounds, which the Phoenician alphabet did not have, and thus created the first truly phonetic alphabet. Because the earliest material evidence for the Greek alphabet comes from the eighth century, it is generally believed that it was developed shortly after 800. Scholars are still debating why the Greeks decided to have a writing system at this time and not earlier. Some propose that the alphabet was adopted for the express purpose of writing down epic poetry, whereas others cling to the older explanation that it was first used for commercial and other utilitarian purposes. Either theory is plausible, although so far no specimen of eighth-century commercial writing has been found.

The earliest known examples of connected Greek words are bits of epic-type verse scratched on vases and dated to the second half of the eighth century. These graffiti do not prove that the alphabet was designed for preserving oral poetry, although they do show that the epics of Homer could have been written down at about the same time as their composition. Whatever the initial motive, once writing was established, it was used to record not only poetry but many other things besides. The earliest known specimen of the civic use of writing is a stone inscription of laws from Dreros in Crete, carved around 650 BC. Writing spread quickly throughout the Greek-speaking world, not as one standard alphabet but as numerous local scripts, with variations in letter form among neighboring locales. The Greek alphabet of twenty-four letters was a huge advance over the cumbersome Linear B syllabic system of eighty-seven signs. Because each letter represented a single spoken consonant or vowel, it was fairly simple to learn to read and even to write Greek. Since reading and writing were accessible to all and fairly easily learned, literacy could not become an instrument of power and control by the rulers over the people, as it was in Egypt and other contemporary

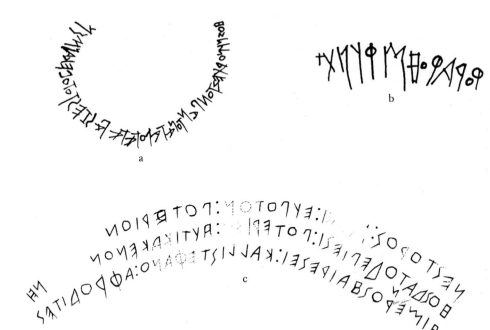

Figure 2.7a. Examples of graffiti on eighth-century pottery. The readable portion of inscription (a) says: "He who, of all the dancers, now dances most gracefully" [? will win this pot?]. Inscription (b) identifies the owner: "I am the cup of Qoraqos." Inscription (c) reads: "I am the drinking cup of Nestor, good to drink from. Whoever drinks this cup, immediately the desire will seize him of beautiful-crowned Aphrodite."

Figure 2.7b. Late Geometric *oinochoe* (jug) from Athens (c. 740 BC), on which graffito (a) was inscribed. Athens, National Archaeological Museum.

Figure 2.8. Middle Geometric crater from Athens (c. 800 BC) with meander, zigzag, and other geometric patterns. Note the flanking horses, which enliven the severe geometric decoration, and the jug-shaped knob on the lid. Paris, The Louvre.

empires, where literacy was an arcane skill confined to an elite group of officials, priests, and scribes.

The impact of literacy on Greek cultural development was enormous. Many of the achievements for which the Greeks are most famous—history, drama, philosophy, mathematics, science, medicine, law, and scholarship—could not have evolved without writing. Later Greeks reverently preserved the writings of earlier Greeks and held constant dialogue with the minds of the past. Progress toward general literacy, however, was slow. Greece in the eighth and much of the seventh century was almost as completely oral-aural as it had been in the earlier Dark Age. Orality coexisted with literacy throughout Greek history; even in the Classical and Hellenistic periods, when literacy was most widespread, most information passed from mouth to ear.

Other Cultural Developments

Development in artistic expression, of which pottery is the best example, as usual, is another index of the creative energy of the Late Geometric period. The stylistic transition from Middle Geometric pottery (c. 850–750) to Late Geometric (c. 750–700) was smooth, but clearly represents a new direction in vase painting. As we have seen, aside from showing an occasional horse or a bird, or, even rarer, a human figure, Greek vases were essentially without images from the eleventh to the eighth century. Pictures of animals and humans suddenly became frequent after 800 BC. The major decorative innovation, however, was the reappearance, after an absence of 400 years, of group scenes that told a kind of story, such as battles, shipwrecks, funerals, and chariot processions.

In Attic pottery, which had long been the style setter, this development occurred just as the Geometric style reached a peak of complexity. On a massive amphora from about 750 BC, commissioned as a grave marker for a wealthy woman, a scene of the woman lying in state occupies the prominent area of the belly of the monumental vase, while the rest of the surface is covered by a masterly composition of abstract geometric designs. The silhouette figures of the corpse and mourners are themselves geometric in execution, as are the bands of repeating, identical deer and birds on the neck (Figure 2.9). Yet it is clear even in this bravura display of the Geometric style that the picture is the focal element. Inevitably, static geometric shapes became mere decorative borders for the pictorial narrative, which soon covered most of the pottery surface. As the repertoire of subjects and scenes expanded, the figures of animals, humans, and objects became increasingly more naturalistic.

Another artistic innovation was the depiction of scenes from Greek legends, painted on vases and engraved on metalwork. These scenes inaugurated the rich and lasting tradition of pictorial narrative in painting and sculpture (see for example Plate III). The unrestrained exuberance (if not always excellence) of this new artistic spirit is also evident in the increase of distinctive regional, local, and even individual styles, as craftsmen from all over Greece experimented with,

Figure 2.9. Late Geometric amphora (c. 750 BC) that was used as a monument on the grave of a woman in the Dipylon cemetery at Athens. At the level of the vase's handles is a scene with human figures: mourners surrounding the body of the deceased woman, who is lying on a funeral bier. Height 61 inches. Athens, National Archaeological Museum.

mixed, copied, adapted, and abandoned, in rapid succession, both homegrown and imported styles and techniques. Near Eastern influence on art appears especially prominent from around 730 or 720 BC and for about a century thereafter. Like the borrowing of the alphabet, the "Orientalizing period" of Greek art exemplifies the importance of Near Eastern models in the development of Greek culture. As in the case of writing, what the Greeks learned from the East they increasingly transformed into a distinctively Hellenic expression.

The monumental temple, which is the signature Greek architectural form, emerged in the eighth century. The earliest known examples from around 800 BC were small, with mud-brick walls, wooden columns, and thatched roofs, and looked very much like regular houses (Figure 2.10). A rectangular temple to Hera on the island of Samos, constructed a few decades later, was the first to make a clear distinction between divine and human houses. Although still made of the same materials as earlier models, it was several times larger: 100 feet long compared with 25 feet. When, later in the century, a wooden colonnade, or peristyle, was built all around the long but narrow shell, the building assumed the form of the Greek temple as we know it. By 700, there were dozens of major and minor temples, built along similar lines, in all parts of the Greek world.

The appearance of large temples shows that people wanted to and were able to spend their wealth, time, and labor on projects that gave honor to the whole community; the community's temple began to replace the chief's house as the focal point of the settlement. In Athens at this time, expensive votive offerings placed in the temples of the gods—most notably bronze tripods and cauldrons, figurines, and bronze dress pins—greatly exceed the amount of metal wealth found in upper-class burials. Giving to the community rather than expressing family pride in the traditional manner was a new form of conspicuous display by the elite, establishing a pattern that was to hold throughout the life of the Greek city-state.

A number of the sanctuaries were located in the countryside away from the population centers. Many see this as a sign of growing civic unity, a deliberate strengthening of the religious bonds for the purpose of more firmly uniting the demos. Religious processions from the central town to the rural sanctuaries symbolically connected urban dwellers with the inhabitants of the outlying villages and hamlets. The temples at the borders of the territory also served to stake out the territory of the demos against any territorial claims from a neighboring demos, especially as populations grew and territories expanded towards one another.

Thick brick and stone defensive walls, another major architectural feature of Greek towns, first appear in Greek Asia Minor and the Aegean islands. Old Smyrna (now Izmir) had an impressive circuit wall by around 850; Iasus, down the coast in Caria, was walled before 800. A number of Cycladic island sites were also fortified in the ninth century. On the mainland, however, the earliest circuit walls date to a little before 700. The increasing numbers of defensive walls possibly indicate that all-out warfare between communities, as opposed to raiding expeditions, was growing more frequent, and also attest to the growing wealth and civic pride of the communities.

Panhellenism

The eighth century also saw the rise of religious sanctuaries and festivals that were not merely local but Panhellenic (*pan*, "all"), attracting worshippers from all over the Greek world. Panhellenic shrines and festivals celebrated and reinforced the idea that Greeks everywhere belonged to a single cultural group sharing the same heritage, language, customs, and religion. The most famous early Panhellenic sanctuaries were those of Zeus and Hera at Olympia and of Apollo

Figure 2.10. Clay model of house or temple from Argos (c. 725–700 BC). Athens, National Archaeological Museum.

and Artemis at Delos, and the oracles (places of divine prophecy) at the shrines of Zeus at Dodona and of Apollo at Delphi. All these sites, as well as others, show evidence of intermittent cult activity from the Late Bronze Age on, but they emerged as Panhellenic centers only in the eighth century. Eventually they would become large complexes of temples, treasure houses (for the depositing of gifts), and holy precincts.

The worshippers who came to the Panhellenic festivals participated in common rituals and sacrifices to the gods, and at some sanctuaries they took part in athletic contests as well. The first and the most prestigious of these athletic games were those held every four years at the great festival of Zeus at Olympia, a rather remote site in northwestern Peloponnesus. The games were inaugurated, according to later Greek computations, in 776 BC (the archaeology does not disagree with this date). At first, Olympia and the Olympian games attracted contestants and visitors only from the vicinity, but by the end of the century costly dedications were being deposited in the sanctuaries of Zeus and Hera by Spartans, Athenians, Corinthians, and Argives. By the sixth century, contestants and spectators would be drawn from all over the Greek world.

The rise of Panhellenism coincided with increased contact with the eastern world, which made the Greeks more conscious of the cultural differences between themselves and non-Greeks. When Homer describes the Carians, allies of the Trojans, he calls them *barbarophōnoi* (strange-speaking), indicating the odd sound of foreign languages to Greek ears. This is the first occurrence of the word **barbaros**, which the Greeks later employed as the general term for foreigner. Contrast between Greeks and "barbarians" would be most strongly expressed in the early fifth century, when the Greeks united to fight against the Persian empire.

The Heroic Revival

Closely related to Panhellenism were activities, at both local and national levels, that centered around the recovery of the world of the Bronze Age ancestors. Quite suddenly, around 750, Greeks everywhere began to express their connection to the heroic past in new and dramatic ways. Numerous ancient tombs (mostly Mycenaean) that had been ignored throughout the Dark Age began to receive votive offerings, an indication that their anonymous inhabitants were now worshipped as "heroes." Hero cults of other kinds came into being during the late eighth century. They were celebrated not at graves but at new shrines set up in honor of legendary heroic figures, for example, the precincts sacred to Agamemnon at Mycenae and to Menelaus and Helen near Sparta. The impetus behind hero cults was the belief that the great men and women of the Heroic Age had power in death to protect and to help the people. Like gods, they were accorded animal sacrifices and other divine honors, though on a smaller scale.

Wealthy Greeks of the later eighth century also expressed an urge to connect with the past through heroic-style burials, most notably in Attica, Euboea, and Cyprus. These burials somewhat resemble the funerals of heroes in epic poetry. As in the funeral of Patroclus (the close hetairos of Achilles) in the *Iliad*, the corpse was cremated and the bones put in a bronze urn; weapons were placed in the grave, and occasionally the bodies of sacrificed horses. Also around this time, vases depicting events from the Heroic Age begin to turn up in these graves. There is additional evidence from Athens that wealthy families had begun to group their graves in enclosures that not only held contemporary graves but also took in Mycenaean graves, as if to convert the inhabitants of the ancient burials into family ancestors. All this suggests that the leading families were proclaiming descent from the heroes of old.

As the eleventh to the eighth centuries come more clearly into view, it becomes increasingly apparent that the Dark Age was the cradle of the city-state society and culture that was to follow. The basic structures and institutions of later Greek society were firmly in place well before 800 BC. And so it was during the eighth century that Greece emerged from the Dark Age into the renaissance of the Archaic period. This cultural watershed, which not so long ago was seen as a sudden and revolutionary phenomenon, appears now more like a rapid evolution in response to rapidly changing conditions. The swift transformation of the traditional chieftain government into the city-state government and the turbulent history of the early city-states are the subjects of the next chapter.

KEY TERMS

alphabet	Hesiod	oral composition
barbaros	Homeric epics	Phoenicia
basileus	Ionian migration	polytheism
chiefdom	iron	Protogeometric style
Cyprus	kleros	thetes
Dark Age	Lefkandi	timē
Geometric style	Nichoria	
guest-friendship (xenia)	oikos	

SUGGESTED READINGS

Bryce, Trevor. 2006. *The Trojans and Their Neighbors*. London: Routledge. Lucid history of Troy in the context of second-millennium BC Anatolia by an outstanding Hittite historian.

Burkert, Walter. 1985. *Greek Religion*. Cambridge, MA: Harvard University Press. A classic history of ancient Greek religion from the Minoan–Mycenaean Age to the Hellenistic period.

Carter, Jane B., and Sarah P. Morris, eds. 1995. *The Ages of Homer*. Austin: University of Texas Press. Informative collection of essays on the historical and literary background of Homer.

Coldstream, J. N. 2003. *Geometric Greece*. 2d ed. London: Routledge. A comprehensive presentation and analysis of the archaeological evidence from 900 to 700 BC.

Edwards, Mark W. 1987. *Homer, Poet of the Iliad*. Baltimore and London: Johns Hopkins University Press. A reliable, general treatment of Homeric poetry and the epic style, with commentaries on selected books of the *Iliad*.

Finkelberg, Margalit, ed. 2011. *The Homer Encyclopedia*. Oxford: Blackwell. Massive, comprehensive collection featuring work by leading specialists writing for specialists and nonspecialists alike.

Finley, Moses I. 1978. *The World of Odysseus*. 2nd ed. New York: Viking Press. First published in 1954, this book revolutionized the study of Dark Age society and institutions.

Griffin, Jasper. 1980. *Homer on Life and Death*. New York: Oxford University Press. An insightful literary exploration of the Homeric characterization of the epic hero.

Hurwit, Jeffrey M. 1985. *The Art and Culture of Early Greece, 1100–480 B.C.* Ithaca, NY: Cornell Univerity Press, chaps. 1–3. A highly readable and insightful discussion of Dark Age art in relation to the changing social scene. Chapters 4 to 6 are also recommended reading for art and culture in the Archaic period.

Latacz, Joachim. 2004. *Troy and Homer: Towards a Solution of an Old Mystery.* Oxford, UK: Oxford University Press. A new effort at finding history embedded in the traditions of the Trojan War and the documents from the Ancient Near East.

Lord, Albert Bates. 1991. *Epic Singers and Oral Tradition.* Ithaca, NY: Cornell University Press. A collection of articles and papers (some not published before), offering an overview of oral-traditional epic songs and singers, spanning the long career of one of the founders of oral-formulaic theory.

Morris, Ian, and Barry Powell, eds. 1997. *A New Companion to Homer.* Leiden: Brill. A valuable collection of thirty articles, covering all areas of Homeric studies, literary and historical, written by specialists for a nonspecialist audience.

Snodgrass, A. M. 1971. *The Dark Age of Greece: An Archaeological Survey of the Eleventh to the Eighth Centuries.* Edinburgh: University of Edinburgh Press. Remains the standard treatment of the archaeological evidence for the whole of the Dark Age.

Thomas, Carol G. 2005. *The Trojan War.* Westport, CT: Greenwood Press. Lucid introduction to the problems concerning the Trojan War and its aftermath.

Thomas, Carol G., and Craig Conant. 1999. *Citadel to City-State: The Transformation of Greece, 1200–700 B.C.E.* Bloomington and Indianapolis: Indiana University Press. Written with the general reader in mind, this book traces the processes of change that led from the destruction of Bronze Age civilization to the emergence of the city-states. Each chapter is devoted to a specific site, among which are Nichoria and Lefkandi.

Whitley, James. 1991. *Style and Society in Dark Age Greece: The Changing Faces of a Preliterate Society 1100–700 BC.* Cambridge, UK: Cambridge University Press. Clear and concise overview of the changing social circumstances of Dark Age Greeks.

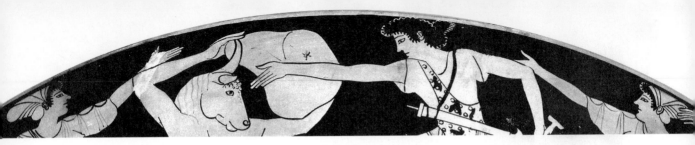

CHAPTER THREE

Archaic Greece
750/700–480 BC

The seventh and sixth centuries belong to the **Archaic period** (750/700–480 BC). During those 200 years, the pace of change and development accelerated rapidly, continuing and surpassing the progress made in the eighth century as Greece emerged from its Dark Age. Once neglected by historians as being merely the prelude to the glorious and tragic fifth and fourth centuries—the Classical period—scholars now consider the Archaic period to be the formative era of the intellectual, cultural, and political achievements of Greece's Golden Age.

The city-state form of government, which came into being with the demographic and economic changes of the eighth century, grew to maturity during the seventh and sixth. A steady movement of overseas colonization, starting in the later eighth century and continuing into the sixth, spread the Greek language and culture across the lands of the Mediterranean and Black seas. Trade dispersed Greek goods far beyond the limits known to the Bronze Age traders. Literature and art flourished; new genres of artistic and intellectual expression were invented, and women participated in their creation. The Panhellenic shrines, festivals, and oracles grew in importance, further nourishing the ideal of the cultural unity of all Greeks even as the Greek world expanded to distant shores. Within the Greek city-states, new ideas began to form, two of which would shape the history of the western world: a rational view of the universe, which replaced supernatural causes for natural events with scientific explanations, and the concept of democratic government, in which all freeborn males were equal under the laws and the laws were made directly by the majority rule of male citizens.

The Archaic period also had its dark side. Wars of one demos against another became much more frequent, and warfare itself much more lethal. Worse, civil strife within a demos became commonplace, as leaders, with their armed followers, fought among themselves over power sharing and poorer citizens fought for economic relief and their civic rights. Widening economic inequality caused much human misery and produced serious tensions between the few rich and the many poor, which occasionally erupted in actual class warfare. Political instability gave rise to a new type of leader, the tyrant, whose absolute rulership in turn led to further turmoil. All this movement, for good or bad, took place within a new social and political structure, the city-state, which by 700 BC had replaced the old chieftain system in many parts of Greece.

SOURCES FOR THE SEVENTH AND SIXTH CENTURIES

Even though we are separated from the Archaic Age by over two millennia, we can apprehend what was happening all across the Greek world as the eighth-century renaissance turned into the "Greek miracle," as it has been called, of the seventh and sixth centuries. For the first time we can speak of actual events, with dates and names, and even connect events into a coherent historical narrative. That is possible because beginning in the seventh century the Greeks produced copious amounts of texts written on papyrus, the "paper" of antiquity. Surviving examples of texts on papyrus rolls were laboriously copied and recopied by hand until papyrus was replaced first by parchment, which was made from animal skins, and then by paper, which was invented in China in the second century AD and adopted in the Middle Ages in the West; the copying continued using these simple technologies until replaced by the invention of the printing press in the fifteenth century AD.

Only a small fraction of what the ancient Greeks wrote has survived the centuries of selection and chance. That enough survived to fill several library shelves is the ultimate testimony of the continuing value of Greek literature to the western world. The writings of the Archaic Age did not fare as well as the literature of the later periods. Other than the works of Homer and **Hesiod**, only bits and pieces of the volumes of poetry and philosophical treatises from the seventh and sixth centuries have come down to us. Some of the fragments are preserved as quotations in the extant writings of later Greeks, who greatly admired the poets and thinkers of the Archaic period. Other fragments come from papyri of the Hellenistic and Roman periods luckily preserved in the hot dry sands of Egypt. Though pitifully few, the precious remnants of Archaic literature provide valuable insights into contemporary life and thought in the seventh and sixth centuries. (See Plate V.)

Most of our information about the events of the period is found in the works of later historians, who had some access to earlier writings and records. They wrote long after their sources had been composed, however, and their accounts are often untrustworthy because much of their knowledge was based on orally transmitted narratives. Public and private inscriptions carved on stone and the images and letters on coins, which were first minted in the sixth century BC, supplement the evidence given by the ancient historians. The amount of inscriptional material (mostly laws posted in the centers of communities) before the fifth century is small.

The archaeological evidence follows the upward trajectory begun in the Geometric period. The number of manufactured items found now increases markedly, a natural result of the growth in population and wealth. Architectural finds are also much more numerous. Moreover, because the temples and other monumental buildings were now constructed mostly of stone, much more can be learned from their foundations, which are often all that survives. Enough homes have now been excavated to allow us to compare houses of the Archaic period to houses before and after: on average, sixth-century houses are about 40 percent larger than the houses of the previous three centuries and about half the size of Classical houses. An important new source of evidence is sculpture, life-sized and larger figures in stone and bronze.

By comparison with the Classical period, the evidence for the seventh and sixth centuries is in general rather meager. Nevertheless, despite the large gaps in our knowledge it is possible to put together a reasonably clear picture of Greek society and culture in the early city-states.

THE FORMATION OF THE CITY-STATE (POLIS)

The city-state form of government came into existence during the eighth century. By the early seventh century, dozens of Greek communities all across the Greek world, from Ionia in the east to Sicily and southern Italy in the west, had formed themselves into city-states. The **polis**, as the Greeks called it, served as the characteristic social and political organization for Greeks until at least the Roman period. As an ideal, the polis has had enormous significance in the history of later nations. The very words "political" and "politics" are derived directly from *polis*.

What is a city-state? A simplified definition is this: a geographical area comprising a city and its adjacent territory, which together make up a single, self-governing political unit. The essential elements of the city-states were in place during the later Dark Age. The capital cities of what became city-states existed all through the Dark Age, and most of them had been the major centers of their regions during the Mycenaean period. The territorial community, the demos in its joint sense comprising the land and the people, appears fully developed in the Homeric epics; within the demos there was a collective identification—"the Ithacans" or "the Pylians"—and a communal worship of the same gods. The two primary governmental organs of the city-state, the assembly of men of fighting age and the council of "elders," are also present in Homer. All that was lacking to make the demos-communities of 800 BC into the polis-states of 700 BC were certain necessary formalities: formal political unification of the demos and the creation of a central government.

Political Unification (Synoecism)

In all city-states, from ancient Mesopotamia to Renaissance Europe, the capital city is the focal point of the state. The original meaning of the Greek word *polis* (plural *poleis*) was "town" or "city," and that is how it is used in the Homeric epics. In most city-states, all male members of a city's territory, both those who lived in the capital and those who lived in the countryside, were called *politai* (members of the polis), as if they all lived together in the polis (the city).

Later Greeks referred to the process of political unification of states as *synoikismos*, "uniting the oikoi." **Synoecism**, to use the anglicized term, was the process by which every town, village, and hamlet of a demos accepted a single political center. Whatever local autonomy they had formerly enjoyed, whatever freedom of action they had exercised separate from the capital and the other settlements, was given up. Moreover, they identified themselves by the name of the capital city. Thus, all those who lived in the territory of Attica, of which Athens was the capital city, referred to themselves (and were referred to by others) as "the Athenians," even if they lived 25 miles from the city of Athens. The Athenians even attributed their synoecism to the mythic Attic culture hero Theseus, thus dressing the new event in old, comfortable clothes.

Synoecism took different forms depending on the size of the territory. Synoecism of a small demos made up of a single main town and its adjacent plain, holding a couple of subsidiary villages, was a very simple process. In those cases, polis (the state) and polis (the town) were almost identical entities. For example, the polis (city-state) of Sicyon, in the northern Peloponnesus, occupied a small plains region (Sicyonia) of about 140 square miles, which even in the fifth century contained only a few villages in addition to the main town, called Sicyon. Because everyone lived within a few miles of everyone else, and most of the few hundred families in the demos were interrelated, drawing them together as a single political unit was merely a matter of making formal the ancient ties of kinship and neighborliness and precisely defining the territorial boundaries of the demos. Most of the several hundred city-states that came into existence during the Archaic period were of the Sicyon variety, a single town and its small plain; the majority, in fact, were even smaller in territory than Sicyon.

Synoecism of the regional territories, those that contained several important towns and villages besides the central town, was a more complex process and is not well understood. Scholarly opinion is that the unification of the regional states was a drawn-out development, beginning possibly in the ninth century and crystallizing between about 750 and 700. Archaeology provides a hint of how religion may have been used to promote unity within regions. As we saw in Chapter 2, it is thought that during the eighth century, temples and shrines to the gods and heroes of a regional demos were built in the countryside to connect the center symbolically to the outlying villages, with religious processions from the main polis to the outer sanctuaries fostering and strengthening the people's sense of being a single nation. A border sanctuary also would clearly indicate to neighbors where the boundary was located.

In some regions, unification was voluntary and peaceful, as in Megaris under the leadership of Megara and in Corinthia under Corinth. There is evidence, however, that in other mainland regions intimidation and even force was used to integrate the towns and villages into a single polis. The village of Amyclae, three miles south of the original four villages of Sparta, was absorbed into the unified Spartan polis against the will of the Amyclaeans, and the more distant settlements of Laconia were reduced to a dependent status. Synoecism was also incomplete in some regions. Argos, for example, never fully succeeded in unifying the whole of the large region of Argolis, and a number of small, separate, independent city-states continued to exist in the plains outside the Argive plain. Even within the plain of Argos itself, some villages retained a good deal of local autonomy. Other regions were never united into a single polis. Although Thebes had been the principal settlement in the large, fertile region of Boeotia since the Early Bronze Age, the Thebans controlled only their local area and had to deal on more or less equal terms with ten other district poleis.

As this brief sketch shows, there was no single model of synoecism. Each region experienced its own kind of city-state development, which was determined by local factors that are hidden from us. The important fact is that by around 700 BC, the permanent boundaries of the Greek poleis were pretty well established. Of course adjustments continued to be made here and there—a small polis absorbed by a larger neighboring polis—but the political map of 700 BC remained much the same throughout the Archaic period and beyond.

THE ETHNOS

The history of Greece between 700 and 400 BC was primarily the history of city-states, for they were the main makers of Greek history. Huge areas of Greece, however, had a different form of political organization. The Greek name for these regions was *ethnos*, variously translated as "tribe," "nation," or "people." An ethnos was a regional territory and people (a demos) without a single urban center or a central government or formal political union.

The city-state Greeks tended to regard the *ethnē* (plural) as politically and culturally backward. In fact, the ethne of the seventh and even sixth centuries were at a stage very much like that of the regional demoi in the Dark Age. Each ethnos had a strong sense of being a single people occupying a specific territory. The people were united in worship of the gods of the ethnos. They had institutions for reaching common decisions and for acting as a unit. No single town, however, was the official capital of the ethnos, and, as in Homeric society, united action occurred infrequently, mostly in situations of common defense against an outside enemy. Within this general description, however, the ethne varied considerably. Boeotia, for example, was a single ethnic region with separate small city-states. It differed from the synoecized region of Attica in one significant way: all the inhabitants of all the towns and villages of Attica considered themselves Athenians, whereas in Boeotia they identified themselves as Thebans, or Plataeans, or Orchomenians first, and only secondarily as Boeotians.

What really mattered in ancient Greece was cohesive military force. The Athenians could call on manpower from a region of a thousand square miles, whereas the Thebans had only the men who lived in the city of Thebes and its few square miles of adjoining plain-land. To be militarily powerful, the Thebans had to form alliances with their neighboring poleis, who might or might not contribute troops to a military enterprise and might or might not see it through to the end. The ethne of the Peloponnesus—Arcadia, Achaea, and Elis—were similarly divided into separate, small poleis and were similarly second-rank powers until they formed effective alliances among their constituent city-states.

A purer form of the ethnos existed north of the Peloponnesus. Those regions contained no large urban centers. Instead, the population lived mostly in small villages spread thinly across the territory. The districts were not synoecized into poleis; rather, each village was independent and autonomous. Even an ethnos of this type, however, had some kind of communal government through which it could take concerted action in times of national crisis. The fifth-century historian Thucydides suggestively reveals how well a large ethnos could respond as a unit. In 426 BC, the Athenians, who were a great power at the time, were campaigning in central Greece. They were told that "The ethnos of the Aetolians was indeed large and warlike, but as they lived in unwalled villages which were widely dispersed, and were also lightly armed, they could be easily crushed before they could gather their forces" (3.94.4, adapted). Counting on this fragmentation, the Athenians planned to attack and defeat the villages one by one. A few days into the campaign, however, Aetolian warriors assembled from every part of the territory and drove the Athenians out with heavy losses.

GOVERNMENT IN THE EARLY CITY-STATES

Political union could not have occurred unless the local basileis, the leaders of the districts, towns, and villages of the demos, wished it. These men, the new landowning **aristocracy**, were the planners and architects of the new centralized governments of the emerging city-states. The key decision was to eliminate the position of the paramount basileus and rule collectively, a relatively easy matter, since no one chief had power over the other chiefs to begin with. The same small group became the planners and architects of the new central governments. The governmental structures of the individual city-states, as we first glimpse them in the early seventh century, differed in specifics, yet all followed a similar pattern: (1) the office of paramount basileus was either abolished completely or greatly reduced in power; (2) the governing functions formerly exercised by the basileus were distributed among several officials; and (3) the importance of the council of aristocratic "elders" increased, while that of the assembly of the people decreased. Of course, these decisions were not arrived at in a single year or even a single generation. The sources make it clear, however, that the process of determining which villages and districts were to be included in the polis and what kind of government it would have probably took no more than two or three generations.

For a unified polis to be strong and to compete successfully against other unified poleis, it had to create a more powerful and more intrusive central government than it had possessed before unification. A more complex system of organization and social control was a necessary response to the new conditions of rapidly growing populations, greater exploitation of the land and resources, increasing productivity and wealth, expanding trade, and more complicated relationships with neighboring states. Especially pressing was the need for ways to mobilize manpower and resources efficiently for warfare, for as population increased and land became scarcer, poleis fought each other over territory, a more serious business than the raids and counterraids for animals and booty that had characterized "war" in the Dark Age. Firm control from the center was therefore both necessary and good for a polis as a whole, but it was especially good for the large landowners who made up the government and, like all dominant groups in human history, were highly motivated to preserve their economic and political power.

The basileus did not disappear completely. In a few poleis, a type of the traditional hereditary chiefdom, with severe limits on the paramount leader's power, appears to have continued on through the Archaic period. The Spartans retained the chieftain system the longest, though in a unique form, with two hereditary, lifelong basileis ruling as equals. In this "dual kingship" the Spartan basileis exercised considerable authority, especially in the military sphere, but their powers were curbed by five annually elected magistrates, called ephors ("overseers"). Their job was to make sure that the basileis ruled lawfully and to prosecute them if they did not.

In most poleis, however, the title "basileus" became just the name for one of a number of officials who made up the collective leadership of a city-state. The powerful families divided up the spheres of authority—administrative, military, religious, and judicial—among themselves, creating magistracies and boards. Later Greeks called this kind of government an **oligarchy** or "rule by the few" (*oligoi* = few). The ruling oligarchs referred to themselves as *aristoi,* the "best men"; hence the term "aristocracy." Although the terms *oligarchia* (oligarchy) and *aristokratia* (aristocracy) do not occur in literature or inscriptions before the fifth century, the idea that the few best were the fittest to rule was certainly promoted assiduously by the wealthy, wellborn families who controlled the Archaic city-states.

Each of the city-states developed its own system of magistracies according to its own needs and circumstances. Larger states, such as Athens, required more officers, while small city-states needed few. As poleis grew in population and complexity, they added more officials, with more specialized functions, such as treasurers and supervisors of public works. By the end of the sixth century in Athens, for example, there were several dozen officeholders; by the late fifth, the number had grown to around seven hundred. The number of important magistracies, however, remained small.

In general, there was no hierarchy among the major offices, although many states did have a principal official who was regarded as the chief administrator. The most common names for the chief officer were *archōn* (e.g., at Athens and elsewhere in central Greece) and *prytanis* (e.g., at Corinth and poleis in Ionia). Both are very general titles: *archōn* (like *archos*) means simply leader, and *prytanis* means something like "presiding officer." The chief magistrate sometimes retained the old title of basileus. In some poleis—Athens, for example, and Megara—an officer called the *polemarchos* ("war leader") was in charge of military operations. Supervision of religious activities fell to another official or, more often, a board of officials, which also judged crimes having to do with religion, such as homicides, which polluted the community. The common use of the title basileus to designate these officials is evidence of the reverence still attached to the name. Many other city-states, especially the smaller ones, were governed by small boards or colleges of magistrates, who divided the functions of government among them without stipulating the specific duties. By the middle of the seventh century in most states, the term of office was limited to a single year, and a retiring incumbent could not hold the same office again until a stipulated number of years had passed. These measures had the dual purpose of curbing the power of any single magistrate and of distributing honors among the whole of the aristocratic community.

In many city-states the power and authority of the basileus were also perpetuated through self-styled royal clans. The **Bacchiads** of Corinth are a good example. A legendary Corinthian basileus named Bacchis founded a new line of chiefs called the Bacchiads, the descendants of Bacchis. According to the tradition, the Bacchiad basileis ruled in succession for several generations until 747 BC, when the last of them was killed by his own kinsmen. These collectively took over the leadership of Corinth, retaining the family name Bacchiads. The Bacchiads, said to number more than two hundred, chose one among themselves every year to be prytanis and distributed among themselves other offices as well. Their assertion of common descent from Bacchis was pure fiction, but it was very useful as a way of legitimizing their control of the government. In actuality, they were a narrow oligarchy of prominent, wealthy oikoi. To ensure their exclusivity as a clan, the families married only among themselves. Their rule lasted three generations until 657, when they were overthrown by the tyrant Cypselus.

Similar royal clans appeared in many other poleis, especially in the eastern Aegean. At some point in the early seventh century, a small group of aristocratic families who called themselves the Penthilids took over the government of Mytilene, the largest polis on the island of Lesbos, and ruled for nearly a century. They derived their name and claim to rule from Penthilus, who was grandson of Agamemnon and son of Orestes as well as the mythical founder of Mytilene. In like manner, the Ionian polis of Miletus was ruled for a time by the Neleids, who claimed descent from Neleus, the father of Nestor of Pylos. In several other city-states, the ruling families simply assigned themselves the generic name of Basilids, that is, descendants of the basileus. All these royal clans, which appropriated for themselves the authority and power of the basileis on the basis of their direct descent from them, were deeply resented by the other wealthy families. By the middle of the seventh century, most of them had been displaced, either by a broader oligarchy or by a tyrant.

The royal clans notwithstanding, the true center of power in the government of the early city-states was not in the officials and boards but in the council of elders. The *boule* in the Archaic poleis had even more power than the *boule* in Homeric society. The members were normally recruited from the highest magistrates, who entered the council after the expiration of their terms of office. Membership in the council might be for a long term or even for life. The council thus had a natural supremacy over the archons and other magistrates, who had limited terms and would hesitate to oppose the august body of prominent men whose ranks they wished some day to join. The aristocratic council met more frequently than in the prestate period and assumed for itself the task of making policies and drafting laws for the polis.

Corresponding to the increased power of the council, the limited power of the assembly of adult male citizens to influence policy was further reduced in the oligarchic city-state. Some states excluded the poorest citizens from membership in the assembly by imposing a property qualification. Some restricted the number of assembly meetings and the business to be brought before it; others curtailed free discussion of the issues. The total sovereignty of the aristocratic council, however, was short-lived; as time went on, the inclusiveness and authority of the assembly to decide policy would increase. In fact, before the end of the sixth century, even in oligarchic city-states the assembly had gained the ultimate decision-making power.

The Colonizing Movement

The emergence of the polis system in Greece coincided with the beginning of an extraordinary emigration of Greeks from the Aegean homeland. This emigration began about the middle of the eighth century BC and continued for over two centuries. When it ended, around 500 BC, the Greek world extended from Spain in the west to Colchis at the furthest point of the Black Sea in the east and from the northern littoral of Africa in the south to Ukraine in the north. As was pointed out in Chapter 2, the primary causes of this remarkable expansion were twofold: the search for sources of metal to satisfy the Greeks' growing need, and the hope of acquiring the land required to live the life of a citizen in the new poleis as opportunities for land at home dwindled.

The decision to found a **colony** was one of the earliest and most difficult political actions taken by a polis, and one that helped determine its future identity. A mother city (*mētropolis*) had to choose a site for the colony, obtain divine approval for it, make plans for the new settlement, and choose its *oikistēs* (founder). Moreover, as the foundation oath for Cyrene reveals, the decision to found a colony involved the whole community and was backed by communal sanctions. Founding a colony also indirectly defined the citizen body of a **metropolis**, since those who joined a colony gave up their citizenship in the mother city. Nevertheless, it is also becoming clear to modern historians that the sponsorship of a colony is often to be interpreted loosely, as there appear to be colonies that are in all likelihood private enterprises; although most of the individuals involved may have come from one particular city-state, there is manifestly no city-state driving the foundation.

DOCUMENT 3.1

Foundation Oath of Cyrene, Libya (late seventh century BC)
Inscription from Cyrene containing the oath sworn by the Theraeans and the colonists of Cyrene.

Resolved by the Assembly. Since Apollo spontaneously told Battus and the Theraeans to found a colony in Cyrene, the Theraeans decided to dispatch Battus as the founder of the colony and basileus. The Theraeans shall sail as his comrades. They shall sail on equal terms; and one son shall be enrolled from each family. Those who sail shall be adults, and any free man from the Theraeans who wishes may also sail.

If the colonists secure the settlement, any colonist who sails later to Libya shall have a share in the citizenship and honors. He also shall receive an allotment from the unassigned land. But if they do not make the settlement secure, and the Theraeans cannot come to their aid and they suffer troubles for five years, the colonists may return without fear to Thera. They may return to their own property and become citizens of Thera.

If anyone is unwilling to sail when sent by the city, let him be subject to the death penalty and let his property be confiscated. Whoever receives or protects such a person—whether a father his son or a brother his brother—shall suffer the same punishment as the person who refused to sail. On these terms oaths were sworn by those remaining at Thera and those sailing to found the colony. They also cursed those who transgressed these conditions and did not abide by them, both those settling in Libya and those staying here.

They formed wax images and burned them while they uttered these curses, all of them together, men and women, boys and girls. The person who does not abide by these oaths, but transgresses, shall melt and flow away just as these images, he and his descendants and his property. But may there be many things and those good ones to those who abide by these oaths, both those sailing to Libya and those remaining in Thera, to themselves and their descendants.

Supplementum Epigraphicum Graecum 9.3

Once the decision to found a colony had been made, it was the oikist who was responsible for its success. Homer (*Odyssey* 6.7–10) clearly describes his task: to lead the colonists to their new home, lay out the colony's defenses, locate the sanctuaries of the gods, and assign house plots and farmland to the settlers. If the oikist fulfilled his duties wisely, he would become the ruler of a new polis and its guardian hero after his death. The colony itself would remain linked to its metropolis by bonds of kinship and cult, symbolized by the fire the oikist brought from the metropolis' hearth to kindle the hearth of the new polis. So that the cults of the gods would be properly observed in the colony, priests and priestesses also migrated from the metropolis. Otherwise, however, the colony was a new and completely independent polis, as the Greek term for a colony, *apoikia*, indicates: "a home away [from their old home]" for the colonists.

Reconstructing the history of the colonizing movement is difficult. The literary tradition concerning Greek colonization is encumbered with legends intended to connect various colonies to the Heroic Age and to establish divine sanction for their foundation. Stripped of these legendary accretions, the Greek sources preserve little more than a bare skeleton of dates of colonial foundations, names of founding cities, and, sometimes, of oikists as well.

Archaeology has made it possible for historians to overcome the limitations of the written sources by confirming the general chronology of colonial foundations, revealing the details of colonial city planning, and providing evidence for relations between the colonists and their non-Greek neighbors and the trade routes that linked the colonies to the Greek homeland. Archaeological evidence also indicates that the colonizing movement had two phases, each lasting a little over a century. The first began about the mid-eighth century BC and was directed to Italy and the western Mediterranean; the second started about a century later and was concentrated on the north Aegean and the Black Sea.

The pioneers in the colonization of Italy were Euboeans from Chalcis and Eretria, the same peoples who had helped maintain contact between Greece and the Near East during the Dark Age. Following routes that probably had been blazed by Phoenician traders, they founded their first settlement on the island of Pithecusae in the Bay of Naples in the early eighth century BC. Pithecusae conformed to the picture of an ideal colonial site described in the *Odyssey* (9.116–141): a deserted island, with "meadows, well-watered and soft; the grapevines would grow there endlessly; and there is level plowland...and the soil is deep and rich. There is also a harbor giving safe anchorage with no need for mooring cables or anchor stones..." Pithecusae was also well located to exploit the iron deposits on the nearby island of Elba and to trade with the Italic populations of the mainland. The settlement grew rapidly, attracting settlers not only from the Aegean but even from Phoenicia. The Euboeans followed up their success at Pithecusae with additional settlements both on the Italian mainland at Cumae (757 BC), near modern Naples, and in northeastern Sicily, where they founded Naxos (734), Leontini (729), Catana (729), and Rhegium (after 716).

Meanwhile, Italy and Sicily also attracted the attention of the Dorian poleis of the Peloponnesus. Wracked by the problems of unequal distribution of land at home, these cities sought out sites for their colonies that had good agricultural potential. Achaeans from the northern Peloponnesus moved first, founding in the late eighth century Sybaris and Croton on the instep of Italy. Sparta quickly followed, establishing its only early colony, Taras (called Tarentum later by the Romans) (706 BC), in the corner of the heel of the Italian peninsula. The Bacchiad rulers of Corinth also sought a solution to their internal problems in the west, founding Corcyra in the southern Adriatic Sea (c. 734 BC) and, most importantly, Syracuse (733), which

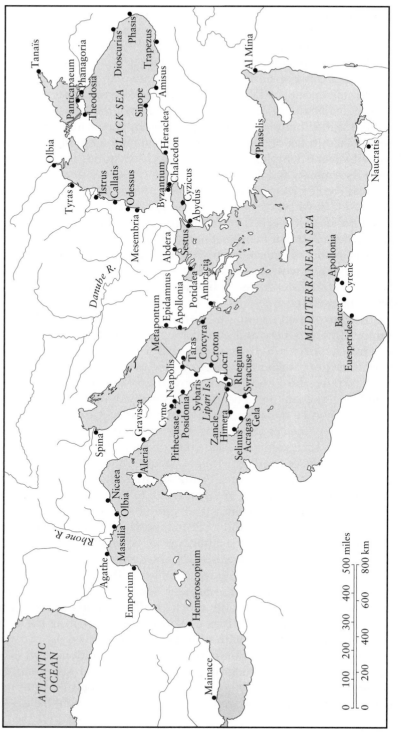

Figure 3.1. Greek colonization: 750–500 BC.

would ultimately dominate the whole of southeastern Sicily and play a major role in the struggle for power in the central Mediterranean between Rome and Carthage.

Greek colonial activity in the Mediterranean was not limited to Italy and Sicily. Thera founded Cyrene in Libya in the late seventh century BC (c. 630). Cyrene prospered from the export of silphium, a now extinct plant that was believed to have medicinal value. (See Plate IV.) Around 625, Greeks from western and southern Anatolia founded Naucratis on the Canopic branch of the Nile in Egypt, about 45 miles from the sea. Although it is often described by modern historians as narrowly a commercial outpost under strict supervision by the Egyptians, Naucratis nevertheless had several temples devoted to Greek divinities (and also one for the Egyptian gods Ammon and Teuth). In the sixth century, a great temple called the Hellenion was erected cooperatively by nine different Greek Anatolian states. It was the far west, however, that offered the greatest possibilities. According to Herodotus, Greeks first learned of the opportunities offered by the western Mediterranean when a Samian merchant named Colaeus returned from the kingdom of Tartessus in southwestern Spain with a fabulously rich cargo. It was not Samos, however, but the west Anatolian city of Phocaea that took advantage of Colaeus' discovery, founding Massilia (modern Marseilles) at the mouth of the Rhone River in about 600 BC.

Massilia quickly exploited its superb location, trading with the Celtic inhabitants of the upper Rhone Valley and establishing a series of trading posts along the northeastern coast of Spain. By the early sixth century, however, opportunities for further Greek expansion in the central and western Mediterranean were disappearing. The powerful Phoenician colony of Carthage in modern Tunisia— probably founded in the late ninth century BC—also had ambitions in the region and established its own colonial empire in western Sicily, Corsica, Sardinia, and southern Spain. When the Carthaginians and their Etruscan allies forced the Phocaeans to evacuate their colony at Alalia on Corsica in the mid-sixth century BC, Greek colonization in the central and western Mediterranean came to an end.

As colonizing opportunities shrank in the Mediterranean, Greeks turned to the north and the northeast for new areas to settle. In the seventh century, many states, especially from Aeolis and the islands, founded colonies on the coast of Thrace, the northern boundary of the Aegean, and the Thracian Chersonnesus, the modern Gallipoli Peninsula. In the latter part of the seventh century, attracted by the rich fishing and agricultural wealth of the Hellespont and Black Sea region, various Ionian and Aeolian states founded colonies in the area. The most active of these was Miletus, credited by the ancient sources with seventy colonies, though the actual number was probably much smaller. Among Miletus' numerous colonies were such important cities as Cyzicus (679 BC) near the entrance of the Hellespont, Sinope (late seventh century) on the north coast of Anatolia, Olbia (c. 550) at the mouth of the Southern Bug River in southwestern Ukraine, and Panticapaeum (shortly after 600) in the Crimea. Megara also colonized in this area, occupying the important sites of Chalcedon (685) and Byzantium (660) on both sides of the Dardanelles as well as founding the city of Heraclea Pontica

Figure 3.2. Limestone gorgon pediment from the temple of Artemis on Corcyra (c. 580 BC). Maximum height 9.25 feet. This early triangular pedimental relief focuses on the Gorgon Medusa, originally shown with her offspring, the winged horse Pegasus and her son Chrysaor, and flanked by a pair of fearsome panthers. This monument from the Corinthian colony of Corcyra (the modern island of Corfu) exemplifies the tendency of colonies to embrace recent cultural trends in the Greek homeland, such as the construction of large stone temples with ambitious sculptural decoration.

(560 BC) on the coast of northwest Anatolia near one of the reputed entrances to Hades. Whereas the Greeks had rivals in the Mediterranean basin, they had none in the Black Sea area, and thus were able to establish new colonies throughout the Archaic and Classical periods until the Black Sea was almost entirely ringed by Greek poleis.

The colonizing movement is often viewed primarily as the story of the spread of Greek life and culture. Support for such reconstructions exists in the ancient sources. The new poleis proudly proclaimed their Greekness by building monumental temples, patronizing Panhellenic institutions such as the Delphic oracle and the Olympic games, and eagerly trying to keep abreast of cultural developments in the Aegean. The earliest example of the Greek alphabet is from the town of Gabii near Rome, and the earliest surviving hexameter verse in fact comes from Pithecusae. Nevertheless, the creation of new poleis is only part of the story of Greek colonization.

Relations with the people in whose lands the colonists settled were anything but simple. On the one hand, the colonies were gateways through which various peoples of southern Europe and the Black Sea areas obtained access to the products and culture of the Greeks and other Mediterranean societies. The Etruscans in Italy, for example, adapted the Greek alphabet and avidly embraced Greek art and even religious cult. On the other hand, the Greeks were intruders and conflict with the native inhabitants occurred frequently. A few new cities, such as

Syracuse, Byzantium, and Heraclea Pontica, ultimately succeeded in expelling or enslaving their non-Greek neighbors. For the most part, however, the minority colonists made accommodations with their non-Greek neighbors, trading and intermarrying with them, and sometimes even sharing their territory. Nor, indeed, was the cultural exchange all in one direction. For instance, cults such as those of the Thracian goddess Bendis and the divine musician Orpheus spread throughout the Aegean and beyond.

Economic and Social Divisions in the Early Poleis

Many who left their homes to emigrate abroad in the late eighth century were lured chiefly by the prospect of the equal lot of farmland (*klēros*) promised to new settlers. The colonizing movement was both the sign of inequality in landownership in Greece and a partial remedy. Not every family could emigrate, however, and as population continued to grow, land became scarcer. The result was a widening of the social and economic distance between the top families and the rest of the people.

The rich landowners cultivated an image of themselves as a true aristocracy, far superior to all the groups below them. They claimed exclusive entitlement to the term **hoi agathoi**, "the good," purely on the basis of their birth into illustrious and wealthy families, and labeled as **hoi kakoi**, "the bad," those who were not born into the landed nobility. This presumptuous arrogance was a large leap from the justified self-esteem of the warrior-chiefs whom the aristocrats boasted of as their ancestors. For Homeric heroes, descent from great warriors, though a matter of pride, was not automatic proof of personal excellence, and they did not demand honors or privileges on that basis. Their claims to be called "good" (*agathos*) and "best" (*aristos*) were measured solely by their performance as warriors and leaders. In the same way, the term *kakos* also acquired social connotations in the seventh century. In Homer, *kakos* had meant unskilled in warcraft or cowardly; in the aristocratic lexicon it referred to anyone who was not a member of the closed group of the wealthy and wellborn. Similarly, the wealthy families signaled their separateness from the rest of the community by narrowing the term *dēmos* from its inclusive usage designating the whole people to mean the masses or the poor, whom they also referred to disparagingly as *hoi polloi,* "the many."

The Rich, the Poor, and the Middle

The powerful aristocrats' arrogance was rooted in their hereditary control of the land. Generations of aristocratic houses had inherited a disproportionate share of the total agricultural land in the demos and an even greater share of the good land, including lush meadows for grazing their horses and cattle. They became even richer through improved farming techniques that increased crop yields and through concentration on specialty crops, such as wine and olive oil. Most significant for their incomes was their ability to exploit the labor of the poorest farmers, who were eking out a precarious existence on small plots of land or on marginal land. Many scholars believe that some of those poor families rented land from the rich as sharecroppers in return for a portion of the harvest, while others mortgaged their land to the rich and were compelled to hand over a stipulated amount of the crops as payment on the debt. Small farmers fell easily into debt. One bad year meant borrowing next year's seed from a wealthy neighbor; a run of lean years could put a family so deeply into debt that it lost its land. We may assume also that the number of *thētes*—those who contracted to work as hired hands in return for food, clothing, and shelter—increased considerably. The attitude of the land-owning class toward those whom they exploited combined contempt, mistrust, and dislike.

Conjectures about the size of the noble class—defined as those whose land-holdings provided them a leisured lifestyle—range between 12 and 20 percent of the families; for the lower class—those with insufficient land to support themselves—estimates are on the order of 20 to 30 percent. (Of course, the percentages would have varied from polis to polis.) These figures allow for at least 50 percent of the families to have been neither rich nor dependent upon the rich. The fourth-century philosopher Aristotle in his *Politics* calls this group "the middlers" (*hoi mesoi*), the portion of the polis that was between "the very rich and the very poor" and possessed a moderate amount of wealth.

These three divisions were not monolithic, of course; within each there were gradations of wealth and social rank. The small number of aristocratic households was dominated by a smaller number of families that were preeminent because of their nobler bloodlines and greater wealth, an aristocracy within an aristocracy. Moreover, the hierarchy was naturally subject to change; one family might rise into the ranks of the upper nobility while another might drop down into the lesser nobility. Nevertheless, the propertied class as a whole remained clearly marked off from the groups below them. The agathoi protected and extended their economic and social exclusiveness by marrying only within the group. The ideal was to maintain class solidarity and at least the facade of equality among the families.

Within the middle group, there was greater economic and social gradation. Some non-noble oikoi shared in the rising prosperity of the Archaic Age and were fairly well off; at the other end of the spectrum were those barely keeping out of debt. The difference in economic status—and therefore in social status—among the independent farmers and craftsmen prevented them from perceiving themselves as a class with their own interests, as the rich landowners did. Upward mobility, though not impossible, was not easy. If a commoner became wealthy enough, he could marry into the nobility. But the aristocrats resisted assaults on their exclusiveness, as when the sixth-century aristocratic poet Theognis complains that although men take pains to make their animals "wellborn" by careful breeding, a "good man" will not hesitate to marry the daughter of a "kakos man," if she brings with her a good dowry. "Wealth," he says, "corrupts a lineage" (*Theognidea* 183–192). Downward mobility, on the other hand, was much more common, as unmanageable debt frequently reduced farmers to the condition of a thete. The erosion of the independent farmer group in the seventh century became a serious problem within the city-states.

Within the lowest group, gradations would have been only in the degree of abjectness, as the chances for economic betterment for the very poor were slight. It was not just poverty that made the lives of thetes miserable. They lacked even the limited protection slaves received from belonging to an oikos. Worse still, they had to endure the stigma of working for others, which for the Greeks connoted loss of freedom. Not surprisingly, when Homer wished to emphasize the utter misery of death he had the dead Achilles tell Odysseus that he would rather be alive and the thete of a landless man—the poorest of the poor—than king of the dead (*Odyssey* 11.489–491).

Citizenship

Although all free-born members of the polis were citizens (*politai*), they were far from equal in their citizen rights. Aside from their public role in religion, female citizens were denied any participation in political, judicial, or military affairs. These were exclusively the domain of adult (over age eighteen) male citizens. Among the men, the share of civic responsibilities and rights—to vote and speak in the assembly, to hold office, to serve as judges, to fight in the army—was divided unequally along mainly economic lines. In the early city-states, as we have seen, only the rich and wellborn possessed the full range of citizen privileges. Non-noble citizens of moderate means were barred from holding office, and in many cases the poorest citizens had no vote in the assembly. Full participation by all citizens in their governance of their poleis would be achieved only at the end of the Archaic period, and then only in democratic states; in oligarchic states, the poorest members would continue to be second-class citizens.

Women always played important roles in the Greek state. Religion was an integral part of the polis, where the proper worship of the gods was key to good order, prosperity, and success in battle. Many priesthoods were held by women. From an early date, the polis counted on women for the stability of individual households (oikoi) in terms of the bearing and rearing of children, the production of clothing, and in the case of the more affluent households, the management of slaves. Besides women, other categories of free persons living in a polis territory were denied citizen rights, chiefly resident aliens and former slaves. And in some states (mainly Doric), whole villages and towns were regarded as nonmembers of the demos, and their members were given the status of half-citizens. We will have more to say about these *perioeci* ("dwellers round about") in the next chapter. By far the largest groups of rightless inhabitants, however, were slaves and semislaves.

Slaves and Serfs

During the seventh century, there was some increase in the number of chattel slaves (persons captured or bought and legally classed as property), but rich landlords generally used the labor of farmers who were in debt or otherwise obligated to them, which was in many respects economically better for them than keeping multitudes of slaves. The real upsurge in slaveholding came in the sixth century when political reforms and measures in the city-states limited or abolished debt bondage, forcing the rich to use slave labor on their lands.

The Spartan "helots" provide an example of another category of agricultural laborers in Greece, whose status was characterized as "between free persons and slaves." The helots were the inhabitants of parts of Laconia and most of Messenia who were conquered by the Spartans in war and then made to work for Spartan citizens as serfs on what had been their own land. (The importance of the helots to the Spartan way of life will be discussed in the next chapter.) Similar serflike groups existed in other Greek states, especially in the areas where the Doric dialect was spoken. The origins of these subjugated peoples is very obscure. One theory is that they were the people dwelling in the lands that were taken over by the Dorian immigrants in the early Dark Age. Because they were ethnically different from the newcomers, they could be treated as an inferior subclass, permanently stigmatized as "other." They were compelled to work the land as sharecroppers and to provide other labor (including some military service), in return for which they were granted certain minimal protections, such as the right to marry and raise a family and the guarantee that they would not be expelled from the land they farmed.

Thessaly also had a huge population of unfree agricultural workers, called "the toilers," and, as we saw earlier, a few of the colonial city-states in the west and around the Black Sea reduced the nearby native populations to forced labor. It is not certain, however, whether other impoverished and exploited groups that we are told of were subjugated disenfranchised people or just the poorest class of citizens. That they were socially and economically inferior, however, is certain from the slang terms for them: "the naked ones" (in Argos), "dusty-feet" (in Epidaurus), "wearers of sheepskins" (in Sicyon), "wearers of dogskin helmets" (in Corinth).

Resentment from Below and the Beginnings of Social Change

There was strong popular resentment against the wealth, power, and arrogance of the self-styled agathoi in the seventh century. The rallying cry among the have-nots must have been "redistribution of the land!" The middling oikoi—those who produced enough to live on or enough plus some extra—also had cause for resentment. Because the aristocratic groups successfully held on to most of the fertile soil, the independent farmers had few opportunities to acquire good land. Their alternatives were to emigrate abroad, which many did, or to seek marginal land far from their villages, which yielded poorer return for extra labor and increased travel time. The middle group also chafed at being shut out of positions of power and prestige by the oligarchy's lock on the magistracies, boards, and particularly the council, where the political decisions were formulated. The well-off farmers were just as liable to be cheated in the law courts as the poorer ones and were just as helpless against "crooked judgments." In the assembly, the one organ of government to which they were admitted, the people's voice carried little weight against the concentrated power of the rich.

Yet, in spite of the strength of the ruling oligarchs and the apparent weakness of the rest of the demos, the absolute domination by the former was destined to be short-lived. By the early sixth century, oligarchic rulership had broadened to include numerous families outside the exclusive club of hereditary agathoi, and in some states even broader governments were emerging that would eventually give political power to the mass of people, including the poor. Spearheading the protest against aristocratic excess was the middle group of independent farmers, over whom the oligarchs had the least control. We are fortunate to have a very early voice for this group, Hesiod.

HESIOD: THE VIEW FROM BELOW

In addition to the *Theogony*, Hesiod is credited with another long hexameter poem (828 lines), about farming, called *Works and Days*. Unlike the Homeric epics, which are set in a distant Age of Heroes and tell of the triumphs and tragedies of great warrior chiefs, *Works and Days* is set in the present and tells about ordinary people and their ordinary lives. In the *Iliad* and the *Odyssey*, common folk are visible only as part of the social background. They are given collective roles as the mass of soldiers or citizens in the assemblies, or they appear in vignettes about farmers, housewives, shepherds, and craftsmen. These Hesiod puts in the foreground.

Hesiod also differs from Homer and the other epic poets in that he purports to be speaking of his own experiences: "I, Hesiod." As noted earlier, many scholars maintain that the poet adopted a *persona,* or poetic character, and that the details he provided about his own life are fictitious. Whether "Hesiod" was a real person and was giving his own autobiography matters little. No one doubts that his account of rural life in the early Archaic period is accurate.

Hesiod tells us that he and his brother, Perses, lived in the small Boeotian village of Ascra (part of the polis of Thespiae, five miles away), and when their father died a dispute arose over the division of the kleros. Perses cheated or tried to cheat Hesiod of a portion of the inheritance by bribing the judges (basileis). After the judgment, Hesiod intimates, Perses became a loafer and a spendthrift and reduced himself to such poverty that he found it necessary to go to his poet brother for help. Whether this is the literal truth or a fiction, such family situations must have been common.

The quarrel provides the pretext for the poem's form—a sermon to his erring brother. Sermonizing poetry, so different from that of the Homeric narrative, was clearly influenced by the ancient genre of Near Eastern "wisdom literature," which consisted of exhortations, instructions, and admonitions addressed to a son or other relative, or even to a king, and was spiced with stories and proverbs about right and wrong. Though ostensibly Hesiod was advising Perses, the real audience was the whole group to which he and Perses belonged, namely, the upper level of the independent farmers. At other points in the poem, however, he speaks on behalf of his peers and directs his sermonizing to the ruling group, whom he calls basileis. This might have been their actual title as a board of magistrates or judges in the city-state of Thespiae, but it is more likely that Hesiod was using the term in the generic epic sense of the leaders of any community.

Hesiod addresses the basileis very sternly, not at all deferentially. He calls them "gift-eating" basileis and accuses them straight out of habitually rendering their verdicts "with crooked judgments." He tells them that Zeus himself is watching over his daughter, Dike ("Justice"), and avenges unjust acts against her committed by those in power. Thus, the basic civic moral that justice through law is the foundation of good government appears already fully formed in Hesiod.

DOCUMENT 3.2

Hesiod lectures the aristocrats.

O basileis, you too observe well this judgment, for the deathless ones, who are near among people, observe all those who wear each other out with crooked judgments, paying no attention to the vengeance of the gods.... There is the virgin Dike, born from Zeus, majestic and revered among the gods who hold Olympus. And whenever somebody hurts her by scorning her crookedly, she straightway seats herself at the side of father Zeus, the son of Cronus, and tells him about the unjust thinking of people, until the demos atones for the outrages of the basileis who, by thinking pernicious thoughts, veer off the right track by pronouncing judgments crookedly.... O basileis, straighten your words, gift-eaters, and forget entirely crooked judgments.

Works and Days 248–264; Tandy, adapted

A moralistic tone pervades the entire poem. Hesiod has a whole litany of proverbial dos and don'ts that we could find in any peasant society in the world. He counsels a strict reciprocity in all dealings. When you borrow from a neighbor, he says, "pay it back well, with the same measure, or better if you can, so that you may later find him reliable should you need him" (349–351).

At the core of Hesiod's moral program is the ethic of work, arduous manual labor:

> It is from work that men are many-sheeped and rich, and the man
> who works is much dearer to the deathless ones. Work is no reproach;
> idleness is a reproach. If you work the idler will quickly envy you as
> you become wealthy. Success and renown attend upon wealth.
> (*Works and Days* 308–313; Tandy)

Here, Hesiod asserts that through work the ordinary farmer may win the three prizes that in the Homeric epics could be attained only by heroes: wealth, the special favor of the gods, and glory. Thus unremitting toil in the farm fields becomes a virtue equivalent to great deeds on the battlefields. Of course, the prizes are pared down to suit the humble life of a rural village. To Hesiod and his neighbors, wealth meant "having their granaries full of the sustenance of life" at harvest time and not having to borrow; renown was being admired and respected by all the folk in the village. This pragmatic and non-aristocratic system of values, the motto of which was "work with work upon work," can be detected throughout the Archaic period.

As a social document of the peasant-farmer's values, *Works and Days* also allows us to appreciate class differences in outlook toward institutions such as marriage. Among the upper class, marriage was primarily a means of establishing alliances and enhancing family prestige. Noble families often sought advantageous matches outside their polis, and, as in Homer, suitors competed against one another with expensive gifts and shows of manliness in athletic contests. Aristocratic women, though they lived highly circumscribed lives, had a high status and were treated with great respect by the men. The different, much narrower view of the farmer class shows through in Hesiod's advice on marriage:

> Marry a virgin so that you may teach her devoted ways, and marry especially one who resides near you, lest you marry a source of laughter for the neighbors. For a man carries off nothing better than a good wife, and in turn there is nothing else more chilling than an evil one....
>
> (*Works and Days* 699–703; Tandy)

Prestige, though just as important as in an aristocratic marriage, is here confined to the village and expressed in negative terms. It is not a wife who will bring advantageous connections that the farmer seeks, but one who will not cause him to lose respect if she should turn out to be a glutton or lazy or unfaithful—typical faults that Hesiod attributes to women.

The misogyny expressed in Hesiod was a common attitude during the Archaic period and continued throughout Greek antiquity. The best-known illustration of this way of thinking is the myth of Pandora, the first woman, as it is told in both the *Theogony* (571–612) and *Works and Days* (60–105). Zeus, Hesiod says, commanded this "beautiful evil" to be created as a punishment for the crime of Prometheus, who stole fire from the gods and gave it to humans. Pandora opened the lid of a jar containing all the plagues and diseases of the world and let them out. All womankind inherited Pandora's "shameless mind and deceitful nature," her "lies and coaxing words." Women, the poet says, live off men like the drones among the bees. "Do not let a woman wiggling her behind deceive you in your thinking by chattering wheedling words. She is after your granary. The man who trusts a woman trusts thieves" (*Works and Days* 373–375).

The members of Hesiod's economic class resembled the wealthy class in one respect: they exploited the labor of others. The difference was that the ordinary farmer had only a few workers and labored alongside them. Hesiod takes for granted that the farmers he is addressing can afford to own at least one slave woman or man, take on a hired hand (thes), and employ day workers at busy times. The farmer keeps his eye on the bottom line. The day's food for a hired plowman is carefully measured out—just enough to keep up his energy level. Hesiod advises hiring a thes who has no oikos (he will work for less) and a childless female worker ("a worker with a child at her breast is a bother").

The *Works and Days* clearly reveals Hesiod to be a middler. There are ten to twelve people living on his farm, and to feed them he would need ten to fifteen acres under grains if he used a three-field rotation or twenty acres if he used an alternate fallow system. Bear in mind that Hesiod's father's farm had been twice that size. Farms would be smaller in the Classical period, but there were more people by then.

However much he railed against the wealthy and powerful, then, Hesiod was not a "champion of the oppressed," as some historians have called him. Rather, his was the indignant voice of the middle: Zeus will look favorably on those who are pious, hard-working, and just, and in the end will punish those who are not. A hundred years later in Athens, another thunderous voice would be raised against the evil greed and violent actions of the aristocrats—this time not from below but from a member of the aristocracy, the statesman Solon, whose reforms would pave the way for Athenian democracy.

THE HOPLITE ARMY

Warfare took on a different character in the Archaic period. Between about 725 and 650, the Greeks made major changes in military equipment and tactics. Henceforth, all Greek battles were fought by heavily armored foot soldiers called **hoplites**, arranged in a tightly packed formation called the **phalanx**. Many now believe that the phalanx evolved from an earlier, looser type of mass formation. In this "protophalanx," as it is sometimes called, the fighting men were grouped in regular units arranged in straight rows or ranks. The protophalanx is depicted in the *Iliad*, though for dramatic effect the poet concentrates on encounters between individual warrior-heroes, largely ignoring the mass of soldiers who fought around them. This clouds our understanding of the actual deployment of the formation in battle. It appears, however, that the hostile ranks in Homer move into spear range, hurl their pair of short throwing spears, and then fight hand to hand with their long swords.

As the phalanx evolved, it became progressively more compact, with the soldiers lined up almost shoulder to shoulder and each rank almost treading on the heels of the one in front of it. Phalanx fighting was simple in the extreme: the two close-packed phalanxes charged at one another and collided. The more ranks, the more effective the charge. In its developed form (by 650 at the latest), the phalanx was normally eight rows deep, fewer if circumstances required the phalanx to widen. Weapons and armor evolved in tandem with the compact phalanx, to make it more effective. The hoplite's main weapon was his long heavy spear, which he used as a thrusting weapon. After the initial collision, when there was no room to jab with the spear, the hoplite used his secondary weapon, a short

Figure 3.3. Detail of Corinthian polychrome *olpē* (wine jug), known as the Chigi Vase, with a rare depiction of a battle between phalanxes of hoplites (c. 640 BC). Rome, National Etruscan Museum of the Villa Giulia.

slashing sword. In a hoplite battle the soldiers needed better protection than they had had earlier. Helmets, upper-body armor (breastplates), and shin-and-knee protectors (greaves), all of which had been used in earlier warfare, were redesigned to be thicker and stronger (bronze replaced other materials, such as padded wool or linen), and to cover larger areas of the body.

The most innovative item of equipment was a new type of shield called the *hoplon*, after which the hoplite was named. Designed specifically for the phalanx formation, it was round, made of wood covered with a thin sheet of bronze. It was the hoplon that made the phalanx an effective fighting force. Larger than all the earlier round shields (about three feet in diameter), it was held by inserting the left arm through a central band and gripping a strap at the rim. (See Figure 3.3.) The hoplon was large enough to cover the man on the left, allowing hoplites to fight shoulder to shoulder with half of their body protected by the next man's shield. Seen from the front, a phalanx presented nearly a solid wall of shields, helmeted heads, and spears.

A hoplite battle was a ferocious affair. At a signal from a trumpet, the phalanx advanced at a fast walk, sometimes at a trot; when they came close, the front ranks

Figure 3.4. Bronze votive offering, first quarter of the seventh century, said to have been found near Thebes. Height: 8 inches. This hoplite has lost his right arm and spear, as well as his shield, which would have been attached to his left forearm. The inscription on his legs is two hexameter lines: "Mantiklos dedicated me to the far-shooter, silver-bowed Apollo from his share; and may you, too, Phoebus [=Apollo], give a generous return." Boston, Museum of Fine Arts.

raised their spears, stabbing overhand at the enemy, aiming at vulnerable spots unprotected by armor. Meanwhile, the ranks behind literally shoved against those in front—the maneuver was called "the pushing"—using their weight to break the enemy's ranks. Enormous courage was required of every single warrior, for success depended on every man holding his place in the formation. To flee the fight brought the contempt of the whole demos; thus men as a rule stood their ground, "biting their lip with their teeth," as the Spartan poet Tyrtaeus (c. 650 BC) says.

The conditions of hoplite battle were awful. In the Archaic period, the equipment weighed about seventy pounds, almost half the weight of an average man. It was unbearably hot inside the armor; vision was restricted by the dust and the helmet; the noise was incessant and terrifying. Everyone was spattered with blood; wounded men were trampled underfoot. Tyrtaeus describes an old hoplite "breathing out his brave spirit in the dust, holding his bloody genitals in his hands." The battles were fairly brief, however, seldom more than an hour. Casualties were relatively light for the losers as well as the victors, rarely over 15 percent. Once the enemy broke ranks and fled, there was not much pursuit, so that massacres were rare. Campaigns, too, were brief; usually, a single set battle ended the fighting for the summer. Farmer-hoplites, whether winners or losers, could not stay long away from their fields and animals.

Not all citizens fought in the phalanx, however. Because hoplites had to furnish their own arms and armor, which were fairly expensive, the poorest men were disqualified and served instead as light-armed troops. Modern estimates of those who did qualify vary considerably. Given the importance of the phalanx to the survival of the polis, and taking into consideration that captured armor would be distributed and that some of the hoplites' gear would be donated, a reasonable estimate is that at least half of the broad group of *mesoi* were able to serve.

The Hoplite Army and the Polis

It is in the hoplite army that we most clearly observe the polis ideology that the citizen is the slave of the common good. The poems of Tyrtaeus of Sparta and Callinus of Ephesus, both from around the mid-seventh century, reveal a shift in values from the individual to the polis. Although Homeric warriors faced death willingly as the price of their glory, they nevertheless saw it as an unmitigated evil. In Tyrtaeus, dying in battle had acquired a positive value. "It is a noble thing for a good man to die, falling among the front ranks, fighting for his fatherland," he tells his fellow Spartans, and again, "Make life your enemy, and the black spirits of death dear as the rays of the sun." Bravery in battle was still the highest virtue, but it too had become a cooperative value—not the heroics of individual champions but simply keeping your place in the phalanx.

> This is the highest worth, the finest human prize
> and fairest for a bold young man to win.
> It benefits the whole community and state,
> when with a firm stance in the foremost rank
> a man bides steadfast, with no thought of shameful flight,
> laying his life and stout heart on the line,
> and standing by the next man speaks encouragement.
> (Tyrtaeus fr. 12.15–19; West)

Similarly, honor, glory, and fame are sought just as eagerly by the citizen-soldier as they were by the Homeric hero, but these rewards could be earned only in service to the polis.

Distinctions of wealth and birth vanish in the ranks of the phalanx. Thus, Callinus says, though a man may have "immortal gods as his ancestors," he is despised by the demos if he flees the "thud of spears," while the stout-hearted man who dies in battle is mourned by both the "great and the small; in death he is missed by the whole people and in life he is treated as a demi-god" (i.e., as an epic hero). Tyrtaeus, too, shows how the hoplite ideal was eroding the Homeric notions of excellence that the aristocrats laid claim to as proof of their exclusive worth. In the elegy just cited, Tyrtaeus lists all the things the *agathoi* valued—skill in athletics, strength and beauty, great wealth, political power, eloquence in speaking—and says that he would not even mention in his poems a man who "had every kind of fame except a fighting spirit."

The reality of strict equality in the ranks, where high-born men and men from the middle fought side by side, would make it increasingly difficult for the agathoi to claim that they alone were competent to wield power and formulate policy for the poleis. Already in Hesiod and Tyrtaeus we see the concomitant growth of an anti-elitist ideology that challenged elitist pretensions of natural superiority and substituted the leveling notion that non-aristocrats were equal to aristocrats off the field of battle as well as on. Throughout the Archaic and Classical periods, the non-aristocratic hoplites would play a key role as the independent variable in the power relations within the city-state.

This class, comprising fairly well-off farmers and craftsmen, was the pivotal group in determining where a polis stood on the continuum from narrow oligarchies to full democracies. If they were content with an uneven distribution of power and agreed to or abetted the exploitation of the weak, oligarchic regimes reigned secure. If, on the other hand, they opposed the status quo and sympathized with the bottom half of the citizenry, the balance of power shifted from the elite to the mass. Because the well-off farmers tended toward conservatism, most Greek poleis in the Archaic and Classical periods were moderately oligarchic, granting citizen rights in accordance with economic status. But in city-states in which the upper level of the middle group came down firmly on the side of the poor, there was complete legal and political equality between the classes. The rapid swings from oligarchy to democracy (and vice versa) that occurred so frequently in the history of a polis are best explained by the shifts in attitude of the nonaristocratic hoplites. They also played a major role in the political phenomenon the Greeks called **tyranny** (*tyrannis*).

THE ARCHAIC AGE TYRANTS

Hardly had the aristocrats rid themselves of the position of basileus when a new type of one-man rule arose in the form of the *tyrannos* (tyrant). Between about 670 and 500 BC, a great number of city-states throughout the Greek world went through a phase of tyranny. The words *tyrannos* and *tyrannis* (tyranny) were borrowed into the Greek language (perhaps from Lydia in Asia Minor) to describe a form of government for which the Greeks had no word: rule by a man who seizes control of the state by a coup and governs illegally. The Archaic Age tyrant was what we call today a dictator or strongman. At first the word *tyrannos* had no real negative connotation. It eventually came to mean a wicked and oppressive despot, in part because of propaganda spread by the aristocrats, who naturally hated the men who had overthrown their regimes, but also because later generations perceived that dictatorial rule by one man not accountable to the demos threatened the freedom of all. Yet there are ample indications that the non-aristocratic contemporaries of the early tyrants viewed them in a more favorable light. Unfortunately, only a few of the dozens of tyrants who grabbed power in their poleis are known in any detail. Still, we can see a general pattern in their rise and fall.

Tyrannies were short-lived. Although all the tyrants tried to form dynasties by passing on the rulership to their sons, no tyranny lasted more than three generations and most collapsed after one or two. Despite aristocratic hate propaganda that described some tyrants as lowborn, it appears that all were members of the aristocracy. For example, Pheidon of Argos was the hereditary basileus before he turned himself into a *tyrannos*. Not all tyrants, however, were from the top-ranked families. Cypselus of Corinth, for instance (c. 657–627), was marginalized within the "royal clan" of the Bacchiads, because his mother, a Bacchiad, had married outside the clan.

In addition to their membership in the elite, would-be tyrants were distinguished in their poleis for their individual achievements. Cypselus, prior to becoming a tyrant, had held the post of polemarch (military commander). Orthagoras of Sicyon (mid-seventh century) had also been polemarch and had compiled an outstanding battle record. Cylon of Athens, whose attempted coup in 632 failed, had won fame as a victor in the Olympic games.

Vicious infighting among the aristocratic families in the polis for honor and precedence was a major factor contributing to the emergence of the tyrants. Rivalry among the aristocrats, though it was channeled to some extent into competition for offices and control within the council, was particularly nasty in the seventh and sixth centuries because the struggles for power were waged among "clans" (*genos;* plural *genē*). Like the royal clan, an aristocratic genos—the word essentially designated a lineage—was composed of a preeminent family that extended the umbrella of fictive kinship over less prestigious noble oikoi, whose members supported the leader-family in its political ambitions. Disputes among these factions—gangs of hotheaded young aristocrats—frequently erupted in bouts of violence and bloodshed, as the *genē* morphed into political clubs. For example, at Mytilene on Lesbos, in around 600 BC, Aristotle tells us that aristocratic violence intolerably overflowed into the general population when the Penthilids "went about striking people with clubs."

The Greeks called formal conflict between groups within the city-state *stasis* ("taking a stand"). Opposition of this sort was integral to the Greek political process of every period. The stasis between aristocratic factions in the Archaic period, however, was much more frequently violent than afterward (when the power of the *genē* had declined), and was highly disruptive of the society; in addition to violence in the community, the factional strife also regularly led to exile and property confiscation for the losers. Worse, because membership in a genos was hereditary, this kind of civil war could keep flaring up for generations. The intervention of a strongman who could stop, or at least check, the feuds of the noble families, though anathema to the nobles, was welcome to the rest of the people.

To climb to power, these "renegade aristocrats," as some call them, needed resources and manpower. One potential source was disaffected aristocrats within the polis who were frozen out of the ruling circle. This band of followers might be supplemented by a mercenary force from outside the polis. Such aid was sometimes supplied by a friendly tyrant (for his abortive coup at Athens, Cylon

Figure 3.5. Gold libation bowl dedicated by the Cypselids (sons of the Corinthian tyrant Cypselus) made of spoils from the city of Heraclea, a polis on the west coast of mainland Greece. c. 630 BC. Height 6.7 inches. Inscribed in the Corinthian version of the Greek alphabet, this precious bowl is the only votive offering of the Cypselid dynasty that has been preserved. Boston, Museum of Fine Arts.

received some troops from his father-in-law, Theagenes, tyrant of Megara), or, in the case of many of the Ionian tyrants in the late sixth century, by the Persian empire. The best known tyrant, Pisistratus of Athens (who made three attempts before succeeding), availed himself of a variety of resources, including local bodyguards, mercenaries, and troops donated by powerful outsiders. His story will be told at greater length in Chapter 5.

Yet no tyrant, however, no matter what his resources, could have succeeded without the tacit support of the citizens themselves, particularly the heavily armed farmer-hoplites. There is no evidence that any tyrant came to power at the head of a hoplite army, but such active intervention would not have been necessary. An oligarchy could not have been overthrown if it had the loyalty of the non-aristocratic hoplites, whereas all that a would-be tyrant needed was their passive refusal to defend the nobles. Among the many reasons for the hoplites' disaffection with oligarchic rule, not the least was that the incessant infighting among the aristocratic families was harmful to the good order of the state. As for the lowest citizens, they naturally would have been very supportive of a coup against the group that was exploiting them.

All later writers judged that the tyrants were viewed as champions of the demos against the oligarchs. In the fourth century, Aristotle put it concisely:

> A tyrant is set up from among the *dēmos* and the multitude against
> the notables, so that the *dēmos* may suffer no injustice from them. This
> is clear from [human] events. For nearly all tyrants have arisen from

among the demagogues, so to speak, after gaining trust by slandering the notables.

(Aristotle, *Politics* 1310b 3–4)

After seizing power, the tyrant usually attacked the rich. Cypselus killed or banished many of the Bacchiad aristocrats and confiscated their lands (presumably some of them went to poorer Corinthians), and other tyrants did the same. Tyrants made laws to limit aristocratic power and privilege, including "sumptuary laws," which curbed aristocratic luxury and ostentation. They also protected the existing institutions; Aristotle said of the Orthagorid dynasty of Sicyon that "in many ways they were slaves to the laws."

Under tyranny, many poleis thrived and reached new heights. Extensive building and improvement projects—stone temples and other major buildings, harbors and fortifications, and urban amenities like the water supply, streets, and drainage systems—turned the capital towns into real cities, and also provided work to poor citizens.

Moreover, trade, commerce, and crafts were encouraged and supported under the tyrants. Pheidon of Argos, for example, standardized weights and measures for the Peloponnesus, an enormously important advance in the commercial economy of the area. And Cypselus' son and successor, Periander, built a stone trackway across the narrow Isthmus of Corinth, where a canal runs today, allowing ships and cargoes to be hauled between the Saronic and Corinthian gulfs. (It was still in use as late as 883 AD.) Tyrants also instituted new religious cults and festivals that celebrated and strengthened the unity of the polis, and they supported all cultural activities, competing to attract the best artists, architects, poets, and thinkers in Greece to stay at their city.

The sons of dictators are seldom as successful as their fathers. The Archaic tyrants had gained popular support for their takeover because of their personal charisma and achievements. Their sons, however, were heirs to a nonexistent office, and so were extremely vulnerable. A few succeeded on their own merits, but most found themselves resorting to increasingly "tyrannical" measures to repress opposition, which naturally exacerbated resentment against them. Tyrants were overthrown, and they and their families were exiled or killed. Usually, the aristocrats who had been banished by the tyrants returned and reestablished an oligarchy. Aristocratic rule was never the same, however, after a tyranny. The farmer-hoplites were no longer willing merely to vote for their leaders without being able to hold them accountable. Nor could the nobles now refuse their inclusion in the process of public decisions, or take away from the poor the benefits that the tyrants had bestowed on them to make their lives easier. So it is paradoxically possible to view tyranny as a transitional structure that led to democracy.

ART AND ARCHITECTURE

In art as well as in literature, philosophy, and science, Archaic Greece experienced a burst of creative energy unsurpassed in any comparable time period of the ancient world. Building on the achievements of the Late Geometric period, the craftsmen of the seventh and sixth centuries attained new heights of excellence in all the forms of visual art. With the development of the city-state, differences in style between the various poleis became more distinct. This is most evident in the pottery, which continues in the Archaic period to be the most ample source for measuring artistic evolution. The "Orientalizing" tendencies of the eighth century reached a peak in the seventh, with more extensive artistic borrowings from the ancient Near East, including floral designs and friezes of real and fantastic animals that replaced the earlier geometric patterns. In addition, artists enhanced narrative depictions of myth with more sophisticated representations of the human body.

Under the leadership of the tyrant Cypselus (c. 657–627), Corinth emerged as the leading commercial center of Greece and dominated the trade in finely painted pottery. Corinthian pottery workshops specialized in perfume flasks exquisitely decorated in the Orientalizing style, two to three inches high, which they filled with scented olive oil and exported in huge quantities throughout the Greek world. The enterprising Corinthians also invented a widely imitated technique called "black figure," which permitted the rendition of minute details. In this technique, the vase painter first applied to the pale yellowish Corinthian clay a slip composed of clay particles suspended in water; on this field, he created silhouetted figurative and decorative forms. He then used a sharp point to incise linear details into the clay surface. The decoration was generally further enhanced with red and white colors. When the vase was fired, the areas covered with the clay slip turned black. Corinthian black figure was enormously popular, but as often happens, success led to mass production and a consequent decline in quality, as the famous animal motifs were monotonously and carelessly repeated.

By 550, Athenian black-figure pottery, featuring differently shaped and larger vessels, had driven Corinthian vases from the export market. Around 530, the Athenians, in turn, invented a new technique of vase painting called "red figure," which reversed the black-figure technique. The artist drew outlines first and then painted the background with a gloss (clay slip) that fired black, leaving the outlined areas in the orange-red color of the Attic clay itself. Afterwards he painted on the details with a fine brush. This allowed a more subtle and refined rendering of detail than the incised black-figure technique.

Seventh- and sixth-century vase paintings most commonly depicted episodes from mythology and the heroic sagas. (See Plate VIa.) On Athenian vases of the later sixth and early fifth centuries, depictions of contemporary life became more common, and many of these focused on the activities of upper-class males. Typically portrayed were athletics, horsemanship, and rowdy drinking parties, as well as school scenes, music lessons, and homosexual courtship. The depictions of drinking parties often included non-Athenian female slaves and prostitutes (*hetairai*), who sometimes provide musical entertainment by playing the double pipes. Upper-class Athenian women, represented less often than men, were occasionally shown in a domestic setting or else participating in weddings or funerals. Archaic potters and painters, who appear to have been proud of their work, frequently

(a) **(b)**

Figure 3.6a–b. Two views of an Attic bilingual amphora (storage jar) showing the heroes Achilles and Ajax playing a board game, attributed to the Andocides Painter and to the Lysippides Painter (c. 520 BC). This special vase is called "bilingual" because it is decorated in the new red-figure technique on one side and in traditional black-figure on the other. Boston, Museum of Fine Arts.

signed their vases employing different verbs that signified their individual creative roles ("Euxitheus made me," "Euphronius painted me") and occasionally including a taunt to a rival potter. (See Plate VIa.)

Monumental sculpture (life-sized or larger) in both marble and bronze was an innovation of the Archaic period. Egypt was a source of both aesthetic and technical inspiration for the first large Greek marble statues. The first large marble statues appeared around 650; larger bronze statues were first produced in the sixth century but did not became common until the fifth century, after which they far outnumbered those made of marble and other stone. While the Greeks continued to employ marble for architectural sculpture, they preferred bronze for freestanding sculpture. (See Plate X.)

Two important types of freestanding stone statuary in Archaic Greek were a naked male figure, now called a **kouros** ("youth"), and a clothed young female known as a **kore** ("maiden"). Throughout the Archaic period, these statues conformed to the original rigid Egyptianizing pose, staring straight ahead, with arms pressed against

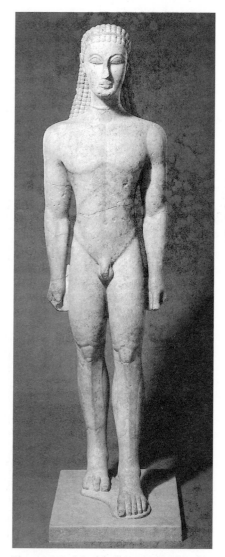

Figure 3.7. Statue of an Egyptian nobleman. Early seventh century BC. Boston, Museum of Fine Arts.

Figure 3.8. Marble kouros, said to be from Attica (c. 600–480 BC). Height without plinth, 6 ft. 9/16 in. While the stiff and stylized pose as well as the carving methods employed in Egyptian stone statuary were sources of inspiration, the Archaic Greek sculptor has created a free-standing nude male figure. New York, Metropolitan Museum of Art.

Figure 3.10. Late Archaic kore from the acropolis of Athens (c. 490 BC), dedicated by Euthydicus.

Figure 3.9. Marble kouros with inscribed base that stood upon the grave of Aristodicus in Attica (c. 510–500 BC). Although naturalistically proportioned and fluidly modeled, this statue of a short-haired athletic youth still conforms to the traditional kouros pose. Athens, National Archaeological Museum.

their sides, one foot stepping forward. As time went on, they became increasingly less rigid and blocklike, and by the end of the sixth century they both had been given more accurate bodily proportions and were more natural-looking. The conventional "Archaic smile" had disappeared, and the stylized treatment of hair had relaxed. From the very beginning, these images of youths and maidens as well as other Archaic Greek sculptures were brightly painted, enhancing their lifelike qualities. (See Plate VIIIa and VIIIb.) Kouroi and korai were commonly set up by wealthy families as grave monuments or as offerings in the sanctuary of a god or goddess. Often bearing an inscription with the dedicator's name, they were highly public advertisements of a family's or an individual's status in the community.

Another type of Archaic sculpture consisted of reliefs depicting mythological scenes, carved on the triangular pediments and along the entablatures of late-sixth-century

temples. Relief sculpture was increasingly successful at showing figures in movement and action. By contrast, the stylized freestanding kouroi and korai must
have appeared rather old-fashioned by the end of the century.

The architecture of the Archaic period still centered on religious buildings, the
monumental temple and (beginning in the sixth century) smaller edifices, such
as the "treasuries," which housed dedications to the gods. A significant advance
in temple architecture occurred around the middle of the seventh century, when
limestone and marble replaced mud brick and wood. Here again, the Greeks
were indebted to the Egyptians, from whom they learned the engineering skills

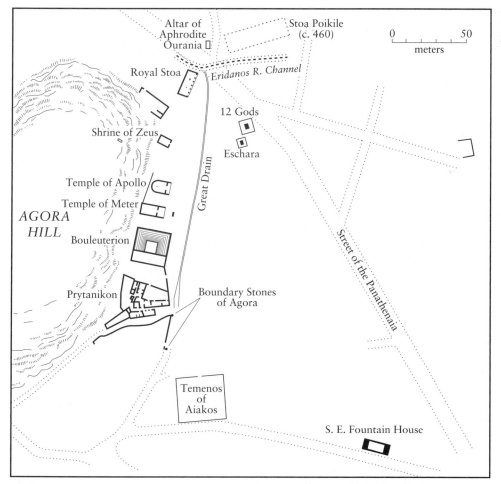

Figure 3.11. Plan of the Athenian agora as it looked at the end of the Archaic period
(c. 500 BC), showing the earliest public buildings. (After J. Travlos, 1971.)

necessary for handling huge stone blocks. The temple plan, however, was a continuation of the Greek Geometric model, and most of the architectural features, such as the low-pitched roof covered with terra-cotta tiles (replacing the old thatched roof), were purely Greek. By the early sixth century, the two main types or "orders" of architecture, the Doric and the Ionic (see later: Figure 7.6), were well established. Greek temples looked much as they would for the next five hundred years—but the extant ruins of these structures are somewhat deceptive. Like the freestanding stone statues, portions of Greek temples and their sculptural decoration were painted in strong bright colors, presenting a rather different impression from the bare, gleaming marble we see today.

During the sixth century, other carefully constructed permanent structures appeared in the main cities. Most of these were built in and around the **agora**, or gathering place, a large open space at or near the center of the city. The Dark Age agora had been only the place where the assembly met; in the Archaic period, it became the marketplace and public space of the city and therefore of the whole city-state. Male citizens congregated to do business, gossip, and make political deals. By about 500 BC, the agora contained one or more open colonnaded passageways called stoas, which provided shade and shelter and space for market stalls. Enhancing its dignity and importance were official buildings such as the council house and offices. Sanctuaries, fountain houses, and public sculptural monuments also graced the agora. In addition to the agora, Archaic poleis contained open spaces with specified functions: the *gymnasium*, where men exercised, and the *palaestra*, a wrestling ground.

The agora and other public spaces would not receive numerous or splendid public buildings until the fifth and fourth centuries. Nevertheless, by about 550 all the major poleis except Sparta merited the title of true urban center. An aerial view of Corinth or Athens or any other major center would have revealed a dense concentration of buildings, most of them private houses, connected in blocks along narrow streets, broken up by patches of garden plots. The houses were larger than those of the Dark Age—three or four rooms rather than one or two—but still quite modest compared to the houses that would be built later in the Classical period. Even the homes and furnishings of the elites, including the tyrants, remained unpretentious throughout the Archaic and well into the Classical period.

The modesty of private homes and the relative modesty even of secular civic buildings underscore the basic fact that efforts toward architectural and sculptural distinction in ancient Greece were directed primarily toward sanctuaries; the gods received the lion's share of a city-state's surplus wealth, both at home and in the Panhellenic sanctuaries.

Lyric Poetry

In literary expression as well, the Archaic period was one of innovation. Archaic poetry is markedly different from the poetry of Homer and Hesiod. Many poets did continue to compose lengthy epic narratives (the epic cycle of heroic sagas

and the Homeric hymns described in Chapter 2 are examples). But the most original Archaic poets chose not to follow in the giant footsteps of Homer, who by the
early seventh century had already been canonized as the supreme poet of all time.
They turned their talents instead to other poetic genres, which we lump together
under the rubric of **lyric poetry**.

The roots of lyric poetry extend far back in time to folk songs created for specific occasions such as harvests, weddings, funerals, and coming-of-age rituals,
or to hymns, fables, drinking songs, and love songs—everything, in other words,
that pertained to communal and private life. With the advent of literacy, such
poems could be preserved and circulated; poets could attain not merely local but
Panhellenic fame, by competing with their more carefully crafted songs composed
and polished in writing.

Each of the several genres commonly grouped under the name "lyric" had its
own metrical pattern, subject matter, occasion, tone (elevated and serious or low
and scurrilous), and musical accompaniment. Like epic poetry, lyric poetry was
"song" and was presented in performance. Some types were accompanied by a
stringed instrument, the lyre (*lyra,* hence "lyric"), others by a wind instrument,
the *aulos,* consisting of a pair of pipes. And some were simply recited or chanted
without musical accompaniment.

A major distinction is made by modern scholars between solo songs and songs
performed by a chorus of young men or women, who sang and danced to the
music of the lyre. Choral poetry and some kinds of solo poetry were presented
before large public audiences at festivals, whereas others were performed in small
private gatherings such as, usually, a drinking party (*symposium*). Unlike the two
Homeric epics, which ran to 12,000 and 16,000 lines, lyric poems were short—from
a few lines to several hundred lines (in the case of choral songs).

Most Archaic lyric poetry was not choral; it was personal, sometimes extremely
so, in subject and tone. The poets sang about drinking, friends and enemies, sexual love, old age and death, politics, war, and morality. The poet's tone could
vary from lighthearted to bitter to contemplative. As we saw earlier with Hesiod,
"personal" need not mean "autobiographical." Yet the lyric poets went far beyond
Hesiod in revealing their own (or their persona's) emotional and mental states.
They therefore not only give us rare insights into feelings about private matters
but also, because private life and polis life were so closely intertwined, reflect sentiments and attitudes about their society. Further, with the exception of Sappho's
work the poetry presents (from a strictly male point of view) the social attitudes of
both the elite and the middle strata. Although we have fragments from about two
dozen lyric poets of this period, we can sample only a few of them here. Three
major lyric poets, Simonides, Bacchylides, and Pindar, whose careers were mainly
in the fifth century will be discussed in Chapter 6.

Some Lyric Poets and Their Social Attitudes

Archilochus of Paros (mid-seventh century) was particularly known for his
mordant wit, which he often directed against the old heroic ideal. According to

tradition, Archilochus was the son of a nobleman and a slave mother. His voice is highly personal and passionate. His poems are about drinking and carousing, his sexual adventures, the pain of losing comrades in shipwrecks, hatred of his enemies, the uncertainties of life, written in alternating tones of tenderness and cruelty, deep seriousness and obscene levity. He stresses his twofold role: soldier of fortune as well as inspired poet. "I am a servant of the lord god of war, and one versed in the Muses' lovely gifts." And again, "On my spear's my daily bread, on my spear my wine from Ismarus; and drinking it, it's on my spear I recline."

Where Tyrtaeus and Callinus, whom we met earlier in the description of hoplite warfare, transvalue the epic-heroic conventions, Archilochus pokes fun at them. The Spartans found the following mock complaint so outrageous that they forbade the recitation of Archilochus' poetry at Sparta.

> Some Thracian sports my splendid shield:
>   I had to leave it in a wood,
> but saved my skin. Well, I don't care—
>   I'll get another just as good.
>   (Archilochus fr. 5; West, adapted)

This is not the boast of a Homeric hero. The irony and the humor lie in the incongruity between the poet's cynical stance and the Homeric ideal. Archilochus also uses humor to puncture the pretentiousness of the aristocratic equation of physical beauty and manly excellence.

> I don't like an army commander who's tall, or goes at a trot,
> or one who has glamorous wavy hair, or trims his beard a lot.
> A shortish sort of chap, who's bandy-looking around the shins,
> He's my ideal, one full of guts, and steady on his pins.
>   (Archilochus fr. 114; West)

The ostentatious display of luxury by the aristocrats was another thing that met with the censure of poets who reflected the sentiments of the ordinary yeoman farmers. For example, the Ionian philosophical poet Xenophanes (570–475 BC) criticized the upper class of his native Colophon who went to the agora in their all-purple cloaks, "proud in the splendor of their finely coiffured hair and sleek with unguents of the choicest scent." An earlier contemporary, Asius of Samos, registered similar displeasure at the elites who swept into the precinct of Hera in their snow-white robes, their long hair tied up in golden clasps and fancy bracelets on their arms.

At the same time as it deplores ostentation, the popular poetry promotes the practical wisdom and commonsense values held by the ordinary citizen of moderate means. A collection of homespun maxims from the first half of the sixth century, attributed to Phocylides of Miletus, is made up of sayings such as "Many things are best in the middle; I want to be middle (*mesos*) in the *polis*" and "What good is noble birth for those who lack grace in words and counsel?" In a similar vein, Xenophanes devalues the aristocratic pursuit of honor and prestige through athletic competition (only the wealthy could afford to compete), asserting that it is "small joy for the polis" when athletes win at the Olympic games, "for these things do not fatten the treasury of the polis" (Xenophanes fr. 2.20-23; West)

Perhaps the most colorful representative of the nonelite perspective was Hipponax of Ephesus (sixth century), who adopted the persona of an urban hustler, always broke and engaging in drunken brawls and escapades. Hipponax wrote in a vernacular full of street slang and obscenity, savagely lampooning his enemies and making fun of himself and his poverty. "And Wealth—he's all too blind—he's never come to my house, never said, 'Hipponax, here's three thousand silver drachmas, and a heap of other stuff besides.' No, he's a dimwit" (Hipponax fr. 36, West).

But most poets present the world from an elitist perspective. Their poems are directed to an audience that has wealth and leisure. Most of this poetry was composed specifically for recitation at *symposia,* male drinking parties, which were an exclusively aristocratic form of entertainment. Symposiastic poetry, as it is called, covered a range of subjects, from the lofty (patriotic songs and retellings of ancient myths) to the playful (riddles and jokes). Partisan politics was a favorite topic. The commonest themes, however, were personal musings on the pleasures of wine and love (both heterosexual and homosexual) and the sad necessity for these joys to fade with old age.

Typical is this short poem by the seventh-century Ionian poet Mimnermus (from Smyrna or Colophon).

> What's life, what's joy, without love's heavenly gold?
>   I hope I die when I no longer care
> for secret closeness, tender favors, bed,
>   which are the rapturous flowers that grace youth's prime
> for men and women. But when painful age
>   comes on, that makes a man loathsome and vile
> malignant troubles ever vex his heart;
>   seeing the sunlight gives him joy no more.
> He is abhorred by boys, by women scorned:
>   So hard a thing God made old age to be.
>   (Mimnermus fr. 1; West)

Another Ionian poet was Anacreon of Teos (mid-sixth century), who was invited to Samos by the tyrant Polycrates, and after Polycrates' murder joined the court of the Pisistratid tyrants of Athens. The consummate aristocratic court poet, he particularly celebrates the pleasures of wine and love. For Anacreon these are the proper topics for symposia, not the worn themes of war and bloodshed:

> I like him not, who when he drinks by the full bowl
> tells only of disputes and tearful war,

but rather him who blends the Muses' boon with Love's,
and turns his mind to good cheer and delight.

(Anacreon Elegy 2; West)

Similar in style and tone to Anacreon was his contemporary Ibycus, from
Rhegium in Italy, who also spent years at Polycrates' court. Some of Ibycus'
poems are long choral narratives in lyric meters, on traditional epic and mythological themes. Most of his extant work, however, is homoerotic poetry, full of
sensuous imagery. In one poem, Eros (Love) comes like the north wind from
Thrace, and with "parching madness, dark and fearless, shakes me to the bottom
of my heart with his might." In another poem, on falling in love again, he com-
pares himself to an old champion racehorse that unwillingly drags his chariot to
the contest.

Mytilene, the dominant polis of Lesbos, produced two prominent poets,
Sappho and Alcaeus, at the end of the seventh century. Both were from leading
aristocratic families. Sappho is the only known woman poet from the Archaic
period, in fact, one of the few in all ancient Greek literature (women were not
encouraged to write). Her poetry was greatly admired throughout antiquity—
she was hailed as the "tenth Muse." Unfortunately, very little of Sappho's poetry
has survived. Most of what we have consists of solo songs, highly personal in
tone, whose main theme is erotic love between women. It appears that Sappho
was the leader of a close-knit circle of young upper-class women in Lesbos
(hence the modern term "lesbian"), who shared their lives for a brief period
before marriage. Sappho also wrote weddings songs performed by choruses of
young girls.

DOCUMENT 3.3

*Nine "books" (i.e., papyrus rolls) of Sappho's poetry were collected in the Alexandrian peri-
od, but only two complete poems survive, along with several substantial portions of poems
and a number of very short fragments. Here is a selection of shorter fragments.*

Honestly I wish I were dead.
She was covered in tears as she went away,
   left me, saying "Oh it's too bad!
   How unlucky we are! I swear,
Sappho, I don't want to be leaving you."
   This is what I replied to her:
   "Go, be happy, and think of me.
You remember how we looked after you;
   Or if not, then let me remind. . . ."

Sappho fr. 94; West

Atthis, you've come to hate the thought of me,
You fly to join Andromeda.

Sappho fr. 131; West

> I have a pretty child, like flowers
> Of gold her form, my precious Cleis;
> Whom I would not exchange
> for all of Lydia, or the lovely land. . . .
>
> Sappho fr. 132; West

Previously unknown texts, as well as some known only through fragments, still turn up among the papyri. In 2004, scholars deduced that part of a papyrus roll from Egypt in the collection of the University of Cologne contained fragmentary poems of Sappho. Like Mimnermus, Sappho talks of growing old. But the girls who remain in her circle for a few years are always young and desirable, for younger ones replace their elders who leave for marriage. She cites the mythic example of Tithonus, who had been granted immortality in response to the prayer of Eos, the dawn goddess who loved him. Since Eos forgot to ask that Tithonus be given eternal youth, he grew older and more frail without being able to die, while she remained forever young.

> You for the fragrant-bosomed Muses' lovely gifts
> be zealous, children, and the clear melodious lyre:
>
> but my once tender body old age now
> has seized; my hair's turned white instead of dark;
>
> my heart's grown heavy, my knees will not support me,
> that once on a time were fleet for the dance as fawns.
>
> This state I oft bemoan; but what's to do?
> Not to grow old, being human, there's no way.
>
> Tithonus once, the tale was, rose-armed Dawn,
> love-smitten, carried off to the world's end,
>
> handsome and young then, yet in time grey age
> o'ertook him, husband of immortal wife.
>
> Sappho, fr. 58 + P.Köln 21351; West 2005, adapted

All the noble families of Lesbos, during the lifetimes of Sappho and Alcaeus, were embroiled in vicious power struggles. Some of Sappho's fragments reflect this state of affairs. Alcaeus, however, puts us right in the center of the complicated intrigues, the political deals and betrayals, and the partisan hatreds and violence, which he relates in great detail. Alcaeus' venom was directed primarily at another aristocrat named Pittacus, a bitter enemy who had been a former ally. Predictably, Alcaeus levels at Pittacus the worst insults an aristocrat could muster:

"base-born" (*kakopatridēs*; literally "son of a *kakos* father") and "tyrant" (he had been elected by the people to serve as a temporary dictator to end the incessant aristocratic feuding). Alcaeus is best known for this invective poetry, but the other symposiastic themes, such as love, legend, and wine, occupy his verses just as much. Indeed, he stresses that love, wine, and the pleasures of the drinking party offered him and his companions welcome repose from the factional strife that sent him into exile at least twice. Here is his description of his predicament, separated from his society and his family's lands:

> Plunged in the wild chaste-woods I live
> a rustic life, unhappy me,
> longing to hear Assembly called
> and Council, Agesilaidas!
>
> From lands my grandfather grew old
> possessing, and my father too,
> among these citizens who wrong
> each other, I've been driven away
>
> an outland exile....
>   (Alcaeus fr. 130b.1–9, West)

The largest chunk of symposiastic poetry that we have is a compilation of fourteen hundred lines of poetry, all attributed to Theognis of Megara (mid-sixth century) but actually containing poems written by a number of different authors, dating from the late seventh to the early fifth century. This anthology, called the *Theognidea,* includes the usual aristocratic themes, but it goes further in revealing the class prejudices of the elite and their antagonism toward the lower classes. The collection reads like a moral handbook for aristocrats, praising the values of the wellborn *agathoi* and vilifying the base-born *kakoi,* who are represented as incapable of any sort of excellence. This intensified contempt is the reaction of a frustrated aristocracy, who realized that they were losing their status and privilege while a significant number of nonelites were making economic and political gains.

Conveyed again and again in verses such as these (addressed to the young lover of "Theognis") is a sense of helplessness mingled with bitter resentment at the intolerable reversal of station:

> Cyrnus, those who were *agathoi* once are now *kakoi,* and those who were *kakoi* before are now *agathoi.* Who could bear seeing this, the *agathoi* dishonored and the *kakoi* getting honor?
>   (*Theognidea* 1108–1111)

Although aristocrats would continue to proclaim their innate superiority, the movement toward political leveling that had begun in the seventh century was essentially completed by the early decades of the fifth.

PHILOSOPHY AND SCIENCE

Like lyric poetry, philosophy (literally "the love of wisdom") arose with the awakening of the Greek world in the Archaic period. The earliest Greek philosophers, some of whom were the first to write in prose, are called the Presocratics to distinguish them from the disciples of Socrates, who lived in Athens in the Classical period. The Presocratics are also clearly differentiated from the Socratics in that the former concentrated on the structure and development of the physical universe, while the latter were more interested in ethics, in the role human beings play in relation to one another and to the larger society.

Cosmos: The Visible Sky

Because they did not have telescopes, the Greeks knew only the stars and the five planets they could see with the naked eye. But they were much more familiar with the night sky than most city dwellers are nowadays. Since there were no streetlights, smog, or tall buildings, their nights were filled with stars. They named the planets and constellations after their gods and characters in their myths, like Orion the hunter and the girls he pursued and never caught, the Pleiades. In *Works and Days,* Hesiod's agricultural calendar is addressed to farmers who learned when it was time to perform their seasonal chores by the position of the constellations. When Greeks sailed, they plotted their location by the position of celestial objects.

In the Archaic period, colonization, travel, and the development of trade and commerce spurred the growth of astronomical thinking. Contact with other civilizations in Asia, especially Babylonia, where astronomical records of phenomena such as eclipses had been kept from as early as 1600 BC, showed that the movements of the stars and planets exhibited some regularity and predictability.

The Search for Origins

Unlike the Babylonian record keepers, early Greek astronomers tried to find explanations for the celestial motions. They attempted to develop scientific models that not only would explain what had been observed but would predict future events. Then as now, the same scientists who were interested in understanding the universe searched for its origins. Then as now, the search often took as its first axiom that at the beginning there was only one substance, or very few, out of which all matter evolved.

The earliest Greek scientists we know of lived in Miletus in the sixth century. Their thoughts have been transmitted to us because they were quoted by later Greek philosophers and scientists such as Aristotle. The Milesians were the first to abandon supernatural or religious explanations for natural phenomena and instead to seek purely physical causes. Thales, traditionally the first of the three great Milesians, was able to predict a solar eclipse and the solstices, thereby demonstrating that occultation of the sun and the length of days were not determined by divine whim. He also believed that the single origin of matter was water (for it could be transformed into both gas and solid forms) and that the earth was flat and floated on water. In contrast, his fellow Milesian, Anaximander, called the original principle "the Boundless" or "the Indefinite"; this limitless entity contained all matter, including such opposites as wet and dry and cold and hot. He postulated that the earliest creatures arose from slime warmed by the sun's heat, and he was also the first Greek to draw a geographical map. Another Milesian, Anaximenes, thought that everything had evolved from air: it became fire when it was rarefied, could change to wind and cloud, and when condensed was transformed into solid substances. Like Thales, Anaximenes believed that the earth was flat, but he thought that it floated on air.

Pythagoras, one of the most influential cosmologists, is familiar to us because of the theorem that bears his name. He was born in Samos, but left around 531 BC because of the tyranny of Polycrates. Pythagoras settled in southern Italy and lived an ascetic life with a group of disciples. The original Pythagoreans and their successors followed strict rules in their daily lives. Women were included in the Pythagorean communities and were imbued with the philosophical doctrines that regulated the conduct of daily life. For example, the Pythagoreans followed strict dietary rules, at least partly because they believed in transmigration of the soul. Nevertheless, they were interested in worldly matters like politics and geometry. Geometry (literally "taking the measure of the earth") was a theoretical and practical science of special importance in the ancient world, where land was the most valuable commodity; the founding of new cities included the careful measurement of land into plots of equal size and its distribution to colonists.

It is difficult to assess Pythagoras's own contributions to the practices and ideas associated with his name. The followers of Pythagoras believed that arithmetic also held the key to understanding the universe. They postulated that the earth was a sphere in the center of a series of hollow spheres. The stars were fixed on the outer spherical shell, and the planets on smaller shells within. Each day the stellar sphere rotated from east to west while the planetary spheres rotated from west to east at various rates. Their movement created a sound, but since the sound is always with us, we are unable to hear it. The Pythagorean theory of the musical harmony of the heavenly spheres is an example of an attempt to find, or even to impose, an aesthetically pleasing mathematical explanation for the movement of celestial bodies. More than a century later Plato, who was much influenced by Pythagoreanism, also sought to explain the universe in terms of arithmetical abstractions and asserted that all celestial bodies move at the same rate in a circular path.

DOCUMENT 3.4

Xenophanes on the Gods

His radical stance on anthropomorphic religion is seen in these six fragments, each of which comes down to us through quotation by later Greek authors.

Homer and Hesiod assign to the gods everything that is blameworthy and disgraceful among human beings: stealing, committing adultery, and deceiving each other (fr. 11).

But mortals think gods are born and have clothes, voices, and bodies like their own (fr. 14).

The Ethiopians say that their gods are snub-nosed and black and the Thracians that their gods have light blue eyes and red hair (fr. 16).

But if cattle and horses and lions had hands or drew with their hands and completed works like men, horses would draw images of their gods that were like horses and cattle like cattle, and they would make their bodies like the bodies each of them had (fr. 15).

There is one god and he is the mightiest among gods and men, resembling mortals in no way at all in either form or thought (fr. 23).

All of god hears, all of him senses, all of him hears; but with no effort at all he controls all things with the thought of his mind (fr. 24-25).

Xenophanes fragments 11, 14–16, 23-25 Diels-Kranz

Like Pythagoras, Xenophanes of Colophon, whom we just met as representative of the lyric poets, moved from the eastern Mediterranean to Magna Graecia, where he traveled about as an exile. Fragments of his poems criticizing conventional religious and ethical beliefs are extant (Document 3.4). Xenophanes' ideas about the development of the cosmos were based on personal observation. For example, when he noticed fossil imprints of marine life and seaweed in three different locations inland, he theorized that they were produced long ago when the earth was covered with the mud produced by a mixture of seawater and earth.

An important characteristic of early Greek science is that ideas circulated widely through the writing of books. Because the city-states were nontheocratic, the early philosophers could freely criticize each other's theories. Heraclitus, who lived in Ephesus in the second half of the sixth century, was a fierce critic of Pythagoras and Xenophanes. Rejecting Pythagoras' worldview, which emphasized regularity and order, Heraclitus maintained that everything was constantly changing like a river: you cannot step into the same river twice. The world consists not of one or more material substances but of processes governed by what Heraclitus calls "logos," a rational principle or statement that people must understand in order to understand the world in which they live. Heraclitus taught that the world is not what it appears to be. A similar idea was at the core of Parmenides' philosophy. He lived in the Greek colony of Elea in southern Italy and wrote a poem in which he tried to analyze what it means to say that something is or exists. According to Parmenides, all you can say and think is that "being" exists but "nonbeing" does

Figure 3.12. Aerial view of the sanctuary of Apollo at Delphi. See also Plate IX.

not exist. Change is logically impossible, because if something changes it is no longer the same and does not exist. For the rest of antiquity, Greek philosophy struggled with these questions: What do we mean when we say that something exists, and what is the relation between the world as we experience it and what it "really" is?

Some of the speculations of the Presocratics appear to be uncannily consistent with the hypotheses of modern cosmology. As we nowadays search distant planets for signs of life "as we know it" and delude ourselves that earth is the center of our galaxy when we view the pageant of the stars overhead, we can better understand the anthropocentric and geocentric arrogance of the Greeks and appreciate these early scientists, whose only tool for exploration was their own intelligence.

PANHELLENIC INSTITUTIONS

The ease with which poets, thinkers, artists, and ideas moved from city to city across the wide expanse of Greek occupation indicates how culturally unified the Greek world was even as it remained politically divided. The Panhellenic gatherings played a prominent role in forging a common Hellenic identity, as ever greater numbers came to worship, consult oracles, and attend musical and athletic competitions.

The oracle of Apollo at Delphi drew Greeks and non-Greeks from all over the Mediterranean world. For a fairly hefty fee, an individual could consult Apollo for advice on marriage, careers, voyages, and so on. Poleis sought the god's guidance and sanction on serious matters of state, such as colonizing, religion, and laws. Apollo responded through a priestess, called the Pythia, who, in a self-induced trance, divulged his messages. These were put into coherent (though frequently ambiguous) form by "interpreters" (*prophētai*). Because so many tyrants, foreign kings, and aristocratic leaders consulted the oracle, the sanctuary became a storehouse of information about political conditions across the Mediterranean.

The greatest attraction, however, was the sanctuary of Zeus at Olympia. By the end of the seventh century, the quadrennial games in honor of Zeus were drawing spectators and contestants to Olympia from the entire Greek world. Shortly thereafter, three new Panhellenic games were instituted at other sanctuaries: the Pythian games for Apollo at Delphi (582 BC), the Isthmian games for Poseidon near Corinth (581), and the Nemean games for Zeus at Argos (573). The new games were integrated into the four-year Olympiad to form an athletic "circuit" (*periodos*). The festivals were staggered so that there would be one major set of games every year, with the Olympics always the premier event. Other Panhellenic festivals modeled on the Olympic games were inaugurated at Athens, Thebes, and elsewhere during the sixth century.

The Panhellenic contests and rituals brought Greeks together in peaceful celebration. For the month in which the Olympic games were held, for example, poleis observed a sacred truce that guaranteed safe passage for all participants and spectators while traveling to and from Olympia. The sacred precincts themselves became places for poleis to flaunt their wealth and achievements with costly dedications of statues and marble "treasuries," which commemorated both athletic and military victories.

There were no team events, only individual contests. Thus, the games kept alive the ancient ideal of the individual hero: to be declared best (*aristos*) by gaining victory over a worthy opponent. The content and spirit of the Panhellenic games had changed little from the games described in the *Iliad*. The events still tested speed, strength, dexterity, and endurance, precisely the qualities desired in a Homeric warrior.

The main events at the Olympic games were the foot races, the most prestigious of which was the short sprint, called the stade (*stadion*, hence "stadium"), a distance of about 210 yards; at Olympia, the winner of the stade race was listed first in the summary of all victors. At the end of the sixth century a new race run by contestants in full armor was inaugurated, in recognition of hoplite fighting. Male athletes competed in a variety of events, including wrestling, boxing, and the *pankration*, a vicious combination of boxing and wrestling with no holds barred except biting and eye gouging. In the pentathlon, opponents competed in five events: the stade, javelin and discus throws, the long jump, and wrestling. Most

Figure 3.13. The stadium in the sanctuary of Zeus at Olympia. The preserved stadium dates to the mid-fourth century BC, but it follows the Archaic form in which spectators sat on the ground surrounding the race course to observe the events instead of in seats, as in later stadia.

spectacular of all was the four-horse chariot race, a contest dating back to the Late Bronze Age. (The wealthy owner of the horses and chariot, not the charioteer, was declared the winner.) A number of festivals also featured competitions in choral and solo poetry and in musical performances.

Separate sets of contests were held for boys (under age twenty) and for men. Women did not compete at the major games, nor were they permitted to attend as spectators, although maidens raced in honor of Hera at Elis. The young women did not race completely nude, as the males did, but their tunics barely reached the knees and covered only one side of the chest. (See Chapter 4, Figure 4.5.) The prizes were just tokens of glory, wreaths of foliage: at Olympia olive leaves, at Pythia laurel, at Nemea wild celery, and at Isthmia pine. (Much more substantial prizes were offered at the several less prestigious Panhellenic games that sprang up during the sixth century at Athens, Thebes, and elsewhere.) On their return home, however, victors reaped lavish rewards: triumphal processions, civic honors, statues, and even prizes of money.

RELATIONS AMONG STATES

Cultural exchange was only one means of interaction among the Greek poleis. Throughout history states have interacted in two additional areas: trade and warfare.

Trade was brisk in archaic Greece, with many products traveling by sea. Yet money as we know it was largely absent. Both at home and away, Greeks continued to rely on the barter system familiar from earlier eras. Wealthy traders might pay for their purchases with solid pieces of gold, silver, bronze, or iron, but of course these always had to be weighed and their purity verified, which was burdensome. Had nobody thought to mint coins? In fact, someone did. A twentieth-century find in the kingdom of Lydia in western Anatolia turned up coins that date to the late seventh century. They were made of **electrum**, an alloy of gold, silver, and a trace of copper, and stamped with a symbol that indicated their weight and hence their value. The idea soon caught on in Greece as well. Most early coins, however, were of such high value as to be of limited use in the commerce undertaken by ordinary persons, and it is likely that the principal function of the earliest coins was to declare the authority and independence of the government that issued them. It was not until the classical period that coins were issued in a wide variety of denominations and began to play a large role in commercial life.

With the emergence of the city-state, the external problem of coexistence became much more complicated. What had been raids among neighboring communities turned into serious warfare. There were several reasons for the heightened tensions. As states began to run out of land, they attempted to extend their boundaries, and disputes often erupted over borderlands that had not required strict definition when populations were still small. Moreover, quarrels of mother-cities were often taken up by their colonies, with new enmities among poleis hundreds of miles away. On the mainland, territorial wars between poleis began as early as the late eighth century, when Chalcis and Eretria in Euboea fought over possession of the rich Lelantos River plain that lay between them. In the Lelantine

Figure 3.14. Electrum coin from Ephesus or Halicarnassus in eastern Greece with a stag on the obverse and a punch mark on the reverse. Early sixth century BC. The earliest inscribed Greek coin, it was made from the natural alloy of gold, silver, and copper known as electrum before the precious metals themselves were used for coinage. Athens, Numismatic Collection.

War, as it is called, both sides were said to have had distant allies from much further away—possibly indicating the involvement of rival colonial networks.

Interstate tensions were especially high in the Peloponnesus, which contained three of the major Greek city-states—Sparta, Argos, and Corinth. After their conquest of Messenia in the late eighth century, the Spartans warred against their rivals, the Argives, with some success, although they were badly beaten in 669 BC in a battle at Hysiae in Argolis. (It has been suggested that the Argive victory encouraged the revolt of the Messenian helots in the Second Messenian War.) The Argives in the meantime were trying to expand their own landholdings and influence within the Peloponnesus, particularly around Corinth; the Corinthians themselves were fighting over territory with their smaller neighbors, Megara and Sicyon. Such costly and deadly squabbles over land continued in the Peloponnesus until the middle of the sixth century, when the Spartans began using diplomacy and forming alliances to maintain their supremacy in southern Greece.

Diplomacy and Alliances

In the sixth century, Greek states began in earnest to establish formal mechanisms for avoiding war. Most of these cooperative institutions had their genesis in the prestate period, but it was not until the later Archaic Age that they were refined and regularized. At the same time that formal means were being instituted, diplomatic relations were still being conducted much as they had been in the Dark Age, through personal relationships among the leading men. This was especially so in the tyrannies. Tyrants conducted foreign policy as sovereigns, making pacts of friendship or marriage alliances with other tyrants or with the top aristocrats. For example, Periander (c. 627–587), who succeeded his father, Cypselus, as tyrant of Corinth, developed a political friendship with Thrasybulus, tyrant of Miletus, which ended an enmity between the two poleis that went back to the Lelantine War. The pact aided Corinthian traders in Egypt and the Black Sea and Milesian traders in the west. Periander was also asked by Athens and Mytilene to arbitrate a dispute over control of Sigeum, an important way station on the route to the Black Sea.

Personal diplomacy became institutionalized in the form of **proxeny**, whereby a resident of one city-state acted as a semiofficial representative of the interests of another. Proxeny was a formalized version of the Dark Age institution of "guest-friendship" (*xenia*), observed in Homer. As we saw in Chapter 2, when Agamemnon and Menelaus arrived in Ithaca to recruit Odysseus and his followers for the Trojan War, they stayed at the house of their *xenos*, or "guest-friend," at Ithaca while they conducted their embassy. In the Archaic version, when an Athenian, say, came to Corinth on public or private business, the *proxenos* of the Athenians at Corinth would aid him in his mission.

Temporary military alliances between communities, both offensive and defensive, were as old as war. In the Archaic period they became more formal and longer-lasting. States began to make written treaties, pledging friendship and nonaggression for a stipulated time. The earliest formal pact we know of is on an inscription dating to between 550 and 525, between the polis of Sybaris in southern Italy, its allies, and another polis. It reads: "The Sybarites and their allies and the Serdaioi made an agreement for friendship, true and guileless, forever. Guarantors, Zeus, and Apollo, and the other gods, and the polis of Posidonia." There were also several new types of multistate alliance. One was the amphictyony, or association of neighbors, in which several independent city-states cooperated to maintain and protect a common sanctuary of a god. Such associations may have gone far back in time, although we know of them only from the sixth century forward, when they had taken on a more political character than merely protecting the common sanctuary. Although an amphictyony did not prevent its members from warring against one another, at least it mitigated hostility. Member states might pledge, for example, not to destroy each other's cities or cut off a member's water supply.

It was also in the sixth century that ethne began to form loose unions of their separate towns and villages for the purposes of foreign relations and warfare. These differed from the amphictyonies in that they had an overarching governing body for coordinating communal action. Nevertheless, the authority of central governments over the independent entities would remain relatively feeble until the creation in the fifth century of true "federal states."

One of the most successful federations in the Archaic period was that of the ethnos of Thessaly. As early as the seventh century, this vast, rich northern region was loosely united for military action under the headship of a war leader, called either *archōn* (leader) or *tagos* (military commander). Thessalian unity allowed them to become the major power of northern Greece for a period of time in the sixth century, until the confederacy was weakened by quarrels among the local chiefs. The ethnos of the Phocians, under pressure from the unified Thessalians, quickly developed a federal union of their own in the sixth century, complete with federation coinage and army. Similarly, the need for some unity against both Thessalian and Athenian pressure at this time prompted the rival poleis of Boeotia to form a confederacy under the leadership of Thebes. This early Boeotian league, too, proved fractious and unstable, because of opposition by the other city-states to Theban hegemony.

The mid-sixth century also saw the first of the mega-alliances, the Peloponnesian League created by Sparta. The history of the fifth century would be shaped by the rivalry and then the hatred between the Spartans and the Athenians. They would conduct their wars and diplomatic skirmishes as the hegemons of two huge alliances, the Peloponnesian and Delian leagues, respectively, which together comprised most of the Greek world.

At the beginning of the Archaic period (c. 750 BC), the Greeks were still a relatively isolated and economically backward people, organized politically in low-level chiefdoms. By the late sixth century, they lived in a culturally advanced state-society that had spread across the entire Mediterranean zone, and they were major players in the complex international economy.

The supreme political achievement of the Archaic Age Greeks was the polis, which in the course of the period at different rates at different places evolved from narrow oligarchy to tyranny to a more broadly based polity in which the majority of male citizens participated in its governance. Because the people, not just the elite, had a stake in the polis, the sense of loyalty and dedication to the "commonality of citizens," as Aristotle called the polis, was profound. It was this polis–citizen bond that made the Greek city-state unlike any other form of state in the ancient world. This fierce loyalty translated into a deep conviction that no persons from outside the state could be allowed to violate its independence.

Civic pride was the cement of the city-state and was largely responsible for the cultural flowering of the Archaic period. The Greeks' passion for autarchy, however, was a permanently divisive force, which in the second half of the fifth century would cause the poleis to exhaust themselves in the great Peloponnesian War between the Spartans and the Athenians and their respective allies. That would be the start of the slow decline of the polis as an autonomous political unit. But at the beginning of the fifth century, the Greek states were at the height of their proud independence and had no inkling that their unyielding self-interest would drive them into such a calamitous war.

Yet, in a seeming paradox, the growing awareness during the Archaic period of a shared Greekness (what the historian Herodotus called *to hellēnikon*, "the Greek thing") also gave rise to a strong cultural identity and sense of kinship. The shining moment of Panhellenic solidarity would come in the early fifth century, when the Greek poleis subordinated their individual loyalties to unite against the attempts of the Persian empire to conquer Greece. In the Persian wars (490–479), the Greeks would equate the freedom of their individual city-states with the "freedom of the Greeks" against the "slavery" of the Persian "tyrant."

The glow of Panhellenic unity would soon fade, however, and for the next century and a half the poleis and ethne of Greece would continue in their old ways, despite a growing realization among many observers that wars of Greeks against Greeks were tantamount to civil war within a city-state. For most of that period, diplomatic and military activity would center on the two great powers of Sparta and Athens.

KEY TERMS

agora	Hesiod	metropolis
Archaic period	*hoi agathoi*	oligarchy
aristocracy	*hoi kakoi*	phalanx
Bacchiads	hoplite	polis
colony	kore	proxeny
electrum	kouros	synoecism
ethnos	lyric poetry	tyranny

SUGGESTED READINGS

Andrewes, A. 1956. *The Greek Tyrants*. New York: Harper & Row. Though written more than a half century ago, it remains the best introduction to the *tyrannoi*.

Aubet, Maria Eugenia. 2001. *The Phoenicians and the West: Politics, Colonies, and Trade*. Translated by Mary Turton. 2nd ed. Cambridge: Cambridge University Press. Comprehensive account of the colonizing activities of the Greeks' chief rivals in the Mediterranean.

Boardman, John. 1974. *Athenian Black Figure Vases*. London: Oxford University Press.

———. 1975. *Athenian Red Figure Vases: The Archaic Period*. London: Oxford University Press.

———. 1978. *Greek Sculpture: The Archaic Period*. London: Oxford University Press. These three volumes make up a valuable set of handbooks on Greek art of the Archaic period, lavishly illustrated, with concise and informative commentary.

———. 1999. *The Greeks Overseas: The Early Colonies and Trade*. 4th ed. London: Thames & Hudson. Comprehensive account of Greek colonization based primarily on archaeological evidence.

Burkert, Walter. 1992. *The Orientalizing Revolution: The Near Eastern Influence on Greek Culture in the Early Archaic Age*. Translated by Margaret E. Pinder and Walter Burkert. Cambridge, MA: Harvard University Press. Illuminating analysis of the interaction between Greek and Near Eastern culture in the Archaic period.

Edwards, Anthony T. 2004. *Hesiod's Ascra*. Berkeley and Los Angeles: University of California Press. Reconstruction, on the basis of Hesiod's *Works and Days*, of life in a Greek town in the Archaic period.

Forsdyke, Sara. 2005. *Exile, Ostracism, and Democracy: The Politics of Expulsion in Ancient Greece*. Princeton: Princeton University Press. An excellent survey of the political instability generated by aristocratic violence and its legacies into the Classical period.

Hanson, Victor Davis. 1995. *The Other Greeks: The Family Farm and the Agrarian Roots of Western Civilization*. New York: Free Press. A wide-ranging, meticulously detailed study of the "yeoman" farmer-hoplite and his role in the formation of the city-state.

Mitchell, Lynette G., and P. J. Rhodes, eds. 1997. *The Development of the Polis in Archaic Greece*. London and New York: Routledge. A good collection of articles on various aspects of the development of the Greek city-state.

Ridgway, David. 1992. *The First Western Greeks*. Cambridge, UK: Cambridge University Press. Lucid survey of the archaeological evidence for early Greek settlement in Italy.

Snodgrass, Anthony. 1980. *Archaic Greece: The Age of Experiment*. Berkeley and Los Angeles: University of California Press. The first major book on Archaic Greece written by an archaeologist, and an important reappraisal of the importance of the Archaic period to Greek history.

Tandy, David W. 1997. *Warriors into Traders*. Berkeley and Los Angeles: University of California Press. An innovative revisionist analysis of the economic history of Greece in the Archaic period.

——— and Walter C. Neale, eds. 1996. *Hesiod's Works and Days: A Translation and Commentary for the Social Sciences*. Berkeley and Los Angeles: University of California Press. A specialized commentary incorporating the perspectives of sociologists, anthropologists, and social economists.

van Wees, Hans. 2004. *Greek Warfare: Myths and Realities*. London: Duckworth. Brilliant reinterpretation of the development of Greek warfare in the Archaic period.

Sparta

Admired in peace and dreaded in war, for much of the Archaic and Classical periods Sparta was the most powerful city in the Greek world. Although the Spartans are the specific subjects of only one chapter of this book, their role in Greek history should not be minimized. Sparta was different from other poleis. To be sure, the Spartans shared many basic institutions with other Greeks: their society was patriarchal and polytheistic; servile labor played a key role; agriculture formed the basis of the economy; law was revered and martial valor prized. Nonetheless, Sparta was unique in many important ways. No other Greek state ever defined its goals as clearly as Sparta or expended so much effort in trying to attain them. While the intrusion of the state into the lives of citizens was substantial in all Greek states, no state surpassed Sparta in playing an invasive role in the daily life of women and men alike. Spartans took enormous pride in their polis, and other Greeks were impressed by the patriotism and selflessness the Spartan system entailed. The Spartans' denial of individuality fostered a powerful sense of belonging that other Greeks envied, and Sparta continues to cast a spell over historians, philosophers, feminists, and political scientists.

SOURCES FOR SPARTAN HISTORY AND INSTITUTIONS

Despite the interest the Spartans sparked in their contemporaries, it is surprisingly difficult to write the history of Sparta and of its surrounding territory, Laconia. The problem is not lack of sources. Though unfortunately all the sources concentrate on upper-class and royal Spartans and provide little information about the majority of the population of the territory of Laconia—the servile masses known as

Figure 4.1. View over Sparta to Mount Taygetus from the Shrine of Helen and Menelaus (the Menelaum).

helots and the large disfranchised free class known as **perioeci**—still the volume of ancient writing on Sparta is large and includes unusually detailed information about women. The two greatest Greek historians, Herodotus and Thucydides, reveal a great deal about Spartan history, but the bulk of our information comes from two authors who wrote works focusing specifically on Archaic and Classical Sparta: Xenophon and Plutarch.

Xenophon was born in Athens around 430 BC, and he knew the Spartans at first hand. With other young men, Xenophon left Greece in 401 to serve as a mercenary in the army of Cyrus the Younger, pretender to the Persian throne. In the course of this expedition and subsequent campaigns in Asia, he met many Spartans, including the king, Agesilaus II, whom he came to admire. In the late 390s, with Athens and Sparta at war, Xenophon was exiled for favoring the Spartans against Athens. Relocating in the Peloponnesus, he wrote a treatise called *The Spartan Constitution*. Since Xenophon was an eyewitness and knew many leading Spartans personally, his work is our best source for Spartan social, political, and military institutions.

Plutarch, who lived from 46 to 126 AD, a thousand years after the earliest events at Sparta that he describes, also prefers many customs and institutions of the Spartans to those he found elsewhere, both in Greece and Rome. He was a Greek living in a Roman world, since by his day his native Boeotia had been incorporated into the Roman Empire. Although his writings contain large quantities of information, Plutarch was influenced by nostalgia for a happier past when Greece was not ruled by foreigners. Plutarch's writings on Sparta, more than those of any other ancient author, have shaped later views of Sparta, but Plutarch was a biographer and a philosopher of ethics, not a historian. His works on Sparta include five biographies: the lives of **Lycurgus**, Lysander, Agesilaus, Agis, and Cleomenes (the latter two combined in a single essay). The *Sayings of Spartans* and the *Sayings of Spartan Women* are also included among Plutarch's works. Despite the centuries that separated him from the people he depicted, Plutarch's work is of value because he visited Sparta and also read books that are now lost or survive only in fragments. One of the important works that he must have read, but that no longer exists, is Aristotle's *Constitution of Sparta*. Some of the surviving works of Aristotle, however, do provide some important information on Sparta, and Aristotle's reports are consistent with the data supplied by Xenophon and Plutarch.

One of the major controversies among today's scholars of ancient history is whether to take the primary sources at face value or to be skeptical. Some believe that the sources generally reflect an actual historical situation, while, at the other extreme, others argue that they present a picture of a utopian society so idealized that it has consequently been labeled "the Spartan mirage." Since Spartans did not write historical literature before the Hellenistic period, reports about Sparta must have been disseminated orally at first and in literature written by non-Spartans. Even Sparta's laws were preserved in the memory of Spartans rather than committed to writing. Except for some fragmentary verse by the seventh-century poets Alcman and Tyrtaeus, much of our written evidence for Sparta originated after many of the events described. Thus, some scholars argue that much of what we regard as the Spartan way of life was actually created in the Hellenistic period by reformers who convinced the Spartans and other Greeks that they were merely restoring the archaic constitution attributed to their venerable lawgiver Lycurgus. This scenario, however, posits that the Spartans and other Greeks were quite gullible. To some scholars it seems more reasonable to assume that the well-known Spartan way of life developed in the Archaic period, that it had changed by the end of the fifth century, and that the original lifestyle was revived by reformers, perhaps in an enhanced or exaggerated form, in the Hellenistic period.

Unfortunately, archaeological evidence only partly remedies the deficiencies of our written sources. In commenting on the need for historians not to be deceived by superficial impressions, the Athenian historian Thucydides observed:

> If, for example, Sparta were to be deserted and only the temples and the foundations of the buildings remained, I imagine that people in the distant future would seriously doubt that Sparta's power ever approached its fame.... The Spartans never developed one metropolitan area or built lavish temples and buildings but rather live in scattered settlements in the old-fashioned Greek way.
>
> (*The Peloponnesian War* 1.10)

The calculated austerity of Spartan life meant that domestic dwellings were extremely simple, even by Greek standards. This is bad news for archaeologists.

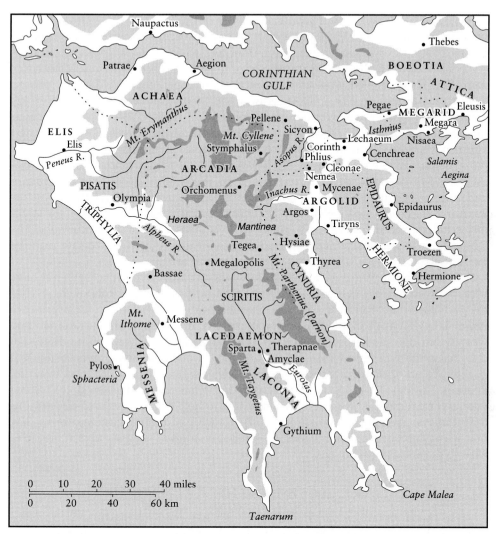

Figure 4.2. Peloponnesus.

Furthermore, modern Sparta has not been the subject of extensive excavation as has Athens, where the efforts of scholars as well as haphazard finds due to the construction of subways and the expansion of the capital city of Greece have led to major discoveries. In Sparta, public construction was limited to a few government buildings, gymnasiums, and temples, and for our knowledge of most of these we currently depend less on excavations than on the descriptions of Pausanias, who wrote a guide to Greece in the second century AD. By then, the Romans had built monuments and buildings on top of the earlier structures. Inscriptions concerning public or private matters are likewise scarce. Even tombstones, which are ubiquitous in the rest of the Greek world, are rare; at Sparta only men who had died in battle or women who had died in childbirth were permitted to have inscribed epitaphs. Nor did Sparta coin gold or silver money until well after the Classical period. Because lavish grave offerings were also forbidden, archaeologists have not unearthed the quantities of pottery, mirrors, weapons, and personal items that have been discovered in other parts of the Greek world and exploited in historical research. The only exception is a large number of votive offerings made of clay, amber, lead, bronze, gold, silver, and ivory dating from as early as the beginning of the seventh century BC and continuing through Roman times. These have been found at the site of the temple of Artemis Orthia ("Upright," or "Protector of the ordering of the life cycle"). These rich finds from the earliest period of the sanctuary are important for the evaluation of Spartan religion and culture, because they prove conclusively that in the early Archaic period the Spartans were on a par artistically and commercially with their neighbor states in the Peloponnesus. It was only later, in the course of the sixth century, that the famed Spartan austerity made art and other cultural refinements a low priority. Nevertheless, the Spartans continued to be known for their piety.

The number of offerings to Artemis was enormous: over 100,000 items have been recovered. This material record is witness to the central role of the cult of the goddess in religious and civic life. Ritual ceremonies enacted in the precinct of Artemis Orthia appear to have revolved around the passage of Spartan men and women through the key stages of their lives. Choruses of girls sang and danced at the presentation of a new robe for the archaic statue of Artemis, an occasion that probably also celebrated the passage of their age group from girlhood to womanhood. Plaques depicting textiles may likewise have been dedicated at the time when women passed from one life stage to another. There were also dedications to Eileithyia, the spirit of childbirth and protector of young girls and boys. The many lead figurines of hoplite soldiers probably marked the graduation of young men to the status of warriors.

The Dark Age and the Archaic Period

Despite these obstacles, painstaking research has made it possible to trace the broad outlines of Spartan history. Laconia was an important center in the Bronze Age. Archaeological evidence indicates that there was a large settlement at Therapne, east of the Eurotas River, with shrines to King Menelaus and his wife, Helen. Like much of the rest of Greece, Laconia experienced a sharp drop in population at the end of the Mycenaean period. Most of the settlements that had been inhabited during the second millennium BC were abandoned, and the popularity of cattle and sheep figurines as dedications in sanctuaries in the region suggests that stock raising became a mainstay of the local economy. Sometime in the tenth century BC, Dorian newcomers entered the territory. By the eighth century, trends similar to those documented elsewhere in Greece had begun to appear in Laconia as well. New villages were founded as population gradually increased, and four of those villages near the Eurotas in the center of the Laconian plain united to form the city of Sparta. Early in the eighth century, the town of Amyclae, three miles south of the original four villages, was added to the city. Thus, the Spartan polis comprised the city center plus the territory of the plain. Increased contacts with the rest of Greece were reflected in the emergence of a distinctive Spartan version of geometric art.

Like other early Greek poleis, Sparta (or **Lacedaemon**, as it was often called in antiquity) began to experience difficulties in satisfying its needs from its own territory. Sparta was located inland, with the nearest port, Gythium, 27 miles to the south. This atypical location encouraged the city to seek a novel solution to the need for land to feed a growing population, a solution that would determine the course of future Spartan development. Unlike other Archaic Greek cities, which repeatedly founded colonies overseas in an effort to alleviate the pressure on resources caused by population expansion, the Spartans founded only one colony, Taras (now known as Taranto), a prosperous and influential city, and home of many Pythagorean women and men in southern Italy. Instead of looking abroad for a solution to their difficulties, the Spartans sought a military answer to their problem through conquest of their neighbors, and by the end of the eighth century, they had gained control of the whole of the Laconian plain. The details of how this was accomplished are lost, but the results can be detected in the social structure of historical Sparta.

Helots and the Social Hierarchy

Sparta primarily needed to support its population. Consequently, to ensure control of the Laconian plain, its inhabitants were reduced to the status of helots, hereditary subjects of the Spartan state. The rest of the inhabitants of Laconia, who occupied the area surrounding the city of Sparta, became perioeci ("dwellers round about [Sparta]"). Little was written about these "neighbors" in antiquity. Unlike the helots, who were enslaved, the perioeci remained free. Even though they were obligated to serve in the Spartan army in their own units under a Spartan commander, and did so in large numbers, they were not permitted to participate in the Spartan government. They did enjoy some local autonomy, however, and in many ways lived like the majority of Greeks who were not Spartans, working as farmers, craftsmen, and merchants. Unlike the Spartans, the perioeci were permitted to handle money and precious metals. Thus, despite their name, which implies that this populace was peripheral, the perioeci constituted an essential part of the Spartan economic system.

Success only whetted Sparta's appetite for expansion, and this expansion in turn increased the institution of helotry significantly. As a result, early in the conquest of neighboring regions the helots outnumbered Spartan citizens by a ratio that may have been at least as high as seven to one. This phenomenon would play a dramatic role in the evolution of the Spartan way of life. As a result of the conquest of Laconia, the western reaches of Spartan territory abutted those of another emerging Dorian state, **Messenia**. The Spartans coveted the fertile Messenian lowlands, and at some time in the third quarter of the eighth century they invaded Messenia, beginning what modern historians call the First Messenian War. The fighting centered around the formidable natural fortress of Mount Ithome in northern Messenia. The details of the war itself are lost. Tradition, however, made the war last twenty years and placed its conclusion about 720 BC. This dating is corroborated by the disappearance of Messenians from the Olympic victor list about that time. If the course of the First Messenian War is unclear, its results are not: Messenia became subject to Sparta. Like the Laconians, some of the Messenians became perioeci, but most became helots, bound to their land and obliged to work it for their Spartan masters with no consolation but the understanding that, unlike chattel slaves, they could live in family groups, would not be sold out of Messenia, and could not be manumitted by their masters, only by the state. The Spartan poet Tyrtaeus described them working like donkeys suffering under heavy loads, forced to bring their masters half of all the produce that the soil brought forth.

The conquest of Laconia and Messenia made Sparta one of the largest of all Archaic Greek states, controlling an empire of over 3,000 square miles (about three times the size of the Athenian state). Compared with Athens, Sparta was never densely populated, and some centers of habitation were quite remote. Sparta was also one of the richest states. Spartan pottery and metalwork were among the finest in Greece. (See Plate IV.) The beauty of Spartan women was widely celebrated, and Sparta's female choruses were famous. A vivid impression of the wealth and elegance of Spartan life is provided by a few surviving fragments of the works of the seventh-century poet Alcman, whose hymns, written for choruses of unmarried Spartan girls to sing on ceremonial occasions, mention luxury items including racehorses, purple textiles, and gold jewelry in the shape of serpents.

> There is no abundance of purple sufficient to protect us, nor our
> speckled serpent bracelet of solid gold, nor our Lydian cap, adornment
> for tender-eyed girls, nor Nanno's hair, (70) nor Areta who looks
> like a goddess, nor Thylacis and Cleesithera. Nor will you go to
> Ainesimbrota's and say "I wish Astaphis were mine," and (75) "I wish
> Philylla would look at me, and Demareta, and lovely Vianthemis"—
> No, it is Hagesichora who exhausts me with love. . . .
>   (Alcman, *Partheneion*, fr. 1.65–78; Pomeroy 2002, pp. 6–7)

Spartan prosperity, however, rested on insecure foundations. Though civil unrest was probably a serious problem in the late eighth and early seventh centuries in the immediate aftermath of the First Messenian War, civil war over the division of the conquered territory was avoided by exiling the dissidents, who founded Sparta's only colony, Taras. The growing desperation of the Messenians was a more serious threat. Greek political theorists considered it a mistake to enslave people in their own home territory, especially when the enslaved significantly outnumbered their masters, as the Messenians did the Spartans. Not surprisingly, the Messenians rebelled in the wake of a major Spartan military defeat by the Argives at the Battle of Hysiae around 669 BC.

As is true of the First Messenian War, little is known of the details of the Second Messenian War. Tyrtaeus, whom we also quoted in Chapter 3, celebrated Spartan courage in the war in poems that became Sparta's classics.

> This is the man of worth in time of war.
> Soon he turns back the foemen's sharp-edged battle lines
>   And strenuously stems the tide of arms;
> His own dear life he loses, in the front line felled,
>   His breast, his bossed shield pierced by many a wound,
> And of his corselet all the front, but he has brought
>   Glory upon his father, army, town.
> His death is mourned alike by young and old; the whole
>   community feels the keen loss its own.
>
> (Tyrtaeus fr. 9; West))

In the end Sparta prevailed, and the surviving Messenian rebels were exiled to Sicily. There they eventually gained control of the city of Zancle, which they renamed Messene. As for the rest of the Messenians, they had no choice but to resign themselves to the rigors of their former helot status.

The Second Messenian War had been a terrifying revelation of the potential risks of the helot system, and the possibility of a repetition haunted Spartans and their enemies alike. One certain way of avoiding such a catastrophe, abandoning Messenia, was unthinkable. Consequently, the Spartans were forced to find another way to preserve their domination over their helots and the prosperity it

Figure 4.3. "Laconian Rider." Cup depicting rider on horseback, waterbirds, and a winged demon or figure of Victory. London, The British Museum.

brought. The solution they found was drastic, and its implementation gradually transformed Sparta and eventually created the unique regimented society known to us from Classical sources. Simply stated, the Spartans realized that if all potential hoplites could be mobilized and trained to the highest degree of skill possible, Sparta would enjoy an overwhelming military advantage over its helots and other enemies. Therefore the Spartans redesigned their institutions with a view toward achieving two goals: freeing male citizens of the five villages that constituted the polis of Sparta from all but military and civic obligations, and socializing them to accept the regimentation and discipline required of a Spartan soldier. Until the fourth century and the Hellenistic period, the Spartans were the only Greek men whose life work was military service. In effect, they waged a perpetual war against the helots and were consequently always prepared to engage in other acts of defense or aggression.

THE SPARTAN SYSTEM

Little is known about the actual development of the Spartan system. Greek historians followed Spartan tradition and ascribed its creation to **Lycurgus**, a shadowy figure who may or may not really have lived. Thucydides dates Lycurgus' reforms to the end of the ninth century BC; other Greek historians place him as early as the tenth. In that case, he would have lived before the conquest of Messenia, and his reforms could not have been an attempt to deal with the problems that arose in the eighth and seventh centuries. Scholars today are agreed that many of the institutions whose creation Greeks credited to Lycurgus, such as men's dining groups, organization of both the female and male components of the population by age cohorts, and the use of iron money, had, in fact, once existed in other Greek communities. They survived at Sparta because their place in Spartan life had been redefined to create ideal Spartan hoplites and women who would give birth to them.

However this evolution occurred, the evidence indicates that the main features of the Spartan system were in place by the end of the seventh or the early sixth century BC. The Great Rhetra (statement), said to have been given to Lycurgus by the Delphic oracle, was in existence early in the Archaic period, perhaps by the eighth or the beginning of the seventh century. This Rhetra—at least as preserved in Plutarch—deals with religious, military, and political issues, such as the meetings and the roles of the citizens' assembly, and the power of the kings and the gerousia to reject the decisions of the assembly. The Rhetra includes the following provisions:

> After dedicating a temple to Zeus ... and Athena..., forming *phylai* [tribes] and creating *ōbai* [divisions relating to the distinction between the five villages], and instituting a Gerousia of thirty including the kings, then hold an Apella from time to time. Thus bring in and set aside [proposals]. The people are to have the right to respond, and power .... But if the people speak crookedly, the elders and kings are to be setters-aside.

The Spartan regime may be called totalitarian, for it touched on almost every aspect of life, including those we in modern western society consider private: how to wear one's hair, the choice of whether and when to marry, the conditions of conjugal intercourse, and the decision whether to rear a child.

The Education and Upbringing of Boys

As the poetry of Tyrtaeus made plain, the Spartan ideal for a man was to be skilled and courageous in battle, neither to run away nor surrender, but to stand his ground even if it meant giving up his life. The system was designed to produce men who conformed to this pattern alone. The Spartan was liable for military service to the age of sixty and needed to stay fit; hence he never was trained for any other profession or way of life. The educational system, like much else that was unique to Sparta, received legitimacy from the insistence that it was created by Lycurgus. In the Hellenistic period it was referred to as the **agoge**.

The process of creating invincible warriors began at birth, for the state took upon itself the right to determine a newborn baby's viability. Whereas other Greek poleis left the decision to the father, at Sparta officials appointed by the government examined the newborns. The vitality of male infants and their potential as soldiers determined whether they would be raised or abandoned in a place near Mount Taygetus designated for that purpose. (Female babies, apparently, were not subjected to official scrutiny, for their physical prowess did not directly affect the outcome of battles.) Fathers did not decide how to raise their sons. Rather, all boys received the same education under state supervision. Education in Sparta, as elsewhere, was organized by age groups: children, boys, youths (**ephebes**), young men, and adults. From the age of seven, boys left home to be trained in groups called herds according to principles designed to encourage conformity, obedience, group solidarity, and military skills.

The emphasis in the boys' education was not on reading, writing, and the liberal arts, but rather on practicing to endure hardships and to fend for themselves, as would be necessary when they became hoplite soldiers. To toughen their feet, they went barefoot, and they often went naked as well. When they were twelve, their hair was cut short. They never wore a tunic and were each allocated only one cloak yearly to wear in all kinds of weather. Unlike the rest of the Greeks, who made war only in the summer, the Spartans were perpetually at war with the helots and therefore needed to be prepared to fight year-round. Magistrates called **ephors** ("overseers") inspected the boys daily and examined them in the nude every ten days. Spartans, unlike other Greeks, were so well nourished that there was concern lest they become fat. The boys slept in groups on rough mats that they had made themselves. To develop cunning and self-reliance, they were encouraged to supplement their food rations by stealing. Physical punishment was a common means of disciplining children in Greece, and whipping awaited any Spartan boy who revealed his lack of skill by getting caught.

The harsh toughening process was ritually enacted at the altar of Artemis Orthia every year. One group of youths would try to steal cheese from the outdoor altar, which was defended by a group of older youths with whips; blood was supposed to splatter on the altar. It is a sad irony of history that what began as a solemn test of manliness, witnessed only by the goddess and the community, became a tourist attraction in Roman times. The show was so popular that in the third century AD, a stone theater was built in the sacred precinct. Sightseers could view the spectacle of Spartan youths exhibiting their legendary endurance of pain without flinching or crying out as they were brutally flogged, sometimes to death, in front of the altar, egged on by the priestess of Artemis holding a statue of the goddess. In old Sparta, competition was also encouraged in the form of athletic contests and other public displays of prowess, but a spirit of cooperation was considered essential as well, and it was instilled by forming groups of boys and creating rivalries between them.

These group activities served to identify the most talented among the youths and to prepare them to become leaders in the army. From the ages of fourteen to twenty, the ephebes performed their preliminary military service. At twenty they grew their hair long (unlike men in other parts of the Greek world) and shaved themselves in the distinctive Spartan style—a long beard and no moustache. When they reached twenty they were permitted to marry, but had to continue to live with their army groups until the age of thirty.

Acceptance into a **syssition** ("dining group" or "mess") was an essential stage in reaching adulthood. The Spartan man ate his meals with about fifteen members of his army group, an experience that fostered the loyalty, solidarity, and cooperativeness essential to successful hoplite warfare. Each member of the syssition was obliged to contribute a fixed quantity of food and drink, but the wealthier soldiers could supplement the menu by providing such items as better grain than was required, or meat from animals they had hunted or sacrificed. The Spartan ideal of austerity dictated that the cuisine be nutritious and served in portions that were adequate but hardly generous. In some cases, small portions may have been a blessing. The staple of the common mess appears to have been a dish known as black broth. Composed of pork cooked in blood and seasoned with vinegar and salt, black broth was apparently an acquired taste, and the few foreigners who made their way to Sparta were repelled by it.

The *syssitia* (plural) were in some ways analogous to the *symposia* (drinking parties) enjoyed by Greeks elsewhere, but the fact that the Spartan was purposely schooled to drink in moderation points to an important difference. Though Greeks usually mixed their wine with water, helots were brought in and forced to consume undiluted wine and to perform vulgar and ridiculous songs and dances. Young Spartans, who were invited to the syssitia as part of their education, were encouraged to laugh at the spectacle of the drunken helots. The lesson was a double one; from this experience youths were expected to learn both to be wary of drinking to excess—for inebriation could lead to death in conditions of perpetual warfare—and to view the helots as pathetic creatures, patently inferior to the Spartan soldiery. In this way, the older Spartans reinforced the young in their sense of a yawning gulf between themselves and the helots, and headed off any qualms about treating helots as subhuman.

Figure 4.4. Spartan hoplite, so-called Leonidas. Third quarter of fifth century BC, found in temple of Athena of the Bronze House. Archaeological Museum of Sparta.

Inevitably, the success rate in forging soldiers according to the prescribed mold was less than 100 percent. Though the harsh treatment of those perceived as cowards discouraged failure, some boys failed to develop as expected. Since martial valor offered the sole path to the honor and respect of one's peers, life was wretched for boys who were unable to cope with the rigors of military life. When cowards were identified they were stigmatized and called "tremblers." Their ridiculous appearance announced their disgrace: they were obliged to wear cloaks with colored patches and to shave only half their beards. Mocked and humiliated in public, they were despised even by their own kinsmen, whom they were believed to have dishonored. They could not hold public office, nor was it likely that a woman would be given to them in marriage or that anyone would marry their sisters. The long Peloponnesian War and the shrinking of the Spartan population eventually made fighting to the death and severe punishment of soldiers who had surrendered their shield less useful for the ultimate survival of the state. Thus the changing needs and goals of the state caused the Spartan discipline and way of life to evolve over time.

Figure 4.5. Bronze statuette of a Spartan girl running, wearing a racing dress that exposes her right breast. From Prizren or Dodona (c. 525–500 BC). London, The British Museum, 208.

Becoming a Spartan Woman

Sparta's military ethos had implications for females as well as males. Just as boys were brought up to become brave fighters, girls were raised to bear stalwart soldiers-to-be and future mothers of soldiers. Spartans were the only Greek women whose productive life work was essentially bearing children. Furthermore, they were the only Greek women whose upbringing was prescribed by the state and who were educated at state expense. Unlike other Greek females, who spent most of their time indoors and were regularly given less food than men, Spartan females exercised outside, and were well nourished. They drank wine as part of their daily diet, and mixing wine into their water helped to purify it. They were also forbidden to wear cosmetics; since archaeologists have discovered that lead was a component of Greek cosmetics, the Spartans were fortunate in their lack of artifice. The beauty for which they were famous must have been, at least in part, a result of exercise and good nutrition. Childbearing was women's only civic obligation. Though, like all Greek women, they did know how to weave, like Spartan men they were free from the obligation to engage in any form of domestic or money-making labor.

Specific lines of development were prescribed for Spartan girls much as they were for boys. The educational system for girls was also organized according to age classes. We are aware of fewer stages than marked the corresponding system we have described for boys; perhaps there really were fewer, or, as is usually the case in the study of ancient history, perhaps we simply have less information about female activities. Girls were divided into the categories of children, young girls, maidens who had reached puberty, and married women. Hairstyles distinguished maidens from the newly married women, for the latter (unlike adult women in other parts of the Greek world) wore their hair short. As with so much else in their way of life, Spartans ascribed the customary upbringing of Spartan girls to Lycurgus:

DOCUMENT 4.1

Excerpt from Plutarch's *Life of Lycurgus*

He made the girls exercise their bodies by running and wrestling and throwing the discus and javelin so that their children in embryo would have a strong start in strong bodies and would become stronger, and the women themselves would also have the strength to bear their pregnancies and to experience childbirth more easily. He did away with prudishness, sitting indoors, and all kinds of effeminacy. He made it customary for young girls no less than boys to be nude when they walked in processions, and when they danced and sang at certain festivals with the young men present and looking on. Sometimes the girls would make fun of individual young men, helpfully criticizing their mistakes. On other occasions they would sing the praises which they had composed about those deserving them, so that they inspired them with great enthusiasm and love of glory....

There was nothing shameful in the girls' nudity. They were modest, and not wanton. Nudity encouraged simple habits and an enthusiasm for physical health, as well as giving the female sex a taste of noble feelings.... Therefore the women tended to speak and think in the way that Leonidas' wife Gorgo is reported to have done. When some woman, probably a foreigner, said to her "You Spartans are the only women who rule men," she replied "That is because we are the only ones who give birth to men."

Plutarch, *Life of Lycurgus*, 14.2–4

As is the case in many warlike societies, the perpetual absence of men on military duty created a division of labor in which women managed domestic affairs. Aristotle, writing in the fourth century BC and considering some 400 years of Spartan history, complained that for this reason Spartan women enjoyed altogether too much freedom, power, and prestige. The constitution of Lycurgus, he believed, was flawed from the start because only men conformed to it, while women escaped its regulations. He was convinced that Spartan women indulged in "every kind of luxury and intemperance," promoting greed and an attendant degeneration of the Spartan ideal of equality among male citizens. He also maintained that the Spartans' freedom to bequeath their land as they wished and to determine the size of dowries led to two-fifths of the land in his own time having fallen into the hands of women. This land was acquired through dowry and inheritance. Spartan daughters received as dowries one-half the amount of their parents' property that their brothers received as inheritance. (In contrast, at Athens daughters received approximately one-sixth the amount that their brothers inherited.) Yet Aristotle no doubt exaggerates when he complains that Sparta was ruled by women, for they had no share in the government. Nevertheless, they did have a public voice, praising and blaming men. Furthermore their ownership and control of property gave Spartan women far more authority than their counterparts in the rest of Greece.

Since Aristotle's strong convictions about the need for men to control women clearly played a role in shaping his perceptions of Spartan society, it is hard to

Figure 4.6. Laconian bronze mirror with a handle in the form of a nude female figure standing on a lion; the winged griffins on her shoulders help support the mirror's originally shiny and reflective disk (c. 520 BC). Such unusual portrayals of nude young women made at Sparta may depict the goddess Artemis Orthia or celebrants of her cult. Because female nudity is rare in early Greek art, mirror handles like this one have also been associated with Aphrodite, the goddess of love. New York, The Metropolitan Museum of Art.

know just what to make of his criticisms. Opinions vary according to whether one believes that Spartan women enjoyed a good, healthy life within a totalitarian, militaristic state.

Sex and Marriage

As elsewhere in Greece, marriages in Sparta might or might not entail a close emotional attachment between wife and husband. The Spartan requirement that married men continue to live in barracks until the age of thirty meant that young couples did not live together even in peacetime.

Nevertheless, heterosexual intercourse in marriage was essential to the production of Spartan warrior-citizens. Since women married at about the age of eighteen and men before the age of thirty, Spartan spouses were closer in age than their counterparts at Athens, where it was common for a fourteen-year-old girl to marry a thirty-year-old man. Plutarch mentions that Spartan men were reluctant to marry and that the state provided incentives for marriage and the production of children. An array of unique wedding customs are attributed to the Spartans, including marriage by capture:

DOCUMENT 4.2

Excerpt from Plutarch's *Life of Lycurgus*

They used to marry by capture, not when the women were small or immature, but when they were in their prime and fully ripe for it. The so-called "bridesmaid" took the captured girl. She shaved her head to the scalp, then dressed her in a man's cloak and sandals, and laid her down alone on a mattress in the dark. The bridegroom, who was not drunk and thus not impotent, but was sober as always, having dined with his mess group, then would slip in, untie her belt, lift her, and carry her to the bed. After spending only a short time with her, he would depart discreetly so as to sleep wherever he usually did with the other young men. And he continued to do this thereafter. While spending the days with his contemporaries, and going to sleep with them, he would cautiously visit his bride in secret, embarrassed and fearful in case someone in the house might notice him. His bride at the same time was scheming and helping to plan how they might meet each other unobserved at a suitable time. They did this not just for a short period, but for long enough that some might even have children before they saw their own wives in the day. Such intercourse was not only an exercise in self-control and moderation, but also meant that partners were fertile physically, always fresh for love, and ready for intercourse rather than being satiated and impotent from unlimited sexual activity. Moreover some lingering spark of desire and affection always remained in both.

Plutarch, *Life of Lycurgus* 15.3–5; Pomeroy 2002, p. 41

In addition to the secret marriage, other reported customs include the random selection of spouses by cohorts of potential brides and bridegrooms groping in a dark room. In a system of aristocratic endogamy (marriage within the group), the haphazard selection of spouses is a symptom of equality, for one spouse is as good as the next. Since the sole purpose of marriage is reproduction, the secret, or trial, marriage permits the couple to find other spouses if their union proves to be infertile. If these customs were ever practiced, they apparently had died out by the Classical period. The absence of adultery at Sparta, however, continued to evoke comment among non-Spartans. Xenophon also mentions a combination of practices that satisfied both the private desires of individual women and men as well as the state's eugenic goals and insatiable need for citizens:

DOCUMENT 4.3

Excerpt from Xenophon's *Spartan Constitution*

If, however, it happened that an old man had a young wife—seeing that men of that age guard their wives—he [Lycurgus] thought the opposite. He required the elderly husband to bring in some man whose body and spirit he admired, in order to beget children. On the other hand, in case a man did not want to have intercourse with his wife but wanted children of whom he could be proud, he made it legal for him to choose a woman who was the mother of a fine family and wellborn, and if he persuaded her husband, he produced children with her. Many such arrangements developed. For the wives want to get possession of two oikoi, and the husbands want to get brothers for their sons who will share their lineage and power, but claim no part of the property.

Xenophon, *Spartan Constitution* 1.7–10; Pomeroy 2002, p. 40

Homosexuality and Pederasty

Ancient Greeks lacked the binary division modern society tends to impose between people who are considered homosexual and those who are viewed as heterosexual, and same-sex erotic relationships did not prevent their participants from entering into heterosexual marriages, with which the homosexual relationship might exist simultaneously. Ancient homosexuality differs from the modern version in several respects. The origins of many same-sex relationships lay in the educational system. Erotic relationships between members of the same sex were considered potentially educational for both women and men as long as the element of physical attraction was not primary. Single-sex education was the norm in the Greek world, and older men and women often functioned as "teachers" or informal guides to younger members of society. The disapproval that attaches today to romantic connections between teachers and students or between old and young would have puzzled the Greeks, who viewed the erotic element in the teacher–pupil relationship as a constructive building block in the education and upbringing of the young. The attraction of teachers to their youthful, beautiful pupils was considered to have social utility, encouraging the enamored teacher to work hard at educating the student, who in turn was offered an inspiring role model in an older, wiser, more accomplished suitor. The pupils in question were generally in early adolescence. Their age would cause them today to be considered children and hence entirely unfit for the erotic attention of adults, but the Greeks saw things differently. This pattern of same-sex relationships was evident not only in the context of education but in life as a whole. How much physical sexual activity actually was involved is unclear, since many Greek intellectuals who left written records of social customs tended to be prudish and were eager to stress the cerebral element in same-sex romantic connections. Xenophon, while making plain the frequency of homosexual relationships with a physical dimension, insisted that this was not accepted in Sparta:

> I think I ought to say something about loving boys, since this also has a bearing on education. In other Greek states man and boy live together like married people; elsewhere they become intimate with youths by giving them gifts. Some, on the other hand, entirely forbid suitors to talk with boys. The customs instituted by Lycurgus were the opposite of all these. If someone, being himself an honest man, admired a boy's soul and tried to make him a blameless friend and to associate with him, he approved, and believed in the excellence of this kind of education. But if it was clear that the attraction lay in the boy's body, he considered this most shameful. Thus he caused lovers to abstain from sexual intercourse with boys no less than parents abstain from their children and brothers from their sisters. I am not surprised, however, that some people refuse to believe this. For in many states the laws do not oppose desire for boys.
>
> (Xenophon, *Spartan Constitution* 2.12–13; Marchant)

We know less about the homoerotic bonds between women, but Plutarch in his *Life of Lycurgus* reported that "sexual relationships of this type were so highly valued that respectable women would in fact have love affairs with unmarried girls," and the erotic element in the songs of female choruses (like the poem of Alcman quoted earlier) is not hidden.

For males and females alike, liaisons with members of the same sex provided much of the companionship, sexual pleasure, and sense of spiritual well-being that many people in modern western society nowadays associate with marriage. Homosexuality was so thoroughly integrated into the system that the ephors punished a boy's adult lover for infractions committed by the boy. Furthermore, the idealized model of the same-sex relationship involved an older person and an adolescent and consequently was time-limited. With boys, it was considered inappropriate to continue the relationship after the teenager's beard began to grow. Nevertheless, some relationships did develop between companions of the same age and endure throughout life.

Figure 4.7. Laconian cup, attributed to the Naucratis Painter (c. 570–560 BC). These five reclining men served by a naked boy holding a wine pitcher are probably shown at a syssition, the Spartan version of the Greek symposion. Two winged male demons and two sirens hover above them. Paris, The Louvre.

DEMOGRAPHY AND THE SPARTAN ECONOMY

By their conquests of Laconia and Messenia, the Spartans created a situation in which they never constituted more than a small fraction—perhaps a twentieth—of the total population of their territory. Hence, as is often the case with ruling aristocracies, their numbers were never deemed to be sufficient. Furthermore, unlike other Greek states, at the very start the lack of trade and colonization limited the growth of Sparta's population, because it had no colonies to which it might in the future export a population that could no longer be supported at home. Xenophobia also restricted Sparta's numbers. Unlike the Athenians, for example, at no time did Spartans marry foreigners, nor did they recruit large numbers of new citizens of non-Spartan origin, although manpower losses during the long war with Athens during the fifth century known as the Peloponnesian War did move them to take some exceptional measures. Coping with this emergency, they allowed members of several out-groups to be trained for service in the Spartan army—some sons of impoverished Spartiates who had fallen below the census requirement for full citizenship, non-Spartiate boys living in Sparta, or the offspring of helot women and Spartiate fathers. These boys were raised as foster children in prosperous Spartiate families, eventually served in the army alongside their Spartan "brothers" and enjoyed some modified form of citizenship. The Spartans also freed some helots as a reward for military service, and appointed perioeci to some positions of command. Some of these practices continued into the Hellenistic period, when the population problem was even more acute. Thus the requirements for citizenship changed over time, and various levels of citizenship developed as the Spartans recruited new citizens from the previously unenfranchised.

Sparta's Shrinking Population

The Spartan lifestyle exacerbated the population decline. Sparta was the only Greek state in which male infanticide was institutionalized. Moreover, many deaths can be explained by the Spartan soldier's obligation to stand his ground and give his life for his country rather than surrender when his situation was patently hopeless. This ideal was reinforced by peer pressure, epitomized by statements attributed to Spartan women such as that of the mother who told her son as she handed him his shield to come home "either with this or on this." (Spartan soldiers who were not buried on the battlefield were carried home on their shields.)

The reduction in the number of Spartans was gradual. In addition to the high rate of infant and juvenile mortality found throughout the ancient world, the Spartan problem was aggravated by their unusual marriage practices. Women married only several years after they became fertile; opportunities for conjugal intercourse were limited; husbands were continuously absent at war or sleeping with their army groups when wives were in their peak childbearing years; and both sexes engaged in a certain amount of homosexual, nonprocreative sex. As if these obstacles to maintaining the population were not sufficient, some women also declined to bear children. Spartans, like other Greek women, probably had access to contraceptives including the use of herbs, douches of vinegar or water, and mechanical barriers made of wads of wool soaked in honey or olive oil. Control over fertility is often indicative of high status for women, and Aristotle noted that Spartan women were in charge of domestic matters, managing households that constituted a significant portion of the family's fortune. The risks of maternity were considered equal to those soldiers faced on the battlefield, and so the state offered incentives; as we have said, the only Spartans who earned the distinction of having their names inscribed on tombstones were those who had died in childbirth or in battle. Sparta's population problem was also accelerated at times by natural disaster, economic problems, and the emigration of men. There were nine thousand male Spartans in the Archaic period. In 479 there were eight thousand male citizens, five thousand of whom served at the battle of Plataea. There, according to Herodotus, each Spartan hoplite was accompanied by seven helots who served as light armed forces and performed the menial jobs. Though these figures are probably not exact, they do give an idea of the proportion of Spartans to helots in the army. In 464, a devastating earthquake killed many Spartans. The entire cohort of ephebes was among the fatalities. Early in the fourth century an unknown number of men left Sparta to serve as mercenaries in Asia Minor; some never returned. In 371, approximately seven hundred Spartans fought against Thebes at Leuctra, and of these four hundred perished. In 330, Aristotle reckoned the number of Spartans at one thousand. By 244, there were no more than seven hundred. By Roman times, very few Spartans were left to perform their hoary rituals and tests of endurance for tourists. We have no information either on the absolute number of female Spartans or on their numbers relative to the number of males.

Helots and the Spartan System

The Spartan economic system was designed to enable citizens to devote all their time and energy to the defense and welfare of the polis. The state saw to it that they always had everything they needed as measured by a standard of austerity, not luxury. Though the perioeci, who conducted business with the rest of the Greek world, used silver and gold coins, Spartans themselves were permitted to use only iron money; these small bars or cakes made of iron had no value beyond the boundaries of Spartan territory. The Spartans used iron until the end of the fifth century, when there was a vast influx of gold and silver after their victory in the Peloponnesian War, but they did not mint their own coins until the Hellenistic period.

The goal for men was economic equality, which was, in reality, a minimum income for all that would allow them to follow the Spartan way of life. The Spartans referred to themselves as **homoioi** ("peers," or "men of equal status"). As we shall see, however, economic equality was an illusory ideal. When Messenia was conquered, the territory was divided into nine thousand equal *klēroi* ("portions"). At birth, each boy was allocated a **kleros** by the state, and a group or family of helots came with the land. The institution of helotry was inextricably tied up with the Spartan system, essential as it was to releasing Spartan men and women from the need to produce or purchase their own food and clothing.

The owner of each kleros was entitled to receive a specified amount of produce annually from the helots who worked it. The helots' burden seems to have varied over the centuries. Tyrtaeus describes them as sharecroppers, forced to give their masters half their yield, but Plutarch mentions a fixed rent of 70 bushels of barley for each Spartan man and 12 for his wife, in addition to oil and wine. Though they were not free, helots were not the same as slaves elsewhere in Greece. They belonged to the state, not to individuals, and could not be sold abroad. Unlike many slaves elsewhere, the helots were natives of Greece and spoke Greek. Some of the men served in the military. Historians, both ancient and modern, have ignored helot women because they were women, low-class, and had no perceptible influence on political and military history. We assume that helot women worked for the Spartiates as domestic servants. Since Spartan women did not weave, except for ritual purposes, helot women must have produced all the clothing, ground the grain, carried water, and performed the work done by slave women in other Greek cities. If they did not live with their masters or with the army, the helots lived in stable family groups on a farm assigned to them. They were obliged to provide sustenance for the owner of the plot of land, to serve as auxiliaries in the army, and to mourn at the death of kings and magistrates. They were rewarded for good productive work by being permitted to sell excess crops in the market and to accumulate some money in that way. So that they should never forget that they were enslaved, the helots were subjected to an annual beating. They were also obliged to wear a primitive and humiliating costume that identified them immediately, including animal skins and a leather cap. Submitting to the rule of others but living in their own territory, the helots did not lose their desire for freedom. The service they performed in the Spartan army, moreover, provided them with useful knowledge in their ongoing struggle against their masters. In 464, some of them took advantage of the earthquake that had devastated Sparta and staged a decade-long rebellion at Ithome. In 455, the Spartans agreed to let the rebels depart on condition that they never return to the Peloponnesus. The Athenians settled many of them at Naupactus, on the northern side of the Corinthian Gulf. Finally, in 369, Messenia regained its independence with the aid of Thebes and other Boeotian enemies of Sparta.

The system of helotry distinguished Sparta sharply from other Greek states, making it the only polis with an economic system totally dependent upon geographical and social distance between landowners and workers on the land. Despite the prevalence of slavery in the Greek world, nowhere else was the labor of the lowest class so essential to survival. In other states, inhabitants were located at many points on a sliding scale of privilege; in Sparta, a clear line of demarcation separated haves from have-nots. As Plato's relative Critias observed, nowhere else were the free so free or the enslaved so enslaved. Furthermore, though agriculture remained the basis of the domestic economy throughout the Greek world, other sources of gaining a livelihood were customarily developed; at Sparta alone among major states, agriculture remained the sole basis of the citizens' economy. The Spartan system was a remarkably successful experiment in what is now called social engineering. To be sure, despite the ideology of equality among citizens that was associated with their polis, disparities of wealth did not disappear. Many Spartans had only the kleros to support them, whereas rich Spartans who owned additional land could afford, for example, to enter chariots in the Olympic games. In fact, Cynisca, the first woman to own horses that won at Olympia, was a sister of a Spartan king. Except for the members of the royal families and the group elected to the council of elders, however, the role played by differential wealth in determining status and power was far smaller in Sparta than in other Greek poleis. The Spartans called themselves the "men of equal status" for good reason. Rich or poor, they all had survived the same judgment at birth, they had endured the same training, and they wore the same uniform and fought side by side with the same weapons in the phalanx.

SPARTAN GOVERNMENT

Like its social and educational system, Sparta's government was much admired by contemporaries. It consisted of monarchical, oligarchic, and democratic elements;

these constituted the kind of system political theorists like Aristotle called a mixed constitution. Spartan conservatism made for a reluctance to abandon traditional institutions like the monarchy and the council of elders when other Greek poleis had abolished these institutions and had decreased the importance of hereditary power in government. As later on in the Roman republic, the various organs of government and shared offices were designed to serve as checks and balances to one another, minimizing the danger that the government would take too rapid, radical action.

Dual Kingship

The executive office was divided between two men. Two kings (*basileis*) served as the head of government; one each was drawn from the prominent families of the Agiads and the Eurypontids. This system probably reflects an effort to resolve the tensions that arose when the villages united to form the town of Sparta; perhaps these kings had originally been chiefs of the two most powerful villages. The succession was hereditary and usually passed to the oldest son born after the king's accession. When a king's marriage had not produced a son, the king was urged to take a second wife to help ensure the continuity of the male line. Despite these exceptions, and despite the report about wife sharing for reproductive purposes, the Spartans, like other Greeks, were monogamous. Now was the value of the Spartan dual ideology of competition and co apparent than in the kingship. The two kings, who were both competitive with one another and were equal in authority, ser check on the power of the monarchy. Sparta, moreover, was n leader, and thus avoided what the Greeks called anarchy (absenc or of government).

Like the Dark Age basileis, the Spartan kings exercised milit and judicial powers; in many ways, their manner of rule resembled Homeric chiefs. One king served as commander-in-chief of the ar while the other supervised domestic matters and took charge if his co was killed in action. (This division of labor came about when history taught the Spartans the harsh lesson that it was risky to send two kings out in command of a single campaign. Herodotus tells of the crisis that arose shortly before 500 BC, when King Demaratus changed his mind about attacking the Athenians and abandoned his co-king Cleomenes just as battle was about to be joined. For this reason, the Spartans passed the law mandating that one king remain in Sparta while his colleague was away on campaign.)

The kings were not mere figureheads but were important leaders who contributed to the political cohesiveness and military effectiveness of the country. As the Great Rhetra states, they attended meetings of the gerousia, and—like the ephors and members of the gerousia—were permitted to address the Spartan assembly. Considered descendants of Zeus through his son Heracles, the kings functioned as the chief priests and conducted all the public sacrifices on behalf of Sparta. Their interpretations of the sacrificial omens influenced their decisions in military matters. The royal compensation for fulfilling the office of priest included a supply of animals for a bimonthly sacrifice to Apollo and consequently the special favor of the god. The kings were given the skins of animals that were sacrificed, and double portions of the meat that was distributed. They did not consume the extra meat themselves but gave it away as gifts, a practice that reflects the common Greek aristocratic system of demonstrating and consolidating one's power by showing signs of generosity. They were also expected to serve as moral exemplars. Thus, the courage and self-sacrifice of King Leonidas and his troops, who obeyed the command of the Spartans to fight at Thermopylae in 480 BC against all odds in the war against the Persians, became legendary and enhanced the image of the invincible Spartans. (See Plate VIIa.)

Gerousia

The kings shared their judicial functions with the other members of the **gerousia**, the Council of Gerontes ("Elders"). In addition to the two kings, the gerousia was composed of twenty-eight men over the age of sixty who served for the rest of their lives. Sixty was also the age at which military service terminated. Though all male citizens were eligible, gerousia members were usually wealthy, influential men. Consequently, the gerousia constituted an aristocratic, oligarchic component. Election to the gerousia was the highest honor to which a Spartan could aspire. Candidates appeared in an order determined by lot. The winners were chosen by acclamation in the assembly. Those who received the loudest shouts were considered elected, a procedure Aristotle later criticized as "childish." The gerousia possessed the crucial right of legislative initiative: no bill could be brought before the assembly until it had first been discussed by the gerousia, and the gerousia could decline to accept a decision of the assembly by summarily declaring an adjournment. It also served as a criminal court for cases of homicide, treason, and other serious offenses that carried the penalty of disenfranchisement, exile, or death.

Ephors

Every year the Spartans elected five ephors by acclamation from candidates over the age of thirty. These overseers supervised the kings and represented the principle of law, precious to the Spartans as it was to many Greeks. Since Spartan laws were unwritten, it was particularly useful to have officials whose role was to serve as judicial watchdogs. When the office of ephor came into being is unclear: it is not mentioned in the Great Rhetra.

The ephors took a monthly oath to uphold the office of the kings as long as the monarchs behaved in accordance with the laws. They shared some of the kings' executive powers, but they were also empowered to impeach kings and depose them. Ephors monitored the kings in Sparta, and two of them always accompanied a king who was on campaign. The ephors presided over the gerousia and assembly and dealt with foreign embassies. They also exercised judicial powers in civic matters and in cases involving perioeci.

One ephor was always "eponymous"; that is, his name was used at Sparta to signify the year. For example, Thucydides dates a treaty of 421 as follows: "The treaty is effective from the 27th day of the month of Artemisium at Sparta, when Pleistolas is an ephor; and at Athens from the 25th day of the month of Elaphebolium, when Alcaeus is an archon" (5.19). As a check on the ephors' power, these officials served for only one year, could not be reelected, and were subject to an audit by their successors. Thus, they were both a democratic and an oligarchic constituent of government.

The ephors exercised total control over the education of the young and enforced the iron discipline of Sparta. They were in charge of the **kryptea** ("secret police"), a force recruited from the young and designed to control the helots. This feature of government was unique to Sparta among Greek cities, though the Persian empire also had an elaborate spy system. Some of the most talented young men were sent out for a year to spy on the helots and were encouraged to kill any helots they caught, especially the best of them who might be most prone to rebel. The ephors declared war against the helots annually, thus making it possible for the Spartans to kill them without incurring the religious pollution that usually accompanied acts of homicide. Plutarch gives a vivid picture of the doings of the kryptea. The magistrates, he wrote,

> would send those who gave them the impression of being the most intelligent out into the countryside—to different districts at different times—with nothing more than a dagger each and a bare minimum of supplies. By day the young men spread out and found remote spots where they could hide and rest, but at night they came down to the roads and murdered any helots they caught. They also often used to walk through the fields and kill the helots who were in the best shape and condition.
>
> (Plutarch, *Life of Lycurgus* 28; Waterfield)

Assembly

In terms of its membership, the assembly (ecclesia) was the most democratic organ of Spartan government, since it included all male citizens over the age of thirty. It met once a month at full moon, outdoors. Though, when invited, citizens occasionally did express opinions in the Assembly, they usually listened to a proposal made by the gerousia and simply voted to accept or reject it. This ethos gave rise to the English word "laconic" (derived from *Lakōn* "Spartan"), which is used to describe a spare style of speech or someone who talks very little. This inhibition, however, applied to men only; Spartans were the only Greek women whose witty remarks were quoted and collected (by Plutarch in *Sayings of Spartan Women*).

The Mixed Constitution of Ancient Sparta

Since antiquity, many political theorists have admired Sparta's government, believing it to confirm the basic principle that the best guarantee of stability lies in a blend of monarchic, oligarchic, and democratic elements. Certainly Sparta had kings, and the strong ideology of economic equality among male citizens fostered an egalitarian spirit. In reality, however, the oligarchic element considerably outweighed the other two. Power lay predominantly with the gerousia. As time went by, moreover, the five ephors also gained increasing power over the kings and frequently took the lead in framing foreign policy. Even if we discount the 95 percent or so of disfranchised residents of Laconia—perioeci, helots, and Spartan women—the truth is that even within the subgroup of male citizens, active participation in government was limited to a small group.

SPARTA AND GREECE

In the sixth century, Sparta repeatedly became involved in the politics of other Greek states, often to suppress tyrannies. Philosophically, this hostility originated in an aversion to any government that was innovative and extraconstitutional. Tyrants, moreover, were generally supported by the poor, and in return for this support they expanded the nonagricultural economies of cities and adorned them with public works. This power structure and urban style of living were the precise inverse of the Spartan ethos, and it was understandable that the Spartans, who never developed an urban center, should look for allies in other states among men who were landed aristocrats like themselves. From time to time, of course, self-interest overrode principle: not long after helping the Athenians expel their tyrant Hippias in 510 BC, the Spartans tried unsuccessfully to set up another politician, Isagoras, as head of an oligarchy who would be friendly to them.

The Peloponnesian League

Until the Roman conquest of Greece, Sparta itself was never subject to the ongoing rule of non-Spartans. In the seventh century, Sparta tried to expand northward against Arcadia and Argos, with varying results. After the defeat of Argos in 546 BC, Sparta had become the most powerful state not only in the Peloponnesus, but in all Greece. With Peloponnesian states other than Messenia, Sparta adopted a policy of alliance, rather than conquest. Sparta had gradually assumed a position of leadership. Sparta's first important ally was nearby Elis; this alliance had been gained in return for supporting Elis's bid to gain control of the influential and lucrative Olympic games around 570. Eventually (c. 510–500 BC), "Sparta and its allies," or the **Peloponnesian League**, as historians today call the Spartan alliance, was organized. The League included all the states in the Peloponnesus except Argos and Achaea, as well as key poleis that lay outside the Peloponnesus, such as Thebes.

One of the first united actions of the League was its defeat of Argos at the Battle of Sepeia in 494. Because Sparta depended on its hoplites, the membership of cities like Corinth, Aegina, and Sicyon, which had fleets, was of particular value to its defense. Such an alliance protected Sparta against foreign invaders, who not only posed a threat to Sparta itself but might also foment rebellion amongst the helots. The purpose of the League was mutual protection. Each state pledged to contribute forces in case of war and swore an oath "to have the same friends and enemies, and to follow the Spartans wherever they lead." The allies also pledged not to support the helots against Sparta. Nevertheless, the League was not an empire but an alliance; no tribute was paid except in wartime. Furthermore, Sparta did not dictate the policy of the League; the other member cities were influential, and Sparta could not force the League to go to war if the allies were opposed to it.

The government of the League was bicameral, consisting of the assembly of Spartans and the congress of allies, in which each state had one vote. Only Sparta could convene a meeting of the League, and only Spartans served as commanders of its armed forces. Sparta's own reputation for distinction in military matters, along with the existence of the League—the most powerful military alliance in the Greek world in the early fifth century—made Sparta the natural leader of the Greeks in their war against the Persians. Foreigners, including Lydians, Scythians, and Greeks in Ionia, sought the Spartans as allies in their struggles against the Persians. The League remained in existence until the 360s, when Corinth and other member states were obliged to quit it after Sparta's defeat by Thebes.

League members were bound by treaty only to Sparta, and they had no bonds with one another. Although they might rise to the occasion and band together for mutual defense in a crisis, as was the case when Persia invaded Greece shortly after 500 BC, in general, Greek states had difficulty developing really warm ties. The states in the Peloponnesian League, consequently, were not especially concerned about one another's well-being; the Spartans wanted assistance in the event of a helot uprising and backing in their ongoing quarrel with Argos, and the other states were interested in the guarantee of protection by Sparta. Just how much power League members other than Sparta really enjoyed depended largely on how much Sparta needed them. Thus, for example, Corinth was a cherished ally because of its fleet, and Corinthian rage at Athens would play a large role in the League's fateful decision to declare war on Athens in 432 BC.

HISTORICAL CHANGE IN SPARTA

Because there are no witnesses to the full operation of the Spartan community as described by Plutarch, and Xenophon states that the laws of Lycurgus were no longer enforced in his own time, we must admit the possibility that some features of the legislation attributed to Lycurgus were observed only briefly, or partially, or not at all, and that they changed over time. There are twentieth-century parallels

Plate Ia. A diver carefully excavates amphoras, the standard transport containers from the Bronze Age well into the Roman Empire, from a ship that was wrecked before 1300 BC off the coast of modern Turkey near Uluburun. The ship was probably carrying a Mycenaean passenger. See Chapter 1.

Plate Ib. At the same wreck, divers inspect some of the metal ingots that comprised most of the ship's cargo: ten tons of copper and one ton of tin, the ingredients of bronze.

Plate IIa. Sophie Schliemann, née Sophia Engastromenou, decorated at Troy by pieces of "Priam's Treasure," which turned out to be hundreds of years older than Schliemann had asserted. Heinrich's marriage to Sophia enhanced his reputation for eccentricity, acquired from his business adventures in Russia and in California during its gold rush; that the Schliemanns' marriage was arranged by the Archbishop of Greece at Heinrich Schliemann's request did nothing to diminish that reputation. The photograph was taken in 1882, the color added later. See Chapter 1.

Plate IIb. Gold-plated silver diadem from the "Treasure of Priam" excavated at Troy by Heinrich Schliemann and modeled in the photograph above by Mrs. Schliemann. Staatliche Museen Berlin: Museum für Vor- und Frühgeschichte.

Plate IIIa. Terra-cotta chest (c. 850 BC), covered by a lid with five model granaries, found in the same grave as the jewelry in Figure 2.3, p. 70, and accompanied by two other free-standing granary models. The chest testifies to the agricultural wealth of the deceased woman's family. Athens, Agora Museum. See Chapter 2.

Plate IIIb. Proto-Attic amphora from Eleusis, attributed to the Polyphemus Painter (c. 675–650 BC). This masterpiece of Athenian Orientalizing art ambitiously depicts two different heroic myths, the Gorgon sisters of the beheaded Medusa chasing Perseus on the vase's body and Odysseus and his men blinding the Cyclops Polyphemus on its neck. The monumental vase, 4.75 feet high, was used for a child's burial. Eleusis Museum.

Plate IV. Laconian cup attributed to the Arcesilas Painter (c. 560 BC). On the interior of this drinking cup, King Arcesilas II of Cyrene is depicted supervising workmen weighing and carrying bales of silphium, a plant used for medicine and seasoning. The monkey atop the scales, the tame wildcat under the king's seat, and the lizard behind him are the Spartan vase painter's way of indicating the scene's exotic African location. This cup provides evidence of close commercial ties between the two poleis. Paris, Bibliothèque Nationale de France.

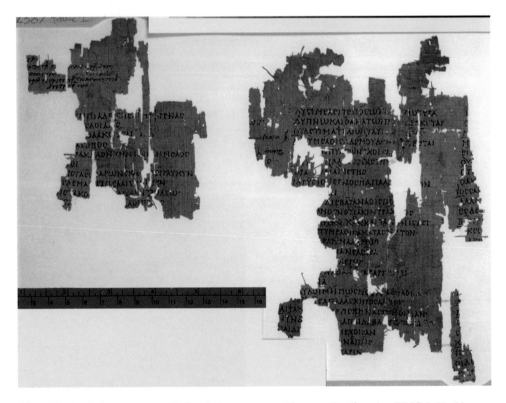

Plate V. Archaic poetry on Hellenistic papyrus. Alcman, *Partheneion PMG* 3.61–64. *Oxyrhynchus Papyrus* xxiv 2387. Late first century BC or early first centuy AD. These fragments of a papyrus roll containing poems by Alcman and works by other authors found in Oxyrhynchus, Egypt, illustrate the fragile nature of many of our texts from antiquity. The top line of the section on the right is: *lusimelei te posōi takerōtera*. The first four lines of this text as reconstructed: "With limb-loosening desire and more meltingly than / sleep and death she gazes toward... / nor is she sweet in vain. / But Astymeloisa does not answer me." See Chapters 4 and 12.

Plate VIa. François Vase. This fine black figure volute crater of the mid-sixth century, inscribed with the names of the painter Clitias and the potter Ergotimus, was exported from Athens to Italy and found in an Etruscan tomb. Horizontal friezes on both sides depict epic myths. Inscriptions give the names of the characters. The side shown here illustrates, from top to bottom, the Calydonian Boar Hunt, showing Meleager administering the death blow to the monstrous beast; the funeral games of Patroclus, companion of Achilles; gods attending the wedding procession of Peleus and Thetis, who became the parents of Achilles; Achilles chasing the Trojans Troilus and Polyxena at the fountain house; animals and sphinxes; pygmies fighting cranes (foot). See Chapter 5.

Plate VIb. François Vase detail depicting Thetis. The clothing on this vase displays the intricate weaving produced by women. The skin of women is shown as white and the skin of men black. See Chapter 6.

Plate VIIa. *Leonidas at Thermopylae*, Jacques-Louis David, 1814. Oil on canvas, 395 × 531 cm. This painting, in the classical style popular in David's time, perpetuates the Spartan legend. In this segment of the larger work, the Spartan general Leonidas stands with two warriors on his right who embrace before meeting certain death. See Chapter 5.

Plate VIIb. Procession of life-size guards from the palace of Darius the Great, Susa, Iran; glazed brick, late sixth century BC. Bearded guards carrying bows, quivers, and spears, wearing earrings, gold bracelets, fillets, and patterned garments. The uniform but majestic style in which these warriors are portrayed may be compared with the individuals in Greek art. See Chapter 5.

Plate VIIIa. Marble statue of a female figure (c. 530 BC) from the Athenian Acropolis traditionally called the "Peplos Kore." Athens, Acropolis Museum. See Chapter 6.

Plate VIIIb. Reconstruction of the statue in Plate VIIIa as a depiction of Artemis, the goddess of the hunt. Originally brightly polychromed, the statue on the Acropolis still contains numerous traces of red color that suggest that her garment might have been decorated with animal friezes.

Plate IX. Temple of Apollo at Delphi. The temple of Apollo whose remains are visible today on the slopes of Mt. Parnassus dates from the fourth century BC. Two earlier temples on the same site were destroyed. The temple at this Panhellenic sanctuary was surrounded by thirty-eight Doric columns of Corinthian limestone, six along the front and back and fifteen along each side, and was a little over half the size of the Parthenon at Athens. Considered the center of the earth and widely consulted throughout antiquity on all matters from marriage to warfare, the oracle at Delphi was abolished in 393 AD by the emperor Theodosius when he made Christianity the official religion of the eastern Roman Empire. Photo: Eliot Porter, 1970. See Chapters 5 and 6.

Plate X. This bronze charioteer was dedicated in the sanctuary of Apollo at Delphi in the 470s BC by the tyrant of Syracuse Hiero's brother Polyzalus after one of his victories in the chariot races at the Pythian games. The statue, which originally stood in the car of a bronze four-horse chariot, has survived because an earthquake cast it into an ancient drain. The charioteer's colorful inset eyes with bronze eyelashes have been preserved. His teeth and the inlaid design on his headband are made of silver. Delphi, Museum. See Chapter 6.

Plate XI. Lucanian calyx crater attributed to the Policoro painter. This vase, made in southern Italy and currently in the Cleveland Museum, dates from about 400 BC and offers a spectacular depiction of the last scene of Euripides' *Medea*. Here Medea is shown escaping in her chariot drawn by serpents; they are encircled by the rays of the sun god Helios. The desolate Jason stands below looking up on the left; on the right are the bodies of the murdered children and, mourning them, their nurse and tutor. See Chapter 6.

for the transformation of similar totalitarian dystopias or utopias. One reason it is difficult to trace historical development in Sparta is the Greeks' essentially negative view of change. Modern historians follow the general model traced by Aristotle of drastic change over time in Spartan society, dating the "normalization," or loss of distinctiveness, to the later fifth century. Such a change may be observed in the public behavior of male Spartiates, but it is not at all clear that women's lives had been fundamentally altered, for, as Aristotle pointed out, women had never completely submitted to the Lycurgan system.

Some change, however, is plainly discernible. One area in which development is apparent is that of land tenure. Land was the most valuable commodity in the ancient world. Two systems of land tenure, a public one and a private one, existed in Sparta. When a man died, his kleros reverted to the state and then was allocated to another Spartan baby, who was not necessarily related to the previous owner. At the end of the fifth century or early in the fourth, a certain

Figure 4.8. Edgar Degas, *Young Spartans Exercising* (1860). In this painting, Lycurgus stands among the mothers in the group of adults in back. Degas stated that his source for his interpretation was Plutarch. Thus the painting reveals the power of the utopian, naturalistic view of Sparta. Compare the costume of the girls in this painting with the dress on the Greek bronze statuette in Figure 4.5. London, National Gallery.

Epitadeus made a proposal to abolish the Lycurgan system regulating public property. Thenceforth a man could give his kleros and his house to anyone he wished, or bequeath them by testament. The change undermined the ideal of economic equality and eventually led to the concentration of great wealth in the hands of a minority. This shift created an impoverished underclass, who failed to meet the economic requirements for full citizenship, for they could not make the necessary contribution to a syssition. They were no longer "men of equal status" but known as "inferiors."

By the Classical period (if not earlier), in addition to the land designated for distribution as kleroi, some land was held as private property. Though women had probably been excluded from the distribution of kleroi, they owned a larger proportion of the private land than women in any other Greek city. Land came into women's possession as dowry and inheritance. It seems likely that before the free bequest of land was introduced, daughters automatically inherited half as much as sons. Some families, of course, had daughters but no sons. Sparta was always plagued by a lack of men, for men were continually lost in battle; others left Sparta for mercenary service, and still others failed to meet the census requirements for full citizenship. Moreover, though male infanticide was systematically practiced, it seems unlikely that female babies were eliminated in this way. Plutarch, who supplies details about the official elimination of male infants, says nothing about girls, though his interest in the rearing of girls is noteworthy. If this deduction is correct, then these factors probably created a substantial imbalance in the sex ratio. A woman could inherit all her father's land, and many women became extremely wealthy by this means. Thus Aristotle's statement that in his day women owned two-fifths of the land of Sparta is credible.

THE SPARTAN MIRAGE IN WESTERN THOUGHT

The admiration writers like Xenophon and Plutarch felt for Spartan society led them to exaggerate its monolithic nature, minimizing departures from ideals of equality and obscuring patterns of historical change. Sparta was also attractive to subsequent thinkers for whom a static, conservative society seemed to offer the stability lacking in a more dynamic state (such as democratic Athens). Luminaries of the Renaissance like Niccolò Machiavelli and Thomas More preferred seemingly stable Sparta to volatile, changeable Athens. The cult of Sparta reached its peak in the eighteenth century, which was an era, not coincidentally, when the popularity of Plutarch was at an all-time high. The philosopher and educational theorist Jean-Jacques Rousseau considered Sparta a "republic of demigods rather than of men," and many of the patriots caught up in the French Revolution modeled themselves self-consciously on the Spartans of antiquity, emulating their readiness to give their lives in a good cause.

The fascination with Sparta in modern political thought also owes much to Plato. Already in antiquity, Sparta served as "the other" vis-à-vis Athens and its democracy, as intellectuals unsympathetic to Athens exaggerated the differences between the two societies. In their writings, Sparta became a paradise of *eunomia*—a Greek word meaning governance by good laws. The most dramatic instance of this concept is probably found in the blueprint for the utopian state in Plato's *Republic,* where many features of the constitution attributed to Lycurgus appear. They are evident, for example, in Plato's description of the life of his philosopher-rulers, the "guardians." Central to both social systems are commonality and totalitarian control. Women and men of the top class are given the same education, including physical training. The private family, with its emphasis on women's monogamy and the transmission of property to legitimate male heirs, is eliminated among Plato's guardians. Sexual intercourse is guided by eugenic considerations. The only gender-related task of female guardians is giving birth to children; they do not have to perform domestic labor, for members of the lower classes do the work usually accomplished by Greek women. Marriage is dispensed with, since the state educates all children. Private property and money are likewise outlawed, to minimize the envy and class conflict that perpetually threatened to dissolve the fabric of Greek society.

⟫———⟪

Controversy about Sparta and its critics, both ancient and modern, continues to the present day. For the past 2,400 years, historians and philosophers have put forward views that vary radically, though they are based on readings of precisely the same texts. Readers have widely differing reactions to the plethora of anecdotes that has survived from antiquity, embodying the underpinnings of the Spartan ethos. Several of these are collected in Plutarch's *Sayings of Spartan Women.* A Spartan mother burying her son, Plutarch reports, received condolences from an old woman who commented on her bad luck. "No, by the heavens," the mother replied, "but rather good luck, for I bore him so that he could die for Sparta, and this is precisely what has happened." Another woman, seeing her son coming toward her after a battle and hearing from him that everyone else had died, picked up a tile and, hurling it at him, struck him dead, saying "And so they sent you to tell us the bad news?"

The notion of a people whose response to stimuli is the very opposite of what we nowadays define as natural has exercised a hold on the imagination. Critics of western capitalist society have idealized the Spartans as highly virtuous, patriotic people produced by a stable noncapitalistic society. Some, however, who cherish individual freedom and social mobility saw in Sparta a forerunner of totalitarian regimes such as Nazi Germany, and in fact some Nazis did identify with Sparta. Furthermore, the blueprint for twentieth-century communism had many affinities with the Spartan utopia. Nevertheless, even today, the old preference for Sparta has reappeared in the works of some feminist theorists, who have noted that the lives of women in Sparta appear to have been more conducive to good health, enjoyable, and in many ways superior to those of women in democratic Athens.

Although Athens was no more a typical Greek polis than was Sparta, examining Athens and Sparta together is a useful way of understanding the ancient Greek view of life. Many Greeks shared the Spartan dislike of change and associated it not with progress but with decline. For example, powerful cities like Sparta, once victorious in war, were eventually humiliated. Consequently, much of what has come down to us about changes in Spartan society consists of laments about the falling off from the virtuous days of Lycurgus. A similar pattern can be traced at Athens, where historians tell a story of virtue and decline, leading to efforts to restore earlier laws and institutions. It is to Athens that we now turn.

KEY TERMS

agoge	kleros	Peloponnesian League
ephebe	kryptea	perioeci
ephor	Lacedaemon	Plutarch
gerousia	Laconia	syssition
helots	Lycurgus	Xenophon
homoioi	Messenia	

SUGGESTED READINGS

Cartledge, P. A. 1979. *Sparta and Lakonia. A Regional History 1300–362 BC.* London, Henley, and Boston: Routledge. One of the standard surveys of Spartan political and military history. Cartledge tends to reject the testimony of Xenophon, but accepts Aristotle's reports about Sparta.

Gray. Vivienne J. (ed.) 2010. *Xenophon.* New York, Oxford University Press. A collection of essays by many scholars on Xenophon's life and major works, including his historical narratives, his portrait of Socrates, his views on Spartan society, democracy, women, slavery, and heterosexual and homosexual love.

Kennell, Nigel M. 2010. *Spartans: A New History.* New York, Oxford, Chichester: Wiley-Blackwell. Kennell offers a complex picture of Spartan military and political history that shows contradictions in the traditional view. He also presents Greek history from the Spartan rather than from (as is usual) the Athenian perspective.

Lamberton, Robert. 2001. *Plutarch.* New Haven. Yale University Press. Readable survey of the life and major works of Plutarch.

Page, Denys L. 1951, 1979. *Alcman. The Partheneion.* Oxford: Oxford University Press, 1951. Reprint New York: Arno, 1979. A scholarly edition, essential for understanding this fragmentary poetry.

Pomeroy, Sarah B. 2002. *Spartan Women.* New York: Oxford University Press. The first full-length historical study of these distinctive women, covering the Archaic through the Roman periods, presenting and analyzing both the sources and ancient and modern assessments of these women.

Powell, A., ed. 1989. *Classical Sparta: Techniques Behind Her Success.* London and Norman: University of Oklahoma Press. A collection of essays including Ephraim David, "Laughter in Spartan Society," and Robert Parker, "Spartan Religion." Of the essay collections emanating from the ongoing conferences on Sparta organized by A. Powell and S. Hodkinson, this volume is most appropriate for students.

Rawson, Elizabeth. 1969. *The Spartan Tradition in European Thought.* Oxford: Oxford University Press. Reprint 1991 with a new introduction by Keith Thomas. The history of the idea of Sparta from Classical Greece through the Renaissance, Whig England, and Nazi Germany, with a short note on the United States.

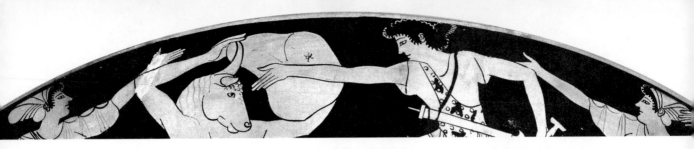

CHAPTER FIVE

The Growth of Athens and the Persian Wars

During the Archaic period, numerous Greek city-states struggled with a variety of problems—factional quarrels among aristocratic families, tension between aristocrats and the people, and tyranny. Sparta found a unique solution to the Archaic crisis, and so did Athens. By 500 BC, Athens' problems had been largely resolved. The last tyrant had been expelled, Athens had a democratic government, and aristocratic competition was largely confined to running for office and addressing the assembly. Because of their relative harmony, wealth, and great numbers, the Athenians had become the second most powerful Greek polis; they were poised to play a major role in the great war that was about to begin. For while the Greek city-states were evolving, the Persian empire was growing into an ambitious power that would threaten to engulf the Hellenic world. A strong Athens would be vital to the defense of Greece against invasions by the Persian kings Darius I and Xerxes.

SOURCES FOR EARLY ATHENS

Written sources for early Athenian history are almost as meager as they are for Sparta and the other Greek states. Hellanicus of Lesbos, who was born around 500 BC, was the earliest in a series of chroniclers known as Atthidographers, that is, people who wrote about Athens. (The other Atthidographers were Athenians, and they wrote during the fourth and third centuries BC.) To the surviving fragments of the Atthidographers we can add the valuable treatise *The Athenian Constitution*, written by Aristotle (384–322 BC) or by one of his students, as well as Plutarch's lives of early figures such as Theseus and Solon, which made use of sources that are now lost. Aristotle, Plutarch, and other later authors also preserve substantial fragments of the poetry of Solon, the great Athenian statesman and lawgiver. Solon's poems, written around the beginning of the sixth century, constitute our earliest direct evidence for Athenian society at a crucial time in its development. The histories of Herodotus and Thucydides, though dealing mainly with fifth-century events, also contain some valuable information about early Athens.

ATHENS FROM THE BRONZE AGE TO THE EARLY ARCHAIC AGE

Literary evidence and physical remains show that during the Late Bronze Age, Athens was the largest and most important settlement on the Attic peninsula and one of the major palace centers of the Mycenaean world. Athens probably was the premier power in Attica, exercising a loose control over the other fortified palace centers in the region, which remained, however, largely independent of the wanax and his palace on the steep hill called the Acropolis. The tradition that the upheavals at the end of the thirteenth century BC spared Athens is confirmed by archaeology. As we saw in Chapter 2, legends told that Attica served as the safe haven and point of departure to Ionia for refugees from southern Greece. If the story about the Achaean refugees is true (modern opinion is divided), they would have found in Attica the same collapse of the centralized ruling structure, drastic depopulation, and dispersal into small village communities as in the regions from which they had fled.

Recovery was heralded by the appearance of Protogeometric pottery, apparently an Athenian invention, around 1050 BC. Athenian pottery would continue to set the style in Greece throughout the rest of the Dark Age. Though reduced to a cluster of villages around the Acropolis, Dark Age Athens continued without interruption as the central place of Attica. It is likely that by 900 BC, if not earlier, the basileus of Athens was the paramount basileus of the regional demos of Attica. The appearance of rich graves in the ninth century reveals a significant growth in wealth and overseas trade during the later Dark Age. (See Plate IIIa.) The population around Athens rose sharply during the eighth century, and new settlements appeared throughout the sparsely populated countryside of Attica, perhaps through "internal colonization" from the plain of Athens.

Significantly, Athens did not take part in the overseas colonizing movement of the late eighth century. Given the extent of Attica (roughly 1,000 square miles), the synoecism of the towns and villages of Attica into a political unity under the leadership of Athens probably was a gradual process, beginning perhaps in the late ninth century and completed around the middle of the eighth. The Athenians ascribed the unification of Attica to their greatest hero, Theseus, whom myth linked with his companion, the Dorian hero Heracles (known to the Romans as Hercules). Theseus' adventures with Heracles, and his solo exploits, such as defeating the Minotaur in Crete and the Amazons (mythical women warriors from Asia) in Athens, were enshrined in Athenian art and literature. In the

Athenian account of synoecism, Theseus created a political unity by proclamation, abolishing the governments of the other towns and villages and forging a single government in Athens. Later on, the unification of Attica was celebrated in a festival called the Synoikia, believed to have been instituted by Theseus. In making Theseus the founder of the polis, the Athenians followed the common Greek practice of attributing important events of the preliterate period to some great figure from the legendary past. (The Spartans, as we saw, credited their laws and military and political institutions to the semimythical early lawgiver Lycurgus.) Yet the tradition that the formal unification was voluntary was probably correct; the inhabitants of Attica cherished a belief that they were autochthonous (sprung from the land) and thus had always lived in Attica, sharing a common kinship.

We may be fairly certain, at any rate, that by the end of the eighth century every town, village, and hamlet in Attica considered itself "Athenian," and there was never an attempt by any one of them to declare itself a separate polis, as happened in the Argolid and other regions. Nor was there ever in Attica, as in some Doric states, a subjugated population of helots, or communities with second-class citizenship, such as the perioeci. Exercising citizenship in a region as large as Attica presented difficulties of time and travel that citizens of smaller regional city-states did not encounter. Although any citizen of any Attic town could participate in the government of Athens on the same footing as residents of Athens itself, in reality people whose communities were closest to Athens found it easier to vote than those who lived farther away. A farmer who lived, say, 10 miles out of town could expect to lose about three hours of his day walking into Athens and another three

Figure 5.1. Detail of Attic red-figure cup by Epictetus (c. 510 BC) showing the Athenian hero Theseus killing the bull-headed Minotaur, who here wields a large stone. London, The British Museum.

walking back, while a man whose home was 15 or 20 miles away would probably have to arrange to stay overnight. Only the very wealthy owned horses, and not every man could afford even a donkey to ride. Although some people preferred the stimulation of living directly in Athens, most continued to live on the land that had been in their family for generations. When the Peloponnesian War began in 431 BC and Pericles urged the population of Attica to withdraw in its entirety within the walls of Athens, most people, Thucydides reports (2.16), were still accustomed to their lives in the country and found the move painful.

The early government of the Athenian city-state was strictly aristocratic. Its beginnings, however, are very obscure. It was probably during the later eighth century that the chiefs of Attica replaced the position of paramount basileus with three civic officials who divided the leadership roles among themselves and were called collectively the archons, that is, "the leaders." The old word *basileus* was retained in the title of the archon basileus, whose official duties were to administer the cults of the polis and to judge lawsuits pertaining to cult property and other religious matters. The polemarch (*polemarchos*) commanded the Athenian army, which was composed of units from all over Attica. The leading office, which carried the most prestige and power, was that of the eponymous archon, thus called by modern scholars because he gave his name to the year: Athenians identified a given year as "the archonship of so-and-so." He had overall supervision of public affairs, including the duties of presiding over the council and the assembly and judging nonreligious cases. Subsequently (perhaps early in the seventh century), six judicial officials called *thesmothetai* ("layers down of the rules") were added, making up the governing body of the "nine archons." The nine archons were elected for terms of one year from candidates who came from the small circle of wealthy and well-known families known as the Eupatrids ("people with good ancestors").

The archons did not rule alone. Rather, they worked in concert with the council that met on the hill (*pagos*) sacred to the war god Ares and was called for that reason the Council of the Areopagus. Because former archons made up the membership of the council, sitting archons whose short terms in office would be followed by a lifetime of council membership would think twice before flouting its wishes. In addition, citizen males participated in the public assembly, but the precise roles of the assembly and the ordinary men of the polis in the government at this time are unknown; Aristotle in his *Politics* claimed that the assembly elected the archons (2.1274a1–2 and 15–17). What is clear is that policy was made primarily in the council by members of the aristocratic Eupatrid families.

Alongside these official state institutions were other forms of social organization that shaped the lives of the citizens. In Attica, as in the rest of Greece, the basic social units—the individual households (oikoi)—were grouped into larger kinlike associations: tribes, phratries, and clans. Every citizen family in Attica belonged to one of four *phylai* ("tribes") and to another smaller group within their tribe, called a phratry ("brotherhood"). Although treated as if very ancient, the four tribes, found in all Ionian peoples, were in fact invented as the earliest poleis and Ionian identity began to take shape in the eighth century. It is possible that in the early city-state they served as political and military divisions—each tribe, for example, being responsible for furnishing a contingent to the army. The phratry may originally have designated a "brotherhood of warriors," another name for the warrior bands led by Dark Age chieftains that we see in Homer. By the seventh century, however, the phratries had become quasi-official social groups concerned with matters of family and of descent. Membership in a phratry, for example, was the necessary proof that a man was a citizen of Athens; in cases of unintentional homicide, the members of the victim's phratry were obligated to support the family of the victim, or, if the victim had no family, to take the place of the family in pursuing the case. The "clans" (*genē*), as we saw in Chapter 3, were associations of several noble households dominated by a top oikos and claiming descent from a common ancestor. It is possible that some nonnoble families also belonged to a *genos*, as subordinate members. These aristocratic clans were politically very powerful in Archaic Athens. It was within this framework of oligarchic and aristocratic control of the polis that the events of the seventh and sixth centuries unfolded.

The Conspiracy of Cylon

Only two events of Athenian history are known from the seventh century, both connected with unrest of some kind. About 632 BC, an Olympic victor named **Cylon** took advantage of his marriage connection with Theagenes, the tyrant of nearby Megara, to seize the Acropolis and attempt to become tyrant of Athens, only to find himself and his supporters besieged by the Athenians. Cylon and his brother escaped, but his supporters, who had taken refuge at the altar of Athena, surrendered to the nine archons on condition that their lives be spared. The conspirators even tied a thread to the statue of Athena, and descended while holding onto it, trusting in the protection sanctuaries were traditionally understood to afford suppliants. When the thread snapped, however, the archon Megacles and his supporters killed them, perhaps alleging that the goddess had rejected them. The Athenians, however, believed that Megacles had committed sacrilege, and soon his family was exiled, including dead relatives, whose bodies were exhumed and cast beyond the Attic frontier.

Although Cylon's coup failed, it played a significant role in future Athenian history because of the prominent family to which Megacles belonged. The **Alcmaeonid** genos would contribute important politicians to Athens, including **Cleisthenes** and Pericles, two of the most prominent Athenian statesmen of the sixth and fifth centuries. Politically motivated demands for the expulsion of the "accursed" repeatedly sent shock waves through the body politic in a world in which people believed that the family's shared responsibility for its members' impious actions might call the wrath of the gods down on the state.

Draco and Early Athenian Law

Much more is known about the next drama, the formulation of a complex of laws by an otherwise unknown man named **Draco** around 620 BC. Because *drakōn* is

Greek for snake and the Athenians worshipped a sacred snake on the Acropolis, it has been suggested that the laws of "Draco" were in fact laws devised by priests on the Acropolis and promulgated on the authority of the local serpent. It seems more likely, however, that Draco was the name of a real person; if Britain can accommodate a politician named Mr. Fox, why deny Athens Mr. Snake?

Most of what is known about Draco's laws concerns homicide. Their thrust was to replace the family and kin with the state as the arbiter of justice in cases of both intentional and unintentional killings. Whereas previously many Athenians viewed intentional and unintentional killings as identical with respect to the "blood guilt" they entailed, Draco distinguished between them. Before Draco was commissioned (we are not sure just how) to revise the laws, bereaved family members customarily took it upon themselves to avenge the deaths of slain relatives. Often the women in the victim's family lamented incessantly until they goaded the men to take vengeance. Those believed responsible for a death could take refuge in a sanctuary while arranging terms with the kinsmen of the slain. Frequently these terms entailed monetary compensation. Draco transferred the adjudication of these disagreements to the government; the next of kin could still prosecute, backed by the victim's phratry, but bodies of magistrates would determine the appropriate outcome.

Most cases that came before Athenian judges did not concern homicide. About Draco's other laws, little is known except that they were severe, naming death as the penalty even for such offenses as the theft of a head of lettuce. Though the fourth-century Athenian orator Demades quipped that Draco's laws were written not in ink but in blood, such measures must be understood in the context of a farming community where food was often scarce. What was significant about Draco's laws was their role in developing the authority of the state at the expense of that of the family, a process that would continue for well over a century.

Just as Draco's laws limited the authority of the family, they also curtailed the opportunities of individual magistrates to shape their decisions in accord with their social and professional ties to particular litigants. Altogether, Draco resembled other early lawgivers in his desire to establish fixed principles of justice that would override the personal preferences of judges. Since judges all came from wealthy families, Draco's system had something of an equalizing effect, although the rich never entirely lost the advantages wealth affords in matters of law. The inequities that were causing unrest in Athens, however, were both economic and political, and reforms that focused entirely on the justice system could not soothe the tensions that seemed to be inviting tyranny. Besides, Draco's laws continued to permit enslavement for debt, a practice that by then had become a principal grievance of the poor.

THE REFORMS OF SOLON

Solon's legislation, generally dated to the 590s, provides the best evidence for the problems of his time. Solon tried to strengthen the fragile agricultural base of the Athenian economy by grafting onto it a thriving commerce. Because of the poor soil of Attica, the Athenians could not raise enough grain to feed their increasing population. Consequently, they obtained wheat from abroad by bartering crops suited to their soil—olives, grapes, figs, and barley. High-quality olive oil was their most significant export. Athenian pottery for drinking wine was also prized by the Etruscans, whose tombs have provided some of the finest examples of this ware. (See Plate VIa.) Athens even seized the strategic city of Sigeum in northwest Asia Minor shortly before 600 BC, a location that allowed it to threaten shipping entering the Hellespont. Besides oil, wine, and pottery, the Athenians had at their disposal silver produced in the mines at Laurium in southeast Attica. Mount Pentelicum in the northeast provided an additional resource in the form of marble.

Although the Athens of 600 had great potential for economic development, many sharecroppers were losing the struggle to survive independently. Nevertheless, there was much hope for the economy in a region with valuable natural resources and inhabited by people with many gifts, including a talent for making pottery. For a second time the Athenians staved off civil war by commissioning a respected individual to address the problems that threatened to spark violence. In 594—though some scholars would put it some twenty years later—the Athenians empowered Solon, an aristocrat with a reputation for wisdom, to draw up laws that would develop this potential by alleviating the sufferings of the poor majority without entirely destroying the privileges of the rich minority. In economic terms, what the poor wanted was the abolition of debt and the redistribution of land; what they got was the abolition of debt slavery. It is harder to say what they wanted in the political arena. Probably Attica's poorer inhabitants were open to any number of strategies for loosening the stranglehold of the rich. Solon did in fact devise numerous innovative and effective ways of undermining the division of Attica into haves and have-nots. His reforms created a sliding scale of privilege that contained something for everyone and ensured that his work would not be rejected out of hand.

Solon composed poems justifying his reforms. Long quotations from these poems survive today and reveal something of the rationale for his work. Decrying both the selfishness of the rich and the leveling revolutionary inclinations of the poor, he frequently identified desire for wealth as a problematic force in human affairs and was quick to remind listeners (for early poets had more listeners than readers) of the transience of riches: "There are many bad rich men," he wrote, "while many good men are poor"; but, he went on, he would not exchange his virtue (*aretē*) for the riches of the wealthy, "for virtue endures, while wealth belongs now to one man, now to another" (quoted in Plutarch, *Solon* 3). In his emphasis on the mutability of human affairs, Solon looked ahead to the writings of the fifth-century historian Herodotus, who would use the early lawgiver as a mouthpiece for his own ideas. Although Solon urged justice for the people, he was also committed to defending the rights of the elite both to their land and to the lion's share of participation in government:

> For I granted the people an adequate amount of power
> And sufficient prestige—not more nor less.

> But I found a way also to maintain the status
> Of the old wielders of power with their fantastic riches.
> I stood protecting rich and poor with my stout shield,
> And saw that neither side prevailed unjustly.
>   (Quoted in Plutarch, *Life of Solon* 18.4; Waterfield,
>   and in *The Athenian Constitution* 12)

Solon's view of the demos as in effect a lobby, a special-interest group similar to that of the rich, reflected the orientation of early Greek political thinking. Later in Greek history, champions of democracy would identify the demos as all the voters; antidemocrats, however, continued to identify the demos as the poor.

"In large things," Solon wrote about his endeavors, "it is hard to please everybody." His rueful lament that in trying to please everyone he pleased no one is ironic in view of the adulation that developed after his death. Because politicians of all stripes sought to co-opt him into their camps, Solon came in time to be credited with a wide variety of programs; democrats and antidemocrats alike claimed him as their ideological ancestor, and reformers at least 200 years later alleged that their programs merely embodied a revival of Solonian legislation. Although the earliest surviving sources for Solon's reforms—aside from his own poems—were written many generations after his death, it is possible to reconstruct the outlines of his thoughtful and original programs that were imitated by other Greek lawgivers.

Solon's first act addressed the sufferings of Attica's poorest people. These included sharecroppers, who were called ***hektēmoroi*** ("sixth-parters"), perhaps because they owed a sixth of their produce to a wealthy landowner to whom they were in debt, perhaps because they were forced by debt or custom to pay this portion for protection, and also those who had fallen so deeply in debt that they had sold the members of their family and then had themselves become the slaves of their creditors. Solon not only made it illegal for loans to be secured by anyone's property or person but also freed those who had already fallen into slavery through debt and canceled the debts of the hektemoroi. More important for the future, he also ended what we now call the hektemor system. The sources do not explain what happened to the former hektemoroi, but the fact that Athens became primarily a land of free small farmers suggests that Solon allowed them to retain the land they occupied at the time of his reforms.

This bold measure was known as the *seisachtheia,* the shaking off of burdens, and for many generations was commemorated by a festival of the same name. To redress the evils perpetrated by debt slavery in the past, Solon tracked down as many Athenians as he could who, because they could not pay their debts, had been sold as slaves outside Attica. He then bought them back, establishing them as free Athenians once more. None of this should be construed as an attack on slavery per se; Solon had no problem with Athenians enslaving non-Athenians.

Solon's other economic measures were less dramatic but equally important. Revising the weights and measures of Attica, he facilitated trade with other states by switching from the Aeginetan standard to the more widely used Euboeic.

Seeing that the future of thin-soiled Attica would lie in oil and in crafts, he encouraged the cultivation of the olive and made it illegal to export grain, which was needed at home. To attract craftspeople from other regions, moreover, Solon offered citizenship to those exiled from their own cities. Solon also settled non-exiled outsiders as metics. Since the Greeks took a narrow view of citizenship, regarding it as closely bound up with religious associations and membership in phratries, this measure was a radical one. (Later on, in the fifth century, when the state and the economy had undergone a long and successful process of development, the Athenians reversed Solon's liberal policy and reverted to restricting citizenship to individuals with two Athenian parents.) Solon was also credited with demanding that all sons be taught a trade; sons whose parents had neglected to instruct them in this regard were freed from any obligation to look after their mothers and fathers in old age. He was also said to have empowered the Council of the Areopagus to inquire into every man's means of supporting himself and to punish those who could show none. Solon's insistence that male citizens earn their living makes a dramatic contrast with the Spartan ethos, where the full-time work of male citizens was military service.

Easing the sufferings of the poor addressed only one source of tension. Solon also tried to deal with the ambitions of the new rich, prosperous nonelite families who resented the Eupatrid monopoly on privilege. His solution to this difficulty was a constitution in which participation in the political process was allotted in accord with income. He used well-established property classes to divide the citizens into tiers, with the addition of a special class at the very top. Classes were ranked according to agricultural wealth. The new class, the **pentakosiomedimnoi**, or "500-measure men," consisted of those whose estates produced at least 500 *medimnoi* (bushels) of produce; any combination of oil, wine, and grain would do. Below them came the *hippeis* ("horsemen," since they were the men who could afford to keep a horse for the cavalry), whose income was between 300 and 499 medimnoi, followed by the *zeugitai*, men who could afford to own a team of oxen, with 200 to 299 medimnoi, and finally the thetes, poor people—farmers and landless workers—who produced fewer than 200 medimnoi. Members of the first class were eligible to fill the office of *tamias* (state treasurer); archonships and the other higher magistracies were restricted to members of the two upper classes; zeugitai could compete with the two higher classes to fill the lower offices; and the thetes could join the others in the assembly (the *ecclēsia*), which was to meet regularly. The zeugitai had sufficient resources to purchase hoplite arms; they constituted the majority of the phalanx. Most of the thetes served as light-armed troops or as sailors in the Athenian fleet. Three categories of persons were excluded from the system. Many residents of Attica were slaves, and many were resident aliens called metics. Women were considered citizens, but they were passive, not active, for they were excluded from the body politic.

Citizen men from all classes could participate in the *hēliaia*, a pool of prospective jurors. These people would serve in courts established to receive appeals from the judicial decisions of the archons and try the cases of magistrates whom someone wished to accuse of misconduct in office. One of Solon's most revolutionary contributions to the Athenian justice system was his insistence that any male citizen—not just the victim or the victim's relatives—could bring an indictment if he believed a crime had been committed. Once the concern of families, justice was now the business of the community of male citizens as a whole.

Filled as it was with former archons, the Council of the Areopagus remained an aristocratic body unsympathetic to the concerns of the poor, and although magistrates were responsible to the people and could be prosecuted for malfeasance, members of the Areopagite Council could not. It seems likely that Solon created a counterweight in the form of the Council of Four Hundred, composed of one hundred men from each Athenian *phylē*. This body served a probouleutic function, that is, it prepared business for the assembly. This council is evident in Athens not long after Solon's time, and it probably dates from his reforms.

Solon left Draco's homicide laws more or less as he found them, but he reduced the penalties for other crimes and decreed an amnesty for everyone who had been exiled for crimes other than homicide or attempted tyranny. It was probably under this amnesty that members of the notorious Alcmaeonid family returned to resume their involvement in factional politics. Like Draco, Solon was concerned that too much power in the hands of a few dominant families was antithetical to the program of state building. It was probably for this reason that he made a law permitting men with no children (like himself) to bequeath their property as they wished; previously, the property of a childless decedent had automatically reverted to his relatives. (Despite Solon's law, juries frequently awarded property to families who contested wills.)

Solon's numerous laws regarding sex and marriage reflect a sense of the state as composed of properly regulated oikoi whose stability was very much the concern of the government, for they were the means by which new citizens were added to the population. Solon brought many hitherto private matters into the public realm. He was concerned to erase the visible distinctions between wealthy and poor, which were divisive in the community. Thus, many of his rules were sumptuary, and since women often served as the means of displaying the wealth of the family, the restrictions fell heavily on them. Funerals provided an opportunity for the rich to flaunt their wealth. The legislation attributed to Solon included the following provisions:

> The *prothesis* [laying out of the body] must be held indoors;
> The *ekphora* [transporting the corpse to its place of burial] must be held before sunrise on the succeeding day, with men walking in front of the cart, and women behind;
> Only women over the age of sixty or related to the deceased within the degree of second cousin are permitted to participate;
> Women must not wear more than three *himatia* [cloaks], nor must the dead be interred in more than three;
> Food and drink brought in the procession must not be worth more than one obol [a relatively small sum].

These laws seem aimed at curbing these occasions for ostentation. Several of Solon's policies, however, had a significant impact on women's lives over many generations. Though he had abolished debt slavery and had forbidden fathers as a rule to sell their children into slavery, he made an exception for a man who had discovered that his unmarried daughter was not a virgin.

Solon's work stands out across the ages as remarkable for its scope and creativity. Like the Lycurgus of Spartan tradition, with whom he would be compared throughout European history, Solon was given an unusual opportunity to think long and hard about what a community is. Like the Spartan system, Solon's program was characterized as eunomia ("governance by good laws," or "law and order"). His laws established the principle that the Athenian state would be guided by all citizens working together. Indeed, in many respects he established the notion of citizenship itself. His law demanding that in a time of civil strife every man take a stand on one side or another demonstrates his determination to involve all male citizens in affairs of state, in fact, to define a citizen as someone who is involved in public concerns. His laws also made plain that while the regulation of women's behavior was essential to a well-ordered society, nonetheless, with the exception of the religious sphere, their role was to be confined to private life. Solon's laws were inscribed on wooden tablets called *axones* and put up in the agora where everyone could see them—though not everyone could read them, since literacy was not widespread in early sixth-century Greece. When the Athenians had agreed to keep his laws in effect for a hundred years and each archon had been compelled to swear that he would dedicate a gold statue at Delphi if ever he violated any of them, Solon left Attica and began traveling, partly from a desire to see the world and partly to forestall any attempts to persuade him to alter his legislation.

Solon was not a democrat, nor did he intend that his reforms should alter the relationship among the classes in Athens. There was some justice, however, in the claims made in fifth- and fourth-century Athens that Solon was the father of the democracy. For by abolishing the hektemor system and debt slavery, Solon not only helped create the free peasantry that formed the basis of the democracy, he also established the distinction between freedom and slavery that was to be central to the Athenian concept of citizenship.

PISISTRATUS AND HIS SONS

Solon's reforms alleviated considerable suffering in Attica. By intensifying the competition for political office, however, they probably played a role in fostering the civil strife that led to the tyranny of Pisistratus, which must be placed in the context of the tensions that survived Solon's labors—and of the spread of political thinking inevitable in an age of experiment. The inhabitants of sixth-century Attica were loosely divided into three factions known as the Men of the Plain, the Men of the Coast, and the Men of the Hill. Historians are puzzled about exactly who comprised each group. It may be that the Men of the Plain were primarily large landowners, while the Men of the Coast were craftsmen, and the poorer inhabitants of the Attic highlands comprised the Men of the Hill; perhaps the city-dwellers were in this last group as well.

Pisistratus Seizes Power

Around 560, Pisistratus, a distant relative of Solon from northern Attica who had made a name for himself earlier in the century by capturing the port of Nisaea in nearby Megara, carried out a successful coup. Pisistratus' backers included not only the Men of the Hill but also some of the poorer city dwellers. Herodotus tells how Pisistratus wounded himself and his mules and then appeared in the agora demanding a bodyguard to protect himself from fictitious enemies. Back from his travels, Solon tried to warn the Athenians against being duped by his kinsman, but to no avail. Packed with his supporters, the assembly voted Pisistratus his bodyguard, whereupon Pisistratus seized the Acropolis and with it the reins of government.

After about five years, the parties of the plain and the coast united against Pisistratus and drove him out, but Megacles, the leader of the coastal party, quarreled not only with the party of the plain but also with his own faction. His base thus eroded, Megacles decided to ally with Pisistratus and agreed to reestablish him in Athens, provided the once and future tyrant consented to marry the coastal leader's daughter. Herodotus marveled at the tale that was circulating in his day about how Pisistratus' return to Athens was accomplished. Pisistratus and Megacles, he reported,

> came up with what is far and away the most simpleminded plot to put him back in power that I have ever heard of, considering that from the very earliest times the Greeks have been distinguished from the barbarians by their intelligence and freedom from simpleminded foolishness—if, that is, these two actually did play this trick on the Athenians, who are said to be the foremost of the Greeks when it comes to brains.
>
> There was a woman in the village of Paeania whose name was Phya. She was tall—about five ten—and good-looking in other ways also. They decked this woman out in full battle gear, and after showing her how she should pose to seem the most beautiful, they put her in a chariot and drove toward the city with heralds sent running on ahead. As they approached the city, the criers, as ordered, shouted, "Athenians! Give a warm welcome to Pisistratus! Athena has honored him above all other men and is herself bringing him back to her own acropolis!" The heralds went from place to place saying this. Word immediately spread from village to village that Athena was bringing Pisistratus back, and even the city dwellers, in the belief that this woman was the goddess herself, worshiped a human being and welcomed Pisistratus.
>
> (*The Histories* 1.61)

Pisistratus' alliance with his new father-in-law did not endure. Pisistratus had two grown sons by a previous marriage. Not wishing to undermine their position by fathering any children with Megacles' daughter (whom in accord with Greek custom Herodotus declines to name), he had intercourse with his wife *ou kata nomon*—"not according to the accepted norm." (Herodotus is hard put to explain just how Megacles found out; he suggests that perhaps the bride's mother had asked her daughter some pointed questions.) Outraged, Megacles

Figure 5.2. Attic black-figure *hydria* (water jar) attributed to the Priam Painter (c. 520 BC), showing women using such vessels to get water at a fountain house constructed during the reign of Pisistratus.

Figure 5.3. This silver coin worth four drachmas and thus known as a tetradrachm was minted at Athens in the late sixth century (c. 520–510 BC). The obverse displays the portrait of Athena in an Attic helmet; the verso shows her attributes the owl and olive branch. On the right, the first three letters of the word "of the Athenians" appear.

made common cause with Pisistratus' enemies, and together they succeeded in driving him out a second time.

Pisistratus' next return to Athens was less picturesque than his first. During the exile that lasted from about 555 to 546 BC, he assembled a force of mercenary soldiers using wealth drawn from the gold and silver mines of Mount Pangaeus in northern Greece. Supported by the wealthy Lygdamis of Naxos and the cavalry of Eretria, he landed at Marathon and defeated the opposition in a battle at Pallene. He then governed Athens for nearly twenty years until he died of natural causes in 527. Although Solon had not succeeded in sparing Athens from tyranny, his reforms played a large role in determining what form that tyranny would take. Solon's system continued to function while Pisistratus guided the city through a period of enormous growth and development. Though Pisistratus' regime has sometimes been described as a "law-abiding tyranny," it should be remembered that Pisistratus packed the archonships with his friends and relations, kept a standing force of mercenaries for his personal use, and held the children of potential opponents hostage. When the last of Pisistratus' sons was expelled in 510, the way lay open for the development of the democratic institutions that are still associated with the city of Athens. It might seem at first that the creation of a governing dynasty would roll back all the work Draco and Solon had done to undermine the power of families. In reality, however, when the ascendancy of the Pisistratids had passed into history, the development of democracy was served by the tyranny's equalizing effect: under the rule of a single family, all non-Pisistratids, rich and poor, found themselves in surprisingly similar circumstances.

Pisistratus' Policies

Strengthening the economy was a major focus of Pisistratus' program, and in this regard too he carried forward much of Solon's work. Like Solon, he was concerned about both agriculture and commerce. He offered land and loans to the needy. He encouraged the cultivation of the olive, and the growth of Athenian trade sparked by Solon's policies became yet more conspicuous under the tyrant's regime. Already during the seventh century, some Athenian pottery had found its way to the Black Sea and even to Italy and France, but quantities were quite small. During the first half of the sixth century, however, Athenian exports begin to be noticeable throughout the Mediterranean and Aegean, and it is difficult to believe that this explosion was not due at least in part to Solon. Under Pisistratus, fine Attic pottery traveled even farther than it had in Solon's day—to Ionia, Cyprus, and Syria in the east, and as far west as Italy and Spain. Black-figure painting reached its apogee shortly after the middle of the century, and around 530 potters began to experiment with the more versatile red-figure style.

The growth of commerce went hand in hand with an ambitious foreign policy. Building a network of alliances in the central Aegean, Pisistratus installed his ally Lygdamis as tyrant at Naxos; Lygdamis in turn installed Polycrates in Samos. Sigeum, which at some point after its foundation had slipped from Athenian

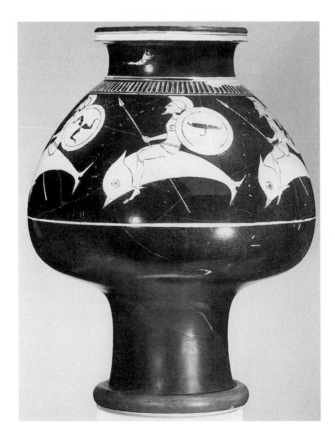

Figure 5.4. Attic red-figure *psyktēr* (wine cooler) attributed to Oltos (c. 520–510 BC), showing armed warriors riding on dolphins, probably representing the chorus of an early theatrical production. The vessel was made for use at drinking parties (symposia) and, therefore, depicts a wine cup as the device on the central warrior's shield.

hands, was recaptured, and Pisistratus sent one of his sons to govern it. Pisistratus also established a foothold in the Thracian Chersonese (the Gallipoli peninsula in western Turkey), sending Miltiades, who belonged to the rival Philaid clan, to establish Athenian power there. Under either Pisistratus or his sons, Athens issued the first of its silver coins, known as owls from the bird with whose image they were stamped (see Figure 5.3). The owl symbolized the goddess of wisdom, Athena, and the Athenian owl immediately became the soundest currency in the Aegean.

In Athens, Pisistratus' public building projects served several ends at once. They provided jobs to people who badly needed them, while at the same time focusing energy on the city as a cultural center. Replacing the private wells guarded by aristocrats with public fountain houses not only meant construction jobs for the short term but also signaled a long-term shift from private to public patronage. Pisistratus also constructed the first aqueduct in Athens, which served the city until another was added in the fourth century BC. This reliable water supply enabled Athens to sustain a large permanent population as well as transients coming for commercial purposes or to attend festivals. Certainly, the aqueduct assured the city dwellers of a healthier source of water than the wells, where archaeologists have found human and animal bones, as well as all sorts of pottery and other debris. With expanded opportunities for jobs and housing in the city, more people could live in the city center, and those who lived in the urban area found it easier to vote. Under Pisistratus' regime, the Athenians rebuilt the temple of Athena on the Acropolis and began a huge temple to Olympian Zeus, which was left unfinished at his death and completed only seven centuries later by the Roman emperor Hadrian.

Pisistratus' support of religion and the arts enhanced both his own reputation and that of the city of Athens. He commissioned a definitive version of Homer's *Iliad* and *Odyssey* and made Homeric recitations a regular part of the Panathenaic festival, which was celebrated at Athens every four years in great pomp and annually on a smaller scale. Pisistratus also instituted new festivals, the greater and lesser Dionysia. State festivals such as the Dionysia and the Panathenaea were lavishly celebrated, and around 534 BC competition in tragic drama became part of the Dionysia (see Chapter 6). The worship of Dionysus flourished in Pisistratid Athens, and Dionysiac scenes of drinking and unrestrained merrymaking were popular subjects of vase painting. At the Dionysia, the god was honored by a choir of "satyrs" wearing goat skins and holding conversation with their leader in the form of a "goat song" or *tragōdia* that evolved into the great Attic tragedies of the fifth century. An expanded Panathenaic festival was celebrated, culminating in a procession bringing to Athena's temple the woolen dress (*peplos*) woven for her by Athenian girls. This was not a small piece of fabric like the cloak the Spartan girls wove for their small archaic wooden figure of Artemis; Athenians were experienced weavers. The robe of Athena was carried up to the Acropolis hung like a sail on a boat-shaped wagon, to be admired by spectators and worn by a much larger than human statue of the goddess. Ironically, the procession up the Acropolis at the Panathenaea would serve as the occasion for the murder of Pisistratus' son Hipparchus in 514.

The Collapse of the Tyranny

Patronage of the arts became still more conspicuous after Pisistratus' death in 527. The historian Thucydides believed that Pisistratus' son **Hippias** ruled alone, but he complains of many others who claimed that Hippias' brother **Hipparchus** was an equal partner in the government. In any event, Hippias and Hipparchus adorned their court with celebrated writers—Simonides of Ceos, whose choral odes were famous; the love poet Anacreon of Teos; and Lasus of Hermione, known for composing novel "hissless hymns," that is, poems in which the sound *s* was never heard. But the prestige of their glittering court did not keep the hereditary tyrants secure in their position. In 514, Hipparchus, finding himself rejected in his romantic attentions to a young man by the name of **Harmodius**, prevented Harmodius' younger sister from serving as a basket bearer in the Panathenaic procession. This rejection was an unforgivable insult, since only virgins were qualified to carry the baskets that held the knife and other equipment for the sacrifice. Just as when Pisistratus mistreated Megacles' daughter, once again an insult to a woman had dire political consequences. Harmodius and his lover **Aristogiton** then plotted to assassinate both Hippias and Hipparchus on the day of the procession. When one of the conspirators was observed chatting with Hippias, the others, wrongly believing the plot had been betrayed, panicked and immediately killed Hipparchus. The results were devastating for Athens: a fundamentally benign government of two aristocrats now gave way to the overbearing and paranoid autocracy of Hippias.

The fall of Hippias four years later in 510 was in large measure the work of the exiled Alcmaeonids. Determined to return to Athens, they did everything in their power to foster good relations with Delphi, where the old sanctuary of Apollo had recently burned to the ground. The Alcmaeonids underwrote the contract to rebuild the temple, and in addition to honoring its terms also threw in a frontage of first-class Parian marble where the terms had called only for ordinary stone. (See Plate IX.) After this, whenever the Spartans went to Delphi for advice about future projects they always received the response: "First free Athens." Since the Spartans enjoyed their reputation as the enemy of tyranny, they were receptive to this suggestion. In 510, the Spartan king Cleomenes blockaded Hippias on the Acropolis. When Hippias' children were captured, the tyrant capitulated in order to get them back and departed with his family to Sigeum. A pillar was set up on the Acropolis recording the condemnation of the Pisistratids to *atimia* (loss of civic rights).

The Athenians chose to remember the heroism of Harmodius and Aristogiton more vividly than the Spartan intervention. The couple was cited as a shining example of the beneficial effects of a homosexual relationship between an older

Figure 5.5. The tyrannicides Harmodius and Aristogiton were commemorated in a lost bronze statue group (c. 477–476 BC) that replaced an earlier group, which was taken to Susa during the Persian wars. These Roman marble figures are a copy of the replacement group. Naples, National Museum.

Figure 5.6. Attica.

and a younger man. Drinking songs began making the rounds in aristocratic circles like the one that went

> I will carry my sword in a bough of myrtle
> The way Harmodius and Aristogiton did
> When they killed the tyrants
> And restored equal laws to Athens.

But the Spartan intervention of 510 had a price: Athens was compelled to join the Peloponnesian League, a development that would have important consequences for the future.

THE REFORMS OF CLEISTHENES

The Athenians did not have long to wait for the Spartans to intervene in their domestic affairs again. Predictably, the departure of the Pisistratids from Athens was followed by a resurgence of factional strife. The aristocrat Isagoras first gained the upper hand when he was elected archon in 508 BC. His popularity was due in part to his platform of revoking the citizenship of those whose ancestors had received it under Pisistratus and his sons. His rival Cleisthenes prudently opposed the plan, thus bringing the masses over to his side. Because Cleisthenes belonged to the Alcmaeonid clan, Isagoras, who had the backing of Sparta, dredged up the ancestral curse that had originated at the time of Cylon's conspiracy, and Cleisthenes withdrew from Athens. In his efforts to aid Isagoras, however, Cleomenes was not able to repeat the success he had achieved on his last Athenian campaign, when he had helped to drive out Hippias. This time he overplayed his hand. Returning to Attica, he expelled seven hundred families pointed out to him by Isagoras and tried to establish an oligarchy. Now it was his turn to be blockaded on the Acropolis. The indignant Athenians rose up en masse, forced Cleomenes and Isagoras to capitulate, and welcomed Cleisthenes and his supporters back to Athens. In their haste to find allies against an anticipated Spartan attempt to avenge this humiliation, the Athenians made a momentous decision: they agreed to become subjects of the Persian empire. When the Spartan threat did not materialize, the Athenians ignored their promise of submission to Persia; the Persians did not.

Cleisthenes, meanwhile, seeing that the rivalries of the wealthy families could not continue without peril to the state, resolved to overhaul the Athenian constitution in a way that would once and for all curb the power of rich families (other than his own). His methods were ingenious. Abolishing for all practical purposes the four ancient Ionian phylai—they remained in existence for ceremonial purposes only—he established ten new tribes on an extraordinary basis. First he divided Attica into three geographical areas: the city, the shore, and the inland (overlapping only partially with the old divisions of the hill, the coast, and the plain). He then subdivided each area into ten *trittyes*, or "thirds" (though actually they were thirtieths), composed of a number of the existing units known as demes—villages or townships of Attica. Since the demes were of unequal size—there were over a hundred in all—the number of demes in each trittys varied. He then took one trittys from each geographical area and put the three together to make a tribe; one tribe, in other words, would contain three trittyes, one from each of the three areas, made up of an irregular number of demes. To signal the weakening of family loyalties in favor of political ones, men were to begin identifying themselves by their demotic, that is, the name of their deme, rather than by their patronymic, the name of their father. It may be that Cleisthenes designed this shift in part to conceal the non-Athenian origins of some of his supporters, but its long-term result was to weaken the force of prestigious lineage in politics. Generations of tradition were not so easily cast aside, however, and the custom was employed only intermittently; we still think of Pericles as the son of Xanthippus and the historian Thucydides as the son of Olorus, and (following the same pattern), Chairestrate is identified on her epitaph as the daughter of Chairephanes.

The new base of ten tribes sparked the creation of a new body, the **Council (Boule) of Five Hundred**, with fifty members chosen annually by lot from each of the ten tribes. Recognizing the principle of proportional representation, the fifty slots for the boule were distributed among the demes in accordance with the population of each. The use of the lot in determining the composition of each year's boule was a key democratic feature of the Cleisthenic system. The boule replaced the old Council of Four Hundred, taking over its probouleutic functions of preparing business for the ecclesia (assembly) and also managing financial and foreign affairs. Because five hundred was an unwieldy number, each tribe was in charge for a tenth of the year. During one period of service, the fifty presiding members of the council were called *prytaneis*, and the prytany came to be used as a measure of time, rather like a month. The chair and secretary each changed every day. The use of the lot and the revolving leadership were intended to prevent any political faction or individual from gaining too much power, and would also discourage bribery.

The archons retained their administrative duties, but a new board of executives was created which—though Cleisthenes may not have anticipated it—would eventually surpass them in importance. The army was reorganized on the basis of the ten tribes, each tribe electing a *taxiarchos* (infantry commander), *hipparchos* (cavalry commander), and, most important, a *stratēgos*, or chief general. Unlike archons, strategoi could serve as many consecutive terms as they liked. In time, the board of ten strategoi became the most prestigious executive body in Athens. They were elected, not chosen by lot, because their jobs required specialized knowledge and political skills, especially in wartime.

Because Cleisthenes was not granted extraordinary powers such as those with which Solon had been invested, his measures needed to be passed in the assembly. His reforms, consequently, were in themselves the product of democratic action. Around 500 BC, a meeting place for the ecclesia was carved out of the rock on the hill called the Pnyx, and from then on the assembly met there regularly and framed policy for the state.

The new Cleisthenic tribes were constituted on artificial lines. Yet it was their very artificiality that made them work, for tampering with the old ties of sentiment and obligation opened the door to framing a new network of alliances. Some noble families, however, remained in control of important (and profitable) cults such as that of Demeter and Persephone at Eleusis. Whether Cleisthenes actually steeled himself to break the power of his own family along with that of the other families is unclear; it should occasion no surprise that the Alcmaeonid power base seems to have survived his elaborate redistricting of Attica, whereas the bases of other families were undermined.

THE RISE OF PERSIA

While the Greeks were struggling to create workable governments in their numerous small city-states, a rich and powerful state of a different character was taking shape to the east, where the Persians had built the largest empire known to that time.

Sources for Persian History

The sources for Persian history are principally Persian and Greek, though there are some records in Elamite, Akkadian, Aramaic, Egyptian, Hebrew, and Babylonian. The Persian sources include inscriptions written in Old Persian found in major archaeological sites such as the capital cities Persepolis and Susa. In addition, scholars have been able to detect a Persian oral tradition glorifying the kings. Archaeological evidence includes monumental buildings decorated with relief sculpture depicting historical events, as well as seals picturing a wide range of activities, yielding information on military, athletic, agricultural, and religious practices and often showing the flora and fauna of the empire. The historical sources emanating from Persia are, of course, biased in favor of the kings and their government. Inscriptions written in Old Persian are all official documents, and give a picture of prosperity, fertility, and security. The Greek sources include the historical writings of Herodotus and Xenophon. The works of the former, in particular, tend to stress differences between Greeks and Persians, between East and West. Although as we have noted, the Greeks called the Persians, as they did all peoples who did not speak Greek, *barbaroi*, the Persians should not be considered barbarians in the modern sense, for their political and artistic achievements were admirable by any standard.

Persia Before Darius

Like the Greeks, the Persians were originally an Indo-European people who came from the north. By the Dark Age they had occupied the territory now known as the Iranian plateau, a place rich in natural resources, including gold, silver, copper, minerals, and semiprecious stones. Not much is known of Persian history before the seventh century BC. After a struggle for domination between the Persians and the Medes, a people related to them, the two groups came to be unified, perhaps under the king Cyaxares, whose capital was at Ecbatana.

At a time when most Greek states had eliminated hereditary basileis from their governments and were wary of one-man rule, which they equated with tyranny, Persia was ruled by kings, each of whom, with the exception of Darius, inherited his throne directly from his father. Because the kings often had more than one wife, there was never a lack of candidates. At first the Persians were subject to the Medes, but around the middle of the sixth century **Cyrus II** of Persia (ruled 559–530 BC), a member of the Achaemenid family, took control and made Media the first of many **satrapies** (provinces) of the Persian empire. Henceforth, members of the Persian dynasty known as the Achaemenids were to rule the Medes, though the Greeks considered Medes and Persians the same and described the act of favoring the Persians as "medizing."

Cyrus' conquest in 546 of the Lydian king Croesus brought Asia Minor into the empire and was one of the events that led ultimately to the war between the Greeks and Persians in the fifth century. Croesus had brought the Greek cities in Ionia under his domination about 560. His wealth was proverbial; the first coins, which were made of electrum, were minted in Lydia. Croesus' prosperous empire provided an Asian outlet on the Mediterranean and the Hellespont that was indispensable for trade with the West. Herodotus portrays him as a philhellene (a lover of things Greek), who enjoyed entertaining Greek philosophers such as Solon and who sought the advice of Greek oracles, sending envoys laden with gifts; but he also reports that Croesus' vanity and self-absorption led him to misconstrue what he was told. Pleased to hear from the oracle at Delphi that "if he made war on the Persians he would destroy a mighty empire," Croesus proceeded against Cyrus.

Apollo spoke the truth, of course, but Croesus had misunderstood. The great empire he destroyed was his own. In 546 BC, Cyrus conquered Lydia, and the Lydian capital Sardis became the chief administrative center in Asia Minor for the Persians. Via the cities of Ionia, Cyrus' conquest brought about the first official contact between Greeks and Persians. Cyrus also conquered Babylonia, Assyria, Syria, and Palestine. These lands and their people were heterogeneous; differences between Greeks of various city-states pale in comparison with differences between parts of the Persian empire. The variety of languages, customs, laws, religions, and manners of waging war was vast. Cyrus' great achievement was that he managed to unify the empire. Communication was facilitated by constructing roads and creating a postal system staffed by royal messengers on horseback. Herodotus reported that "Neither rain, nor snow, nor sleet, nor hail stays these couriers from the swift completion of their appointed rounds" (8.98). Cyrus also permitted his subjects to practice their own religions.

Greek and Asian sources alike praised Cyrus as a benevolent and talented ruler. Whereas the preceding Neo-Assyrian and Neo-Babylonian empires had deported entire populations and had sown conquered territory with salt so that it could never again become fertile, Cyrus' policies enhanced the prosperity of his empire and the well-being of its inhabitants. Cyrus was hailed by the Jews for allowing them to return from exile in Mesopotamia under the Babylonian captivity to Jerusalem and to rebuild their temple there and worship freely. The Old Testament records the declaration of the prophet Isaiah to the Hebrews:

> Thus says the Lord to his anointed, to Cyrus,
> whose right hand I have grasped
> to subdue nations before him and strip kings of their robes,
> to open doors before him—and the gates shall not be closed:
> "I will go before you and level the mountains,
> I will break in pieces the doors of bronze and cut through the bars of iron,
> I will give you the treasures of darkness and riches hidden in secret
> places...."
>
> (Isaiah 45:1–3 New Revised Standard Version)

Cyrus' son Cambyses succeeded him as king and reigned from 530 to 522 BC. In 525, after fighting against an army that included Greek mercenaries, he added Egypt to the empire. Always fascinated by the dangers attendant on wealth and power, Herodotus takes care to depict his degeneration from capable ruler into despotic madman.

The Achievements of Darius

Darius I seized power in 521 BC and reigned until 486. He created an administrative and financial structure that remained unchanged for almost 150 years. He centralized the government and moved the capital to Persepolis. The imperial buildings begun there were completed by his son, Xerxes. Building inscriptions and administrative documents record that Greeks, both men and women (including women with children), were among the workers drawn from all corners of the empire to build and work in the royal buildings. Darius facilitated travel for commercial purposes in many ways, even building a canal linking the Nile and the Red Sea. Darius was the first Persian king to mint his own coins of silver and gold. The gold coins, Daric staters or "darics," demonstrated the king's talent at archery, a skill highly prized by the Persians, who, Herodotus reported, were taught three things—to ride, to shoot straight, and to tell the truth.

The empire under Darius was divided into provinces, or satrapies. These sometimes consisted of people of the same ethnicities or the inhabitants of a single region who had been conquered at the same time. Within each satrapy, authority was divided between civil and military officials: the civil authority furnished supplies to the military, and the military provided protection in return. Each province was obliged to pay an annual tribute to the king. The Persian monarchs wisely refrained from imposing a uniform system of administration throughout the empire and declined to uproot existing governors and procedures that were functioning well. In some areas—for example, Lydia—satraps governed fairly independently. Rebellions were discouraged through a system of spies known as the "eyes and ears of the king." Supreme political power was unified only in the person of the king. The king, as commander-in-chief, defended his subjects against intruders, and in return they paid him taxes, gave him gifts, and paid him tribute. His income was stored in the royal treasury and much of it was lavished on monumental building projects. The labor of the subjects of the empire was exploited on a large scale through taxation, forced labor, and mandatory military service. The king exercised absolute authority and wielded the power of life and death over his subjects, who knelt or even lay prostrate in obeisance. Rather than envying the Persians for enjoying hundreds of years of peace, the Greeks pitied the subjects of the Persian king, considering them his slaves.

THE WARS BETWEEN GREECE AND PERSIA

Around 512, Darius campaigned against the European Scythians, who lived on the shore of the Black Sea, and thus became the first Persian king to enter Europe. Although he failed to conquer Scythia, Thrace was subdued and became a satrapy. Darius' westward expeditions piqued his curiosity about the mainland Greeks, and a rebellion in his empire brought him into direct contact with them.

The Ionian Revolt

In 499 BC, revolt broke out among the Ionian Greeks. Discontent in Ionia was considerable; taxes had gone up when the Greek cities were transferred from Lydian to Persian hands, and the Greeks resented the system of puppet tyrants the Persians had imposed. Violence might not have erupted, however, had it not been for the ambition of Aristagoras, the tyrant of Miletus. Hoping to add Naxos to his domain, Aristagoras had persuaded the Persians to join him in a larger effort to subdue the whole Cyclades island chain in the Aegean and perhaps move on to mainland Greece. When the plan failed, Aristagoras, noticing the restlessness of the Ionians, decided to recoup his failing fortunes by uniting them in revolt.

After resigning his tyranny and accepting a constitutional office instead, he set about overthrowing tyrants in other Greek cities in Asia Minor. Most of this seems to have been accomplished without bloodshed, but the tyrant of Mytilene was so unpopular that he was stoned to death. The rebellious cities showed their unity by issuing coinage on a common standard. Herodotus' account of Aristagoras' attempts to gain support from King Cleomenes was geared to demonstrating the Spartan character as most Greeks imagined it—cautious, conservative, and leery of foreign adventures; the tale also illustrates the assertiveness of Spartan women and the respect that they commanded. Aristagoras, Herodotus maintains, carried with him a bronze map of the whole world—probably the work of the celebrated Milesian geographer Hecataeus. He pointed out to Cleomenes the people whose wealth would fall into Greek hands in the event of a victory, and he exhorted the king to liberate the Greeks of Ionia. Capitalizing on the Spartans' dislike of foreign customs, he suggested that they could easily defeat men who fought in trousers and wore peaked caps on their heads, "so easy are they for the beating." Cleomenes asked for a couple of days in which to make up his mind. When the two days were up, Herodotus says,

> Cleomenes asked Aristagoras how many days it took to travel from the Ionian sea to the seat of the Great King. Now Aristagoras was in general a shrewd man and had so far succeeded in deceiving Cleomenes, but he blundered here. He ought never to have told the truth—by saying that the journey inland lasted three months—not if he wanted to lead the Spartans into Asia. Cleomenes cut short the rest of what Aristagoras had to say about the journey and said: My dear Milesian guest, leave Sparta before sundown, because it doesn't matter how smoothly you make your case to the Spartans if what you want is to lead them away from the sea for three months.
>
> (*The Histories* 5.50)

Not yet willing to abandon his quest, Aristagoras followed Cleomenes to his house, carrying with him the customary sign of supplication—an olive branch, covered with wool—and as he sat in Cleomenes' home as a suppliant, he noticed young Gorgo, who was eight or nine years old, standing by her father. He asked that Cleomenes send his daughter away, but

> Cleomenes told him to speak freely and not to hold anything back on account of the child, whereupon Aristagoras began by promising him ten talents if he did what was asked of him. When Cleomenes refused, Aristagoras kept upping the amount of money until he was offering fifty talents. At this point, the child cried out: Father! If you don't get up and leave, this stranger will corrupt you! Pleased with his child's advice, Cleomenes went into another room and Aristagoras left Sparta once and for all, without ever getting to speak at greater length about the journey inland to the seat of the Great King.
>
> (*The Histories* 5.51)

The Athenians were more receptive to Aristagoras' designs. A more adventurous people than the Spartans, they were not constrained by fear of a slave rebellion in their absence. They were made nervous by the Persians' connection with Hippias, who had found his way to Persia, since they rightly feared that he was planning to return with Persian backing. The Athenians agreed to send twenty ships; the Eretrians, who lived north of Athens on the island of Euboea, were willing to send five.

The unsuccessful rebellion of the Ionian Greeks ended in a major naval defeat off the island of Lade near Miletus in 494 BC. Greek morale had fallen, the tyrants whom Aristagoras had expelled were spreading pro-Persian propaganda, and

Figure 5.7. Detail of the Achaemenid Persian relief from the Apadana at Persepolis (c. 500–480 BC), showing delegations bringing tribute to the Persian king, who received in tribute a wide variety of goods from the subjects of his empire.

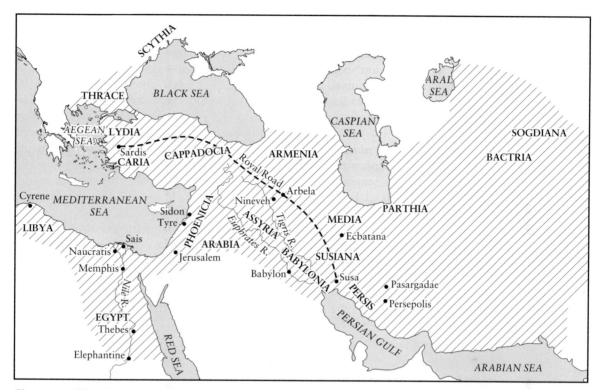

Figure 5.8. The Persian empire in the reign of Darius.

before the battle was over the Samians and Lesbians had deserted. Miletus was defeated, its women and children enslaved, and the men relocated to the mouth of the Tigris. Early in the rebellion, however, the capital city of the western Persian empire, Sardis, was burnt, whether accidentally or on purpose.

Darius would not forget the burning of Sardis, but neither would the Greeks forget the annihilation of Miletus. Home of the philosophers Thales, Anaximander, and Anaximenes, and more recently of the geographer Hecataeus (who had warned Aristagoras of Persia's overwhelming superiority), Miletus had been one of the most cultured cities in the Greek world. When the poet Phrynichus produced a tragedy on its fall entitled *The Capture of Miletus*, the Athenians fined him one thousand drachmas for reminding them of their misfortune. The story of the Athenians' outrage reveals a growing sense of identity among the Ionians and perhaps among the Greeks more broadly. The Athenians had withdrawn from the rebellion in its early stages, after the burning of Sardis, so that Athenian soldiers had not been involved in the collapse of Miletus; yet they identified passionately with the city in its final hour.

There was reason to believe that the fate of Miletus could soon be that of cities in mainland Greece. Under the leadership of a rising politician named **Themistocles**, who had just been elected archon, the Athenians began to fortify the three rocky harbors of Piraeus and convert them into a naval and commercial base. Unlike most Athenian politicians, Themistocles lacked family connections beyond those he had garnered by a prudent marriage, and unlike most earlier politicians, who had drawn support from the leisured landowning class, he seems to have enjoyed the backing of those who made their living by trade. Acutely sensible to the Persian threat—Thucydides praised him for his ability to foresee what the future held (1.138)—Themistocles served Greece well at this critical time.

Darius' Invasion of Greece

Darius had been interested in expanding west since his unsuccessful invasion of Scythia. Furthermore, the Greeks' involvement in the burning of Sardis focused his attention on them. In 492 BC, he sent his son-in-law Mardonius west at the head of a large force. Though Mardonius successfully restored Persian prestige in northern Greece, conquering Thrace, Thasos, and Macedonia, he was forced to turn back when his fleet was wrecked off Mount Athos on the Chalcidic peninsula. Darius

Figure 5.9. Portrait of Themistocles. This Roman copy was probably modeled after a bronze image of Themistocles erected about 460 BC. With its thick neck and coarse features, the head may be the earliest known example of individualized portraiture in Greek art. We should perhaps associate the unusual physiognomy with the tradition that Themistocles' mother was not Greek.

Figure 5.10. Athenian dedications at Olympia commemorating the Battle of Marathon (Olympia Museum). *Top:* Greek bronze helmet inscribed "Miltiades." *Bottom:* Assyrian bronze helmet inscribed "To Zeus from the Athenians who took it from the Medes."

promptly began mobilizing for another expedition, one that would sail straight across the Aegean, avoiding the treacherous promontories of the north. Mindful of the fate of Miletus, many Greek cities yielded to the demand of Darius' heralds for earth and water, the proverbial tokens of submission that signaled recognition of the king's supremacy on land and sea. The islanders felt they had little choice, and Argos and Thebes, on the mainland, went over to the Persians. Sparta and Athens, however, remained steadfast in their opposition.

Darius' first order of business was to punish Athens and Eretria for their role in the Ionian rebellion and to force Athens to live up to the terms of the submission it had made over a decade earlier. In the summer of 490, his fleet arrived in Greece, commanded by his nephew Artaphernes and Datis, a Mede. The figure given by Herodotus of six hundred ships is probably exaggerated, but Datis and Artaphernes may have had twenty thousand men with them, one of whom was the aging Hippias, the exiled ruler of Athens whom they hoped to reinstall as both Athenian tyrant and Persian vassal. En route, the Persians burnt the town and temples of Naxos, deporting their captives; elsewhere, they pressed men into service and seized children as hostages. After a siege of less than a week, Eretria was betrayed from within. The Persians burnt the Eretrians' temples in revenge for those destroyed at Sardis and deported the population in accordance with

Figure 5.11. The tumulus for the 192 Athenian dead at Marathon.

Darius' orders. (Centuries later Apollonius of Tyana, the peripatetic prophet of the Roman Empire, reported finding the descendants of the deported Eretrians at Ardericca near Susa in Cissia, still speaking their native Greek.) From Eretria the Persians moved down on **Marathon** in the old Pisistratid stomping ground of northern Attica.

The Athenian assembly immediately voted to dispatch their forces to Marathon, and a runner, Pheidippides (or perhaps Philippides), was sent to Sparta, covering, so the story went, fully 140 miles by the next day. The Spartans, however, could not take advantage of the speed with which the message was delivered, for, they explained to the breathless Pheidippides, they were celebrating a festival of Apollo, the Carnea, and were forbidden to march until the full moon. Since the Spartans were deeply religious and no cowards in war, this explanation for their refusal to mobilize immediately may have been sincere.

The Battle of Marathon

Herodotus' figures are probably erroneous, but it is likely that the Athenians were outnumbered, if not as outrageously as he suggests, then by at least two to one. The Persians had the more versatile force, with cavalry, archers, and skirmishing troops, but the Athenian force, consisting essentially of hoplites, was more heavily armed. The most serious problem faced by the Athenians was the lack of a commander, for all decisions lay with the ten strategoi (the board of executives created by Cleisthenes) deliberating as a body. As some wanted to wait for the Spartan reinforcements expected after the full moon and others thought delay risky, there was danger that a deadlock in the Athenian camp would throw the victory to the Persians and Greece would be overrun. When the Athenians learned that some of the Persian troops and cavalry were missing and suspected that part of the Persian forces were heading for Phaleron, it seemed to several generals that the moment to strike had come, even though the moon was full and the Spartans could be expected shortly; any delay could be fatal. At this crucial juncture the strategos **Miltiades** stepped in to play a key role in saving Athens.

A nephew of the Miltiades whom Pisistratus had dispatched to protect Athenian interests in the Chersonese (thus conveniently disposing of a potential rival), Miltiades the younger had inherited his uncle's power and had spent much of his life in the remote outpost. In part because he was a member of the prominent Philaid clan and indeed a distant relative of Pisistratus himself, he became the victim of Athenian factional politics in 493 BC, when he returned to Athens, only to be prosecuted for alleged tyranny in the Chersonese. Since it is impossible to see why the Athenians would worry about one of their own citizens tyrannizing abroad, Herodotus is surely right to ascribe the trial to the machinations of Miltiades' enemies (6.104); alternative rumors ascribed the attack to Themistocles or the Alcmaeonids. In any event, Miltiades was acquitted and went on to take the lead in the Greek victory over Darius, persuading the polemarch Callimachus and several of the other strategoi to let him direct Athenian strategy. Herodotus offers a stirring rendition of his speech:

> Callimachus, it is up to you, *right now*, to enslave Athens or to make her free, and to leave for all future generations of humanity a memorial to yourself such as not even Harmodius and Aristogiton have left. *Right now*, Athens is in the most perilous moment of her history. Hippias has already shown her what she will suffer if she bows down to the Medes, but if this city survives, she can become the foremost city in all Greece. Now, I'll tell you just how this is possible, and how it is up to you—and only you—to determine the course of events. We ten generals are split right in two, with half saying fight and the other half not. If we don't fight now, I am afraid that a storm of civil strife will so shake the timber of the Athenian people that they will go over to the Medes. But if we fight now, before the cracks can show in some of the Athenians, and provided that the gods take no sides, why then we can survive this battle. All this depends on *you*. It hangs on your decision—*now*. If you vote with me, your fatherland will be free and your city be first in all of Hellas, but if you choose the side of those who urge us not to fight, then the opposite of all the good I've spoken of will fall to you.
>
> (*The Histories* 6.109)

And so, early one morning in late September 490, under Miltiades' command, the Athenians, flanked by some Plataeans, ran down the hill on which they had encamped, covering the mile or so that divided them from the Persians at double speed despite the weight of their hoplite armor. Aristides and Themistocles commanded their tribal contingents in the center, while Callimachus commanded on the right wing and the Plataeans held the left. Knowing they were outnumbered, the Athenians packed their wings as tightly as they could, concentrating as many men as possible on the outer ends of their formation, even though it meant leaving the center thin. Despite their numerical superiority, the Persians were unable to withstand the disciplined and determined hoplites fighting in defense of their freedom, who had, in addition, the advantage of better armor and longer spears. While fleeing to their ships, many of the Persians became bogged down in the marshes and died.

Arriving too late to participate in the fighting, the Spartans visited the battlefield and surveyed the Persian corpses. Herodotus maintained that the Athenians lost 192 men, the Persians 6,400. The Greek statistic is probably correct, for the names were inscribed on the battlefield; they included Callimachus. The dead were cremated where they had fallen, and a monument was subsequently erected on the site. Some Plataeans and some Athenian slaves also died, but their numbers are unknown. The playwright Aeschylus himself fought at Marathon. The epitaph he composed for himself makes no mention of his stupendous achievements as a tragic dramatist but speaks only of his service in this battle for freedom: "The glorious grove of Marathon," he wrote, "can tell of his valor—as can the long-haired Mede, who well remembers it." Throughout the next decades, the *Marathōnomachoi*—men who had fought at Marathon—enjoyed singular prestige in Athens and came as time went by to represent the simple virtues of the older generation in an increasingly luxurious and complex society.

About a quarter-century after the battle, the Greek victory was memorialized in a painting in the Stoa Poikile (painted portico) at the north end of the Athenian agora; Callimachus, Miltiades, Datis, and Artaphernes could all be identified, as well as Aeschylus' brother Cynegirus hanging onto the Persian ship, to which he clung intrepidly until his arm was cut off with an ax. Gods and heroes were present at the battle as well—Heracles, Athena, and Theseus, who many believed had offered phantom aid on the battlefield as Homeric gods had done at Troy.

Not all Greeks rejoiced in the defeat of Persia. A shield signal was apparently flashed from Athens after the battle advising the Persians that the city was prepared to surrender. Any connection between the Alcmaeonids and the signal was indignantly denied by Herodotus, who tended to favor the Alcmaeonids and seems to have used Alcmaeonid sources in his writing, but just such a connection was common gossip at the time. In any event, someone at Athens wished the Persians well. Over the years, accusations of Persian sympathies would dog aspiring Athenian politicians and offer an easy route to damaging a controversial figure's reputation.

Greek Leaders and Their Misadventures: Miltiades, Cleomenes, and Demaratus

Athenians held their leaders to high standards. Although the history of the fifth and fourth centuries would provide numerous examples of the exacting temperament of the demos, the earliest are among the most interesting. Shortly after the battle of Marathon, Miltiades was impeached in the assembly and condemned to pay a stiff fine. He died in disgrace before he could pay, and his son Cimon discharged the debt. The circumstances were curious. Because of his heroic standing after the victory of Marathon, the Athenians had granted ships to Miltiades on his promise that he would make them rich. He had set out to attack the island of Paros, but the venture had ended in failure and embarrassment—Herodotus claims the wound that eventually killed him was sustained while violating the sanctuary of Demeter. At the impeachment trial, which Miltiades had to attend on a stretcher because his wound was becoming gangrenous, the Athenians considered putting him to death. Although it is impossible to know just how much the voters in the assembly had known about the object of Miltiades' expedition—security considerations would have argued against openly naming Paros, which had sided with the Persians during the war—what is clear is that the demos had developed the confidence to hold its leaders accountable. Throughout the decades that followed, interaction between the demos and its leaders would be characterized by a changing dynamic that helped define the nature of the democracy as history unfolded.

It was not only in Athens that political leaders tended to come to bad ends. Spartan kings had a habit of getting into difficulties as well. After winning a decisive victory over Sparta's inveterate enemy Argos at Sepeia, Cleomenes was accused by the Spartans of sparing the city as a consequence of bribes. A couple of years later, when he had enlisted the Delphic oracle in machinations to engineer the deposition of his fellow king Demaratus, further accusations of bribery followed. If Herodotus' sources are correct, he lost his mind and perished horribly while displaying the Spartans' proverbial endurance of physical pain. He had never been quite right in his head, Herodotus maintained, and finally,

> Cleomenes was gripped by a frenzy of madness. Whenever he met a Spartan, for example, he would hit him in the face with his royal scepter. After he went out of his mind and did this sort of thing, his family confined him in the stocks. He, pilloried as he was, watched for his guard to be left alone by the others and demanded a knife....Slicing lengthwise through his skin and muscles, he proceeded from his shins to his thighs, from his thighs to his hips, and from his hips to his sides until he reached his stomach, which he slashed in strips. And in this way he died.
>
> (*The Histories* 6.75)

The exiled Demaratus fared better. Some of his conflict with Cleomenes had been over his sympathy with the pro-Persian party at Aegina, and so he found a warm welcome in Persia, served as an adviser in the wars with Greece, and was rewarded for his services with the grant of four cities in Asia Minor.

Figure 5.12. Numerous *ostraka* have been discovered in the Athenian agora. These bear the names of Aristides, son of Lysimachus, and Themistocles, son of Neocles, of the deme Phrearrhioi.

Athens After Marathon

The nature of political leadership in Athens changed shortly after the Battle of Marathon in a very specific manner. Events surrounding the campaign had impressed on the Athenians the importance of sound military leadership. Shortly afterward, they signaled this awareness by a change in the method of selecting archons, who as primarily judicial officials had come to seem less important in comparison with the strategoi, who had life-and-death military responsibilities. In 487, the Athenians began choosing archons by lot from a large pool (perhaps a hundred men in total?) contributed by the various demes—the method already used for selecting members of the Council of Five Hundred. This shift ensured that men of ambition would stand not for the archonship, a nonrenewable office, but for the *stratēgia* (generalship). It also served gradually to undermine the status of the venerable Council of the Areopagus. Because it was composed of former archons, as time went by the council came more and more to be filled by men who had been chosen by lot. It seems likely that the originator of this move was the feisty Themistocles. Not only was Themistocles hostile to the aristocratic ethos that granted special power and prestige to the Areopagites; as a man who had already served his archonship and was eligible to repeat only his general-ship, he had a more immediate interest in enhancing the role of the strategoi at the archons' expense. Selection by lot was a procedure commonly associated with democracy in Greece. It worked to discourage the machinations of special-interest groups and to ensure that a significant proportion of the men eligible for each office would participate in politics, and it seemed to offer the gods a role in choosing officials. The Athenians were no fools, however. They subjected all would-be officeholders to an interrogation known as *dokimasia*, and they declined to employ the lot to select commanders for the state's armed forces. As a consequence, the generalship became the most prestigious office in the government, and the ten strategoi outranked all other Athenians in authority.

At the same time, the Athenians began deploying an unusual procedure for preventing any one individual from taking over the state, although the rapid disappearance of several of Themistocles' opponents serves as a reminder that the method was not foolproof. One of the innovations attributed to the reformer Cleisthenes was **ostracism**, a system whereby every spring the Athenians had the option of voting to send one of their fellow citizens into exile for ten years. The peculiar process took its name from the broken pieces of pottery known as *ostraka* on which the voters inscribed the name of the man they wanted to banish. No accusation was lodged; no shame attached to the departure; the exile's rights of citizenship and his material possessions would be waiting for him upon his return. But the man who was identified as dangerous by receiving the most votes would be compelled to withdraw from Attica for a ten-year cooling-off period. Inevitably historians have wondered why, if this procedure was really developed by Cleisthenes, the first man to be exiled in this fashion—a Pisistratid named Hipparchus—was not ostracized until 487, fully twenty years after Cleisthenes' ascendancy. The answer may lie in the minimum of six thousand votes that the Athenians demanded be cast; perhaps the ostracism of Hipparchus was not the first attempted ostracism but just the first one in which the quorum was met, the first that "took." It is probably no coincidence that the first man known to be ostracized bore such an unfortunate name; one common explanation of ostracism was that it was designed to ward off tyranny. Whenever ostracism was first devised, it should perhaps be seen as a means of replacing the expulsion of whole family groups, like the Alcmaeonids, with the less sweeping exile of a feared individual. Several prominent men were ostracized in the 480s—Megacles, leader of the Alcmaeonids, in 486; Xanthippus, the father of Pericles, in 484; and Themistocles' great rival Aristides in 482.

What role Themistocles played in the first three ostracisms is a matter of speculation, but his conflict with Aristides is indisputable, and the ostracism of 482 compelled the Athenians to choose between two distinct policies. Civil war might be averted by the safety valve of ostracism, but the danger of another contest with Persia also had to be addressed. Darius raised taxes in the summer of 486, thus arousing suspicion that he was gathering resources to finance a new invasion of Greece. He would probably have some support in northern Greece—Thessaly,

Figure 5.13. A trireme at sea. Working in England and Greece, twentieth-century scholars and naval architects reconstructed the Athenian trireme of the Classical period.

for example—and no doubt in the south as well. By this time the Persians were well aware of how divided Greek cities were among themselves—they knew of the rivalry of Argos with Sparta, Aegina with Athens—and how racked by internal conflict. In the event, Thessaly, Locris, and all of Boeotia except Plataea and Thespiae would in fact give the requisite earth and water to the Persians after they learned Persian forces had crossed the Hellespont. Darius' project had to be delayed, however, because of a rebellion in Egypt sparked by the increase in taxes. In the fall of 486 BC, the Persian king fell ill and died.

The Invasion of Xerxes and the Building of Triremes at Athens

Darius' son and successor, **Xerxes** (Cyrus' grandson on his mother's side), was at first ambivalent about carrying out the invasion, but by 484 BC he had made his decision, and the Greeks learned that ships were being built in large numbers throughout the ports of the extensive Persian empire from Egypt to the Black Sea. Engineers and laborers were dispatched to the Hellespont, where they bridged the crossing with boats, and to northern Greece, where they cut a canal across Athos so that the shipwreck Mardonius had suffered in 492 could be avoided.

Fortuitously, at this very time the Athenians working the silver mines of Laurium in southeastern Attica for their modest yield discovered an extraordinary lode of silver, from which they extracted well over two tons the first year alone. In Athens, voters were divided about what to do with the valuable ore. Aristides led those who wanted to partition it among the citizens, but Themistocles advocated building ships. Well aware that gloomy prognostications of war with Persia were likely to make him unpopular, he reminded the Athenians of their constant warfare with the neighboring island of Aegina, which had just inflicted a serious setback on Piraeus trade by a major naval defeat. The ostracism of 482 decided the issue: Aristides left Athens, and the fleet that would save Greece was built. It is difficult to imagine how history might have turned out had the vote in that ostracism been different.

The ships the Athenians built with their windfall from Laurium were **triremes**, light, fast, maneuverable warships with three banks of oars. Although the first triremes had been built, presumably in Corinth, as early as the seventh century, they were expensive vessels to construct, and it took some time for the trireme to replace older, less efficient models as the Greek warship par excellence. By the fifth century, however, the trireme had established itself as an indispensable tool of war. A long, slender vessel, the trireme was about nine times as long as it was wide, about 120 feet by 15 feet, and was powered by 170 rowers. Whereas Greek oared ships had originally been designed simply to transport soldiers to the theater of war, by the fifth century naval warfare had evolved to make ramming tactics crucial to success, and for this the trireme was ideal. It was triremes that would defeat the Persians, and the triremes would come from Athens. As the Athenian navy grew in power and prestige, the trireme came to be identified with Athens; in Aristophanes' play *The Birds,* an Athenian traveler, asked for his polis of origin, replies, "Where the fine triremes come from."

While the Athenians busied themselves constructing warships, Xerxes' heralds arrived in Greece seeking earth and water, and many states complied. Thessaly, Thebes, and Sparta's inveterate enemy Argos could not be counted on. Athens and the Peloponnesian League would have to take the lead, and in concert they called a congress of delegates at Corinth in 481 BC to plan the defense of Greece. There the thirty-one states that were determined to resist the Persians formed an alliance historians generally call the Hellenic League. In the crisis, Aegina and Athens were reconciled and Aristides was recalled, along with other Athenian exiles. The high command on both land and sea was conferred on Sparta. Troops would be sent north, though not so far north as to be in territory bound to go over to Persia, but the Greeks probably placed their greatest hope in their fleet. After an abortive expedition to Thessaly, they established their ground forces at the pass of Thermopylae on the Malian Gulf while the fleet settled in at nearby Artemisium off northern Euboea. At the instigation of Themistocles, the Athenians evacuated Attica and waited out the war on the island of **Salamis** and in nearby Troezen in the Peloponnesus. A third-century copy of the decree discovered on Troezen in 1959 may be a reasonable facsimile of the original text:

> The Gods
> Resolved by the Council and People
> Themistocles, son of Neocles, of Phrearrhioi, made the motion
> To entrust the city to Athena the Mistress of Athens and to all the other Gods to guard and defend from the Barbarian for the sake of the land. The Athenians themselves and the foreigners who live in Athens are to send their children and women to safety in Troezen, their protector being Pittheus, the founding hero of the land. They are to send the old men and their movable possessions to safety on Salamis. The treasurers and priestesses are to remain on the Acropolis guarding the property of the gods.
> All the other Athenians and foreigners of military age are to embark on the 200 ships that are ready and defend against the Barbarian for the sake of their own freedom and that of the rest of the Greeks along with the Lacedaemonians, the Corinthians, the Aeginetans, and all others who wish to share the danger.
>
> (Jameson, modified)

The information center of the Greek world, the Delphic oracle, knew enough about Persian might to discourage resistance—the combined forces of the rich king contained many thousands of men, perhaps as many as a quarter-million—and both the Spartans and the Athenians had received glum oracles. Themistocles argued that the "wooden wall" that Delphi conceded might save Athens was in fact the navy; Spartans were told that their only chance lay in the death of a king. The oracle may in part explain King Leonidas' tenacity in holding the **Thermopylae** pass against all odds. It is also true, though, that hard calculation called for a land operation, however unpromising, to buy time for Greece while

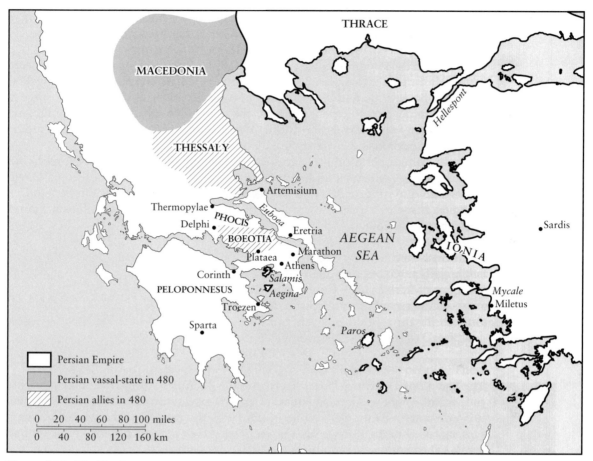

Figure 5.14. The Persian wars.

the fleet off Artemisium could cripple the Persian navy. As luck would have it, a storm did much of the Greeks' work for them, and the Persians lost many ships even before the indecisive fighting at Artemisium.

The Battle of Thermopylae

Leonidas marched into **Thermopylae** with about seven thousand men, a fairly small force; possibly the Spartans were ambivalent about taking a stand so far north. But for their dependence on the Athenian fleet, some of them might have been content to limit their defense to the Peloponnesus. The Phocian contingent, which was most familiar with the local terrain, was charged with defending the hidden road over the mountains against the chance that Xerxes would be lucky enough to find it. Lucky he was: a Greek traitor revealed the existence of the road and led Xerxes' commander Hydarnes up it with the crack troops known as the

Immortals. For some reason, Leonidas dismissed the bulk of his forces. He may have doubted their loyalty, or perhaps he knew his position was hopeless and wished to save as many soldiers as he could for future battles while still inflicting damage and delay on the enemy. Only the small force of four hundred men sent by the Thebans, the Thespians, and three hundred Spartans remained—as well as the many helots who had been pressed into service, their families held hostage at home. Leonidas and his men defended the pass heroically and fell fighting, having slain many "Immortals," including two brothers of Xerxes. On Xerxes' orders the body of Leonidas was decapitated and displayed on a cross.

The holding operation at Thermopylae not only bought time for Greece but went down in history as an extraordinary act of heroism. Jacques-Louis David painted his famous *Leonidas* in 1814 (see Plate VIIa). Lord Byron's long poem *Don Juan* included these impassioned lines in support of the Greek revolution against Turkish domination:

> Must we but weep o'er days more blest?
>   Must we but blush?—Our fathers bled.
> Earth! Render back from out thy breast
>   A remnant of our Spartan dead!
> Of the three hundred grant but three,
>   To make a new Thermopylae!
>   (Byron, *Don Juan* III.86.7)

The legend of Thermopylae even crossed the Atlantic. Texans routinely compare the defenders of the Alamo against superior Mexican forces in 1836 to the Spartan defenders of Thermopylae, while in the 1970s the futility of the war in Vietnam was captured in the film *Go Tell the Spartans,* which took its title from the epitaph for the Thermopylae dead attributed to Simonides:

> Go tell the Spartans, stranger passing by,
> That here, obeying their commands, we lie.

Consistently history has eulogized the 300 Spartans at the expense of the back-up troops—and the helots.

The Battle of Salamis

The victory at Thermopylae opened central Greece to the Persians, whose confidence was boosted by the knowledge that they had killed a Spartan king. Swiftly they moved their land forces down on Athens. From Salamis just off the western coast of Attica, where the opposing fleets had taken up their position, the Athenians could see the smoke of the burning Acropolis all too easily, and those who had regarded the fortifications on the hill as the saving "wooden wall" touted by Delphi were forced to admit their mistake. Dissent racked the navy. Some of the Peloponnesians wanted to cut back to the isthmus, while the Athenians were determined to stay where they were and fight in the narrows. Xerxes was tricked into taking action by a message from Themistocles, who purported to be on his side and urged immediate attack before the demoralized Greeks could disperse to their various homes. In reality, many Greeks were thinking of doing just that, and Xerxes' decision to attack was a foolish one. Herodotus, who came from Halicarnassus in Ionia, took delight in telling how Xerxes' prudent adviser Artemisia, queen of Halicarnassus, counseled him in vain against engaging battle when all the evidence suggested he could win by default. By arranging for the contest to be decided in the narrows, Themistocles maximized the chances that the heavier and less maneuverable Greek ships could worst the more numerous Persian vessels with their more experienced crews. From his high perch on the shore, Xerxes watched the course of the battle, in which the Greeks had the additional advantage that, as nearly all of them had grown up near water, they could swim; many of Xerxes' sailors could not. By sundown the Persians had lost two hundred ships and the battle. Rather than confront the foolishness of his decision to fight, Xerxes reacted to the defeat by executing his Phoenician captains for alleged cowardice in the battle, thus depriving himself of Phoenician naval support for the future.

Retreating with his navy to Persia to secure control of the Hellespont, Xerxes left Mardonius in Greece, where in the spring of 479 he faced the largest Greek army ever to have taken the field. Theban support bolstered the Persian cause, but it was insufficient to ensure victory. At the town of Plataea near the border between Attica and Boeotia, Mardonius ended his long years of service to Persia. Led by the Spartan Pausanias, nephew of Leonidas and regent for his infant son, the Greeks managed to win the hard-fought battle, and in the fighting Mardonius fell. The Theban leaders who had "medized," that is, gone over to the Persians, were subsequently executed without trial. Around the same time—tradition claimed that it was the very same day as the battle at Plataea—the Greek fleet that had pursued the Persians eastward defeated their navy at the Battle of Mycale off the coast of Asia Minor, in part because the Ionian Greeks deserted from the Persian side.

The Persian Invasion in Greek Eyes

Victors usually record the history of their triumphs. The vanquished reduce the same events to trivial, easily forgotten incidents. Until the work of Iranologists in the twentieth century following the decipherment of Old Persian in the 1800s and the excavation of archaeological sites, our views of the Persian empire were shaped largely by Greek historical sources and by scholars who preferred the western, European democratic tradition to what they saw as "Oriental despotism." In other words, the sources have been overwhelmingly Hellenocentric. Foremost among the ancient literary sources that established this perspective has been the *Histories* of Herodotus, who highlighted the unexpectedness of the Greek victory against all odds and searched for the causes in the fundamental institutions of Greek and Persian society and government. Although Herodotus portrays the early Achaemenids as virtuous and constructive, he depicts Xerxes as a dangerously arrogant ruler, who was responsible for initiating the decline of Persia.

Xerxes' chief character flaw, in Herodotus' view, was hubris (arrogance). Like Croesus, Xerxes imagined himself on the same level as the gods. He dared to bridge the formidable Hellespont. Thus the gods were thought to have aided the Greeks in defeating Xerxes, and he was thought to have earned his humiliation. The playwright Aeschylus, who fought at Salamis as well as at Marathon, also portrays Xerxes as responsible for the death of many noble Persians because of his folly. In 472 BC he produced a tragedy, *The Persians,* in which he reminded the Athenians of their role in defeating the Persians and celebrated the values for which they had fought—liberty as opposed to slavery, responsible democratic government as opposed to capricious autocracy and monarchy.

The play also contains a vivid description of the battle itself. In reconstructing the events of the Persian wars, Plutarch's lives of Aristides and Themistocles are also of some value, dependent as they were on sources now lost to us. By far the bulk of our knowledge, however, comes from Herodotus' sweeping *Histories.* The first continuous extant prose narrative in the Greek language, Herodotus' work, rich in detail and resonant with many important themes, traced the conflict between East and West to before the Trojan War. The author's researches extended far in both time and space, dealing in depth with the consolidation of Persia, the growth of Greece, and even the customs of Egypt (which may originally have been contained in a separate work). Born of the marriage of Ionian inquisitiveness with the creativity of the Athenian enlightenment, the *Histories* was only one reflection of the extraordinary burst of energy that erupted among the Greeks after their surprising victory over the wealthy and powerful empire that had sought to bring them into its orbit.

DOCUMENT 5.1

The chorus from Aeschylus's *Persians* (472 BC)

Aeschylus used the occasion of his drama about Salamis to stress the differences between eastern despotism and what he conceived as Greek freedom. Here the chorus of Persian elders laments Persia's defeat by Greece:

> They throughout the Asian land
> No longer Persian laws obey,
> No longer lordly tribute yield,
> Exacted by necessity;
> Nor suffer rule as suppliants,
> To earth obeisance never make:
> Lost is the kingly power.—
> Nay, no longer is the tongue
> Imprisoned kept, but loose are men,
> When loose the yoke of power's bound,
>   To bawl their liberty.

But Ajax' isle, spilled with blood
Its earth, and washed round by sea,
Holds the remains of Persia.

> Aeschylus, *The Persians* 584–596; Benardete

The Athenians later celebrated their triumph over the Persians in the relief sculptures of the Parthenon, the temple built to honor their goddess Athena. The reliefs on the four sides of the building showed battles: the gods against the giants; the Greeks against the Amazons; the Lapiths (a Greek people) against the half-human, half-horse males known as centaurs; and the Greeks against the Trojans, a reference to the struggle against the Persians, who also lived in the east. Thus the Athenians elevated their victory to mythical status, perhaps becoming guilty of hubris themselves.

THE OTHER WAR: CARTHAGE AND THE GREEK CITIES OF SICILY

In Herodotus' account, Athens, Sparta, and their few allies faced the might of Persia virtually alone. He emphasized their isolation by telling how they rebuffed the demand of Gelon, the tyrant of Syracuse and the most powerful Greek ruler of the time, for a share in the command of the Greek forces despite his offer of two hundred ships and over twenty thousand troops. Their refusal was timely, because the Greek cities of Sicily faced a massive attack from the North African city of Carthage simultaneously with the Persian invasion of Greece.

The Greek cities of Sicily had prospered from the beginning of Greek settlement of the island in the eighth century BC, gradually spreading along its north and south coasts as they subdued or pushed into the interior its native Sicel, Sican, and Elymian populations. The construction of some of the greatest temples and theatres in the Greek world bear witness to their prosperity. Athletes from the Sicilian cities also competed in the Olympic games and had their exploits celebrated by the finest sculptors and poets of the Greek homeland. Prosperity, however, was not accompanied by political stability. While tyranny was declining in Aegean Greece, it flourished in Sicily, reaching a climax in the late sixth century, when Gelon, the tyrant of Gela, seized Syracuse and then, in alliance with Theron, tyrant of Acragas, brutally conquered most of the cities of Sicily, sometimes transferring or selling into slavery whole populations to ensure his control. Only Messina and Selinus remained independent, and in desperation they sought help from Carthage. Fearful for the safety of their colonies in western Sicily, Carthage responded in force, allegedly invading Sicily with an army of three hundred thousand men and a fleet of two hundred ships in 480 BC. The decisive battle took place at Himera and ended in a total Carthaginian defeat and the suicide of the Carthaginian commander, who jumped into the sacrificial fire when he learned of the Greek victory.

Gelon celebrated his victory by dedicating a huge golden tripod and a statue of Nike (Victory) to Apollo at Delphi. His triumph was short-lived. Gelon died in 478 BC, and his empire disintegrated soon after; but the significance of his victory at Himera lived on, ensuring the safety of the Greeks of Sicily for the rest of the fifth century BC. It is understandable, therefore, that Greek legend maintained that the Battle of Salamis and the Battle of Himera were fought on the same day.

>>> ———— <<<

Although Greek historical sources tend to depict Persian history as the gradual degeneration of the mighty empire established by Cyrus the Great, as we shall see in Chapter 11, the Persians were not decisively defeated by European forces until their conquest by Alexander the Great (from 334 to 323 BC). They continued to play an influential role in Greek politics, both in civic disputes and in rivalries between Greek states, favoring now one side, now another, and providing refuge for exiles and soldiers of fortune, including the Athenians Hippias, Themistocles, Alcibiades, and Xenophon and the Spartans Demaratus and Pausanias. The Spartan victory in the Peloponnesian War of the late fifth century would have been impossible without Persian backing, and the relations of the poleis during the fourth century are impossible to understand without understanding Persian involvement in Greek affairs. Persia held special attractions for exiled Spartans, not only because it offered a luxurious way of life but because of some similarities in social structure. Xenophon admired both the Persian and Spartan educational systems. Persia and Sparta were stable, hierarchical societies in which social mobility was virtually impossible. Both societies depended upon economic exploitation of vast numbers of people by the relatively few members of the upper class. This way of life, however, was anathema to the volatile, mercurial Ionians. The unanticipated successes of the Greek city-states over Persia in the east and Carthage in the west had little impact on these two great empires, but in Greece it would give birth to a civilization of extraordinary brilliance and originality. The unity the Persian empire had sparked, however, would prove short-lived, and its fragility would place limits on how long this civilization could endure.

KEY TERMS

Key Terms
Alcmaeonid
Cleisthenes
Council of Five Hundred
Cylon
Cyrus II
Darius I
Draco
Gelon

Harmodius and
    Aristogiton
hektēmoroi
Hippias and Hipparchus
Marathon
Miltiades
ostracism
Pisistratus
pentakosiomedimnoi

Salamis
satrapies
Solon
Themistocles
Thermopylae
trireme
Xerxes

Suggested Readings

Briant, Pierre. 2002. *From Cyrus to Alexander: A History of the Persian Empire*. Winona Lake, MN: Eisenbraun. Perceptive and massively detailed history of the Persian empire.

Cartledge, Paul. 2006. *Thermopylae: The Battle that Changed the World*. Woodstock & New York: Overlook. Brilliant account of the Battle of Thermopylae and its significance.

Cawkwell, George. 2005. *The Greek Wars: The Failure of Persia*. Oxford: Oxford University Press. A detailed study of relations between Greece and Persia written from the perspective of Persia.

Cook, J. M. 1983. *The Persian Empire*. London: J. M. Dent. A history that provides vital background in understanding fifth-century Persia.

Dillon, Matthew. 2002. *Girls and Women in Classical Greek Religion*. London: Routledge. A comprehensive, well-organized, and readable survey of the roles of women of all statuses in public and private religion.

Green, Peter. 1996. *The Greco-Persian Wars*. Berkeley and Los Angeles: University of California Press. Vividly written account of the Persian wars.

Lenardon, Robert. 1978. *The Saga of Themistocles*. London: Thames & Hudson. The life of the innovative and irreverent politician.

MacDowell, Douglas M. 1978. *The Law in Classical Athens*. Ithaca, NY: Cornell University Press. A comprehensive account of Athenian law with emphasis on its relationship to Athenian society.

Ober, Josiah, and Charles W. Hedrick, eds. 1993. *The Birth of Democracy: An Exhibition Celebrating the 2500th Anniversary of Democracy*. American School of Classical Studies at Athens. Well-illustrated exhibition catalog with a valuable set of essays on Athenian democracy.

Ostwald, Martin. 1969. *Nomos and the Beginnings of the Athenian Democracy*. Oxford: Oxford University Press. Important study of Cleisthenes' goals and tactics.

Pomeroy, Sarah B. 1997. *Families in Classical and Hellenistic Greece: Representations and Realities*. Oxford: Clarendon Press. Comprehensive history of the family drawing on a wide range of sources, including literary texts, inscriptions, papyri, and archaeological evidence.

Romm, James. 1998. *Herodotus*. New Haven, CT: Yale University Press. A lucid introduction to Herodotus and his place in Greek literature.

Strauss, Barry S. 2004. *The Battle of Salamis: The Naval Encounter That Saved Greece—and Western Civilization*. Readable military history including analysis of the texts and discussion of the cultural differences between Greeks and Persians. London: Simon & Schuster.

CHAPTER SIX

The Rivalries of the Greek City-States and the Growth of Athenian Democracy

In the struggle to prevent a Persian takeover of Greece, a powerful sense of Hellenic identity was forged. Eager to avoid a third invasion, a number of Greek states entered into an alliance, the **Delian League**, led by the Athenians, whose naval strength had been instrumental in winning the war. Tribute from the League enabled Athens to offer state pay for public service such as jury duty, thus expanding the number of men who could afford to participate in government. Moreover, the lower-class citizens who rowed the triremes were becoming increasingly pivotal to the city's well-being, making it difficult for the rich and wellborn to maintain their monopoly on political power. Democratic reforms consequently reduced the advantage aristocrats enjoyed in politics, though nothing was done to remove the civic disabilities of women or to abolish slavery. Indeed, Athens' imperial ventures probably increased the number of slaves in Attica, and the status of women declined with the growth of equality among citizen males.

During the decades that followed Xerxes' defeat, moreover, Athens became a major cultural center. Tourists came from all over Greece to watch the tragedies performed in honor of the god Dionysus, and Athens used some of the money it received to police the seas to celebrate religious festivals and erect magnificent public buildings, such as the temple to Athena called the Parthenon; for the Greeks' deliverance from Persian autocracy, the gods received ample thanks. The tragedians **Aeschylus**, **Euripides**, and **Sophocles** were all Athenians, as were the comic dramatist **Aristophanes**, the sculptor Phidias, and the historian **Thucydides**. Many Greek thinkers, like the historian **Herodotus** and the philosopher Anaxagoras, came from elsewhere to participate in—and enhance—what Athens had to offer.

Athens was not the only site that could boast major attractions. At Delphi, for example, donors grateful for deliverance from Persia dedicated splendid monuments and works of art. Olympia remained a vital religious center as well; the games were extended to five days, and after its completion in 456, participants could also admire the altar by the imposing temple of Zeus. Democracies similar to that evolving at Athens developed in a number of places, most prominently Syracuse in Sicily, and throughout the Greek world, intellectuals could be found bringing new ideas to birth. While Socrates was asking questions about justice and the human community in Athens, on the island of Cos Hippocrates was investigating medicine and the human body.

SOURCES FOR THE DECADES AFTER THE PERSIAN WARS

Although Greek culture flourished throughout the Aegean, tensions between Athens and Sparta marred the scene. No Spartan writers of the Classical period have left us records of their view of the world or even of the history and habits of their country. For fourth-century Sparta, **Xenophon**, a disciple of Socrates, provides considerable information, since his personal inclinations were in many ways Spartan rather than Athenian, and he lived for many years in the Peloponnesus after being exiled from Athens. Of course, some of what he had to say about Spartan society is applicable to the fifth century as well. But in terms of foreign policy and domestic development, the story of classical Sparta can be reconstructed only in part, using archaeological evidence and snatches from contemporary Athenian authors such as Xenophon and Thucydides or from later writers like Plutarch.

Sources for Athens are fuller. Though there is no detailed history of the decades that followed the defeat of Persia, a wealth of inscriptions survive that illuminate both domestic and foreign policy, and the sections dealing with this period in the first book of Thucydides' history of the Peloponnesian war, though sketchy, are enormously useful. Herodotus sheds light on the first months after the end of the Persian invasion. Some information can also be gleaned from the *Library of History* composed by Diodorus of Sicily, who lived shortly before the birth of Christ and made use of the fourth-century Greek historian Ephorus, whose work is now lost. Constitutional developments at Athens are traced in the *Constitution of Athens* ascribed to Aristotle. Facts preserved from the work of Ephorus and of other lost historians who wrote during the fifth and fourth centuries sometimes pop up in Plutarch's lives of Themistocles, Aristides, **Cimon**, and **Pericles**.

Literary sources for day-to-day life and popular culture during the fifth century are meager indeed. Much of what we know has been inferred from the comedies of Aristophanes and the ancient commentaries on them by editors known as scholiasts. Art and archaeology also offer insights into how people lived and what they cherished; vase painting, for example, depicted not only mythological episodes but also scenes from daily life. The organization of public and private space reveals a great deal about civic and family life. Much of what we know of customs

Figure 6.1. The bronze dedication from the Sanctuary of Apollo at Delphi known as the "serpent column," made after the Greek victory over the Persians in 479 BC, was moved by the Roman emperor Constantine to his new capital Constantinople (the former Byzantium), where it stands today in a square in Istanbul known today in English as the Hippodrome, the former site of a Roman racetrack.

and norms in the fifth century, however, has to be extrapolated from the rather fuller evidence for the fourth. About the lives of women, slaves, and poor people, we know less, because their activities usually did not attract the interest of upper-class male writers. Women philosophers and a few poets were found in Greek cities; the largest group of women philosophers consisted of Pythagoreans who lived in Croton, Metapontum, and other cities in southern Italy. Their writings are not extant, but their witty and astute remarks were quoted by later authors. Only one Athenian woman in the classical period—Plato's mother Perictione, to whom a Neopythagorean treatise "On the Harmonious Woman" is attributed—has left us a written record of her thoughts. Athenian red figure vase paintings, however, do portray women reading papyrus rolls.

The Aftermath of the Persian Wars and the Foundation of the Delian League

After their victory over the Persians at Plataea in 479 BC, the Greek allies set up a monument at Delphi made of three intertwined bronze serpents (Figure 6.1). On the coils were inscribed the names of the thirty-one Greek states that had stood fast against the Persians. The Greeks agreed that Plataea should henceforth be considered sacred land, dedicated to Zeus the Liberator in gratitude for the victory over Persia. First among the thirty-one states listed on the **serpent column** were Sparta and Athens. The role of the Athenian navy in beating back the Persians had radically altered the balance of power in Greece, and only time would tell how the Spartans would accommodate this shift.

The Continuing Persian Threat: Conflicts Over Greek Leadership

Despite the preponderance of Athenian ships, by custom a Spartan still commanded the fleet of the Hellenic League. While the League's fleet was at Byzantium in 478 seeking to consolidate Greek power in the east, the Greeks under the command of **Pausanias**, regent for Leonidas' underage son Pleistarchus, began to complain bitterly about the Spartan's conduct. They alleged that Pausanias acted like an eastern potentate, dressing like a Persian and fortifying his position with a bodyguard of Medes and Egyptians. He was also accused of exchanging treacherous letters with King Xerxes. Pausanias may or may not have been guilty of treason; what is certain is that his lack of tact alienated the Greeks serving under him, particularly the Ionians, who had only recently been freed from the Persian king and were especially sensitive to the trappings of despotism. Having appealed to Athens to take over the leadership of the fleet, the Greeks were unmoved by the arrival of Dorcis, whom the Spartans had optimistically sent out to replace the disgraced Pausanias. In this way the leadership of the fleet passed into willing Athenian hands—a development many people in the allied states would come to regret.

Inevitably the Spartans were divided about this turn of events. To some the containment of Persia without undue Spartan exertion was an appealing prospect. Throughout Classical history, the underlying threat of a helot rebellion inhibited Spartan ambitions in the east. Others, however, were stung by the blow to Spartan prestige and found the Athenians' growing power ominous and unsettling.

In Athens, on the other hand, there was little cause for ambivalence. Because a shortage of fertile land made the Athenians depend on grain imported from the northern Aegean and the Hellespont, safeguarding the region from Persia was of supreme importance. In addition, the Athenians enjoyed a sentimental attachment to their cousins the Ionian Greeks, and abandoning them to Persian rule would both feel bad and look bad. Athens, moreover, had seen its territory ravaged by the Persians, an experience Sparta had been spared. For all these reasons, the Athenians considered it in their interest to assume leadership of the naval forces.

The Delian League

An alliance was consequently formed which, though it had no name at the time, is called the Delian League by modern historians because its treasury was originally located on the island of Delos in the Aegean. In 477, representatives from Athens and dozens of other states met at Delos and took oaths binding themselves into an organization designed to fight the Persians. The allied states entered into a treaty with Athens, which agreed in exchange for annual contributions in ships or money to lead the League in military operations against Persia while simultaneously respecting the internal autonomy of each polis in the alliance. Policy was to be established by a League assembly (in which each state had one vote regardless of its size). It would be executed, however, by an Athenian high command that would also control the treasury. Thus from the beginning, power in the League was concentrated in Athenian hands. The small size of Greek states is reflected in the number of poleis that enrolled in the alliance—probably about 150. Numerous states also declined to join, particularly those whose fear of the Athenians outweighed any apprehension about Persia and those that decided to rely for their security on their membership in the Peloponnesian League. As was customary in Greek alliances, all states swore to have the same friends and enemies. The association, moreover, was conceived as permanent. Whereas the goals of the Peloponnesian League had never been defined, those of the Delian League were fairly clear—containment of Persia, the gathering of booty as compensation for damages done to Greece during the war, and simple revenge.

In view of the personality problems that had brought down Pausanias (and with him Spartan naval leadership), it was fortunate for the Athenians that they had Aristides as their leader, a man famous for his probity. It was he who was charged with assessing each state's appropriate contribution to the League treasury. Some of the larger states, such as Lesbos, Samos, Chios, Naxos, and Thasos, chose to make their contributions in ships; most preferred to pay cash. As time passed, some of the bigger poleis converted to cash payments, and periodically the tribute assessment was revised. Funds were in the care of ten Athenian magistrates known as *hellēnotamiai* (treasurers of the Greeks). Although records of the tribute paid in the League's first years are lacking, it is possible to track the history of payments beginning in 454 through the inscriptions that today are

Figure 6.2. Section of the Athenian Tribute List inscribed on a marble slab showing payments for 433–432 BC by the citizens of Myconos, Andros, Siphnos, Syros, Styra, Eretria, Grynchae, and Rheneia. Athens, Epigraphical Museum.

called the Athenian Tribute Lists (Figure 6.2). Since these list one-sixtieth of each contribution that was dedicated to the goddess Athena Polias (of the City), the size of each state's contribution in a given year can be determined by multiplying the respective figure by 60.

From Delian League to Athenian Empire

For over a quarter century, the League fought against Persia, and, led by Miltiades' son Cimon, the Athenians and their allies expelled the Persians from Europe and prevented them from establishing naval bases in Ionia. In 476, Cimon set out with the League's navy for the northeast. His aims were to expel the Persians from all Thrace, banish troublesome pirates from the island of Scyros, and clear the route to the Hellespont of any obstacles. He took the fortress of Eion on the Strymon River with little difficulty. The Athenians then moved against Scyros, a rocky island east of Euboea inhabited by pirates. Enslaving the pirates and their families, they established on the island the kind of colony that was known as a **cleruchy**. Unlike most Greek colonies, which were fully autonomous and independent of the mother city, cleruchies were in effect part of Athenian territory, for all their inhabitants (called cleruchs) retained their Athenian citizenship. Generally chosen by the government from among poor Athenians, each cleruch was granted a parcel of land (a *klēros*, hence the word "cleruch") adequate to maintain him in Solon's third class, that of the zeugitai, and hence qualify him for service as a hoplite infantryman. Cleruchies filled a double function: they provided an outlet for the disaffected and potentially dangerous poor, and they operated as garrisons in the empire to discourage rebellion from Athens.

While in Scyros, Cimon also organized a search for the bones of King Theseus, who according to Greek tradition had died there, because the Delphic oracle had commanded that the Athenians retrieve these remains and honor them as sacred relics. Cimon's triumphant announcement that he had indeed managed to find the king's remains won him enormous popularity in Athens. Plutarch tells the tale in his life of Theseus:

> [Cimon] caught sight of an eagle, at a place which had the appearance of a mound, pecking at the ground with its beak and tearing it up with its talons, and by some divine inspiration he concluded that they should dig at this place. There they found a coffin of a man of gigantic size and, lying beside it, a bronze spear and a sword. When Cimon brought these relics home on board his trireme, the Athenians were overjoyed and welcomed them with magnificent processions and sacrifices, as though the hero himself were returning to his city.
>
> (Plutarch, *Life of Theseus* 36; Scott-Kilvert)

Theseus became the object of a thriving hero cult, and from then on Cimon made a point of boasting of his connection to the legendary ruler whenever possible.

Shortly afterward, the Athenians and their allies sailed against Carystus in southwestern Euboea, compelling the city to join the Delian League, and when the island of Naxos decided to leave the League, the Athenians forcibly prevented its withdrawal and in fact confiscated its fleet, ordering the Naxians thenceforth to pay their tribute in money rather than ships. These two developments highlight the problematic nature of the Delian League. A strong case could be made—and was made—that since all Greek states benefited from the existence of the League, all should pay tribute and support its fleet. Against this argument, however, resentful poleis adduced the right to make their own determinations about the extent of the Persian peril.

Because the League's existence was justified only by the need for continued protection of Greece from the Persians, the Athenians would have a problem if Cimon and his navy did too good a job of squelching any designs Persia might have on Greece; success in this endeavor would eliminate the need for an expensive anti-Persian alliance. This is precisely what happened around 467, when the Persian forces were badly beaten by those of Cimon at the mouth of the Eurymedon River in southern Asia Minor. After destroying the two hundred Phoenician ships fighting on the Persian side, Cimon's men landed and defeated the Persian army; they then captured eighty ships that were coming from Cyprus as reinforcements. Cimon was now the hero of the hour, and his supporters in Athens were quick to identify his exploits at the Battle of the Eurymedon as the newest chapter in the conflict between East and West that had begun with the Trojan War—another contest that had culminated in a Greek victory in Asia.

Greek Leaders in Trouble Again: Themistocles and Pausanias

Though his stunning victory at the Eurymedon did much for Cimon's popularity in Athens, it also encouraged defections from the League. Cimon's success probably played a role in the revolt in 465 of the important island of Thasos, located just off Thrace, but economic considerations also contributed to tensions between the Thasians and the Athenians, for both hoped to control the mines of Thrace. The revolt of Thasos was quelled only after a siege of two years. When the Thasians finally surrendered to Cimon, they were compelled to yield the mines and their ships, paying tribute henceforth in cash—cash that could not be raised from the mines, which were now back in Athenian hands. Athenian activities in Thasos also gave rise to an interesting political trial in Athens. Despite his reputation for incorruptibility, Cimon was impeached by his enemies on the grounds that bribes from King Alexander of Macedon were responsible for his decision not to use his base in the north to invade Macedonia. Cimon was apparently acquitted, but one of the public prosecutors chosen to argue the case against the popular admiral was Pericles, a young man who would become the most distinguished statesman of Classical Athens.

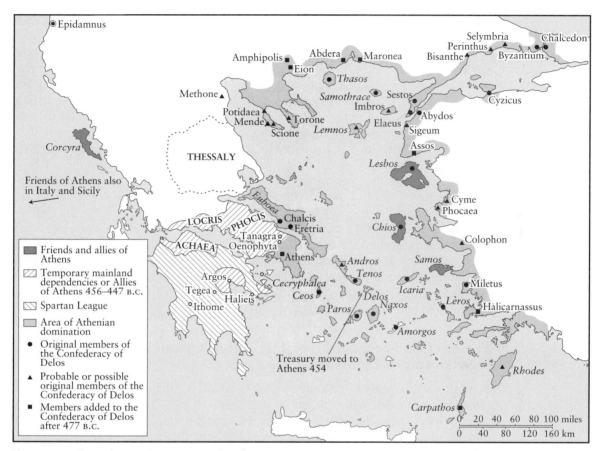

Figure 6.3. The Athenian empire at its height.

The Athenians' refusal to permit states to remain aloof from the League, combined with the gradual conversion of tribute payments from ships to money, made it clear that Athens ruled the sea and was converting the naval alliance into an empire. Yet if Athenian leaders were of one mind about the merits of naval imperialism, they were divided about Athens' proper relationship to Sparta. These conflicts were tied to disagreements about the further democratization of Athenian political life. Although sources for Athenian politics during these decades are sparse, some underlying fault lines are discernible: Themistocles encouraged competition with Sparta and the development of democracy, whereas Cimon favored Sparta and opposed any further democratization.

Sparta had helped Isagoras in his battle with Cleisthenes for the privilege of redefining the Athenian body politic, plotting to disband the boule (the Council of Five Hundred) and entrust the government to three hundred oligarchs. But Sparta had also driven out the Pisistratids, and many Athenians viewed Sparta as their natural ally. Commanded by King Leonidas, Spartans had bought time for Attica at Thermopylae, laying down their lives so that Greece might remain free. In both fact and memory, the union of Athens and Sparta had played an important part in the defeat of Persia. The forces in Athens favoring warm relations with Sparta and opposing the increasingly democratic trend in the government were strong. So was Themistocles' personality; his sharp tongue and quickness to claim credit for his achievements played into the hands of his enemies, and it seems that he was ostracized around 471. Probably he used his enforced absence from Athens to foment discontent and perhaps some democratization in the Peloponnesus, hoping to undermine the position of Sparta. In the 460s, the Spartans and Athenians united against him, and the Spartans provided evidence purporting to show that he and Pausanias were engaged in treasonable correspondence with the Persian king. In all likelihood, Pausanias was guilty and Themistocles innocent, but when the Athenians recalled the latter from Argos to stand trial and he found no place in Greece that would harbor him, Themistocles fled to Xerxes' successor, Artaxerxes. He died in Persia about ten years later, substantially outliving Pausanias, whose enraged countrymen had walled him up to starve to death in a temple of Athena in which he had taken refuge.

Further Conflicts at Athens: The Fall of Cimon and the Reforms of Ephialtes

Having rid themselves of a keen and colorful politician in Themistocles, the Athenians were left with the genial and gentlemanly Cimon. Themistocles and Cimon were opposites in every way. The pro-Spartan Cimon named his son Lacedaemonius, while Themistocles cast his eyes further westward and named his daughters Sybaris and Italia. Slow where Themistocles had been quick and courteous where Themistocles had been insolent, Cimon was no intellectual, but he had a flair for generalship. Because of his military reputation, he continued to command a good deal of respect in the Athenian assembly even after the development of a calculating and determined coalition led by Ephialtes, whose purpose was to break with Sparta and further the growth of democracy.

For some years Ephialtes and his associates had been making attacks on individual members of the venerable and aristocratic Council of the Areopagus; Cimon's trial needs to be placed in this context. In 462, not long after Cimon's return from Thasos and impeachment by Pericles, matters came to a head. Two years earlier, when an earthquake in Sparta killed thousands of people and destroyed most houses, the helots had seized the moment and revolted. Unable to dislodge the rebels from their stronghold on Mount Ithome, the Spartans appealed for aid to the cities with which they were still technically allied by the terms of the Hellenic League formed in 481 for the defense of Greece during the Persian wars. The Athenians looked like promising associates, for they were reputed to be better than most at siege warfare, though standards of excellence in this branch of tactics were low in Classical Greece, where sieges were generally prolonged and tedious.

Sparta's request touched off a vigorous debate in the Athenian assembly. Cimon, it seems, defended the time-honored alliance between Athens and Sparta, imploring the Athenians "not to allow Greece to go lame, or their own city be deprived of its yoke-fellow," while Ephialtes exhorted his fellow citizens to "let Sparta's pride be trampled underfoot" (Plutarch's *Cimon* 16.8; Scott-Kilvert). Cimon carried the day, and he marched off to Sparta with four thousand hoplites. But something about the way the Athenian soldiers conducted themselves in Sparta sparked panic in the conservative and fundamentally xenophobic people they had come to help. Alone among the allies, the Athenians were sent home. Their abrupt dismissal imperiled what harmony had been achieved among the Greek states. Athens now made an alliance with Sparta's enemy Argos; Cimon was ostracized for his miscalculation, leaving an open highway for Ephialtes and his associates. If the Spartans were alarmed by the Athenians' innovative and forward-looking ways of construing the world, they did a bad job of squelching them. The end of Cimon's ascendancy marked the beginning in Athens of full-blown democracy, taking democracy in the Greek sense of diffusing political power throughout the male citizen body, with no votes for women, no citizenship for immigrants, and slaves in abundance. Ironically, moreover, the naval ascendancy that Cimon had done so much to develop played a large role in fostering the democratic reforms he opposed. Cimon seems to have supported a moderate hoplite democracy, that is, government by those who could afford to provide their own weapons and armor. The success of his naval operations, however, underlined the increasing importance to the state of the men who rowed the triremes (some moderately poor, some indigent), a development that served to undermine the old-fashioned system of power following property and contributed to its replacement by a more broadly based form of government.

With the discrediting of Cimon's policies, some significant moves in the direction of democracy became possible, as represented by the **reforms of Ephialtes**. Though the details remain obscure, we know that Ephialtes substantially diminished the power and prestige of the ancient Council of the Areopagus. Time had already done some of Ephialtes' work for him; because the Areopagus consisted of former archons, it had been growing increasingly less aristocratic with each year that passed since the Athenians had begun selecting archons by lot in 486. Its members, however, held power for life, and the newer, poorer Areopagites may well have been co-opted into the value system of their aristocratic elders. At the instigation of Ephialtes, the assembly passed measures constricting the jurisdiction of this body, transferring many of its functions to the boule, the ecclesia, and the body of prospective jurors known as the heliaia. Ephialtes was careful, however, to show respect for its venerable history and long traditions by leaving it with jurisdiction over homicide and some religious matters.

Shortly after these reforms were enacted, men who presumably disliked the turn the government was taking arranged for Ephialtes' assassination. With

Ephialtes' death, his associate Pericles seems to have assumed leadership of the loosely organized political group to which we give the somewhat misleading term "party." With the exception of two years, Pericles remained the leading politician in Athens from roughly 461 to his death in 429, being elected repeatedly as one of the ten strategoi.

THE FIRST (UNDECLARED) PELOPONNESIAN WAR (460–445 BC)

Pericles took the lead in shaping Athenian policy throughout the decade during which Athens chose to wage war simultaneously with the Persian empire and the Peloponnesian League. The period from 460 to 445 BC is sometimes known as the First Peloponnesian War, an undeclared war between the Athenian and Spartan leagues that consisted of a series of battles often punctuated by considerable intervals of peace. (The famous Peloponnesian War, which was fought fairly steadily between 431 and 404, was really the Second Peloponnesian War.) The fact that historians have labeled the earlier war as "Peloponnesian" is an indication that the principal sources are Athenian; just as we know the Trojan War and the Persian wars from the Greek standpoint and do not normally call them the Greco-Trojan or Greco-Persian wars, the Atheno-Spartan War has come to be known as the Peloponnesian War, though Thucydides himself called it the war of the Athenians and the Peloponnesians.

Athens' Conflicts with Its Neighbors

Sitting between Corinth and Argos, the commercial state of Megara played an important role in the outbreak of both Peloponnesian wars. Around the time of Ephialtes' death, the Megarians decided to bolt from the Peloponnesian League and ally themselves with Athens to obtain protection from the designs of Corinth. Not surprisingly, the Corinthians were alarmed by the Athenians' possession of the Megarian port of Pegae on the Corinthian Gulf, from which it was easy to sail to the west. They became more agitated still at the upshot of the helot rebellion that had followed the earthquake in the Peloponnesus, for when the helots on Mount Ithome finally surrendered on condition that they be permitted to leave the Peloponnesus, the Athenians settled them at Naupactus, near the mouth of the Gulf. This bold action drove an additional wedge into the Corinthians' sphere of influence. With the two states locked in trade rivalry, moves that promised to expand the territory easily accessible to Athenian shipping were found to spark hostility in Corinth, and it was predictable that the tension between Athens and Corinth would play a large role in determining the diplomatic relations of the Greek states.

In 459, Corinth and Aegina combined against Athens. The Athenians not only repelled a Corinthian invasion of Megara but also built the so-called Long Walls, linking Athens to the port of Piraeus. This prudent strategy had the effect of making the whole town complex impossible to besiege by land, since supplies could always be brought in by boat. Around the same time, the Athenians engaged Hippodamus of Miletus, the earliest Greek town planner, to design the port area.

The Spartans' decision to enter the war against Athens in 457 did more harm to them than to their designated enemy. Fighting the Athenians in Boeotia, what the Spartans chiefly accomplished was to draw Athens into Boeotian affairs. By 456, the Athenians had come to control the whole region with the exception of Thebes, and Athenian influence had made democratic governments the norm in the Boeotian poleis. West of Boeotia, Phocis and Locris joined the Delian League, as did the vanquished island of Aegina, and Athens also gained two states in the Peloponnesus itself, Troezen on the east coast and Achaea on the Corinthian Gulf.

Disaster in Egypt and the Transfer of the League Treasury to Athens

Athens' land empire now stood at its maximum extent. Determined to continue operations against Persia, Pericles persuaded the Athenians to send ships both to Cyprus, where they hoped to inflict damage on the Phoenician fleet, and to Egypt, which had rebelled against King Artaxerxes. The Egyptian campaign dragged on for years, ending in a wretched debacle in 454 after an eighteen-month siege in which Artaxerxes' general Megabazus penned in the Athenians on the island of Prosopitis. Ultimately, Megabazus drained the channels around the island, leaving the ships high and dry, and marched across on foot to capture the Athenian sailors. Thucydides reports that nearly all the Athenians were killed. In addition, a relief force of fifty ships that arrived ignorant of the disaster was attacked by the Persian infantry and the Phoenician fleet, and only a small number of these ships escaped. Although the size of the original force is uncertain—Thucydides says two hundred ships, the historian of Persia Ctesias only forty—the loss in morale was enormous, surpassed only by the loss in life.

In 454, meanwhile, the Athenians transferred the treasury of the Delian League from the island of Delos, vulnerable to pirates and Persians alike, to Athens itself. Though their ostensible purpose was security, Delos was probably no more endangered than it had been previously, and the Athenians' decision to move the treasury was primarily a power play designed to demonstrate their supremacy. Historians therefore have taken 454 as a convenient date to stop referring to the Delian League and begin speaking of the Athenian empire, though in reality the transformation had been going on for some time.

A Brief Hiatus: Athens at Peace with Persia and Sparta

Returning from his ten years' exile in 451, Cimon seems to have come to an understanding with his rival Pericles; he would resume his efforts to make war on Persia and peace with Sparta but would not interfere with any domestic policies Pericles might wish to implement. In 451 Cimon negotiated a truce of five years between Athens and Sparta and abandoned Athens' alliance with Argos. Argos in turn signed a thirty-year treaty with Sparta. When Cimon died campaigning in Cyprus in 450, the Athenians seem to have made peace with Persia. We do not, however, have the text of this agreement, the so-called Peace of Callias, named after Cimon's former brother-in-law, who was later said to have negotiated it. Because the only sources that mention the treaty date to the fourth century, some scholars doubt that such a document ever existed, while others believe it should be dated substantially earlier or later. What is certain is that Athens and Persia ceased fighting at this time, treaty or no treaty.

Peace with Sparta followed in 445 when the Athenian land empire collapsed. After sixteen years of imperialism within mainland Greece, the Athenians had lost hundreds of lives and had no more territory than they had possessed in 461 when the fighting began. Just as the five-year truce between Athens and Sparta expired in 446, Euboea revolted, probably because it resented the cleruchies the Athenians were establishing there. While Athens was frantically trying to put down the Euboean rebellion, the Megarians took the occasion to defect, slaughtering their Athenian garrison. When Pericles returned from Euboea to Attica, King Pleistoanax of Sparta had already invaded the land. Delicate diplomacy—and probably bribery as well—enabled Pericles to persuade Pleistoanax to return home, but terror had been struck in the Athenians' hearts. Though in time Pericles subdued Euboea, Megara reverted to the Peloponnesian League, and Athenian influence in Boeotia crashed to a close as Thebes assumed leadership of an anti-democratic Boeotian League.

The peace the Athenians made with Sparta in 445 was optimistically named the **Thirty Years' Peace**, though it would not last even half that long. The Athenians had overextended themselves by fighting simultaneously with the Persian empire and the Peloponnesian League, and their naked imperialism had also made them unpopular. The key terms of the peace were five: neither state was to interfere with the allies of the other, neutrals were free to join either side, disagreements were to be settled by arbitration, no allies were permitted to switch sides, and each **hegemon** (alliance leader) was free to use force to resolve conflicts within its own alliance.

Pericles and the Growth of Athenian Democracy

The guiding spirit of Athenian imperialism was Pericles, who owed his position at Athens in part to his repeated election to the post of strategos and in part to the high regard in which the Athenians held him. Though he always served concurrently with nine other strategoi, none of the other generals exercised a comparable influence in the ecclesia. This outdoor assembly meeting made policy in fifth-century Athens, backed by the large juries of hundreds of citizens selected from the heliaia. Although Pericles occasionally campaigned—commanding, for example, the troops that regained rebellious Euboea—his skills lay primarily in formulating policy and in persuading members of the ecclesia to vote his proposals into law.

Figure 6.4. The hill of the Pnyx, showing the *bema,* or speaker's platform. From here speakers would address their fellow Athenians, rich and poor, meeting in assembly in all kinds of weather to vote on questions ranging from small financial matters to whether or not to go to war. The surviving structure dates from about 340 BC.

The Athenian Assembly

The assembly met in the open air on the hill known as the Pnyx—a magnet for the many men of Attica who wished to play a role in determining the peninsula's future (see Figure 6.4). In the early decades of the fifth century, the assembly met only about a dozen times a year, but the number of meetings soon expanded, and in Pericles' time ten days rarely went by without at least one meeting. Assemblies that promised discussion of serious problems were likely to be attended by about six thousand—the quorum for certain important actions such as ostracism. This number was probably about an eighth of all adult citizen males in Attica during Pericles' career; when the population dropped later on, in part as a consequence of the ruinous Peloponnesian War of 431–404, the quorum of six thousand accounted for a higher proportion of the populace. During the first half of the fifth century, children with at least one Athenian parent would be enrolled in their demes as citizens at the age of eighteen, but in 451 Pericles persuaded the Athenians to limit citizenship to those whose parents were both Athenians. This was evidently an anti-aristocratic measure aimed at affluent men who made marriage alliances with noble families from other states, following the example of Megacles, the father of Cleisthenes, for instance, whose wife was the daughter of the tyrant of Sicyon in mainland Greece. The **citizenship law of 451** may not have been entirely retroactive, but probably children who had not yet reached the age of eighteen were excluded from citizenship. Citizenship was important for girls as well as boys; though Athenian women could not vote or hold offices, they were now the only women who could bear Athenian children.

The consequences of this legislation were profound. The insistence that Athenians marry citizens of their own state eliminated a powerful source of connectedness among poleis and fostered a sense of separateness that frequently led to war. Social problems were also created within the polis. Limited in their choice of marriage partners to Athenian women, married Athenian men frequently opened the door to domestic tensions by maintaining sexual relationships with the exotic "foreign" women whom they could not marry if they wanted civic rights for their sons and grandsons. A double irony awaited Pericles in his own family life: unhappy in his marriage, he divorced the mother of his legitimate children (who was also his cousin) and lived instead with the hetaira Aspasia, a highly intelligent immigrant from Miletus who was one of the most cultivated women of the century. When his legitimate sons died, he implored the assembly to pass a special decree conferring citizenship on the son he had with Aspasia. Admitted to citizenship, the younger Pericles served as strategos in 406 and was one of the six generals executed after they failed to retrieve sailors in a storm off the Arginusae islands in Ionia.

The prytaneis alone—the fifty members of the boule whose turn it was to be in charge for the month—had the privilege of calling a meeting of the citizens' assembly, though sometimes they did so at the behest of the strategoi. Theoretically, no motion could be put at the assembly that had not been drafted by the boule and posted at least five days before the day of the meeting, but this restriction did not mean that only council members could frame legislation. Sometimes the boule's motion was deliberately couched in such vague terms that a private citizen would reframe it at the assembly meeting; frequently an original motion wound up amended beyond recognition. Besides, most people who burned to put motions could suggest them to a neighbor, relation, or friend of a friend who happened to be serving on the boule.

Those who attended the assembly might be lifelong advocates of certain policies and could well be followers of a popular politician, but they were not members of political parties as we know them today, for there was no such thing in Athens. Instead people used expressions like "those around General So-and-So" to identify political groups. The degree to which citizens chose to participate varied widely even among those who attended meetings of the assembly. As at gatherings of academic faculties today (or town meetings in New England), some never spoke, some spoke occasionally, and a core of engaged citizens spoke frequently. Generals had the privilege of speaking first, in order of age; among private citizens, originally those over age fifty took precedence over younger men. Some people spoke extemporaneously; others brought notes or even a text. Speakers had to be prepared for their remarks to be interrupted periodically by laughter, applause, or heckling. Once the debate was concluded—assembly meetings rarely went past early afternoon, for some time had to be reserved before supper for the daily meeting of the boule—voting was conducted by show of hands.

Who attended the meetings of the assembly? Common sense would suggest that those who lived in the city center or close to it were more likely to turn up than those who lived far away, and no doubt the walk in from distant villages discouraged some citizens. Nonetheless it seems that people did take the trouble to make the trip when vital matters like whether or not to go to war were slated for discussion.

Athenian Officials

Athens had no president or prime minister; the generals exercised power in politics only by virtue of the esteem in which they were held. Until Pericles' death, men who lacked military reputations did not generally become distinguished politicians. The converse tended to be true as well—military heroes expected to be rewarded with political careers. In addition, though any man from the upper two classes of pentakosiomedimnoi ("500-measure men") and hippeis ("horsemen") might stand for office, the Athenians usually voted for fairly rich men from prominent families. All this changed after Pericles' death, when politics and the military began to diverge as careers and it became somewhat more customary for a man to be just a general or just a politician; concomitantly, the government ceased to be dominated entirely by the scions of famous clans. Throughout Athenian history, however, wealth and lineage remained important factors, and generals continued to involve themselves in politics more than they do in many countries today.

The board of ten generals on which Pericles served was only one of many bodies the Athenians established. Including jobs entailed by the administration of the empire, there may have been as many as seven hundred official positions all told in Classical Athens, and most offices were held, like the strategia, by boards of several men, all serving one-year terms. Many, like the archons, were selected by lot. Most citizen males by the time they died had held public office at one time or another, and a good number had held several. By diluting power in this way, Athenian voters believed they could inhibit the growth of an identifiable class of permanent officials with interests different from those of the populace at large. The interests of the disfranchised—of women, **metics** (resident aliens), and slaves—did not strike them as material to the body politic. The fruits of empire, fifth-century voters believed, were being shared by all.

The Judicial System and State Pay for State Service

In the absence of a chief executive, the Athenians considered sovereignty to be vested in the people. By the time of Pericles, they had come to call their form of government *dēmokratia*, a government in which the *kratos* (power) was in the hands of the *dēmos* (the people), by which they meant the male citizens in their capacity as voters in the assembly—and as jurors in the courts. The large size of Athenian juries—several hundred, sometimes as many as 1,501—facilitated the legal fiction that a decision of a jury was a decision of the demos, and the participation of large numbers of citizens in the judicial system was a hallmark of Athenian democracy.

To ensure that the privilege of serving on juries would be spread as widely throughout the citizen body as possible, not long after Ephialtes' death Pericles introduced a measure providing pay for jury service. It was a small amount, less than a day's wages for an average laborer, but not trivial, and no doubt this legislation bolstered Pericles' popularity at the polls. In time, Athenians came to be paid for serving on the boule and even for attending the assembly; for many years during the fifth century, magistrates were also paid. As elsewhere in Greece, voters gained some free time as a consequence of the labor done by women and slaves, but even a citizen with a wife and a couple of slaves generally had to work hard to survive, and the sums men received for participating in government made a difference. Today it seems natural to compensate people for the time spent serving the community, and state pay for state service is now the norm. Many Athenians, however—mostly affluent men who could afford to serve without remuneration—viewed this system as a discreditable attempt on the part of democratic politicians to buy popularity and votes. In the aristocratic value system, it was acceptable for Cimon to court popularity by inviting passersby to pick fruit from his orchards and by holding banquets for the hungry at his home, but it was manipulative and underhanded of Pericles to introduce measures in the assembly providing for compensation to those who served the state.

Despite a variety of innovations and constitutional reforms designed to maximize popular participation in civic life, rich Athenians continued to enjoy substantial prestige. Democratic politicians cleverly harnessed the wealth of the elite into the service of the state by establishing the public services known as liturgies. Even though these politicians themselves belonged to the elite and hence were creating a system that would oblige them to spend their own money, they considered the liturgies to be good investments in public relations. Liturgies included major outlays such as maintaining a trireme and training its crew (the liturgy known as the trierarchy), leading and financing a delegation to a religious festival in another Greek state, paying and training a team of runners for the intertribal torch races at festivals in Athens, or offering a banquet to all members of one's tribe on the occasion of a religious festival. Some of the most elaborate (though not as expensive as the trierarchy, which remained the costliest liturgy) involved training choruses for performances at Attic festivals. The fifteen members of a tragic chorus, the twenty-four members of a comic chorus, and the fifty members of a chorus that would recite the verses known as dithyrambs all needed to be selected, paid, and trained. Often the rehearsal period extended for months. The citizen who performed this liturgy might or might not know anything about sailing, running, or poetry; often he provided the funds and delegated the work to skilled experts. In addition to dozens of trierarchies, about a hundred civilian liturgies were performed each year. Everyone profited from this system. Those who lacked the means to offer such services benefited from the generosity of those who provided them, and the rich could garner prestige while simultaneously performing vital military, cultural, religious, and civic functions for the community. A competitive element also fostered excellence, for prizes at contests went to the victorious choragus as well as to the successful poet.

LITERATURE AND ART

In nearly every respect, we know more about life in the bustling city of Athens than we do about how people lived in the other Greek poleis, but energy and talent were dispersed widely throughout the Greek world, and much of it went into literature and the arts. The word most commonly attached to the art and literature of the earlier fifth century is "grandeur." Poets, painters, architects, and sculptors carried the traditions of the sixth century throughout the wider Greek world, while in Athens the defeat of Persia was marked by innovations in tragic drama so striking as to constitute a new art form.

Lyric Poetry

Lyric poets were among the most distinguished writers of the fifth century. Simonides (c. 556–468 BC) is remembered chiefly as the unofficial poet laureate of the Persian wars. Born on the Ionian island of Ceos, he spent time at the court of Hipparchus in Athens, among the royal families of Thessaly, and in Sicily, where he was esteemed by the warring tyrants Hiero and Theron and was able to effect at least a brief peace between them. He was probably in Athens during the wars with Persia, and his epitaphs for the war dead (such as the one cited in Chapter 5) became to Greek literature what the Declaration of Independence and the Gettysburg Address are to Americans (only easier to remember, since they were more concise and in verse).

Sicilian tyrants were famed for their interest in culture, and Simonides' nephew Bacchylides accompanied him to Sicily. Both were accomplished poets in the genre known as epinician odes, that is, poems written *epinikē* (upon [an athletic] victory). Bacchylides composed a poem for Hiero's victory in the chariot race at the Olympics in 476. He had a gift for gripping narrative, and Hiero was drawn to his work, but the verdict of posterity went to his rival **Pindar**, who competed with him for the favor of the Sicilian rulers.

Born into an aristocratic family in Boeotia, Pindar traveled widely and enjoyed the patronage of the powerful; some of his poems honored the Sicilian tyrants Hiero and Theron. Like Theognis, Pindar assumed that merit was inherited and that victors spring from illustrious families that can trace their origins ultimately to divine ancestors. Writing numerous epinician odes, he also associated physical prowess with all-around virtue. Connecting recent achievements with divine blood and tracing the ancestry of his subjects, he elaborated his poems with myths about gods and heroes and interspersed traditional moral and ethical comments for human beings.

DOCUMENT 6.1

Excerpt from Pindar's Seventh Olympian Ode

The family of Diagoras of Rhodes was one of the most illustrious and successful families in athletics. All their victories were in combat events. Diagoras won the men's boxing at Olympia in 464 and was victorious at the Isthmian, Nemean, and Panathenaic games, as well as at competitions in other cities, including his native Rhodes. Diagoras' oldest son Damagetus was victorious twice in the pancratium, and another son, Acusilaus, won in boxing. Dorieus, the youngest son of Diagoras, won thirty-six victories as a boxer and pancratiast. Like his father, he was a periodonikēs *("winner of the crown at all four major pan-Hellenic festival in one Olympic cycle," comparable to a modern "grand slam" in tennis). Two of Diagoras' grandsons also won victories in boxing at Olympia. A daughter of Diagoras became the first woman (who was not a priestess) to view the Olympic games. She disguised herself as a gymnastic trainer. When she was detected, she gained admission on the grounds that she was daughter, sister, aunt, and mother of Olympic victors.*

For Diagoras of Rhodes, winner, boxing, 464 B.C.

As when a man takes from his rich hand a bowl
foaming inside with dew of the vine
and presents it
to his young son-in-law with a toast from one home
    to another—an all-golden bowl, crown of possessions—
as he honors the joy of the symposium
    and his own alliance, and thereby with his friends
present makes him envied for his harmonious marriage,
so I too, by sending the poured nectar, gift of the Muses
and sweet fruit of the mind, to men who win prizes,
gain the favor
of victors at Olympia and Pytho.[1]
    Fortunate is the man who is held in good repute.
Charis, who makes life blossom, looks with favor
    now upon one man, now another, often with sweetly
singing lyre and pipes, instruments of every voice.
And now, to the accompaniment of both,
    I have disembarked with Diagoras, singing a hymn
To Rhodes of the sea, the child of Aphrodite
    and bride of Helios,
so that I may praise, in recompense for his boxing,
    that straight-fighting man of prodigious power,
who won a crown by the Alpheos[2]
and at Kastalia,[3] and may praise his father,
    Damagetos, who is favored by Justice;
they dwell on the island with its three cities near
to the jutting coast of broad Asia among Argive spearmen.

I intend, in proclaiming my message, to set forth truly
for them from its origin, beginning with Tlapolemos,

the history they share as members of Heracles'
mighty race, for they claim descent from Zeus
   on their father's side, while on their mother's
they are Amytor's descendants through Astydameia.
   But about the minds of humans hang
numberless errors, and it is impossible to discover
what now and also in the end is best to happen to a man....
There [in Rhodes]...
is established for Tlapolemos, the Tirynthians' colony-founder,
as if for a god,
a procession of rich sacrificial flocks and the judging
   of athletic contests, with whose flowers Diagoras
has twice crowned himself. Four times did he succeed
   at the famous Isthmos,
and time after time at Nemea and in rocky Athens.

The bronze[4] in Argos came to know him, as did the works
of art[5] in Arcadia and Thebes, and the duly ordered games
of the Boiotians
and Pellana; and Aigina knew him victorious
   six times, while in Megara the record in stone
tells no other tale. But, O
   father Zeus, you who rule Atabyrion's[6]
slopes, honor the hymn ordained for an Olympic victory
and the man who has won success at boxing,
   and grant him respectful favor
from both townsmen and foreigners,
   for he travels straight down a road
that abhors insolence, having clearly learned
   what an upright mind inherited from noble forbears
declared to him. Keep not in obscurity the lineage
they share from the time of Kallianax,[7]
   for at the celebrations of the Eratidai[8]
the city too holds festivals. But in a single portion of time
the winds shift rapidly now here, now there.

Pindar, Olympian 7; Race

[1]Delphi. [2]Olympia. [3]Delphi. [4]A shield awarded as prize. [5]Perhaps tripods. [6]The highest peak in Rhodes, crowned by a temple to Zeus. [7]Diagoras' ancestor. [8]Diagoras' clan.

The Visual Arts

Greek painters and sculptors were fascinated with both the human and the divine. Throughout the decades of change that mark the fifth century, both drama and the visual arts reveal a powerful drive to organize the world in accord with harmony, balance, and proportion. During the fourth century, Plato, in the blueprint for the ideal society that he described in his dialogue *The Republic*, would identify justice as the condition that obtained when all parts of the soul and state are in balance. The connections Plato posited between beauty and truth underlay much of the Greek view of the world throughout the Classical period.

Like dramatic poets, Greek painters and sculptors achieved what they did within the constraints posed by a variety of conventions. One popular vehicle for painting was the vase, which was produced in a wide variety of sizes and shapes, each affording distinctive challenges and opportunities. (See Plates IV, VIa, and XI.) The smaller vessels called for particular ingenuity and skill. Bronze and marble, however, the customary materials for sculpture, were difficult to work with and did not lend themselves to naturalism. The two generations or so that followed the Persian wars mark a period of transition during which Greek artists begin to emancipate themselves from the formulas of the Archaic period. Some of the change may have had to do with a rejection of eastern influences in the wake of the bitter conflict with Persia; the ties with the Near East that were so conspicuous in Archaic styles now seem more tenuous. As tragedy became more dramatic with the addition of a second actor, so the visual arts grew less static during these decades, and action became important. Conveying a strong sense of movement in a still medium is no small achievement. Some of the most outstanding artists of these decades managed despite the constraints of their craft to build a sense of anticipation and excitement.

A freestanding sculpture that conveys a dramatic sense of movement to come was the *Discobolus* (discus thrower) of the Athenian sculptor Myron, who was known for his realism; admirers commented that a bronze cow of his on the Acropolis could easily be mistaken for the real thing. Though the bronze statue Myron made around 460 does not survive, Roman copies enable us to appreciate the pent-up energy the athlete is about to unleash as he thrusts his arm back in preparation for the throw (see Figure 6.6).

The relief sculpture with which Greeks adorned their temples offered still greater opportunities for storytelling. Like tragedy, relief sculpture focused on mythological themes grounded in conflicts embroiling gods and mortals in tortuous scenarios. Tales involving animal-like figures also offered wonderful opportunities to visual artists. Thus the half-horse, half-human race of centaurs figured in the sculptural programs of two temples of the fifth century, the Parthenon at Athens, to be discussed in Chapter 7, and the **temple of Zeus at Olympia**.

When we think of Greek sculpture, both relief and freestanding, we usually assume that it was a uniform pale color as it is today. For us, the stark whiteness or beigeness or grayness is a large part of what makes it "classical." This misunderstanding gives us a very false impression of what a Greek city looked like. In fact, Greeks painted their buildings and statues with bright colors. Surviving bits of paint have made it possible for modern scholars to restore these colors to a number of works (see, for example, Plates VIIIa and VIIIb).

The temple of Zeus at Olympia was completed between 470 and 456 BC, just when the dramas of Aeschylus were defining the Attic stage. Beginning in AD 1876, excavations brought to light sculptural groups on the portions of the temple

Figure 6.5 Statue of a Warrior. Mid-fifth century BC. This statue is one of a pair of well-preserved bronze statues of warriors—possibly from a victory monument—recovered from the seabed near Riace in southern Italy. The statue is larger than life-size, and the warrior is depicted wearing a diadem, symbolic of victory. The teeth and eyelashes are made of silver, the eyes of bone and glass, and the lips and nipples of red copper. Some of the curls were sculpted separately and soldered. Reggio, Museo Archaeologico Nazionale.

known as the pediments—the elongated triangular spaces under the roof that sat atop the columns and cried out for decoration (see Figure 6.7a–c). In the temple of Zeus, each pediment extended horizontally for over 80 feet and rose in the center to a height of 10 feet. Libon was the chief architect for the project, although many artisans labored to create the elaborate sculptures. The west pediment celebrated the triumph of order and civilization over the animal-like barbarism represented by the centaurs, who in their characteristic drunkenness had sought to disrupt the wedding of the hero Pirithous to Deidamia, only to find themselves worsted in the melee by Pirithous and his friend Theseus. In the center of the relief stands a figure that most scholars identify as Apollo upholding the principles of civility.

The east pediment portrayed a more complicated story—an episode in the life of Agamemnon's ancestor Pelops, who won his bride, Hippodamia, in a chariot race arranged by her father, Oenomaus, an event associated with the beginning of the Olympic games. Oenomaus was accustomed to defeating her suitors in such races with the special equipment he had obtained from the god Ares. Hippodamia, however, fell in love with Pelops and arranged for the charioteer

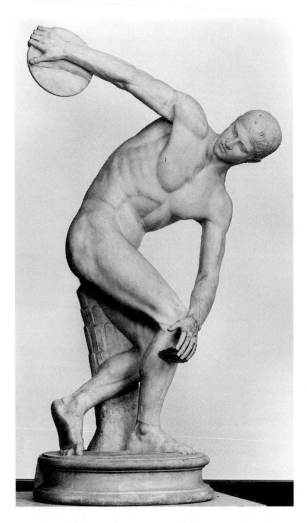

Figure 6.6. Roman copy of the *Discobolus* (discus thrower) by Myron. Scholars recognized that Myron's lost bronze statue was the model for Roman marble copies by means of a passage in the second-century AD author Lucian, who describes the original work in detail. Rome, National Museum.

Myrtilus to sabotage her father's chariot by substituting wax linchpins for the customary metal ones. In the ensuing accident, Oenomaus was killed. Though Pelops won the race, married Hippodamia, and fathered several children, Myrtilus, who was also in love with Hippodamia, placed a curse on him that Greeks connected with the subsequent misfortunes of his descendants, including Agamemnon and his family. Numerous figures in the scene depicted on the temple have survived, including one of the most remarkable individuals depicted in relief sculpture, a pensive seer who even before the race has begun knows what is going to happen (Figure 6.7c).

Grave stelae also provided an important medium for relief sculpture. One of the best-preserved funerary reliefs portrays a little girl holding her pet doves. This poignant reflection of the dead child makes clear that for all their preoccupation with war and civic engagement, the Greeks could also feel private losses deeply.

Our insight into the private lives of the Greeks owes much to the scenes that appear on surviving vases. Unlike sculpture, painting was as likely to treat mundane scenes of daily activities as it was to portray deeds of epic proportions. In painting as in sculpture, we are often ignorant of the identity of the artist whose work stands before us. Painters are often known simply by the subject matter of their most memorable works or the places they were or can be found (e.g., the Pan Painter, the Berlin Painter). Greek wall painting of the Classical period has not survived to be placed beside the vivid frescoes of Bronze Age Crete; what we have are thousands of vases and vase fragments. As in the Archaic period, the painters frequently took their subject matter from mythology, as in the fine vase in the Museum of Fine Arts in Boston depicting on one side the murder of Agamemnon and on the other that of Aegisthus (see Figure 6.8).

Daily life might also be represented, and scenes depicted on vases provide social historians with a wealth of information about how people spent their time at work and at play, showing women and men in a variety of activities; shoemakers, blacksmiths, agricultural workers, and other laborers are portrayed going about their tasks. We are indebted to vases for numerous scenes from women's lives and images of domestic space (Figure 6.13).

Like sculpture, vase painting of the earlier fifth century focused on the human figure, to which the curving surfaces of the vessels lent a sense of movement and grace. Even more than in drama, the possibilities of facial expression are limited by the medium, and character portrayal is weak; we are often given a clear sense of what the dramatis personae of the vase are experiencing at the moment in time the artist has chosen to capture, but little understanding of who they have been over their lifetimes, or what their driving anxieties or concerns might be. The figures on Greek vases are portrayed in action, not contemplation—they almost never appear to be posing for the artist—and we ask ourselves not only, "What are they thinking? What are they feeling?" but also, "What has just happened, and what will happen next?" But the focus always remains the human being. Landscapes are rarely developed in any substantive way, and though animals often appear as the companions of humans, they are rarely the center of attention as they had once been.

Although Greek wall painting has not survived the ravages of time, ancient critics suggest that facial expression was rather more varied in this medium, particularly after Cimon's friend Polygnotus of Thasos liberated it from traditional Archaic constraints, depicting, for example, open mouths and even teeth. Polygnotus was much admired in antiquity for the character portrayal in his vivid and complex murals—the Roman rhetorician Quintilian advised serious students of painting to begin with Polygnotus—but what we know of his work comes largely from descriptions by Pausanias, a traveler of the second century AD, whose *Description of Greece* offers descriptions of many artworks that no longer survive today; Polygnotus' paintings are lost. The Roman polymath Pliny the Elder

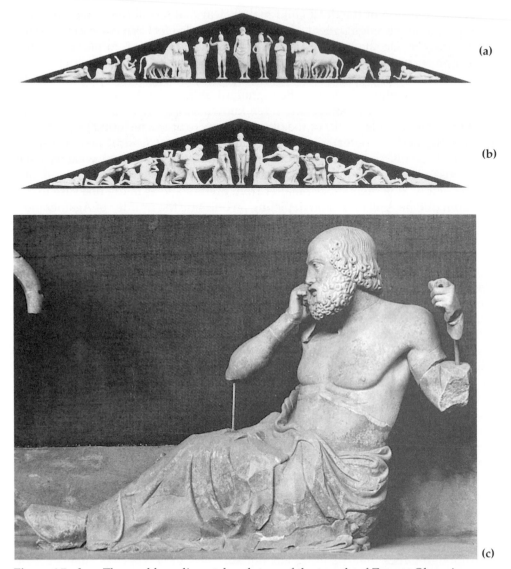

(a)

(b)

(c)

Figure 6.7.a,b,c. The marble pedimental sculpture of the temple of Zeus at Olympia (c. 460 BC) represents scenes from Greek mythology. Reconstructions show (a) the east pediment, telling the story of the chariot race between Pelops and Oenomaus, king of Pisa, and (b) the west pediment, depicting the melee that ensued when Peirithous made the mistake of inviting the barbarous centaurs to his wedding. Olympia, Museum. (c) This unusually naturalistic marble statue of an elderly seer is the third figure from the right in the reconstruction of the east pediment in Figure 6.7a. This male figure's half-reclining pose enables him to fit into the narrower space toward the side of the triangular pediment. Olympia, Museum.

(a)

(b)

Figure 6.8.a–b. Attic red-figure calyx-crater (mixing bowl for wine and water) attributed to the Dokimasia Painter (c. 470 BC). This vase, which was probably painted shortly before the production of Aeschylus' *Oresteia*, depicts both the murder of Agamemnon (a) and Orestes killing his father's murderer, Aegisthus (b). Boston, Museum of Fine Arts.

reported that Polygnotus was the first to portray women draped in transparent clothing, the "wet T-shirt" look.

Other painters active at Athens in the first half of the fifth century included Micon, who also seems to have enjoyed Cimon's patronage. Pliny the Elder records that Micon's daughter Timarete was also an artist and painted an image of Diana (the Roman counterpart of Artemis) on a mural in Ephesus. Micon was one among several artists who were drawn to the theme of Theseus fighting the Amazons, placing it in the context of the ongoing conflict between West and East, Greek and alien. Theseus was also depicted around the same time fighting centaurs. The association of women with foreigners and animals and the notion that Greek male identity could and should be asserted by setting oneself against them would be repeated in Greek art and thought throughout the Classical period. Because Greek writers were often reticent in discussing women, visual images provide important clues to how women were thought of in ancient Greece. Vase paintings depict women of all social classes. Vases that were used for mixing and drinking wine at drinking parties frequently show prostitutes entertaining men. Some women are shown playing pipes, others are engaged in various stages of flirtation, and some scenes are frankly pornographic. Common prostitutes were often slaves. A woman of higher status who nevertheless mingled with men and received pay for her services was known as a *hetaira*. Such women were likely to be metics, either former slaves or freeborn, who—like male metics—gravitated to Athens because it was a commercial center. A few of these women, like Aspasia, the common-law wife of Pericles and the most famous hetaira of all, participated actively in the intellectual life of their male associates. In contrast, many paintings on vases used by respectable women depict wedding scenes, or women visiting tombs or sitting at home spinning wool or adorning themselves, often in the company of other women.

Oikos and Polis

As in most cultures, respectable women in Greece spent most of their time with the family, which was also the primary focus of their energy. We have much more information about family life in Athens than in any other Greek polis. The wide range of evidence includes not only vase painting but tomb sculpture and epitaphs, laws and courtroom speeches delivered in cases of family disputes, and portrayals of family life in comedy and tragedy. The material from drama, however, must be used with special caution. In any society, comedy both reveals much about social norms and distorts for the sake of humor. Tragedy poses problems peculiar to Athens; though the authors were fifth-century Athenians, they use mythological plots and characters inherited from the Bronze Age, when values were different. All this material, moreover, was filtered through the imagination of the male poet. Sometimes the result seems misogynistic, as in Aeschylus' *Oresteia*; later in the fifth century, authors like Sophocles and Euripides appear sympathetic to women's plight in Athenian society. One thing is clear: daring, outspoken women like Clytemnestra were not normally found in Classical Athens, where initiative (not to mention violence) was a male prerogative and political power never shifted into female hands. In fact, all the actors were men, wearing masks. All the historical evidence from Classical Athens was created by men and (at least in the immediate sense) financed by them. So, for example, even vases designed for women's use and depicting women's daily activities were painted by men, then bought by men and given as gifts to women. Greek society was male-dominated, or "patriarchal."

The Greek polis was made up of oikoi (families, estates, or households). The oikos was the primary unit of production, consumption, and reproduction. Citizens became members of the polis not directly as individuals, as they do in most modern states; rather, they first had to be accepted as members of an oikos.

Family Membership

When a baby was born in Attica (in the home, and sometimes with a midwife in attendance), the father decided whether to raise or expose it. He doubtless evaluated the newborn's health as well as the financial impact of raising another child. Most sons were raised, because male heirs were the normal means of perpetuating the lineage, and it was of great importance that families not die out so that the cults of the ancestors would continue. A woman's offspring were legally members of her husband's family, not her father's. As boys grew up, their labor was considered valuable. Moreover, they were expected to support their aged parents, bury them, and look after their tombs. At the scrutiny for public office known as the *dokimasia*, the areas investigated included proper treatment of parents and of the family tomb. In a state in which the government took minimal responsibility for those whom age or other infirmity prevented from working, proper bearing toward parents was crucial for the smooth functioning of society. Parents placed less value on girls, who lacked earning power and whose children would belong to a different family. Though the eldest child was normally raised regardless of its sex, some historians have conjectured that as many as 20 percent of newborn Athenian girls were abandoned in places like the local garbage dump. Slave dealers collected a few of the exposed infants and turned them over to wet nurses to be raised and sold as slaves. Most exposed infants, however, died, and exposure quickly became infanticide, without the stigma and pollution attaching to murder.

In Athens, after a baby boy was accepted as a member of his father's family he needed to be approved by his father's quasi- or pseudofamily; a boy inherited membership in his phratry (brotherhood) and deme (city district or country village) from his father. Enrollment in the father's phratry was a desirable, if not essential, step toward becoming a full-fledged Athenian citizen. The father introduced and enrolled his infant in his phratry and vouched for him as being legitimate and his own, born of an Athenian mother.

Names

Names revealed family membership. Children were identified by their own name and the name of their father; it was usual to name the first son after his paternal grandfather and the second after his maternal grandfather. Because rules of etiquette required the suppression of respectable women's names, at least while they were living, the quantity of evidence available for the study of their names is far less than for men's names. Nevertheless, the data indicate that, like a boy, a girl was given a name that was derived from those in her father's family, skipping a generation. Thus the first daughter would be named after her paternal grandmother. This repetition of names within the family sometimes makes it difficult for historians to determine when a particular person lived.

Demography and the Life Cycle

Scholars have calculated that the average age at death in Classical Athens for adult females was 36.2 years and for adult males 45 years. An average woman bore 4.3 children, 2.7 of whom survived infancy. The death ratio for infants was 500 per 1,000 adults. Athenian men married at approximately the age of thirty and women around the age of fifteen. Women were often widowed as a consequence of war, and the age difference heightened the likelihood of widowhood overtaking a woman before old age; on the other hand, men lost young wives in childbirth. Marriages could also be ended by divorce, which was not stigmatized unless a scandal was involved. Widowed and divorced people often remarried, and children of divorced parents lived with their fathers or their father's family, to whose oikos they belonged. It may be that only a minority of children reached adolescence living with both their natural parents; many had lost one or both parents at an early age. Children whose fathers had died were considered orphans even if their mothers were still living, and generally lived with their fathers' families.

Childhood

It is difficult for historians to reconstruct what life was like for Greek children, although we have detailed descriptions of the education of Spartan girls and boys. Throughout the Greek world, children's lives depended on their parents' circumstances, much as they do today. Child exposure was practiced by all classes, and we can only guess at the impact on siblings of mothers' pregnancies that ended in the disappearance of the newborn. Girls and boys from wealthier families might spend a great deal of time in the care of slave nurses and nannies. Most children were breast-fed, either by their mothers or by a wet nurse, but archaeologists have found some clay feeding bottles. Poorer children—including slaves and helots—probably began helping to work the land at an early age. Children of both sexes also participated in the religious activities of the family, such as performing sacrifices of food or animals.

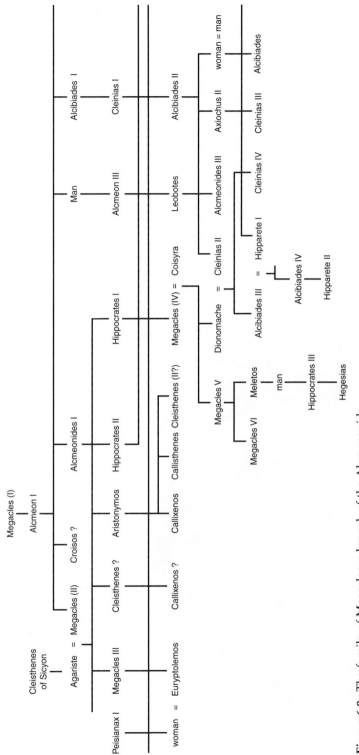

Figure 6.9. The family of Megacles, a branch of the Alcmaeonids.

We know of a number of children's games, often involving balls, hoops, and tops. References in literature describe a number of standard games. *Khytrinda* combined elements of monkey-in-the-middle and tag, while *posinda* was some sort of guessing game. Not surprisingly, social realities were reflected in some games: in *drapinda* the child who is "it" has to get others, who play the part of runaway slaves. Physical remains also tell us about children's lives. Babies had various sorts of bells and rattles, such as hollow animal forms with loose pebbles inside. Vases depict children with pet birds, dogs, rabbits, goats, and occasionally cats or monkeys (see Figure 6.10). Older boys kept hunting dogs. Swings and seesaws also appear on vases. Schooling was only for the rich, and mostly for the male rich; the rhythm of the school day and the school year did not define children's lives.

Figure 6.10. Attic red-figure *chous* (wine jug) (c. 425–420 BC) depicts a little boy holding a cake for his pet bird. A toy roller leans on the wall behind him. Athenian children had their first taste of wine from jugs like this one at the Anthesteria festival celebrating the new wine, and they are often depicted on these jugs. Boston, Museum of Fine Arts.

Marriage

Marriage was the social institution that sustained the oikos, and its principal purpose was reproduction (see Figure 6.10). At the time of betrothal, the bride's father or other guardian declared in the presence of witnesses, "I give you my daughter to sow for the purpose of producing legitimate children." After the bridegroom agreed, "I take her," he and his fiancée's father agreed on the size of her dowry. For respectable girls, there was no alternative to marriage, and the obligation to dower each daughter was doubtless a prime motivator in female infanticide.

Before her marriage, it was customary for a girl to dedicate her dolls and other toys to Artemis to mark her transition to adulthood. Traditionally, an Athenian wedding took place at night, and the central event was the procession in which a chariot driven by the bridegroom carried the bride to the home of her future husband (see Figure 6.12). Torches lit the way, and relatives bearing gifts followed the couple on foot. Some gifts would also be brought the following day, when it was the custom of the bride's friends to visit her in her new residence, perhaps to cushion the blow of the radical break she was forced to make with her past. We have no way of knowing how many married women found their home lives rewarding. Speeches placed in the mouths of wives by tragic playwrights like Sophocles and Euripides certainly suggest that many women felt trapped in their marriages.

DOCUMENT 6.2

In this surviving fragment from his lost play Tereus, Sophocles shows Procne, the wife of Tereus, describing the trauma of marriage to a man chosen by a girl's parents.

> But now outside my father's house, I'm nothing.
> How frequently I've thought of women's nature
> In this very regard, how we are nothing.
> When we are young, still in our fathers' homes,
> I think we live the sweetest life there is;
> For ignorance, alas, breeds happiness.
> But when we've gained maturity and understanding,
> Then suddenly we find ourselves thrust out,
> Sold far away from our ancestral gods,
> Parted from parents. Some to go to foreigners,
> Some to barbarians, some to homes filled with sorrow,
> Others to hostile houses. Finally,
> When just one night has joined us to a man,
> We have to make believe that all is well.
>
> Sophocles fr. 583 Radt

Although there was a double standard for sexual conduct, and husbands might have additional sexual partners of either gender, Greeks could be legally married to only one spouse at a time. Marriages between close relatives such as first cousins or uncle and niece were common. In a family with no son or in

Figure 6.11. Detail of Attic red-figure *lebēs gamikos* (wedding bowl) attributed to the Washing Painter (c. 425–400 BC). A bride displays a baby boy, the hoped-for result of her marriage. A standing woman toward the right is holding a *loutrophoros*, a wedding vase used to transport water for the prenuptial bath. The flying Nike (winged Victory) on the far right holds a vase for perfumed oil.

Figure 6.12. Attic red-figure *pyxis* (cosmetic box) (c. 430 BC), attributed to the Marlay Painter. A typical gift for a bride, this pyxis bears appropriate subject matter for its intended owner: a wedding procession leaving the bride's house. The groom mounts the chariot onto which he has lifted his bride, whose head is veiled. London, The British Museum.

which a son or sons had died childless (in war, for example), the obligation to perpetuate the oikos fell on the daughter, called an *epiklēros* (someone "attached to the estate," sometimes translated "heiress" for convenience, though she herself inherited nothing). The epikleros was required to marry the closest of her father's male relatives who was capable of procreation, usually her uncle or first cousin. If the two were married to other spouses, they had to divorce them. A son born of the union with the epikleros would be considered his grandfather's heir, and to encourage the production of heirs, the laws of Solon required men who married epikleroi to have sex with them at least three times a month. Men without any children at all would try to adopt a male relative so that their lineage would not die out.

The wife's dowry plus the husband's contribution constituted the economic foundation of the oikos at the start of a marriage. At Athens, dowries consisted of cash and movable property. The husband provided the land and the house with most of its contents. The ideal, at least for those who farmed their own land, was to furnish most of the basic necessities of life for the family without needing to depend on purchasing supplies at the market. The division of labor was by gender: women's work was indoors and men's outdoors. The husband brought into the house agricultural products such as fruit, grain, vegetables, and raw wool, and the wife and domestic slaves transformed these products into textiles and food ready for consumption (see Figure 6.13 and Plate VIb). Wives were also responsible for storing the household contents safely so that there would always be enough to eat and wear, and even to sell if the family fell on hard times.

DOCUMENT 6.3

The customary division of labor in the oikos is spelled out in Xenophon's Socratic dialogue the Oeconomicus, *in which Socrates' friend* Ischomachus *explains to him how he taught his fourteen-year-old bride to manage the household.*

He told me he said to her: "Wife, the gods seem to have shown much discernment in yoking together female and male, as we call them, so that the couple might constitute a partnership that is most beneficial to each of them....

"Those who intend to obtain produce to bring into the shelter need someone to work at the outdoor jobs. For plowing, sowing, planting, and herding is all work that is performed outdoors, and it is from these that our essential provisions are obtained. As soon as these are brought into the shelter, then someone else is needed to look after them and to perform the work that requires shelters. The nursing of newborn children requires shelters, and so does the preparation of bread from grain, and likewise, making clothing out of wool. Because both the indoor and the outdoor tasks require work and concern," he said, "I think the god, from the very beginning, designed the nature of women for the indoor work and concerns and the nature of man for the outdoor work....

"For the woman it is more honorable to remain indoors than to be outside; for the man it is more disgraceful to remain indoors than to attend to business outside."

. . . .

"And how did you arrange things for her, Ischomachus?"

"Well, I thought it was best to show her the possibilities of our house first. It is not elaborately decorated, Socrates, but the rooms are constructed in such a way that they will serve as the most convenient places to contain the things that will be kept in them. So the rooms themselves invited what was suitable for each of them. Thus the bedroom, because it was in the safest possible place, invited the most valuable bedding and furniture. The dry store rooms called for grain, the cool ones for wine, and the bright ones for those products and utensils which need light. I continued by showing her living rooms for the occupants, decorated so as to be cool in summer and warm in winter. I pointed out to her that the entire house has its facade facing south, so that it was obviously sunny in winter and shady in summer. I also showed her the women's quarters, separated from the men's quarters by a bolted door, so that nothing might be removed from them that should not be, and so that the slaves would not breed without our permission. For, generally, honest slaves become more loyal when they have produced children, but when bad ones mate, they become more troublesome."

Xenophon, *Oeconomicus* 7.18, 20–22, 30, 9.2–5; Pomeroy

Figure 6.13. Attic black-figure *lēkythos* attributed to the Amasis Painter (c. 550–540 BC), showing women producing cloth. The woman at the left is spinning yarn, while two women weave cloth on a vertical loom at the center. New York, Metropolitan Museum of Art.

The fundamental division of domestic space was between men and women. Even in a small house with only two rooms, one upstairs and one on the ground floor, the upper room was the women's quarters and the lower room the men's. Socializing took place in the men's quarters, so a visitor to the Greek home would meet only male members of the family; when strangers were in the house, women and girls would withdraw to the secluded parts of the home and not even be mentioned by name. The females in the household, both free and slave, slept in the women's quarters. They also produced textiles there, though in warm weather they might move their looms into an interior courtyard and work outdoors, protected by the surrounding walls. Women could express their creativity by weaving figured textiles. (See Plates VIb and VIIIb.)

Citizen women not compelled to work by poverty rarely ventured far from the house except for festivals and funerals. In this way, they avoided encounters with strange men who were not their relatives and who might compromise their respectability either by actual sexual contact or by the rumor of it. Only women in straitened circumstances would shop for groceries or household items themselves; wherever possible, slaves and husbands did the marketing and other errands that required leaving the immediate environs of the home.

The prevalence of slavery, in fact, shaped gender roles in a variety of ways. The availability of slaves even for families of fairly modest means was vital, for example, in perpetuating the social ideal of the virtuous woman who never left the house. Though some poor oikoi had to rely on the labor of family members, most oikoi had at least one or two female slaves. The division of labor among the very poor and among slaves was not as strictly gender-based as it was for the middle and upper classes. Under the wife's supervision, slaves performed domestic labor, working at food preparation, child care, and textile manufacture. They were also liable to be compelled to provide sexual services to their masters. Some evidence suggests that this practice caused strain in Greek households and that tactful husbands restricted their extramarital dalliances to locations outside their own homes.

A few free fifth-century Greeks questioned the propriety of slavery. Crates' comedy *The Beasts*, which survives only in fragmentary form, evidently sported a character who envisioned a topsy-turvy world in which nobody is permitted to have a slave:

> Everything will come to people as soon as they call for it. "Table, put yourself down right here next to me.... Fill up, jug.... Get moving, fish!" "But I'm not toasted on the other side yet!" "Well then, why don't you turn yourself over—and cover yourself with oil and salt while you're at it!"
>
> (Quoted in Athenaeus, *Deipnosophists*, 267e–f)

In the real world, however, slavery was a fact of life throughout Greece, as elsewhere in the ancient world.

Death and Beyond

Slave or free, all Greeks died sooner or later, but customs regarding burial, funeral rites, and commemorative markers varied depending on status, as well as from one polis to the next and across time periods. For those who survived early childhood, death in battle and death in childbirth were common occurrences. As a rule, soldiers killed in battle were carried home for burial, with the notable exception of the Athenians who were buried where they died after the battles of Marathon and Plataea during the Persian wars. Funerals for Athenian citizens generally began with women washing the body and anointing it with oil, then dressing it in special garments, usually of white, and placing it on a bed, covered with a cloth.

The house was adorned with wreaths, and the family held a vigil. Female family members would rend their cheeks, tear their hair, and sing laments (see Figure 6.14). In accordance with the legislation of Solon, women under sixty were not permitted to participate in the mourning unless they were close relatives of the deceased, but women aged sixty and above could be hired as professional mourners to add to the drama. The burial then took place before dawn on the following day, when the body was transported to its intended burial place accompanied by the music of the aulos, a sort of flute.

A wide variety of passages from Greek literature attest to the importance of burying a body; even a few handfuls of earth could prevent it from polluting the altars of the gods and permit the deceased to enter the underworld. For this reason it was common for a battle to be followed by a truce during which each side could retrieve its dead for burial; it was very bad form for one side to try to prevent the return of bodies to the other. "Burial" might be of the intact body enclosed by a coffin, or of the cremated remains. Ancient Greeks practiced both cremation and inhumation, but by the Classical period inhumation was more common. To avoid the pollution attributed to dead bodies, burial often took place just outside the city walls, although Spartans took a different view and buried their dead inside the city, sometimes even near temples.

At Sparta, only men who had died in battle or women who had died in childbirth were allowed to have inscribed epitaphs, but other Greek states were more liberal. A wide variety of grave markers survive from throughout Greece, ranging from simple stelae to carved reliefs to vases. Although at one time a wide variety of goods had been buried in graves for use in the afterlife, by the Classical period this was less common, although archaeologists have occasionally found such items as shoes and lamps.

Greeks were not of one mind about just what they might expect in the afterlife, but the general view was not very encouraging. Bad deeds on earth might lead to eternal punishment in the house of Hades; everyone had heard the story of Sisyphus, forced to push a rock up a hill until, just as he reached the top, it would roll back to the bottom so that he had to start over, and Tantalus, who was surrounded by enticing fruit and cool water but found that both retreated whenever he reached for them (hence our word "tantalize"). Good deeds, on the other hand, were not usually rewarded. The "Elysian Fields" were reserved for famous heroes like Achilles, not poor potters who were kind to others. Religions like Orphism, however, or the mystery cult celebrated at Eleusis outside Athens, did hold out some hope of rewards beyond the grave.

Like weddings, Greek funerals were essentially secular events. Once the dead had been buried, however, their tombs acquired religious significance for the family, who were expected to visit the burial site at regular intervals, bearing offerings of food, drink, and oil. This obligation was frequently discharged by the women of the household. To keep the price of piety down while still making a favorable impression on the neighbors, some Athenians dropped off vases outfitted with a small internal container that would cut down on the amount of oil they actually had to contribute.

Figure 6.14a–b. Attic red- and black-figure *loutrophoros-amphora* attributed to the Cleophrades Painter (c. 480 BC). The main scene on the body of this vase depicts the *prothesis* (lying in state) of a deceased youth surrounded by female mourners. The small black-figure frieze below shows a commemorative procession of cavalrymen. Such vases normally were employed for holding water to anoint the body of the deceased, but this exceptionally tall example has no bottom and would have been used for libations at the grave. Paris, The Louvre.

THE GREEK ECONOMY

All but the poorest oikoi had at least one female slave. The work of slaves, however, did not always take place in the context of the oikos. The extent to which slaves were engaged in agricultural labor is controversial. Some scholars believe that large numbers of male slaves worked on farms, especially when a wealthy owner had large plots of land that were not contiguous but scattered about Attica. Others stress the grounding of the agricultural economy in the small family farm worked by the independent peasant farmer. Like women, slaves were a "muted group";

although they were numerous, their names and thoughts were not recorded, and few have left their mark on the historical record.

There is no doubt that large numbers of slaves were employed in the craft industries, some working for their owners and others rented out by them. Their jobs tended to be gender-specific. Men worked in factories making swords, shields, furniture, pottery, and other items, while women often worked in textile-related industries. Some trusted slaves, who worked as bankers, however, became very wealthy after they were manumitted. Inscriptions recording expenses incurred in construction on the Athenian Acropolis show the labor of slaves had the same value as that of free workers. Many female slaves who were not engaged in domestic labor worked as prostitutes. Of course, the wages of slaves who were rented out were paid to their masters.

Figure 6.15. This marble grave relief from Paros, depicting a young girl with her pet doves, predates the mid-fifth century, when luxurious funerary monuments with figural images appear to have been forbidden in Athens. The relief's white Parian marble was originally colorfully painted; some details rendered solely in paint, such as the girl's sandal straps and her doves' feathers, are now entirely lost. New York, Metropolitan Museum of Art.

By no means were all craftspeople slaves; Aristotle, in fact, contended that most craftsmen were rich. Greeks whose economic status allowed them some choice shunned work that made them subject to the commands of another person, and this included most craft fields. Such a life, they believed, was demeaning to a free male citizen. Unlike farming, to which a certain nobility always attached, manual work performed indoors was despised by many wealthier Greeks and known by the name "banausic" labor, which means literally work performed over a hot furnace, and distinctions between skilled and unskilled labor were often ignored. It may be that the leisured classes disdained indoor work because of its connection with slaves and women. Litigants in Athenian courtrooms enjoyed making snide remarks about their opponents (or their opponents' relatives) ever having held any kind of job or even having run a business, and political theorists—who always came from the upper classes—often contended that strenuous indoor work should disqualify people from voting on the grounds that it damaged the mind as surely as it compromised the body. Most Greeks, however, had limited choices about how to support themselves and their families, and there is no reason to believe that those who worked for others or performed indoor manual labor were embarrassed about their professions. Some craftspeople, both citizens and metics, achieved high status as a consequence of their technical abilities and economic success. Tombstones frequently boasted of craft skills; surviving examples include epitaphs of a woodcutter and a miner. As elsewhere, the ideology of literate elites was at odds with the daily practice of ordinary people.

The disdain with which some Greeks regarded paid labor did not prevent a great deal of work from getting done or a good bit of money from being made. Sometimes, however, revenue was the product of imperialism and other forms of exploitation. It might come as war booty (slaves included), or it could take the form of tribute. The size and wealth of the Athenian empire played a large role in defining the character of the fifth century. Without the tribute paid by subject allies, it would have been difficult for the Athenians to initiate the system of state pay for state service, and thus expand the proportion of citizens able to participate in the business of government. Democracy was not entirely dependent on empire; the Athenians lost their empire in 404 BC but continued to have democratic government for several generations until their conquest by Philip of Macedon in 338 (and democracy persisted even after that). The practice of democracy, however, seems to have received its impetus from the surplus funds generated by imperial tribute. The splendid buildings with which the Athenians adorned the Acropolis after relocating the treasury in Athens owed their existence to imperial revenues: no empire, no Parthenon. In addition, the empire's maritime nature meant that it served as the fulcrum of Greek trade. The centrality of the Athenian empire to commercial life became obvious in the late 430s when the Athenians banned Megarian merchants from trading in imperial ports, claiming they were simply making rules for their own sphere of influence as stipulated by the Thirty Years' Peace. The consequences of this move were fatal to Megarian trade, and outrage over the prohibition was one cause of the long Peloponnesian War (431–404).

Especially after the defeat of Aegina in 457, Athens' most formidable commercial rival was Corinth. Possessing ports both on the Saronic Gulf, which divided Attica from the Peloponnesus, and on the Corinthian Gulf to the northwest, the Corinthians hauled ships overland from the one harbor to the other and thus enjoyed a unique position in Greek commerce.

Agriculture and Trade

Before the nineteenth century, most people in the world made their living by agriculture, and fifth-century BC Greeks were no exception. It was trade, however, that united the far-flung states that ringed the seas, and the routes over which material goods traveled also served as vital conduits for the exchange of ideas. Trade rivalries like that between Athens and Corinth accounted for a good deal of tension among Greek poleis. Most trade went by boat, land traffic being slow and expensive over rocky roads; the cost of carting heavy goods by land might well exceed the price of the goods themselves. Few roads were really suited for wheeled vehicles, and some parts of Greece (including Attica) lacked sufficient oxen to draw them.

Lacking sophisticated navigational instruments, Greek vessels avoided the open seas when possible, preferring to hug the shore. Mariners limited long voyages to spring and summer, though some determined speculators insisted on winter runs as well. Speeds, however, had increased considerably since Homeric times, and travel times had been halved or better. Merchant vessels as large as 250 tons ranged the Mediterranean, and Athenian determination cleared the waters of the piracy that had been such an important factor in Greek life; for this, at least, Athens' subject allies were grateful. The widespread use of coinage, mostly silver, facilitated trade, and Athens pressured its allies to adopt its own currency. Litigation arising from sea trade was so widespread that the Athenians established a special court of *nautodikai,* or marine judges, to handle cases brought to Athens. On the whole, however, the embryonic state of international law offered little hope to victims of dishonest business practices.

The diversity of natural resources in the ancient world made trade a necessity; no polis had everything, and some poleis had very little indeed. Athenian commerce especially was driven largely by the need for grain to feed a large population. Grain might come from north or south. One crucial source was the Black Sea region, which also provided hides, cattle, fish, hemp, wax, chestnuts, iron, timber, and slaves. For these commodities, the Athenians exchanged wine and oil, sometimes in decorated vases. The exports were themselves often resold elsewhere; the Phoenicians often sent Attic vases to Egypt, and a good deal of secondhand pottery from Athens has been discovered in Etruria in Italy. Italians also bought Attic pottery firsthand. Another key granary lay in Egypt, where Attic olive oil was also traded for papyrus, ivory, glasswork, slaves, and exotic animals. Carthage provided textiles; Etruria fine bronzework and boots; Sicily pigs, cheese, and grain; and Phoenicia purple dye and dates. Corinth exported its own wares as well as serving as an intermediary between East and West, sending out tiles and metalwork. Already in the fifth century, some silks from China made their way to Greece via Scythian intermediaries. Arabia exported perfumes, and Persia carpets. Important sources of metals were identified early: Cyprus for copper, Spain for tin, Laconia as well as the Black Sea for iron, Thasos and Mount Pangaeus in northern Greece for gold. All these goods flowed throughout the Greek world, but most of all they flowed into Piraeus.

Throughout Greece, however, agriculture remained the most common source of income. Athens was by far the largest city, with a population that normally varied between 200,000 and 300,000. Most people in Attica who participated in political life were independent farmers who worked fairly small plots of land. Generally unaware of the value of rotating crops to maximize the productivity of the soil, farmers often allowed their land to lie fallow in alternate years, so the poorest were indeed quite poor; those who were doing a little better were able to buy a female slave or two to help out around the house and outdoors at harvest time. Some, of course, owned a great deal of land and did very well. Because only citizens could own land, even the neediest farmers took pride in their way of life.

Metics in Classical Athens

Many rich residents of Athens did not own land because they could not legally do so without special dispensation. These were the resident aliens known as metics, and they played a key role in the economy. Craftspeople and entrepreneurs who had come from all over the Greek world to conduct business in Athens, metics accounted for a significant proportion of the Athenian population. They could not vote or hold office; neither could their children or their children's children. They lived in rented homes. But they suffered no social disabilities, and metic families mingled comfortably with families of citizens. A number of the characters in Plato's works were metics, and the most famous Platonic dialogue, *The Republic*, was set at the home of the wealthy metic Cephalus, whom Pericles had invited to Athens from Syracuse. Citizens, metics, and slaves often worked side by side, sometimes for the same pay; a list of workers at one construction site included eighty-six laborers whose status can be determined—twenty-four citizens, forty-two metics, and twenty slaves. In a crisis, metics could be drafted into the armed forces. Ironically, the Greek thinker who wrote most extensively about citizenship was a metic, Aristotle, who lived much of his life in Athens.

Many of Athens' most distinguished intellectuals were metics, including the philosopher Anaxagoras from Asia Minor and the rhetorician Gorgias from Sicily. Pericles' common-law wife, Aspasia, belonged to the metic class, and their children became citizens only after the assembly, at the behest of Pericles, so decreed them. The inability of metic women to produce children who could enjoy Athenian citizenship played a large role in shaping the contours of Athenian society, creating two classes of women available as long-term partners to citizen men—metic mistresses and citizen wives. (In addition, a variety of prostitutes, both slave and free, were available for briefer encounters, and male owners enjoyed the privilege of sexual access to their slaves, both male and female.) Most metic women, of course, were housewives married to metic men. Slaves who were granted their freedom became metics rather than citizens. Metics lived in other poleis as well, but almost nothing is known of metics outside Athens.

⇛———⇚

The cultural achievements of sixth- and early fifth-century Greece were substantial, but the difficulties the city-states experienced in getting along with one another (and their aversion to uniting into a single political unit) was to have a profound impact on the future direction of Greek civilization. The Thirty Years' Peace held a great deal of promise, but it was problematic in many ways. Dividing the Greek world openly into two spheres of influence—a Spartan land empire in mainland Greece and an Athenian naval one in the Aegean—was a dubious enterprise. From one standpoint, by drawing lines clearly the agreement seemed to hold out the hope of peace, but it also fostered a potentially dangerous bipolarity. The notion of submitting disputes to arbitration was quite civilized in the abstract, but with every state of any reputation allied with one side or the other, just who was going to act as mediator? No treaty, moreover, could change the fact that Megara still sat uneasily on the Attic border, or could diminish the commercial rivalry between Athens and Corinth. In 445, it was impossible to predict whether the Peace would last.

KEY TERMS

Aeschylus	First Peloponnesian War	Pindar
Cimon	hegemon	reforms of Ephialtes
citizenship law of 451	Ischomachus	serpent column
cleruchy	metics	temple of Zeus at Olympia
Delian League	Pausanias	Thirty Years' Peace
Discobolus	Pericles	Thucydides

SUGGESTED READINGS

Cohen, David. 1991. *Law, Sexuality, and Society: The Enforcement of Morals in Classical Athens.* Cambridge: Cambridge University Press. What the framing and application of law reveal about sexual values and practices.

Cohen, Edward E. 2002. *The Athenian Nation.* Princeton, NJ: Princeton University Press. An iconoclastic study of Athens that envisions it not as a descent group of male voters but as a broadly conceived nation in which many different groups had important roles to play.

Ehrenberg, Victor. 1973. *From Solon to Socrates.* 2nd ed. London: Methuen. This remains a sensitive and thoughtful study of the evolution of Greek culture during the sixth and fifth centuries.

Fantham, Elaine, Helene Foley, Natalie Kampen, Sarah B. Pomeroy, and H. A. Shapiro. 1994. *Women in the Classical World: Image and Text.* New York and Oxford: Oxford University Press. An examination of the written and visual evidence for the lives of ancient women, placed within their historical and cultural context.

Hanson, Victor. 1989. *The Western Way of War: Infantry Battle in Classical Greece.* New York: Alfred A. Knopf. A gripping account of the experience of hoplite battle.

Hesk, Jon. 2000. *Deception and Democracy in Classical Athens.* Cambridge: Cambridge University Press. A thoughtful examination of Athenian literature that explores the ways in which the telling of lies was a problem for the Athenian democracy, with modern parallels.

Meiggs, Russell. 1972. *The Athenian Empire.* Oxford: Oxford University Press. A richly detailed examination of Athenian imperialism and the world that came under its sway.

Pollitt, Jerome J. 1972. *Art and Experience in Classical Greece.* Cambridge: Cambridge University Press. A fine survey of Greek art that grounds it firmly in its historical context.

Pomeroy, Sarah B. 1998. *Families in Classical and Hellenistic Greece: Representations and Realities.* Oxford: Clarendon Press. An account of the Greek family as a productive, reproductive, and social unit.

CHAPTER SEVEN

Greece on the Eve of the Peloponnesian War

Avoiding war was particularly important when the Greeks had such precious achievements to protect in so many areas. From Sicily to Anatolia, temples to the gods proclaimed the grandeur of Hellenic civilization. Greek ships sailed in all directions, enabling men and women hundreds of miles away to exchange their wares and to profit from a wide variety of resources and skills. Novel experiments in government were in progress. The same diversity that fostered the dynamic creativity of the Greeks, however, also fragmented their world. The world of the polis, moreover, was in many ways a narrow one. Despite the growth of what the Greeks called democracy, ultimately each polis was grounded in the rule of an elite of free male citizens over everyone else, and the inability of the poleis to get along boded ill for the future of Greece. Inevitably, prospects for the future were clouded by intermittent suspicions that the peace between the Athenian and Spartan camps might not endure.

SOURCES FOR GREECE ON THE EVE OF THE WAR

The principal source for the decades that preceded the outbreak of the great war between Athens and Sparta is Thucydides' *History*. Thucydides served as a general in the war, and this history is the primary source for the period from 479 to 411 BC, but his account of the years before 433 is not as detailed as his narrative of the war itself and the tensions that immediately preceded it. A good number of inscriptions survive, although nowhere near as many as we would like. Diodorus' *Library of History* remains useful. Though he was not a great historian and does

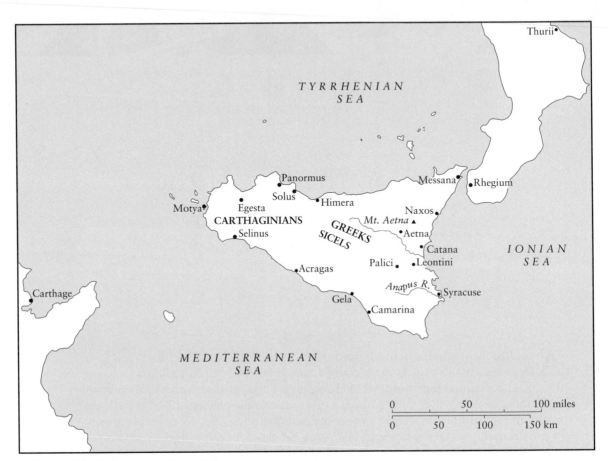

Figure 7.1. Sicily and southern Italy.

not add to our understanding of the war when he is using Thucydides as his only source, Diodorus did sometimes draw information from other writers. Plutarch is helpful as well; biographies like that of Pericles incorporate a great deal of information from fifth- and fourth-century historians whose work is lost. All the intellectuals who have left records of their thoughts, from the historian Herodotus to the physician Hippocrates, have contributed to our understanding of how Greeks viewed their world at this fertile period in their cultural history. Finally, a great debt is owed to the visual artists who left us a wide array of pottery, sculpture, tombstones, and architecture. Unfortunately, however, Greek writers were hardly representative of the whole population. In many states, artists worked at the behest of elites. To be sure, in some democratic poleis like Athens successful dramatic poets had to speak to the people, but it is important to remember that what we call history is in fact an image of the world reconstructed primarily from what seemed worthy of creation or transmission to the minds of that tiny fraction of the human race who were urban, literate males.

GREECE AFTER THE THIRTY YEARS' PEACE

In 445, after the signing of the peace, many Greeks were optimistic, convinced that Athens and Sparta had put their differences behind them. The knowledge that this optimism was misplaced makes it hard for historians to avoid seeing the years before the Peloponnesian War of 431–404 as anything but a prelude to hostilities. Though it is important to try to understand events as they unfold rather than assessing them only in terms of their consequences, hindsight also has some value. Looking back from the vantage point of the war that followed, certain events of the 440s and 430s take on particular significance.

During this period, the Athenians showed a marked interest in the west and in the northeast. Athens had multiple motives for accepting Megara into its alliance in 460, but the desire for access to the port of Pegae on the Corinthian Gulf was

Figure 7.2. This idealized portrait of Pericles survives in a Roman copy of the head of a lost Greek bronze statue by Cresilas (c. 430–420 BC). Wearing a Greek helmet of Corinthian type pushed up atop his head, Pericles is depicted in his role as general. Berlin, Staatliche Museen.

certainly one factor, and the new settlement of the Messenian helots at Naupactus provided a convenient stopping place for ships heading west. It was probably also in the 450s that Athens contracted an alliance with Egesta in northwest Sicily. Alliances with Rhegium in the toe of Italy and with another Sicilian city, Leontini, followed shortly afterward; it may be significant that tensions marked the relationship of Leontini with Syracuse, a colony and ally of Athens' trade rival Corinth. Commerce with the western Greeks played a key role in the Athenian economy. Large quantities of red-figure pottery were exported to Etruria, and Athenian ships returned from Italy laden with grain and cheese from Sicily and metalwork from the mainland. Gradually, the Greek cities of Sicily adopted Athenian currency.

That Athens had a growing interest in the rich lands to the west is confirmed by the decision to found a colony in the instep of southern Italy in 443. Thurii, however, was to be no ordinary establishment, for the Athenians invited the other Greek states to share in founding a Panhellenic colony, thus demonstrating their commitment to a spirit of cooperation and goodwill. The colony was sent out under the guidance of Pericles' good friend Lampon the seer, whom many people believed to have a special relationship with the gods. Lampon obtained oracles regarding the city's founding from Delphi to guide the colonists in selecting precisely the right site for the town. Laid out according to the plans of the same Hippodamus who had designed the Piraeus, Thurii became home to a number of non-Athenians, including the historian Herodotus. Although the constitution of Thurii was democratic and the local coins were stamped with the head of Athena, the city adopted the laws of Zaleucus, an esteemed lawgiver from Locris, and when a disagreement led the colonists some years later to go to Delphi to ask to whom they belonged, the Delphic oracle claimed them for Apollo, not Athens. Pericles' intentions for Thurii remain uncertain. Was his determination to cast the colony as Panhellenic a sincere disclaimer of Athenian meddling in the west, or was he simply hoping to head off Corinthian resentment by cloaking western imperialism in **Panhellenism**? In any event, the Attic element in the population was greatly diluted with the passing of time, and the Corinthians do not appear to have taken offense.

Athens' immediate interest, however, lay in the area around Thrace and the Black Sea region. From here the Athenians imported hides, dyes, and, more importantly, grain and timber, and the routes to this part of the world also gave access to the caravan route through the Ural Mountains to Central Asia and ultimately to the Chinese frontier, whence the West could expect furs, gold, and perhaps even silk. Around 445, the Athenians founded the Thracian colony of Brea, and some years later Pericles himself sailed with an Athenian squadron to the Black Sea.

While the Athenians were engaged in expanding their sphere of interest to the north and the west, an alarming revolt broke out in the east. In 440, Samos rebelled. Spreading to Byzantium, the uprising threw terror into the Athenians, for it seemed to threaten the very continuation of their Aegean empire. Years later, according to Thucydides, Greeks looked back and observed that Samos "had almost managed to wrest from the Athenians their control of the sea" (8.76.4). An oligarchy, Samos had quarreled with the democratic government the Athenians had recently established in neighboring Miletus, and the Milesians who complained to Athens were joined by some Samians who wished to overthrow their government. One of three privileged allies (along with Lesbos and Chios) who were still contributing ships rather than tribute money to the Athenian league, Samos took umbrage at the Athenian directive to submit the matter to arbitration, whereupon the Athenians sent forty ships to depose the government and replace it with a democracy. It was at this juncture that the Samian oligarchs seized control of the government by force and revolted from Athens, aided by Pissuthnes, the satrap of Sardis.

The spread of the conflagration to Byzantium imperiled Athenian access to the Black Sea and raised the specter of a general revolt along the coast or even throughout the empire. The determined campaign that followed involved all ten of the Athenian strategoi and over 200 ships—160 from Athens and 55 from the remaining allies in the navy, Lesbos and Chios. The siege of Samos lasted nine months. When the city fell, the Athenians confiscated the Samian navy, established a democracy, imposed an indemnity, and took hostages. The text of Plutarch preserves the contention of Duris, a local historian, that Pericles bound the Samian commanders and marines to posts in the marketplace and left them there for ten days; he then gave orders, so Duris wrote, that their heads be beaten in with clubs and their bodies tossed on the ground to rot (*Pericles* 28). Most scholars doubt the accuracy of this claim, but the existence of the story reflects the extreme bitterness of the feelings on both sides. About the subjugation of Byzantium we know nothing except that the Byzantines agreed to return to the empire.

Meanwhile Athens kept a hand in the northeast, planting the colony of Amphipolis at a strategic point on the Strymon River by the border of Macedonia and Thrace in 437. In addition to protecting Athens' access to grain, timber, and minerals, Amphipolis helped the Athenians monitor activities in the recently organized kingdom of the Thracian Odrysians to the north and east as well as in Macedonia to the west. But the town drew much of its population from neighboring towns, undermining its identification with Athens, and during the war with Sparta it failed to serve as a rallying point for Athenian loyalties in the north. Less than fifteen years after its founding, Amphipolis was in Spartan hands.

Virtually nothing is known about how Spartans looked at the world during the years between the signing of the Thirty Years' Peace in 445 and their declaration of war on Athens in 432. A hint is provided, however, by Thucydides' account of the Corinthians' claim that they dissuaded the Spartans from attacking Athens at the time of the Samian rebellion: "We did not cast the deciding vote against you," he depicts them as saying, "when Samos revolted from you, and when the Peloponnesians were evenly divided over whether to help them. We openly opposed it, saying that any city could punish its own allies" (1.40). If the story is true and not fabricated for the purpose of scoring points with the Athenians, then some Greeks who participated in meetings of the Peloponnesian League saw merit in attacking Athens in 440, and Spartans may well have been among them. The Corinthians' claim also suggests that many, indeed most, people in Corinth were untroubled by the foundation of Thurii, or at least not so troubled that they wished to make war on Athens. The chances for peace, therefore, were probably still fairly reasonable during the early 430s. A series of interrelated crises later in the decade, however, brought the peace to an end, and in these crises Corinth played a large part.

THE BREAKDOWN OF THE PEACE

In the absence of a strong commitment to amicable coexistence, the terms of the Thirty Years' Peace contained the seeds of war. Arbitration was meaningless when all the major states were lined up on one side or another; rules made in one sphere of influence might well have an impact on the other; and some states enjoyed an ambiguous status, with one foot in each camp. On all these fronts the peace was vulnerable, as the events that began in 435 in a remote corner of the Greek world were to prove.

Trouble at Epidamnus

Itself a Corinthian colony, Corcyra off the western coast of Greece had planted its own colony at Epidamnus in the north, on the coast of what is now Albania. There a civil war broke out between the democrats and the oligarchs, moving the democrats to seek assistance from Corcyra. When their mother city turned them down, for reasons we do not know, they were encouraged by Delphi to hand themselves over to their "grandmother" Corinth instead. Since colonies that established colonies of their own took an oikist from the original founding city, a Corinthian, Phalius, was the technical founder of Epidamnus, and the Corinthians agreed to assist the Epidamnian democrats, in part because of a long-standing feud with Corcyra. The Corcyreans, however, scored a conspicuous victory over the Corinthian fleet that sailed to the aid of Epidamnus. The appalled Corinthians set about building a more substantial fleet with which to humble Corcyra and retain their predominance in western waters.

The Alliance of Corcyra and Athens

Because the Corcyreans belonged to neither the Peloponnesian League nor the Athenian alliance, they had much to fear from the growing Corinthian navy. With the prospects of a Spartan alliance cut off by Sparta's relationship to Corinth, they determined to ally themselves with the Athenians, sending ambassadors to Athens in the summer of 433. Though the Thirty Years' Peace specified that neutrals might join either side, the Athenians were understandably nervous about allying with Corcyra, the enemy of the most powerful naval state in the Peloponnesian League; but they were even more apprehensive about what would happen if mighty Corinth defeated and absorbed Corcyra's substantial fleet. Better, they decided, to gain those ships for Athens, and so, after a debate that extended over two days, they voted to make an alliance with Corcyra. Presumably Pericles was one of those who argued in favor of the alliance. Though the Athenians sought to avoid provoking the Peloponnesians by terming the alliance merely a defensive one, this technicality fooled nobody. It was plain that Corinth was about to attack Corcyra and that Athenians and Corinthians would soon be fighting, and so they were. In the late summer of 433, the Corinthians attacked the Corcyrean fleet of 110 ships off the island chain known as Sybota. The Peloponnesian force consisted of 90 Corinthian ships and 60 more supplied by Elis, Ambracia, Anactorium, Leucas, and—significantly—Athens' neighbor Megara. Though at first the Athenians hung back cautiously, when it was clear that the Corcyreans were getting the worst of it they began to give them increasing support. Thus, Thucydides points out, a situation inevitably came about in which Corinthians and Athenians were fighting each other openly. Both Corinth and Corcyra claimed victory in the battle, and it was unclear what would happen next.

The Problem of Potidaea

Chances of a war between the Athenians and the Peloponnesians had now increased, and in the months following the Battle of Sybota, Athens issued problematic decrees against two members of the Peloponnesian League. The city of Potidaea, on the Chalcidic peninsula, occupied two positions in the Greek world simultaneously: it was both a Corinthian colony and a member of the Athenian alliance. Because Greek colonies were fully autonomous, there was nothing illegal about this, but in a climate of escalating tensions, Potidaea's ambiguous identification was likely to be a source of strain. The potential difficulties were aggravated by the fact that Potidaea's relationship to its mother city was everything that Corcyra's was not. Corcyra was the proverbial bad colony, acting independently from Corinth in all things—excluding the Corinthians from the customary privileges at public festivals, and boasting of its financial and military superiority to its mother city. Potidaea, on the other hand, was exceptionally attached to its mother city and went so far as to accept its annual magistrates from Corinth. During the winter of 433–432, the Athenians ordered the Potidaeans to dismiss their Corinthian magistrates, reject any future officials from Corinth, tear down their seaward defenses, and give hostages. In all likelihood, the Athenians' motives included the desire to take vengeance on Corinth and fear of Corinthian interference in the Athenian sphere of influence. The proximity of Potidaea to Macedonia complicated an already difficult situation, for Macedonia was a valuable source of timber for shipbuilding—not only for Athenian ships but for Corinthian ones as well.

With Corinthian help, the Potidaeans extracted a promise from at least some Spartans that Sparta would invade Attica if Potidaea were attacked. The first to involve themselves in the Potidaean affair, however, were not the Spartans but the Macedonians. Once an Athenian ally, Macedonia's king Perdiccas had been alienated by Athens' support of two relatives who challenged his right to

Figure 7.3. Alliances at the outset of the Peloponnesian War in 431.

ODRYSIAN KINGDOM

THRACE

Abdera
Neapolis
Maronea
Thasos
Thasos
Aenus
Cardia
Samothrace
Sestos
Lampsacus
Imbros
Abydus
Sigeum
Troy
Lemnos
Tenedos
Antandrus
Adramyttium

Selymbria
Perinthus
Byzantium
Chalcedon

PROPONTIS

Cyzicus
Dascylium

PHRYGIA

MYSIA

Methymna
Lesbos
Mytilene

Scyros

*AEGEAN
SEA*

Cyme
Phocaea

LYDIA

Sardis

Chios
Erythrae
Clazomenae
Teos
Colophon
Notium
Ephesus

Carystus
Andros
Tenos
Myconos
Delos
Paros
Siphnos
Naxos

Samos
Priene
Miletus

CARIA

Iasus

Halicarnassus
Cos
Caunus
Cos
Cnidus

Melos

Thera

Ialysus
Rhodes
Rhodes
Camirus
Lindus

the throne. Perdiccas not only encouraged the Spartans to move against Athens and urged the Corinthians to raise a revolt in Potidaea, he also persuaded the peoples of Chalcidice and Bottiaea to join with Potidaea in revolt against Athens. Athens then attacked Macedonia, while Corinth entered a secret alliance with the Bottiaean and Chalcidian states. Two thousand men called "volunteers"—some Corinthians, some Peloponnesian mercenaries—entered Potidaea. The Athenians defeated this force and laid siege to Potidaea. The siege would last for two years, costing the Athenians much in men and money.

Athenian Decrees Against Megara

Around the same time, the Athenians took action against Megara. Because Thucydides did not discuss the decrees relating to Megara in any detail, we understand much less about this third crisis than we do about the Corcyrean alliance and the conflict with Potidaea. The time frame is uncertain and the causes of the friction vague. Bordering poleis often quarreled. The Athenians accused the Megarians of harboring escaped slaves and of cultivating some sacred and undefined land that lay between Eleusis and Megara. They were probably angry, too, at the assistance Megara had given Corinth at the Battle of Sybota. At least one decree against Megara, passed probably in 432, excluded Megarian merchants from all ports of the Athenian empire. This decree enabled the Athenians to inflict considerable harm on a member of the Peloponnesian League without technically infringing the terms of the Thirty Years' Peace. Since there were few Greek ports outside the Athenian empire, their claim that they were simply regulating their own sphere of influence was disingenuous. Plainly the Megarian economy would be devastated by these economic sanctions, and the Athenians could hardly have expected the Spartans to sit idly by while their ally suffered so conspicuously.

Even more than the other actions taken by the Athenian assembly during the years that preceded the outbreak of the Peloponnesian War, the **sanctions against Megara** (and the subsequent refusal to revoke them) are associated with the name of Pericles. Aristophanes' plays and Plutarch's biography of Pericles make it plain that some people considered the friction with Megara pivotal in bringing on the war and blamed Pericles for the outbreak of hostilities. Scattered references in Thucydides confirm this. In the autumn of 432, the Corinthians denounced the Athenians before the Spartan assembly. Though the Spartan king Archidamus urged caution and tried to convince his fellow Spartans to postpone taking any action until they could build up their resources for war, his arguments did not prevail, and the Spartans voted that the Athenians had violated the Thirty Years' Peace. They then summoned delegates from the Peloponnesian League, who duly voted to go to war with Athens.

Last-Ditch Attempts to Avert War

Archidamus was an old family friend of Pericles, but he was by no means the only Spartan hesitant to fight Athens, and for several months after the formal decision for war had been taken, the Spartans sent embassies to the Athenians demanding concessions that could preserve peaceful relations. These included "freeing the Greeks" (abandoning the empire), expelling any cursed Alcmaeonids in the city (Pericles was an Alcmaeonid on his mother's side), and rescinding the Megarian decree. The Athenians responded with demands of their own. They requested, for example, that the Spartans purify "the curse of the goddess of the Brazen House," a reference to the impieties involved in the death by starvation decades earlier of Pausanias, who as we have seen had taken refuge in the temple of Athena. Though some of these exchanges involved nothing more than pious posturing, others were probably sincere, particularly on Sparta's behalf. What these interchanges make clear are, first, that Pericles was firmly entrenched as the leader of the Athenians and as the framer of Athenian policy; second, that the Megarian decree was of considerable importance to the Spartans; and third, that both Athens and Sparta were split about the desirability of war. When negotiations had been going on for several months, the impatient Thebans forced ambivalent Sparta's hand by attacking Athens' ally Plataea. Because Plataea enjoyed a special position in Greece as the site of the great victory against Persia in 479, this assault was considered particularly heinous. Afterward nobody could question that the Peloponnesians and the Athenians were at war.

RESOURCES FOR WAR

Thus ended the period of a half century between the Persian and Peloponnesian wars to which Thucydides gave the name the Pentacontaetia, "the Fifty Years" (technically forty-seven years). In the jockeying for position that went on during the months leading up to the Theban attack on Plataea, the Spartans seem to have come out ahead. Though it was they who had declared war, the Greek world was inclined to see imperialist Athens as the aggressor—and some Athenians agreed, censuring Pericles for his combative stance and advocating the nullification of the Megarian decrees. Sparta did not keep as tight a hold on the members of the Peloponnesian League as did Athens on those of its empire. In a culture that prized autonomy as much as Greeks did, consequently, it was possible for Sparta to put itself forward in opposition to Athens as the champion of freedom—as the state that had never itself endured a tyrant and that opposed tyranny throughout Greece. When war broke out, Thucydides writes,

> Popular opinion shaped up in favor of the Spartans by far, especially since they had proclaimed that they were going to liberate Greece. Everywhere, city and citizen alike were eager, if at all possible, to join with them in word and deed, and everyone felt that any plan would come to a standstill if he himself could not take part in it. That is how angry most people were at Athens—some because they wanted to rid themselves of Athenian rule, and others because they were frightened lest they fall under that rule.
>
> (*The Peloponnesian War* 2. 8)

Thucydides also lists the principal combatants at the time of the attack on Plataea in 431. On the Peloponnesian side were Corinth, Boeotia, Megara, Locris, Phocis, Ambracia, Leucas, Anactoria, and all the states in the Peloponnesus itself except for Argos and Achaea (though in Achaea the state of Pellene did join the Spartans). Ranged on the Athenian side were an assortment of allies, some no doubt enthusiastic but many reluctant, expecting to gain nothing from the war and imagining that they would enjoy autonomy if Sparta could bring an end to Athens' imperial pretensions. (Those who believed this were mistaken. The Spartan hegemony that followed the war proved so distasteful that numerous states were eager to join the naval confederacy the Athenians established in the fourth century.) The Athenians' allies at the time war broke out were Chios, Lesbos, Plataea, Zacynthus, the Messenians of Naupactus, most of Acarnania, Corcyra, and some cities that paid tribute on the Carian coast, in Ionia, in the Hellespont, in Thrace, among what Thucydides calls the islands that lie between the Peloponnesus and Crete toward the east, and most of the Cyclades.

The belligerents differed not only in temperament but also in the nature of their military strengths. The Athenians had a great deal more money than the Peloponnesians, and their navy was incomparably superior. Athens itself possessed over three hundred ships and could count on a hundred or so more from its allies Chios, Lesbos, and, of course, Corcyra. The Peloponnesians relied principally on the Corinthian navy and could not put many more than a hundred ships in the water. Their crews, moreover, could not compare in skill and experience with those of the Athenians. But the Peloponnesian infantry was formidable. An advancing phalanx of Spartan hoplites wearing their distinctive red tunics and sporting the dreaded letter "lambda" for Lacedaemon on their shields (our letter L) threw terror into Sparta's enemies. The combined infantry of the Peloponnesians outnumbered that of the Athenians. Moreover, a good number of their soldiers were Spartans who had spent their entire lives training for war while helots and perioeci attended to the other business of life. For these, the citizen farmer-soldiers of the average Greek state were a dubious match. Accordingly, Athens hoped to conduct as much of the war as possible at sea, while the Spartans would focus on the land. The Athenians were fighting essentially a defensive war, whose goal was to preserve the empire which the Spartans sought to destroy. For Athens, a stalemate would amount to victory. Sparta needed something more.

Intellectual Life in Fifth-Century Greece

As Pericles lay dying, Plutarch maintains, he spoke with pride of what he considered his greatest achievement—"that no living Athenian ever put on mourning because of me." The inaccuracy of this peculiar boast became increasingly clear with every passing year. The war Pericles had encouraged his fellow Athenians to fight with the Peloponnesian League would sap the strength of one of the most extraordinary civilizations the world has ever seen. Throughout the Greek cities, people had begun to explore new ideas about the universe and humanity's place in it.

Speculating About the Natural World

Greeks of Hesiod's day had viewed the earliest state of the universe as a formless void they called *chaos*. Out of chaos, they believed, the order of their own world had emerged—*kosmos*, a Greek word meaning both "order" and "beauty" (hence the word "cosmetics" for makeup, or "cosmetic" surgery to improve appearance). Mythology grounded the growth of cosmos from chaos in various actions taken by the gods. The great contribution of the sixth-century Greek thinkers of Ionia had lain in their determination to abandon this mythological and religious framework and attempt instead to explain the world by material processes alone.

As we saw in Chapter 3, the Ionian rationalists had focused on the natural world rather than on the values of the human community. Their speculations, however, like those of Charles Darwin in the nineteenth century, raised inevitable questions about relations between gods and mortals, for the Ionians sought to enthrone human reason as the tool for understanding the universe and to replace divine plan (or caprice) with material forces. Anaxagoras from Clazomenae in Asia Minor (c. 500–428 BC) was one of many intellectuals who were drawn to the glittering city of Athens. There he became a trusted friend of Pericles, whom he served as a mentor for many years. Anaxagoras viewed material objects as composed of infinitely divisible particles and conceived of their organization as the work of a force he called *nous* (intellect); from this came his nickname, Nous ("the Brain"). The sun, he claimed, was not a deity but rather a white-hot stone a little larger than the Peloponnesus. When Pericles' political enemies sought to undermine his position in the 430s by bringing his known associates to trial, Anaxagoras provided an easy target and was forced to flee for his life.

The workings of the universe also intrigued other fifth-century thinkers throughout the breadth of the Greek world. Empedocles (c. 493–c. 433 BC), who lived in Acragas in Sicily, propounded a cosmogony based on the idea of four primary elements—earth, air, fire, and water. Physical substances, he argued, were produced when the twin forces of attraction and repulsion that he called "love" and "strife" acted upon these elements, combining them in various proportions. Maintaining that these combinations were randomly produced, Empedocles conjectured that monstrous forms had probably been created early in history but had perished through their failure to adapt.

An alternative view of how the world is made was put forward by Leucippus and Democritus. Like Anaxagoras, Leucippus, who seems to have been active around the middle of the fifth century, believed that matter was created of tiny particles, and his ideas were further developed by his pupil Democritus, from Abdera in Thrace (c. 460–370 BC). In their view, moreover, the tiny particles were *atoma* (uncuttable). Ironically, then, the word for "atom," which has been split in our own age with such devastating consequences, originally meant "that which cannot be divided." In addition to atoms, so the theory had it, there was "void"; falling through void, atoms collided in a variety of ways to form visible matter. What determined the manner of these collisions was a little uncertain—Leucippus insisted it was necessity and not chance, though other atomists disagreed—but the atomic theorists agreed on one thing: whatever was active in shaping the form of matter was a natural force and no divine being.

Though they certainly looked around them for models and paradigms, thinkers like Anaxagoras, Empedocles, Leucippus, and Democritus were essentially philosophers, not scientists. A mix of observation and systematic thinking formed the basis of Greek medicine. Nevertheless, prayer probably remained the most common Greek response to illness in antiquity. During the sixth century BC, Greeks in Asia Minor began learning about anatomy from the observations Mesopotamians had made on animal entrails used in divination. By 500 BC, medical centers had been established on the island of Cos off the coast of Asia Minor and on the nearby peninsula of Cnidus. Some instruction also took place within the family; often the medical profession was passed down from father to son. Women were prohibited from practicing as doctors, but they frequently functioned as midwives.

Case studies formed the basis of the doctrines of Hippocrates of Cos (c. 460–c. 377 BC). The body of writings associated with Hippocrates' school included over a hundred works composed over a long period, and there is no way to know which of these might have been written by Hippocrates himself. Greeks did not develop many cures for diseases. The principal contribution of the Hippocratics lay not in any specific discoveries about medicine but rather in the commitment to seeking rational explanations of natural phenomena. Epilepsy, for example, had been labeled "the sacred disease" by the Greeks; in their treatise *On the Sacred Disease*, the Hippocratics took a different view, claiming that this notion was put forward by anxious charlatans who "having no idea what to do and having nothing to offer the sick...labeled the disease sacred in order to conceal their ignorance" (*On the Sacred Disease* 2). Another treatise, *Airs, Waters, Places*, examined the impact of climate on health, laying the foundations for epidemiology.

The largest group of Hippocratic texts deals with gynecology. Along with the general devaluation of women in Greek culture, women's reticence about speaking to male physicians sometimes cut doctors off from information vital to understanding female reproductive processes. In the absence of real data concerning symptoms and sexual practices, where women were concerned speculation often substituted for the careful observation on which the Hippocratics prided themselves:

> If suffocation occurs suddenly, it will happen especially to women
> who do not have intercourse and to older women rather than to
> young ones, for their wombs are lighter. It usually occurs because
> of the following: when a woman is empty and works harder than in
> her previous experience, her womb, becoming heated from the hard
> work, turns because it is empty and light. There is, in fact, empty
> space for it to turn in because the belly is empty. Now when the
> womb turns, it hits the liver and they go together and strike against
> the abdomen—for the womb rushes and goes upwards towards the
> moisture, because it has been dried out by hard work, and the liver

is, after all, moist. When the womb hits the liver, it produces sudden suffocation as it occupies the breathing passages around the belly.

(Hippocrates, *Diseases of Women* 1.7; Hanson)

HISTORICAL AND DRAMATIC LITERATURE OF THE FIFTH CENTURY

In the verbal realm, the principal achievements of the Athenians during this period lay in history and in tragedy. Dozens of tragedians were active in fifth-century Athens. History was the less common genre, but the two works that survived in their entirety were remarkable in their scope and depth—Herodotus' history of the Persian wars and Thucydides' history of the Peloponnesian War. Between them, Herodotus and Thucydides enshrined in historical writing the model of the war monograph that has remained popular to this day.

Herodotus

Like the early Greek philosophers, Herodotus sought to challenge traditional ways of looking at the world. Born in Halicarnassus in Ionia, Herodotus inherited the traditions of Ionian rationalism and had a passionate curiosity about causes and origins. Why the Persians and the Greeks fought, what accounted for the Greek victory, how Darius came to rule Persia, where the Nile began, how the priestesses at Dodona came to be thought of as birds with human voices, where the Greeks got their gods—Herodotus used the Greek word *historia* ("inquiry") to describe his quest for understanding, and this word has given English and numerous European languages their word for the investigation and analysis of the past: "history." Herodotus reports in the opening sentence of his work that he has set forth the results of his inquiry "so that the actions of people shall not fade with time, so that the great and admirable monuments produced by both Greeks and barbarians shall not go unrenowned, and, among other things, to set forth the reasons why they waged war on each other" (1.1).

Born shortly before Xerxes' invasion of Greece in 480, Herodotus was not old enough to remember the Persian wars, but he was able to interrogate informants of his parents' generation closely. His interests were not confined to a particular series of historical events; like his somewhat younger contemporary Thucydides, he was fascinated by what history revealed about human nature and the way the world works. What he learned from his study of history was that power goes to people's heads, and that the mighty rarely contemplate their condition with sufficient judiciousness and reflection—that rulers hear what they want to hear, and collaborate in their own destruction. In many ways the *Histories* is a meditation on power, and not only the power of Eastern potentates; as Herodotus was writing, the Athenians were busy flexing their muscles in the Aegean heedless of the consequences, consequences which before Herodotus' death overtook them in the form of the ruinous Peloponnesian War.

Herodotus' paradigm for the perils of wealth, power and self-absorption appears early in his history in his imaginative reconstruction of a conversation between Solon, the Athenian lawgiver, and Croesus, the fabulously wealthy king of Lydia who has given his name to an expression still current today, "rich as Croesus." During his travels, Herodotus maintains, Solon came to Croesus' palace, where the king made a point of having attendants give Solon a tour that would highlight Croesus' prosperity. Afterward, Croesus asked Solon if there was anyone in the world who struck him as particularly fortunate. Feigning ignorance of Croesus' purpose in asking this question, Solon named a little-known Greek who had died fighting for his city and was buried with honors, leaving children behind him. When Croesus was dissatisfied with this response, Solon offered an alternative example. Two young Argives, he related, when their mother needed to attend a feast of Hera and the oxen had not yet returned from the field, yoked themselves to the family wagon and pulled it several miles to the temple. Amidst the great words of praise lavished upon the young men and on her for having such fine sons, their mother prayed to the goddess to bestow on her children whatever was best for humankind. Lying down to sleep in the temple, the youths never awoke. The Argives dedicated statues to them at Delphi in commemoration of their excellence.

Resentful at not being named the most fortunate of men, Croesus spoke harshly to Solon, voicing his indignation at the notion that the Athenian should consider ordinary citizens more fortunate than a rich king like him. Solon in turn counseled him to think harder about what it means to be truly fortunate, cautioning him not to make facile judgments without waiting to see how things turn out in the end. "To me," he tells Croesus,

> it is obvious that you have great wealth and that you rule over many
> people, but it will be impossible for me to answer your question until
> I learn that you have happily ended your allotted life. After all, the
> rich man is not really happier than the man who lives from day to
> day unless good fortune stays with him and he dies painlessly, and in
> possession of all the good things life has to offer.... You have to con-
> sider how everything ends—how it turns out. For god gives many a
> glimpse of happiness and then withers them at their very roots.
>
> (*The Histories* 1.32)

Croesus, however, does not listen. By carelessly misinterpreting a series of oracles, he loses his empire before he comes to recognize Solon's wisdom.

It is not likely that Solon and Croesus really met. Solon's travels evidently preceded Croesus' accession to the throne around 560 BC. Herodotus has crafted this vignette to demonstrate the superiority of Athenian over Persian ways of thinking—of the western dependence on the solid citizen over the eastern reverence for the powerful autocrat. Similar points are scored in Herodotus' characterization of the overconfident Xerxes. The implications of this are plain enough: for all their virtues, the Persians, like other eastern peoples, were dragged down by their habit of according immense power to a single individual, the king. Encouraging him in his childish self-confidence, they became slaves to someone who exaggerated his own importance not only vis-à-vis other mortals but, more dangerously still, in relation to the gods. In comparison, Greek civilization held all the promise inherent in free institutions, in the rule of law, in respect for gods and the acceptance of human limitations.

In all this Herodotus was a typical Greek, but in other respects he sought to undermine knee-jerk assumptions he saw in the world around him—assumptions about the insignificance of non-Greek cultures and the low intellect of women. Greeks, in Herodotus' view, needed to think harder and longer about their place in the world. To assist them in this project, he included in his history many stories about the intelligence of clever queens (such as Queen Artemisia of his native Halicarnassus) and a detailed account of the accomplishments of the Egyptians, stressing the greater antiquity of Egyptian culture in relation to Greek and suggesting Egyptian origins for the Greek gods. Herodotus has been called not only the Father of History but the Father of Anthropology as well. Some of the most memorable portions of his *Histories* were embedded in his accounts of non-Greek cultures—the Atlantes, who never dream; the Getae, who believe they are immortal; the Argippaeans, who are bald from birth; the Gyzantes, who eat monkeys; and the Callatian Indians, who eat the dead bodies of their parents. This distinctly un-Greek funerary practice appears in a dialogue that Herodotus sets at the court of Darius:

> When Darius was king he summoned the Greeks who were in his court and asked them how much money it would take to get them to eat their dead fathers. They answered that they would never do it for any amount of money. Next, Darius summoned some Indians known as the Kalatiai, who eat their dead parents, and asked them in the presence of the Greeks, who understood what was said through a translator, how much money it would take for them to permit their dead parents to be cremated on a funeral pyre. The Indians made a loud commotion and begged Darius not to so much as speak of such a thing. So settled, then, is custom, and Pindar was right, I think, when he wrote in his verses that "custom reigns over all men."
>
> (*The Histories* 3.38)

To Herodotus the wide variety of customs in the world was a source of endless fascination.

To learn about the world outside Greece, Herodotus had to travel, and he did so extensively, relying both on what he himself saw and on what his various native informants told him. Twice in the *Histories* he observes that he only reports what he has heard and considers himself under no obligation to believe it (2.123, 7.152). In this way, he is able to offer not only a political and military history of the Persian Wars but a broader account of the then known world in which tall tales retailed by his informants had their place. For Herodotus was also a skilled raconteur, and the *Histories* are full of lively anecdotes: the poet Arion is rescued by a dolphin; the pharaoh Rhampsinitus goes down to the underworld and returns to earth with a gift from the goddess Demeter; Themistocles lures Xerxes into a trap at Salamis. A hybrid genre that blended sober research with folk motifs and fairy tales, the *Histories* gives great pleasure. Indeed, it was this aspect of the *Histories* which disturbed Thucydides, who boasted that his own work would be not an entertaining display for the moment but a possession for all time.

Thucydides

As a historian Thucydides faced less of a challenge than Herodotus, for he wrote largely about his own day—about a war, indeed, in which he himself participated. Many intellectual currents of the fifth century flowed through Athens as Thucydides was coming to maturity and during the years when he composed his history. Some were plainly important to him, others apparently not. Careful observation, rational deduction, and a tragic view of the world can all be discerned in his history, just as they can in that of Herodotus. Both were influenced by the work of the Hippocratics. Like many thinkers of the later fifth century, Thucydides construed the world as fundamentally human-centered. Whereas Herodotus, born a generation earlier, had conceived history as an interaction of divine and human forces, both vitally important, Thucydides saw the actions of people as pretty much exclusively responsible for how things turn out. Belonging to a later generation, moreover—and being an Athenian citizen—Thucydides had been exposed to a great deal of rhetoric in the assembly and perhaps the law courts as well, and speeches, both straightforward and manipulative, are prominent in his work.

Almost nothing is known of Thucydides' life. Since he served as a general in 424, he must have been at least thirty in that year, and historians conjecture he was born around 460. He came from an aristocratic family with kinship ties to two of Pericles' best-known rivals, Cimon and Thucydides, son of Melesias, but he had enormous admiration for Pericles. His opportunities for research took an unexpected turn when he was exiled after failing to keep the Spartans from taking Amphipolis. From then on, he was able to gather a great deal of information from non-Athenian sources but could no longer attend meetings of the Athenian assembly. He lived long enough to see Athens lose the war, just as Herodotus had lived long enough to see the Greeks squander their victory over Persia and become embroiled in internecine warfare. He claims to have begun writing as the war broke out, foreseeing its importance, and to have written up each year as it happened. Even if this is true in its outlines, however, he certainly made some revisions based on hindsight; in Book 5, for example, dealing with the events of 421, he refers to the fall of Athens in 404 and identifies the duration of the war as twenty-seven years.

Thucydides himself discusses his methodology at the outset of his history, stressing the lengths to which he went in his quest to determine the truth—and expressing impatience with those less committed to the search for knowledge. Most people, he complains, "expend very little effort on the search for truth, and prefer to turn to ready-made answers." His own approach will be different.

DOCUMENT 7.1

Thucydides explains his methodology in his history of the Peloponnesian War, contrasting himself with less reliable reporters—including, it seems, Herodotus, as well as rhetoricians given to virtuoso public displays.

One will not go wrong if he believes that the facts were such as I have related them, based on the evidence, and not as they are sung by the poets—who embellish and exaggerate them—or as they are strung together by popular historians with a view to making them not more truthful but more attractive to their audiences; and considering that we are dealing with ancient history, whose unverified events have, over the course of time, made their way into the incredible realms of mythology, one will find that these conclusions, derived as they are from the best known evidence, are accurate enough. Even though people always think that the war they are fighting is the greatest there ever was, and then return to marveling at ancient wars once theirs have ended, it will be clear, after we examine the events themselves, that this actually was the greatest there has ever been.

As to the statements the participants made, either when they were about to enter the war or after they were already in it, it has been difficult for me and for those who reported to me to remember exactly what was said. I have, therefore, written what I thought the speakers must have said given the situations they were in, while keeping as close as possible to the consensus about what was actually said. As to the events of the war, I have not written them down as I heard them from just anybody, nor as I thought they must have occurred, but have consistently described what I myself saw or have been able to learn from others after going over each event in as much detail as possible. I have found this task to be extremely difficult, since those who were present at these actions gave varying reports on the same event, depending on their sympathies and their memories.

My narrative, perhaps, will seem less pleasing to some listeners because it lacks an element of fiction. Those, however, who want to see things clearly as they were, and, given human nature, as they will one day be again, more or less, may find this book a useful basis for judgment. My work was composed not as a prizewinning exercise in elocution but as a possession for all time.

The Peloponnesian War 1.22.

Many readers regard Thucydides as the finest historian of the Greco-Roman world. This is reasonable. He is less disposed to see divine justice as a force in history than Herodotus, who had the luxury of writing up a war which, in his view, the good guys won; the Peloponnesian War, on the other hand, was a war that everyone lost. He does not moralize like Plutarch. In comparison with the famous historians of Rome, he is less jingoistic than Livy, and his partisanship is better concealed than that of Tacitus. He has often been described as the world's first scientific historian, and his work has been cited for its objectivity. This characterization rests on a misunderstanding of what the writing of history really involves. History is not a science, and it cannot be objective because it entails humans writing about other humans. Every omission, every connection, requires a judgment call.

One example will illustrate the choices all historians must make. In analyzing the outbreak of the war, Thucydides downplayed the Megarian decree to a remarkable degree, saying almost nothing about it. He did this, presumably, either because he really believed the decree was unimportant or because he wished to deflect criticism from Pericles, who was commonly blamed for the decree and for the war. It would be impossible to construe this decision as objective or scientific. The result of Thucydides' choice is that it is now very difficult for students of the past to reconstruct what really happened. If the Megarian decree really was unimportant, then presumably Thucydides did a good thing, but if he was wrong, then he did his readers a great disservice. There is no limit to the number of similar decisions that confront historians. Herodotus was more disposed to put everything in and let his readers sort it out. As one consequence of this decision, however, he has been criticized for being less analytical than Thucydides.

The Birth of Tragedy

Drama played a central role in the spiritual and intellectual life of Athens. Wealthy citizens vied for honor and acclaim by undertaking the expense of training choruses, and during the festival of Dionysus in March, actors and audience alike needed enormous stamina. Each dramatic poet presented three tragedies and one shorter ribald play called a satyr play in which the chorus dressed and behaved like the satyrs who were part of the cult of Dionysus. Spectators had not only to follow the intricate poetry of the choruses but also to turn up for six days for the religious rites to view lyric performances, another three days of tragedies and satyr plays, and then one more day in which five comedies were performed. A significant proportion of men—and probably women as well—attended the plays and no doubt continued among themselves a lively dialogue about the issues the dramas had raised. Even in eras of comparatively high literacy, Greek culture remained oral to a considerable degree, and absorbing the complex imagery of tragic and comic choruses was not so difficult for people trained to listen and remember as it would be nowadays. Nonetheless, the popularity of performances that demanded serious intellectual work on the part of the audience tells

us something about the richness of Athenian culture. Over thirty complete tragedies and eleven comedies have survived. In tragedy, only the plays of Aeschylus,
Sophocles, and Euripides have survived, and of these only a fraction of their
works—seven each of Aeschylus and Sophocles, and nineteen of Euripides. (We
will look at comedy more closely in Chapter 8.)

Even female parts in drama were played by men. Masks facilitated the dis-
guise and also made it possible for one actor to play several parts. They were
shaped at the mouth rather like megaphones and so made for good acoustics.
To be sure, they discouraged the nuanced portrayal of personality. This was
not, however, a great loss, for tragedy was never intended to be naturalistic.
Characters in tragedy represented humankind in all its aspiration—and frailty.
They are not easy to like or dislike, for they were not intended to be lifelike, flesh-
and-blood individuals.

Nor was the material of tragedy a "slice of life." Tragedy was meant to be heroic and grand, far removed from the mundane. Plots were generally taken from
myths of the Heroic Age, but exceptions could be made for major events such as
the Persian wars. Even here, though, Aeschylus achieved a certain distance by sit-
uating his *Persians* in faraway Asia, where people dressed exotically. Formalities
of several kinds limited the dramatist in his choice of material. No violence was
permitted on stage, and all action had to take place within a twenty-four-hour
period. Finally, the author had to contend with the challenges posed by the intricate meters of tragic verse.

Dramatic Performance and the Polis: Aeschylus and the *Oresteia*

Aeschylus (525–456 BC) was the first of the famous tragedians of fifth-century
Athens. He died in Sicily after a long life, during which he wrote perhaps seventy
plays. Only seven of these survive. After his death the Athenians paid homage
to his talent by decreeing that the archon should grant a chorus to anyone who
wanted to produce one of his plays, though until the fourth century it was customary to produce each play only once. Already in the time of Pisistratus, Thespis
had expanded the range of the choruses honoring Dionysus by adding an actor
who could carry on a dialogue with the chorus; now Aeschylus added a second
actor. This innovation made possible real conflict and moved tragedy beyond
tableau into the realm of drama. At the same time, drama remained grounded
in poetry, and throughout antiquity verse remained the vehicle for both tragedy
and comedy.

Aeschylus' greatest surviving achievement is the trilogy known as the *Oresteia*,
which treats the difficulty of understanding and obtaining a just social and religious order. Although the sets of four dramas that playwrights entered in the
competition generally comprised three tragedies followed by a satyr play, the
three tragedies did not need to treat the same theme, and frequently they didn't.
In the case of the *Oresteia*, however, the three plays form one grand and complex
drama, and this work is the only Attic trilogy that survives.

The point of departure for the *Oresteia* was evidently Ephialtes' curtailment of the powers of the Areopagus, for the trilogy culminates in precisely the sort of trial that remained within the council's purview—a murder trial. It seems likely that Aeschylus supported the reforms and chose this plot as a vehicle by which to reassure conservative Athenians that the trying of homicide cases, the privilege with which Ephialtes had conspicuously not tampered, was in fact the ancient mission of this venerable body. In this way he could draw attention away from the limitations that had been placed on its jurisdiction. The material with which Aeschylus chose to convey his message was the familiar tale of the cursed house of the hero Pelops and his descendant Agamemnon king of Mycenae and commander-in-chief of the legendary expedition against Troy.

The first play, *Agamemnon*, portrays the king's murder upon his victorious return from the Trojan War. Agamemnon's murder by his faithless wife, Clytemnestra, and his cousin Aegisthus, who has become Clytemnestra's lover, poses an agonizing dilemma for his children Orestes and Electra, who are faced with a choice between killing their mother and allowing their father's death to go unavenged. Their pain and Orestes' eventual murder of Clytemnestra and Aegisthus form the subject matter of the second play, *The Libation Bearers*. As the play closes, Orestes is pursued by the avenging earth goddesses known as the Furies. His suffering ends in the final play, *The Eumenides*. This play is set in Athens, where Orestes has taken refuge, hoping that a responsible government will afford him a fair trial. Athena's charge to the jury proclaims the glories of the Areopagus, the importance of justice, and the centrality of law. The goddess saves Orestes by casting her vote for him, and her grounds are revealing. Following Apollo's proclamation that it is the male and not the female who is the true parent, and bearing in mind her own birth (fully developed from the head of her father Zeus), she decides that the claims of the father trump those of the mother, justifying Clytemnestra's death. Now tamed, the Furies are given a new name, the Eumenides ("Kindly Ones"). Plainly, Aeschylus conceives the creation of responsible government in Athens as the antithesis not only of tyranny but also of a primitive, chaotic universe in which emotional and female forces of vengeance were paramount. The new world ruled by the Olympic gods will be governed by orderly, rational institutions in which vengeance is replaced by justice, but not only that: it will be planned and staffed by males.

The choruses celebrated the awesome power of the gods while also exploring the nature of the human condition. "Sing sorrow, sorrow," the chorus chants toward the opening of *Agamemnon*, "but good win out in the end":

> Zeus: whatever he may be, if this name
> pleases him in invocation,
> thus I call upon him.
> I have pondered everything
> yet I cannot find a way,
> only Zeus, to cast this dead weight of ignorance

finally from out my brain.

…

Zeus, who guided men to think,
who has laid it down that wisdom
comes alone through suffering.
Still there drips in sleep against the heart
grief of memory; against
our pleasure we are temperate.
From the gods who sit in grandeur
grace comes somehow violent.

(Aeschylus, *Agamemnon* 160–166, 176–183; Lattimore)

The genre perfected by Aeschylus would become one of the defining art forms of Greek civilization. Tragic drama, as it evolved throughout Aeschylus' career and in the hands of his successors Sophocles and Euripides, was in many ways the hallmark of Athenian greatness. Through Shakespeare and other great tragedians of Europe, this remarkable testament to the heroic struggle against human limitations forms an important part of a legacy that has endured to our own time.

Sophocles

Herodotus' warnings about the vicissitudes of fortune and the impossibility of judging a man's life until it is over are echoed in *Oedipus Tyrannus,* the most famous tragedy of antiquity. It was written by the poet Sophocles (c. 496–406 BC), author of over a hundred plays. Like Aeschylus and other tragic poets, Sophocles reworked the familiar plots of Greek mythology, with their emphasis on agonizing family discord, to express his view of the world.

Not long after Herodotus' departure for Thurii, Sophocles produced the first of three surviving dramas about the unfortunate house of Oedipus, the legendary ruler of Thebes who was fated to kill his father and marry his mother. Though Sophocles' plays that deal with the family of Oedipus were not presented as a trilogy, we will discuss them together following the chronological sequence of the myth. In *Oedipus Tyrannus* we meet the hero—the highly intelligent and respected ruler of Thebes in the Heroic Age—only later to witness his life disintegrating as he learned that he was fated to kill his father and marry his mother.

The *Oedipus at Colonus,* which was produced posthumously, portrays the blind hero, having learned much through suffering, finally finding asylum in the Athenian suburb of Colonus. In the *Antigone* we contemplate the painful tensions that arise in Oedipus' family after his death. One of his sons, Polynices, has died fighting to take the throne of Thebes from his brother; Polynices' sister Antigone wishes to fulfill her religious obligation and bury his body. But their uncle Creon, now king of Thebes, forbids anyone to take up this project on the grounds that Polynices was a traitor. Like many characters in Greek tragedy, Antigone now finds herself confronted with a painful choice. She must decide whether to honor her obligation to her brother and to the gods, which means facing death herself, or to obey the laws of the state and keep herself safe. She is headstrong and defiant; Creon is rigid and insensitive.

Though Sophocles is a conventional Athenian in his respect for the gods and their power to guide human life, in other regards he challenged conventional mores. Antigone's situation paralleled that of the Athenian girl known as an *epiklēros*, a girl with no surviving brothers, and it is hard to doubt that Sophocles' sympathies lie with the fatherless, brotherless girl who experiences all the helplessness that fell upon Athenian women who lacked male protectors. Sophocles, as his other plays confirm, sympathized with the plight of Greek women. Creon, however, makes a good case for the importance of a law that makes no exceptions for family members, and as an Athenian democrat, Sophocles certainly saw the need to uphold the rule of law. But is the decree of an autocrat really law, especially when the populace is on Antigone's side? Sophocles fully recognizes the complexity of the tortuous choices Antigone and Creon must make, and he sees in their confrontation proof of the wondrous complexity of humankind and the communities humans have struggled to develop.

DOCUMENT 7.2

The chorus of Theban elders celebrates the achievements of the human beings:

> Many the wonders but nothing walks stranger than man.
> This thing crosses the sea in the winter's storm,
> making his path through the roaring waves.
> And she, the greatest of gods, the earth—
> ageless she is, and unwearied—he wears her away
> as the plows go up and down from year to year
> and his mules turn up the soil.
>
> Gay nations of birds he snares and leads,
> wild beast tribes and the salty brood of the sea,
> with the twisted mesh of his nets, this clever man.
> He controls with craft the beasts of the open air,
> walkers on hills. The horse with his shaggy mane
> he holds and harnesses, yoked about the neck,
> and the strong bull of the mountain.
>
> Language, and thought like the wind
> and the feelings that make the town,
> he has taught himself, and shelter against the cold,
> refuge from rain. He can always help himself.
> He faces no future helpless. There's only death
> that he cannot find an escape from. He has contrived
> refuge from illnesses once beyond all cure.
>
> Clever beyond all dreams
> the inventive craft that he has

> which may drive him one time or another to well or ill.
> When he honors the laws of the land and the gods' sworn right
> high indeed is his city; but stateless the man
> who dares to dwell with dishonor. Not by my fire,
> never to share my thoughts, who does these things.
>
> Sophocles, *Antigone* 332–372; Wyckoff

Like Herodotus, Sophocles combined profound reverence for the gods with a compelling interest in the human dimension of life. In his plays, dialogue—the talking back and forth of humans—was expanded at the expense of the chorus; he also added a third actor where Aeschylus had used only two (not counting silent actors, who appeared on the stage but did not speak).

Euripides

In the spring of 431, Athenians and foreign visitors gathered in the theater of Dionysus to see Euripides' *Medea*. Plays by Euripides (c. 485–c. 406 BC) had been produced before, so the playwright was already known to the audience, but the subject matter for this drama was singularly shocking. Although the plots of Greek tragedy derived from familiar myths, Euripides enjoyed innovation, and there is reason to believe that the ending of the play came as a surprise to the enthralled onlookers.

The questions Sophocles posed about the society in which he lived seem tame compared with the more searching critiques of Greek values that appear in Euripides' plays. In *Medea*, Euripides used the tale of Jason, the celebrated leader of the Argonauts in their quest for the Golden Fleece, to undermine conventional views of what makes a hero. In the course of his adventures, Jason has married Medea, a sorceress from Colchis, at the far end of the Black Sea, who has helped him in his quest. He has such confidence in the excellence of the Greek way of life that even when he has decided to abandon his wife to marry a Corinthian princess, he boasts of the benefits he has conferred on Medea by rescuing her from a barbarian land and transplanting her to Greece. Predictably, these arguments do not sit well with a highly intelligent woman who has the advantage of a non-Greek perspective. The bitter laments of Medea enable the audience to see things differently as she details the constraints on her life as a woman in a Greek city:

> We women are the most unfortunate creatures.
> First, with an excess of wealth it is required
> For us to buy a husband, and take for our bodies
> A master; for not to take one is even worse.
> And now the question is serious whether we take
> A good or bad one; for there is no easy escape
> For a woman, nor can she say no to her marriage.
>
> (Euripides, *Medea* 231–238; Warner)

Jason's shameful rationalizations for his actions, moreover, raise serious questions about a society that makes heroes of such men. Greek tragedies, however, were not morality plays, and when in the play's horrifying conclusion Medea decides to take vengeance on Jason by killing their children, even those in the audience who were sympathetic to her plight probably shifted their sympathy to the bereaved father. (In the same way, Sophocles' audience felt for the harsh Creon when his actions led to the death not only of Antigone but of his own wife and son as well.) *Medea* was only one of the plays in which Euripides explored the dynamics of the conflict between reason and passion—reason, which could justify Jason in deserting the wife who had risked her life for him in her youth, and passion, which could move a mother to kill her offspring. Inevitably the agonizing conflict that marked plays like *Antigone* struck a particularly resonant chord with the audience in *Medea*, which was produced just as war was breaking out between two very different states with opposing views of the world.

CURRENTS IN GREEK THOUGHT AND EDUCATION

The verses in which Euripides' Jason defends his action as calculated to improve his children's lives (won't it be wonderful for them to have royal stepsiblings?) show the influence of the itinerant intellectuals who gravitated to Athens during the second half of the fifth century, the men who came to be known as the **sophists**, from the Greek word *sophistēs*, which means something like "practitioner of wisdom." Unlike the philosophers, who sought to understand the world, the sophists contented themselves with teaching eager, paying pupils how to get by in it. Many of the sophists were important, iconoclastic thinkers whose keen analysis pierced pretensions. Though their works do not survive except in fragments, it seems clear that they rejected facile assumptions about the connections between noble birth and true merit. Because of this, and because they enabled young men from newly rich families to learn to speak effectively, they aroused suspicion among Athens' entrenched elite.

Formal and Informal Education

The origins of the sophistic movement lie in the haphazard and informal nature of Greek education, in its literary and aristocratic bias, and in its ultimately superficial and stultifying nature. Since Homer's day, Greek children had learned primarily by watching the world around them and imitating respected elders. Few people in antiquity or the Middle Ages knew how to read, and "book learning" played a minor role in the educational system of Archaic Greece, where most formal education involved listening and reciting from memory. Girls were rarely sent to school. Neither were most boys. The problem was not simply that poverty usually compelled children to stay home and work on the farm; rather, Greek states did not provide public schools. Parents of the upper classes, however, paid for their sons to be instructed in what was called *mousikē*, a word that means literally "having to do with the Muses." Mousikē included the memorization of poetry, and since ancient poems were sung, it also involved learning to play the stringed instrument known as the lyra, hence our word "lyrics"—verses designed to accompany lyre playing—and of course our word "music." Beginning in the sixth century, more and more children also learned to read and write. Vases from the sixth and fifth centuries show these skills being taught to boys and occasionally to girls as well; parents sometimes had daughters instructed in basic reading and writing skills in case they needed this knowledge to supervise household accounts or to manage temple properties if they became priestesses. Some instruction in math was also offered to children by private tutors and in schools, though not much was offered in the way of science. The curriculum included little of what we would call social studies, and the young were generally thrown back on family and friends for the answer to questions like, "How far is it to Sparta?" and "What kind of government do they have in Corinth?" By the time boys progressed to the age at which adolescents today would enter college, moreover, they had ceased to be students and had become soldiers and citizens, and their sisters were mothers of two or three children.

Most education went on in less formal settings, however, and this sort of education would continue throughout life. In childhood, girls would absorb the norms of appropriate social behavior from their mothers and aunts, boys from their fathers and uncles. As in many societies, the upbringing of the two sexes was designed to cultivate very different skills for males and females. These differences were most pronounced in the upper classes, for poor children of both sexes were likely to learn farming and craft skills from parents. Among the elite, however, a sharp differentiation occurred in adolescence, for at this juncture girls married and reproduced. Their education in home management continued at the hands of older relatives, and probably older slaves, who had considerable experience of child rearing. In addition, husbands sometimes took it upon themselves to give their wives vocational training in household management. In the *Oeconomicus*, highlighted in the preceding chapter (see Document 6.3), Xenophon describes how Ischomachus was obliged to train his young wife to be a successful estate manager:

> [Socrates] said, "I would very much like you to tell me, Ischomachus, whether you yourself trained your wife to become the sort of woman that she ought to be, or whether she already knew how to carry out her duties when you took her as your wife from her father and mother."
>
> "What could she have known when I took her as my wife, Socrates? She was not yet fifteen when she came to me, and had spent her previous years under careful supervision so that she might see and hear and speak as little as possible. Don't you think it was adequate if she came to me knowing only how to take wool and produce a cloak, and had seen how spinning tasks are allocated to the slaves? And besides, she had been very well trained to control her appetites,

Socrates," he said, "and I think that sort of training is most important for man and woman alike."

(Xenophon, *Oeconomicus* 7.4–5; Pomeroy)

While teenage girls might receive such instruction from their husbands, adolescent males were exposed to important influences of another kind. Books were expensive, and though literacy increased throughout the sixth and particularly the fifth century, learning still went on primarily in the interaction between two or more human beings, not in the interaction of a person with a written text. Relationships with somewhat older mentors formed a key element in the education of teenage boys. Just as younger teachers today often serve as role models for adolescents, so young men in Greece offered examples of manhood to those who were just developing into men. The one-on-one nature of these friendships, however—untrammeled by any need for a teacher to be evenhanded with an entire class of students—combined with different attitudes to sexuality to produce a significantly different dynamic. The bond between a Greek male teenager and his adult mentor was often profoundly erotic. What we know about these relationships is somewhat compromised by a reticence about sex in the written sources and by the need many Greeks felt to stress the intellectual and spiritual bond at the expense of the sexual one. In Plato's dialogue on love, the *Symposium*, the character Phaedrus praises this bond for its value in the moral improvement of both the individual and society as a whole:

> The greatest benefit, to my mind, that a young man can come by in his youth is a virtuous lover, and a virtuous boyfriend is just as good for a lover too. Anyone who wants to live a good life needs to be guided throughout his life by something which love imparts more effectively than family ties can, or public office, or wealth, or anything else. What is this "something"? The ability to feel shame at disgraceful behavior and pride in good behavior, because without these qualities no individual or community could achieve anything great or fine.
>
> (Plato, *Symposium* 178C–D; Waterfield)

The bond between the older lover (the *erastēs*) and the younger beloved (the *erōmenos*) shored up the stability of society by encouraging each generation (or half-generation) to imitate the one that had gone before.

Erotic bonds, of course, that had begun in school might also be strong between men of a similar age. Xenophon portrays Socrates describing the passion of Critobulus for Cleinias:

> This hot flame of his was kindled in the days when they used to go to school together. It was the discovery of this that caused his father to put him into my hands, in the hope that I might do him some good. And without question he is already much improved. For a while ago he was like those who look at the Gorgons—he would gaze

at Cleinias with a fixed and stony stare and would never leave his presence....It does look to me as if he had also kissed Cleinias; and there is nothing more terribly potent than this at kindling the fires of passion. For it is insatiable and holds out seductive hopes. For this reason I maintain that one who intends to possess the power of self-control must refrain from kissing those in the bloom of beauty.

(Xenophon, *Symposium* 4.23–24; Todd)

Finally, participation in the life of the city as a whole afforded an ongoing education to growing men. The poet Simonides put it well: *Polis andra didaskei* ("The polis teaches a man"). To some extent, women, particularly those who served as priestesses, and all women who attended state-sponsored festivals, benefited as well. In general, the purpose of Greek education was a blend of indoctrination and socialization calculated to foster the perpetuation of traditional values. Poetry was more likely to be memorized than analyzed, and despite the originality with which the Greeks are rightly credited, the culture did not as a whole prize innovation. What Greek youth was taught above all was to copy approved models.

All this changed when the sophists burst on the scene during the second half of the fifth century, sparking powerful tensions between the generations. Athens acted as a magnet for the philosophers and teachers of rhetoric who had sprung up throughout the Greek world as speculation about both the natural universe and the human community became increasingly popular among intellectuals. Democracy was grounded in skill in speaking and reasoning—in the ability to dissect and demolish the arguments of political opponents. The goal was to speak

Figure 7.4. This drinking cup depicts a mature, bearded man courting a very young, barely adolescent boy. Oxford, The Ashmolean Museum (1967.304).

persuasively in the assembly and courts. The sophists offered to teach these skills. Sophists filled other needs as well, since they delighted in exploring tricky questions about the workings of the world. Not everyone had been satisfied by the conventional pieties about the awesome powers of the gods and the concomitant need to revere authorities of all kinds, and for the dissatisfied the sophists' speculations provided an opportunity to flex both their intellects and their rhetorical skills. No common belief system marked the thinking of the various sophists, but they shared an enthusiasm for the kind of exercises in argumentation that are central to much higher education today.

The Sophists

Like the formal education that had gone before, the instruction offered by sophists benefited only a fairly small class of affluent students who could afford to pay. What the sophists had to offer, however, differed sharply from earlier education, for the sophists questioned the notion that deferential emulation of one's elders and betters was the noblest of achievements. They challenged conventional beliefs in other ways as well. One object of their explorations was the notion of ***nomos***.

Herodotus had shown in his history the centrality of nomos to society. The meaning of the word varied according to time and place. It meant both "law" and "custom"; Spartan society and the legislation of Solon were both considered to display ***eunomia*** ("good laws" or "good customs"). In many poleis, there were state-sanctioned nomoi forbidding burglary, but there were also social nomoi regarding what to wear at your wedding and religious nomoi about how to worship Apollo. In a society that had existed for centuries without written law, only a blurry line divided a legal nomos and a conventional nomos based on tradition. The two began to diverge, however, the harder people thought about the problem. Herodotus' *Histories* demonstrated two different sides of nomos. On the one hand, the Greeks had fought the Persians in order to live by nomos rather than at the whim of a despot. On the other hand, the multiplicity of nomoi in different cultures reveals a diversity that suggests that local customs are the product of tradition rather than of abstract, unchanging principles of right and wrong. It was to demonstrate the force of nomos in society that Herodotus had told the tale of Darius' conversation with the Greeks and the Callatian Indians about the proper disposal of the dead—cremation, or consumption. Each society, he concluded, considers its own customs to be best.

When this idea was assimilated to the speculations of the natural philosophers, an opposition evolved in many minds between the concepts of ***physis*** ("nature") and *nomos* ("convention"). The relationship between physis and nomos became central to Greek thought around Herodotus' time, for it carried powerful implications for the legitimacy of authority. If nomos was not the natural outgrowth of physis but actually existed in opposition to it, then the laws of the community were not necessarily to be obeyed, for they might have grown up randomly, endorsed by generations of unthinking traditionalists who had given no thought to their grounding in physis.

This concept of law varied conspicuously from the usual view that law ultimately came from the gods, and in fact the new ways of looking at the world had serious implications for relations between gods and mortals. One of the most renowned of the sophists who came to teach in Athens was Protagoras (c. 490–420 BC) of Abdera in northern Greece, who moved to Athens around 450 and spent most of the rest of his life there. He is best known for two sayings with religious implications. "Each individual person is the measure of all things—of things that are, that they are, and of things that are not, that they are not." Nobody, in other words, can tell you what is real or true—no state official, no parent, and no god. Another contention was still more provocative: it is impossible to know, Protagoras is said to have observed, "whether the gods exist, or how they might look if they do. Numerous obstacles stand in the way, such as the shortness of life and the difficulty of the subject matter."

Not all sophists had unconventional ideas about politics or society or religion. Plato represents Thrasymachus arguing that justice is nothing but the interest of the stronger, but Plato plainly did not like Thrasymachus. Xenophon reported that Hippias maintained that certain natural laws were common to all societies; if this is true, then Hippias did not see a conflict between nomos and physis. Some of what the sophists taught was simply practical knowledge that would be useful to an aspiring politician; they probably did know facts such as how far it was from Athens to Sparta and what sort of government ruled Corinth. Many sophists were highly esteemed in their birthplaces and in Athens, where they tended to wind up, but they also sparked hostility in many quarters. Their ideas about religion and authority seemed subversive, and people tended to associate them with thinkers like Anaxagoras, who, after all, had said that the sun was not a divinity but rather an extremely hot stone. In fact, those who associated the sophists' speculations in moral and social philosophy with developments in scientific thought were on to something, for behind both lay the same commitment to open-minded, rational inquiry into basic structures, the same interest in the connection of appearance to reality, the same curiosity about the relationship between the eternal and the changing. Parmenides' contention that motion was illusory had something in common with the questions the sophist Antiphon raised about the validity of distinctions between aristocrat and commoner, Greek and barbarian, and his conclusion that all grew alike by nature. (Similarly, Alcidamas argued that nature had made nobody a slave.)

More, however, lay behind the mistrust the sophists inspired. Some affluent Athenians were suspicious of people who took fees for anything, since inherited landed wealth was viewed as the most respectable form of income, followed by wealth earned by farming one's own land. Some of those who were less well off resented the sophists precisely because they could not afford to pay what the sophists charged. It was unclear, moreover, just what skill these people were teaching, and by what right they were charging their fees. It was easy to see how an experienced flute player could teach flute playing or how a gifted boxer could teach boxing, but it was harder to understand who was qualified to offer instruction in getting ahead in politics and in life. In many ways, the sophists were the "consultants" of ancient Greece, inspiring many people to wonder grouchily (and enviously) just what they were selling that was making them so rich.

There was an answer, however, to the question, "Just what do these people teach, anyway?" That answer was rhetoric, and not everyone liked it. No parent who has gone head to head with a smart-alecky teenager can fail to sympathize with middle-aged Athenians who found themselves confounded at every turn by the smugness of a new generation that had studied the arts of argumentation from experienced masters. Concern that clever speaking was coming to substitute for serious thinking about right and wrong, moreover, was not limited to the stodgy and the stuffy. Euripides, in his unsettling portrait of Jason in *Medea*, and Thucydides, in his representation of the dynamics of power politics, show a painful awareness of the problems created when rhetoric is deployed to distract the listener from plain old-fashioned principles of fairness. Protagoras himself, who won respect as an honorable man even from the antisophistic Plato, was reputed to be the first person to write a treatise in the techniques of argument and to claim that he knew how to make "the weaker argument the stronger." Works ascribed to him included *Contradictions* and *The Knockdown Arguments*.

Another popular sophist was Alcidamas' teacher Gorgias (c. 485–c. 380 BC), a native of Leontini in Sicily who visited Athens in 427 on an embassy that sought to persuade the Athenians to become involved in Sicilian affairs. Gorgias' name is associated almost exclusively with rhetoric; it is unclear whether he thought much about philosophy. One of his more famous pieces was a rhetorical tour de force in which he defended Helen against the charge of having caused the Trojan War by eloping with Paris. Gorgias lists three possible reasons for Helen's action, each of them exculpatory: "Either she did what she did because of the will of fortune and the plan of the gods and the decree of necessity, or she was seized by force, or persuaded by words," or, he later suggests, captured by love. All these possible explanations, he argues, get Helen off the hook:

> If she left for the first reason, then any who blame her deserve blame themselves, for a human's anticipation cannot restrain a god's inclination. For by nature the stronger is not restrained by the weaker but the weaker is ruled and led by the stronger....
>
> If she was forcibly abducted and unlawfully violated and unjustly assaulted, it is clear that her abductor, her assaulter, engaged in crime; but she who was abducted and assaulted encountered misfortune....it is right to pity her but hate him.

He then takes the occasion of discussing persuasion to expatiate on the charms of fine speaking, arguing that

> If speech persuaded and deluded her mind, even against this it is not hard to defend her or free her from blame as follows: speech is a powerful master and achieves the most divine feats with the smallest

and least evident body. It can stop fear, relieve pain, create joy, and increase pity. How this is so, I shall show; and I must demonstrate this to my audience to change their opinion....

How many men on how many subjects have persuaded and do persuade how many others by shaping a false speech!...The power of speech has the same effect on the disposition of the soul as the disposition of drugs on the nature of bodies. Just as different drugs draw forth different humors from the body—some putting a stop to disease, others to life—so too with words: some cause pain, others joy, some strike fear, some stir the audience to boldness, some benumb and bewitch the soul with evil persuasion.

("Encomium of Helen"; Gagarin and Woodruff)

Many Greeks believed there was no limit to what sophists would use rhetoric to defend. The anonymous treatise known as *Dissoi Logoi* (Double Arguments) reveals the moral relativism that many associated with sophists. Can sickness ever be good? Certainly, if you are a doctor. But what about death? Death is good for undertakers and gravediggers. The author goes on to demonstrate that no act is intrinsically good or bad by enumerating the many examples of cultural difference found in Herodotus. A mental universe in which nothing was purely good or patently evil was not one in which all Greeks wished to dwell.

For all these reasons, the sophists drew to themselves a considerable amount of odium. They found themselves under attack not only in conversation but on the stage. In 423, Aristophanes produced *The Clouds,* in which the intellectuals of Athens—the "eggheads"—are derided as teaching a corrosive rhetoric that made a mockery of decent, sensible values. The man Aristophanes identifies as running the "think shop" was not, however, a sophist. Like some of Aristophanes' other characters, he was a real person, but not one who taught rhetoric or accepted fees. He was Socrates, and the disposition to identify him with the sophists contributed in no small measure to his execution just after the end of the war.

THE PHYSICAL SPACE OF THE POLIS: ATHENS ON THE EVE OF WAR

The Greek world was both one and many: though common features tied the city-states together, each polis was unique in culture. As so often in attempts to recover the world of Classical Greece, however, the bulk of our knowledge about the development of the polis during the later decades of the fifth century comes from Athens. Even during the war, Athenian dramatists continued to produce masterpieces. Some of our best evidence about fifth-century Athens is physical, since the revenues of empire helped to adorn the imperial city with splendid buildings, many of which still impress and intrigue visitors today.

The Acropolis

A hill was a distinct advantage to a city-state. Though most people today associate the word "acropolis" with the Acropolis of Athens, in fact it was a feature common to many poleis, which relied for protection on a fortified citadel from which lookouts could see far into the distance. In Athens, the Acropolis was the spiritual focus of the polis. Because of its height and steeply sloped sides, this naturally fortified area had been the residence of early rulers and had always been home to the chief gods and legendary figures of the Athenians. The sixth-century tyrant Pisistratus, like Pericles later, initiated an ambitious building project on the Acropolis, because he understood not only that such work would provide steady employment to the restless urban poor, but also that a beautiful city would create still more jobs, foster patriotism among all citizens, and attract wealthy, talented metics. It would be, as Pericles would later say in the pages of Thucydides, "the school of Greece." The Persian invasion of 480 BC destroyed the monuments and statues of Pisistratus's time. This rubble, in turn, was used as the foundation of the buildings constructed in Pericles' day on the Acropolis, largely financed by funds from the Delian League.

Figure 7.5. This model of the Acropolis in the late fifth century BC shows the Panathenaic procession proceeding through the front gates (Propylaea), which are flanked on the right (south) by the temple of Athena Nike (Victory). The largest building is the Parthenon. The Erechtheum is on the left (north) of the Parthenon.

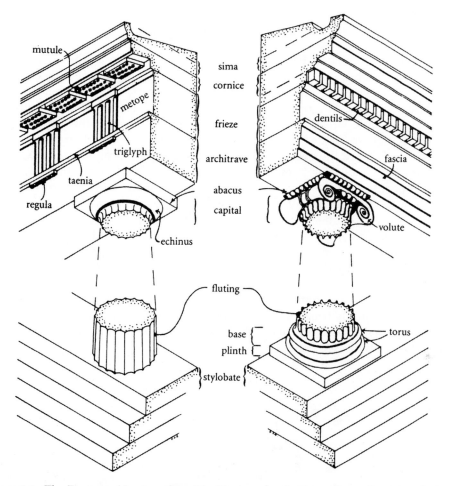

mutule

sima

cornice

metope

frieze

dentils

triglyph

architrave

fascia

taenia

abacus

regula

capital

volute

echinus

fluting

base

torus

plinth

stylobate

Figure 7.6. The Doric and Ionic orders. The Doric order (left) may be a direct translation into stone of building elements that were originally made of wood. The more complex capital of the Ionic order is a spiraled form known as a volute.

In the Classical period, the two principal architectural styles or orders were the Doric and Ionic. (The ornate Corinthian capital, though invented in Classical times, did not become popular until the Hellenistic period.) Both orders were used for the same building purposes, but they differed in details such as the shape of the columns and of their bases and capitals and in the features of the entablature, the structure that supported the roof. Architects strove to design buildings according to the principles of each order rather than to invent new or highly individualized styles. The pleasure they took in their work was not the sort of delight one might take today in striking out in original and startling directions.

Rather, Greek architects took from their work that special kind of satisfaction that comes from exercising creativity within the limits posed by an elaborate code of restraints. In this they resembled the tragedians.

The temple of Athena Parthenos ("the virgin"), known as the Parthenon, is the best known building of classical Greece. Replacing an older temple of Athena that was destroyed by Xerxes during the Persian Wars, it was a blend of Doric and Ionic elements. The rectangular structure with a ratio of eight columns on the front and back ends to seventeen on the sides was both aesthetically pleasing and appropriate to its commanding site on the acropolis. Greek architects knew that from a distance the eye would perceive straight vertical elements as thin in the middle and appearing to fall outward, and a horizontal foundation (stylobate) would appear to droop toward the center. As the Roman architect Vitruvius, who worked in the second half of the first century BC, explains, architects countered these illusions by subtle swelling (entasis) of the midportion of the columns, by tilting the columns and interior walls toward the interior lest they seem to be falling outward, and by increasing the height of the floor and steps toward the center. These refinements increase the impressions of solidity and height and some add strength to the building. Although except for the roof, the Parthenon was built of marble, like other Doric temples it preserves elements of earlier wooden construction, especially in the frieze, where the triglyphs imitate the ends of three planks standing on their sides and follow the rule that all the corners of the frieze must end with a triglyph (see Figure 7.6).

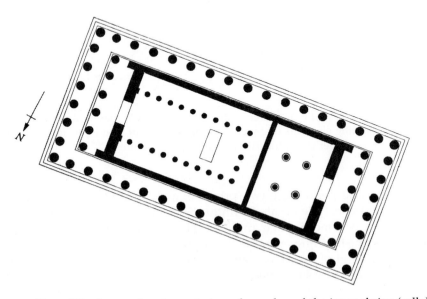

Figure 7.7. Plan of Parthenon showing exterior colonnade and the inner shrine (cella). The cult statue of Athena was kept in the cella, and the state treasury was stored in the back room.

Sculpture was an important feature of Greek architecture. The sculpture of the Parthenon depicted myths and history of Athena and Athens. The east pediment showed the birth of Athena, while the west pediment illustrated the contest between Athena and Poseidon over primacy in Athens. A sculpted frieze running around the top of the exterior wall of the cella, or inner shrine, showed human figures, horses, sacrificial animals, and the twelve Olympian gods. Probably the array of human figures and animals depicts the procession at the Great Panathenaic festival that was held every four years and the presentation of a new dress for the goddess by young girls who had helped weave it.

The temple was not a place where worshippers congregated, but rather the private home of a divinity, whose image was placed inside, and a storehouse for the cult's belongings. Thus, within the cella of the Parthenon was a tall figure of Athena constructed by fitting sheets of ivory and gold over a wooden scaffold. Locked in a back room were the goddess' possessions, among which were the treasury of the city of Athens and, after the middle of the fifth century, that of the Delian League as well. In front of the Parthenon on the west stood a huge bronze statue of Athena Promachus ("Athena the warrior who fights in the front"). The goddess was portrayed standing, with her left hand holding her shield and her

Figure 7.8. The Parthenon, constructed between 447 and 432 BC. In 1687, during the Ottoman Turkish occupation of Greece, an ammunition dump in the building was ignited by Venetian bombardment, and the resulting explosion did considerable damage to the structure and its sculptures.

Figure 7.9. Parthenon east frieze, slab V, a section of the continuous frieze running along the top of the exterior cella wall. The frieze probably shows the presentation of the dress known as the peplos for the old olive-wood cult image of Athena at the Panathenaea. Other portions show a cavalcade of horsemen, religious officials, sacrificial animals, and the Olympian gods. London, The British Museum.

right arm holding her spear. The statue was nearly 30 feet tall; sailors rounding Cape Sunium could see the welcome glint of sunlight off the tip of the spear. Like the statue inside the temple, it was the work of the sculptor Phidias. Viewed by his contemporaries as the greatest sculptor of gods, Phidias also created a huge gold and ivory statue of Zeus at Olympia that was considered to be one of the seven wonders of the ancient world.

In contrast to the Doric, which was massive, solid, and plain, the Ionic order gave a slender, graceful, ornate impression. The Erechtheum, sacred to Poseidon Erechtheus, was purely Ionic. The building consisted of three Ionic porches. To support the roof, the south porch, which faced the Parthenon, employed six figures of maidens, called caryatids, instead of plain columns. The building was begun in 421 BC, and because of the Peloponnesian War the decorations may never have been completed. Many other buildings, temples, statues, and votive offerings adorned the Acropolis. Though little remains of these monuments nowadays

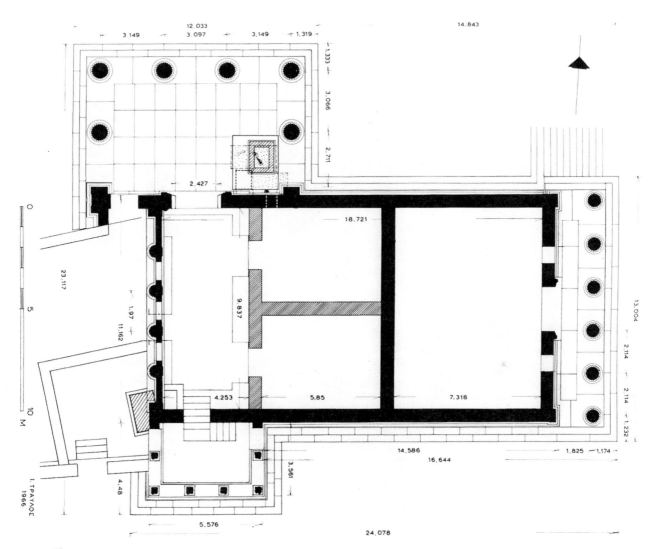

Figure 7.10 Plan of the Erechtheum (421–406 BC). This graceful temple was sacred to Athena, Poseidon, and the legendary Athenian king Erechtheus. The complicated shape was the result of needing to skirt Athena's sacred olive tree and to enclose Poseidon's trident mark and perhaps the tomb of Erechtheus.

except the bare marble framework of the major ones, in antiquity they were much more colorful; some of the architectural and sculptural features were painted red and blue and were covered with gold leaf. Below the Acropolis, dramas were staged in honor of the god Dionysus. Spectators sat in the open air in a semicircle on the bare hillside watching the performances that took place below in the orchestra ("dancing place").

Figure 7.11. The Erechtheum, built between 421 and 406 BC. Detail, showing the Porch of the Maidens (Caryatids), which faces the Parthenon. The statues have since been moved indoors to protect them from pollution; they were replaced with copies.

The structures that comprised Pericles' building program confirmed most Athenians in their support for the empire, for without the tribute pouring in from subject states, such lavish public monuments would have been difficult to finance. They also enhanced Pericles' popularity, providing jobs as well as beautifying the city. At the same time, they provided an opening for Pericles' enemies—personal rivals or those who disliked the march of democracy—to undermine him by calling into question the propriety of diverting League funds to the aesthetic improvement of the hegemonic city. Athenians countered this criticism by pointing out that they had virtually sacrificed their city during the Persian wars.

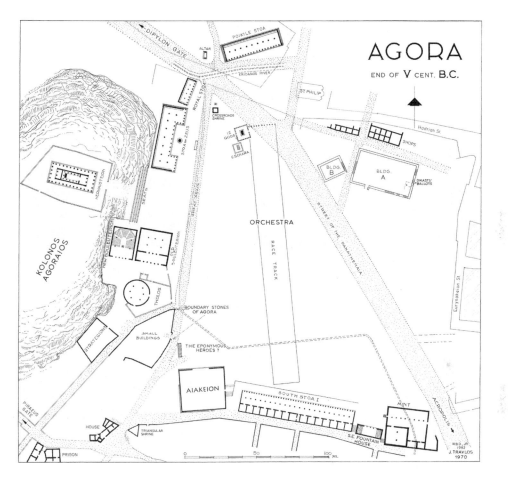

Figure 7.12. Plan of the Agora in the Classical period. Courtesy of American School of Classical Studies at Athens: Agora Excavations.

The Agora

The part of a Greek city known as the **agora** was principally a center for secular human activity, though the gods, who were never excluded from human activities, also had their place. The agora served as a market, as a meeting place for the exchange of goods and of news, and as a focus of social, political, and judicial activities. Daily life for women was ideally indoors and for men outdoors. Men who stayed indoors were suspected of being effeminate and antisocial, and women who ventured outdoors except for festivals and funerals were likely to have their chastity questioned. In the *Laws,* Plato noted that the greatest good in the polis is that the citizens be known to each other, as the men (certainly not the

Figure 7.13. Official standard weights and measures were available in the agora as a protection for the purchaser. These are examples of dry measures. American School of Classical Studies at Athens: Agora Excavations.

women) would be if they saw one another every day in the agora. Aristotle distinguished human beings from other living creatures by their use of speech (though, again, women were placed in a different category and are characterized as ideally silent). Speaking was essential for the activities that took place in the agora.

DOCUMENT 7.3

Aristotle in his Politics *explored the nature of political association and of the polis.*

From these considerations it is evident that the polis belongs to the class of things that exist by nature, and that man is by nature an animal intended to live in a polis. He who is without a polis, by reason of his own nature and not of some accident, is either a poor sort of being, or a being higher than man: he is like the man of whom Homer wrote in denunciation: "Clanless and lawless and heartless is he." The man who is such by nature [i.e., unable to join in the society of a polis] at once plunges into a passion for war; he is in the position of a solitary advanced piece in a game of draughts.

The reason why man is a being meant for political association, in a higher degree than bees or other gregarious animals can ever associate, is evident. Nature, according to our theory, makes nothing in vain; and man alone of the animals is furnished with the faculty of language. The mere making of sounds serves to indicate pleasure and pain, and is thus a faculty that belongs to animals in general: their nature enables them to attain the point at which they have perceptions of pleasure and pain, and can signify those perceptions to one another. But language serves to declare what is advantageous and what is the reverse, and it therefore serves to declare what is just and what is unjust. It is the peculiarity of man, in comparison with the rest of the animal world, that he alone possesses a perception of good and evil, of the just and the unjust, and of other similar qualities; and it is association in [a common perception of] these things which makes a family and a polis.

We may now proceed to add that [though the individual and the family are prior in the order of time] the polis is prior in the order of nature to the family and the individual.

Aristotle, *Politics* 1253a 9–12; Barker

The Athenian agora was a large level space at the foot of the Acropolis on the road from the main city gate. The area was cluttered with public buildings, of which the most easily identified is the round structure called the Tholos, which housed the boule and was where official weights and measures were stored. The agora was also the site of law courts, altars, shrines, statues, inscriptions, fountains, drains, and trophies of war. On the western border stood a Doric temple that was dedicated either to Hephaestus, the god of crafts, or to Theseus, the legendary hero and king of Athens. It has withstood the ravages of time far better than the Parthenon and is still in remarkably good condition. Roofed, multipurpose colonnades called stoas flanked the agora. Sandwiched between the permanent structures and within the stoas as well were shops, bankers' tables, booksellers, wholesale merchants, schools, and people buying and selling the necessities of life.

One important place in Athenian life was not a building. The hillside of the Pnyx, where the assembly met, towered above the city. Throughout the fifth century, citizens sat either on cushions or directly on the rocky ground that sloped from south to north, filling an area of 15,000 square feet. Around 400 BC, the meeting place was evened out and enlarged, and benches seem to have been added. The adult male citizens of Attica gathered in all kinds of weather to listen to speeches and debates, to make motions, and to hold high officials to account. In voting (which was by show of hands) they not only took into consideration what they had heard on the Pnyx but also made use of all the information they had garnered in the agora.

Rural Life in Attica

The growth of the urban center was not at the expense of rural areas. Public buildings were also located away from the city. Gymnasiums and stadiums that required plenty of level space were often found in the suburbs, which were cooler and shadier and closer to plentiful supplies of water than any venues that could be found in central Athens. Plato in one of his dialogues depicts Socrates and his friend Phaedrus conversing about philosophy and love as they walk barefoot through the countryside: "It's lucky I happen to be barefoot," says Phaedrus, "the way you always are. This way we can easily walk along the stream with our feet in the water, and it will be particularly pleasant at this time of year and at this time of day" (*Phaedrus* 229A). Cult centers and markets (as well as fortresses and other structures for defense) were scattered throughout Attica. The religious festivals that dotted the calendar year and were generally linked to the various phases of agricultural labor were often celebrated in the country as well as the city. The women's festival of the Thesmophoria, for example, could be enjoyed in the countryside in December. For some Athenians, it was an easy walk from city to country.

In the fifth century, probably three-quarters of the citizens, rich or poor, owned some rural property. Farming could be a part-time occupation and still produce enough food to provide sustenance for a family. Many people still lived in villages, were intensely identified with their rural demes, and depended on their family farms. Except for the spaces set aside for public activities, Athens was neither a beautiful city nor a comfortable one, and many propertied citizens were happy to leave it to artisans, to the urban poor, and to metics, who were not permitted to own land in Attica. Housing in the city center was flimsy, and sanitation poor. The city had merely grown up in the Archaic and Classical periods without conforming to a town plan. Streets were irregular, narrow, and filthy. These problems were exacerbated when the entire population withdrew inside the city walls during the Peloponnesian War. As Thucydides says,

> The Athenians for the most part belonged to independent homesteads throughout the countryside despite having united into a single city; and, because the ancients and their descendants had this ethos—lasting right up to the present war—of living all their lives on their lands, it was not easy for them to uproot their households, especially since they had recently finished restoring their property after the Persian Wars. They took it very hard and were deeply saddened to abandon the homes and family shrines which had been theirs since before the union of the Attican cities, and to be faced with giving up their way of life, and with having, each and every one, to forsake nothing less than his native city.
>
> (*The Peloponnesian War* 2.16)

The joys of country life were a common theme in the plays of Aristophanes. In his *Acharnians*, the farmer Dicaeopolis, sick of war, comes grudgingly to the city to work for peace, but all the time he yearns for home:

> I am always the first to come here
> And I sit alone, alone in the wide Assembly.
> ...but always I gaze

Out over the fields, craving for peace,
Hating this city, aching for my village
Where the cry isn't always *"Buy, haggle,* and *fleece,"*
But where there is give-and-take and a living for all.…
        (Aristophanes, *Acharnians* 28-29, 32-36; Dickinson)

Sentiment aside, however, not everyone could make a living in the countryside. Lean years could push a family to the edge of starvation. A speaker in an Athenian courtroom had painful things to say about a particularly bad season: "my land not only yielded no crops," he reported, "but that year, as all of you know, even the water dried up in the wells, with the result that not a single vegetable grew in the garden" (pseudo-Demosthenes, *Against Polycles,* 50.61). The wealthy owned estates and purchased slaves to exploit their land. They were able to store a surplus of supplies to tide them over in the lean years, and they certainly did not want their slaves to die of starvation. Even a small farmer was usually assisted by at least one slave, who constituted a major investment. Thus, a paradox of Athenian slavery is that sometimes slaves fared better than the free. In addition to the widespread use of slaves on the farmsteads, however, there were some twenty thousand slaves eking out short and wretched lives in the silver mines.

⇛————⇚

Thucydides, as we saw in Chapter 4, commented on the lavishness of Athens' monumental architecture and revealed his suspicion that its physical remains might lead observers to exaggerate its greatness vis-à-vis Sparta, where public space was filled by humbler structures. Certainly the substantial funds collected in imperial tribute made it possible for the Athenians to deck out their city with edifices of unusual elegance, but the underlying principles governing the allocation of space obtained in other poleis as well. Throughout the Greek world from Ionia to Sicily stood bustling city centers adorned with temples, government buildings, and agoras; some, like Olympia, had special connections to religion, whereas others, like Corinth, were great ports. Some cities, like Thurii, were carefully laid out; most just sprang up little by little, with streets at odd angles making it easy to get lost. Everywhere, the city and its surrounding countryside were interdependent, and residents traveled back and forth comfortably between the two areas. Commerce and agriculture were both central to the functioning of each polis.

Although commerce entailed a good deal of specialized labor, throughout Greece one sort of work was diffused throughout the male population, and that was fighting. Except in Sparta, Greek men generally worked on their the land (or, less often, in trade) in the winter and were available for military campaigns in the summer, serving in the infantry if they belonged to the propertied class or, in the case of poor men, rowing in the fleet. When fighting broke out between the Athenian and Spartan camps in 431, warfare began to claim an increasingly large share of people's time, energy, and worry. The ensuing social upheaval caused women to assume some responsibilities previously exercised by men. In time, the comfortable division of the year into fighting and nonfighting seasons evaporated, and during the last decades of the fifth century Greece found itself consumed by a protracted and debilitating war of unprecedented scope. Fighting, always an important element in Greek civilization, now came to be the organizing principle of life in the city-states.

Key Terms

Aeschylus	erōmenos	Panhellenism
agora	eunomia	Parthenon
Corcyra	Euripides	physis
Epidamnus	Hippocrates	Potidaea
epiklēros	mousikē	sanctions against Megara
erastes	nomos	sophist
Erechtheum	*Oeconomicus*	Sophocles

Suggested Readings

Beard, Mary. 2003. *The Parthenon*. Cambridge, MA: Harvard University Press. The history of the building from temple to medieval cathedral to mosque and armory, the transfer of the Elgin Marbles to Britain in the nineteenth century, and the twentieth-century restoration.

Boedeker, Deborah, and Kurt Raaflaub, eds., 1998. *Democracy, Empire and the Arts in Fifth-Century Athens*. Cambridge, MA: Harvard University Press. Collection of essays dealing with the relationship between empire and cultural achievements.

Camp, John M. 2001. *The Archaeology of Athens*. New Haven, CT: Yale University Press. A thorough discussion of this important subject by a scholar who has spent many years in Athens.

Camp, John M. 2010. *The Athenian Agora Site Guide*. 5th ed. Princeton, NJ: The American School of Classical Studies at Athens, 2010. A practical and detailed guide for visitors designed in the form of a tour and including both the history of the agora itself and the history of its excavation.

Foley, Helene P. 2001. *Female Acts in Greek Tragedy*. Princeton and Oxford: Princeton University Press. Nine essays dealing with the apparent contradiction between the depiction of tragic heroines and the actual role and status of Athenian women, with particular attention to women as moral agents.

Guthrie, W. K. C. 1971. *The Sophists*. Cambridge: Cambridge University Press. A brilliant study of the issues regarding the sophistic movement, excerpted from the author's six-volume *History of Greek Philosophy*.

Harris, William V. 1989. *Ancient Literacy*. Cambridge, MA: Harvard University Press. A survey of the evidence for literacy and the lack of it in ancient Greece and Rome.

Hurwit, Jeffrey M. 1999. *The Athenian Acropolis: History, Mythology, and Archaeology from the Neolithic Era to the Present*. New York: Cambridge University Press. An eminently readable history of the most famous hill in the Greek world.

Jones, Nicholas F. 2004. *Rural Athens Under the Democracy*. Philadelphia: University of Pennsylvania Press. A study of settlement patterns, rural homes, deme centers, rural festivals; the habits and religion of country dwellers, their image in literature, and their relationship to urban dwellers.

Kagan, Donald. 1969. *The Outbreak of the Peloponnesian War*. Ithaca, NY: Cornell University Press. The first installment in Kagan's four-volume history of the war.

Marincola, John. 2006. *The Greek Historians*. A highly readable survey of recent work on Herodotus and Thucydides as well as a study of their themes, sources and narrative methods.

McGregor, Malcolm. 1987. *The Athenians and Their Empire*. Vancouver: University of British Columbia Press. A history of the Athenians' dealings with their allies that takes a sympathetic view of imperialism.

Neils, Jenifer, ed. 1992. *Goddess and Polis: The Panathenaic Festival in Ancient Athens*. Hanover, NH: Hood Museum of Art, Dartmouth College. A collection of essays by Neils and others dealing with the history, performance, and artifacts associated with this festival.

Roberts, Jennifer T. 2011. *Herodotus: A Very Short Introduction*. Oxford, UK: Oxford University Press. A concise introduction to Herodotus's thinking about Greeks, Persians, and the many other peoples who made up the world he knew.

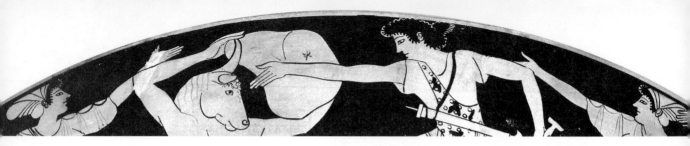

CHAPTER EIGHT

The Peloponnesian War

When war broke out between Athens and Sparta, few Greeks foresaw that it would be different from any war they had ever experienced or even imagined. The twenty-seven-year conflict cost thousands upon thousands of lives and proved a stern teacher. It enhanced many of the worst features of Greek society: competitiveness, jingoism, lack of compassion, and gross disregard for human life. At the same time, a number of extraordinary thinkers focused attention on the problems people face in their attempts to live together; the writings of Thucydides, Sophocles, and Euripides showed vigor and spirit throughout the war years, and the comic dramatist **Aristophanes** continued to produce enchanting plays through three decades of fighting and for a generation afterward—though a biting sorrow is often evident beneath the madcap facade. The Peloponnesian War would alter the world the Greeks knew in many respects. Comfortable assumptions about the citizen-fighter and his role in the polis would break down, and conventional morality and piety would face many challenges. Much, however, would stay the same, such as the polis as a political unit, the primacy of agriculture, the rivalries of the city-states, and the worship of the Olympian gods. The trauma occasioned by the war and its aftermath was also strikingly fertile, for the war supplied the impetus for many of the social, political, and intellectual changes we identify with the fourth century and the period after the death of Alexander in 323 BC that we call the Hellenistic Age.

SOURCES FOR GREECE DURING THE PELOPONNESIAN WAR

Thucydides writes with such eloquence and certainty that historians have had to struggle to challenge his conclusions and strike out on their own paths. His *History* is our principal source for the war. Although Thucydides tried to write each year up as it happened, understandably he began to fall behind as the war progressed, and at the time of his death around 395 BC he had gotten only as far as 411. Rumor had it that his daughter preserved the unfinished manuscript and gave it to Xenophon to edit. Whatever the truth of this, Xenophon picked up where Thucydides left off and wrote the history of Greece through the end of the war down to the year 362 (in the work called the *Hellenica*). Shortly after the war, Xenophon had the advantage of friendship with leading Spartans, including their king, Agesilaus. In the course of the trek through Asia Minor that he described in the *Anabasis,* he certainly would have heard war stories of soldiers and officers from cities other than Athens. After he returned to Greece, moreover, he was exiled from Athens and was settled by Agesilaus in Scillus near Olympia. His sons were apparently educated according to the Spartan system; thus Xenophon certainly understood the Spartans' methods of training soldiers and waging war.

The workings of Athenian democracy were explored in a pamphlet called *The Constitution of the Athenians*, whose unknown author is sometimes called the Old Oligarch; he is also sometimes called pseudo-Xenophon, since before the twentieth century historians believed he really was Xenophon. Hostile to democracy, the essay makes an interesting contrast with the happier view of Athenian government and society set forth in the famous funeral oration for the war dead that Thucydides ascribed to Pericles, and it offers a keen analysis of the distinctive dynamic of naval imperialism and its relationship to Athenian government.

Diodorus and Plutarch continue to be useful. Diodorus' treatment of the war survives intact, and Plutarch wrote the lives of the Athenian politicians **Nicias** and **Alcibiades** and of the Spartan commander **Lysander**. The sources Diodorus and Plutarch used include the fourth-century historians Theopompus and Ephorus, as well as Timaeus, who lived around 300 BC, and Philistus, who had been a boy in Syracuse at the time of the Athenian siege. Speeches delivered in court—or at least written for such delivery—throw considerable light on the later years of the war. Andocides, who was implicated in the religious scandals of 415, described his subsequent imprisonment in his speech *On the Mysteries*. Lysias, who came from a wealthy metic family and knew **Socrates**, wrote a number of speeches early in the fourth century that touched on events during the war and its aftermath; one (*Against Andocides*) attacked Andocides, and another (*Against Eratosthenes*) detailed his own misfortunes at the hands of the **Thirty Tyrants**, whom Sparta set up in Athens at the end of the war.

Although Sophocles produced *Oedipus Tyrannus* during the first years of the war and continued to write until his death in 406, the two playwrights who reveal most about what it was like to live in Athens during this war were the tragedian Euripides and the comic dramatist Aristophanes. Plays like Euripides' *Trojan Women* dealt with the sufferings occasioned by war through the vehicle of the Trojan War, and several of Aristophanes' wartime comedies made plain the immense deprivation of noncombatant men and women and their yearnings for peace. Some of the flavor of intellectual life in Athens can be gathered from Plato's and Xenophon's dialogues, which offer imaginative reconstructions of conversations Socrates held in Athens during the war with fellow Athenians, with metics, and with visiting luminaries such as the rhetorician Gorgias of Leontini or the sophist Protagoras of Abdera.

Finally, inscriptions continue to shed light on the workings of the Athenian empire, and archaeological and topographical investigations have been of some use in illuminating particular military campaigns—for example, that at Pylos on the west coast of the Peloponnesus in 425. On the whole, however, our ability fully to understand this era is compromised severely by the lack of surviving written evidence about this widespread war from any Greek state except Athens. One consequence of this imbalance has been that the Spartan-Athenian war derives the name by which it is known from the perspective of Sparta's enemy; though most of the battles were fought outside the Peloponnesus, for Athens it was the war against the Peloponnesians, and it has been known since antiquity as the Peloponnesian War. The Spartans' decision not to record their own story about the war has made it necessary for us to reconstruct it for them, working entirely from non-Spartan sources and largely from the writings of Thucydides, who may—or may not—have enjoyed contacts at Sparta after (or even before) his exile. Spartans miraculously brought back to life in our own time might be very surprised to learn how their wartime strategies have been imagined.

The Archidamian War (431–421 bc)

To many Greeks alive at the time, the decade of fighting that stretched from 431 to 421 seemed like a discrete entity in itself, and in fact this war has been given its own name—the Archidamian War, after the Spartan king and commander Archidamus. This is the only portion of the war in which any part was played by the man who was most closely associated with the Athenians' decision to fight, because Pericles died in 429.

The Periclean Strategy and the Plague

Pericles devised an ingenious strategy for winning a war he conceived as essentially defensive, and it is a measure of his influence and eloquence that he was able to persuade his fellow Athenians to do something so conspicuously at odds with human nature. Harassing Peloponnesian territory with their navy, the Athenians declined to participate in hoplite battle with the Spartans. At Pericles' instigation, the Athenian farmers abandoned their land, taking with them what few household goods could be loaded on wagons, and huddled with the city-dwellers inside the Long Walls that linked Athens to Piraeus, making the city, in effect, an

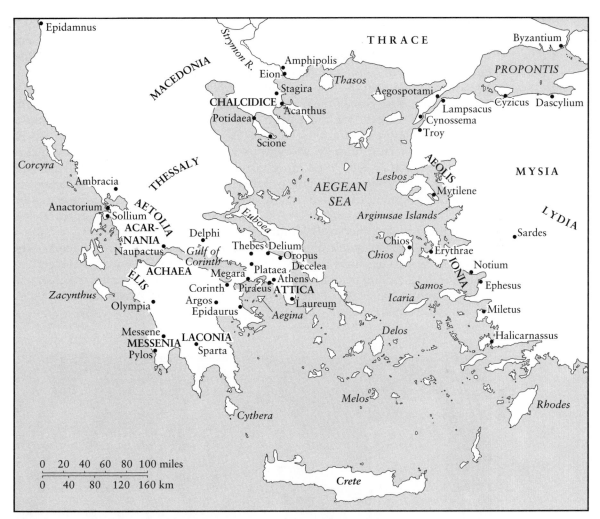

Figure 8.1. Theaters of operation during the Peloponnesian War.

island. Food and other necessary goods would continue to be imported by ship from throughout the empire. The enemy, Pericles calculated, would tire of ravaging the land when nobody came out to fight and would soon sue for peace. The Spartans, meanwhile, conjectured that the Athenians would grow restive cooped up in the overcrowded city throughout the campaigning season and, seeing their land being ravaged, would be unable to tolerate the frustration. They foresaw one of two consequences: the Athenians either would seek peace or would overrule Pericles and come out to fight. In foreseeing that the enemy would give up after a couple of years, both sides miscalculated badly, but there was nothing intrinsically foolish in their thinking.

It was with reluctance and apprehension that the Athenians abandoned their homes and the familiar temples nearby, and when the farmers arrived in Athens only a few were able to find shelter with friends or relatives. Most had to seek out empty space in the city or bunk down in temples and shrines. Some wound up spending summers in the towers along the walls.

Though the first year of the war saw few casualties, by tradition the Athenians held a public funeral for those who had died in war. This much we know: Pericles was chosen to offer the eulogy. How closely the stirring paean to Athens that appears in Thucydides' history approximates what Pericles actually said is another question. We have no other versions of this speech. It could represent Thucydides' accurate recollection of what was said, or a faulty recollection, or even a composition of his own. In any event, the speech we have focuses not on the dead themselves but on the city of Athens and the way of life it represents—a way of life that is defined as the antithesis of everything Spartan.

The organizing principle of the speech reveals much about Greek views of the state, for Pericles assumes that a wise form of government provides the cornerstone for the good life in all its manifestations. In this he is in complete agreement with the political theorists of the fourth century, Plato and Aristotle. Though they

Figure 8.2. Attic red-figure *stamnos* (storage jar), attributed to the Achilles Painter (c. 450–440 BC). An armed warrior, departing for battle, takes leave of family members. London, The British Museum.

disliked democracy, they certainly shared Pericles' conviction that the *politeia* (a kind of government or "constitution") a state chooses will have the widest ramifications for the nature of its citizens and the spirit of its communal life.

The speech has a markedly defensive, indeed jingoistic tone. Its purpose seems to be to counter suggestions that an easygoing polis such as Athens, with its love of words, of ideas, and of beauty, could not compete successfully in war with a highly regulated, militarized society like Sparta, where words are despised as a hindrance to action, people have little choice about how they live their lives, and anxious secrecy is the order of the day. "We love nobility without ostentation," Pericles says,

> and we have a virile love of knowledge. Furthermore, wealth is for us something to use, not something to brag about. And as to poverty, there is no shame in admitting to it—the real shame is in not taking action to escape from it. Finally, while there are those who manage both the city and their own private affairs, there are others, who though wrapped up in their work, nevertheless have a thorough knowledge of public affairs.... For we are the only people who regard a man who takes no interest in politics to be leading not a quiet life but a useless one. We are also the only ones who either make the governmental decisions or at least frame the issues correctly, because we do not think that action is hampered by public discourse but by not learning enough in advance, through discourse, about what action we need to take.
>
> ...
>
> To sum up, I tell you that this city, taken all in all, is the school of Greece, and as far as I am concerned, any man among us will exhibit a more fully developed personality than men elsewhere and will be able to take care of himself more gracefully and with the quickest of wit.
>
> (*The Peloponnesian War* 2.40–41)

Pericles' concluding charge to the women of Athens sat oddly on the lips of a man who lived with a companion far more visible and renowned than many of his fellow politicians:

> And since I must also make some mention of womanly virtue to those who will now be widows, I will define it in this brief admonition: your greatest fame consists in being no worse than your natures, and in having the least possible reputation among males for good or ill.
>
> (*The Peloponnesian War* 2.45)

This is certainly striking advice in a society as loquacious as the one Thucydides depicts in Athens. It is posited on a notion of woman as in every way the opposite of political man, in whose mind reputation counted for practically everything.

The next year saw two entirely predictable events and one unexpected development. The invasion of Attica by the allied forces of the Peloponnesian League and the harassment of the Peloponnesian coast by the Athenian navy were becoming routine, but nobody could have foreseen the horrific plague that attacked the population of Athens. Its origin is unknown, as is its precise nature, though typhus seems increasingly likely. It spread rapidly in the crowded, unsanitary environment of a city packed to capacity and beyond. Probably about a third of the populace died. Thucydides, who himself fell ill but recovered, took pains to record everything he could about the course and symptoms of the illness so that it would be possible for readers to recognize the disorder should it ever reappear.

In many ways, Thucydides' meticulous account of the disease and its behavior is a microcosm of his history as a whole, revealing his passionate interest in chronicling events that seem to him to have broad significance, reflecting as they do patterns in events, and his belief that accurate accounts of such occurrences would be useful in the future. Beginning with a detailed account of the symptoms of the disease—the oral bleeding, the bad breath, the painful vomiting, the burning skin, the insomnia, the memory loss, the often fatal diarrhea—he goes on to describe the way in which people reacted to the disease. Those who recovered from the illness, sensing that they were now proof against it, not only nursed the sick but "in the jubilance of the moment held the vain belief that they would never die from any other disease in the future, either." Most, however, took a darker view of life, as the overwhelming catastrophe seemed to obviate the necessity for observing customary moral and religious norms. The disease, Thucydides wrote, "initiated a more general lawlessness in the city" as people

> decided to go for instant gratifications that tended to sensuality because they regarded themselves and their property as equally short-lived. No one was willing to persevere in received ideas about "the good" because they were uncertain whether they would die before achieving it. Whatever was pleasurable, and whatever contributed to pleasure, wherever it came from, that was now the good and the useful. Fear of the gods? The laws of man? No one held back, concluding that as to the gods, it made no difference whether you worshipped or not since they saw that all alike were dying; and as to breaking the law, no one expected to live long enough to go to court and pay his penalty. The far more terrible verdict which had already been delivered against them was hanging over their heads—so it was only natural to enjoy life a little before it came down.
>
> (*The Peloponnesian War* 2.53)

Demoralized by the plague and frustrated by being forbidden to march out and offer battle, some Athenians tried to open negotiations for peace with the Spartans, defying Pericles' wishes and in fact voting to fine him and depose him from the strategia. Nothing much happened when Pericles was out of office except the long-awaited surrender of Potidaea. Finding that other leaders conducted the war no better, the Athenians returned Pericles to office at the next elections. Then he caught the plague and died, leaving the Athenians to their own devices.

Cleon and Diodotus: The Revolt of Mytilene (428–427 BC)

The 420s saw a change in the character of Athenian government. Though no formal distinctions divided rich from poor or separated social classes, still until the war Athenians had felt most comfortable with political power in the hands of men from old, aristocratic families—men like Cimon and Pericles. Now this ceased to be true. Richer men still had the advantage in elections for the generalship, but increasingly men whose fathers and grandfathers had recently made money in business began to compete successfully with those whose families had been living off their landholdings for generations. New words, moreover, crept into discussions of Athenian politics: *dēmagōgos* and its relative *dēmagōgia*, which first appears in the surviving literature in Aristophanes' *Knights*, produced in 424 BC. It literally means a "leader of the people"—surely there is nothing wrong in that—but in the hands of class-conscious critics the word *dēmagōgos* came to signal a calculating politician who manipulated the voters for his own ends rather than letting himself be guided by patriotism and principle. In reality, however, there is no way to be sure of people's motives, and sometimes the word just betrays the class prejudice of the writer using it. Thucydides described Pericles as leading the Athenian people rather than being led by them. Did this mean Pericles was a demagogue too?

Foremost among the men who came to be identified as demagogues was Cleon. Deliberately cultivating an antiaristocratic persona, Cleon (d. 422) was the brash and outspoken owner of a successful tannery, a messy, smelly sort of place that no gentleman would deign to enter. He was the first of several leading politicians at Athens who commanded respect in the assembly without having held the generalship. Before Cleon, politicians had always served as strategoi even if, like Pericles, they had not greatly distinguished themselves in the field. Cleon, however, who was a talented public speaker, had become influential already in Pericles' lifetime and was probably the most powerful politician in Athens during the years after his death (though he never attained Pericles' stature or exercised comparable authority).

In 428, when the fortunes of war had been shifting back and forth for three years, the Spartans received some very good news. Four of the five cities on the island of Lesbos were revolting from the Athenian empire. Led by Mytilene, the revolt was particularly unexpected since, along with Chios, Lesbos was one of the two remaining so-called autonomous members of the empire, that is, a member that provided its own ships for the navy rather than being assessed in tribute money. The **revolt of Mytilene** indicates how powerful was the desire for independence, even for the most privileged members of the Athenian empire.

The Athenian alliance appeared to be coming apart at the seams, and the Spartans were happy to grant the Mytileneans' request for alliance and assistance. The promised aid, however, never materialized, and in 427 the Mytileneans surrendered. The discussion in the Athenian assembly about what to do with the capitulated rebels first brings Cleon alive in the pages of Thucydides. The Athenians initially voted to put all the men in Mytilene to death and to sell the women and children into slavery, and they dispatched a boat to bring the news to Paches, the general in command on the island. The next day, however, some people at least had second thoughts, and a debate ensued. Cleon shows a cocky self-assurance in the dismissive way he addresses his audience: "I, for my part," he begins, "have often noticed before that democracies cannot rule over others, but I see it especially now in these regrets of yours about Mytilene..." (3.37). Deriding the Athenians for their openness and flexibility, he advocates a policy of harsh consistency. Bad laws that stay the same, he insists, are better than good ones that change. His studied anti-intellectualism contrasts pointedly with the praise of deliberation and debate in Pericles' funeral oration delivered three years earlier: ordinary people, Cleon says, "run their cities far better than intelligent ones, for these want to seem wiser than the laws and to top whatever nonsense is said in public assemblies.... They are the downfall of cities because of this sort of thing" (3.37). In other respects, however, Cleon for all his crassness is plainly Pericles' heir. "You don't understand," he says, "that you hold your empire as a tyranny and that your subjects are schemers who are governed unwillingly" (3.37). Compare Pericles in his last speech: "You hold your empire like a tyranny by now. Taking it is thought to have been criminal; letting it go would be extremely dangerous" (2.63).

Diodotus, who is otherwise unknown, spoke against proceeding with the original plan, making a marvelous argument grounded in human psychology. Deterrence, he contended, was not as effective as commonly believed, because people who undertake risky ventures do so in the expectation that they will succeed, not fail. Furthermore, he argued, there was no merit in killing people even when they had surrendered, for to do so removed any incentive for surrender in future rebellions. He then made a key observation about the dynamics of the empire. "So far," he maintained,

> the populace in all of the cities is well-inclined toward you. Either
> they do not join in rebellion with the oligarchs, or, if they are forced
> to do so, they quickly turn against them. Thus, when you go to war
> you have the populace of the city you are attacking on your side.
> (*The Peloponnesian War* 3.47)

Though some might debate the accuracy of Diodotus' contention, it certainly makes us think twice about Thucydides' claim that the Athenian empire was universally detested in the subject cities.

Diodotus won the day, and a second boat was sent out to overtake the first. Envoys from Mytilene provided extra rations for the rowers and promised a large reward if they arrived in time. As it happened, the rowers on the original boat had been in no hurry to announce the impending doom, and the second boat managed to arrive just as the death sentence was being announced. Instead of putting all the men to death and enslaving all the women and children, the Athenians executed the ringleaders of the revolt—apparently more than a thousand men.

The War Continues

Meanwhile misery and death prevailed elsewhere in Greece. Frustrated in their attempts to unite Boeotia under Theban leadership as Athens had united Attica, the Thebans particularly hated the Plataeans because of their friendship with Athens. In 427 they persuaded the Spartans to destroy Plataea, killing those who had not managed to escape to Athens. At the same time, a particularly vicious civil war broke out in Corcyra. This conflict was so bloody and impassioned that both sexes took part, women throwing roof tiles as the women of Plataea had done in trying to prevent a Theban takeover in 431. As Thucydides points out, the war raging throughout Greece intensified the long-standing tensions between the ordinary citizens, who resented the wealth of the elite, and the aristocrats, who considered a lavish lifestyle to be their birthright, for the former could expect help from Athens and the latter from Sparta. The result was *stasis* ("civil strife") more frequent and ferocious than ever before. Thucydides describes the agony that ensued when the democratic party gained the upper hand and, as allies of the demos, the Athenians under their admiral Eurymedon made no move to curtail the butchery. To avoid death at the hands of the democrats, some oligarchic partisans

> hanged themselves from trees. Others killed themselves in any way they could. Eurymedon remained at Corcyra for seven days with his sixty ships, during which the Corcyraeans ceaselessly slaughtered those among them whom they thought to be enemies.... One saw every imaginable kind of death, and everything that is likely to take place in situations like this did, in fact, take place—and even more. For example, fathers killed their sons; people were dragged from the temples and slaughtered in front of them; some were even walled up in the temple of Dionysus and left to die.
>
> (*The Peloponnesian War* 3.81)

While operating in the west, the Athenians initiated a spectacular project that would not determine the outcome of the war but nonetheless had dramatic short-term effects. Detained by bad weather, the Athenian strategos Demosthenes (not to be confused with the famous fourth-century orator by the same name) decided to build a fort at Pylos, the legendary home of Nestor. This promontory combined with the narrow island of Sphacteria to enclose a body of water known today as the Bay of Navarino.

Fearing that Sphacteria might fall into Athenian hands, the Spartans positioned 420 hoplites on the island. When the Athenians defeated the Spartans in naval

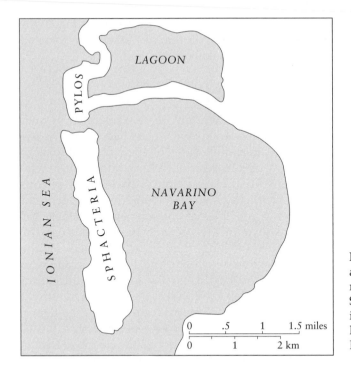

Figure 8.3. The Athenians achieved a great coup by marooning hundreds of Spartan soldiers on the island of Sphacteria, which lies off the west coast of the Peloponnesus.

combat, effectively marooning the hoplites on Sphacteria, the Spartan government panicked and sent envoys to Athens to plead for an armistice. So limited was the number of Spartans that their government was willing to do anything to get those hoplites back—even make a peace that took no account of their allies' interests. On the advice of Cleon, the Athenians refused, whether out of overconfidence or because they feared the fallout from a hasty peace that ultimately excluded key players on the Spartan side like Corinth and Thebes.

The Spartans, then, remained on Sphacteria, and when Cleon made disparaging remarks about the failure of Athens' generals to capture them, he took for his particular target the respected strategos Nicias. A wealthy and pious man, Nicias had impressed many Athenians by the lavish sums he spent on religious festivals, and his base of support lay with Athens' richer and more conservative voters—the sort of men who despised Cleon. Pointing his finger at Nicias, Thucydides reports, Cleon "said scornfully that if the generals were real men they could easily set out with an armada and capture the troops on the island. If he were in command, he continued, that was what he would do" (4.27). Nicias promptly suggested that Cleon himself be given a special commission to go to Pylos and get hold of the stranded hoplites. Against the expectation of upper-class Athenians, the inexperienced Cleon not only accepted the commission but worked well with Demosthenes; and to the astonishment of all Greeks, the Spartan soldiers surrendered rather than fight to the death. Since 128 of the Peloponnesians had been killed in the fighting, the Athenians now had 292 bargaining chips with which to negotiate an end to the war. Of these the most valuable were the 120 full-blooded Spartiates, "equals." Seeing their position strengthened by the possession of hostages, the Athenians resolved to keep fighting rather than make peace. This was probably a mistake, for any peace that Sparta made to regain its men was likely to alienate its allies and foster the disintegration of the Peloponnesian League.

The presence of Spartan hostages at Athens put an end to the annual invasions of Attica, but the war did not end. Now, growing in confidence because they had compelled Spartan hoplites to lay down their arms, the Athenians began experimenting with substantial departures from Pericles' strategy, sending out infantry to face the enemy in battle. A sound defeat by the Boeotians at Delium in 424 dampened the high spirits sparked by the success at Pylos; the philosopher Socrates, fighting in the ranks, might well have been killed had he not been rescued by his admirer, the young Alcibiades. Athenian losses farther north added strength to the Spartan cause even while Spartan soldiers remained captive in Athens. For the Spartans had discovered what they had previously lacked, at least since the loss of Archidamus around 427: a charismatic general. As talented an orator as he was a strategist, Brasidas, by his campaigns in Chalcidice, very nearly won the war for Sparta, just as Demosthenes and Cleon had nearly won it for Athens at Pylos.

Brasidas and Chalcidice (424–422 BC)

Athens' hold on Chalcidice had always been fragile, and when some Chalcidic towns that had requested Spartan aid were joined in their appeal by Athens' on-again, off-again ally Perdiccas of Macedonia, the Spartans promptly dispatched the dynamic Brasidas. Once in Chalcidice, Brasidas was able to persuade the towns of Acanthus, Stagirus, and Argilus of Sparta's sincerity as a liberator and to induce them to revolt from Athens.

Figure 8.4a. This bronze shield found in the Athenian agora bears an inscription identifying it as booty the Athenians took from the Spartans at Pylos in 425–424 BC. Athens, Agora Museum.

Figure 8.4b. Line drawing of the shield in Figure 8.4a showing the inscription.

Though Brasidas had accomplished much for Sparta, the greatest prize lay ahead: the Athenian stronghold of Amphipolis. This was Brasidas' principal target, and he brought it over to the Spartan side in the space of one night. Horrified by this loss, the Athenians impeached one of their generals who had been offshore at Thasos when the catastrophe occurred:, the historian Thucydides. Whether he was exiled or sentenced to death in absentia we do not know, but he was certainly compelled to leave Athens. The events of that snowy December evening in the north played a large role in determining just what form Thucydides' history of the war, already begun, would take. Just as they cut off the opportunity for hearing speeches delivered in the assembly and for picking up the latest scuttlebutt in the agora, they also ensured that Thucydides, freed from civic responsibilities and perhaps more trusted by foreigners now that he was on the outs with the home government, would have more reliable non-Athenian sources. Thucydides seems to know a great deal about Brasidas' thinking, for example; perhaps the two men got to know each other.

The following spring (423) the Athenians and the Spartans signed a year's armistice that was respected in most parts of Greece. Trouble continued in Chalcidice, however, where the city of Scione revolted to Sparta, probably before learning of the truce. When the armistice expired in 422, it was in Chalcidice that fighting resumed. There Cleon, now a regularly elected general, met Brasidas in battle at Amphipolis, deciding not to wait for reinforcements from Perdiccas, who had returned to the Athenian fold. Greek generals fought in the front lines, and in the fighting both Cleon and Brasidas were killed.

The door to peace, then, was opened by the deaths of the men the comic poet Aristophanes called the pestles who were grinding down Greece's cities in the mortar of war. Athens and Sparta had both had enough. Agriculture in Attica had been severely disrupted, and with it the trade between city and countryside that was the foundation of polis life; moreover, the Athenians were unsettled by the patent unrest throughout their sphere of influence in the north. Sparta was nervous about continuing its war with Athens when the Spartan–Argive truce of thirty years was on the verge of expiring. A number of Spartan soldiers had died in captivity in Athens, and the Spartans were extremely eager to recover the survivors. Both sides were disturbed by the degree to which they had been compelled to hire mercenaries to keep the war going; it seemed like a bad precedent, and it was costly. The other key players on the diplomatic scene, however—Corinth, Megara, and Boeotia—had somewhat less to gain from peace in general (although they had also experienced devastation during the war), and nothing to gain from the particular peace on which the Athenians and Spartans agreed. In fact, they refused to sign it. The highly problematic agreement known as the Peace of Nicias (named for the principal Athenian negotiator, Cleon's old rival) was essentially a victory for Athens.

THE RISE OF COMEDY

While Spartan sources for attitudes toward the war are lacking, comic drama supplies considerable evidence for Athenians' feelings. Although comedy may have begun in the sixth century in Athens and to the west (in Megara and even Syracuse), and the first victory accorded to a comic poet at the City Dionysia was recorded in 486 BC, it was only during the Peloponnesian War that the genre we know as Old Comedy erupted on the Athenian stage. (The name distinguishes it from New Comedy, which began in the late fourth century.) Comic dramas were produced twice a year in Athens, both times in competitions among several dramatists at festivals of the god Dionysus. The only complete plays that survive were written by the comic genius Aristophanes (c. 450–385 BC).

Unlike the tragedians, Aristophanes did not take his plots from mythology; rather, his story lines were firmly grounded in the culture and politics of his day. Everything he saw around him was grist for his mill—pretentious teachers, overactive law courts, pompous aristocrats from the horsy set, and self-interested politicians whom he blamed for the chaos and misery of life in Athens during the Peloponnesian War. Not even the illustrious Pericles was spared. In the *Acharnians* he was pilloried for starting the war because some Megarians stole two of his mistress Aspasia's prostitutes! Like many Athenians, Aristophanes dreamed of an earlier day when role models were provided by the "men of Marathon" rather than by silver-tongued sophists, and a number of his plots involved protagonists who felt just as he did. Typical was the madcap scheme hatched in *The Birds*, in which two alienated Athenians take refuge up in "Cloudcuckooland" in the sky, plot out a utopian society, and, with the aid of their newfound feathered friends, come to rule the world in accord with their own principles. Naturally, the chorus sported beaks for the occasion; in *The Wasps*, which parodied the courts, chorus members representing jurors were outfitted with suitably phallic "stings." As in tragedy, all parts in comedy were played by men, so that in the *Ecclesiazusae* (*Women in Congress*), where women disguised themselves as men in order to take over the assembly, what the audience really saw was men disguised as women dressing up as ... men.

Obscene and boisterous, decked out with outlandish costumes (see, for example, Figure 8.5), and packed with mentions of bodily functions and scurrilous sexual conduct, Aristophanes' plays also manifest a tender love of the countryside, a nostalgia for a simpler time, and a sober commitment to peace. Though Aristophanes' comic genius was unique, his values must have been congenial to the community; the decision whether to grant a chorus for training lay with the city magistrates, and of course prizes were awarded by citizen judges.

The Peace of Nicias and the *Peace* of Aristophanes (421 BC)

In 421, with an end to the war in sight, Aristophanes wrote his *Peace*; by the time it was presented, the treaty was close to becoming a reality. Here, parodying a lost play by Euripides, Aristophanes shows his protagonist Trygaeus riding on a huge dung beetle to the house of Zeus (accomplished on stage by a beam and pulley) to inquire why Zeus is destroying Greece by war. There he learns from Hermes that the gods have been alienated by the two sides' childish squabbling. The audience cannot have been entirely comfortable with Hermes' evenhanded allotment of blame. The gods, he says,

> were frequently for peace.
> But you guys wanted war. Laconians,
> when once they got a little piece of luck,
> would say, "By God, those Atticans will pay!"
> Or if it seemed that luck was on your side,
> and then the Spartans came about a peace,
> at once you'd cry: "We're being taken in!
> Athena! Zeus! we can't agree to this!
> If we hang on to Pylos, they'll come back...."
> (Aristophanes, *Peace* 211–219)

He then explains that War has imprisoned Peace in a cave and, having obtained a huge mortar in which to grind down all the Greek cities, has sent his slave Tumult in search of pestles. Tumult, however, has learned that Athens and Sparta have recently lost their pestles—Cleon and Brasidas. Perhaps, then, there is some hope of setting Peace free.

Trygaeus finally persuades Hermes to help him organize the rescue of Peace. This is no mean task, since it is difficult to get all the Greeks to pull together on the necessary ropes even with divine assistance, but in time their efforts are successful. The blessings Peace will bring are celebrated in terms that reflect the concerns of the Athenian farmers in the audience:

> Trygaeus: Fellow farmers! Stop and listen! Can you hear these wondrous words?

Figure 8.5a. Attic red-figure *chous* (wine jug), attributed to the Nicias Painter (c. 410 BC). Old Comedy and its costumes appear to be reflected on this vase, which depicts Nike (Victory) driving Heracles in a chariot pulled by centaurs. Paris, The Louvre.

Figure 8.5b. Other side of the same vase, showing that the centaurs are preceded by a comic actor carrying two torches. Paris, The Louvre.

No more spears, men, no more javelins, no more fighting with our
    swords!
We've got peace with all its gifts now, we can trade in all that arming
For a happy, happy song as we march home to do some farming.
Chorus: What a day, not just for farmers but for anyone worthwhile:
What a yearned-for, hoped-for vision! See how joyously I smile
As I think about how soon I'll see the vines upon my land;
And the fig-trees that I planted as a youth with my own hand!
                    (Aristophanes, *Peace* 551–558)

The terms of the real-life peace were to be observed for fifty years. Athens was
to keep the empire with which it had entered the war; the treaty contained the
expression "the Athenians and their allies." Sparta was to return Amphipolis,
while Athens would abandon Pylos and the island of Cythera, which it had seized
in 424, and release all prisoners of war. Though at tremendous cost in money
and human lives, the Athenian war goal had been met: the Spartans had failed to
destroy the empire. Without even trying, the Athenians had done much to weaken
the Peloponnesian League. After a grueling war of ten years Sparta had suffered
loss of life and loss of prestige, and now it was about to lose its allies as well.

The disintegration of the Peloponnesian League might have proven helpful to
the Athenians, had the terms of the limited peace been respected. When Argos
decided not to renew its treaty with Sparta and the Spartans responded by nervously signing a fifty-year alliance with Athens, the position of the Athenians
seemed quite enviable. But Sparta had exaggerated its ability to control its allies.
Angry that no substantial damage had been done to the Athenian empire and
that two cities on the west coast, Sollium and Anactorium, remained in Athenian
hands, Corinth refused to sign the peace. Megara would not sign an agreement
that allowed the Athenians to retain its port Nisaea—as the Spartans should have
foreseen. The Boeotians, furious at the order to relinquish the border fortress of
Panactum to the Athenians, not only declined to sign the treaty but demolished
Panactum rather than give it back. The Amphipolitans refused to return to the
Athenian empire and even began revering Brasidas as their founder rather than
their actual founder, the Athenian Hagnon. In retaliation, the Athenians held on
to Pylos, and in the end, the chance for a productive alliance between the two
most powerful states in Greece was lost. The years that followed were tense,
and Thucydides viewed the Peace of Nicias as a false peace, a troubled interlude
before the resumption of hostilities.

BETWEEN PEACE AND WAR

Though the Athenians and Spartans who desired peace wanted it very badly
indeed, they had to contend with formidable countervailing forces. Effectively
excluded from the peace of 421, Sparta's most powerful allies posed a serious
threat to the welfare of Greece. Danger also came from individuals within the hegemonic states. Two ephors, Cleobulus and Xenares, schemed with the Corinthians

and Boeotians to bring Argos over to the Spartan side and set the stage for continuing the war. In Athens, the ambitions of one memorable Athenian had a powerful impact on the course of events. As a rule, it is dangerous to accord too large a role to high-profile individuals in shaping the course of history. At times, however, a particular person does seem to bear an extraordinary share of the responsibility for the way things turn out. Such was the case with the flashy Athenian aristocrat Alcibiades. Strategos for the first time in 420, Alcibiades had little prospect of making a name for himself in a tranquil world. His future glory was contingent on the disintegration of the fragile peace. To Alcibiades, even more than to the average Greek aristocrat, a life without glory was no life at all.

Alcibiades, Renegade Aristocrat

Alcibiades had been three years old when his father died, and he was raised in the home of his relative Pericles. Handsome, witty, athletic, charming, and sensuous, he was eagerly courted by lovers of both sexes. His rakish personality and flamboyant lifestyle were conducive to anecdote, and Plutarch tells several stories illustrating the opposition between the responsibility of Pericles and the irresponsibility of his irreverent ward. One day, it seems, when Alcibiades had grown up and wished to speak to Pericles, he

> went to his house, but was told Pericles was unable to see him, as he was considering how best to present his accounts to the Athenian people. "Would it not be better," Alcibiades asked, "for him to spend his time considering how to avoid presenting accounts to the people at all?"
>
> (Plutarch, *Life of Alcibiades* 7)

Alcibiades never did like rules. His passions included his teacher Socrates, the breeding and racing of horses, and indeed competition in all its forms, on and off the track. His wealthy family (whose genealogy we have diagrammed in Chapter 6, Figure 6.9) had connections abroad, and despite his relationship to Pericles, his grandfather had been the Spartan *proxenos* at Athens—the man charged with representing Spartan interests in his home state. To the family connections that were his by birth, he added a marriage connection: his wife, Hipparete, belonged to one of the most prominent and wealthy families in Athens.

At first it appeared that Alcibiades' interest in reactivating the war would come to nothing. Although Elis and Mantinea joined the alliance Athens had formed with Argos, Sparta managed to defeat the new grouping in battle, scoring a decisive victory at Mantinea in 418 BC, and also succeeded in mending fences with its disaffected allies Boeotia and Corinth, thus in effect restoring the Peloponnesian League. Meanwhile, tensions ran high among the various would-be leaders in Athens. An ostracism might have decided the rivalry of Alcibiades and Nicias, the hawk and the dove, but the two men seem to have panicked and mobilized their supporters to turn on a third man, Hyperbolus, instead.

This was not what the Athenians had had in mind when they first employed the system of ostracism. Cheated in their attempt to be rid of a truly powerful politician (preferably from a distinguished family), they endorsed the sentiment of a contemporary comic poet who quipped, "The man, indeed, deserved the fate, but not the fate the man," and they never held another ostracism. Instead, they turned to a different, less peculiar strategy for ensuring democratic control on government. Around this time they begin utilizing the *graphē paranomōn* ("indictment for illegal proposals") to punish politicians who brought forward proposals in conflict with existing laws. Like ostracism, however, this procedure was often used politically—a development that is not surprising, since, without a written constitution or bill of rights, only a highly subjective judgment could determine what new laws were and were not in harmony with the old.

The Destruction of Melos (416 BC)

The years that followed were marked by conflict in Athens and chaos in the Peloponnesus. Argos switched alliances more than once, and both Alcibiades and Nicias had sufficient support to be elected two of the strategoi for 417–416. A disturbing Athenian naval expedition stands out from these troubled years, memorialized in some of the most frequently read pages in Thucydides. In 416, probably at the instigation of Alcibiades, the Athenians decided to bring the little island of Melos under their control. The only island in the Cyclades that had stood aloof from their alliance, Melos had technically remained neutral in the war but had given Sparta a small sum for the war effort. A Spartan colony, Melos definitely leaned to the Peloponnesian side, but Athens and Sparta were not really at war any longer, and **Melos** was of no strategic significance. It is unclear what Athens had to gain by subjugating Melos besides the satisfaction of making an example of the uncooperative Melians; but for whatever reason, Athenian ships were dispatched to Melos to order its inhabitants to enter their alliance. Hope of Spartan assistance moved the Melians to turn Athens down. The episode plainly made a deep impression on Thucydides, who chose to include in his history a chilling rendition of the conversation between the Melians and the Athenians. How did he know what was said in such detail? He didn't, of course. In the set piece known as the Melian Dialogue, Thucydides was experimenting with an art form closer to drama than to history. There he showed the Athenians articulating the philosophy that has become known by the German word *Realpolitik*, or political realism. "Given what we believe about the gods and know about men," he portrays the Athenians as saying,

> we think that both are always forced by the law of nature to dominate
> everyone they can. We didn't lay down this law, it was there—and
> we weren't the first to make use of it. We took it as it was and acted
> on it, and we will bequeath it as a living thing to future generations,

knowing full well that if you or anyone else had the same power as
we, you would do the same thing.

(The Peloponnesian War 5.105)

As so often, Spartan aid did not materialize, and as punishment for their recal-
citrance, the Athenians killed all the Melian men and sold all the women and children into slavery. To treat an enemy this way was not unheard of in Greece; this
is precisely what the Athenians had done to the inhabitants of rebellious Scione in
421. But the Melians had not been enemies of Athens, and what the Athenians did
to them tarnished the city's reputation well into the next century.

Thucydides was not the only Athenian alive at the time who used his verbal
talents to showcase the horrors of war and to explore its corrosive effect on morality. The following spring (415 BC), Euripides confronted the Athenians with his
anguished *Trojan Women*. No one could seriously doubt that this exquisitely painful drama, ostensibly set in Troy in the aftermath of the city's fall, was designed
to illustrate the dreadfulness of war in general and the current war in particular.
"Toddlers," sang the men in the chorus dressed as women,

> in terror pressed against their mothers' skirts
> as soldiers burst from ambush, poised to strike.
> Pallas Athena's work, this killing was.
> The altars of the gods ran red with blood
> and desolation reigned in every bed—
> the murdered men a glory to the Greeks,
> the women taken to breed Argive sons,
> and only sorrow left for fallen Troy.

(Euripides, Trojan Women 557–567)

The specter of the enslavement of the wives and sisters and daughters of the
Trojan heroes and the execution of the young Astyanax, Hector's son, thrown to
his death from the city walls, was all too evocative of recent developments; many
of those sitting in the audience had themselves done the killing at Melos. It also
proved prophetic of events to come.

THE INVASION OF SICILY (415–413 BC)

While a small number of men met daily to practice singing the unsettling choruses
in Euripides' sobering drama, a large number busied themselves preparing for the
largest military expedition in Athens' history. In the winter of 416–415, temptation had appeared to the Athenian assembly in the form of ambassadors from the
Sicilian city of **Egesta**, an old ally. Since the Carthaginians' defeat by Gelon, tyrant
of Gela, in 480, much had changed in Sicily. Tyranny had ceased to be the dominant form of government; many states, in fact, were democracies. While peace
among the various cities often prevailed, inter-polis warfare was by no means

unknown, and the relationship between Egesta and Selinus was notoriously strained. The year 416 found them quarreling over border territory. As Syracuse, the most powerful city on the island, was supporting Selinus, Egesta actually appealed for help to Carthage. Receiving no response, the Egestans then turned to Athens, where their request for assistance in the war with Selinus provided a springboard for hawks like Alcibiades, as well as other Athenians who yearned for new adventures. Pericles had warned the Athenians that attempts to expand their empire would undermine their chances of winning the war, but Pericles was long dead, and his strategy had died with him. When Alcibiades advocated full support for Egesta and Nicias argued with equal passion against involvement in Sicily, the Athenians resolved on a peculiar compromise. Alcibiades would indeed be sent west with a large force, but he would be accompanied by two other strategoi—Lamachus, an experienced general, and Nicias himself, whose presence they hoped would serve as a check on Alcibiades' rashness.

The idea that Nicias' prudence would counter Alcibiades' impulsive nature was singularly wrongheaded. Shortly before the expedition was to sail, moreover, a bizarre nocturnal escapade in Athens sparked a scandal of extraordinary proportions that spilled over from religion to politics. Outside the entrances of Athenian homes, as well as religious shrines and public spaces, stood images known as herms—squared shafts topped by archaizing heads of the god Hermes and sporting erect phalluses on their front surfaces (see Figure 8.6). These were believed to bring good luck and protection from danger. One morning not long before the expedition was to set sail, the Athenians awoke to find that nearly all these herms had been defaced—and quite possibly dephallused as well.

Cultural differences make it hard for us fully to understand why Athenians reacted to this sacrilegious prank with utter terror and became convinced that a plot was afoot to overthrow the government, but this is exactly what happened. Though many were punished, responsibility for the project has never been determined. It may have been the work of one or more of the organizations known as *hetaireiai*. Drinking clubs composed of upper-class young men, often with oligarchic leanings, hetaireiai involved themselves in a variety of social and political activities. To democrats they seemed sinister and potentially treasonous.

Not surprisingly, fingers were pointed at Alcibiades, precisely the sort of irreverent individual who would set his drinking companions on such an enterprise, whether they belonged to a hetaireia or not. Fuel was added to the flames by accusations that Alcibiades had staged a burlesque mocking the mystery rites celebrated at Eleusis, violating their secrecy by enacting them in front of the uninitiated. Since he had solid support among the adventurous sailors bound for Sicily, Alcibiades wisely demanded that he be tried at once, before the fleet left. Instead, his opponents waited to bring charges until the expedition had sailed.

The fleet the Athenians dispatched for Sicily was entirely out of proportion to the size or importance of its intended objective. It consisted of 134 triremes with 130 supply boats, a total of over 25,000 men. Dozens of merchant vessels decided to accompany the navy, hoping for profits. Both citizens and foreigners crowded the shore ogling the armada, which Thucydides says was the most expensive any

Figure 8.6. This fragmentary fifth-century herm found in the excavations of the Athenian agora may have been one of those mutilated in 415–414 BC before the Athenians sailed for Sicily. Athens, Agora Museum.

Greek city had launched until that day. A trumpet proclaimed silence, and a herald recited the prayers. On every deck both officers and marines offered libations to the gods in vessels of gold and silver. The crews raised the paean, and when the libations were finished, put out to sea, sailing first in single file and then racing one another as far as Aegina. From there they hastened to Corcyra to rendezvous with the rest of their allies.

Of the many who sailed for Sicily, few returned. The Athenians received less support from the cities of Sicily and southern Italy than they had expected, and even the eager Egestans turned out to lack the resources they had claimed. Envoys dispatched to Egesta, it proved, had been duped into believing the city was rich

Figure 8.7. Set on the edge of a canyon amid imposing mountains, this temple at Egesta was never finished, and today birds nest in the unfinished Doric capitals.

when in fact it was poor. Thucydides tells how the various Egestans received the crews of the Athenian ships in their homes, rounding up as many gold and silver cups as they could find in town and in the neighboring cities and presenting them at parties as if they belonged to the household:

> They all used the same goblets, for the most part, and they showed so much of it everywhere that it absolutely awed the Athenian crewmen, who, when they returned to Athens, spread the news about the great wealth they had seen. Those who had been deceived in turn misled others, and they were all held responsible by the troops when word got out that Egesta did not have any money.
>
> (*The Peloponnesian War* 6.46)

Just about everything that could have gone wrong with the Sicilian enterprise did. Lamachus died fighting. Alcibiades was recalled to stand trial, and on the journey managed to jump ship and defect to Sparta. When in the winter of 415-414 envoys from Syracuse and Corinth came to seek Spartan aid for the Sicilian campaign, Alcibiades warned the Spartans that the Athenians were planning to conquer Sicily and Italy, attack Carthage, and then go after the Peloponnesus. The dispatch of a Spartan general to Sicily, he suggested, might be necessary if the Spartans wanted to prevent an Athenian takeover of the entire Greek world.

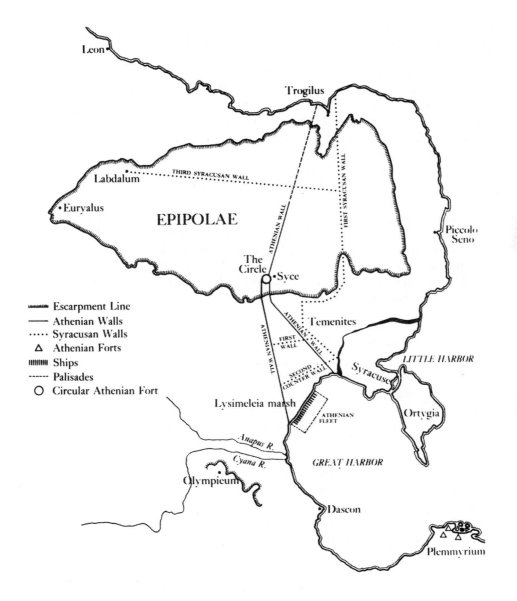

Figure 8.8. Diagram of Syracuse and Epipolae. After D. Kagan, 1974.

Nicias and Lamachus had occupied the plateau known as Epipolae west of Syracuse and had begun building a north–south wall with the idea in mind of blockading the city. Now in sole command, Nicias successfully moved the Athenian fleet into Syracuse's harbor, creating a real possibility of blockading the city, but the Spartans were determined to prevent an Athenian takeover of Sicily. Though the numbers of full-blooded Spartiates had dropped, talent was not lacking, and the reinforcements that arrived in Syracuse were led by Gylippus, a gifted commender from a new class known as *mothakes*—the offspring of a Spartan father and a helot mother. The arrival of Gylippus with reinforcements changed the situation dramatically. Gylippus scaled the Epipolae heights via a pass the Athenians had carelessly left unguarded—the same pass they themselves had used a few months before. The Syracusans, moreover, built a counterwall that destroyed Athenian chances for a blockade.

Nicias was now suffering acutely from kidney disease and asked the Athenians to recall him. They refused. Convinced the situation was hopeless, he tried to dissuade them from continuing their efforts in Sicily by a long letter to the assembly maintaining that only a force as large as the original expedition could have any chance of success. To his horror, the Athenians sent Demosthenes out at the head of the proposed reinforcements. Upon his arrival with the second fleet, followed promptly by a serious reverse on the Epipolae heights, Demosthenes advocated immediate withdrawal. At that point, however, religious anxiety once more intruded into the secular sphere. When everything was ready for the Athenians' departure, Thucydides related,

> and just as they were about to sail, there was an eclipse of the moon, which happened to be full. The event made most of the Athenians feel uneasy, and they urged their generals to stay; and Nicias, who was too inclined to believe in the interpretation of omens and that sort of thing, refused even to discuss a move until after they had stayed for "three times nine days," as their seers decreed. This was the reason the Athenians stayed on after all their delays!
> (*The Peloponnesian War* 7.50)

On learning that the Athenians had been planning to leave, the Syracusans attacked the Athenian fleet and blocked the exit from the harbor. A fierce battle ensued, with some two hundred ships rammed together in a tight space. The din made it impossible to hear the calls of the coxswains.

Unable to make their escape by sea, the Athenians resolved to depart overland, abandoning their sick and wounded. About forty thousand men set out on the dismal trek, the Syracusans hot on their heels. Nicias and Demosthenes became separated; the Syracusans caught up first with Demosthenes, who surrendered in the hope of saving his soldiers' lives. The Syracusans then overtook Nicias' army.

DOCUMENT 8.1

Thucydides is at his narrative best in portraying the final collapse of the Athenian effort in Sicily.

The Athenians pushed on to the Assinarus river, all the while being devastated by the spears, arrows and stones coming from everywhere and by the hordes of cavalry and other troops. They thought that if they could just get across the river, things would be a little easier for them. They were desperate to stop the pain, to drink some water. When they got to the river, they broke ranks and ran into it, every man struggling to make the brutal crossing first as the enemy bore down. Driven to cross all together, they fell onto one another and trampled each other down. Some were killed immediately by their own spears; others got tangled up in their equipment and with each other and sank into the river. Syracusans positioned on the other bank, which was steep, hurled down spears at the Athenians, most of whom were jumbled together ravenously drinking from the nearly dry riverbed. The Peloponnesians went down into the river after them and did most of the killing there; and though it quickly became fouled, the Athenians nonetheless fought among themselves to gulp the muddy water clotted with blood.

Finally, with dead bodies heaped atop each other in the riverbed, and the army decimated, some in the river and others—such as got across—by the cavalry, Nicias surrendered himself to Gylippus, trusting him more than the Syracusans. He told Gylippus and the Spartans to do with him what they wanted, but to stop slaughtering his men. After this, Gylippus ordered his troops to take prisoners, whereupon the surviving men were brought in alive, except for the large number who had been hidden by individual Syracusan soldiers. They also sent a search party out after the three hundred who had broken through the sentries by night and captured them.... A large number, of course, were killed, for there was a great slaughter at the river, greater than any which occurred in the whole war.

The Peloponnesian War 7.84–85

The triumphant Syracusans celebrated their victory by presenting Apollo with lavish offerings at Delphi. The Athenians, on the other hand, had lost tens of thousands of men and accomplished nothing. For them, the outcome of the campaign was so horrific that they at first refused to believe the appalling news. Plutarch claims that word of the disaster first reached Athens by way of a hapless man who had reported it matter of factly to a barber in Piraeus, as if it were common knowledge: the agitated barber promptly ran the five miles to Athens, where he repeated the tale. He was in the very process of being tortured as a troublemaker when messengers arrived to confirm the astonishing story. As Thucydides was later to write, "All was lost. Ships. Men. Everything" (7.87).

THE WAR IN THE AEGEAN AND THE OLIGARCHIC COUP AT ATHENS (413–411 BC)

By their defeat at Syracuse, the Athenians stunned the Greek world as much as they had by their victory at Marathon. The myth of naval superiority that had held the Delian League together was shattered. Athens' fighting force was vastly smaller than it had been in 431. Money was in short supply; previously, one trierarch had been appointed for each ship, but soon after the disaster in Sicily, the Athenians introduced the syntrierarchy, allowing two men to share the expense. For Athenian subjects, suddenly revolt became not merely an option but a powerful temptation. Alcibiades cruised the seas on Sparta's behalf, fomenting rebellion where he could. Meanwhile, in Attica some twenty thousand slaves deserted to the Spartan king Agis, who at Alcibiades' instigation had established himself in a fort at Decelea in northeast Attica. The disappearance of the slaves from the mines prevented the continued tapping of the silver veins, and the strength of the encampment at Decelea interfered gravely with Athenian agriculture. Now the Spartans could ravage Attica all year, killing farm animals as they went and keeping Athens in a perpetual state of siege. Seeing success well within their grasp, the invigorated Spartans set about building a new naval force of a hundred triremes and began negotiating for Persian support.

Incredibly, it took Sparta eight years to bring Athens to its knees—eight years during which the Athenians, crippled by devastating losses in Sicily, survived the loss of the huge island of Euboea off the Attica coast and an oligarchic coup in the city. The history of these eight years is crowded with shifting alliances, plots and counterplots, murders and lies. Within Athens, lines between democrats and oligarchs appear blurred as key players in the political arena move back and forth between the parties, and a new creature appears, the "moderate"—a politician whose motives for keeping one foot in each camp are often impossible to determine: sincere patriotism becomes increasingly difficult to distinguish from unprincipled time-serving. Spartans are divided about how seemly it might be to barter the Ionians' freedom in exchange for Persian gold. Persians cannot decide which side, if any, to support. Through it all Alcibiades remains a wild card, cagily shifting position to suit the rapidly altering international situation—and to keep himself safe from the wrath of Agis, whose wife he appears to have seduced in a moment of imprudence. The fortunes of battle swing wildly back and forth. In 413, Athens seems to be finished; by 410 the Spartans sue for peace. Athens wins a stunning victory in 406 only to lose the war by 404 (really by 405).

Civil Strife in Athens

The burst of Peloponnesian energy that erupted in the wake of Athens' defeat in Sicily was short-lived. The Spartans' efforts would have come to little had it not been for the dynamic energy of Alcibiades and the tensions that erupted in Athens, setting the hoplite infantry and the aristocratic elite against the thetes who manned the fleet.

For nearly a century after the clash between Cleisthenes and Isagoras, Athens had been free from the danger of civil war. The debacle in Sicily, however, gave an opening to would-be oligarchs who wanted to reconstitute the government on less democratic lines. The first rumblings of discontent were mild, though ominous: in 413 BC, the Athenians placed decision making in the hands of ten older men called *probouloi*. Despite the undemocratic nature of such a board, however, the individual probouloi were men of impeccable democratic credentials; one was the playwright Sophocles. The Athenians now tapped the emergency reserve fund they had been storing on the Acropolis since the beginning of the war and used it to rebuild the fleet and train new crews. With the new ships, they were able to prevent the secession of Chios from the empire and win a few victories on the coast of Asia Minor.

Unrest continued, however, as men of oligarchic inclinations played on the Athenians' anxieties about the failure of their democratic leaders to bring the war to a successful conclusion. Alcibiades' machinations provided a catalyst for a more substantial change in the government. Alcibiades had rendered signal service to Sparta in encouraging rebellions in a number of cities, including Erythrae, Rhodes, Ephesus, Chios, and Miletus. Having fallen foul of Agis, however—whether because of the alleged affair with his wife or for some other reason—he had begun to plot a return to Athens. The entry of Persia into the equation provided the springboard he needed. In the years that followed the Athenian defeat in Sicily, Persian policy toward Greece was determined not primarily by the king, Darius II, but by the coastal satraps—Pharnabazus (the satrap of Dascylium) in the north, and Tissaphernes (the satrap of Sardis) in the south.

Tissaphernes in particular had a lively interest in Greek affairs, and indeed in Greek culture as a whole. At first he leaned toward Sparta, and in fact negotiated a series of treaties in which the Spartans, who had entered into the war posing as the liberators of Greece from Athenian tyranny, uncomfortably but unmistakably agreed to sell out the freedom of the Greek cities of Ionia in exchange for Persian gold. Sparking Persia's interest (however vacillating) in their cause was pretty much Sparta's only achievement during these years, and even this the Spartans owed in good part to Alcibiades. Not long afterward, however, Alcibiades persuaded Tissaphernes that it might be better for Persia to let Athens and Sparta wear each other down. When Tissaphernes' support for the Spartan cause began to waver, Alcibiades sent word to Athens that he had it in his power to bring the Persians into the war on the Athenian side—but that their support would be contingent on replacing the democracy with an oligarchy. His support, of course, would be contingent on his recall. By the time it became clear that the Persian support Alcibiades had promised was illusory, the wheels had been set in motion for a change in government and his return.

It is an indication of how deeply the long war had shaken the Athenians that in 411 the assembly, some members intimidated and others just demoralized, voted itself out of existence and placed the safety of the state in the hands of a new, provisional council known as the **Four Hundred**, which, it was understood, would soon give way to a larger body of five thousand. Despite the way the war had undermined confidence in the democratic government, this vote was made possible only by the absence of the fleet, based now at Samos; for sailors, who were generally poor men, could be counted on to oppose any reforms that had the effect of limiting the franchise to property owners.

Experiments in Oligarchy

Neither of the reformers' notions was entirely new. Solon was believed by many people to have created a council of four hundred—certainly such a body dated from approximately his time—and the five thousand were thought to correspond to the hoplite class. Sailors were right to be alarmed by such projects. What was really at issue here was their disfranchisement. The notion of "hoplite democracy" had been Cimon's ideal, and he was not alone. From this moment many Athenians of antidemocratic tendencies began to make use of a new watchword, "the ancestral constitution," that is, a democracy limited to landowners, which they insisted was more traditionally Athenian than the upstart democracy that included the poor men who served as rowers in the fleet. This issue, which had seemed to be settled in 508 with Cleisthenes' victory over Isagoras, was now once again on the floor.

Under the oligarchy of 411, consequently, the clock was in fact turned back. Pay was abolished for most state offices. Though this did serve the purpose of concentrating money on the war effort, it also effectively limited participation in government to those who could afford to spend time in unremunerated labor. Carrying arms and flanked by an additional 120 men, moreover, the Four Hundred also entered the Bouleuterion where the council met, paid the councilors the balance of what was owing to them, and dismissed them. Their own despotic rule was made easier by the ominous suspension of the *graphē paranomōn*, the indictment for illegal proposals.

There were now two Athenian governments—the oligarchy of the Four Hundred in the city and the democratic fleet stationed at Samos, which functioned as the assembly. Considering themselves the real government of Athens, the sailors on Samos deposed the incumbent generals and appointed new ones, including the trierarch Thrasybulus, a champion of the democracy. Those who had always suspected Alcibiades of designs on the democratic constitution proved to have much justice on their side. Not only had he suggested constitutional innovation directly, indirectly he had brought it about by fomenting rebellions in the east that kept the democratic fleet away from Athens. His support, however, did not come entirely from antidemocratic quarters. Thrasybulus was just one of the democrats who backed him, and soon after his arrival on Samos, Alcibiades too was elected general.

Back in Athens the Four Hundred were undermined by two powerful divisions in their camp. Some wanted to prosecute the war vigorously, but others with different plans prevailed and sent an embassy to Sparta seeking peace at any price. In addition, some fully expected the implementation of the government of the Five Thousand, while others understood that larger body was nothing but a fiction calculated to bring about the abdication of the assembly. Meanwhile rumors circulated among the fleet at Samos that the Four Hundred were exercising a reign of terror, that no wife or child was safe from their outrage. At this juncture, it appears, Alcibiades rose to statesmanlike heights and dissuaded the furious sailors from sailing to Athens to overthrow the Four Hundred. Their departure would have left the east at the mercy of Athens' many enemies, and their intervention at Athens proved unnecessary, as the Four Hundred were self-destructing anyway.

The belief that Athens' foreign affairs would do better under oligarchic guidance suffered serious setbacks when the peace with Sparta failed to materialize—and Euboea successfully revolted from the Athenian empire. The hoplites whom the Four Hundred had set to fortifying the promontory of Eetionia at Piraeus mutinied, and the Five Thousand were promptly installed. They then recalled Athens' exiles, including Alcibiades, and governed Athens for eight months, from September 411 to June 410. Not a great deal is known about their government, though they seem to have limited the franchise to the hoplite class (cutting out the thetes who manned the triremes). Thucydides, who was frequently impatient with democracy, praised the government of the Five Thousand as a laudable blending of democratic and oligarchic elements.

The vigor the Athenians showed in rebuilding their fleet and carrying on the war despite acute domestic conflict was remarkable. After a victory in the Hellespont at Cynossema, the Athenians, led by Alcibiades, scored a still more striking one not far away at Cyzicus, where the Spartans lost their admiral-in-chief, Mindarus. The battle is memorable for the "laconic" dispatch the Athenians intercepted on its way to Sparta afterward: "Ships lost; Mindarus dead; men starving; can't figure out what to do." It is also memorable as the first major encounter of the war not described by Thucydides: the historian's account breaks off shortly after Cynossema. From this point on, the principal sources are Xenophon and Diodorus.

The victories in the east had been won by the cooperation of the Five Thousand in Athens and the fleet at Samos, and in June the democracy was formally restored at Athens. A number of the leaders of the Five Thousand remained powerful under the democracy. Among these was Hagnon's son Theramenes, who seemed to find a place for himself in any group. Animosity and suspicion were not entirely gone, however, and the restored democracy, as one of its first official acts, administered a loyalty oath, requiring each citizen to swear: "I will do my best to kill by word and by deed, by my vote and by my hand, anyone who overthrows the Athenian democracy, holds office under an undemocratic regime, or seeks to establish a tyranny either for himself or for someone else. If anyone else kills such a person, I will consider him clean in the eyes of gods and spirits" (Andocides, *On the Mysteries*, 97).

The Spartans sought peace from the restored democracy, but only on the basis of the status quo. That the Athenians had regained their confidence is indicated by their refusal. In retrospect, many Athenians must have regretted their rejection of the Spartan offer, but at the time it did look as though they might win back their lost possessions.

The Last Years of War (407–404 BC)

In 407, however, the union of two powerful men dramatically altered the situation in the Aegean. Alcibiades was not the only Greek with charm. An enthusiastic friendship sprang up between Cyrus, son of the Persian king, and Lysander, the ambitious mothax who served as chief admiral of the Spartan navy. Ultimately, their association spelled doom for Athens.

That same year, Alcibiades, having raised a hundred talents for Athens by looting the coast of Caria, decided it might finally be safe to return home. It was an extraordinary circumstance—a man with so many friends that he was repeatedly elected to the board of generals but with so many enemies that he feared to set foot on Attic soil. Even after his ship had sailed into Piraeus in June, he stood motionless on the deck surveying the huge crowd that had assembled on the shore until he saw a party of his friends waiting to escort him. Only then did he disembark.

His ascendancy, however, was remarkably brief. Within a matter of months, the Athenians lost twenty-two ships to Lysander at a naval engagement off Notium, where Alcibiades had left his personal pilot Antiochus in charge with orders under no circumstances to engage the Spartans. Antiochus, a friend of Alcibiades, probably had no business in a position of such authority, since he was not a trierarch, and Alcibiades had not acquitted himself well, but the strength of the Athenian reaction attests to the continuing agitation of his enemies. Alcibiades' career at Athens was finished. It is certain that he was not reelected to the strategia, and it is likely that he was actually deposed before his term was out. Rumors circulated that he had fortified a castle in the Gallipoli peninsula as a refuge in case of emergency. Now that the emergency had materialized, he promptly withdrew to this very fortress. He never saw Athens again.

That spring, the Athenians offered freedom to slaves who would join the navy that was about to set out for the area of Lesbos. There they scored an impressive victory in a huge naval battle off the **Arginusae** islands, sinking fully seventy-five Peloponnesian ships. Some twenty thousand Greeks lost their lives, including the Spartans' chief admiral, Callicratidas, another mothax who had taken over from Lysander. A noble and generous young patriot, Callicratidas represented the best elements in Sparta—those willing to risk their lives to prevent the imperialist Athenians from tyrannizing over the weak, and committed to doing it without Persian help—whereas Lysander represented the worst. The loss of Callicratidas boded ill for the future of the Greek world.

The aftermath of the battle witnessed a bizarre frenzy of self-destruction. Though the Athenians were heartened by their victory at Arginusae, they knew that their admiral Conon and his fleet were blockaded at Mytilene. While the Athenian strategoi were debating whether to set about retrieving the sailors in the water or to sail to Mytilene to rescue Conon's force, a sudden storm came up that made rescue impossible. When news of the casualties reached Athens, people began anxiously to cast blame on one another. The generals blamed the trierarchs Theramenes and Thrasybulus, and the trierarchs blamed the generals. Whether the men in the water were dead or alive is uncertain, but for Greeks the recovery even of bodies was important, since the souls of those left unburied would wander eternally in Hades, unable to find a resting place. The eight generals in command were summoned home for trial, and six chose to return. In violation of customary procedure—and over the protests of the philosopher Socrates, who happened to be chairing the assembly meeting that day—the generals were tried on a single slate, condemned, and executed. Ironically, after the death of his legitimate sons, Pericles had implored the Athenians to confer citizenship on his sons by Aspasia, and Pericles the Younger was among the generals executed.

The Final Battle

Again, the Spartans offered peace on the basis of the status quo (though they were willing to evacuate Decelea); again, the Athenians declined. Time, however, was running out, as was the pool of talented commanders—and of money. It seemed that the next major battle would be Athens' last stand, and in fact it was. Late in the summer of 405, Lysander, making good use of the subsidies he had obtained from his friend Cyrus, established a base at the city of Lampsacus in the Hellespont. In August the Athenians Conon and Philocles stationed their fleet two miles across the channel at **Aegospotami**. Alcibiades, seeing that the Athenians' position was highly vulnerable, descended from his fortress and advised his countrymen to move, but they disregarded his cautions. After the fleets had been in these positions for five days, and the Athenian crews had gone ashore to gather provisions, Lysander gave the signal for attack. The Spartans captured 171 ships, and their infantry overwhelmed the camp. Understandably, the Athenians' carelessness gave rise to rumors of treachery. Only a handful of Athenian vessels escaped, one of them the official state trireme the *Paralus*, another commanded by Conon. Remembering the fate of the victors of Arginusae, Conon took refuge in Cyprus and did not return to Athens until he had engineered a victory over the Spartans at Cnidus in 394, ten years after the end of the war.

Lysander then called a meeting of the allies to solicit their thoughts about the proper treatment of the prisoners. In the discussion speakers brought up

> both the many deeds [the Athenians] had already done that were contrary to custom and law, and the many resolutions they had passed in their Assembly concerning how they would treat their enemies if they had won the battle—in particular, the vote to cut off the right hands of those they captured. It was also noted that the Athenians, when they had captured a Corinthian and an Andrian trireme, had thrown all the men on those ships overboard. (Philocles was the Athenian general who had sent these men to their deaths.) Many other accusations were made against the Athenians, and it was finally decided to kill all those of the prisoners who were Athenians, with the exception of Adeimantos, who alone had attacked the decree in the Assembly about the cutting off of hands. He was, however, charged by some with betraying the ships. Philocles, who had thrown overboard the Corinthians and the Andrians, was first asked by Lysander what

he thought he deserved for having begun uncustomary and illegal actions against the Greeks, and then had his throat cut.

(Xenophon, *Hellenica* 2.1.31–32)

The Spartan victory at Aegospotami had cut off Athens from its principal source of grain; to make sure there would be no slipups, Lysander also decreed death as the penalty for anyone caught bringing grain to Athens. Lysander knew that the war was now over, and the Athenians would know it soon enough, for the *Paralus* was en route to Piraeus with the dismal tidings. The ship arrived at night, and as the news was reported, Xenophon relates, "a cry arose in the Piraeus and ran up through the Long Walls and into the city itself as one man imparted the calamitous news to the next. As a result, no one slept that night as they mourned not only for the men destroyed but even more for themselves" (*Hellenica* 2.2.3). Late in the fall Lysander sailed victorious for Piraeus. Along the way he accepted the surrender of Athens' former allies and replaced their democracies with oligarchic governments beholden to Sparta. He also ensured still further stress on the Athenians' dwindling food supply by encouraging Athenian garrisons to return home. Samos persisted in its loyalty to Athens, in recognition of which the Athenians uncharacteristically granted the Samians citizenship. Agis, whose occupation of Decelea had played its desired part in the starvation of the city, moved down to the walls of Athens, where he was joined by Pausanias, his co-king. Miserable and terrified, the Athenians, Xenophon wrote, were at a loss for what to do and saw no future for themselves but to suffer "the same evils that they themselves had unjustly inflicted against the citizens of smaller states. They had done these things not for the sake of avenging wrongs but simply to display their arrogance, for the only offense of these states was that they had allied themselves with the Spartans" (2.2.10).

The mutability of fortune had been a commonplace in Greek literature, and the Athenians gathered in the theater in 415 had been given the opportunity to contemplate the cruelty of war's chances in Euripides' *Trojan Women*. Of those who prosper, the Trojan queen Hecuba had suggested, "consider no one blest until he's dead" (509–510). This notion, so reminiscent of Solon's warning to Croesus in Herodotus' cautionary tale, was developed later in the play, as Hecuba underlines the foolishness of those who believe prosperity is secure:

like someone who's gone mad, in changing moods
fortune leaps wildly, now this way, now that:
nobody ever prospers all the time.

(Euripides, *Trojan Women* 1204–1206)

In the end, Athens was spared. The Thebans, Corinthians, and other Spartan allies advocated doing to Athens precisely what had been done to Melos—killing all the adult men and selling all the women and children into slavery. The Spartans declined, pleading Athens' noble service to Greece during the Persian wars. The brutality of Lysander's temperament makes it more likely that the real motive was fear of the power vacuum into which Corinth or—more likely—Thebes could be counted on to rush.

Early in the spring, however, the Athenians finally agreed to a treaty negotiated by Theramenes on the Spartans' terms: Athens would not only become Sparta's ally but would agree to the destruction of the Long Walls and of the fortifications of Piraeus and would surrender all but a dozen ships. Exiles would also be recalled; these were largely men of oligarchic sympathies. The walls were pulled down, Xenophon says, to the merry accompaniment of flutes, for people believed that "that day would be the beginning of freedom for all of Greece" (2.2.23). The Spartans' actions, however, presaged ill for freedom. The willingness to sell out the Ionians to Persia and the establishment of pro-Spartan oligarchies in cities formerly in the Athenian empire were bad signs, and worse was to come.

FALLOUT FROM THE LONG WAR

As we have seen, it sometimes happened that men who did not belong to the entrenched aristocracy became wealthy through industry—Cleon, for example, whose family owned a tannery. It was also true, however, that the tendency to keep land in the family constricted social mobility in Greece, limiting opportunities for improving one's lot in life. The frustrations of the poor resulted in frequent stasis, with the poor likely to favor democracy and the rich oligarchy, although there were always some aristocrats among the partisans of democracy, men like Pericles and Cleisthenes at Athens. The natural disposition of Greek city-states to factionalism and civil strife had been intensified during the war. Predictably, his interest in human nature and the drive to power focused Thucydides' attention on this development, which he captured in his description of events occurring early in the war.

> ### DOCUMENT 8.2
>
> *In one of the most memorable passages in his History, Thucydides took the occasion of the bloody events at Corcyra in the 420s to comment on the way the three decades of war intensified conflict within the polis.*
>
> Later, virtually all of Greece was in a frenzy, with dissension everywhere, and the leaders of the people trying to bring in the Athenians, and the oligarchs, the Spartans. In peacetime, there would have been neither pretext nor inclination for inviting their intervention; but in war, where alliances are at one and the same time a way to hurt your enemies and gain something for yourself, inducements came easily to those who wanted radical change. Events struck these strife-torn cities as they always do and always will for so long as human nature remains the same, hard and fast with more or less violence, quickly changing shape as change keeps pace with happenstance. In times of peace and prosperity, both cities and individuals can have lofty

ideals because they have not fallen before the force of overwhelming necessity. War, which robs the ease of every day, is a harsh teacher and absorbs most people's passions in the here and now.

. . .

The cause of all this was power pursued for the sake of greed and personal ambition, which led in turn to the entrenchment of a zealous partisanship. The leadership in the cities on both sides advanced high-sounding phrases like "The equality of free men before the law," or "A prudent aristocracy," but while serving the public interest in their speeches, they created a spoils system. Struggling with one another for supremacy in every way they could, they kept committing the most horrible crimes and escalated to ever greater revenges, never to promote justice and the best interests of the city, but— constantly setting the limit at whatever best pleased each side at any given moment—they were always prepared to glut their partisanship by either rigging votes or by seizing power with their bare hands. Thus, neither side observed the rules of piety: they were more respected for the high words with which they got away with performing their base actions. As for the citizens who tried to be neutral, they were killed by both sides either because they did not join in the fighting or out of envy because they were managing to survive.

(*The Peloponnesian War* 3.82)

Of the hegemons, only one had remained immune to this disease. A unique state, Sparta managed throughout the war to confine internal bloodshed to the usual suppression of helots (or at least to keep word of murderous civil conflict from leaking beyond the Peloponnesus). Throughout the war, it remained for many Greeks a model of stable government. Athens, however, was not free from civil strife. From Cimon to Theramenes, selected Athenian politicians had always had serious reservations about democracy, and the democracy's failure in the theater of war always carried with it the danger of an oligarchic coup. The takeover of 411 had been short-lived, but Lysander's victory in 404 would spark a second and far bloodier episode.

The Thirty Tyrants (404–403 BC)

Throughout the Aegean Lysander set up **decarchies**, that is, boards of ten pro-Spartan officials charged with ensuring that Athens' former allies would be governed in accordance with oligarchic principles and with Spartan interests. Ten men would not be enough for Athens; the intimidated assembly had no choice but to accede to Lysander's request and ratify a new government to be run by a board of thirty (the **Thirty Tyrants**). Athenian citizens, these thirty were sympathetic to Sparta and willing to sacrifice democratic principles, but they were not all committed oligarchs. Theramenes, who was among them, became a controversial figure not only among Athenians of the fourth century, but among modern historians as well. His propensity for landing on his feet in any crisis has suggested to some that he was a flexible man who saw merit in a variety of regimes, whereas others have seen him as an unprincipled timeserver. The most prominent of the Thirty, however, left no doubt as to his political convictions. Plato's relative Critias was a memorable figure—a pupil of Socrates, a brilliant intellectual, an avowed atheist, a passionate antidemocrat, a long-time admirer of the Spartan constitution, and, as events were to show, a man who would order murders by the hundreds without a qualm. Banished after the fall of the Four Hundred, to which he had belonged, Critias was now back with a vengeance.

The Thirty did not establish the "ancestral constitution," although they did abolish the organs of democratic government such as the popular assembly and the people's courts and appoint a new boule of five hundred antidemocrats. What they did do was to put to death anyone conspicuous for affluence or birth or reputation, confiscating property liberally in order to build up their own wealth. No less than fifteen hundred men were executed. To protect themselves from the popular uprising they rightly feared, they requested from Lysander seven hundred soldiers and a Spartan **harmost** (garrison commander) similar to those Sparta had established throughout the Aegean in states it had "liberated" from Athenian hegemony. They also surrounded themselves with three hundred whip-bearers and set up a board of ten to keep an eye on Piraeus, rightly considered a hotbed of democratic radicalism.

The execution of enemies began. Under protest from the alarmed Theramenes, Critias and his clique agreed to broaden the oligarchy by establishing a citizen roll of three thousand whose members would be entitled to trial by the boule. The consequence of this, however, was the opposite of what Theramenes intended. Now it appeared to the Thirty that the existence of this protected Three Thousand gave them carte blanche in treating all others as they wished, and a bloodbath commenced. Not all victims were citizens who could possibly have been imagined as political enemies; many were wealthy metics whose property the Thirty coveted.

Understandably, so many Athenians were appalled—and frightened—that the Thirty came to fear that Theramenes might organize a resistance movement, and they summoned him for trial in the boule—a "trial" at which young oligarchs with concealed daggers had been stationed by prearrangement. When it appeared that Theramenes' impassioned defense of moderate government had moved the councilors, Critias struck his name from the roll of the Three Thousand, thereby obviating the need for a trial. Dragged off to prison from the altar where he had taken refuge, Theramenes was executed by being forced to drink hemlock, the poison later used to execute Socrates. Heroic at least in his final hours, Theramenes went out in style and not without irony, toasting Critias' health with the last drops.

Ultimately the Thirty were undone by their own abandon. By forbidding those not on the list of the Three Thousand to enter Athens and confiscating many of their farms, they created a dangerous body of exiles. Though Sparta had forbidden neighboring states to receive refugees from the Thirty, the murderous conduct of the Athenian oligarchy had alienated many Greeks from Sparta, and neither Thebes nor Megara was disposed to turn away Athenians fleeing the brutal Spartan-backed oligarchy. It was in Thebes that the Athenian exiles mounted their campaign to regain their city, making their move in January of 403. Led by Thrasybulus, seventy of the exiles seized Phyle, a stronghold on Mount Parnes on the Athenian side of the Attic/Boeotian boundary. There they waited until their numbers rose to seven hundred; in spring they moved down to Piraeus, joining the dissidents there and establishing themselves on the hill of Munychia. Critias and his men attempted to dislodge them in an uphill charge, and in the attempt Critias died.

Thrasybulus' call for peace and union between the two camps was rejected by the oligarchs, who expected Spartan aid. In Sparta, however, the murderous arrogance of Lysander and his associates was making many powerful men nervous, including the kings Agis and Pausanias. Marching into Attica, Pausanias took the lead and masterminded not only the reconciliation of the various Athenian parties but also the temporary eclipse of Lysander. Under his aegis the Athenians agreed on the first recorded amnesty in history. Under its terms, only the Thirty and their chief officers could be brought to justice for crimes committed before 403; all others were compelled to renounce the many bitter grievances that had accumulated. In September Thrasybulus led his men unopposed to the Acropolis, where they sacrificed to Athena in gratitude for the salvation of the city and their own safe return. The work of reestablishing the democracy then began.

The Trial of Socrates (399 BC)

The Athenians came close to respecting the terms of the amnesty upon which they had agreed. Nonetheless, decades of war followed by months of terror under the Thirty had taken a heavy toll, and there was no lack of people eager to assign blame for Athens' problems. The colorful Socrates had annoyed jealous parents whose young sons had lionized him, and though the Athenians were averse to breaking the amnesty law, some were open to bending it. Raw from the devastating war and frustrated by the change they saw in the world around them, three Athenians—Anytus, Meletus, and Lycon—zeroed in on the eccentric old philosopher who haunted the public spaces of Athens confuting the careless in argument. Socrates (470–399 BC) had been quick to identify the drawbacks of democracy, and he had also been the teacher of (at least) two men who in different ways had harmed Athens: Alcibiades and Critias. The amnesty prevented his accusers from charging Socrates with inciting his pupils to treason, so instead they brought a three-pronged accusation of a kind somewhat unusual in Athens. Socrates, they claimed, did not believe in the gods of the state; he taught new gods; and he corrupted the young.

Figure 8.9. This Roman copy reflects the head of a Greek portrait statue of Socrates from the third quarter of the fourth century BC that may have been created by the sculptor Lysippus. It depends on an earlier fourth-century portrait type that depicted the philosopher with the ugly face of a satyr and a bald head. Paris, The Louvre.

Though this sort of charge was not common at Athens, precedents were not lacking. Athens had no constitutional principles separating church and state or protecting free speech. Because of his naturalistic explanation of the universe and his sophisticated conception of divinity as Nous, Anaxagoras had been forced to leave Athens to avoid prosecution for atheism. This accusation, however, was plainly political in its motivation and constituted an indirect attack on Pericles; indeed, Aspasia was brought to trial for impiety at the same time. The charges against Socrates were also politically motivated, though no doubt the ironic manner that charmed some and infuriated others played a role as well.

Since Socrates never wrote anything, we depend for our conception of him on the dialogues of his admirers Plato and Xenophon. Plato's pupil Aristotle observed about Socrates that the two things one could be certain of attributing to him were inductive reasoning and universal definition. We can be sure of a few other things. Socrates, an Athenian citizen, performed conventional civic services in Athens, fighting as a hoplite at Potidaea, Delium, and Amphipolis in the Peloponnesian War and serving as president of the assembly on the day of the Arginusae trial in 406. His avocation was discussing interesting philosophical questions with young men, questions that focused on the best way for humans to think and live; at least in his mature years, he was not particularly excited by natural science. He believed that the best way to develop ideas was in the give and take of conversation, and that the best way to educate people was to ask them a series of questions leading in a particular direction (now named "the Socratic method"). However painful it might be to find oneself the object of injustice, he was firmly convinced that doing wrong oneself was the only real misfortune that could befall a person. He had a keen wit and an engaging personality, and pupils flocked to him eagerly, though he had nothing that could be called a school. He was not a sophist; he became poor through his refusal to charge fees, and his goal was to inculcate moral excellence, which he viewed as the particular virtue of a human being. Like the sophists, however, he used clever arguments and subjected conventional notions to rational analysis, and like them he disrupted the customary bond that placed education in the context of the family, wounding Athenian parents whose sons preferred his company to theirs—and who gave his ideas greater credence. Whom, Socrates asks Meletus in Xenophon's rendition of his defense speech, do I corrupt? "By God," Meletus replies, "I know some—those you've persuaded to obey you rather than their parents" (Xenophon, *Apology of Socrates* 20). It is not peculiar, therefore, that he was mistaken for a sophist, or that the sophists' shady reputation should have rubbed off on him. He was parodied in Aristophanes' *Clouds*, which showed him carried across the sky in a crane in a flaky educational establishment known as a "think shop."

He also spoke sharply about democracy. Whether it is fair to say that he opposed it and would have liked to see a different regime instituted at Athens is another question. Socrates enjoyed puncturing illusions. But if anything can safely be gathered from Plato's dialogues, then Socrates was troubled by the notion of amateur government, in which anyone's opinion counted for as much as the next man's and in which a volatile assembly was swayed this way and that by rhetorical displays. Most people, he pointed out, aren't terribly thoughtful or analytical, so why should "most people," that is, the majority, make the life-and-death decisions that affect the polis?

This is a question any advocate of democracy must ask, and Socrates' insistence on asking it need not be taken as implying that he wanted decisions made by a minority. Combined with his association with Alcibiades and Critias, however, his pointed remarks about the foibles of democracy seemed downright unpatriotic, and he could easily enough be cast as a purveyor of dangerous ideas.

By Athenian custom, Socrates' trial took only one day. It is painful for many readers of Plato's *Apology of Socrates* to believe that the words written down by Plato were not actually spoken at Socrates' trial. Perhaps they were, and perhaps they weren't; Xenophon's account of Socrates' speech, also called the *Apology*, is less inspiring and much shorter, and may or may not be close to what Socrates actually had time to say. (The Greek word *apology* does not connote "apologizing" in the modern sense but rather means a refutation or defense.) Plato's rendition contains the famous dictum that "the unexamined life is not worth living" and constitutes an extraordinarily moving paean to intellectual freedom and the life of the mind. Shunning the strategy that he identifies as standard procedure in an Athenian courtroom—weeping, pleading, parading his children in front of the jury—Socrates, according to Plato, took the position that the best defense was a strong offense. Using the question-and-answer method for which he was famous and which had apparently gotten him into trouble, he demolished his accusers by demonstrating the inconsistencies in their allegations and then went on to explain in poignant detail the great service provided to the state by his relentless probing. His service to the state, he argues, is precious and irreplaceable. It is, literally, a godsend:

> Know that if you kill me, I being the sort of man I say I am, you will injure yourselves more than you injure me. Meletus and Anytus will not injure me; that would be impossible, for I believe it is not the gods' will that a better man should be injured by a worse.... If you put me to death, you will not easily find another, who, if I may use a rather ludicrous figure of speech, attaches himself to the city as a gadfly does to a great and noble horse, which is sluggish on account of its very size and needs to be aroused by stinging. I believe that I am the gadfly which the god has fastened upon the city in some such capacity, and all day long I go about arousing and persuading and reproaching each one of you, popping up all over. And since you will have difficulty finding another like me, gentlemen, you will take my advice and spare me. Now you might be angry, like someone awakened from a nap, and slap me, as Anytus advises, and easily kill me; then you would pass the remainder of your lives asleep, unless the god, in his care for you, should send someone else to sting you.
>
> (Plato, *Apology* 30C–31A)

Socrates persuaded nearly half the jury of 501 Athenian citizens; he seems to have lost his case by about thirty votes. Meletus, the principal accuser, had proposed the penalty of death.

Athenian procedure called for convicted defendants to recommend an alternative penalty, and it seems clear that Socrates' accusers expected him to propose exile—and would have been quite content to see him leave town. Instead, he provoked the jury by suggesting rather that the Athenians should provide him with free meals at state expense for the rest of his life as their benefactor, just as they did for Olympic victors and for the descendants of Harmodius and Aristogiton; these were the highest honors that Athens bestowed. Xenophon ascribed this strategy to Socrates' wish to end a satisfying life before the sad realities of old age overtook him; it is also possible that Socrates was testing the jury to see if they understood who he really was and what he really provided to Athens. A number of those who had wanted him acquitted had a change of heart and voted for the death penalty. Socrates was then executed by one of the customary Athenian methods, being ordered to down a poisonous draft of hemlock.

At his trial, if we are to believe Plato, Socrates prophesied that the Athenians would bring great odium on themselves for killing him. He was right. Throughout subsequent history, the execution of Socrates is the most common charge that has been brought by the critics of Athenian democracy. Socrates' death also made a deep impression on his brightest disciples, young aristocrats like Xenophon and Plato. Though Xenophon's works are less widely read than Plato's today, they were very popular in ancient Rome and during the Renaissance, and the dialogues Plato began writing soon after his teacher's death, in which Socrates served as a mouthpiece for his own thinking, became the foundation of western philosophy. In this way the strains occasioned by the Peloponnesian War played a dramatic role in the history of ideas.

THE WAR IN RETROSPECT

There was nothing inevitable about the Spartans' ultimate victory in the war. Darius of Persia died in 404. Had the Athenians not been so careless at Aegospotami, the withdrawal of Persian support that probably would have attended on Darius' death would gravely have compromised the Spartans' chances of winning the war. On the other hand, the Spartans—although not as quickly as prudence would have dictated—did in time learn a vital lesson about the centrality of naval power. The anonymous treatise written during the later fifth century by the so-called Old Oligarch (once confused with Xenophon) had judged sea power superior to power on land. The Athenians, the author argued, did well to sacrifice the development of their infantry to that of their navy. For while it is possible, he conceded,

> for small states subject to the rule of a land power to unite and form a single army, those who are subject to a naval power cannot unite, insofar as they are islanders divided by the sea which their rulers control. ... The rulers of the sea, moreover, have the option of doing what a land power cannot always do, namely, ravaging the country of a superior opponent. For they can put in where the enemy forces are few or non-existent, and if these advance to the attack, they can jump on their ships and sail off. In this way they encounter fewer difficulties than those who operate on land. Then again, the rulers of the sea can sail as far as you like from their own territory, but land powers cannot venture far from theirs, for marching is slow going, and it is not possible to take supplies for a long period when traveling on foot. A land force, moreover, is limited to marching through friendly territory or fighting its way through, whereas a naval force

can choose to land only where it feels secure, sailing onward until it arrives at allied territory or encounters inferior forces.

(Pseudo-Xenophon, *The Constitution of the Athenians* 2. 2–4)

When Sparta became a sea power, the Athenians lost this advantage, lost the war, and lost their empire.

The economic consequences of the war were grave. Except in Sparta proper, where helots continued to till the land and no foreign force dared invade, agriculture suffered terribly. The redoubled labor of women and slaves was insufficient fully to compensate for the death or absence of farmers on long campaigns far from home, and a good deal of territory (in Attica on the Athenian side and Megara on the Peloponnesian, for example) was regularly ravaged by the enemy. Livestock and farming implements were destroyed. Vines took several years of nurture before they would produce a rich crop of grapes, and damage wrought by the destruction of olive trees was even longer lasting: though cuttings carefully grafted onto damaged trees or stumps might produce enough olives for a small family in five or ten years, newly planted trees generally took at least fifteen years to produce a salable crop. Commerce by land and sea was disrupted; cities like Corinth suffered immensely.

Unlike the overseas wars of the Roman republic, which enriched the few while impoverishing the many, the Peloponnesian War hurt everyone. Throughout Greece, poverty pushed a significant number of men beneath the hoplite census. Some men took service as mercenaries, an increasingly popular profession. As usually happens in wartime, many women were forced to work outside the home. Population also dropped in many parts of the Greek world, and the loss of thousands upon thousands of soldiers and sailors left many women without husbands. In the play named for her and produced in 411, Aristophanes' protagonist Lysistrata, who has organized the wives of Greece in a sex strike to force an end to the fighting, is scandalized when a magistrate complains about uppity behavior on the part of women "who bore no share in the war":

> None, you hopeless hypocrite?
> The quota we bear is double. First, we delivered our sons
> to fill out the front lines in Sicily....
> Next, the best years of our lives were levied. Top-level strategy
> attached our joy, and we sleep alone.
>   But it's not the matrons
> like us who matter. I mourn for the virgins, bedded in single
> blessedness, with nothing to do but grow old.

Men, the Commissioner protests,

have been known
   to age, as well as women.

No, Lysistrata replies,

   not as well as—better.
   A man, an absolute antique, comes back from the war, and he's barely
   doddered into town before he's married the veriest nymphet.
   But a woman's season is brief; it slips, and she'll have no husband,
   but sit out her life groping at omens—and finding no men.
                     (Aristophanes, *Lysistrata* 587–589, 591–597; Parker)

In Athens alone, as many as fifty thousand people probably died of the plague,
many of them before they could reproduce. War casualties seem to have included
the deaths of at least five thousand hoplite soldiers and twelve thousand sailors
(including some three thousand executed by Lysander after Aegospotami), and
the Thirty Tyrants of 404–403 apparently killed some fifteen hundred citizens,
perhaps many more. Probably the number of adult male citizens in 403 was half
what it had been in 431. Some cities, like Melos and Scione, had been virtually
annihilated. In Sparta, absolute numbers dropped less sharply, but the various
classes began to redefine themselves, as the ranks of commanders as well as soldiers were swelled not only by distinguished mothakes but also by *neodamōdeis*
(new citizens), helot fighters who had been rewarded with freedom and land.

⇛———⇚

Whether Thucydides was right to identify a single war as lasting from 431 to 404
remains an open question, perhaps one that can never be resolved; where one
war stops and another begins may be a subject more for philosophers than for
diplomatic historians. But he was correct to envision something unprecedented
about these decades of conflict. For until this time Greek warfare had observed
a distinct seasonal pattern. When winter came, fighting ceased; using citizens for
fighting in farming season violated both decorum and common sense. There was
a time to plow and a time to fight, and they were not the same time. Previously
in Greek history, important conflicts and even so-called wars had been decided
by brief hoplite encounters on level ground. The growth of Athenian naval power
had begun to change this, but never before the Peloponnesian War had fighting
become the central fact of life in both hot and cold weather. The Battle of Delium
took place in winter, as did the climactic naval battle in the Syracusan harbor.
Thucydides lost Amphipolis to Brasidas in the snow. Brasidas, moreover, had
with him seven hundred helots and numerous mercenaries. The increased use of
mercenaries and the periodic emergency enfranchisement of helots and slaves—
there were one thousand neodamodeis in Sparta by 421 and probably at least
fifteen hundred by the end of the war—blurred the lines that had traditionally
divided citizens from noncitizens, and the frequency of bloody civil strife eroded

the concept of the polis itself. Aristophanes' Trygaeus at the doorstep of Zeus was not the only Greek to inquire how it could be that the gods would allow Greece to be consumed by a war of this scope. At the same time, however, the shattering of faith fostered a questioning spirit that opened the door to the reflections of Socrates, Xenophon, and Plato. The Peloponnesian War transformed the Greek world, but it did not destroy it.

Key Terms

Aegospotami	Four Hundred	revolt of Mytilene
Alcibiades	harmost	Socrates
Aristophanes	Lysander	Sphacteria
Battle of Arginusae	Melos	Syracuse
Cleon	mothakes	Thirty Tyrants
decarchies	Nicias	Tissaphernes
Egesta	Pylos	

Suggested Readings

Cawkwell, George. 1997. *Thucydides and the Peloponnesian War*. London: Routledge. An erudite but highly readable analysis of Thucydides' work that offers original and controversial insights into his account of the war.

Connor, W. Robert. 1992. *The New Politicians of Fifth Century Athens*. Indianapolis: Hackett. A nuanced examination of the changing dynamics of Athenian political life in the fifth century.

De Romilly, Jacqueline. 1988. *Thucydides and Athenian Imperialism*. Trans. P. Thody. Reprinted Salem, NH: Ayer. A classic study of Thucydides and the empire.

Ehrenberg, Victor. 1974. *The People of Aristophanes*. Reprinted New York: Barnes & Noble. A study of the sociology and economics of the Athenian state based on a close examination of data in Aristophanes' comedies.

Green, Peter. 1970. *Armada from Athens*. London: Hodder and Stoughton. A spirited account of the Athenian invasion of Sicily by a distinguished ancient historian.

Hansen, Mogens Herman. 1995. *The Trial of Socrates from the Athenian Point of View*. Copenhagen: Royal Danish Academy of Sciences and Letters. Discussion of the sources, a reconstruction of the trial, and an investigation of the political background of the prosecution.

Hanson, Victor Davis. 2005. *A War Like No Other War: How the Athenians and Spartans Fought the Peloponnesian War*. New York: Random House. A real page-turner that brings the devastating war alive before the reader's eyes.

Hornblower, Simon. 1986. *Thucydides*. Baltimore: Johns Hopkins University Press. A penetrating study of the "historian's historian."

Kagan, Donald. 1974, 1981, 1987. *The Archidamian War* (1974), *The Peace of Nicias and the Sicilian Expedition* (1981), and *The Fall of the Athenian Empire* (1987). Ithaca, NY: Cornell University Press. These three volumes offer a detailed analysis of the war's military and diplomatic history.

———. 2003. *The Peloponnesian War*. New York: Viking. A highly readable one-volume account of the war by its most eminent modern scholar.

Loraux, Nicole. 1986. *The Invention of Athens: The Funeral Oration in the Classical City*. Trans. Alan Sheridan. Cambridge, MA, and London: Harvard University Press. An examination of the key role of the Athenian funeral oration in shaping ideals of civic life and defining what Athens was all about.

McGlew, James F. 2002. *Comedy and Political Culture in the Athenian Democracy*. Ann Arbor: University of Michigan Press. An incisive study of the connection between public and private life as it was revealed in the comedies of Aristophanes.

Meiggs, Russell. 1972. *The Athenian Empire*. Oxford: Oxford University Press. A history of Athens' relationship with its allies from the inception of the Delian League to the end of the Peloponnesian War, with chapters on the judgments made on the empire in both the fifth and fourth centuries and a chart recording tribute payments for the years 453 to 420.

Sage, Michael, ed. 1996. *Warfare in Ancient Greece: A Sourcebook*. London and New York: Routledge. A collection of passages relating to Greek warfare, tied together by thoughtful and detailed commentary that includes critical readings of the sources themselves.

CHAPTER NINE

The Crisis of the Polis and the Age of Shifting Hegemonies

The long Peloponnesian War wrought changes in the Greek world so far-reaching that it is impossible to imagine the course of history without it. To be sure, fourth-century Greeks continued to farm and weave and fight, and the politically aware polis remained the primary unit of government for several generations. Years of futile warfare, however, accompanied by economic difficulties and attendant civil strife, led many people to question their relationship to the world around them. Already around the middle of the fifth century, Greek thinkers had begun to ask key questions about the human community. What was the purpose of civic life? Why had people come together in communities in the first place? Were the laws of the polis in accord with nature or in conflict with it? Why were some people free and others slaves? How were Greeks different from non-Greeks? Should Greeks war with other Greeks and enslave them when victorious?

To these questions others came to be added. Why should some have so much more than others? Did the autonomous city-state provide the best way of life? Did the exclusion of women from decision making go without saying? Was warfare worth the sacrifices it entailed? A smaller group debated larger questions—the nature of justice, of piety, of courage, of love. Though many of these concerns had engaged fifth-century minds, the postwar generations were more prone to this kind of questioning and less confident that they lived in the best of all possible worlds. New genres took the place of the old as the search for meaning in life moved forward on different paths; whereas the painful issues of human existence had been explored during the fifth century in tragedy and history, fourth-century thinkers developed the philosophical dialogue and treatise.

While many Greeks were subjecting their traditional values to scrutiny, others perpetuated the squabbles of the fifth century. The Peloponnesian War had solved nothing. In many poleis, the economic problems arising from the war exacerbated existing class tensions and sparked bloody civil conflict, though Athens and Sparta remained free of major stasis. Interpolis warfare continued to be the order of the day, and civil strife—often bloody—was extremely common. Persia's eager involvement heightened an already chaotic situation. When an extraordinary individual arose to the north in the form of Philip of Macedon, the inability of the Greeks to work together productively had dramatic consequences, and the autonomous polis ceased to be the defining political institution of the Greek world.

SOURCES FOR FOURTH-CENTURY GREECE

In almost all respects, the sources for the political history of the fourth century are richer than for the fifth. An abundance of inscriptions sheds light on both international relations and domestic policy, and Aristophanes' *Ecclesiazusae* (*Women in Congress*) and *Plutus* (*Wealth*) provide valuable information about Athens' troubles in the generation after Aegospotami. Plutarch wrote biographies of the Spartans Lysander and **Agesilaus** and of the Theban **Pelopidas**. Much can be gleaned from the vast body of miscellany gathered together in Plutarch's *Moralia*.

Attic oratory provides a vital window into the lives and thought patterns of fourth-century Athenians. Unfortunately, no comparable body of texts has survived from any other polis. Dozens of speeches written for delivery in Athens—sometimes to the courts, sometimes to the assembly—reveal the political, social, and economic situation in the city. Numerous speeches have been preserved under the name of the metic Lysias, though some of them may really be by others. The speech Andocides gave when he served as ambassador during the **Corinthian War** is very useful. Of the many speeches attributed to Isocrates (436–338 BC), about half of the twenty-one that survive were composed during the period between the end of the Peloponnesian War and the rise of Macedon. Those written later also contain useful perspectives on the preceding decades. Indeed, orators active primarily after the accession of Philip of Macedon in 359 provide some of our most precious information about the half century after the end of the Peloponnesian War. Most prominent among these is Demosthenes (384–322 BC), dozens of whose speeches survive. (He is of course a different person from the fifth-century Athenian general of the same name who was executed in Sicily.) Even the speeches that seem to have been wrongly attributed to him comprise a valuable compendium of detail about Greek law.

Speeches, however, must be used with even more caution than is generally exercised with sources. Though a priceless index to the values of the community, and dotted with allusions to historical events, they aimed at persuasion, not truth, and their content must be regarded with some skepticism. Moreover, there were no professional lawyers in Athens; those who had to appear in court often hired trained rhetoricians to write speeches for them. Not surprisingly, the laws embedded in these rhetorical displays were often quoted partially or inaccurately, since the speech writers could not be held to account for their misrepresentations. Even as late as the fourth century, Greek culture was largely oral, and the notion of verification by reference to documents was not as firmly entrenched as it is today.

No history of the fourth century survives that can match that of Herodotus or Thucydides in either painstaking research or depth of analysis. One gifted historian wrote during the fourth century, but his work is almost entirely lost; a little on the Peloponnesian War and on the years 397 to 395 is all that survives of the writer known as the Oxyrhynchus historian because the fragments of his work were found amidst other papyri at the Egyptian village of Oxyrhynchus.

Fortunately, works of Xenophon survive, although his unswerving partiality for Sparta sometimes mars his account of Greek history. We are indebted to his *Hellenica* for much information that would otherwise have been lost; the same is true of his encomiastic biography *Agesilaus*. His *Ways and Means* provides valuable insight into Athens' economic difficulties in the fourth century. The *Anabasis,* the account of his experiences with fellow mercenaries in Persia, is an incomparable eyewitness source for Greco-Persian interaction. The *Cyropaedia,* a historical romance based on the life of Cyrus the Great, tells us a great deal about Greek perceptions of Persia. Various dialogues in which Socrates appears reveal a good deal about the values of Xenophon's social class, and may even tell us a bit about Socrates.

Socrates, like Jesus, expressed himself in speech and wrote nothing. Most of Plato's work and some of Xenophon's consist of conversations imaginatively "reconstructed," in which someone named Socrates leads one or more young men to a greater understanding of some subject. Aristotle was still more prolific. Ancient estimates of Aristotle's prodigious output ranged from four hundred to a thousand different works. Though many are lost and some are thought to be the work of his students, the Aristotelian corpus fills several volumes.

POSTWAR GREECE AND THE STRUGGLE FOR HEGEMONY

Spartans were noble in death but insufferable in victory. Plutarch, as we have seen, described the disappointment Spartan mothers professed if a son made the mistake of surviving a losing battle, and Xenophon narrated the heroic fortitude of the Spartans in hearing about their resounding defeat at the hands of the Thebans in 371: the next day, he wrote, "one could see the relatives of those who had died going around with bright and happy faces, while you would have seen on the street only a few of those whose relatives had been reported as still alive, and these few were making their way with gloomy expression and downcast faces" (*Hellenica* 6.4.16). The protocol for dealing with victory, however, was more elusive. Though at first their hoplites continued to do well on the battlefield, a graceless diplomacy regularly led the Spartans to lose the peace after winning the war. In time, Sparta's aggressive foreign policy would spark a counterattack that would also end the myth of Spartan invincibility on the battlefield, much as Athens' conversion of the Delian League into a tribute-paying empire of subject states had led to the city's defeat at the hands of other Greeks.

Jubilant after bringing Athens to its knees in 404, Sparta housed significant imperialist factions that supported the aggressive policies of Lysander and King Agesilaus. In 395, Sparta's alienated allies combined against it. The resulting Corinthian War ended in 387, but continuing high-handed behavior on Sparta's part caused existing resentments to fester. By 377, Agesilaus' provocative policies resulted both in the formation of a new Athenian naval confederacy and in the alliance of Athens and Thebes. By 371, Thebes was strong enough to defeat Sparta on the battlefield, and the years that followed saw the Thebans cripple Sparta still further by the liberation of Messenia. The Thebans' ascendancy died, however, when their charismatic leader **Epaminondas** was killed in battle, and revolts during the 360s and 350s gradually weakened the **Second Athenian Confederacy**. The resulting vacuum would be filled by Macedon under the resolute leadership of Philip.

The New Imperialists of Sparta

Though details about their collapse are lacking, the murderous decarchies Lysander established in the wake of Aegospotami seem to have been short-lived. Sparta's interference in the domestic affairs of its allies, however, continued. Alarmed by this proclivity, the Thebans declined to help their Spartan allies when King Agis II marched on Elis around 400 to compel the democratic government there to grant independence to the outlying cities in its control. Bad feeling increased when Agis died and Lysander engineered the succession of the king's brother, his friend Agesilaus. When Agesilaus, planning to invade Asia, tried to lend legitimacy to his crusade by sacrificing at Aulis, just as Agamemnon had done en route to Troy, the Boeotian cavalry was dispatched to stand in his way. Agesilaus never forgot the insult, and he lived a long time. The next decades saw frequent warfare between Sparta and Thebes.

The genesis of Agesilaus' journey to Asia is significant in a number of respects. Sparta's relations with Persia began to deteriorate when Lysander's ally Cyrus the Younger became enmeshed in a quarrel over the succession. When his brother Artaxerxes succeeded Darius II in 404, Cyrus mounted a rebellion for which he engaged thirteen thousand Greek mercenaries. Though Cyrus' army was successful at the pivotal battle of Cunaxa near Babylon in 401, in the hour of victory Cyrus caught sight of his brother and, losing control, attempted to kill him. He was promptly cut down in the ensuing melee. This unexpected development left his Greek soldiers in an extraordinarily vulnerable situation, deep in the heart of a huge empire whose king they had just attempted to overthrow. Under the leadership of Xenophon the Athenian, among others, the Greeks miraculously completed the arduous march back to the sea and returned by ship to their homes in Greece. Xenophon's lively account of their adventures in this "march up-country" (*Anabasis*), filled with his psychological insights, survives intact and has provided entertainment and excitement for generations of intermediate Greek students (as well as anthropologists and zoologists). Xenophon's contemporaries also found news of the Greeks' experience in Asia to be profoundly instructive, but along different lines: from it they learned that the Persian empire was by no means as formidable an adversary as Greeks had imagined. In time, this knowledge would issue in the campaigns of Alexander, campaigns that would transform the civilizations of Greece, Egypt, and western Asia. In the short run, it prompted Agesilaus to invade Asia.

While Agesilaus and his men fought in Asia Minor, the Spartans continued to alienate their allies in mainland Greece by intervention in their domestic affairs. When nearly a decade had passed since the end of the Peloponnesian War and the economies of the mainland states had managed a partial recovery, Sparta's long-time allies Thebes and Corinth were open to allying with their old enemy Athens against Sparta. In a remarkable political reversal, the new coalition was aided by money the Persian king Artaxerxes II gave them in the hopes of getting Agesilaus off his back.

The Corinthian War (395–387 BC)

The conflict that ensued was known as the Corinthian War, since much of the fighting took place in the area of the isthmus. It pitted Sparta against a coalition of Athens, Thebes, Corinth, and Argos. The first consequence of this futile war was the death of Lysander, who was killed fighting. The Persians then got their wish: Sparta recalled Agesilaus from Asia. Meanwhile the Persian navy commanded by the satrap Pharnabazus and the Athenian admiral Conon won a decisive victory over Sparta at Cnidus (394 BC) in southwest Asia Minor. Feeling secure at last from the odium that had attached to all who had been present at Aegospotami, Conon now returned to Athens and played a large part in rebuilding the Long Walls there. In this project also he was assisted by Persian ships and money.

To the hoplite warfare of these years was added a crucial new element—a variety of lightly armed troops, including archers, slingers, and javelin throwers. A particularly useful brand of javelin thrower was the man known as the **peltast**, named for the small round wicker shield he carried, the Thracian *peltē*. Enjoying a mobility unthinkable for the hoplites with their heavy shields and armor, peltasts and other lightly armed soldiers expanded the possibilities of warfare. They could be deployed to forage for supplies, to seize and defend passes, to ambush enemy troops, and to ravage enemy territory. They also played key roles in what were basically hoplite confrontations, for harassment at a distance by javelin-throwing peltasts made it difficult for the heavily armed enemy hoplites to retreat. A hardy band of peltasts backing up a hoplite force could easily turn the tide of battle.

Perhaps because of their history of success at hoplite warfare, the Spartans never really learned to make use of light-armed troops—and this despite a harsh lesson administered in 390, when harassment by peltasts in the command of the Athenian **Iphicrates** enabled the Athenians to destroy an entire

Figure 9.1a. This beautiful monument, dating to 394 BC, commemorates the death of Dexileus, a cavalryman who died fighting in the Corinthian War, though the relief depicts him as victorious. Athens, Ceramicus, Oberländer Museum.

Figure 9.1b. Many striking monuments line the south side of the so-called Street of the Tombs in the Ceramicus cemetery. Further along the street a cast stands in the original location of the monument of Dexileus.

Figure 9.2. These remains of the walls built by Conon and other Athenians after the Battle of Cnidus in 394 BC are still visible in Piraeus.

Spartan regiment at the Corinthian port of Lechaeum. The Spartan commander, Xenophon reports,

> ordered [the soldiers in the first age group, from twenty to twenty-nine,] to chase away the assailants, but when these men pursued, they could capture no one, since they were hoplites pursuing peltasts and could not come within a spear's throw of them. (Iphicrates had ordered the peltasts to retreat before the hoplites could come to close quarters with them.) When the Spartan hoplites retired from the pursuit, however, they were scattered about, since each man had individually pursued his target as swiftly as he could, and at this point Iphicrates' men would wheel around and again throw their javelins at the hoplites in front of them, while other peltasts would run alongside the hoplites and throw javelins at their unprotected side....
>
> [Finally] they gave way and fled, some throwing themselves into the sea, while a few made it safely to Lechaeum with the cavalry.
>
> (Xenophon, *Hellenica* 4. 5. 14–15, 17)

This remarkable achievement stunned the Greek world. It also made the reputation of Iphicrates. Subsequently elected on numerous occasions to the strategia, Iphicrates became one of Athens' best-known generals. In time he introduced longer swords and light, comfortable boots that came to be called Iphicratides. Mercenary service and the popularity of light-armed troops frequently went hand in hand; the lesser cost of the light wicker shield made service as a peltast more appealing to the impoverished landless men who chose to support themselves as soldiers of fortune. Like mercenaries, lightly armed soldiers had been used throughout the later fifth century. Having learned of their potential from his painful experiences with the Aetolians, Demosthenes had made sure to deploy them at Pylos and Sphacteria, where they were crucial to the Athenians' success. As in so many areas, what appear as distinguishing characteristics of the fourth century in fact had their roots in the Peloponnesian War.

In 387 the exhausted Greeks agreed to a peace negotiated in Persia. This agreement was the first of several fourth-century attempts at what Diodorus, following Ephorus, called a *koinē eirēnē* (common peace), a peace applicable to all poleis and whose overriding principle was that of autonomy. Throughout the fourth century, intellectuals and politicians expressed longing for such a peace. The form this particular peace took, however, was calculated to drive home to the Greeks the Persian king's clout in Hellenic affairs. The text appears in Xenophon's *Hellenica:*

> King Artaxerxes believes it to be just that the cities in Asia should be his, as also the islands Clazomenae and Cyprus, but that the rest of the Greek cities, both small and large, should be autonomous, except for Lemnos, Imbros, and Scyros, which should, as of old, belong to the Athenians. Whichever of the two parties does not accept this peace, I will wage war on them by land and by sea, with ships and money, taking with me those who accept my views.
>
> (Xenophon, *Hellenica* 5.1.31)

Greece After the King's Peace

The guarantor of the peace was to be Persia's ally Sparta—most ironic, since Sparta was getting a well-deserved reputation for meddling in the internal affairs of other states. In the guise of enforcing autonomy, Sparta promptly set about using force to dismantle a variety of existing arrangements. Mantinea, composed of five villages, was compelled to tear down its fortifications and dissolve itself into the five original communities. The Boeotian League was dissolved, and in 382 the Spartans occupied the Theban acropolis and installed a pro-Spartan government. The Spartan government then executed the head of the pro-Athenian faction at Thebes on the grounds of conspiring with Persia. Sparta's record of collaboration with Persia made this turn of events particularly scandalous throughout Greece.

Sparta, Athens, and Thebes

Spartan control of Thebes was short-lived; in 379, Theban democrats staged a coup and, with Athenian assistance, killed the oligarchs and expelled the Spartan garrison. Not long afterwards, the Athenians allied with the Thebans for mutual protection against Sparta. They also moved forward with their plans to establish a new naval confederacy known as the Second Athenian League. The establishment of the league was commemorated in a decree which proclaimed that all allies "will remain independent and autonomous, enjoying the form of government they wish, admitting no garrisons or magistrates and paying no tribute." League policy was to be controlled by two bodies of equal weight, the Athenian assembly (*ecclēsia*) and the assembly of the allies (*synedrion*). Although no tribute was specified, a system of *syntaxeis* ("contributions") was set up to finance League operations. Periodic defaults make clear the ambivalence of some league members, but the fact that about half the league's seventy-odd members were former members

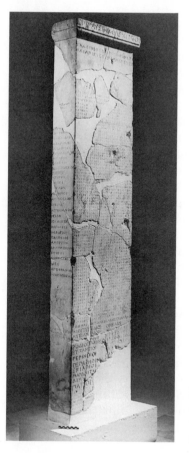

Figure 9.3. The Decree of Aristoteles, 377 BC. The names of the cities that joined the alliance were inscribed on the same stone as the decree. As new states joined, their names were added.

Figure 9.4. Hypothetical reconstruction of the Mausoleum. Its construction was overseen by Mausolus' widow, Artemisia, after his death (c. 350 BC).

of the Delian League certainly needs to be thrown in with the other evidence concerning the popularity of Athens' earlier experiment in league leadership.

From this point on, the history of Greece involves a dizzying sequence of shifting alliances marked by two notable military victories and by outside interventions on the part of eastern potentates such as Mausolus of Caria, technically a Persian satrap but de facto an independent ruler who operated from Halicarnassus (the home town of Herodotus), where he engaged Greek sculptors to construct the huge tomb for him that has given us our English word *mausoleum*. Mausolus saw the Athenian League as a serious obstacle to his ambitions, and he was quick to encourage any unrest he could detect; it was after receiving promises of Carian backing that Rhodes, Cos, and Chios revolted from Athens.

In mainland Greece, the Spartans and the Thebans met twice on the battlefield, with dramatic results on both occasions. In the 370s, Thebes was stronger than ever, led by two intimate friends, Epaminondas and Pelopidas, both of whom had been involved in the liberation of Thebes from the Spartans in 379. On the plain of Leuctra, Epaminondas packed his left wing (normally the weaker side of a Greek formation) fully fifty shields deep. He also advanced in an oblique line so as to hold back the center and right wing while overpowering the enemy with the left at the point where he could expect the Spartan king Cleombrotus to be.

The cutting edge of the Theban line was provided by the elite corps known as the **Sacred Band**, 150 pairs of select hoplites. Plato was probably thinking of the Sacred Band when he wrote that "in view of their mutual emulation and their fear of dishonoring themselves in front of one another, there could be no better organization for a state or an army than for it to consist entirely of pairs of lovers. A handful of such men, moreover, fighting at each other's sides, could defeat practically the entire world" (*Symposium* 178–179). The Sacred Band and the novel tactics of Epaminondas carried the day, killing nearly half the Spartans present, including their king Cleombrotus. The remainder of the Spartan army withdrew, the legend of Spartan supremacy in hoplite warfare forever shattered.

When the Spartans' weakness became apparent to their allies, democratic revolutions broke out in many cities, and a league was formed consisting of Mantinea, Tegea, and the communities of southern and central Arcadia. Arriving in the Peloponnesus to give support to the league, Epaminondas' army was unable to take the city of Sparta, but it ravaged Laconia—and succeeded in the liberation of Messenia. Helots were now to be citizens, and the new capital city of Messene was founded on Mount Ithome. Epaminondas also founded a new capital for the Arcadian League, Megalopolis. This new foundation became the meeting place for the Council of Fifty that represented the communities of the league in proportion to their population, and of the Assembly of the Ten Thousand, open to all citizens. This development indexed a growing interest in experimenting with thoroughly amicable federations, a new phenomenon in Greece.

Within a few years and with comparatively little loss of life, Thebes under Epaminondas and Pelopidas managed to accomplish what generations of Athenians could not. Sparta was finished as an international power. This did not mean, however, that the Thebans achieved their goals. Pelopidas was killed fighting in Thessaly. Epaminondas' support in the Peloponnesus began to wane, and a number of Arcadian communities allied with Sparta—and Athens—against Thebes. Epaminondas met the alliance on the plain of Mantinea in 362 BC. Deploying the same strategy as at Leuctra and outnumbering the enemy by some ten thousand men, the Thebans were victorious. But Epaminondas himself was killed and with his dying breath counseled his countrymen to make peace.

Epaminondas and Pelopidas seemed to have had no plan for Greece beyond replacing Athenian and Spartan imperialism with Theban imperialism. Ultimately, Thebes gained nothing for itself, or for Greece, by its decade of military ascendancy. Though the liberation of Messenia offers great satisfaction to the enemies of slavery in all times and places, by knocking out Sparta as a military power Thebes performed a great service to Philip of Macedon, the future conqueror of Greece, something for which not all Greeks would ultimately be grateful. Philip was also the beneficiary of the agitation of Mausolus, who did so much to foment disaffection in the Second Athenian League. Beginning in the mid-350s, several key states broke away from the confederation. The sanitized Delian League had not endured more than a generation.

Law and Democracy in Athens

The survival of so many speeches and inscriptions from the fourth century enables us to see Athenian democracy in action more vividly in this period than was possible for the fifth century. In some ways, the democracy changed after the restoration of 403, particularly in the constitution of various ad hoc boards of *nomothetai* (creators of laws) to approve and review legislation. The fundamental principles, however, remained the same. All free adult males had a theoretically equal right to participate in government, regardless of differential prestige and economic standing. Women and slaves were excluded, and it was difficult for resident aliens or their children to become citizens. Only men with two citizen parents could vote. Wealth and illustrious ancestry were distinct advantages in seeking public office or pleading your case in court. Although Solon's four classes were never formally abolished, it is clear that at least by the middle of the fourth century, public offices were open to men of all groups. Many thetes and zeugitai were selected for offices chosen by lot, such as service on the boule. Thus participation in government was widely diffused throughout the community of citizen males.

Jokes in Aristophanes' plays reveal a change in the dynamics of assembly attendance. The *Acharnians* (425 BC) alludes to the habit of roping citizens in with a cord covered with red paint that would smear the clothes of the recalcitrant, but when women dress as men and pack the assembly in the *Ecclesiazusae* (392 BC) until a quorum is reached, the real men of Athens complain that they arrived too late to get their pay. The carrot replaced the stick shortly before 400, when a salary of three obols was instituted for attendance at the assembly. By Aristotle's time it had been raised to a drachma (six obols) for an ordinary assembly and a drachma and a half for the *kyria ekklēsia*, that is, the principal assembly of a prytany. At the level of assembly attendance, then, the government of the fourth century was somewhat more democratic than the fifth, for a higher number could afford to take time away from work, though it remained the case that attending meetings was easier for those who lived close by and for those who worked for themselves. The large number of political issues ultimately decided in the courts (when an official was impeached, for example, or when a citizen was indicted via the graphe paranomon) was another democratic element.

As in the courts, where even criminal cases depended on volunteer prosecutors to set them in motion, the voluntary principle played a key role in the assembly. In the absence of organized political parties, concerned citizens took it upon themselves to initiate legislation. No well-defined group of officeholders saw itself—or was seen by others—as clearly marked off from the rest of the populace. By "politicians," people simply meant those who most enjoyed making proposals in the assembly and giving speeches in their support. The importance of oratory and debate to the functioning of the democratic system is attested in the Greek word that comes closest to our word "politician," *rhētōr*. Since *rhētores* shared common interests and habits, no doubt people were comfortable identifying a particular citizen they might see walking down the street as "one of the rhetores." It is important to remember, however, that there was no official "board of rhetores" to which such men belonged. Today it would be peculiar to identify someone who did not hold public office as a politician, but the Athenians saw nothing strange about it. It was precisely because of the power private citizens could gain through skillful oratory that the Athenians made sure that the graphe paranomon was thoroughly entrenched to ensure the accountability even of those who took part in public affairs without holding office. Those convicted of proposing something illegal were generally fined; three convictions deprived a citizen of the right to make further proposals.

The frustrations of Athens' imperialist ventures, the exacerbation of class tensions, and the rise of individualism all played a role in the creation of a new phenomenon at Athens: a large class of wealthy men like the philosopher Plato who chose not to involve themselves in politics. Though this is common enough today, when even among the elite participation in national affairs tends to be limited to a small fraction, this development was noteworthy in fourth-century Athens, for during the preceding century men from affluent families normally had chosen to stand for the high offices they considered appropriate to their status. Now, after the ruinous Peloponnesian War, the quietism some had always chosen became more widespread. The Athenian system, however, still guaranteed that civic responsibility would be shared by a large group—the hundreds who sat on the boule (still a one-year term), the thousands who served as dicasts (jurors) and attended meetings of the ecclesia, and the hundreds who sat for a day in the new body that was periodically constituted to inspect and pass laws, the nomothetai. Socrates was certainly onto something important in the ideology of Athenian democracy when he complained that it meant government by amateurs; Athenian democracy was run largely by people who devoted only a fraction of their time to politics. Nevertheless, the ignorant and untalented were discouraged from involving themselves in public affairs by the Athenians' relentless use of the machinery of accountability against anyone who chose to mount the speaker's platform, let alone hold a state office. The principles of selection by lot and frequent rotation in office, moreover, meant a good deal of hands-on training in the business of government.

One reason Solon was revered as a founder of the democracy was his establishment of courts on which even the poorest citizen could serve. These courts, known as dicasteries (*dikastēria*), formed a key building block of the democracy. In the minds of contemporaries, the notoriously litigious Athens was inseparable from its courts. Aristophanes' play *Clouds*, known primarily for its lampooning of Socrates, gives a feel for the Athenians' sense of humor about themselves; when a student in Socrates' "Think Shop" shows one of his fellow citizens, Strepsiades, a map of the world and tries to point out Athens, Strepsiades replies, "Athens? No way. I don't see any courts in session" (*Clouds* 207). Unlike societies in which vendettas were carried out through violence, with one killing following another, the Athenian democracy offered its courts as tools of revenge; plaintiffs were never squeamish about identifying the quest for vengeance as their motive in bringing a case. Aristotle described its dynamics well when he quoted Homer's account of the anticipation of revenge as "sweeter by far than honey, dripping down the throat and spreading though the heart" (*Iliad* 18.109).

In the hands of unscrupulous politicians, court cases also became tools of factional strife. Trials of impeached officials—strategoi in particular—were frequently of a political nature, for impeachment at Athens was often used as a forum for a debate on foreign policy. Since decrees proposed in the assembly could be challenged by the graphe paranomon, it can be argued that in fourth-century Athens the dicasteries rather than the ecclesia were the ultimate arbiters of policy. In the absence of a supreme court or a body of jurisconsults, dicasteries were also the arbiters of law. Courts were also used, of course, in the adjudication of private lawsuits and criminal cases with no political ramifications.

The Functioning of Dicasteries

All male citizens over the age of thirty were eligible to serve on dicasteries, and dicasts were chosen each year by lot from those who voluntarily presented themselves for service. Because only one day was allotted to each case and juries voted without deliberation, there was no danger that jury service would drag on, interfering with work and home life. Many cases offered spellbinding entertainment, as jurors heard tales of poisoning, embezzlement, conspiracy, and, not infrequently, treason. Frequently, jurors would be in a position to decide whether someone lived or died. As executions were generally carried out the same day as the verdict—Socrates' case was exceptional—a man might well relish the power to see the defendant before him dead by sundown. As we saw in Chapter 6, to ensure that the composition of the courts would reflect the voters of Athens, Pericles had instituted pay for jury service. The three obols a day was only half the average wage of a laborer, but it probably attracted the poor, who could not earn three obols another way, as well as comfortably retired older men who did not need to worry about the consequences of being away from their farms or workshops. Perhaps, then, the jury system was not as representative as Pericles had hoped; nor, of course, did juries include women, slaves, or resident aliens.

The number of dicasts allocated to a given case varied usually from 201 to 501 (odd numbers prevented a tie), although a larger body might be used for high-profile trials of a political nature, and some important political trials were held in the assembly itself. Large juries were designed in part to involve large numbers of citizens in decision making, in part to discourage bribery. Further obstacles to bribery included an elaborate mechanism to select juries by lot and the custom of choosing them at the last possible moment before the trial. Small plaques, each inscribed with a dicast's name, were inserted into a *klērōtērion*, an allotment device that distributed the names haphazardly among the daily juries). Voting was by secret ballot. Each dicast was given two pebbles or bronze discs, one of which had a hole punched through it; a herald would proclaim that "the pebble with the hole is a vote for the prosecutor, and the whole pebble a vote for the defendant." To cast his vote, a dicast would throw the pebble he wanted to be counted into a copper receptacle and discard the other into a wooden one. The decision of an Athenian jury was final and often devastating. There could be no appeal to a higher court or to the people, for an Athenian dicastery was both the highest court and the people. Consequently, dicasts functioned as judges as well as jurors.

The kinds of sly machinations we associate with Athenian courtroom antics were already evident during the Peloponnesian War, a time when the sophists, the tragedians, and the historians Thucydides and Herodotus all were also making use of the art of persuasive speech. In 419 a man known to us only as the Choregus (chorus trainer) was tried for murder when one of the boys in the chorus he had agreed to prepare for a festival died unexpectedly.

The Choregus had accepted the liturgy of preparing a chorus of boys to perform at the festival of the Thargelia. He had incurred the hostility of some of his fellow Athenians, however, by trying to impeach a government official who, in conjunction with three private citizens, was embezzling from the state. The case was to be heard in late April. Just a few days before the court date, however, a certain Diodotus, one of the boys in the chorus, was given some kind of special drink to improve his voice. It did not improve his voice. Instead, it killed him.

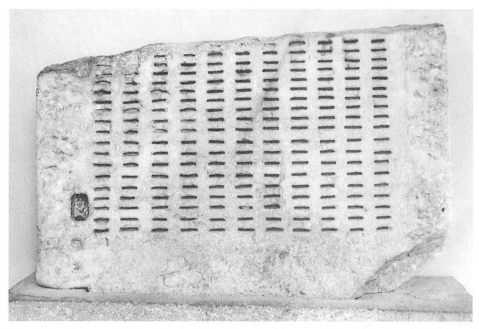

Figure 9.5. This surviving fragment of a kleroterion, or allotment device that assigned jurors to dicasteries, enables us to envision the way it must have functioned. Athens, Agora Museum.

The news of Diodotus' demise was music to the ears of four men about to be tried on the Choregus' accusation, and they pressured the boy's brother Philocrates to lose no time in entering a charge of homicide against the Choregus, who would thus be precluded from appearing in public places until his case had been tried. So much for the impeachment. Unfortunately, the four had overlooked certain fine points of Athenian law that prescribed a pretrial three-month inquiry that had to be conducted by the archon basileus. As it happened, the incumbent was going to be leaving his office in only two months, and he refused to become involved in the case.

The trial of the embezzlers, then, proceeded, and at it they were convicted and heavily fined. Philocrates, brother of the dead Diodotus, apologized to the Choregus (for trying to have him convicted of murder!), and somehow the two men reconciled. A month later, however, the Choregus became a member of the Council of Five Hundred, to which he had been assigned by lot in accordance with Athenian law. No sooner did he take office than it came to his attention that not only were no fewer than three boards of financial officers involved in further embezzlement, but that a number of private citizens were also profiting from the malfeasance—including Philocrates.

Once again, the Choregus brought charges of impeachment, and once again the embezzlers were convicted, but not before Philocrates had lodged a retaliatory charge of homicide against the Choregus. On this occasion the accusation was better timed and the Choregus was brought to trial in November. The verdict in the case is unknown.

Murder and the Courts

The case of the Choregus fell under the Athenian laws concerning homicide. These were the earliest known laws in Athens, going back to the seventh-century lawgiver Draco. Since the Greeks believed that murder offended the gods, there were religious sanctions against homicide, and anyone who killed another person outside of wartime was considered to be polluted. At the same time, a pressing religious and social obligation lay upon the male next-of-kin to avenge a death by killing the perpetrator, even if an act of homicide had been involuntary, say, as the result of a hunting accident. The constant volleys of retaliation upon retaliation that operated in trials of other kinds were particularly evident in homicide trials. The Athenians claimed to have founded the first law court in the world when Agamemnon's son, Orestes, came to Athens from Argos seeking absolution for the murder of his mother, whom he had killed to avenge his slain father. The ancient myth, fleshed out by Aeschylus in his *Oresteia*, had offered the playwright an opportunity to explain how law had come to replace family feud in such a case. The court of the Areopagus in Athens adjudicated the case, marking the historic transfer of jurisdiction from the family to the state.

A personal element, however, remained, for accusations of homicide had to be brought by family members. Throughout Athenian history, self-help remained a central principle in law. It also extended to helping friends and relations in a wide variety of instances. Citizens were expected to show both friendship and civic-mindedness by bringing cases on behalf of otherwise defenseless individuals who were wronged, such as orphans or girls of marriageable age without dowries.

Besides the Areopagus, there were four additional venues for murder trials. The court of the Palladion was used for unintentional killings, the Delphinion for justifiable ones (i.e., homicides committed in self-defense, or by a man who discovered someone in the act of having intercourse with the plaintiff's wife, mother, sister, or daughter). The Prytaneion handled cases of unidentified murderers and cases in which an animal or an object such as a falling roof tile had caused a death. Finally, according to Aristotle, those who were already sentenced to exile for homicide and were on trial for an additional murder had to plead their cases on a boat off the coast of Phreatto (near the port of Piraeus) to avoid polluting the land of Attica.

Conduct of Cases

The seriousness of the charges dictated the amount of time allocated to a trial, and the minutes were measured out by a **klepsydra**, or water clock. Though rules of time were stringently observed, rules of evidence were few. Both plaintiff and defendant were given to boasting about their services to the city, and those in danger of conviction on serious charges did not hesitate to seek sympathy by parading their vulnerable children before a jury. The conduct of cases differed from those in modern western courts in that the Greeks relied heavily on the testimony of witnesses not only about the facts but also about the character of the defendant. It was customary for witnesses to testify to the public services the defendant had performed, and indeed defendants had no hesitation about tooting their own horns. Not atypical was a man who, hauled into court after the end of the Peloponnesian War on a charge of taking bribes, went on at interminable length about his public service, enumerating his endless liturgies, including the two thousand drachmas he had spent when appointed to produce a tragedy at the festival of the Thargelia held in honor of Apollo and Artemis, the dancers for the Great Panathenaea on whom he had spent eight hundred drachmas, the chorus for the Dionysia which had set him back fully five thousand drachmas (including the cost of dedicating a tripod), the seven years during which he equipped warships, at a cost of six talents, and so on and on.

Even after the advent of writing, Greeks remained somewhat suspicious of texts, and jurors usually trusted the testimony given by witnesses under oath more than written evidence; they understood that a document such as a will could be forged. Slaves were often the best witnesses, for they were ubiquitous and often obliged to assist their owners in illicit activities. Theoretically, the testimony of slaves was admissible only if it had been given under torture, but we are uncertain how often such torture was actually inflicted. Following a guilty verdict, prosecutor and defendant proposed alternate penalties, as in the case of Socrates,

Figure 9.6. Modern model of a klepsydra, or water clock. In this device, which was used to time speeches in the law courts, water drained from the upper vessel to the lower one. It took several minutes for a vessel to empty. Ten vessels were allocated for cases involving large sums of money.

and the jury decided between the two. The principle of self-help also meant that in civil cases the prosecutor, who was by custom the same person as the plaintiff, had to execute the judgment himself, something often more easily said than done. When the orator Demosthenes succeeded in convincing a jury that his guardians had dissipated the fortune his father had left, it was his own responsibility to try to collect the missing funds and property.

Crime and Punishment

Monitoring crime in classical Athens was a very different affair from what it is in modern times. There was for all practical purposes no law enforcement agency. The Scythian archers the state engaged as "police" were in fact used primarily for crowd control. If you were hauled into court and charged with a crime, it was often because one of your fellow citizens had dragged you there.

Athenian ideas about what penalties various crimes called for also differed from those of most moderns. Abandoning a helpless newborn to its fate was not a crime at all, but rather an acceptable means of family planning or avoiding embarrassment. Killing a slave was illegal, but if the slave you killed was your own, nobody had the legal standing to take you to court, because the slave's relatives would not be citizens; ritual purification would probably be called for to purge you of blood guilt, but nothing beyond that. Whipping and torture were acceptable punishments for slaves but not for citizens, at least not after the fifth century. Citizen defendants were sometimes slapped with manageable fines, but it was not unusual for Athenian juries to vote for exile, the confiscation of property, the termination of civic rights (such as making proposals in the assembly), truly crippling fines, or death. Crimes that would be considered misdemeanors today could be punishable by death in Athens; we read of a man executed for stealing clothes. Surviving texts claim that the death penalty was mandated in a wide variety of cases ranging from citing a nonexistent law to failing to inscribe the name of a man in debt to the state on the official list. Socrates was put to death for his teachings in 399; Menon the miller was executed for keeping a free boy in his mill, and one Euthymachus was executed for putting a free girl from the town of Olynthus in northern Greece in a brothel. Both the lesser-known cases illustrate the Athenians' determination to uphold the distinction between slave and free: Menon and Euthymachus had treated free people as one would treat a slave. Although many Athenians were in fact executed, self-imposed exile was considered entirely acceptable, and indeed after the first speeches had been delivered at a homicide trial, the accused was free to leave town rather than wait to see how the trial turned out. Even the decision not to turn up for one's court date in the first place was honored, and extradition was not generally practiced.

In a society that relied to a considerable extent on self-help, unofficial executions were not unusual; a man who caught you in his house at night, or in a compromising situation with his wife at any hour of the day, was entitled to kill you on the spot. The Athenians saw no point in paying people to build and oversee large jails, so imprisonment was not a common punishment. People who spent time in jail did so only if they were unable to post bail prior to their trial, if they were unable to pay a fine levied against them, or if they had been condemned to death and there was some unusual reason not to carry out the sentence immediately. These penalties would also weigh heavily on a man's family: a jury that voted to deprive a man of his civic rights would sometimes also disfranchise his descendants. Another penalty, the razing of a man's house, deprived his family of a place to live.

The officials in charge of executions were known simply as the Eleven. Like most other Athenian officials, they were chosen by lot. The methods used to execute criminals varied over the course of Athenian history. There is some evidence that prior to the fourth century those destined for execution may have been hurled into a pit known as the *barathron*, but it may be that the barathron was used simply as a depository for the bodies of the executed. At some point a gruesome means of execution known as *apotympanismos* came into use. We are not certain exactly how this worked, but it was highly unpleasant, guaranteeing a prolonged and wretched death. It involved wooden boards and iron collars. It was similar, in other words, to crucifixion, but without the nails. This nicety is probably due to the Athenians' aversion to shedding the blood of their fellow citizens. In wartime, enemies, even civilians, were regularly killed by the sword, but the blood of fellow citizens was considered to be polluting. Archaeologists have found a mass grave near Athens containing seventeen skeletons with necks, wrists, and ankles encircled by iron bands that were attached to pieces of wood. Probably such people had met their death by apotympanismos. Finally, hemlock came to be used, as in the case of Socrates, although apotympanismos may well have remained in use as well.

The Fourth-Century Polis

Although the bulk of our evidence comes from Athens, most Greeks, of course, lived in other states. In the fourth century as in the fifth, some Greek poleis were governed by democracies, others by oligarchies that varied in their narrowness. As had always been the case in Greece, uneven distribution of wealth fostered tensions that threatened constantly to erupt and disturb the tenuous concord that united citizens, and changes of constitution were frequent. Although warfare remained a fact of life, many people were sick of it and had come to question its efficacy in improving their lives. While some poorer citizens continued to welcome war for the pay it offered to rowers in the fleet, those who had land or commerce to protect were hesitant. No longer did war seem to promise either the tangible rewards of booty or the intangible ones of glory and prestige. The ideal of the citizen-soldier was wearing thin, and mercenaries conducted an increasing share of the fighting. Agriculture remained the basis of the economy, but the devastation of the land during the Peloponnesian War had fostered a drift to the cities. By throwing people together, this development heightened the awareness of economic inequality and sharpened class bitterness. Plato and Aristotle both took it for granted that a polis consisted in reality of two cities, one of the many poor and one of the few rich. The division of citizens into haves and have-nots that had always marked Greek states was exacerbated in the fourth century by the increased poverty of the have-nots, bringing latent tensions to the surface, where they could no longer be ignored.

Stasis

Where the economy was most prosperous and families from the lower classes had the best chance of remaining above the poverty level, stasis might be avoided, as was the case in democratic Athens, the stablest state of the fourth century. Many poleis with large concentrations of poor people, however, were consumed with civil strife; Xenophon's *Hellenica* mentions over thirty instances. Bloodshed was common, and religious pieties were often ignored. In 392, Corinthian democrats violated the sanctity of temples by murdering oligarchs who had taken refuge there. Diodorus reports revolutions in Corinth, Sicyon, and Phlius, and Xenophon recorded serious tensions in Tegea, Phlius, Sicyon, Pellene, and Elis. Diodorus, who shared the antidemocratic orientation of most ancient writers, took a certain satisfaction in relating the torture and murder of the elite by Argive democrats in 371, when class tensions erupted with violence exceptional even by Greek standards. After the execution of twelve hundred influential men, Diodorus contends,

> the people did not spare even the demagogues. For because of the scope of the calamity the demagogues, fearing that some unforeseen turn of fortune might overtake them, desisted from their agitation, and the mob, now feeling that they had been left in the lurch, were angry and put them all to death. Thus these men received punishment befitting their crimes as if some divinity were visiting its just resentment upon them, and the people, purged of their mad fury, were restored to their senses.
>
> (Diodorus, *Library of History* 15.58.4)

Internal strife was exacerbated by tensions among poleis. Thus, for example, a certain Euphron gained power at Sicyon by playing on anti-Spartan feeling in the Peloponnesus. He "told the Argives and the Arcadians," Xenophon reports, "that if the wealthiest men gained control of Sicyon, the city would again take the side of Sparta whenever a suitable opportunity arose. 'But,' he said, 'if the city becomes a democracy, you can be certain that it will remain loyal to you'" (7.1.44). Outside help was available in stasis. In Elis, Xenophon reports, while the Eleans were at war with the Arcadians, the democrats enlisted the Arcadians' help in seizing the acropolis. Assistance might also come from the large pool of available mercenaries, such as those who helped Euphron regain power in Sicyon.

Both Athens and Sparta used the prevailing discord and demoralization to good rhetorical effect in arguing for their own hegemony. Those who would reject Athenian hegemony in favor of the "autonomy" guaranteed by the **King's Peace**, Isocrates argued, should think again:

> For who would want a situation where pirates control the seas and second-rank mercenaries take control of the cities? Instead of making wars against other people to defend their territory, the citizens fight against each other within their own walls, and more cities have been taken captive than before we made the peace; because of the frequency of revolutions, those living in the cities are more disheartened than those who were punished with exile.
>
> (Isocrates, *Panegyricus* 116–117; Papillon)

DOCUMENT 9.1

Isocrates puts similar arguments about Spartan hegemony in the mouth of Archidamus III, the son of Agesilaus. Even allowing for a considerable degree of rhetorical exaggeration, the picture of life in the Peloponnesus is sobering.

I think that the rest of the people in the Peloponnesus in general, especially the democratic faction, who we assume are particularly hostile to us, long for our protection now; they gained nothing that they had hoped for when they revolted, but instead of freedom, they got just the opposite.... Finally, the factionalism that in the past they used to see in other states, they now see breaking out almost daily in their own communities. Their troubles have made them all so equal that no one can tell who is the worst off. No city is unharmed, and no city is without neighbors who would do it harm.... They have so little trust and so much hostility toward one another that they fear their fellow citizens more than their enemies. Instead of the unity of spirit they had during our rule and the prosperity they had from one another, they have become so inhospitable that those who have wealth would rather throw it into the sea than give help to someone in need, while those who are in need would prefer not to find some money by chance but to steal it from the rich.

Isocrates, *Archidamus* 64–66; Papillon, adapted.

Beginning late in the fifth century, Greek intellectuals had begun calling for *homonoia* (concord) among citizens, but the frequency with which the appeal was made reveals the discordant reality; in fact, the slogan caught on during the contentious days of the Peloponnesian War. In praising the rule of law, Socrates had insisted in the pages of Xenophon's *Memorabilia* that throughout Greece homonoia was advocated by the "best men" (the aristoi). Aristotle, however, took a darker and more realistic view. In some states of his own day, he wrote in the *Politics*, the oligarchs in charge took an oath to be hostile to the demos and "plot whatever evil possible against the people" (1310a).

Not all poleis were constantly torn apart by stasis and debilitated by interpolis wars. Since the principal cause of internal weakness and vulnerability to outside attack was the frustrations of the poor, prosperity might act as a powerful deterrent. Megara with its brisk woolen trade flourished throughout the fourth century, and civil strife was rare. The progress of the economy was facilitated by peace with other poleis; the alliance between Corinth and Athens during the Corinthian War eliminated Megara's pivotal position in interpolis diplomacy, and the Megarians seem to have preserved their neutrality throughout that war and for the subsequent decades. Megarian woolens found eager markets throughout Greece. Sheep grazed in abundance, and large numbers of slaves, probably mostly female, turned out well-made and inexpensive garments. The private homes of Megara were known for their elegance, and a variety of monuments decorated the city. The Athenian sculptor Praxiteles (370–329 BC) produced numerous statues of the gods for the sanctuaries of Artemis and Apollo and the temple of Aphrodite there. Scopas, who contributed to the **Mausoleum** in Caria, also worked in Megara. Exactly what kind of government fourth-century Megara enjoyed is uncertain—Plato praised it but did not describe it—but it seems at least to have been fairly stable. Megara was not, however, entirely immune to the endemic stasis of the fourth century; Diodorus reports an abortive uprising in the 370s.

Workers in the Cash Economy

The economy of each polis was different, but throughout Greece prestige attached to some kinds of work more than to others. Because both social status and economic security were associated with self-sufficiency through farming or making money by selling the produce of one's land, free citizens tended to avoid involvement in commerce and banking, turning these activities over to metics and slaves. Such workers became important in the fourth century and often made considerable fortunes, since one phenomenon that distinguished the polis of the fourth century from that of the fifth was the rise of banking.

Bank owners trusted slaves to manage the daily operations of banks independently and even to travel with large sums of cash. Such slaves were highly skilled, usually literate, and very valuable. A slave who managed a bank could be completely responsible for his master's property. Therefore, a master might write a will freeing his bank manager on condition that the former slave marry his former owner's widow and manage the bank on behalf of the couple's minor children. Manumitted slaves became metics. Two of these metics, Phormio and Pasio, were among the wealthiest Athenians of the fourth century. In gratitude for their generous benefactions to the state, Athens rewarded them with citizenship. Thus slaves in banking might experience rapid social mobility.

The stigma that attached to working for someone else was greater for women than for men; few women chose to work outside the home, but many were compelled to do so by poverty. In the fourth century as in the fifth, however, some women did work at service jobs outside their homes. Slave women were sometimes rented out by their owners, and former slaves, metics, and even citizen women in straitened financial circumstances worked at a variety of jobs. Some hired themselves out as nurses for other women's children, some sold goods in the marketplace, and older women often served as hired mourners at funerals. Poor women might work as grape pickers or as vendors of a variety of goods ranging from bread to ribbons. In *Inscriptiones Graecae*, we find various occupations for freed slaves, such as horse tender, salt vendor, perfume vendor, shoe seller, honey seller, frankincense seller, sesame seed seller, and unguent boiler. Gravestone inscriptions commemorate a number of freedwomen listed by profession:

> Good Theoxene, wet nurse
> Good Paideusis, wet nurse
> Good Pynete, wet nurse
> Elephantis, cloak seller
> Thraitta, unguent boiler
> Melitta, salt vendor
> (*Inscriptiones Graecae*[2]. 11647, 12387, 12559, 11254, 11688, 12073)

Although unacceptable for citizen women, prostitution was probably the work done most frequently by women outside the home. A few, like Aspasia, were free-born, but not Athenians. Some were put to work when they were still children. Youthful beauty was prized; older women were least expensive. Though probably most of the profits were made by men, some women profited by running brothels and prostituting other women.

In Corinth, Nicarete, herself a former slave, purchased young girls from slave-holders and trained them for their work:

> Nicarete, who was the freedwoman of Charisius of Elis and the wife
> of his cook Hippias, bought seven girls when they were small chil-
> dren. She was an astute judge of natural beauty in little girls and fur-
> thermore she understood how to bring them up and train them skill-
> fully, for she made this her profession and earned her living from the
> girls. She was in the habit of addressing them as daughters, so that
> by giving the impression that they were free women she could extract
> the highest fees from those who wanted to get close to them. When
> she had reaped the profit of the youthful prime of each girl, she sold
> all seven of them without exception: Anteia, Stratola, Aristocleia,
> Metaneira, Phila, Isthmias, and this Neaera here . . .
>   Neaera . . . was working with her body, although she was still
> extraordinarily young, not having yet reached puberty.
>   (Pseudo-Demosthenes 59.18–20)

Neaera's further adventures are also detailed in this speech, which is included in the corpus of Demosthenes although it was almost certainly written by some-one else. Two of Neaera's clients purchased her from Nicarete to be their slave. In time, they offered Neaera the opportunity to buy her freedom. Neaera borrowed her purchase price from former clients, and repaid them from her earnings as a free prostitute. Her attempt at social mobility was eventually quashed, however, after she had moved to Athens, married a certain Stephanus, and pretended to be an Athenian citizen. Stephanus had brought an indictment for an illegal proposal and another for murder against Apollodorus, son of the wealthy metic Pasio who had been granted Athenian citizenship. Apollodorus in turn brought Neaera to trial for false assumption of citizen rights. He also charged Stephanus with living with a non-Athenian woman as though she were his wife, and with giving Neaera's daughter in marriage to an Athenian citizen as being his own daughter born from a citizen-woman. Although the speech written for Apollodorus makes fascinating reading, Neaera's fate remains uncertain, as the outcome of the trial is unknown.

PHILOSOPHY AND THE POLIS

The changing political situation in the Greek world helped shape Greek thought in each new generation, and the problems of the fourth-century polis were no exception. Philosophy evolved with the polis and survived it when

Philip of Macedon brought the freedom of the independent city-states to an end in 338 BC. The Greek word *philosophos* means a lover of wisdom, and for many years before Plato and Aristotle founded their famous schools in Athens, Greek thinkers had taken delight in searching for the underlying principles that shaped the cosmos and determined the life humans made in it. It was in the realm of social and political theory that philosophy was most closely tied to the polis. Because most surviving texts of political theory were composed in democratic Athens, one might imagine that they praised democracy. In fact, the opposite is true; the principal texts of Greek political theory were the work of intellectuals who were intensely critical of democratic government. Indeed, modern political scientists have observed that political theory—literally, "looking at the city-state"—was invented to show why democracy could not possibly work. It is the workings of democracy itself that reveal the ideology behind it.

Democracy and Political Theory

The Old Oligarch had offered a sardonic "defense" of Athenian democracy with biting irony as a beautifully efficient way of guaranteeing the suppression of one class by another, but no surviving text treats the dynamics of democracy in a positive way. Reconstructing the theory behind democracy from written texts requires assembling patches from a variety of sources that engage the issue only obliquely. Thucydides' version of Pericles' funeral oration gives us a sense of what the Athenians at any rate prized in their government. At Athens, Pericles says, worth is assessed in terms of ability, not wealth or class. Athenians consider remaining aloof from politics a vice, not a virtue. They view debate as an aid to constructive action, not a hindrance.

Just as Thucydides, who was not particularly sympathetic to democracy, included Pericles' speech in his history, so Plato, one of democracy's sharpest critics, included a statement of democratic ideology in his dialogue *Protagoras.* There the famous sophist tells a quaint myth in support of his thesis that all people possess the rudiments of civic-mindedness. In earliest times, Protagoras says, people were unable to live together constructively in cities because of their lack of *politikē technē*, the skill of forming and managing a polis. Seeing this and fearing the destruction of the species, Zeus sent Hermes to bring *aidōs* (shame) and *dikē* (justice) to mortals. When Hermes asked Zeus whether these should be distributed to a select few, as was the case with the arts of medicine and other techniques, or to everyone, Zeus ordered him to give some to everybody, since "cities cannot be formed if only a few share in these skills as they do in the other arts" (322D). It is for this reason, Protagoras says, that when the Athenians come together to make decisions that require the sense of justice that goes into political wisdom "they take advice from everybody, since it is held that for states to exist everyone must partake of this excellence" (322E–323E). Because the politike techne is diffused throughout the community, Protagoras concludes, the Athenians do right to welcome political

Figure 9.7. This portrait of Plato is a Roman copy of the head of a lost fourth-century BC Greek statue. Paris, The Louvre.

advice from anyone who is moved to give it. Nowhere does he suggest that everyone is equally skilled in civics, but everyone, he argues, has at least a little.

Our best clue to the theory of democracy is its practice. The Athenian democracy itself reveals what most men in Athens believed about government: they believed in a democracy of male citizens that required active participation on the part of these citizens, guaranteed by frequent rotation in office, and they believed that the average man was qualified to make political decisions, as evidenced by the use of the lot and the taking of important decisions in the assembly by majority vote. They identified participation in war as a key aspect of citizenship for men. They believed in trial by jury, and they feared the corruption inherent in small groups more than the mob psychology that threatened large ones. They believed that the people had the right to call its officials to account with regularity and on the slightest pretext. They believed in severe punishment for a wide variety of offenses, including military incompetence and the seduction of the wives, daughters, and sisters of citizens. They believed that the stability of the state was so crucial that it was reasonable, under the system known as ostracism, to exile for ten years a man who had done nothing to break the law. They believed in slavery and patriarchy. They believed that the control of women's sexuality was essential to the smooth functioning of the community and that the sequestration of women and girls was a good step in this direction. We know all this not because they wrote it down but because of how they chose to run their government and live their lives.

Although many Athenians identified their democratic constitution with the rule of law, Greek intellectuals sometimes saw things differently. Plato frequently identified democracy with tyranny, and Aristotle complained that the decrees of a democratic assembly were no different from the edicts of the tyrant.

Plato

It is certainly a tribute to Athenian democracy that it produced its own most astute critics. An aristocrat from one of Athens' most distinguished families and a relative of the oligarch Critias, Plato became a disciple of Socrates and was profoundly shaken by his death. Over his lifetime, Plato composed numerous dialogues, in most of which the principal part is played by a character he identifies as Socrates. What is beauty? What is piety? What is justice? What is love? These questions were explored in Plato's Socratic dialogues. As Plato's thinking evolved with the passing of time, this "Socrates" had less and less in common with the historical Socrates and came to serve as a vehicle for Plato's own ideas.

Chief among these was the theory of Forms. Plato's belief in Forms was connected to his passion for definitions, for both depend on a conviction that disparate acts and items can nonetheless be classified in categories—that beautiful objects and acts and ideas, for example, all have something in common. In Plato's view, they all partake of the ideal Form of beauty.

The relationship of appearance to reality in Plato's worldview can perhaps be best grasped in the context of mathematics. A ring or a princely diadem or the perimeter of a hoplite shield might seem to the casual observer to be a circle, but these round objects are not circles in the same sense that the locus of all points in a given plane equidistant from a given point is a circle. They only look like circles; if you were to put them under a magnifying glass you would see that they were not circles at all, merely objects vaguely circular in appearance that bring to mind the Form of the circle. Only the circle depicted in the mathematical definition is a circle. Some people might say that these concrete objects are real circles whereas the geometrical concept is imaginary, but Plato was not one of these people. For Plato, only the concept is real. The tangible objects are debased copies, feeble imitations of the ideal Form. Plato, in other words, was an idealist and a dualist. He believed in an opposition between the physical world of appearances, which are deceptive, and the intellectual universe of ideas, which represent reality and provide the only reliable basis for moral and political action. The first is tawdry and serves only to distract people from ultimate truth; the second is noble, and to contemplate it ennobling.

Plato was a revolutionary. The close connection between appearance and reality was fundamental to Greek civilization. If you are rich and handsome, most of his contemporaries believed, then probably you are also good; if you are poor and ugly, probably you are bad as well. If everyone admires you, then all is right with the world; if you are despised, then you have no reason to go on. For most Greek men, reputation, power, and material success were central to happiness. Like Socrates before him, who preferred being right to being alive, Plato identified values that were more important than being well liked or envied. In *The Republic*, his dialogue on government and education, he raised a key question about justice. Let us say, he proposed, that you had a magic ring that would make you invisible. Would you practice justice, or would you take the opportunity to grab as much power and wealth as you could, practicing injustice in the happy expectation of getting away with it?

As usual, Plato does not appear in this dialogue. His brothers Glaucon and Adeimantus, however, do, and they are quick to point out the customary Greek view that only convention, nomos, holds people back from committing injustice. The behavior that the man-made nomoi of punishment and disgrace discourage, however, is encouraged by physis, the natural instinct that urges people to take whatever they can get away with taking. This was the drive that Thucydides' Athenians at Melos had identified as the customary engine of human conduct; people, they had argued, "are always forced by the law of nature to dominate everyone they can" (5.105). This sort of thing, Glaucon and Adeimantus say, is what the average person believes. It is up to Socrates to show that justice is in fact good for people.

This is a large task, and Socrates decides to shift gears and explore justice in the state in order to discover justice in the individual writ large. In the course of this exploration, he spins out threads that are even more revolutionary. The subject of the dialogue becomes an ideal state of Plato's imagining. It is a state divided into three classes, corresponding to Plato's conception of the tripartite nature of the soul. At the top are the guardians, who represent reason. Their supreme rationality, inculcated by years of education, qualifies them to govern. After them come the auxiliaries, who are characterized by a spirited temperament that suits them for the duties of soldiers. Last come the majority, who correspond to desire in the soul; they are not especially bright or brave and live only to satisfy their own material yearnings. They will do all the jobs in the state other than governing and fighting. Initially, a tricky myth will assign people to classes, and then the three groups will reproduce themselves biologically. A child who seems to have been born into the wrong class will be transferred, but Plato seems to have great faith in heredity, for he plainly expects such cases to be rare.

The only classes that require much education are the top two, and the education and lives of the guardians soon become the focus of Plato's attention. They will study for many years, approaching the understanding of the Forms by applying themselves to mathematics. Plato, Xenophon, and other Socratics believed that the soul has no sex, that women and men have the same potential. In the society envisioned in *The Republic*, the guardians will be of both genders, and Plato advocates a unisex education for them.

DOCUMENT 9.2

Though on the whole, Socrates argues, women are inferior to men in all skills besides weaving and cooking, nonetheless there will always be individual women who are more skilled than individual men. When Glaucon agrees, Socrates launches into his plan for having guardians of both sexes (though he always speaks of guardians and their wives, never guardians and their husbands).

Soc.—There is no aspect of the administration of a state that should be reserved either to a woman just because she is a woman or to a man just because he is a man. Natural gifts are to be found in both creatures alike, and every occupation is suitable for both, so far as their natures are concerned, though the woman is for all purposes weaker than the man.

Glau.—Certainly.

Soc.—Should we then make all functions over to men, and nothing to women?

Glau.—I don't see how we could.

Soc.—The case is rather, I should think, that one woman has the natural disposition of a physician and another not, and one may be naturally musical, and another not.

Glau.—Surely.

Soc.—Can we then deny that one woman may be warlike or athletic, and another not?

Glau.—I think not.

Soc.—And again, one may love knowledge, another hate it; one may be high-spirited, another lacking in spirit?

Glau.—That is also true.

Soc.—It follows that one woman will be suited by her nature to be a Guardian, another will not; for were not these the qualities for which we selected our men Guardians? So for the purpose of the guardianship of the state, women and men have the same nature, save in so far as the woman is weaker.

Glau.—It would appear so.

Soc.—Women of this type, then, must be chosen to share the life and the duties of Guardians with men of the same type, since they are capable of it and of a similar nature, and the same natures must be assigned the same pursuits.

Glau.—Yes.

Soc.—We come around, then, to our previous position, that to give our Guardians' wives the same training for mind and body does not in any way go against nature. The system we proposed, being in accordance with nature, was not impossible or utopian. Rather, the contrary practice which is now in use turns out to be the unnatural one.

Glau.—So it appears.

Soc.—Well, we set out to inquire whether the plan we proposed was workable and also the best. We have acknowledged that it is workable; we must next settle whether it is the best.

Glau.—Plainly.

Soc.—In order to produce a woman who can be a guardian, will we have one education for men and another for women, considering that the nature that we are handing over for instruction is the same?

Glau.—Not at all.

Plato, *The Republic* 455D–456C

The guardians' lives will be unusual in many respects. The acquisitive principle that guides most people's activities will be alien to them, for Plato envisions a communitarian regime within the guardian class: private property, though it exists for the other two classes, will be abolished for the top group. Nor will they have spouses in the conventional sense of the word. In short, they will have no oikoi—something that makes them eminently un-Athenian. To perpetuate the system, however, the guardians must reproduce, even though they will not live in households. An elaborate mathematical scheme will dictate temporary couplings. Children born of these short-term "marriages" will be mixed in with all the other guardian children conceived around the same time and raised in common nurseries. Thus no parent will know his or her own child and vice versa.

Like other utopias, Plato's is designed to demonstrate the shortcomings of real states. Whether he ever planned or even wished to see his Republic established is uncertain. What is clear is his dislike of the existing governments in Greece, and particularly of democracy. Good government, Plato concluded, will never come into being until philosophers and rulers are one and the same. He actively tried to make his dream a reality: twice Plato went to Syracuse and unsuccessfully tried to transform the city's tyrant Dionysius II (see below) into a "philosopher king." In addition, Plato founded a school he called the **Academy** because of its location by the groves of the ancient Greek hero Academus. Putting into practice the principles he expressed in *The Republic,* Plato even took a few female students. Former students at the Academy were politically active throughout Greece and included Plato's friend Dion, who overthrew Dionysius II, and Demetrius of Phaleron, the future tyrant of Athens, as well as Aristotle, who was the tutor of Alexander the Great. Other students became famous as tyrannicides: the assassins of Clearchus, the tyrant of Heraclea in the Black Sea, became the heroes of a philosophical novel written in Roman times. No wonder Athenian democrats were suspicious of philosophers! Besides political figures, however, the Academy also produced many famous philosophers, astronomers, mathematicians, and scientists. The presence of scientists at the Academy is a testament to its breadth, for Plato himself was not drawn to science. How could he be, when he believed that only the eternal mattered—that the Forms were the ultimate and sole reality? Science deals with change and with motion. Like Parmenides, Plato conceived reality as unchanging and unchangeable. Without a mechanism for explaining change, Plato's idealist philosophy was antithetical to science.

Aristotle

Aristotle founded the great institution of scientific learning at Athens, the **Lyceum**. The son of a court physician in Macedon, he had been trained in scientific observation from his youth. He was never happier than in the meticulous observation and classification of species. Scholars in all disciplines, but especially perhaps biologists, will recognize the delight he took in connecting the particular to the general, and in observing nature at work in all its perfection; even in the animals that are not attractive to the senses, he wrote, "the craftsmanship of nature provides extraordinary pleasures to those who are able to recognize the causes in things and who have a natural inclination to philosophy" (*On the Parts of Animals* 645a 7ff). For Aristotle, the dynamic power of change accounted for a great deal of the excitement of mental life. And not only this; he saw movement toward a particular goal—teleology, from the Greek *telos* meaning "end" or "ultimate purpose"—as characteristic of the universe as a whole. In his view, the goal toward which everything was moving was god, but not a god most Greeks would understand. Unlike

Figure 9.8. Roman marble copy reflecting the head of a lost Greek portrait statue of the philosopher Aristotle from the fourth century BC. Vienna, Kunsthistorisches Museum.

the humanlike deities of Greek tradition, Aristotle's god was a perfect being exist-ing outside time and space, one that did not undergo change but was the source of all change in the universe. This god, or, in Aristotle's terminology, the "prime mover," shaped the universe in its ends but was not itself moved. Aristotle's philosophy was very popular in Europe during the Middle Ages, when Thomas Aquinas (1225–1274) adapted it to Christian theology.

Whereas Plato apparently never married or had children, Aristotle was firmly grounded in the customary relations of Greek society. He lived with two suc-cessive women, his wife, Pythias, and then, after Pythias' death, his concubine, Herpyllis; he had a daughter and a son. After Plato's death in 347, when Aristotle had studied at the Academy for nearly twenty years, he left Athens and took up residence in Assos in Asia Minor. Several years later he returned to Macedon, where Philip had summoned him to serve as tutor to the young prince Alexander. Back in Athens in 335, he established the Lyceum. He and his students conversed there while strolling through the colonnaded walks (*peripatoi*, which gave his fol-lowers the name "peripatetics" by which they are still known today). When he was accused of impiety in the burst of anti-Macedonian feeling that erupted after news of Alexander's death arrived in Athens, Aristotle left Attica. Looking back somberly at the trial of Socrates, he observed that he did not want the Athenians to sin a second time against philosophy. He died the following year, in 322.

That Aristotle loved science while Plato loved mathematics reveals a profound difference between the two men and their ways of engaging with the world of ideas. Living things excited Aristotle and inspired in him the desire to categorize them. The same urge would lead him to classify all the political arrangements familiar in his day in the *Politics*. Where Plato had used reason as virtually his only tool in the quest for understanding, Aristotle placed tremendous importance on observation. Though reason was not his only tool, he was the founder of the dis-cipline of logic. To Aristotle we owe the articulation of the fundamental principle of the syllogism—the principle that tells us that if A yields B and B yields C, then A by itself must yield C. If Sneaky is a cat and all cats are mammals, then Sneaky must be a mammal. Since the Parthenon is in Athens and Athens is in Attica, then the Parthenon must be in Attica.

Whereas Plato had developed a framework for discussing politics so theoret-ical that scholars are often puzzled about what real states he might have had in mind, Aristotle approached the question of the human community by amassing and analyzing a tremendous amount of data. In this project he was assisted by his students at the Lyceum, where 158 essays on constitutions of various poleis were drawn up. That all these have disappeared except for *The Athenian Constitution* is an incalculable loss to the study of Greek history.

In his conception of the universe at large, Aristotle differed with Plato on a key point—the existence of Forms. To Aristotle, as to the average person, Forms were not real. Only the combination of form and matter created something real. Plato, Aristotle thought, had failed, like Parmenides, to account for change. In their views of the human community, Plato and Aristotle were quite similar. Both saw the polis as more than a practical arrangement for the exchange of goods and mutual protection; for them, human existence and the existence of the polis were coterminous. The lack of a state structure would make a fully human existence impossible, but a structure larger than the polis seemed unimaginable too. Aristotle identified the largest possible size for the state at ten thousand citizens, the number who could be addressed by a speaker at one time. Aristotle is famous for having said "Man is a political animal." What he actually meant is that people are animals whose nature it is to live in a polis. By so saying, he implicitly denied the full humanity of all non-Greeks. Only in a polis could individuals realize their social natures and grow through the sharing of ideas. This opportunity, however, was limited to men who belonged to a social class that guaranteed them leisure for contemplation. Powerful obstacles prevented the poor from participating in politics—especially the non-farming poor, who did "banausic" labor, arduous jobs that compromised the mind along with the body. The best state, he concludes, will not make common laborers citizens, for citizens must have adequate property to ensure sufficient leisure for goodness and political activity. So much for democracy.

Aristotle's political philosophy differed from Plato's in two key respects. First, Aristotle believed in collective wisdom: a mass of people who are individually unwise, he argues, may surpass the wisdom of the few best men, just as potluck dinners may prove to be tastier than those hosted by a single individual. The masses, he claims, can be perfectly good judges of music and poetry, since "some appreciate one thing, some another, and taken together they appreciate everything" (*Politics* 1281b). For this reason, he is open to a compromise similar to that of Solon: poor people in his ideal state would be allowed to choose officials and hold them to account, but not to hold office. Second, Aristotle had such a powerful belief in natural hierarchies—free over slave, Greek over non-Greek, adult over child, male over female—that he reprised with some frequency the theme of the inferiority of women to men.

Whereas Plato's utopia entailed a unisex education aimed at producing guardian men and women who would govern together, Aristotle was a staunch supporter of patriarchy, which he believed had a solid basis in women's biological and mental inadequacy. Women, he maintained, had colder bodies than men. For this reason, though they were able to provide matter for embryos, only men could provide the soul. In the womb, embryos that stopped short of full development for lack of heat became female. Thus women were literally half-baked. From this came the inferior strength he identified in a variety of species. The female, he contended, "is, so to speak, a deformed male" (*Generation of Animals* 737a). At times, Aristotle's powers of observation deserted him when women were their subject. The twentieth-century philosopher Bertrand Russell quipped that Aristotle would not have claimed that women had fewer teeth than men if he had allowed his wife to open her mouth.

For all their differences, Plato and Aristotle shared a passionate conviction that the goal of philosophy was to work for the creation of a virtuous polis in which enlightenment could flourish. Their thinking contrasts strikingly with that of most moderns, who are more likely to see the state as designed to grant individuals the freedom to pursue their private goals, particularly their economic ones. Though Plato and Aristotle were both intensely critical of democracy, they shared with the

Athenian democrats an eminently Greek belief in the active nature of the polis. Far from an artificial institution whose chief goal was to redistribute goods and prevent crime, the polis was conceived by its residents as a force for the moral and spiritual improvement of its citizens. For this force to operate properly, citizens had to engage eagerly in political life; participation was a duty, not a right. The problems of the fourth century, however, raised serious questions about whether the polis as traditionally conceived was adequate to serve people's needs.

Signs of Despair: Flirting with Monarchy

Aware that his ideal republic would not be realized in his lifetime, Plato framed a second-best state in his late dialogue *The Laws*. Toward the end of his life, however, he also toyed with the notion that rule by a particularly wise individual might be preferable to government by even the best laws. Laws, after all, are inflexible and cannot easily be adapted to individuals. In his dialogue *The Statesman*, Plato gave a blank check to the man of extraordinary wisdom. If such a person can improve the state while acting in accordance with knowledge and justice, he concludes, his rule must be considered to be the only right form of government, "even if he must purge the state for its own good or banish some of its citizens" (*Statesman* 293).

The notion that one gifted man could make an improvement in the life of Greece is apparent in the writings of Plato's contemporaries Xenophon and Isocrates. Each man had something in common with Plato: Xenophon shared Plato's admiration for their teacher Socrates, and Isocrates had his own school. The two men were very different from one another, however; Xenophon was a man of action, a soldier and a practical person who wrote not only about politics and philosophy but also about household management, horsemanship, and hunting, whereas Isocrates was too nervous to feel comfortable speaking in public even though he made his living teaching oratory and writing speeches. Both men, however, were intrigued by the possibilities of a kind of political leadership few Greeks of the fifth century would have dared praise. For different reasons, both were drawn to monarchy.

The concept of a wise monarch ruling by law was central to Xenophon's *Cyropaedia* (*The Education of Cyrus*), a historical romance set in an imaginary, sentimentalized Persia. Cyrus' mother, for example, assures him that Persia is superior to Media in that "among the Persians what is just is defined as what is equal" (*Cyropaedia* 1.3.18). His father, the Persian king, she boasts, is always the first to carry out the orders of the state and to accept what has been decreed, for "his standard is not his own inclination but rather the law" (1.3.18). This, she says, is what distinguishes kingship from tyranny. The just Persia of the *Cyropaedia* is a far cry from the despotism conceived by fifth-century Greeks as the polar opposite of good government. The invasions of Darius and Xerxes left Greeks with a strong feeling that to be themselves they needed to live under some form of nonmonarchic government. By the fourth century, despite the overbearing conduct of Artaxerxes, it seemed more likely that the next invasion would go from west to east. Now memories of the Persian menace served primarily to stir thoughts of revenge, not to shape Greek identity. The world had changed, and increasingly people began to question whether a still more radical shift was not called for.

Isocrates proposed just such a change. His view of monarchy also had to do with Persia, but in an entirely different way. Convinced that the manly and intelligent Greek race had a natural right (not to mention an economic need) to rule over slavish and effeminate barbarians, Isocrates yearned for a man who would unite the Greeks in a holy war against Persian degenerates. Such a project would unify the Greeks by turning their aggression outward against a common foe, enthrone the master race in its appropriate position in world politics, and improve the economic condition of Greece by taking from Persia: "Just imagine," he suggests to his fellow Greeks in his *Panegyricus* of 380, "what a level of prosperity we could attain if we turned the war which now involves ourselves against the people of the continent, and transferred the wealth of Asia to Europe" (*Panegyricus* 187–188).

It was this practical concern that prompted Isocrates to cast about for a strong-man who could save Greece. He considered such disparate personalities as Jason of Pherae and **Dionysius I**, the tyrant of Syracuse, but when Jason and Dionysius died, he turned to Philip and the rising power of Macedon to put the program of the *Panegyricus* in motion. Isocrates did not imagine a Macedonian empire over Greece but rather a league of old-fashioned poleis united under a determined leader. When Macedonia did unite Greece in the year of Isocrates' death, the terms were very different from what he had envisioned. Nonetheless, the hope of a Panhellenic crusade against Persia kept him going until the age of nearly 100. After Philip's conquest of Greece in 338, Isocrates wrote to the Macedonian king assuring him that

> a glory unsurpassable and worthy of your past deeds will be yours when you compel the barbarians ... to be serfs of the Greeks, and when you shall force the king who is now called Great to do whatever you say. For then there will be nothing left for you except to become a god.
>
> (Isocrates, *Epistle* 3.5)

A Real-Life Experiment: Dionysius I of Syracuse

An embryonic experiment in uniting Greece under a charismatic leader had already taken place in the west before Philip acceded to the throne of Macedon. Isocrates was not the only person who had once thought Dionysius I of Syracuse might be destined for greatness. Dionysius thought so too. Had his successors inherited his energy and determination, the empire Dionysius created in Italy, Sicily, and beyond might have changed the Greek world, much as the conquests of Macedon did later in the fourth century. In the event, however, those who came after him lacked his talents and his luck, and in the end all his hard work was rewarded with oblivion.

Although tyranny had pretty much died out in mainland Greece in the sixth century, it continued to flourish in Sicily, whose experience always remained unique in Greek history. Carthaginian invasions provided a springboard for the ambitions of Dionysius. Denouncing his fellow generals for their failure in dealing with the invaders, he persuaded the Syracusans to dismiss his colleagues and place him in sole charge. When a staged assassination attempt (after the manner of Pisistratus) gave credence to the need for a bodyguard, he set himself up as a de facto tyrant (405 BC), using a variety of titles such as basileus and archon of Sicily. As in Pisistratid Athens, much of the day-to-day machinery of democracy continued to function, but Dionysius always had the last word, and his regime was far bloodier than that of his Athenian predecessor. Whatever he called himself, Dionysius owed his power to a mercenary force that numbered between ten and twenty thousand men and effected his restoration whenever popular uprisings ousted him from his office. He remained in power for thirty-eight years, until his death in 367, leading the Sicilians in a series of Carthaginian wars with mixed success. Though he was never able entirely to rid Sicily of Carthaginians, he did succeed in uniting much of the island under his rule. He did not hesitate to make alliances with non-Greek peoples in Europe who were attacking Hellenic cities. His alliance with the Lucanians, who lived in the Italian interior, facilitated his conquest of many coastal Greek cities in southern Italy, and Gallic allies enabled him to ravage the coast of western Italy, establish a naval base on Corsica, and occupy the island of Elba.

Dionysius was the most remarkable military innovator of his day. His advances were conspicuous in the arena of siege warfare. Greek sieges normally ended when hunger forced surrender. Dionysius, however, anticipated Alexander the Great in his ability to take cities by storm, making use of the new device known as the *gastraphetēs* or "bellyshooter" (because of the way its operator used his stomach to activate it). In essence a huge composite bow, the gastraphetes was cocked by a soldier who rested his stomach in a groove and pushed the instrument to maximum extension by pressing forward on it. This device could hurl a projectile about 250 yards. Along with wheeled six-story siege towers with flying bridges, the gastraphetes seems to have been used to good effect in Dionysius' siege of Motya, a key Carthaginian stronghold in Sicily that he destroyed in 397. (Greek inhabitants who had remained loyal to Carthage were crucified.) With the addition of artillery to light and heavy infantry and cavalry, Dionysius' army was the most complex in organization and equipment of any fighting force in Greece down to his time.

DOCUMENT 9.3

Diodorus of Sicily, who often spoke harshly of Dionysius, nonetheless admired his energy and determination. He recounted in his Library of History *the eagerness with which workmen vied to make the best contributions to the war effort. His account also stressed the force of Dionysius' personality.*

After he had collected many skilled workmen, he organized them in groups according to their skills, and set over them the most outstanding citizens,

Plate XII. Praxiteles (c. 400–330 BC), Aphrodite of Cnidus. Roman copy after Greek original (c. 350–30 BC). The female nude began to be depicted in Greek art in the mid-fourth century, mostly portraying Aphrodite preparing to bathe. Here she modestly holds one hand in front of her. With this statue, which was famous for its beauty, Praxiteles established the canonical proportions of the female nude in sculpture.

Plate XIII. The vast Hellenistic world provided new markets for trade and commerce. Alexandria was the center of the flourishing glass manufacturing industry. Luxury pieces and everyday tableware have been found in virtually every Greek settlement in tombs and other locations. See Chapter 12.

XIIIa. Green-yellow glass cup; the inner wall is engraved with circles, 9 × 15 cm. Hellenistic, third–second century BC. MNC27874. Photo: Martine Beck-Coppola.

XIIIb. Glass pyxis. Hellenistic, third–second century BC. From Rhodovani, Crete. Colorless molded glass, 7.0 × 12.2 cm. MNB878. Photo: Hervé Lewandowski. The Louvre, Paris, France.

XIIIc. Small glass cup with widening border and convex bottom, with remnants of decor inscribed in a red circle; a grid of pins and painted lines. Hellenistic. Colorless glass, paint; height 3 cm, diameter 11.5 cm. S2585. Photo: Hervé Lewandowski.

Plate XIV. Hellenistic bronze statuette of an African (known as Ethiopian) youth, possibly an athlete, third–second century BC. The accurate portrayal of the boy's features reflects the presence of Africans, both slave and free, in Alexandria and other cities of the Mediterranean basin. See Chapter 12.

Plate XVa. Wall painting of the myth of the Rape of Persephone, from the Tomb of Perse-phone (Tomb 1) in the Great Tumulus at Aegae, modern Vergina, Macedon, ca. 330s BC. The tomb contained the bones of an adult male, a young female, and an infant, possibly the remains of Philip II and his murdered queen and daughter, Cleopatra and Europa. See Chapters 10 and 11.

Plate XVb. This late Hellenistic mosaic, the Alexander Mosaic from Pompeii, is believed to be a copy of a late-fourth-century BC painting depicting the Battle of Issus by Philoxenus of Eretria for King Cassander of Macedon. Alexander, on horseback toward the left, confronts Darius III, in a chariot on the right. Surprisingly, the focus of attention in this dynamic composition is not Alexander but the Persian king, who is sympathetically depicted as concerned for the welfare of his soldiers instead of fleeing the charge of the Macedonian king. See Chapter 11.

Plate XVIa. Royal tomb at Aegae, modern Vergina, late fourth century BC. The simple architectural facade masks a Macedonian barrel-vaulted tomb that contained the never looted burial of a teenage male believed by some scholars to be Alexander IV, son of Alexander the Great, who would have been buried by Cassander to help legitimize his seizure of power in Macedon. See Chapter 12.

Plate XVIb. This silver *hydria* was discovered in the Macedonian tomb in Plate XVIa, encircled by a gold wreath of oak leaves, holding a teenage male's cremated remains. Sealed with a lid and cut horizontally into two sections, this vase was designed to serve as a funerary urn.

Plate XVII. Tomb of the Hellenizing High Priest Jason (174–171 BC)—Hebrew name Joshua—who was responsible for the reforms that transformed Jerusalem into a polis and laid the foundation for the revolt of the Maccabees. This tomb was built at Jerusalem by his descendants in the first century BC. The design, a pyramid on a square base with a Greek column, may have been modeled on the Mausoleum at Halicarnassus, the tomb of the Carian ruler Mausolus (377–353 BC) and one of the seven wonders of the ancient world. See Chapter 12.

Plate XVIIIa. Head of a greater-than-life-size statue of the Greco-Egyptian god Sarapis, who was created by Ptolemy I; marble, second century BC. This head was discovered underwater in Alexandria harbor, and was probably based on the cult image of Sarapis in the Sarapeum in the Egyptian quarter at Alexandria, which was the center of the god's worship until it was destroyed by Christians in 391 AD. See Chapter 12.

Plate XVIIIb. Sphinx found on the now submerged Antirhodos Island in Alexandria harbor near the Royal Quarter, also submerged as the result of an earthquake about 1,600 years ago. One of a large number of Egyptian monuments that were brought to Alexandria from various sites, but especially from Heliopolis near Memphis, to highlight the Egyptian aspects of the Ptolemaic monarchy. See Chapter 12.

Plate XIX. Basalt statue of Cleopatra VII, Egypt, in Egyptian royal regalia. The queen is portrayed holding a double cornucopia (horn of plenty) with her left arm, illustrating her admiration for her great predecessor Arsinoë II, who was often similarly depicted (see Figure 12.9). See Chapter 12 and Epilogue.

offering large bounties for a supply of weapons. He distributed models of each kind of armor, because he had gathered his mercenaries from all over; for he wanted to make sure to have each of his soldiers armed with the weapons of his people, thinking that this would cause great consternation and that all the soldiers would fight most effectively in the sort of armor to which they were accustomed. And since the Syracusans enthusiastically supported his policy, there was great competition in the manufacture of the arms....

Indeed, it was at this time that the catapult was invented, at Syracuse, since the most skilled workmen had been gathered from everywhere into a single place, their enthusiasm stimulated by the high wages and numerous prizes on offer for those who were judged to be the best. In addition, Dionysius mingled daily with the workers, conversing with them amiably and bestowing gifts on the most zealous of them—as well as inviting them to come dine with him. For these reasons the workmen were amazingly inventive in devising numerous novel and useful missiles and engines of war. He was also the first to think of building quadriremes and quinqueremes and indeed to set about constructing them....The beholder was inevitably filled with great wonder at the sight of so many weapons and ships under construction.

(Diodorus, *Library of History* 14.41.4–43.1)

Dionysius envisioned himself as the founder of a dynasty, and he made a public display of the tyrant's freedom from conventional restraints by marrying two women in a single ceremony. In so doing he borrowed considerable trouble for the future. Upon his death, Dionysius II, the son of one wife, found himself in charge but saddled with an official adviser in the person of Dion, the other wife's brother. The two men had radically different temperaments, and they fought for years. Plato, who had met Dion during a stay in Sicily in the 380s, wound up in the middle when Dion twice invited him back to Sicily in the hope that Dionysius II could be improved by the study of philosophy. The attempt was not successful; Plato returned to Athens, and Dion was assassinated in 354.

The emergence of an imperial tyranny in the west must be seen in the context of the rising individualism of the fourth century, a phenomenon also visible in Athens in the independent ventures many Athenian generals undertook as mercenaries. That the drive to power was strong in talented individuals is also evident in literary works such as Plato's dialogue *Gorgias*, in which the brash young Callicles argues that "The man who is to live rightly should let his appetites become as large as possible and not restrain them, and when they are at their height he should be able to make use of his courage and wisdom to minister to them and to fill each of them up in turn with whatever it desires" (*Gorgias* 491e–492a). People of average abilities, Callicles says, being unable to do this, praise temperance and justice to conceal their own impotence. Dionysius, whom Plato had known in Sicily, would probably have agreed. So would Aristotle's employer Philip of Macedon.

—»»———«««—

The fourth century BC witnessed an explosion of creative energy in many areas. Philosophy, biology, political theory, mathematics, and military science all made significant advances. Where all this fertility was leading is unclear. Solid foundations were established for intellectual traditions that lived and grew for centuries; many of them still flourish in altered—or unaltered—forms. The knowledge generated did not, however, offer salvation to Greece. The increasing specialization of the fourth century led to a division between generals and politicians that resulted in more professional military skills. Consequently, generals in the fourth century were better than those of the fifth. Their weapons and machinery were more versatile and sophisticated. New ways of thinking also led to specialized monographs like Xenophon's treatises on the art of horsemanship and the skills necessary for a successful cavalry commander, and the *Siegecraft* of the author known as Aeneas Tacticus. No good, however, came of these improvements. Greeks simply expanded the repertoire of available methods for killing.

The great texts of Greek political theory continue to be read today. The insight they afforded, however, seems to have had little real-life application in their own day. Plato's students never did take over Athenian government, and Aristotle's influence on Alexander seems to have been negligible. Identifying those who are likely to govern best is always a challenge, and it contributes little to point out the imprudence of according sovereignty to a power-hungry tyrant, a clique of rich men, or an angry mob. It is precisely because wealth and birth have historically been the criteria for inclusion in the elite that democracy has become a popular alternative to oligarchy. It is one thing to advocate an aristocracy of intellect and another to design practical machinery for establishing one. It was a central tenet of Greek intellectuals that most people lacked capacity for growth. Plato and Aristotle worked on the assumption that the secret to reforming government was in nurturing the tiny minority that had this capacity. Their goal was basically to design a constitution that minimized the power prudence must accord to the mindless masses, who might otherwise rise up and slaughter their betters.

To say that the polis ultimately failed because it lacked a truly democratic ideology would nonetheless be ridiculous on several counts. First, mighty empires have flourished for long periods without any democratic ideology whatsoever. Second, we know from the vigor and stability of fourth-century Athens that democracy was alive and well, albeit not in the minds of Greece's intellectuals. Third, the polis did not entirely fail. The collapse of polis ideology before the Macedonian onslaught was certainly noticeable in states like Athens and Sparta that had once enjoyed the privilege of framing their own foreign policies. Smaller poleis, however, had long been accustomed to eking out what dignity they could in the shadow of greater powers. The bustling city in fact remained the core of Greek civilization for centuries to come.

Key Terms

Academy	Iphicrates	Pelopidas
Agesilaus	klepsydra	peltast
Aristotle	kleroterion	Plato
Corinthian War	Lyceum	The Republic
Dionysius I	mausoleum	Sacred Band
Epaminondas	Neaera	Second Athenian
gastraphetes	King's Peace	Confederacy

Suggested Readings

Allen, Danielle S. 2000. *The World of Prometheus: The Politics of Punishing in Democratic Athens*. Princeton, NJ: Princeton University Press. A subtle analysis of Athens' values as a polis grounded in a study of attitudes toward punishment.

Bryant, Joseph. 1996. *Moral Codes and Social Structure in Ancient Greece*. Albany: State University of New York Press. The connection between values and social organization from the Archaic period through the Hellenistic Age.

Cartledge, Paul. 1987. *Agesilaos and the Crisis of Sparta*. Baltimore: Johns Hopkins University Press. A close study of fourth-century Sparta.

Caven, Brian. 1990. *Dionysius I: War-Lord of Sicily*. New Haven, CT: Yale University Press. A readable examination of the sources for Dionysius' rule that seeks to present him in a more favorable light than has been customary.

Cohen, David. 1995. *Law, Violence and Community in Classical Athens*. Cambridge: Cambridge University Press. A detailed exploration of the key role of litigation both in regulating the continual feuding that characterized Athenian society and in keeping physical violence to a minimum.

Edmondson, Jonathan, and Virginia Hunter. 2000. *Law and Social Status in Classical Athens*. Oxford: Oxford University Press. A fascinating collection of essays focusing on the ways in which Athenian law defined and sustained the different social statuses of citizens, metics, and slaves, treating topics such as prostitution, torture, and methods of execution.

Grene, Marjorie. 1963. *A Portrait of Aristotle*. Chicago: University of Chicago Press. A lively summary of Aristotle's thought that grounds his worldview in his enthusiasm for biology.

Hansen, Mogens H. 1991. *The Athenian Democracy in the Age of Demosthenes*. Oxford and Cambridge, MA: Basil Blackwell. An engaging analytical study of Athenian democracy that is crammed with useful facts.

Hunter, Virginia. 1994. *Policing Athens. Social Control in the Attic Lawsuits, 430–320* BC. Princeton, NJ: Princeton University Press. An examination of social control and conflict resolution in Athens, with emphasis on the social matrix and special emphasis on gender relations, slavery, and the role of gossip.

Ober, Josiah. 2010. *Democracy and Knowledge: Innovation and Learning in Classical Athens.* Princeton, NJ: Princeton University Press. A blending of history and theory that explores the role of knowledge and its valuation in establishing a successful, stable democracy.

Salkever, Stephen, ed. 2000. *The Cambridge Companion to Greek Political Thought.* Cambridge University Press. A collection of essays by leading classicists, political scientists, and philosophers that analyze key Greek texts from the point of view of what they have to say about central issues affecting the human community.

Todd, S. C. 1993. *The Shape of Athenian Law.* Oxford: Oxford University Press. A detailed and analytical study of Athenian law dealing with both procedure and substance.

Tritle, Lawrence, ed. 1997. *The Greek World in the Fourth Century: From the Fall of the Athenian Empire to the Successors of Alexander.* London and New York: Routledge. A collection of essays on the problems of the fourth century, including chapters on Thebes, the Greeks of Asia Minor, and the states of western Greece.

Wood, Ellen Meiksins. 1988. *Peasant-Citizen and Slave: The Foundations of Athenian Democracy.* London and New York: Verso. A thoughtful examination of the relationship between agrarian labor and democracy in Classical Athens.

CHAPTER TEN

Philip II and the Rise of Macedon

It is one of the great paradoxes of ancient history that the Greek poleis were able to maintain their independence until almost the last third of the fourth century BC. Their tiny size and constant quarrels made their escape from Persian conquest in the early fifth century BC appear almost miraculous, even in antiquity. It was not surprising when the threat of foreign conquest returned a little over a century later. What was surprising was the source of the threat: not the mighty Persian empire, feared by the Greeks for almost two centuries, but the hitherto insignificant kingdom of **Macedon** located north of Greece in southeastern Europe.

The success of Macedon in conquering the Greek states was due in part to the internal divisions and economic strains that inhibited the evolution of a consistent policy in Athens, in part to the mutual mistrust that stood in the way of an effective united front on the part of the leading poleis—Athens, Sparta, and Thebes. A large part was played as well by the longing many Greeks felt for a radical cure for the ills of Hellas—monarchy, perhaps, and even a crusade such as a monarch could mount against Persia. But credit must also be given to the unique military and diplomatic gifts of the man who became king of Macedon in 359 BC. A man of exceptional talents and indefatigable determination, **Philip II** has fascinated historians of antiquity for over two thousand years.

SOURCES FOR MACEDONIAN HISTORY

Reconstructing the history of Macedon before the reign of Philip II is difficult. The lack of sources that bedevils much of Greek history is an obvious part of the problem. We know the names of several historians who wrote histories of Macedon in antiquity, but only meager fragments of their works survive. The most important of these works, consisting of fifty-eight books, was the *Philippica* of Theopompus of Chios (fourth century BC). A few manuscripts of Theopompus' history were extant in Constantinople in the ninth century AD, but they disappeared soon thereafter. Nevertheless, much of the content of these works survives in general histories such as those by Diodorus of Sicily (first century BC) and Justin (second century AD).

The biographer Plutarch, the geographer Strabo, and several Athenian orators, including Aeschines, Hyperides, and especially **Demosthenes**, also preserve important evidence. In addition, archaeological discoveries constantly supplement the evidence of the literary sources. In recent decades, for example, archaeologists have revealed the remains of the early Macedonian capital of Aegae and the adjacent royal cemetery, the important sanctuary of Zeus at Dion, and an Archaic Age cemetery rich in spectacular gold jewelry at Sindos. The combination of literary and archaeological sources has made it possible for historians to reconstruct the history of Macedon in greater detail than ever before.

This reconstruction is complicated by the threefold biases of the available sources. First and foremost, ancient historians treated Macedonian history prior to Alexander the Great as a mere prologue to Alexander's spectacular reign. Second, many sources originate in Athens and, not surprisingly, view Macedonian actions almost entirely in terms of their putative effects on Athenian interests. The fiercely partisan political conflicts of mid-fourth-century Athens only exacerbate this tendency in some of the most important sources. Finally, the authors of most of our sources were strongly influenced by the fourth-century debate concerning the Greek or barbarian character of the Macedonians. As a result, constructing a chronicle of early Macedonian history is relatively easy, but viewing that history from a Macedonian perspective is not. Only recently have historians attempted to study the history of Macedon from a Macedonian point of view instead of reproducing the orientation of the ancient sources by treating it as an appendix to Greek history.

EARLY MACEDONIA

According to Herodotus, Perdiccas, the first king of Macedon, was promised the land illuminated by the sun as his kingdom. The reality was different. For most of the Archaic and early Classical periods of Greek history, the kings of Macedon ruled a chronically unstable kingdom that was often a state more in name than in fact. Sandwiched between Thessaly on the south, **Thrace** and the Chalcidian League on the east, Paeonia on the north, and **Illyria** and Epirus on the west, Macedonian kings had to struggle to fend off foreign enemies. At the same time, they strove hard to assert their preeminence over the local dynasts, who ruled the various regions that made up the kingdom of Macedon.

Macedonia's geography rendered their struggle even more difficult. Ancient Macedonia consisted of two distinct geographical regions: Lower Macedonia, the great alluvial plain created by the Haliacmon and Axius rivers as they flowed down to the Gulf of Therma, and Upper Macedonia, the horseshoe of rugged uplands and mountains that stretched northwestward toward Illyria and Epirus and was drained by the same two great rivers. The plains of Lower Macedonia formed the heart of the kingdom of Macedon and supported a large agricultural population. Its mountainous hinterlands not only held extensive forests and rich mineral deposits but also sheltered various tribes who jealously guarded their freedom from the control of the lowland Macedonian kings. Uniting these two regions under the authority of the king of Macedon was the essential precondition for the growth and expansion of Macedonian power.

MACEDONIAN SOCIETY AND KINGSHIP

Were the Macedonians Greek? This question is the most contentious issue in Macedonian historiography. In contemporary Balkan politics, conflicting claims to the territory of ancient Macedonia have made the question of the "Greekness" of the ancient Macedonians a burning issue. Modern nationalists may be confident of their answers, but contemporary ideology has little relevance to antiquity. Although recent epigraphic discoveries suggest that "Macedonian" was a dialect of northwest Greek, it was a dialect that most Greeks had difficulty understanding. Language alone, however, does not determine ethnic identity. Equally important are shared culture, tradition, and values, and it is clear that in antiquity neither Macedonians nor Greeks considered the Macedonians to be Greek. Greeks viewed the Macedonians as barbarians like their Thracian and Illyrian neighbors. An exception was made only for the members of the ruling Argead house, who claimed to be the descendants of immigrants from Argos.

Although Macedonian kings encouraged the **Hellenization** of the Macedonian nobility, Macedonian and Greek culture had little in common. While most people in Greece lived by agriculture, cities were the core of what was most distinctive in Greek civilization. Before the reign of Philip II, however, city life in Macedonia was limited to a few Greek colonies on the coast of the Gulf of Therma. The few large settlements in the interior of Macedon, such as Aegae and Pella, were dynastic centers with limited civic institutions. Most Macedonians were farmers or seminomadic pastoralists, living in scattered villages and owing allegiance to local Macedonian aristocrats. Other differences divided the two cultures as well, such as the polygamy of the Macedonian kings, the Macedonians' love of unmixed wine, and their aristocrats' preference for tumulus burial instead of simple cremation or interment. Indeed, the lifestyle of the Macedonian nobility had more in common with that of Homeric heroes than with that of Classical Greeks. War and hunting were central to the life of a Macedonian noble. Before being recognized as an adult, a young man had to spear a boar without the aid of a net and kill an enemy.

The similarities between the Macedonian nobility and the heroes of Homer's poems were not merely matters of lifestyle. Their fundamental values and reactions to violations of those values were also similar. Feuds resulting from heavy drinking, competition for preference at the royal court, and rivalries over the favors of young men were all common. Particularly unforgivable were public humiliations such as beating a superior to the kill during a hunt. The truth is that the slightest hint of an affront, no matter the cause, could lead to explosive violence. Just maintaining peace in their kingdom was a constant challenge for Macedonian kings. Indeed, the history of the Macedonian monarchy is as much about the efforts of Macedonian kings to tame their turbulent nobility as it is about their efforts to expand their territory.

The monarchy was the central institution of Macedonian society. Like Louis XIV of France, the Macedonian kings were autocrats who could well say "I am the state." Although earlier historians held that their powers were limited by an army assembly invested with the right to elect the king and try cases of treason, it is now clear that these hypotheses are groundless. The army might acclaim a new king and witness trials of nobles, but the king and his advisers always made the final decisions. The king made all appointments, all grants of land and privilege, and all responses to petitions. The king alone represented Macedon in foreign affairs. Treaties and alliances were made with him personally, and foreign allies pledged their support to him and his family without reference to the Macedonian people. The king even decided the royal succession. Macedonian kings were polygamous, and, provided only that the new king was an Argead, a king could designate any son by any wife as his successor.

Nevertheless, such a bald summary of the powers of the Macedonian kings is potentially misleading. There were no constitutional limitations on the king's powers, but there were extraconstitutional limits on how these prerogatives were exercised. Greek political theorists usually equated monarchy and tyranny, since they considered the supreme importance of the ruler's personality in public and private spheres alike to be the distinguishing feature of both. This was especially true of Macedon, where no impersonal bureaucracy buffered the king from his subjects. The kings of Macedon spent their lives in the midst of the Macedonian nobles who formed their personal entourage. The kings chose their closest advisers and the members of their bodyguard from these **royal companions**. In war, the companions served in an elite cavalry unit personally commanded by the king. It is not surprising, therefore, that Macedonian kings sat on insecure thrones. Only two of Philip II's predecessors died natural deaths. One, Archelaus, was murdered by a disgruntled male lover. The rest died in battle or fell victim to conspiracies.

The Predecessors of Philip II

Philip II was the beneficiary of almost two centuries of patient state building by his Argead predecessors. In view of the decisive role that Philip II and his son Alexander would play in the destruction of the Persian empire, it is ironic that this state-building process began in the late sixth century BC with Amyntas I's alliance with Persia. The alliance was sealed by the marriage of a Macedonian princess to a high Persian official and lasted for over three decades. The Macedonians proved to be loyal allies. During the Persian invasion of Greece in 480 BC, Amyntas' son and successor, Alexander I, personally led the Macedonian contingents against the

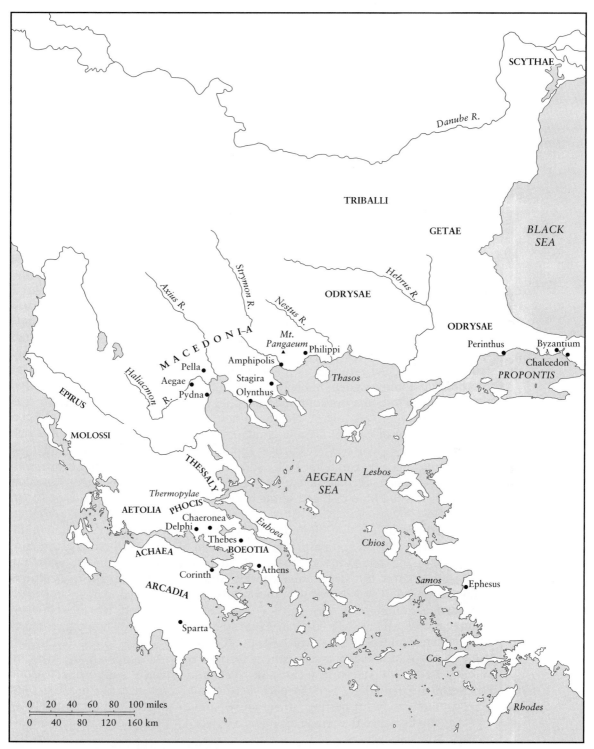

Figure 10.1 Macedonia and its neighbors.

Greeks. Not surprisingly, after the Persian defeat Alexander I encouraged the spread of stories testifying to his covert support of the Greek cause during the invasion.

Persian rule brought Macedon great advantages, even if later Macedonian tradition attempted to conceal the extent of their collaboration with Persia. Shielded from attack by Thracians and Paeonians by Persian power, Macedon flourished. As a result, Amyntas' successors, Alexander I, Perdiccas II, and Archelaus, were able to take advantage of the Persian defeat and expulsion from Europe in the 470s and extend their territory northwestward to incorporate the highlands of Upper Macedon and eastward to encompass the rich silver-mining area between the Axius and Strymon rivers. By the end of the fifth century, Macedon was the strongest kingdom in the region.

Macedon's growing power and its extensive natural resources attracted the attention of Athens and other Greek cities. Macedonian grain helped sustain many of Athens' allies and subjects, and Macedonian timber was critical to the survival of Athens' fleet. For their part, the fifth-century Macedonian kings used their newfound wealth to pursue their twin goals of winning recognition for themselves as Greeks and Hellenizing the life of the royal court. The first steps were taken by Alexander I. Although he may not actually have competed in the Olympic games, Alexander did support Greeks and Greek culture, offering sanctuary to Mycenaean refugees after the destruction of Mycenae by Argos in 462 and commissioning a poem in his honor from the great Theban poet, Pindar.

Alexander I's successors continued his policy of Hellenization. Archelaus was especially active in this regard, creating a new capital at Pella and establishing a festival in honor of Zeus at Dion in emulation of the festival of Zeus at Olympia. Archelaus also supported Greek artists and writers extensively. Greek craftsmen helped build his new capital at Pella, and probably also the system of fortresses and roads that he had constructed. Even Euripides, the last of the great Athenian tragedians, visited Macedon and wrote his last two tragedies at Archelaus' court. One, the lost *Archelaus,* celebrated the alleged Argive ancestry of the playwright's host. The other, the *Bacchae,* offered a terrifying and unforgettable evocation of the power of Dionysus—a god particularly at home in Macedon, where excessive use of alcohol often resulted in violence and tragedy. As a result of the actions of the fifth-century kings, the Macedonian court gradually became the principal cultural center in Macedon and the focus of the social life of the Macedonian aristocracy.

Growing commercial and cultural ties could not avert tension between Macedon and Athens. Macedonian expansion into southern Thrace threatened both Athens' control of its north Aegean allies and its desire to secure the rich gold mines of Mount Pangaeus. Athens responded to Macedonian advances by allying itself with Macedon's Thracian rivals and covertly supporting various Macedonian pretenders. For his part, Perdiccas II protected his predecessor's gains by alternately supporting Athens and Sparta during the Peloponnesian War in a diplomatic dance that made his name a byword for treachery among contemporary Athenian writers.

Nevertheless, the achievements of the three great fifth-century kings were short-lived. When Philip II came to power in 359, Macedon was faced by the

Figure 10.2. Silver tetradrachm of Philip II (359–356 BC). Obverse: head of Zeus. Reverse: Jockey commemorating the victory of Philip's horse at Olympia in 356 BC. Oxford, The Ashmolean Museum.

most severe crisis in its short history. Chronic instability had left the kingdom vulnerable to threats from both Greek and non-Greek enemies. Eight kings ruled Macedon between 400 and 359 BC. Finally, in 359, Philip's brother, Perdiccas III, was killed in a battle against the Illyrians. In addition to the king, four thousand Macedonian troops and numerous members of the Macedonian aristocracy died in the fighting. Macedon's enemies quickly took advantage of this unprecedented debacle and the chaos that resulted from it. The Illyrians and Paeonians prepared invasions, while the Athenians and Thracians offered their support for insurrections in favor of pretenders to the Macedonian throne. The kingdom seemed on the verge of collapse.

THE REIGN OF PHILIP II

Philip II was born about 382 BC, the last son of Amyntas III and his Illyrian wife, Eurydice. Little is known about his early life. According to Plutarch, Eurydice learned to read in order to educate her children. Whatever chance Philip had for education, however, was ended by the turbulent politics of Macedon in the 370s. An unsuccessful attempt by his brother Alexander II to weaken Theban influence in Thessaly led to Philip's spending the years 369 to 367 as a hostage in Thebes. His exile was not all loss. Philip's enforced residence in Thebes, scarcely two years after its victory at Leuctra made it the greatest power in Greece, gave him an insight into Greek politics and military tactics that would later prove invaluable.

Philip's return to Macedon in 367 coincided with the descent of the kingdom into chaos. Three kings ruled Macedon during the middle and late 360s: Ptolemy of Alorus, Pausanias, and Philip's brother Perdiccas III. The instability encouraged Macedon's enemies and apparently foreclosed any hope for a quick restoration of order to Macedonian affairs. It also provided Philip with an unexpected opportunity. The crisis created by Perdiccas' death demanded a ruler capable of taking decisive action. That ruler could only be Philip, since he was the sole surviving adult Argead. Philip quickly assumed control of the government, and by 357 at the latest he had supplanted his infant nephew Amyntas to become king of Macedon.

When Philip took power in 359, his chances of survival seemed slim. Macedon was threatened by formidable enemies on all sides. Worse yet, pretenders challenged his right to the throne. Seuthes II, the powerful king of the Thracians, supported the claims of three of Philip's half-brothers. The Athenians, still hoping to regain their long-lost colony of Amphipolis, backed the claims of Argaeus, a pretender who had briefly ruled Macedon in the 380s before being expelled by Philip's father, Amyntas III.

In the next two years the situation changed dramatically. Through astute diplomacy, Philip persuaded the Thracians and Athenians to abandon the Macedonian pretenders they had been supporting. Free to concentrate all his forces against his other enemies, Philip quickly defeated both the Paeonians and the Illyrians and regained control of western and northwestern Macedonia. Philip's brilliant

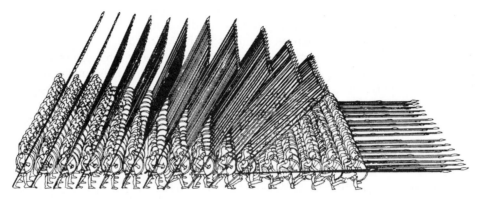

Figure 10.3. Macedonian phalanx.

use of diplomacy to prepare the way for his decisive military victories over the Paeonians and Illyrians in 358 set the pattern for the rest of his reign.

Success followed success during the remainder of the decade. An alliance with the Molossians in Epirus, who also had long suffered from Illyrian attacks, completed the pacification of Macedon's western frontier and freed Philip to turn his attention to the east. In quick succession, Philip seized the Greek cities along the coast of the Gulf of Therma and in southwestern Thrace, together with the rich gold- and silver-mining region of Mount Pangaeus. The same mines provided Philip with the financial resources—one thousand talents a year, according to Diodorus—required to carry out his various plans during the remainder of his reign.

In less than a decade, Philip had freed Macedon from the enemies that had threatened its survival since the sixth century. His military and diplomatic successes in the 350s were accompanied by far-reaching reforms, giving the kingdom unprecedented military strength and political cohesion.

The Reforms of Philip II

Philip II's rise to power coincided with a revolution in military tactics and weaponry that ended the Greek hoplite's dominance of the battlefield. By introducing these innovations to Macedon, Philip transformed it almost overnight into the preeminent military power in southeastern Europe. Some of his innovations were technological. Dionysius I of Syracuse had first demonstrated the potential of the catapult at the siege of Motya in 397. It was Philip, however, who realized that potential by introducing new and more powerful torsion catapults powered by energy stored in tightly twisted ropes. Combined with the creation of an elite corps of military engineers, these new weapons enabled Philip successfully to besiege fortified cities such as Amphipolis. At the same time, the skirmishing and scouting abilities of his army were enhanced by special units of light armed infantry and cavalry recruited from his non-Macedonian subjects and allies.

DOCUMENT 10.1

Alexander's Speech at Opis (324 BC)

In this speech the Roman historian Arrian has Alexander review the changes Philip II brought to Macedonia in an effort to quell the mutiny of his troops at Opis in 324.

In the first place, as is reasonable, I shall begin my speech from my father Philip. For he found you vagabonds and destitute of means, most of you clad in hides, feeding a few sheep up the mountain sides, for the protection of which you had to fight with small success against Illyrians, Triballians, and the border Thracians. Instead of the hides he gave you cloaks to wear, and from the mountains he led you down into the plains, and made you capable of fighting the neighboring barbarians, so that you were no longer compelled to preserve yourselves by trusting rather to the inaccessible strongholds than to your own valor. He made you colonists of cities, which he adorned with useful laws and customs; and from being slaves and subjects, he made you rulers over those very barbarians by whom you yourselves, as well as your property, were previously liable to be carried off or ravaged. He also added the greater part of Thrace to Macedonia, and by seizing the most conveniently situated places on the sea-coast, he spread abundance over the land from commerce, and made the working of the mines a secure employment. He made you rulers over the Thessalians, of whom you had formerly been in mortal fear; and by humbling the nation of the Phocians, he rendered the avenue into Greece broad and easy for you, instead of being narrow and difficult. The Athenians and Thebans, who were always lying in wait to attack Macedonia, he humbled to such a degree … that … those states in their turn procure security to themselves by our assistance.

Arrian, *Anabasis Alexandri* 7.9; Chinnock

Philip's most important military reform was the reorganization of the Macedonian infantry. Philip created a new uniformly equipped **phalanx** to replace the undisciplined militia that had served Macedonian kings so poorly in the past. As in the old general levy, the six divisions of the new phalanx were recruited from each of Macedon's traditional territorial divisions, but they were equipped with new weapons and assigned a new role in battle. Each member of the phalanx wore a metal helmet and carried a small shield and a short sword. His principal weapon, however, was an enormous pike called a **sarissa** that could be as long as 18 feet, allowing the soldier to strike a blow before his enemies could close and use their shorter weapons.

In this way, Philip deprived his Greek opponents of their chief tactical advantage: the ability to concentrate hoplites in close formation against their enemies and destroy them. As a result, the mere presence of the new phalanx in a battle forced Philip's enemies to modify their tactics to cope with this unusual formation. The tactical opportunities thus created could then be exploited by the royal companion cavalry, which would deal a decisive blow to an enemy force already confused by the phalanx and the elite guard units protecting its flanks.

Philip's reforms were not limited to reorganization of the Macedonian army. He also took steps to strengthen the bonds between the army, its leaders, and the king. He freely shared his men's hardships and dangers, as his many wounds (including the loss of an eye) attested. He conferred a new title on the common soldiers, *Pezhetairoi* ("foot companions"), suggesting that they too, like the mounted nobles, were the king's personal companions. A generation later, the rage of Alexander's soldiers at the thought of sharing their cherished new status with the conquered Persians clearly demonstrated the powerful bond Philip had forged with his soldiers.

Philip also made important changes in the nature of the bond between the king and the Macedonian nobility. Perdiccas III's disastrous defeat had caused the deaths of many Macedonian noblemen. Philip used the opportunity thus created to recruit new members for the royal companions, chosen from the Greeks and non-Greeks who flocked to Macedon in search of opportunity and wealth. He also created opportunities for members of the old nobility, who received commands in Philip's new model army. Their sons also became members of a new institution, the **royal pages**. The pages personally served the king and were educated at court. From them Philip recruited his future officers. But at the same time the royal pages served a second purpose: they were hostages for the good behavior of their families.

Theopompus, the moralizing contemporary historian of Philip's reign, sarcastically characterized Philip's expanded corps of companions as composed of men more suited to be "courtesans" than "courtiers." Nevertheless, their personal loyalty to Philip was strong, and for good reason. Philip's victories gave him unprecedented resources in land and treasure, and he used them to reward his followers liberally. Philip's ability to attract and reward loyal supporters was enhanced by land reclamation projects, such as the draining of marshland in Lower Macedonia, combined with the foundation of colonies such as Philippi. As a result, Philip possessed what no previous Macedonian king had had: an extensive and loyal base of support for his policies at home and abroad.

Philip Becomes a Force in Greece

Macedonian kings had long feared the potential danger posed by a united **Thessaly**, with its large population and its strong military tradition. Philip's predecessors had sought unsuccessfully to avert that threat. They repeatedly supported Larisa against Jason and Alexander—Pherae's ambitious tyrants—and their Theban allies. Jason, in fact, nearly reduced Philip's father, Amyntas III, to the status of a vassal in the late 370s, and, as we have already seen, Alexander II's unsuccessful Thessalian campaign in 369 resulted in Philip's Theban exile.

Not surprisingly, developments in Thessaly in the mid-350s led Philip also to intervene in the tangled politics of Macedon's southern neighbor. The primary cause was the conclusion of an alliance between **Phocis** and Macedon's old enemy Pherae. Phocis had suddenly emerged in the mid-350s as one of the major powers in central and northern Greece. The union of Pherae and Phocis threatened the interests of both Larisa and Thebes (Phocis' bitter enemy), forcing them to invite Philip's intervention. Philip initially underestimated the seriousness of the threat posed by the alliance of Pherae and Phocis. He changed his mind after two defeats inflicted by Phocian forces in 353—the most serious he suffered in his entire reign—and returned to Thessaly with overwhelming force the following year, crushing the Phocians at the Battle of the Crocus Field.

This battle transformed Philip's relationship to Thessaly and the rest of Greece. In the immediate aftermath of Philip's victory, Pherae was seized, and its last tyrant fled into exile. Finally freed of the Pheraean threat, the Thessalian League met and appointed Philip archon (commander-in-chief) of Thessaly, effectively uniting Thessaly and Macedon in the person of Philip. The union of Thessaly and Macedon virtually doubled the military forces at Philip's disposal and brought the first decade of his reign to a successful conclusion. It also allowed Philip to expand his influence deep into central Greece.

While Philip was busy extending Macedonian influence in Thessaly, central Greece was convulsed by the conflict historians call the Third Sacred War. Behind the outbreak of the war was Thebes' attempt to consolidate its hegemony in central Greece. Exploiting a favorable majority on the **Amphictyonic council** of Delphi, Thebes arranged to have Phocis severely fined in 357 for cultivating land sacred to Apollo. Phocis' response was unexpected.

Phocis had long been Thebes' chief rival for preeminence in central Greece. Thebes had exploited its victory at Leuctra in 371 to force Phocis to sign a treaty recognizing Theban suzerainty. Phocis had accepted Theban suzerainty grudgingly at best, and in 357 the Phocians made a desperate effort to regain their independence. Instead of submitting to Theban blackmail, they seized control of Delphi and used the treasures of Apollo to recruit a powerful mercenary army. Although the sacrilege outraged Greek opinion, Thebes' attempt to form a united front against Phocis was frustrated by Athenian and Spartan hostility to further expansion of Theban power. As a result, the Phocians quickly brought almost the whole region from the Gulf of Corinth to Thessaly under their sway.

Frustrated at their inability to defeat the Phocians, Thebes and its Thessalian allies appealed to Philip, the new leader of Thessaly, to come to Delphi's aid. Hostilities in Thrace as well as with Athens and Olynthus in the north Aegean prevented Philip from taking action against Phocis for several years. In 346, he finally intervened on the side of Thebes in the Sacred War. Although Macedonian intervention tipped the scales against Phocis, increasing Theban power was not in Philip's interest. Philip, therefore, played a double game. At the same time that he supported Thebes militarily, he also opened negotiations with Phocis over possible surrender terms.

The traditional penalty for sacrilege such as the Phocians had committed against Delphi was the execution of all males of military age. With that dire threat hanging over their heads, the Phocians quickly accepted Philip's offer and surrendered in the summer of 346. As Philip had promised, the terms imposed by the Delphic Amphictyony on Phocis proved to be relatively mild. Phocian cities were broken up into their constituent villages. The Phocians undertook to pay back the treasure they had taken from Delphi at a rate of sixty talents per year. Most important, Phocis' votes in the Delphic Amphictyony were transferred to Philip, who henceforth, thanks to his control of Thessaly, enjoyed a voting majority on the Amphictyonic Council.

As a result of his timely intervention in the Sacred War, Philip had won for himself an important role in Delphic affairs. Just how significant a position he now occupied was made clear to all Greeks in 346 when he became the first Macedonian king to be granted the honor of presiding over the Pythian games supervised by the Amphictyony. Philip's spectacular success in the Sacred War also temporarily halted the growing hostility between Macedon and Athens.

Philip, Athens, and the Peace of Philocrates

Because of the Athenians' vested interest in Chalcidice, their tense relations with Philip dated back to the beginning of his reign. In 359, Philip had induced Athens to withdraw its support from his rival, Argaeus, by promising to restore Amphipolis to Athenian authority. The Athenians quickly learned, however, that their trust in Philip's promises had been misplaced. Philip needed Amphipolitan land to reward his supporters; moreover, its strategic location near the mouth of the Strymon River made the city too significant to turn over to Athens. Two years

Figure 10.4. Polyeuctus' posthumous bronze portrait statue of Demosthenes, erected in the Athenian agora in 280 BC, is reflected in this Roman marble copy. It shows the orator as gaunt, worried, and thoughtful. Vatican, Vatican Museum.

later, in 357, Philip himself occupied Amphipolis after a brief siege. The rapidity with which Philip's new siege engines broke through Amphipolis' defenses gave the Greeks a vivid demonstration of the effectiveness of the Macedonian king's new engineering corps.

Relations worsened a year later when Philip also captured Athens' principal remaining Macedonian allies, Pydna and Methone, as well as Potidaea. In so doing, he eliminated the main centers of Athenian influence in the Chalcidice and on the coasts of the Gulf of Therma. Though many Athenians wanted to fight Philip, and in fact the city declared war, circumstances prevented Athens from mounting serious military operations in the north Aegean.

Athens' slow recovery from the economic devastation caused by the Peloponnesian War restrained the ambitions of all fourth-century Athenian politicians. Financial resources had to be carefully husbanded. Early in the 350s, this meant that Athens ignored Philip's actions in northern Greece to focus its efforts on coping with the threat to the Second Athenian Confederacy caused by the outbreak of the Social War in 357. Athenian foreign policy was further constrained by an important political innovation of the 350s.

Until this time, surpluses from the annual government budgets had been channeled into a fund normally devoted to military expenditures. Eubulus (c. 405–c. 335 BC), however, the leading politician of this era, persuaded the Athenians to pass a law assigning all surplus instead to what is known as the **Theoric Fund**; he himself served as one of the commissioners of the fund. Some of the monies of this fund were to be used for projects such as repairing roads and fortifications. The rest was earmarked for distribution to Athenian citizens at religious festivals; the fund received its name from the "religious embassies" that played a key role in these celebrations.

By mitigating the poverty of Athens' neediest citizens, this arrangement for distributing surplus revenues reduced tensions between rich and poor. For good reason, the orator Demades called it "the glue of the democracy." The Theoric Fund also, of course, encouraged a pacifist foreign policy. Before, the poorer classes might expect to benefit from war, during which they would be paid to row in the fleet, whereas those who had more were sometimes inclined to protect what they had by voting against military involvements. After the establishment of the Theoric Fund, however, this changed, since the outbreak of war would require that funds be redirected to military operations, and the level of the populace's benefits would be reduced.

Eubulus' keen interest in finances had dramatic results. Under his stewardship, Athenian revenues rose from 130 talents to 400, enabling Athens to construct new triremes and improve docks and fortifications. Work at the neglected silver mines at Laurium was renewed, and new inducements lured additional metics to Attica. The wealth of individual citizens grew with that of the state. This situation makes it easy to understand why for most of the decade the Athenians confined their response to Philip's actions to desultory raids, little more than nuisances, into

Macedonian territory. Only the threat of possible direct military intervention by Philip in central Greece induced them to take stronger action.

In 352, with a Macedonian invasion of central Greece seemingly imminent, the Athenians dispatched a large expeditionary force to occupy Thermopylae, to block the Macedonian advance. The motion was made by a close associate of Eubulus. In such a crisis, concern for Athens' security clearly overrode any scruples Eubulus and his supporters may have had about dipping into the Theoric Fund. Otherwise, however, Athens failed utterly to hinder the Macedonian king's growing influence in northern and central Greece.

Athens' actions in the early 340s were similarly ineffective. When Olynthus, increasingly suspicious of Philip's growing power, abandoned its alliance with the Macedonian king and sought to make peace with Athens, Philip turned on his former ally. Athens' responses to Olynthus' desperate appeals for help were too feeble and too late. The Athenians could only watch in dismay when, in 348, Philip captured the city, razed it, and carried off its citizens to become slaves in Macedon. Worse, he dismantled the Chalcidian League, Macedon's only potential Greek rival in the north Aegean.

Athens' restraint in the face of Philip's growing power was prudent. Nevertheless, its inability to regain Amphipolis or to aid its erstwhile allies was humiliating. Not surprisingly, proponents of an aggressive Athenian policy toward Macedon became more insistent in their demands.

The most prominent of these politicians was Demosthenes. The most famous orator of the Greek world, Demosthenes acquired such a reputation for eloquence that the Roman statesman Cicero named his speeches against Mark Antony "Philippics" after the orations in which Demosthenes had sought to rouse the Athenians against Philip. Demosthenes had entered politics initially as a supporter of Eubulus. By 351, however, he had become disenchanted with Eubulus' policies and consequently began to forge a new political identity for himself. In the famous *First Philippic*, Demosthenes revealed his new views by vigorously attacking Philip and berating the Athenians for their sluggish response to the danger the Macedonian posed to Athens. Simultaneously, he urged the Athenians to vote for the establishment and support of a strong naval force to conduct the desired war. Demosthenes continued to advocate resistance to Philip in subsequent years. Still, even he recognized that the fall of Olynthus, combined with Philip's triumph in the Sacred War and the defection of the vital Athenian naval base of Euboea, made peace imperative if Athens was to avoid total disaster.

The Athenian politician Philocrates negotiated peace with Philip in the summer of 346. The process of negotiating the treaty and securing its approval by the Athenian assembly was both complex and contentious. Because the **Peace of Philocrates** quickly collapsed amidst bitter dispute over the responsibility for its negotiation, much remains unclear about the details of the diplomacy that had produced it. The terms of the treaty, however, allow no doubt about its meaning. Faced with the unpalatable alternatives of continuing the war with Macedon or accepting the humiliating terms offered by Philip, Athens chose the latter. Athens publicly renounced its long-cherished claim to Amphipolis, accepted the exclusion of its Phocian and Thracian allies from the protection of the treaty, and agreed that the city and the remnants of the Second Athenian Confederacy would become permanent allies of Philip and his descendants. Athens' impotence in the face of growing Macedonian power and influence in Greece was now revealed for all to see.

The Aftermath of the Peace of Philocrates

By signing the Peace of Philocrates, the Athenians recognized Philip's preeminence in northern and central Greece. Nevertheless, Philip's diplomatic triumph was short-lived. Athens' support for the treaty had been the result of fear of war with Macedon and its consequences. It was therefore no surprise that support dissipated as soon as the threat of war receded. Philip's treatment of Phocis, moreover, not only angered and embarrassed the Athenians; it also cast doubt on the credibility of the ambassadors such as Philocrates and the orator Aeschines, an ally of Eubulus. Along with Philocrates, Aeschines had persuaded the Athenian assembly that no harm would come to the Phocians as a result of their exclusion from the treaty. When Phocis surrendered to him shortly after the conclusion of the agreement, however, Philip, as already mentioned, destroyed the towns of Phocis and resettled their inhabitants in separate villages. The Amphictyonic Council transferred to Philip the two votes at their meetings that had previously belonged to the Phocians. The Athenians and Spartans were so angry at the council's decision that they declined to send their customary deputations to the Pythian games. Aeschines, however, was in attendance, apparently as Philip's guest.

Philip's critics in Athens steadily undermined the Peace of Philocrates and the men associated with it, using the destruction of Phocis to point out the dishonesty of Philip and the questionable competence and integrity of his Athenian supporters. Philip's proposals to strengthen the peace were rebuffed. Indeed, Athens once again demanded that he return Amphipolis. Philocrates, the principal architect of the peace, was indicted for bribery and fled into exile to escape execution. Demosthenes, another of the ten ambassadors who had been sent to negotiate with Philip, nervously sought to protect his position by also impeaching his fellow envoy Aeschines on a charge of accepting bribes.

Aeschines' open partisanship for Philip even after the destruction of Phocis was foolish, and it seems clear that he had accepted gifts from the Macedonian king. Though it was not necessarily a crime in Athens for a politician to receive presents from a foreign head of state unless it could be demonstrated that these gifts had elicited unpatriotic acts, the case against Aeschines looks fairly strong. It is a testimony to the power of his allies that when the case finally came to trial in 343 he was acquitted, though by a very small margin. In his corner he had not only Eubulus, the most prominent politician in Athens and a staunch advocate of peace, but also the strategos Phocion (c. 402/401–318 BC). A biting denigrator of democracy who was elected to the strategia more often than any other man (forty-five times between 371 and 318), Phocion was favorable to Macedon and in fact was executed for his Macedonian sympathies in 318. In addition to harboring many Macedonian partisans among its own citizens, moreover, Athens openly supported or sheltered enemies of Philip from other states.

Only Philip's need for peace in Greece during his Thracian campaign in 342 prevented him from taking strong action against Athens. Philip finally declared war in 340, when Athens in alliance with several other Greek states and Persia frustrated his siege of the Hellespontine city of Perinthus. Athens responded with its own declaration of war.

The actual outbreak of hostilities was delayed for another year. First, Philip unsuccessfully besieged Byzantium; then, he campaigned against the Scythians, who ruled the Dobruja in modern Romania and threatened Macedonian control of Thrace. Nevertheless, he was still able to remind Athens of the potential consequences of war with Macedon. Athens depended for much of its food on grain imported from the Black Sea, so that when Philip seized the whole Black Sea grain fleet in 340, panic broke out in the city.

Philip's long-awaited opportunity to strike directly at Athens finally came in 339, when the Delphic Amphictyony invited him to lead a sacred war against the city of Amphissa, just south of Delphi. He quickly accepted the invitation, and by the end of the year he and his army were securely ensconced in Phocis, within easy striking distance of Athens.

In one of the most famous passages in Greek literature, Demosthenes proudly recalled that only he had had the courage to address the assembly when news reached Athens of Philip's presence in Phocis.

> At dawn the next day the Prytaneis called the Council to the Chamber, and citizens moved into the Assembly.... The Council appeared, announced the news they had received, and brought forward their informant to repeat it. The herald then voiced the question "Who desires to speak?" No one moved. The question was repeated several times without a man standing up, though all the strategoi were there, all the orators, and the voice of Athens called for a word to save her.... I came forward and addressed the Assembly.
> (Demosthenes, *On the Crown* 169–172; Saunders)

The Athenians' despair was understandable. Demosthenes' efforts to form a grand Greek alliance against Macedon had limited success. Only Corinth, Megara, and Messenia, together with a number of other cities in the northern and western Peloponnesus, had heeded Demosthenes' appeal. Sparta, still bitter about the Thebans' liberation of Messenia three decades earlier, remained aloof from the alliance. Throughout history, the Athenians have been censured for failing to respond quickly and vigorously to the growing Macedonian threat, but it is important to remember the role played in the final confrontation by the Spartans' refusal to stand by their fellow Greeks. When fighting finally began in late summer 338, in

Figure 10.5. This monument in the shape of a lion marks the graves of 254 Thebans buried at the site of the Battle of Chaeronea.

the **Battle of Chaeronea** in Boeotia, only the levies of Athens, Thebes, the Boeotian League, and a few Peloponnesian units faced Philip.

A monumental stone lion still gazes over the plain of Chaeronea, marking the site of this pivotal battle in world history. Little is known about the battle itself beyond two facts: Greek casualties were heavy, and the decisive blow was struck by the companion cavalry led by Philip's eighteen-year-old son and heir, Alexander. A thousand Athenians were killed and another two thousand captured; the Thebans' cherished Sacred Band was slaughtered to a man. Philip's triumph over his Greek foes was complete. Whether Philip had planned all along to conquer Greece is unknown. After his victory at Chaeronea, however, any resistance to his authority in Greece would have been futile. All that remained to be determined was the form Macedonian domination of Greece would take.

MACEDONIAN DOMINATION OF GREECE

According to the historian Diodorus, a drunken Philip celebrated his victory by mocking the Greek dead until an Athenian prisoner, the politician Demades, sobered him up with the remark that his conduct ill befitted a great king. Whether the story is true or not, Philip's decisions after Chaeronea reflected careful thought. Exactly when Philip decided to attack Persia is uncertain, but his actions in the aftermath of the battle make it clear that the decision had already been made by the early 330s.

Philip's immediate concern was how to deal with his two principal enemies. The Thebans were treated with exemplary harshness. Inasmuch as Thebes had a long record of collaboration with Persia and was Macedon's chief rival for power in central and northern Greece, Philip took advantage of his victory to break the city's power. Theban and other Boeotian prisoners were released only after payment of a heavy ransom. Thebes' political leaders were either executed or exiled. A Macedonian garrison was installed on the Cadmea, the city's acropolis. Finally, Thebes was stripped of its traditional position of leadership in the Boeotian League.

Philip's treatment of Athens was dramatically different. Athenian support was essential to the long-term pacification of Greece. A difficult siege would be required to capture the city, and in the meantime, its fleet could seriously interfere with his projected Persian campaign. Consequently, Athens escaped significant punishment despite its leading role in the war. Athenian prisoners were returned without ransom, and the bodies of the Athenian dead were escorted back to the city by an honor guard led by Alexander and Antipater, Philip's most trusted general. Nor did Philip object when Demosthenes, his most implacable opponent, delivered the funeral oration over the dead of Chaeronea.

Philip's actions were well received. Few Greeks regretted the humiliation of Thebes, whose arbitrary behavior in the decades since the Battle of Leuctra had bred widespread resentment. Athens, for its part, responded to Philip's unexpected leniency by showering the city's former enemies with honors. Antipater and Alexander were awarded Athenian citizenship, and a cult was established in Philip's honor in one of the city's gymnasia. Needless to say, Athenian suspicion of Philip's intentions or those of his supporters at Athens did not disappear; a law passed in 337 threatened severe penalties for anyone who conspired to overthrow the democracy and establish a tyranny. Some, however, welcomed Macedon as a force in Athenian politics. After Chaeronea as before, all shades of opinion thrived in the city, along with a variety of sentiments toward Philip ranging from reverence to hatred.

Officially, however, relations were amicable. Antipater and Alexander were not the only Macedonian subjects to benefit from the thaw in relations between Philip and Athens. Athenian inscriptions demonstrate that contact between Athens and the Macedonian court became increasingly common in the years after the Battle of Chaeronea. One of those who took advantage of the new relationship between Athens and Macedon was the philosopher **Aristotle**. A close friend of Antipater and the former tutor of Alexander, Aristotle returned to Athens in 335 and remained there until 322, when renewed anti-Macedonian sentiment forced him to flee to Euboea. There he died the same year.

The school that Aristotle founded at Athens, the Lyceum, became the model for the great research institutions of the Hellenistic period. Philip, however, had no such elevated goals in mind when he so dramatically dispatched Antipater and Alexander to Athens in 337. His immediate purposes were to avoid a difficult siege and to win Athens' acquiescence in his plans for Greece; his calculated generosity largely succeeded in achieving those goals. Athens offered no further resistance to Macedonian preeminence in Greece. More important, the Athenians agreed to send representatives to the general meeting of Greek states at Corinth that Philip called in the summer of 337 BC, where Philip revealed his plans for the future.

The Corinthian League

Except for the Spartans, who refused to attend, all the major Greek states sent representatives to Corinth to learn Philip's plans. No account of what transpired at Corinth survives, but the main points of Philip's proposals are known. The centerpiece of the new order was an alliance, traditionally referred to as the **Corinthian League**, which Philip called simply "the Greeks." The purpose of the alliance was twofold: to maintain a common peace in Greece and to retaliate against the Persians for the invasion of 480 BC and other acts of aggression against Greeks. To achieve those ends, the council (synedrion) of the alliance was empowered to pass decrees binding on member states, to arbitrate disputes between them, and to try individuals accused of betraying the goals and policies of the alliance. Member states also received pledges of mutual nonaggression and promises of support against attack or subversion of their respective governments. Not surprisingly, Philip's proposals were approved by the delegates, and he was appointed *hēgemōn* (leader) of the alliance and commander of the war of revenge against the Persians.

DOCUMENT 10.2

Oath of Members of the League of Corinth (338–337 BC)

Fragment of an Athenian inscription recording the oath sworn by the Athenians when they ratified the treaty establishing the League of Corinth.

Oath. I swear by Zeus, Earth, Sun, Poseidon, Athena, Ares, and all the gods and goddesses. I will abide by the peace, and I will not break the agreements with Philip the Macedonian, nor will I take up arms with hostile intent against any one of those who abide by the oaths either by land or by sea. I will not seize in war by any device or stratagem any city or fort or harbor belonging to those who share the peace, nor will I suppress the kingdom of Philip or of his descendants or the constitutions in force among any of those [who share the peace], when they swore the oaths concerning the peace. I will not commit any act that contravenes the agreements nor will I permit any other to do so. If any one breaks the agreements, I will assist those who have been wronged in accordance with their requests and I will fight against those who break the common peace just as the common council and the leader [hegemon] decide....

Inscriptiones Graecae 2.236

Historians have long recognized that the primary purpose of the League of Corinth was to legitimize Philip's domination of Greece, and it did so in a way

Figure 10.6. Theater at the Macedonian capital, Aegae, modern Vergina.

that was all the more effective because it reflected important trends in contemporary Greek thought. Ever since the end of the Peloponnesian War, Greek politicians and thinkers, dismayed by chronic political and social unrest, had sought ways to end the constant warfare that plagued fourth-century Greece. In works like *The Republic* and the *Laws,* Plato and other philosophers offered utopian visions of ideal cities free of stasis that they themselves knew could not be realized. More pragmatic thinkers sought to redefine the place of war in Greek life. They denounced wars between Greeks as civil wars, while insisting that wars against barbarians were inherently just or even desirable as a way of reducing internal tensions in Greece. These ideas were embodied in the repeated attempts to establish "common peaces," such as the King's Peace and its various successors, that are characteristic of fourth-century Greek diplomacy.

The most prominent of the just-war theorists was the Athenian educator **Isocrates**. Isocrates was almost 100 years old when the Battle of Chaeronea was fought. Throughout his long career as a speechwriter and teacher of rhetoric, he had brooded on Greece's chronic social problems. His proposed solution, as we have seen in Chapter 9, was conquering a portion of the Persian empire, providing a place to which economically deprived and potentially dangerous segments of Greek society could emigrate. He had appealed in vain to various Greek rulers, including Dionysius I of Syracuse and Jason of Pherae, to forcibly unite Greece and lead it in a crusade against Persia. To Isocrates, Philip must have seemed his last chance to see his dream realized. Unfortunately, we do not know how Philip responded when the aged Greek invited him to lead such a crusade after his victory at the Battle of Chaeronea. By uniting in the League of Corinth the ideas of a "common peace" and a crusade against Persia, however, Philip was exploiting ideas that had deep roots in fourth-century BC Greece.

The Death of Philip II

The Corinthian League's approval of Philip's plan for a Persian war was well timed. The early 330s were years of severe crisis for the Persian empire. The able but ruthless king Artaxerxes III (358–338 BC) had struggled throughout his reign to rebuild Persian power, and by the late 340s his efforts had been crowned with success. He ended the satrapal rebellions that had disrupted the reign of his father Artaxerxes II (405–359 BC), reestablished Persian authority in Phoenicia and Asia Minor, and even reconquered Egypt, which had been independent since the end of the fifth century.

Artaxerxes' power rivaled that of his great sixth- and fifth-century ancestors. Demosthenes and other enemies of Philip looked to the Persian king for assistance against Macedon. But disaster struck almost as soon as Persia had reemerged as a significant factor in the affairs of the eastern Mediterranean basin. In 338, an ambitious eunuch named Bagoas assassinated Artaxerxes III and precipitated a succession crisis that lasted for almost two years. Only after a relative of Artaxerxes had succeeded in killing the treacherous eunuch and himself ascended the throne of Persia as Darius III did the crisis end and a semblance of stability return.

In 336, Philip quickly took advantage of the chaos at the heart of the Persian empire by sending an expeditionary force across the Hellespont, commanded by his trusted general Parmenion. As the Macedonian army moved southward down the west coast of Anatolia, Philip's supporters in various Greek cities revolted and overthrew their pro-Persian tyrants. At Eresus on Lesbos, the new government signaled its adhesion to the Macedonian cause by establishing a cult to Zeus Philippios; at Ephesus Philip's supporters had a statue of the king placed in the temple of Artemis. The successes achieved by Parmenion and his expeditionary force in 336 augured well for the main campaign Philip was to lead the following year.

Before that campaign could take place, however, fate intervened. In the summer of 336, Philip was assassinated at Aegae by a member of his own bodyguard named Pausanias. Assassination was the climax of the turbulence that had marked Philip's personal life during the last years of his reign, resulting from his seventh marriage in 338. For most of his reign Philip's queen had been his fourth wife, the Epirote princess **Olympias**, who bore his designated heir, Alexander. His other marriages to Thessalian, Thracian, Illyrian, and even Scythian brides had served diplomatic ends without threatening Olympias' position at court. Philip's seventh marriage was different. For the first time, Philip took a Macedonian bride, a young woman named Cleopatra, and allied himself to a powerful Macedonian noble family.

Scholars have been unable to explain Philip's final marriage. Ancient writers saw it as the result of a disastrous infatuation with a younger woman. Some modern scholars have suggested that Philip may have hoped that the new marriage might result in additional sons to strengthen his family's hold on the throne. Whatever Philip's plans may have been, the dramatic consequences of his marriage quickly became evident. In short order, both Olympias and Alexander fell from favor and fled into exile, amidst talk that Philip intended to supplant his son with a "Macedonian" heir.

As it turned out, the threat to Alexander's position ended almost as suddenly as it had begun. In 337, Cleopatra bore Philip a daughter named Europa. The child's name indicated Philip's understandable pride in his accomplishments, but a woman could not succeed to the Macedonian throne. Without a new son to replace Alexander as heir, Philip had no choice but to reconcile with him. A mutual friend, Demaratus of Corinth, effected the rapprochement. Although Olympias remained in exile in Epirus, Alexander returned to Pella and resumed his place at court. The crisis over the succession had ended, it seemed, without serious consequences.

Indirectly, however, Philip's ill-advised marriage to Cleopatra proved to be his undoing. The union inevitably embroiled Philip in the enmities of her family, and one of them involved his assassin, Pausanias. According to Aristotle, Pausanias killed Philip because he had been abused by Cleopatra's uncle Attalus and Philip had done nothing about it. The details are preserved by Diodorus, who makes it clear that the abuse had been extreme. Attalus' servants had raped Pausanias. The motive for this atrocious act was revenge for the death of a young relative of Attalus, whose death had resulted from Pausanias' jealous slanders about his manhood because Philip had not chosen him as his lover. Unwilling to endanger his alliance with his new queen's family, Philip sought to palliate Pausanias' grievance by promoting him to the coveted rank of royal bodyguard.

Philip's efforts to mollify the young man were conspicuously unsuccessful, and Pausanias seized an opportunity for vengeance at the wedding of one of Philip's daughters. The wedding festivities climaxed with a splendid procession led by Philip. As the procession entered the theater at Aegae, Pausanias rushed forward and stabbed Philip to death before the startled eyes of the guests, who had come from all over the Macedonian empire to witness the king's triumph. So ended the reign of the most controversial of all Macedonian kings.

⟫⟫⟫———⟪⟪⟪

Could Greek union and resolve have prevented the Macedonian takeover? Twentieth-century historians sometimes compared Philip with Hitler, casting Demosthenes in the role of Winston Churchill (a construct flattering to Demosthenes, whose efforts failed conspicuously). Leaving aside the validity of the comparison, the analogy raises the question of whether Philip's success was not contingent on Greek vacillation and appeasement, and on the collusion of pro-Macedonian factions in the poleis—it is important to remember Phocion's long-standing affection for Macedon. This question seems ultimately unanswerable, for history is not a laboratory science, and we have no way of replaying the fourth century BC with a healthier, richer, and less divided Greece. What is clear is that Philip II was a remarkable man.

Since antiquity, historians have had difficulty assessing Philip and his achievements. Polybius was bewildered by the opening of Theopompus of Chios' great history of Philip. It began with the observation that "Europe had never produced a man like Philip" and then went on to catalogue Philip's "crimes and follies," including his unbridled sexuality and drunkenness, his betrayal of his friends and allies, and his destruction of Greek cities. As so often in such matters, the problem is partly one of perspective. Polybius wrote two centuries after Philip's death and found it difficult to sympathize with Theopompus, a fourth-century Greek who had viewed Philip primarily as a foreign, malignant force in Greek affairs and not as the founder of Macedonian greatness.

Which point of view is correct? In fact, both have merit. It is impossible to deny that in many ways Philip's influence on contemporary Greek affairs was negative. The destruction of cities including Amphipolis, Methone, Stagira, and Olynthus is well documented. Nevertheless, Philip was first and foremost king of Macedon. His primary concern was the welfare of Macedon, not Greece. In that regard, he succeeded. In the twenty-four years of his reign, Philip transformed Macedon from a kingdom on the verge of dissolution to a unified state, ruling an empire that reached from the Danube to southern Greece. Whether his plans to extend Macedonian power into Asia were as grandiose as those carried out later by Alexander cannot be known. Nevertheless, it is clear that without Philip's legacy of a united, powerful Macedon, the achievements of Alexander and his successors would have been impossible.

KEY TERMS

Amphictyonic Council	**Isocrates**	**royal companions**
Aristotle	**Macedon**	**royal pages**
Battle of Chaeronea	**Olympias**	**sarissa**
Corinthian League	**Peace of Philocrates**	**Theoric Fund**
Demosthenes	**phalanx**	**Thessaly**
Hellenization	**Philip II**	**Thrace**
Illyria	**Phocis**	

SUGGESTED READINGS

Adcock, F. E. 1957. *The Greek and Macedonian Art of War.* Berkeley and Los Angeles: University of California Press. Lucid introduction to Greek and Macedonian ideas of war.

Andronicos, Manolis. 1984. *Vergina: The Royal Tombs.* Trans. Louise Turner. Athens: Ekdotike Athenon. Beautifully illustrated account of the discovery of the Macedonian royal cemetery at Vergina.

Borza, Eugene N. 1990. *In the Shadow of Olympus: The Emergence of Macedon.* Princeton, NJ: Princeton University Press. Insightful history of the kingdom of Macedon from its origin to the reign of Philip II.

————. 1995. *Makedonika: Essays by Eugene N. Borza.* Claremont: Regina Books. Perceptive essays on Macedonian history by a leading scholar.

Carney, Elizabeth Donnelly. 2000. *Women and Monarchy in Macedonia.* Norman: University of Oklahoma Press. Pioneering study of the political significance of royal women in Macedonia.

————. 2006. *Olympias: Mother of Alexander the Great.* New York: Routledge. Perceptive biography of Alexander the Great's mother.

———— and Daniel Ogden (eds.). 2010. *Philip II and Alexander the Great: Father and Son, Lives and Alternatives.* New York: Oxford University Press. Articles by leading scholars assessing various aspects of the relationship between Philip II and his son.

Martin, Thomas R. 1985. *Sovereignty and Coinage in Classical Greece.* Princeton, NJ: Princeton University Press. Important study of the numismatic evidence for Macedonian relations with Thessaly.

Ryder, T. T. B. 1965. *Koine Eirene: General Peace and Local Independence in Ancient Greece.* London: Oxford University Press. Comprehensive account of efforts to establish general peace in Greece in the fourth century BC.

Sealey, Raphael. 1993. *Demosthenes and His Time: A Study in Defeat.* New York: Oxford University Press. Important revisionist biography of the Athenian statesman.

Worthington, Ian. 2008. *Philip II of Macedonia.* New Haven: Yale University Press. Vigorously written, detailed biography of Philip II.

CHAPTER ELEVEN

Alexander the Great

Rarely has an epoch-making reign begun in such uncertainty as that of **Alexander the Great**. In his reign of almost two and a half decades, Alexander's father, Philip II, had transformed Macedon into a strong, centralized monarchy. Philip's military reforms had made Macedon the premier military power in the region, controlling an empire that stretched from the Danube River in the north to Thessaly in the south. By creating the League of Corinth, Philip had extended Macedonian influence deep into southern Greece and gained the public support of his Greek subjects and allies for his projected invasion of Asia. Philip's assassination on the eve of his departure to join his forces in the east threatened to ruin not only his Asian adventure but all of his achievements.

Alexander's reign began, like Philip's, with a succession crisis. Alexander III was only twenty years old at the time of his father's death in the summer of 336 BC. Omens were later said to have forecast his rule. His mother, Olympias, who had much to gain in securing the succession for her son, claimed to have dreamed that lightning struck her womb. The great temple of Artemis at Ephesus was believed to have been destroyed by fire on the day Alexander was born. Although Philip had offspring from several of his wives, Alexander was clearly treated as his father's heir for most of Philip's reign.

Philip and Olympias groomed Alexander carefully for the role he would ultimately play. A series of Greek tutors, including Aristotle, provided him with the education in Greek literature and culture that Philip had lacked. From them Alexander gained his lifelong love of Homer and his determination to equal or excel the exploits of his legendary ancestors, Heracles and Achilles.

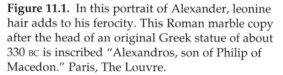

Figure 11.1. In this portrait of Alexander, leonine hair adds to his ferocity. This Roman marble copy after the head of an original Greek statue of about 330 BC is inscribed "Alexandros, son of Philip of Macedon." Paris, The Louvre.

Alexander's practical training in kingship was not neglected. He governed Macedon in Philip's absence and suppressed a Thracian rebellion. Like his father, Alexander founded a city named after himself in Thrace. Finally, he took part in Philip's campaigns, even commanding the companion cavalry in the decisive Battle of Chaeronea that established Macedonian rule in Greece in 338 BC. Nevertheless, Alexander's succession was not assured. He was isolated at court at the time of Philip's death. Olympias and Alexander's friends and advisers remained in exile. Not surprisingly, rumors quickly spread after the death of Philip that Alexander had encouraged Pausanias and that Olympias had even mourned the assassin, who was dispatched on the scene by the king's bodyguard.

There was also talk of other possible successors. The most important of these potential rivals was Philip's nephew, ward, and son-in-law, the former king, Amyntas IV. Only timely intervention by **Antipater**, one of Philip's most senior generals, saved the succession for Alexander. Antipater's presentation of Alexander to the Macedonian troops at Aegae for the traditional acclamation as king, combined with the death of the assassin Pausanias and the rapid condemnation and execution of his alleged fellow conspirators, secured the throne for the young prince. It also changed the history of western Asia.

Sources for the Reign of Alexander

The English poet Chaucer (d. 1400) wrote in *The Monk's Tale* (lines 641–643) that "the storie of Alisaundre is so commune,/ that every wight that hath discrecioun/ hath herd somewhat or al of his fortune." For most of the Middle Ages, the most widely read nonreligious book in the Old World was a romantic biography of Alexander (the so-called *Alexander Romance*) that freely mingled history with fiction. The popularity of his remarkable story has continued to the present, inspiring films and novels. A selective bibliography of works dealing with Alexander contained the titles of almost seven hundred studies published between 1700 and 1970, and dozens of new studies of his reign have appeared every year since. Despite this vast outpouring of scholarship, interpretations of Alexander's character and goals differ widely. Historians have cast Alexander in many roles: as the chief agent in the spread of Hellenism, as an idealistic believer in the unity of mankind, as an Aryan superman, and, more recently, as a brutal conqueror without constructive plans for the future of his empire. The reasons for this lack of agreement on even the most basic issues of Alexander's biography among Greek historians are clear: the limitations of the available sources for his life and reign, and historians' difficulty in transcending their own historical context. Although archaeology has revealed much about the times in which Alexander lived, including the discovery of tombs that may belong to his father and son, historians must still rely on the evidence contained in Greek and Latin literature for the essential details of his life and career.

The ancient evidence concerning Alexander originally was varied and extensive. Alexander himself actively promoted the development of literature about himself and his achievements. In addition to engineers and other technical experts, his entourage included an official historian (a nephew of Aristotle named **Callisthenes**), as well as poets and scholars who were to celebrate his conquests and describe the discoveries made during his campaign. In the two generations following his death, the literary tradition concerning Alexander was enriched by the publication of numerous works—both ephemera, such as political pamphlets, and substantial histories of his reign written by participants in his expedition, including the admiral Nearchus, the Cynic philosopher Onesicritus, and a future king of Egypt, Ptolemy I. These works varied from official *apologiai* (defenses against criticism) to heroic adventure stories. Unfortunately, none of the histories by Alexander's contemporaries survives in original form. Our limited knowledge of their contents is based on the collection and intensive analysis by modern scholars of the few extant quotations, summaries, or allusions to them found in later writers.

The publication in the late twentieth century of cuneiform texts concerning Alexander holds out the hope of the discovery of new sources that would provide a much needed Asian perspective on the Macedonian conquest. Modern historians reconstruct Alexander's life from the five extant accounts of Alexander, namely, those contained in the universal histories of Diodorus (first century BC) and Pompeius Trogus (first century BC), the latter extant only in the form of an abridgment prepared in the second century AD by an otherwise unknown writer named Justin; the *History of Alexander* by Quintus Curtius Rufus (first century AD); Plutarch's *Life of Alexander* (second century AD); and the *Anabasis of Alexander* by Arrian (second century AD). These biographies were all written three hundred to five hundred years after the king's death and reflect the interests and ideas of the early Roman Empire, a period very different from that in which Alexander lived. Their value depends, therefore, on the fact that they drew their information from the now lost works of Alexander's contemporaries. Since no infallible method of evaluating the relative merits of each of the five late biographies has been devised, the variation in modern assessments of Alexander results in large part from the differing judgments of scholars concerning the weight to be assigned to their evidence. On one matter, however, all biographers of Alexander, ancient and modern, agree: Alexander's personal actions were of decisive importance in shaping the remarkable events of his reign.

CONSOLIDATING POWER

Alexander's personal role was never more important than in the critical first year of his reign. The support of Philip's senior commanders had been indispensable in securing the succession for Alexander. In the aftermath of his accession, they urged the young king to proceed cautiously, consolidating his base in Macedon and using diplomacy to conciliate Macedon's northern subjects and allies, even at the risk of losing influence in Greece. Such caution was not to Alexander's taste, and not for the last time he rejected the advice of the Macedonian old guard in favor of decisive action.

Greece first claimed Alexander's attention, and he made a sudden, dramatic appearance there immediately after conducting his father's funeral. Anti-Macedonian politicians at Athens and **Thebes** quickly abandoned plans to free Greece from continued Macedonian rule by exploiting a presumed weakness in Macedon in the wake of Philip's assassination. Alexander was confirmed in Philip's former positions as archon of Thessaly and hegemon of the Corinthian League, and Greek support for the war against Persia was reaffirmed. After a brief stay in Macedon following his return from Greece, Alexander waged an even more wide-ranging northern campaign in the spring of 335, intended to impress on the Thracians and Illyrians that Philip's death would bring no easing of the Macedonian yoke.

Alexander's first major campaign extended as far north as the banks of the Danube. Only sketchy accounts of the course of events survive, but it is clear that Alexander achieved his principal goals in the north. His main target was the Triballi, who had humiliated Philip in 339 during his return march to Macedon after his victory over the Scythians. The Triballi's attempt to hold a key pass against Alexander failed, thanks to the discipline of his Macedonian troops, who were able to clear a path for the wagons their enemies sent careening down the mountain in the hope of breaking their line. Triballian resistance collapsed shortly thereafter when Alexander defeated their main forces and then launched an amphibious assault on an island where the Triballi had placed their women and children for safety. Alexander's dramatic raid in force across the Danube into the territory of the Getae gained the submission of the remaining Thracian tribes. Alexander also concluded a treaty of friendship with a group of Gauls, the vanguard of a migration that was greatly to affect southeastern Europe and Anatolia in the early Hellenistic period.

Having secured his northern frontier, Alexander turned southwestward into Illyria to deal with Philip II's old enemy, King Cleitus. Alexander received the first of his many battle wounds during this phase of the campaign. Only his intuitive understanding of the psychological impact that a display of Macedonian close-order drill would have on the Illyrians enabled him to extricate his army from a potentially disastrous trap. He inflicted a decisive defeat on Cleitus that finally ended the Illyrian threat to Macedon's western frontier that had loomed over so many of his predecessors.

Alexander's long absence in the north sparked rumors of his death in Greece. Hope was mother to the fact. Demosthenes even introduced a supposed eyewitness of Alexander's death to the Athenian assembly. Confident of Athenian aid, the Thebans rose in revolt, besieging the city's Macedonian garrison on the Cadmea, the acropolis of Thebes, and inviting other Greek states to join them in the struggle for freedom. Forced marches by Alexander, who had been informed of the events unfolding in Greece, brought him and his army under the walls of Thebes before the rebellion could spread. The Athenians, who had voted military aid for Thebes, now hesitated. The Spartans, who had failed so stunningly to help at Chaeronea, also held back. When the Thebans nonetheless spurned Alexander's demand for surrender, the city was stormed and sacked. Alexander ordered that Thebes' Boeotian neighbors decide the ultimate fate of the city and its surviving citizens. All too mindful of past efforts by Thebes to subdue them, they decided that Thebes should be destroyed and the remaining Thebans sold into slavery. Alexander carried out the decree, sparing from destruction only Thebes' temples and the descendants and house of its illustrious poet, Pindar.

The destruction of Thebes was remembered for centuries as one of the great atrocities of Greek history. Alexander himself was said later to have given special consideration to personal requests by Thebans. For the moment, his calculated use of terror achieved its purpose. As news of the destruction of Thebes spread, active resistance to Macedonian rule ceased throughout Greece. For the second time in a little over a year, the Corinthian League acknowledged Alexander as its hegemon and affirmed its support for his policies. Now that the example of Thebes' horrible fate had sapped Greek resolve, Alexander could afford to adopt a more generous attitude, abandoning his demands for the surrender of anti-Macedonian leaders at Athens and elsewhere in Greece.

Invasion of Asia

Alexander also took steps to neutralize potential opposition in Macedon. Measures such as freeing Macedonians from all personal obligations except military service won Alexander popularity among his subjects, while potential rivals were eliminated. Unfortunately, the sources conceal the full extent of the purge because they emphasize instead a brutal and unauthorized act by Olympias: the murder of Philip II's last wife, Cleopatra, and her daughter during Alexander's absence in Greece in 336 BC. A spectacular archaeological discovery, however, has illuminated these events.

At the modern village of Vergina, the site of the ancient Macedonian capital of Aegae, archaeologists discovered in 1981 under a tumulus approximately the size of a football field three royal tombs. Tomb 1 was a chamber tomb that had been looted in antiquity but still contained the remains of an adult male, a young female, and an infant. The other two tombs—Tombs 2 and 3—were unlooted barrel-vaulted structures filled with grave goods as spectacular as those discovered by Schliemann at Mycenae a century earlier. Tomb 2 also contained the cremated remains of a middle-aged male and a young woman, and Tomb 3 held the remains of a teenage boy, almost certainly Alexander IV, the son of Alexander the Great. Scholars are divided over whether Philip II and Cleopatra were buried in Tomb 1 or Tomb 2, but in either case the fact remains that as one of the first acts of his reign Alexander buried Cleopatra with full royal honors, probably in the hope of neutralizing the effects of her murder by Olympias. Once Alexander's hold on the throne was secure, however, he dropped all pretense of reconciliation and took decisive action against his enemies. The male members of Cleopatra's family, who had profited from her position as Philip's queen, were wiped out. Likewise, Amyntas IV, whom Philip II had replaced as king of Macedon and who was, therefore, Alexander's only legitimate rival for the throne, was assassinated. Their surviving supporters fled to their only possible refuge, Persia, leaving Alexander as the unchallenged ruler of Macedon. (See Plate XVa.)

In the spring of 334 BC, with his position in Macedon finally secure, Alexander led his forces across the Hellespont to Asia. His formidable army was fully 37,000 strong. Its core consisted of the 12,000 Macedonian troops who formed the phalanx. They were supplemented by 3,000 hypaspists (royal guards) and 1,800 companion cavalry. In addition to his Macedonian troops, his army included special light-armed units from Illyria and Thrace and almost 9,000 allied Greek infantry and cavalry. A fleet of almost 200 ships provided by Alexander's Greek allies supported his troops and maintained his communications with Europe.

Alexander's first actions in Asia were bold, even theatrical. He was the first Macedonian to land on Asian soil, leaping ashore and casting his spear into the land to claim all that he conquered as territory won by the spear. He then went to the traditional site of Troy, where he sacrificed to Athena, asked pardon of the ancient Trojan king Priam for invading Asia, and paid homage to Achilles, who he believed was one of his ancestors.

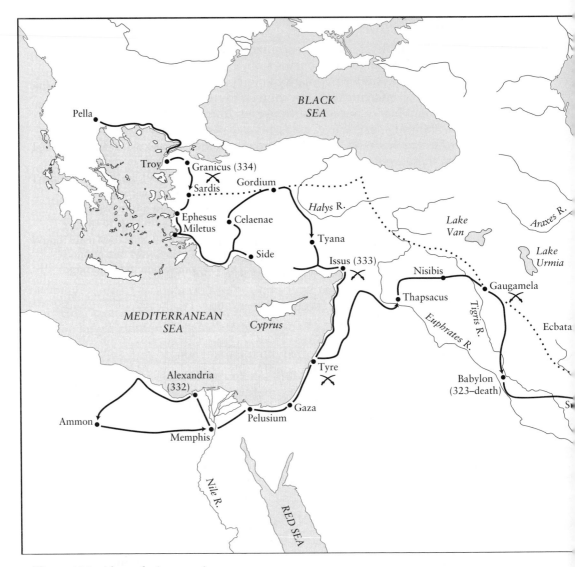

Figure 11.2. Alexander's campaign.

The symbolism suited the leader of the Greek crusade, but serious problems lay behind all the bravado. To maintain his authority in Macedon and Greece, Alexander had been compelled to leave almost half his Macedonian troops behind in Europe with Antipater. In Asia, everything won by Philip's advance guard in 336 except the bridgehead at Abydus had been lost to a vigorous Persian counteroffensive. Worse yet, Alexander had sufficient funds for only a brief campaign, and his friends did not yet hold important positions in the government and army.

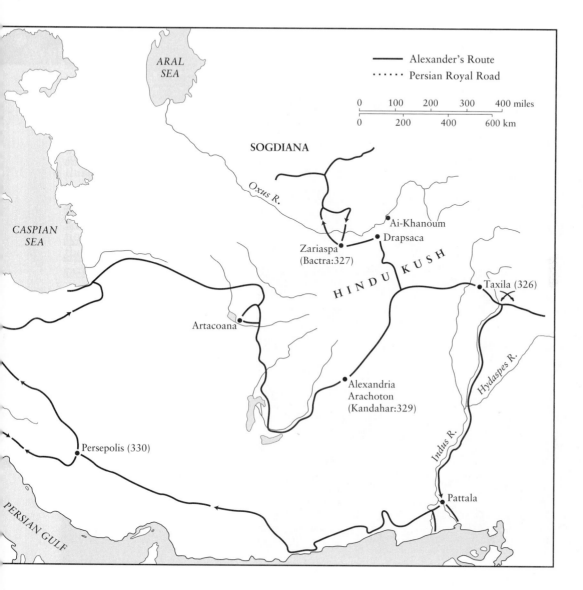

In Macedon, Antipater governed as regent in his name. Alexander's second-in-command in Asia was **Parmenion**, a close friend of Antipater and, until Philip's death, an ally of Cleopatra's family. Moreover, Parmenion's relatives held key commands in the army's critical cavalry units. Alexander needed a quick victory to achieve the goals of his campaign and ensure his freedom from the domination of the Macedonian aristocrats who had made him king. Fortunately for him, the Persians proved to be "convenient enemies."

Figure 11.3. The great tumulus at Vergina during excavation including the supposed tomb of Philip II and the tomb of Alexander IV.

The Battle of Granicus (334 BC)

The vast size of the Persian empire meant that mobilization of its main forces to confront a threat on a remote frontier was always slow. Local satraps, therefore, had to rely on the limited forces stationed in their territories to cope with the initial phases of an invasion. In such circumstances, satraps normally used a defensive strategy that aimed at controlling key strong points while denying the enemy use of local resources until the **Great King** could mobilize the empire's financial and military forces and bring them to bear on the invader. Such a strategy was in fact proposed by Memnon, the Rhodian general who had defended Asia Minor against Parmenion's forces the year before. The Anatolian satraps, however, were jealous of Memnon's high standing with Darius and unwilling to risk having to justify the losses in revenue and the destruction of royal lands that such a strategy would entail. Instead they chose a bolder course, deciding to confront Alexander directly in battle in the hope of killing him.

The strategy almost worked. The Persians met Alexander at the Granicus River, the modern Biga Çayı, in northwest Anatolia. Their position was strong: the cavalry was stationed along the riverbank itself to prevent the Macedonians from successfully crossing the river, while the infantry, including several thousand Greek mercenary troops, were posted behind them as support. The details of the battle itself are unclear. Alexander apparently overruled Parmenion's suggestion that he wait until the next day to attack, to allow the soldiers to recover from their march. Instead, he ordered an immediate attack. The fighting was hard, and disaster was barely averted.

The Persians nearly succeeded in killing Alexander, who stood out clearly in the flamboyant "armor of Achilles" that he had taken from the temple of Athena at Troy. The king was saved from certain death only by the daring action of **Cleitus the Black**, the brother of Alexander's nurse: at a crucial moment Cleitus sliced off the arm of a Persian noble who was about to deal a fatal blow to an already dazed Alexander. Because the Persians had staked everything on killing Alexander, the failure of their plan brought disaster. The bulk of the Persian cavalry, trapped between the Macedonians and their own infantry, was slaughtered. The Persian infantry, which had taken no part in the battle, fled and abandoned the Greek mercenaries who formed the core of the Persian army. Since many of these were exiled enemies of Macedonian rule in Greece, it is not surprising that Alexander ordered all but two thousand of them massacred as traitors to the Greek cause. The survivors were sent to Macedon to work in chains. Alexander boldly announced his victory to the Greek world by sending to Athens three hundred suits of Persian armor as a dedication to Athena with the inscription: "From Alexander, the son of Philip, and the Greeks, except the Spartans." His barbed reference to the Spartans highlighted their refusal to join the League of Corinth and share in the Panhellenic crusade against Persia that he was leading.

Alexander's decisive victory at the Granicus changed the character of the war. Defeat deprived the Persians of a principal advantage; no longer could they mount an effective defense in Anatolia while exploiting their naval superiority and financial resources to harass Alexander's communications with Macedon and foment rebellion in Greece. With most of the Persian commanders dead and much of their best cavalry and Greek mercenaries lost, the Persian position in Anatolia disintegrated. Although the Phoenician fleet freely cruised the Aegean, the Greeks as a whole refused to commit themselves to the Persian cause. Alexander's forces, meanwhile, swept south along the west coast of Anatolia. Fierce resistance by the Persian garrisons at Miletus and Halicarnassus slowed the Macedonian advance but could not stop it. In quick succession the satrapies of Lydia, Caria, and Lycia fell to Alexander. By the spring of 333, Alexander had reached Gordium, the capital of the ancient kingdom of Phrygia, near modern Ancyra in central Anatolia. In less than a year, Isocrates' once seemingly impossible dream of severing Anatolia from the Persian empire had been realized.

The first year of the campaign also exposed the unresolved conflict inherent in Alexander's dual position as hegemon of the League of Corinth and leader of the Greek crusade and king of Macedon. As hegemon he was required to respect Greek opinion and the commitments he and Philip had made to the League of Corinth. Consequently, he punished the Greek mercenaries after the Battle of the Granicus and turned deposed pro-Persian tyrants over to the council of the League of Corinth for trial. As king of Macedon, however, conquered territory was his to do with as he saw fit, and increasingly his interests as king overrode his obligations to the League and his concern for Greek opinion.

Greek Reaction

Alexander made his supremacy clear immediately after his victory at the Granicus. He told representatives of Greek and non-Greek cities that had surrendered to him to obey their new Macedonian satrap and pay to him the same tribute they had paid to the Persians. Alexander retained the existing pattern of satrapal government elsewhere in Anatolia. When it became clear that his previous severity had only stiffened the resolve of Greek mercenaries in Persian service to fight, he eased the terms for surrender offered to them. Similarly, active support for democracy in the Greek cities of Asia became royal policy only when democratic factions offered their support to the Macedonian forces. Cities so liberated, however, found their new freedom hedged about with restraints. They were free of the obligation to pay "tribute" to the Persians, but they now had to make financial "contributions" to the Macedonian military effort and were severely punished if they objected. Moreover, as a series of inscriptions from Chios and other Asian cities reveal, Alexander freely intervened in the internal affairs of the Greek cities of Asia whenever he thought it necessary.

The development of his relations with his new non-Greek subjects was similar. As befitted his position as the hegemon of the League of Corinth, the first new satraps Alexander appointed were Macedonians. In the course of the campaign, however, Alexander took steps to win local support. In Caria, he entrusted the civil administration of the area to Queen Ada, who adopted him as her son and heir. At the same time, control of military affairs remained in the hands of a Macedonian garrison commander responsible to himself.

Alexander pursued the same policy elsewhere in Anatolia, appointing Persian satraps for Cappadocia and Armenia. Although circumstances prevented these latter appointments from becoming effective, the policy was clear. Non-Greek leaders who recognized Alexander could expect royal favor and promotion. Although Isocrates had dreamed of a new greater Greece in

Anatolia, the true situation was more accurately reflected in the symbolism of Alexander's dramatic severing of the "**Gordian knot**." According to a famous legend, rule over Asia was promised to whoever loosed the complex knot that connected the drawpole to the wagon the first Midas had ridden when he became king of Phrygia. While he was at Gordium, Alexander fulfilled the prophecy by slashing through the knot with his sword, allowing no doubt that a new king had arisen in Asia.

DOCUMENT 11.1

Letter of Alexander to the Chians (334 BC)

The tension between Alexander's claim to have "freed" the Greek cities of Asia and the reality of Macedonian power is particularly clear in this letter of instructions concerning the reform of the city's government that Alexander wrote to the citizens of Chios.

All the exiles from Chios are to return and the government at Chios is to be a democracy. Law drafters are to be chosen who shall draft and correct the laws, in order that nothing may be contrary to the democracy or to the return of the exiles. The laws that have been corrected or drafted are to be referred to Alexander. The Chians are to provide twenty fully manned triremes at their own expense. These are to sail as long as the other fleet of the Greeks sails with us. Those who betrayed the city to the barbarians and have escaped are to be exiled from all the cities that share in the peace and are to be liable to arrest according to the decree of the Greeks. Those who have been captured, however, are to be brought back and judged in the *synedrion* [council] of the Greeks. Any dispute which may develop between those who have returned and those in the city is to be judged before us. Until the Chians are reconciled to one another, there is to be a garrison among them from king Alexander. The garrison is to be of sufficient strength; and the Chians are to support it.

Translated by A. J. Heisserer, pp. 80–81.

A severe fever that brought Alexander to the brink of death delayed the departure of the Macedonian army from Anatolia until the summer of 333. The ancient biographies, with their concern for Alexander's heroic stature, focus on his steadfast trust in his personal physician in the face of Parmenion's warning that he had been bribed by the Persians. More important, Alexander's brush with death revealed to everyone his unique importance to the expedition. Without an heir and with no plausible available alternative king, Alexander was indispensable. Only he held the army together and gave its actions force and direction. The army's dependence on Alexander and the power it gave him would only increase as the army's march carried it further and further away from Macedon.

The Battle of Issus (333 BC)

After recovering from his illness, Alexander made a characteristically bold decision. Instead of moving to confront the forces of **Darius III** directly in Mesopotamia, as the young Persian prince Cyrus had done in his revolt against his brother Artaxerxes II almost seventy years earlier, Alexander directed his forces toward the coastal regions of Syria, Palestine, and, ultimately, Egypt. Behind this decision lay a risky calculation. Having disbanded most of his Greek fleet almost a year earlier, Alexander hoped to end Persian naval operations in the Aegean by depriving the Persian fleet of its Syrian and Phoenician bases.

The strategy was daring and almost resulted in catastrophe. Alexander marched south along the Syrian coast during the late summer and fall of 333. At the same time, Darius III, who had completed the mobilization of the Persian empire's main forces, moved northwestward from Babylon along the Euphrates River in the hope of catching Alexander before he succeeded in leaving Anatolia. At one point, the two armies, marching in opposite directions, passed each other

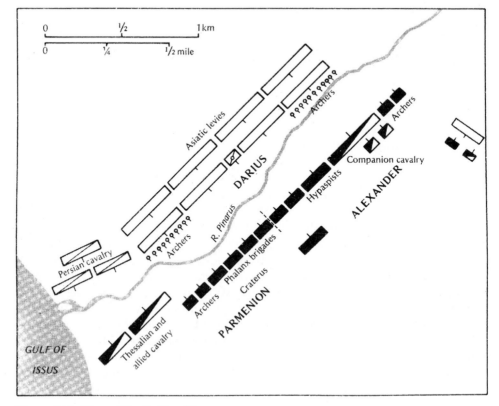

Figure 11.4. Plan of the Battle of Issus.

at a distance of less than a hundred miles. On learning Alexander's location, Darius wheeled his army around the northern end of the Amanus Mountains and hastened southward to take the Macedonian forces in the rear. Having brilliantly cut Alexander's communications with Anatolia and his Macedonian base, however, Darius yielded the initiative to Alexander by allowing him to choose the battlefield. Alexander chose to meet the Persians at Issus in Cilicia, in a narrow coastal plain confined between the Amanus Mountains on the east and the sea on the west. By preventing Darius from fully deploying his forces, this choice of battleground neutralized the significant numerical superiority the Persians enjoyed over Alexander's Macedonians.

When Alexander entered the plain of Issus he found the Persian forces posted along the north side of the Pinarus River, which is probably the modern Kuru Çay. Darius had stationed his cavalry on both wings while he, his royal guard, and his remaining Greek mercenaries occupied the center of the Persian line.

Figure 11.5. The Alexander Sarcophagus (c. 310 BC). Found in the royal necropolis at Sidon, the sarcophagus contained the remains of Abdalonymus, whom Alexander appointed king of Sidon and one of his companions after the Battle of Issus. The side illustrated depicts Macedonians and persons in Persian dress participating in a royal hunt. Many traces of the original colors are preserved. Istanbul, Archaeological Museum.

Figure 11.6. Representation of Alexander as pharaoh before Ammon-Ra and Khonsu-Thoth in the Bark shrine at Luxor temple at Thebes (c. 330–325 BC).

Alexander, for his part, drew up his Macedonians in the unbalanced line that had by now become traditional. Parmenion commanded the phalanx and most of the infantry on the left wing; Alexander placed the bulk of the cavalry on the right wing under his personal command.

The official historian, Callisthenes, whose account is the ultimate source of the several extant narratives of the Battle of Issus, treated it as a Homeric contest between Alexander and Darius III, but we do know the main outlines of the battle. The Macedonian left suffered severely from the Persian assault, until a direct attack by Alexander and his cavalry units on the center of the Persian line forced Darius to abandon his army and flee. This moment was brilliantly depicted in a famous painting of the late fourth century BC, a copy of which appears in a mosaic that was discovered at Pompeii and is now preserved in the Naples Museum. The flight of Darius turned the defeat of the Persian army into a fearful rout. Years later Ptolemy I recounted in his history of Alexander how his units had crossed streams on the piled up bodies of Darius' dead soldiers while pursuing the fleeing Persian forces. (See Plate XVb.)

Alexander's victory at Issus was a fundamental turning point in his campaign. Darius III was in headlong flight. Most of the core of the Persian forces had been destroyed. The royal treasure stored at Damascus quickly fell into Alexander's hands and put an end to the financial problems that had threatened his plans since their inception. In his haste to escape, moreover, Darius had abandoned his family, which, in accordance with Persian custom, had accompanied him during the campaign. Now the Great King's mother, wife, daughters, and son and heir to the Persian throne were Alexander's prisoners.

Alexander had not merely defeated the Great King, he had humiliated him. This humiliation continued, as Alexander summarily rejected Darius' written offer of friendship and alliance in exchange for his family's return. He also accorded the Persian royal family the protection and public deference to which their former station entitled them and which they had lost when Darius deserted them. The symbolism was clear and unambiguous: henceforth, Alexander and not Darius was the arbiter of the fate of the Achaemenids.

The significance of Alexander's victory was equally great for the Greeks. After Issus, all hope of Persian aid against Macedonian rule had to be abandoned. Not surprisingly, the rest of Greece remained passive when Antipater crushed a Spartan rebellion in 331 BC. Finally, and most important, the road to Egypt lay open to the Macedonian army. With the expulsion of Persian power from the shores of the Mediterranean, even the conquest of the empire itself suddenly seemed possible.

From Issus to Egypt: Conquest of the Eastern Mediterranean (332–331 BC)

While Darius fled eastward, Alexander resumed his march south along the coast of Syria. Without hope of Persian support, the majority of the Syrian and

Phoenician coastal cities surrendered, successfully concluding Alexander's plan to defeat the Persian fleet by depriving it of its bases. The situation is less clear with regard to the peoples of the interior of Syria and Palestine, but the surrender of the Samaritans in northern Judaea suggests that they also quickly came to terms with Alexander.

Only at Tyre and Gaza did Alexander meet with resistance, and his response was characteristically ruthless. When the Tyrians, trusting to the strength of their island fortress, rejected Alexander's request to enter the city and sacrifice to his ancestor Heracles in the guise of their chief god Melqart, he laid siege to the city. Rightly seeing in the Tyrians' refusal a rejection of his authority, Alexander pressed the siege of Tyre for almost eight months. The city fell in August 332 and suffered the same brutal fate as Thebes: the slaughter of most of the male population and sale of the surviving women and children. The decision by Gaza's Persian governor, a eunuch named Batis, to maintain his loyalty to Darius in the face of Alexander's demand for surrender resulted in a similarly unhappy fate for his city two months later. The fall of Gaza removed the final barrier between Alexander and the greatest prize of the first phase of his adventure: Egypt.

Alexander in Egypt

Alexander's stay in Egypt dramatically altered his view of himself, but the actual conquest of Egypt was somewhat anticlimactic. Isolated in the midst of a restive population and without hope of aid from Darius, Mazaces, the last Persian satrap of Egypt, surrendered his satrapy without a fight.

Unlike most of the other peoples of the ancient Near East, the Egyptians had never accepted Persian rule. The fifth and fourth centuries BC had been marked by repeated Egyptian rebellions and severe Persian repression; the last episode was only a few years before Alexander's invasion. The Egyptians, therefore, welcomed Alexander and his Macedonians during their march through the delta to the ancient capital of Memphis, where he celebrated his victory by holding Greek-style games and sacrificing to Zeus. At the same time, Alexander sought to conciliate the Egyptians by publicly honoring the Apis bull, the living incarnation of Ptah, chief god of Memphis, and other Egyptian deities. Alexander doubtless accomplished much during the six months he spent in Egypt, but the sources concentrate on only two episodes: his consultation of the famous oracle of **Zeus-Ammon** and the establishment of **Alexandria**, the first and greatest of his foundations.

The oracle of Zeus-Ammon, about 300 miles west of the Nile in the oasis of Siwah in the Libyan desert, was one of the three principal oracles patronized by the Greeks. Because of its impact on Alexander's conception of himself, the ancient sources suitably embellished the tale of his visit to Siwah with miracle and romance. Unseasonable rains provided his party with water, and sacred animals, such as snakes or crows, guided them when they became lost. Unfortunately, Alexander revealed neither his reason for consulting the oracle nor its reply to him. Ancient and modern historians have proposed widely differing explanations for his visit: he may have hoped to equal his legendary ancestor Heracles, who was reputed to have visited the oracle; he may have desired to surpass the Persian king Cambyses, who had failed to conquer the oasis; or he may simply have sought divine approval for the new city he was already planning to found in Egypt.

Whatever Alexander's original reason may have been, all the ancient accounts agree that the decisive moment of his visit came when the chief priest of the oracle greeted him as Son of Ammon. Through the process historians call syncretism (the unification of religious beliefs), Greeks equated Ammon with Zeus. The Greeks, therefore, understood that Alexander was presenting himself as a Son of Zeus. Whether or not the priest was merely according Alexander the welcome traditionally granted a king of Egypt, Alexander clearly took it as a divine sign that, as his mother had always claimed, there was something more than mortal about his birth.

Alexander had probably selected the fishing village of Rhakotis near the western tip of the delta as the site for his new city during his trip to Siwah, but the actual foundation of Alexandria was delayed until his return from the oracle in April 331. The strong Homeric associations of the site played an important role in his choice of Rhakotis. Less than a mile offshore was the island of Pharos, which Homer had mentioned in the *Odyssey*. The site was also ideal for a great commercial center, with Pharos creating a sheltered anchorage for ships and the nearby Lake Canopus affording ready access to the Nile and the interior of Egypt. Understandably, the sources depict Alexandria as marked out for greatness at its inception. They tell how birds consumed the sacred flour with which Alexander was marking its boundaries, thereby indicating that the city would have abundant resources and nourish people from all over the world.

The foundation of Alexandria was Alexander's last major act in Egypt. It is difficult to assess the significance of Alexander's conduct in Egypt. Egyptians considered him their liberator from Persian tyranny, and Alexander acted accordingly, taking care to pay honor to Egyptian gods and ensuring that he was accepted by the priests as Pharaoh. These actions suggest that Alexander hoped to avoid the hostility aroused by the sacrilegious outrages that Greek historians claimed were committed by the Persian kings Cambyses and Artaxerxes III Ochus.

At the same time, consideration of Alexander's actions in Egypt as a whole indicates significant continuity between his policies in Egypt and those he followed in the territories conquered earlier in the campaign. This is particularly clear with regard to Alexandria, which was founded as a Greek polis with citizenship limited to Greeks and Macedonians. Alexander's organization of Egypt itself likewise followed the model he had used in Anatolia. Thus, although he did not appoint a single satrap for all of Egypt, Alexander retained much of the Persian organization of Egypt, including the requirement that Egyptians pay tribute. Natives, both Egyptians and Greeks, exercised only civil authority. Military power remained in the hands of Macedonian officers.

Only in one area was there significant change, but that area was the most important of all: Alexander's self-image. The revelation of his divine parentage at

Siwah struck a responsive chord in Alexander. It confirmed his sense of his own uniqueness and heightened his personal identification with his heroic ancestors Heracles and Achilles. Henceforth, although Alexander never renounced Philip as his earthly father, his unshakable belief in his connection to his divine father Ammon would be the linchpin of his personality. His belief in his divine descent also opened a rift between him and the older Macedonians. They could not accept Alexander's view of his special tie to a "barbarian" god and the implied slight to Philip, the king they believed responsible for Macedonian greatness.

From Alexandria to Persepolis: The King of Asia (331–330 BC)

A few weeks after the foundation of Alexandria, Alexander left Egypt, intent on seeking a final and decisive confrontation with Darius III. While Alexander marched north toward the Euphrates River, Darius made one last desperate effort to avoid battle, offering Alexander marriage to his eldest daughter, cession of all territory west of the Euphrates River, and an enormous ransom for his family. Darius' offer was unprecedented. It involved division of the empire, surrender of

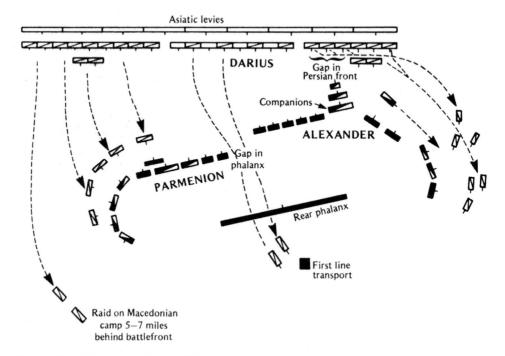

Figure 11.7. Plan of the Battle of Gaugamela.

several of its richest satrapies, and permanent exclusion of Persian power from the shores of the Mediterranean.

Parmenion probably spoke for most of the army when he advised Alexander to accept Darius' proposal. Alexander, however, would have none of it, curtly observing that he would accept it too if he were Parmenion! Faced with Alexander's refusal, Darius had no choice except to hastily gather together another army to face the Macedonians. The two armies finally met on October 1, 331 BC, at Gaugamela, just south of Mosul in northeastern Iraq. Thanks to the capture of the Persian headquarters after the battle, which gave Alexander's historians a unique insight into Persian plans, the **Battle of Gaugamela** is the best documented of all battles in ancient Greek history.

The Battle of Gaugamela (331 BC)

Having learned from his defeat at Issus the preceding year, Darius carefully chose a battlefield that suited the peculiar strengths and weaknesses of his army. Deprived of almost all its Greek mercenaries and other units drawn from the western portions of the empire, Darius' new army was composed primarily of levies drawn from Persia and the eastern portions of his empire. This meant that his forces were more cohesive than most Persian armies and particularly strong in cavalry, but weak in first-line infantry. Darius hoped that the broad plain of Gaugamela would allow him to exploit his superiority in cavalry to outflank and ultimately envelop Alexander's Macedonians, while relying on shock and terror weapons such as scythed chariots and elephants to compensate for his lack of good infantry.

These hopes were disappointed. Alexander employed a modified version of the tactics that had worked so well at Issus. He stationed the bulk of his infantry under the command of Parmenion on his left wing and posted his best cavalry units under his personal command on his right wing. A strong force of allied Greek infantry was held in reserve to prevent the Persian cavalry from encircling his forces and attacking them from the rear. Although the fighting was fierce, particularly on the left wing, where the Macedonian phalanx was hard pressed, the battle ended as at Issus, when the attack of Alexander and the companion cavalry on the center of the Persian army forced Darius to abandon his forces and flee the battlefield.

Alexander's victory was marred only by his failure to capture Darius. The sources characteristically blamed this failure on Parmenion, who was reported to have recalled Alexander from his pursuit of the Persian king to rescue the Macedonian left wing. Otherwise, however, the heartland of the Persian empire was now Alexander's for the taking. With justification, his troops saluted him as king of Asia. In rapid succession, the three westernmost capitals of the Persian empire (Babylon, Susa, and Persepolis) fell to Alexander, while Darius and his immediate entourage sought refuge in eastern Iran.

Alexander's treatment of his three great prizes differed sharply. Alexander entered Babylon in triumph in mid-October, 331. Cuneiform texts leave no doubt that, as in Egypt, he actively sought to conciliate the local population and especially the influential Babylonian priesthood. His troops were ordered to respect property during the march to Babylon. During his stay in the city Alexander offered sacrifice to its chief god Marduk and ordered the reconstruction of Marduk's great ziggurat, Esagila, which the Persians had destroyed a century and a half earlier as punishment for a Babylonian rebellion. Mazaeus, the Persian satrap of Babylonia, had played a key role in the surrender of Babylon, and Alexander rewarded him by confirming him in his former position. As he had done in Egypt, however, Alexander strove to ensure Mazaeus' loyalty by assigning command of the Babylonian garrison to one of his own officers, a Greek from Amphipolis named Apollodorus. In like manner, Abuleites, who surrendered Susa to Alexander with its royal palace and treasure intact, was reappointed satrap of Susiana. Far different, however, was the fate of Persepolis, the third of the Persian capitals to fall into Alexander's hands, and its citizens.

The Destruction of Persepolis

In deciding the fate of **Persepolis**, Alexander could not consider expediency alone, as he had done with regard to Babylon and Susa. Persepolis was the spiritual center of the Persian empire. The central events and rituals of Persian rule, including the ceremonial presentation of their tribute to the Great King by the subjects of the empire, all took place there. It was also at Persepolis that Greek ambassadors had been required to abase themselves before Persian kings since the reign of Darius I. Persepolis was therefore identified with Persian rule in the eyes of Greeks and Persians alike, and its treatment would send a clear message to both peoples. The message Alexander chose to send was one of vengeance for the destruction of the temples of Athens during the Persian wars a century and a half earlier. On the eve of Alexander's departure from Persepolis in April, 330 BC, the Macedonians torched the city's palaces.

The sources heightened the sense of "poetic justice" in the destruction of Persepolis by assigning credit for the burning of the city to an Athenian, the courtesan Thaïs, who was said to have suggested it to Alexander and his friends during a drunken revel. Thaïs may have inspired the actual burning of Persepolis, but there are clear signs that Alexander already had decided four months earlier at the time of its capture that the city was to be destroyed. Despite its surrender, Persepolis suffered all the same rigors of a sack as had Thebes and Tyre. Modern excavations have also revealed that its palaces were completely stripped of their treasures, the accumulated wealth of two centuries of Persian imperial rule, before they were set on fire. With the flames rising over the ruins of Persepolis, Alexander unmistakably signaled the triumphant end of the Greek crusade.

Figure 11.8. Palace of Persepolis, 518–330 BC.

THE HIGH ROAD TO INDIA: ALEXANDER IN CENTRAL ASIA

As Alexander watched Persepolis burn, he could not have anticipated that the next four years would be the most difficult of the campaign. At first, his good fortune seemed to continue unabated. News of the end of the Spartan rebellion had already reached him before he left Persepolis. Meanwhile, Darius had fled eastward from Media, leaving Ecbatana, the last of the Persian capitals, to fall into Alexander's hands with its treasures intact. Having secured Persia and Media, the historical heartland of the Persian empire, Alexander liquidated the last traces of the Greek crusade by discharging his remaining Greek troops. All that was needed to complete his victory was to capture Darius III himself and put an end to the long line of Achaemenid rulers.

The Death of Darius (330 BC)

Leaving Parmenion behind at Ecbatana to secure his communications with the west, Alexander raced toward the Caspian Gates, the gateway to the eastern satrapies. He hoped to intercept Darius before he could reach Bactria, roughly modern Afghanistan, and continue resistance from there. Before Alexander could overtake the fleeing Great King, news reached him that a cabal of eastern satraps headed by **Bessus**, the satrap of Bactria, had arrested and then assassinated Darius III in July 330. Worse yet, Bessus had escaped to Bactria, where he had assumed the throne of Persia as Artaxerxes IV.

The assassination of Darius III changed the dynamics of the campaign. As the sack of Persepolis clearly indicated, Alexander had hitherto acted in Persia as the avenger of past Persian misdeeds. It was a stance that was popular with Greeks but hardly calculated to encourage Persian acceptance of the new regime. Darius' assassination gave Alexander the opportunity to escape from this dilemma. Upon learning of Darius' death, Alexander immediately assumed the role of the Persian king's successor and defender of Achaemenid legitimacy against the regicides. To symbolize his new role, Alexander adopted a new style of dress that combined elements from both Macedonian and Persian royal dress. Darius' body was brought back to Persia and buried with full royal honors at the royal cemetery at Naqsh-e Rustam near Persepolis. A rumor even began to spread that Darius' last wish had been that Alexander avenge him.

Alexander's strategy was clever and effective. While Persian nobles and even some surviving members of the Achaemenid house joined Alexander, Bessus alienated potential supporters by relying on a scorched-earth defense to halt Alexander's advance instead of attempting to confront him directly. As a result, resistance melted away as Alexander moved further and further into eastern Iran. Finally, in the spring of 329, Bessus' fellow regicides, fearful for their own survival, seized Bessus and surrendered him to Alexander in exchange for a pardon and confirmation in their offices, just as they had betrayed Darius III a few months earlier. Alexander remained true to his new role as the successor of the Achaemenids. Bessus was turned over to Alexander's Persian supporters for trial and execution as a regicide.

The Struggle for Bactria and Sogdiana (330–327 BC)

Alexander's ignorance of conditions in eastern Iran almost cost him everything he had gained through his astute dynastic policy. By trying to establish a controlled border between Sogdiana and Scythia at the Jaxartes River (the modern Syr Darya) without understanding the close ties that connected the peoples of eastern Iran with the nomadic Scythian tribes of the Central Asian steppe, Alexander ignited a rebellion that quickly spread throughout much of Sogdiana and Bactria. The revolt was marked by atrocities on both sides. It was led by a guerrilla commander of genius, Spitamenes, a Sogdian noble and one of the regicides, who betrayed Alexander as readily as he had previously betrayed Darius III and Bessus. The revolt lasted almost three years and ended with the murder of Spitamenes by his Scythian allies in the spring of 327. By the time it was over, Alexander had suffered some of the worst military defeats of the entire campaign and had been forced to develop a whole new approach to the control of conquered territory.

Alexander replaced Iranian satraps with Greek and Macedonian officials. He also settled Greek mercenaries and superannuated veterans in a series of military colonies established at strategic sites throughout Sogdiana and Bactria. Most important, the crisis in Central Asia starkly revealed the growing tensions in the army and even within Alexander's court itself.

Macedonian Unrest

No Greek or Macedonian army had ever campaigned for so long or so far away from home, and Alexander's soldiers became ever more reluctant to go on as their march led them deeper into Asia. It had taken all of Alexander's persuasive powers to dissuade his troops from going home as soon as they learned of Darius' death. The miseries of the subsequent struggle against Spitamenes in the forbidding environment of Sogdiana and Bactria only increased their frustration and longing for home. His officers worried more about Alexander's gradual abandonment of the traditionally informal Macedonian style of kingship and the growing prominence of Iranians and Iranian practices at his court. The most dramatic example of the trend was Alexander's marriage in the spring of 327 to **Roxane**, the daughter of a powerful Sogdian noble. The advantages of the marriage were obvious: Alexander gained an important ally in Bactria and Sogdiana. Nevertheless, the fact remained that Alexander's queen and the potential mother of his successor was not a Macedonian or even a Greek but an Iranian!

Tension at court was increased still further by Alexander's unsuccessful demand for the ritual prostration known as *proskynēsis* on the part of all members of his court. Both ancient and modern thinkers have seen a connection between Alexander's attempt to impose proskynesis on his court and his claim to be son of Ammon, but they disagree regarding his intentions. According to Arrian, Alexander desired that people recognize his divine descent:

> The fact is that the report prevails that Alexander desired people
> actually to do him obeisance, from the underlying idea that his father
> was Ammon and not Philip, and as he was now expressing his admiration for the ways of the Persians and Medes, both in his change of
> dress and in addition by the altered arrangements for his attendance,
> and that even as to obeisance there was no lack of flatterers to give
> him his wish.
>
> (Arrian, *Anabasis* 4.9; Brunt)

Plutarch, on the other hand, thought that Alexander hoped to use proskynesis as a means of dominating his eastern subjects:

> He generally behaved haughtily towards non-Greeks and made it
> seem as though he was fully convinced of his divine birth and parentage, but kept his assumption of divinity within reasonable bounds

and did not overdo it when he was dealing with Greeks. All the
same, in a letter to the Athenians about Samos he said, "I cannot
have given you that free and illustrious city; you received it from the
person who was then your master and who was called by you my
father"—that is, Philip. But on a later occasion, when he had been
wounded by an arrow and was in great pain, he said, "What you see
flowing here, my friends, is blood and not 'ichor,' which flows in the
veins of the blessed gods." ... Anyhow, it is clear from what I have
said that Alexander had not actually become affected or puffed up,
but used belief in his divinity to dominate others.

(Plutarch, *Life of Alexander* 28; Waterfield)

Most modern scholars adopt a view similar to that of Plutarch, especially
since it is clear that Persians viewed proskynesis primarily as an affirmation
of the hierarchical order of society and not a recognition of divinity. Greeks
and Macedonians, however, believed that only a god could properly receive
proskynesis, and it is hard to believe that Alexander did not know this. That he
nevertheless went ahead with his plans suggests that he desired such a public recognition of his divinity from his closest followers. Whatever his intentions may
have been, Alexander underestimated the resistance his plans would encounter.
Greeks and Macedonians tolerated the performance of proskynesis by Persians at
Alexander's court, but they bitterly resented his effort to make them also perform
it. It is not surprising, therefore, that the sources for the first time refer to open
resistance to Alexander's policies and even conspiracies against his life during his
stay in Central Asia.

The first sign of trouble appeared late in 330 and involved one of Alexander's
senior commanders: **Philotas**, the commander of the companion cavalry and son
of Parmenion, was executed after failing to inform Alexander of an alleged plot
to kill him. Philotas' guilt has been debated since antiquity. Some scholars even
suggest that Philotas was the victim of a plot devised by Alexander. Whether the
charges against Philotas were true or not, Alexander henceforth took seriously the
possibility of conspiracies against himself and acted accordingly. One of the king's
bodyguards, who was suspected of complicity in the plot, was cashiered, and
Parmenion was assassinated. Alexander of Lyncestis, a son-in-law of Antipater
(Alexander's regent in Macedon), had been held under arrest since the beginning
of the campaign; now he was executed, to remove a potential focus for rebellion.
Alexander also began to censor his soldiers' and officers' correspondence.

These measures muted the rancor at court, but as later events revealed, they
did not eliminate discontent. The most dramatic incident was Alexander's drunk-
en murder in autumn 328 of Cleitus the Black, who had saved his life at the
Granicus and had just been appointed satrap of Bactria and Sogdiana. Cleitus'
offense was criticizing Alexander's efforts to accommodate the Persians and his
unwillingness to recognize the contribution of his officers and soldiers to his successes. More seriously, Alexander barely escaped assassination six months later
by a group of his own pages, who claimed at their trial that they hoped to free

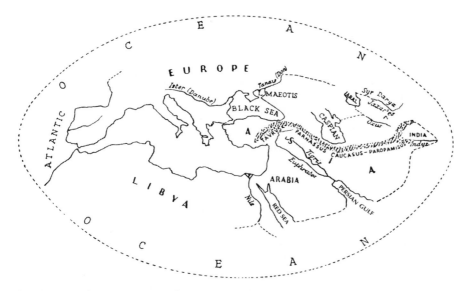

Figure 11.9. The Greek view of the inhabited world.

the Macedonians from Alexander's growing tyranny. As the case of Philotas had revealed, Alexander was implacable in the face of disloyalty by members of his personal entourage. The pages were summarily tried and sentenced to death. Callisthenes, Alexander's official historian and the pages' tutor, whose public opposition to proskynesis was neither forgotten nor forgiven, was arrested and later died under mysterious circumstances.

By the summer of 327, Alexander could consider Sogdiana and Bactria secure. Spitamenes was dead, and open resistance to Macedonian rule had ended. Before that happy outcome, the years of hard fighting and suffering had resulted in major changes. Most obvious were the changes in the army. Forced to cope with a mobile and resourceful enemy and cut off from European reinforcements, Alexander reorganized his army to allow greater flexibility in its use. In particular, he extensively recruited Iranian units to supplement his steadily dwindling supply of Macedonian and Greek troops.

DOCUMENT 11.2

Plutarch's Account of the Murder of Cleitus the Black in 328 bc

The rift that opened between Alexander and his Macedonian officers and soldiers during his campaigns in Central Asia is particularly clear in Plutarch's vivid account of the murder of Cleitus the Black at a dinner party in Bactria.

A vigorous drinking-session was initiated, and songs by a certain Pranichus ... were sung, which had been composed to embarrass and mock the Macedonian commanders who had recently been defeated by an eastern army. The older men protested and rebuked both the poet and the singer, but Alexander and his friends were enjoying the song and told the man to continue. Clitus [*sic*]… was particularly angry. He said that abusing Macedonians in front of non-Greeks and enemies was wrong.… Alexander retorted that for Clitus to make cowardice out to be a piece of bad luck was no more than special pleading. Clitus stood up and said, "Well, this 'cowardice' kept you safe once, for all your divine parentage, when you left your back exposed to Spithridates' sword, and it was Macedonian blood and these wounds of mine that made you grand enough to disown Philip and call yourself a son of Amon [*sic*]!" Alexander was furious, "Damn you!" he hissed. "Do you think you're going to get away with it every time you talk like that about me and set the Macedonians at one another's throats?" "I'm not getting away with it even now, Alexander," Clitus replied. "Look at how I'm rewarded for all my troubles. The lucky ones are those who have already died, to my mind, because they didn't live to see us Macedonians flogged with Median rods and having to beg Persians for an audience with our king." [The argument between Alexander and Cleitus became more heated, and Cleitus' friends hustled him out of the dining area.] He started to come in by another door, insolently and brashly quoting the following lines from Euripides' *Andromache* [line 683]: "Alas! What evil customs rule in Greece…." This was when Alexander grabbed a spear from one of the guards, and as Clitus stepped towards him while drawing aside the curtain which covered the door he ran him through.

Plutarch, Life of Alexander 50–51; Waterfield

Equally important changes occurred in Alexander's court. The Macedonian old guard had largely disappeared in the purges that resulted from the period's various conspiracies and tumults, leaving preeminent men personally tied to Alexander such as Perdiccas, Craterus, Lysimachus, and Ptolemy. These men would play critical roles in the turbulent events that followed Alexander's death. Finally, the relationship between Alexander and his soldiers had altered in a subtle but significant way. Their loyalty remained unchallenged, but after the strains of the Central Asian campaign, as events in India were to demonstrate, Alexander would never again be able to count on their unquestioning obedience.

INDIA AND THE END OF THE DREAM

When Alexander crossed the Hindu Kush mountains in the summer of 327 BC, he believed he was approaching the end of the inhabited world. For Greeks and Persians alike, India was the land of the Indus River, essentially modern Pakistan. Aristotle believed that beyond India there was a great desert and then ocean, which supposedly was visible from the towering peaks of the Hindu Kush.

Although Darius I had conquered India and briefly made it a part of the Persian empire, Persian rule had long since ended when Alexander entered the region. He would be campaigning in a mysterious land that Dionysus, Heracles, and the legendary Assyrian queen Semiramis all had failed to conquer, a land where fact and fiction coexisted, where cannibals and monstrous men and animals lived, where cloth grew on trees, and ants mined gold. What Alexander actually found was almost as remarkable: a vast subcontinent occupied by a complex network of peoples and states, where Alexander was viewed as a new piece to be played in a complex political chess game.

It was virtually a new world that Alexander and his army entered in the summer of 327 BC. Nor can he have remained long in doubt about conditions in India. As the Macedonian army passed along the famous route through the Khyber Pass to the plain of the Indus River in the summer and fall of 327, it encountered some of the fiercest resistance in the campaign. Opposition ended only when the army reached the city of Taxila, whose ruler, called Taxiles, had solicited Alexander's aid earlier, while the Macedonian was still in Central Asia. Taxila was one of the principal centers of Indian religious thought. Throughout antiquity, Greek and Roman moralists continued to be fascinated by Alexander's sojourn there and his meeting with a group of "naked philosophers"—ascetic Indian holy men, one of whom, Calanus, even joined his expedition.

Taxiles had sought Alexander's aid against his eastern neighbors, Abisares, the ruler of Kashmir, and especially Porus, whose kingdom included all the territory between the Jhelum and Chenab rivers. When Abisares offered his submission, Alexander moved against Porus in early 326.

Figure 11.10. Silver five-shekel coin from Babylonia (c. 326–323 BC). Obverse: Alexander attacking Porus on his elephant. Reverse: Alexander holding scepter and thunderbolt, attributes of Zeus. London, The British Museum.

The Battle of the Hydaspes (326 BC)

The two armies met at the Hydaspes River, the modern Jhelum. There Alexander found that Porus had established a strong defensive position, using his infantry and his two hundred elephants to form a living wall along the east bank of the river. Solving this difficult military problem took all of Alexander's tactical skills and involved a daring secret crossing of the flooded river. In the end, however, the outcome was the same as that of his earlier battles: the total destruction of his enemy's forces. Much to the displeasure of Taxiles and his other Indian allies, Alexander did not exploit his victory to destroy Porus. Instead, impressed by the nobility of his defeated opponent, who had asked only to be treated "like a king," Alexander restored his kingdom to Porus and even added new territories to it.

Although Alexander did not realize it at the time, the confrontation at the Hydaspes was to be his last pitched battle. As the army marched further eastward through the Punjab, morale dropped steadily. The crisis came when Alexander reached the river Hyphasis, the modern Beas. Exhausted by the stresses of fighting and marching during the endless rains of the summer monsoon, terrified by rumors of yet another great river valley occupied by great kingdoms possessing thousands of war elephants, and doubtful that they would ever return home, the army mutinied. This time not even Alexander's formidable powers of verbal and moral persuasion could convince his soldiers to go on. Ultimately, Alexander yielded, defeated by his own army, and agreed to return to the Indus, where he had already ordered the construction of a great fleet.

The End of the Campaign

Alexander did not announce his long-range aims to his contemporaries. From antiquity to the present, therefore, historians have speculated about his goals. After he had defeated Darius, avenged the Persian wars, and taken control of the Persian empire and its vast treasures, why did he continue to push ever eastward? Did he have a master plan for world conquest when he left Macedonia, or did his ambitions grow with each new success? Unfortunately, no definitive answer is possible. Whatever Alexander's ultimate intentions may have been, the resistance of his army forced him to adopt a more modest goal: the conquest of the entire Indus River valley to its mouth.

From early winter 326 to midsummer 325, Alexander's army moved steadily southward against heavy resistance. The tale of slaughter told in the ancient sources is unparalleled elsewhere in the campaign. Alexander himself received a near-fatal wound, leading his increasingly reluctant troops in storming a city of the Malli. Finally, in July 325, the army reached the mouth of the Indus and the ocean. On an island near the mouth of the Indus, Alexander made offerings to gods for whom his father Ammon had ordered sacrifices. Then he sailed out onto the Indian Ocean to pray to Poseidon for a safe voyage to Babylonia. Alexander's seemingly endless eastward advance was at an end, and the preparations for the journey home had begun.

Results of the Indian Campaign

Alexander's invasion was the first major incursion into India from the west since the reign of Darius I almost two centuries earlier. Like that of his Persian predecessor, Alexander's campaign resulted in a flood of new information about the Indian subcontinent and its peoples. Also like the Persians, the Macedonians were to remain only briefly in India. Within little more than a decade after Alexander's death, most traces of his campaign and its results had disappeared from the Indian landscape and even Indian consciousness. Indian culture knows only the romantic Alexander of medieval legend, not the Alexander of Greek history.

The ephemeral character of Alexander's achievements in India has led some historians to suggest that he lost interest in the area once his army prevented him from extending his conquests to the Ganges Valley, but this is to confuse results with intentions. Alexander's political arrangements suggest that he intended to maintain control of his Indian conquests after his return to the west. Three Macedonian satraps supported by strong detachments of mercenary troops governed the Indus Valley from its northern approaches to the sea. Local rulers such as Taxiles, who had demonstrated their loyalty, retained their thrones but were placed under the supervision of one of the Macedonian satraps. Three new Greek cities were founded at strategic locations in the northern satrapy, and several foundations were also planned for the other satrapies. Finally, the Macedonian eastern flank was protected by the expanded kingdom of Alexander's ally, King Porus. Alexander had planned carefully for his Indian domain, but the resources available to his agents proved inadequate to maintain Macedonian rule in this remote part of his empire.

RETURN TO THE WEST

Alexander left India for Persia in late August 325. He intended to lead his army through Gedrosia, an arid region in southwestern Pakistan. His purpose was to establish supply depots for his fleet, which was to follow the time-honored route along the north coast of the Indian Ocean from the mouth of the Indus River to the Persian Gulf. Nearchus, the commander of Alexander's fleet and one of his closest friends, later claimed that Alexander, ever the competitor, was also determined to surpass Semiramis and Cyrus the Great of Persia, who were said to have lost their armies in Gedrosia. For almost two months, Alexander's men struggled through the arid wastes of Gedrosia. Including the wives and children the soldiers had acquired in the course of their campaigns and the camp followers that had attached to the group, possibly as many as eighty thousand souls comprised what was virtually a moving city. Before the army finally reached Carmania and safety, thousands died, including most of the soldiers' families, who were swept away together with the bulk of their possessions in a flash flood. Alexander's sense of having barely escaped total disaster was lessened only by news of the safe arrival of the fleet at the head of the Persian Gulf sometime in December 325 after a difficult and adventure-filled voyage that included encounters with whales and exploration of a "haunted" island.

Reorganization of the Empire

Alexander's return from India sparked turmoil throughout his vast empire. In short order, eight satraps and generals—both Macedonians and Iranians—were deposed and executed. One of Alexander's oldest friends, the royal treasurer, Harpalus, fled to Athens with a huge fortune looted from the king's funds and a private army of six thousand mercenaries. The ancient sources argued that the upheaval was caused by the deterioration of Alexander's character. Modern admirers cite his outrage at the reports of corruption and oppression by his officials while he was away. The truth is more complex. Some victims of the king's wrath, such as the governors of the satrapies along his line of march through Gedrosia, clearly were scapegoats for a disaster that was largely of Alexander's own making. Others were victims of court politics and jealousies; but as the Roman historian Curtius Rufus (10.1.7) perceptively noted, most were guilty of the one unforgivable crime: they had assumed Alexander would not survive and had begun to exploit his empire for their own personal benefit.

Alexander's actions were not limited to punishing overly ambitious and corrupt subordinates. He also attempted to prevent similar problems in the future. All satraps were ordered to disband their mercenary forces immediately. When the security of his Asian realm was threatened by roving bands of embittered cashiered soldiers, a further order was sent to the cities of European Greece requiring them to permit their exiles to return home. Fully twenty thousand exiles are said to have heard Aristotle's son-in-law Nicanor read the royal decree at Olympia in the summer of 324 BC. The problems of reintegrating them into the life of their various cities were to cause turmoil in Greece for years to come, sparking a last desperate attempt by the Greek cities to free themselves from Macedonian rule immediately after Alexander's death.

"Unification of Mankind"

Almost as serious a threat to Alexander was posed by the dismay and suspicion of his veteran Macedonian troops at the changes in their relationship to their king. In the early spring of 324, Alexander celebrated the conquest of India in grand style. Decorations were distributed to officers of the army and fleet. The climax of the celebration was a grand marriage ceremony in which Alexander himself took two Persian wives—daughters, respectively, of Artaxerxes III and Darius III. Ninety of his principal officers took noble Persian and Median wives. Gifts were distributed to ten thousand soldiers who had followed Alexander's example and married Asian women, and their debts were paid by the king.

The good feelings quickly dissipated when Alexander introduced into the army thirty thousand young Iranian troops trained to fight in Macedonian style, whom he referred to as his "successors." Their name suggested that they were eventually

Figure 11.11. Silver tetradrachm minted by Ptolemy I. Obverse: Head of Alexander the Great wearing elephant-head helmet with horns of Ammon visible under the helmet. The elephant head recalls Alexander's connection to Dionysus as conqueror of India, while the horns of Ammon identify him as son of Ammon. Reverse: Seated Zeus with eagle. London, The British Museum.

to replace his Macedonians. It is not surprising, therefore, that when Alexander announced at Opis in the summer of 324 that he intended to discharge and send home veterans who were too old or too ill to fight, the army mutinied. The soldiers demanded that the king discharge them all and sarcastically urged that he henceforth rely on his father Ammon. Only after Alexander reassured them that his Macedonians were his only true "companions" did the mutiny subside.

The victory of the veterans was only symbolic. Although Macedonians occupied seats of honor at a great banquet Alexander held at Opis to celebrate the end of the mutiny, he remained steadfast in carrying out his original plans. He discharged the veterans shortly thereafter and sent them back to Macedon, while retaining the children produced by their marriages to Asian women with him as the nucleus of a new generation of soldiers loyal only to himself. In the meantime, the integration of Iranian units into the army continued.

Death in Babylon

The final year of Alexander's reign was full of activity and unfulfilled plans. It began with a personal tragedy. In November 324, Hephaestion, Alexander's most intimate friend, drank himself to death. The grief-stricken king executed Hephaestion's doctor and ordered a monstrous zigguratlike monument to Hephaestion to be built at Babylon. When he believed he had received approval from Ammon, he ordered the Greek cities to grant his dead friend heroic honors. It may also have been at this time that Alexander issued another decree demanding that the Greeks worship him as a god.

Alexander further assuaged his grief with a winter campaign in the Zagros Mountains before returning to Babylon in the spring of 323. There he received a series of delegations bearing congratulations and petitions from the Greeks and other peoples of the Mediterranean. He also began to formulate plans for his next major project, the conquest of the Arabians, who, he claimed, had not sent an embassy to honor him. But omens of his impending death were already being bruited about. In desperation, the Babylonian priests even revived the ancient substitute-king ritual: a criminal was seated on the king's throne dressed in the royal regalia, then executed in the hope of averting the doom threatening the king.

This frantic effort was to no avail. On May 29, Alexander fell ill at a party hosted by one of his officers. After suffering from fever and delirium for almost two weeks, he died on June 10, 323 BC. Legend would later claim that he was the victim of a plot concocted by Aristotle and Antipater, whom he had decided to replace as his regent in Europe. More likely, his body, exhausted by the strain of constant campaigning and numerous wounds, was unable to fight off a disease, possibly malaria, that he contracted during his final sojourn at Babylon. He was not yet thirty-three years old.

On learning of Alexander's death, the Athenian politician Demades remarked that he "could not be dead because the whole world would stink from the stench of his corpse." Alexander had roused strong passions during his life and continued to do so after his death. He had conducted the longest and most far-reaching military campaign in Greek history, and in so doing he had changed forever the world the Greeks and Macedonians knew. From the Mediterranean to India, Eurasia had been linked together and would remain so until the end of antiquity. The cities he established in Egypt and Central Asia provided the foundations for a significant Greek presence in those areas.

Since antiquity, scholars have disagreed about Alexander's plans for the future of his empire. A clear tendency toward increasing autocracy can be detected over the course of Alexander's reign, culminating in actions such as the decrees ordering the return of exiles and his own deification. No clear evidence exists that might reveal how Alexander envisioned the final form of that autocracy or the roles he expected the various peoples of his empire to play in it. In part, of course, this is because Alexander did not expect to die when he did. There is, however, a more fundamental reason. Upon hearing that Alexander had completed most of his conquests by the age of thirty-two and was perplexed about what he should do with the rest of his life, the Roman emperor Augustus is said to have expressed surprise that Alexander did not consider governing his empire a greater challenge than conquering it. Not surprisingly, his papers contained only schemes for grandiose monuments and future campaigns, not plans for the governance of his empire.

In a very real sense, therefore, Alexander's greatest achievement was negative. He destroyed the Persian empire, thereby liquidating a state system that had governed relations in the Near and Middle East for over two centuries. He also ended the role of the Greek states as significant players in the politics of the eastern Mediterranean basin. His successors, however, and not Alexander himself, would shape the new political order that would replace the Persian empire, providing the framework for social and cultural relations in much of western Asia for the rest of antiquity.

KEY TERMS

Alexander the Great	Bessus	Persepolis
Alexandria	Callisthenes	Philotas
Antipater	Cleitus the Black	proskynēsis
Battle of Gaugamela	Darius III	Roxane
Battle of Granicus	Gordian knot	Thebes
Battle of the Hydaspes	Great King	Zeus-Ammon
Battle of Issus	Parmenion	

SUGGESTED READINGS

Andronikos, Manolis. 1987. *Vergina: The Royal Tombs and the Ancient City.* Athens: Ekdotike Athnenon. A beautifully illustrated account of the discovery of the Macedonian royal tombs and their contents by their excavator.

Bosworth, A. B. 1988. *Conquest and Empire: The Reign of Alexander the Great.* Cambridge: Cambridge University Press. Unsentimental and clearly written political and military history of Alexander's reign.

———. 1996. *Alexander and the East: The Tragedy of Triumph.* Oxford: Clarendon Press. A revealing study of Alexander's Indian campaign and its treatment by ancient and modern historians.

Briant, Pierre. 2010. *Alexander the Great and His Empire.* Translated by A. Kuhrt. Princeton: Princeton University Press. Brillian account of Alexander's reign from the perspective of the Persians.

Engels, Donald W. 1978. *Alexander the Great and the Logistics of the Macedonian Army.* Berkeley and Los Angeles: University of California Press. An illuminating account of the practical problems of supplying Alexander's army during its long campaign.

Green, Peter. 1991. *Alexander of Macedon, 356–323 BC: A Historical Biography.* Berkeley and Los Angeles: University of California Press. Vivid and scholarly biography of Alexander the Great.

Heckel, Waldemar. 2006. *Who's Who in the Age of Alexander the Great.* Oxford: Blackwell Publishing. Comprehensive biographical dictionary of the reign of Alexander.

———— and Lawrence A. Tritle (eds.). 2009. *Alexander the Great: A New History.* Malden, MA: Wiley-Blackwell. Thematic history of Alexander's reign.

Holt, Frank L. 2003. *Alexander the Great and the Mystery of Elephant Medallions.* Berkeley and Los Angeles: University of California Press. Illuminating discussion of Alexander's coinage and its contribution to the history of his reign.

————. 2005. *Into the Land of Bones: Alexander the Great in Afghanistan.* Berkeley and Los Angeles: University of California Press. Vivid account of Alexander's Central Asian campaign and its significance for the establishment of Greek culture in Bactria.

Roisman, Joseph, ed. 2003. *Brill's Companion to Alexander the Great.* Leiden: E. J. Brill. Important collection of essays on all aspects of Alexander's reign.

Stewart, Andrew. 1993. *Faces of Power: Alexander's Image and Hellenistic Politics.* Berkeley and Los Angeles: University of California Press. Detailed study of the development and use of the best-known royal portrait image in antiquity.

Stoneman, Richard. 2008. *Alexander the Great: A Life in Legend.* New Haven: Yale University Press. Illuminating analysis of the *Alexander Romance* and its influence.

Wheeler, Mortimer. 1968. *Flames over Persepolis: Turning-Point in History.* New York: Reynal. Illuminating survey of the archaeological evidence for Alexander's campaign.

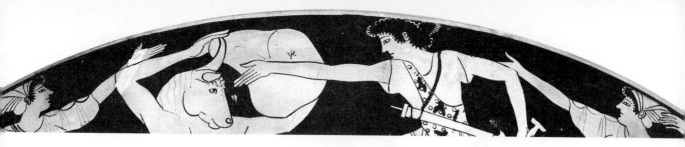

CHAPTER TWELVE

Alexander's Successors and the Cosmopolis

Alexander's conquests changed forever the world the Greeks knew. From citizens of minuscule city-states on the fringes of the Persian empire, the Greeks had become partners in the rule of a vast territory that stretched from the Mediterranean to the borders of India. This enormous "cosmopolis" (literally, a city-state comprising the world) was unified by the use of Greek as the common language of government and culture and by the creation of islands of Greek culture in settlements scattered throughout this broad area. The cosmopolis served as a huge arena for the military and political struggles of Alexander's successors. Against this bloody backdrop, ordinary people, both Greeks and their subjects, attempted to retain traditional values while making innovations that enabled them to live in a world that was vastly different from that of their grandparents.

The Macedonian conquest ended the world known today as Classical Greece. Classical Greece certainly set standards in a number of areas, such as sculpture, architecture, philosophy, and political theory, that shaped the direction of western culture. The modern world, however, is sharply different from the narrow and intensely political universe of the polis; in many respects, its closest affiliation is with the era we call Hellenistic.

A NEW WORLD

The **Hellenistic period** spans the three centuries from the death of Alexander in 323 BC to the death of **Cleopatra VII** of Egypt in 30 BC. That the Hellenistic period is the only era in ancient history defined by the reign of a queen highlights not only the increased independence and visibility of women but also the complexities of life

469

Figure 12.1. Traditionally called the Old Market Woman, this statue of an old woman carrying chickens probably represents an elderly peasant, wearing her finest dress and an ivy wreath around her head, participating in a festival of Dionysus. Roman marble copy of Hellenistic original of the third or second century BC. New York, The Metropolitan Museum of Art.

in this period. Indeed, in many ways the challenges of the Hellenistic Age antici-pated those that faced modern imperial powers. Moreover, in the large multiethnic Hellenistic states, the average man was no longer as intensely invested in politics as he had been in, say, Classical Athens. Private life occupied a larger share of people's energy. Schools of thought like Stoicism, Epicureanism, Cynicism, and Skepticism addressed the same feelings of stress and anxiety that trouble men and women today. Whereas the philosophies of Plato and Aristotle were designed for affluent men who could expect to participate in the government of their poleis, Hellenistic philosophies spoke to wider concerns, including those of women. In the visual arts, the Classical preoccupation with the beautiful young male diminished and the sculptural repertoire expanded to include such groups as the elderly, children, women, non-Greeks, and even the deformed.

SOURCES FOR THE HELLENISTIC PERIOD

The collapse of Alexander's empire generated an extensive historical literature, much of it written by participants in the events. The most important were two great histories that covered the whole period from the death of Alexander to the last conflict of his successors in the late 280s BC. One was written by Hieronymus of Cardia, a diplomat and courtier who served several of Alexander's successors, and the other by Duris, a student of the philosopher Theophrastus and tyrant of the large island of Samos. The written evidence that once existed was not limited to general histories. The two generations following Alexander's death saw the composition of city and regional histories; biographies of rulers, intellectuals, and artists; descriptions of the lands conquered by Alexander; political pamphlets; and even collections of inscriptions.

Unfortunately, virtually all of this extensive body of evidence has disappeared. The modern view of the Hellenistic period as one of the formative eras of history was not shared by the Greeks of late antiquity, who decided what books would be copied and thus would survive into the Middle Ages. In their opinion, these centuries were a time of foreign rule and humiliation that contrasted unfavorably with the Classical period, when Greece was independent and triumphant over its enemies. Their medieval successors, the Byzantines, were likewise uninterested in the history of the Hellenistic period, but for a different reason. Since they viewed themselves as Christians and Romans, the Byzantines' interest in Hellenistic history was limited to the story of Roman expansion in the east and the fate of the Jews in the intertestamental period. As a result, the works of the Hellenistic historians ceased to be copied. In the end, only one detailed account of the three centuries that followed the death of Alexander the Great survived into the Byzantine period—that contained in Books 21 to 40 of the *Library of History* of Diodorus of Sicily—and the last manuscript of Diodorus' work that included those books was destroyed during the Turkish sack of Constantinople in 1453 AD.

For much of Hellenistic history, therefore, modern historians are forced to cobble together their narrative of events from disparate, fragmentary, and often intractable sources. Fortunately, the situation is less desperate with regard to the critical half-century after Alexander's death, when the fate of his empire was decided. Diodorus' account of the last two decades of the fourth century BC survives intact. When his narrative fails, historians intent on reconstructing the history of the next quarter-century still can draw on a variety of sources that include Plutarch's lives of Demetrius and Pyrrhus, Justin's epitome of the *Philippica* of Pompeius Trogus, and inscriptions. Historians are far better served, however, with regard to sources for everyday life and administrative and economic history.

Figure 12.2. Grant exemption by Cleopatra VII. Papyrus with declaration of tax exemption of the Roman citizen Q. Cascellius, probably bearing the signature of Queen Cleopatra VII, February 23, 33 BC. Inv. P 25239. Photo: Margarete Buesing. Location: Ägyptisches Museum, Staatliche Museen, Berlin, Germany.

For most writing, the Greeks and the other peoples of the ancient Mediterranean world used flat sheets woven from strips cut from the papyrus reed. Because of dampness elsewhere, documents written on this material have survived in large numbers only in Egypt, where archaeologists have discovered documents written in Greek, Latin, Egyptian, and Aramaic. These documents illuminate all aspects of the lives of the inhabitants of Hellenistic Egypt. They include private letters, wills, marriage contracts, leases and other financial documents, and even elementary school texts. **Papyri** also often provide our main evidence for activities of the government of Alexander's successors, the Ptolemies, including tax collection, religious affairs, and legal proceedings. This rich documentation gives us unique snapshots of the Ptolemaic government at work, from the royal court to the smallest Egyptian village.

Papyri have also preserved long-lost works of Greek literature, many of which survive only in fragmentary copies discovered in the ruins of Greek towns in Egypt. Thus, some of Sappho's poetry and Aristotle's *Constitution of Athens*, so important for the history of the Athenian democracy, survive only because Greeks living in Egypt had their own copies of these texts. Likewise, the plays of the Athenian playwright Menander and "The Lock of Berenice" by the Alexandrian poet **Callimachus** are extant only in papyrus copies. The vast number of **papyri** that have been discovered in the Egyptian countryside testify to both the use of the Greek language and the spread of Greek culture, one of the most enduring results of Alexander's conquests. Equally important, scholars have just begun to study in detail the numerous Demotic (vernacular Egyptian) papyri, which show that, despite the influx of Greeks, the Egyptian way of life, legal system, and religious institutions all endured and even flourished in the Hellenistic period.

THE STRUGGLE FOR THE SUCCESSION

When Alexander died suddenly in 323 BC, the Persian empire had disappeared, but no regime had emerged to replace it. Only Alexander's charismatic personality had held his empire together. A new king had to be chosen quickly, but there was no heir. Although his wife Roxane was pregnant, only Alexander's mentally deficient half-brother Arrhidaeus survived of his family. A regency, therefore, was inevitable—but who would lead it, and in whose interest?

On his deathbed, Alexander had given his signet ring to his chief minister, **Perdiccas**, and his bodyguards and the cavalry supported Perdiccas' proposal to wait for the birth of Roxane's child. The Macedonian infantry, however, mutinied and demanded that Arrhidaeus become king. Only a bizarre compromise averted civil war: if Roxane's child were male, he and Arrhidaeus would be joint kings! When Roxane gave birth to a son, he and Arrhidaeus were proclaimed kings as Alexander IV and Philip III. Although the immediate crisis was over, events were to bear out Alexander's alleged prophecy that there would be great "funeral games" over his corpse.

For almost half a century Alexander's successors fought over his empire. Only when the last of them died in 280 BC did a new political system emerge dominated by three kingdoms, each ruled by a Macedonian dynasty: the Ptolemies in Egypt, the Seleucids in western Asia, and the Antigonids in Macedon and northern Greece. This arrangement formed the framework for political and social life in Egypt and western Asia for over two centuries and nurtured a vibrant culture that endured through later antiquity and the Middle Ages.

THE REGENCY OF PERDICCAS

More was at stake after Alexander's death than the selection of his successor. Decisions also had to be made concerning the goals of the new imperial government. Conquest and expansion characterized Alexander's reign, and on his deathbed Alexander was planning to invade Arabia. Perdiccas had no interest in such projects. The exhausted soldiers demanded that Alexander's final plans be abandoned. The fantastic career of conquest that had begun a decade earlier was over. The time for consolidation of Macedonian rule and enjoyment of the fruits of victory had arrived, or so the soldiers thought.

With the succession settled, Perdiccas quickly organized the regency, beginning by reallocating the satrapies of the empire. The sources anachronistically highlight the satrapies assigned to Alexander's successors: Cappadocia to Eumenes, Egypt to **Ptolemy I**, Thrace to **Lysimachus**, and much of western Anatolia to **Antigonus the One-Eyed**. Cappadocia, however, had yet to be conquered; and much of Thrace had been lost in a Thracian rebellion. Perdiccas understandably needed to avoid alienating the powerful Macedonian satraps in Asia to survive, so most retained their satrapies.

Perdiccas' other decisions were equally cautious. Three men were to govern the empire in the name of the kings: Antipater, Alexander's strategos in Europe; Craterus, Alexander's most prominent field commander; and, of course, Perdiccas himself. Macedonian unity was preserved, and Perdiccas' principal rivals shared the governance of the empire. Marriages of two of Antipater's daughters, to Perdiccas and to Craterus, were to seal the alliance. Nevertheless, Perdiccas' position began to crumble almost immediately.

Revolts broke out at both the eastern and western ends of the empire. Alexander's Asian subjects had remained quiet during the crisis after his death; not so the Greeks. The Greek settlers in Central Asia revolted first. Bactria was to become home to a remarkable Greek kingdom that would exert a significant influence on the cultures of Central Asia and India, but that was in the future. In 323, twenty-three thousand Greek settlers mutinied and started to march home. Perdiccas responded promptly, forcing the survivors to return to Bactria. The European Greeks revolted at almost the same time.

The roots of the European uprising lay in the decree of 324 concerning the return of exiles, which threatened many Greek cities with social and political upheaval, none more so than Athens and Aetolia. In desperation, Athens hired a mercenary army and launched the strongest naval force mobilized by the city since the Peloponnesian War. Victory initially seemed to be almost within the Greeks' grasp. Antipater was besieged in the Thessalian city of Lamia, from which the revolt gets its name, the Lamian War (323–322 BC). But then events turned against them. The Athenian fleet was decisively defeated at the Battle of Amorgos, while Macedonian reinforcements from Asia freed Antipater and helped him defeat the Greek army at Crannon in Thessaly in 322. Antipater intended that there should be no further revolts. The League of Corinth was dissolved, and with it the last traces of the fiction that the Greeks were allies and not Macedonian subjects. Athens was severely punished, and the democracy was dismantled. Demosthenes committed suicide, and other democratic leaders were executed. Twelve thousand Athenians failed to qualify for citizenship and were disfranchised. Athens was again ruled by an oligarchy maintained in power by a foreign garrison.

The Death of Perdiccas

While Antipater was occupied with the Lamian War, Perdiccas was struggling to control the satraps in Asia, especially Antigonus the One-Eyed, the satrap of Phrygia, who had refused to help Eumenes take control of his satrapy of Cappadocia. To save himself, Antigonus fled to Macedon with the news that Perdiccas was planning to marry Cleopatra, Alexander's sister, despite his promise to wed one of Antipater's daughters. Antigonus' news outraged Antipater and split the regency, but Ptolemy ignited the wars of Alexander's successors by diverting Alexander's funeral cortege to Egypt. Perdiccas could not ignore so direct a challenge to his authority, but his invasion of Egypt in 321 failed when Ptolemy opened the Nile dikes, drowning thousands of Perdiccas' soldiers. Demoralized by defeat and seduced by Ptolemy's promises, the Macedonian officers assassinated Perdiccas.

The victors quickly met at Triparadeisus in Syria to reorganize the regency. Antipater replaced Perdiccas as regent for the kings, and the satrapies were reassigned yet again. Ptolemy and Lysimachus retained their satrapies, and **Seleucus** received Babylon as his satrapy. Eumenes was condemned to death, while Antigonus the One-Eyed, appointed strategos in Asia, was ordered to hunt him down. Antipater himself returned to Macedon with the two kings. For the first time since Alexander had crossed into Asia over a decade earlier, a king would occupy the royal palace at Pella.

At first glance, little had changed. The empire was intact, and Philip III and Alexander IV were still joint kings. Nevertheless, appearances were deceptive. Perdiccas had failed to control the Asian satraps, and Antipater was unlikely even to try. Indeed, by taking the kings back to Macedon, he had made clear that Macedon was central in his view of the empire. The person best situated to exploit the new situation was Antigonus the One-Eyed, who controlled all royal forces and resources in Asia.

The Primacy of Antigonus the One-Eyed

Antigonus' rise to preeminence in Asia was rapid. He quickly expelled Eumenes from Cappadocia and was on the verge of subduing him when Antipater's sudden death in 319 BC set off a new round of conflict. Antipater's son Cassander refused to accept his father's choice of Polyperchon—another survivor from the reign of Philip II—as regent for the two kings and fled to Antigonus, precipitating the formation of a grand alliance of Antigonus, Cassander, Ptolemy, and Lysimachus against the new regent.

The struggle lasted for three years, ending with the collapse of the royal cause in both Europe and Asia and the destruction of the Argead house itself. Polyperchon enjoyed a brief period of success when Olympias joined the struggle on his side—but her passion for her grandson Alexander IV led to the murder of Philip III and his queen, Eurydice, and the alienation of much of the Macedonian aristocracy, which rallied to Cassander. Shortly after the death of Philip III, Olympias met a similar fate at the hands of Cassander, leaving her grandson and Macedon in his control. Although Cassander claimed to be regent for Alexander IV, he was in reality the new ruler of Macedon. Alexander IV and Roxane were confined under house arrest in Amphipolis, never to be seen in public again.

A similar fate befell the royal cause in Asia. Although Eumenes managed to avoid defeat for three years, the end came in 316 when his own soldiers betrayed him to Antigonus, who ordered his immediate execution. As in Europe, so in Asia, a victory won in the name of the heirs of Alexander resulted instead in the usurpation of Argead rule. Antigonus quickly appointed his supporters to key satrapies. Not surprisingly, Seleucus hastily abandoned Babylon and fled to Ptolemy. Although officially only strategos in Asia for Alexander IV, Antigonus actually controlled the child-king's vast Asian territories as securely as Cassander did his European ones.

The "Freedom" of the Greeks

Antigonus' triumph was brief. In 315, his allies demanded that he share the territories that he had captured. Antigonus responded with an ultimatum of his own demanding that his rivals recognize all Greek states as free. Although these ultimatums were propaganda, Antigonus' invocation of the concept of **Greek freedom** was a shrewd attempt to build Greek support. Antigonus never freed the Greek cities he controlled, but he was right to believe that his proclamation would be well received in Greece. Already in 319, when Athens had rebelled, Polyperchon promised to restore democracy and freedom to the Greeks. Antigonus planned to invade Macedon, where he hoped that his proclamation would have a similar effect among Cassander's other embittered Greek subjects. The invasion of Macedon, however, never materialized. Ptolemy defeated Antigonus' son **Demetrius** at Gaza in 312 BC and helped Seleucus return to Babylon, where he incited defections among the eastern satraps. In 311, with his southern and eastern fronts in ruins, Antigonus made peace with his former allies.

In the Peace of 311 Antigonus admitted that his attempt to gain control of all of Alexander's empire had failed. The treaty provided that Cassander would remain as strategos in Europe, Antigonus would continue as strategos over all Asia, Ptolemy and Lysimachus would retain their satrapies, and the Greek cities would be free. In return for an empty pledge to support the principle of Greek freedom, Antigonus had accepted the division of the empire as it had existed at the beginning of the war.

DOCUMENT 12.1

Letter of Antigonus the One-Eyed to Scepsis (311 BC)
The importance of the theme of the "freedom of the Greeks" in the wars of Alexander's successors is reflected in this letter, sent by Antigonus the One-Eyed to the citizens of Scepsis in northwest Anatolia shortly after the conclusion of the Peace of 311 bc and preserved in an inscription discovered at Scepsis.

. . . we exercised zeal for the liberty of the Greeks, making for this reason no small concessions and distributing money besides. To further this we sent out together Aeschylus and Demarchus. As long as there was agreement on this we participated in the conference on the Hellespont, and if certain men had not interfered the matter should then have been settled. Now also, when Cassander and Ptolemy were conferring about a truce and when Prepalaus and Aristodemus had come to us on the subject, although we saw that some of the demands of Cassander were rather burdensome, still as there was agreement concerning the Greeks we thought it necessary to overlook this in order that the main issue might be settled as soon as possible. We should have considered it a fine thing if all had been arranged for the Greeks as we wished, but because the negotiation would have been rather long and in a delay sometimes many unexpected things happen, and because we were anxious that the question of the Greeks should be settled in our life-time, we thought it necessary not to let details endanger the settlement of the principal issue. What zeal we have shown in these matters will I think be evident to you and to all others from the settlement itself. After the arrangements with Cassander and Lysimachus had been completed, to conclude which they had sent Prepalaus with full authority, Ptolemy sent envoys to us asking that a truce be made with him also and that he be included in the same treaty. We saw that it was no small thing to give up part of an ambition for which we had taken no little trouble and incurred much expense, and that too when an agreement had been reached with Cassander and Lysimachus and when the remaining task was easier. Nevertheless, because . . . we saw that you and our other allies were burdened by the war and its expenses, we thought it was well to yield and to make the truce with him also. We sent Aristodemus and Aeschylus and Hegesias to draw up the agreement. They have now returned with the pledges, and the representative of Ptolemy, Aristobulus, has come to receive them from us. We have provided in the treaty that all the Greeks are to swear to aid each other in preserving their freedom and autonomy, think-ing that while we lived in all human expectation these would be protected, but that afterwards freedom would remain more certainly secure for all the Greeks if both they and the men in power are bound by oaths. For them to swear also to help to guard the terms of the treaty which we have made with each other, seems to us neither discreditable nor disadvantageous for the Greeks; therefore it seems to me best for you to take the oath which we have sent. In the future also we shall try to provide both for you and for the other Greeks whatever advantage we have in our power. . . . Farewell.

Orientis Graeci Inscriptiones Selectae 5; Welles, pp. 4–5

Antigonus' Last Gamble

The Peace of 311 was merely a truce that Antigonus and his rivals used to rebuild their strength. War resumed in 307 when Demetrius invaded Greece with a mandate "to free all the cities of Greece." Success was immediate. Demetrius liberated Athens from Cassander and restored the democracy. The next year he occupied Cyprus, seizing Salamis in the first of the epic sieges that would gain

Figure 12.3. Bronze statuette, perhaps a portrait of Demetrius Poliorcetes from Herculaneum. In this portrait, a Macedonian king is shown as a handsome young man with a royal diadem around his head, wearing only a cloak and boots. Youthfulness, nudity, and the distinctive pose elevate him to heroic status, and the horns of Dionysius Taurus (the bull) sprout from his head. Naples, National Archaeological Museum.

him the sobriquet Poliorcetes (the Besieger), and inflicted a crushing defeat on the fleet Ptolemy sent to relieve the city. Demetrius' victory transformed the political world. Alexander's successors had maintained they were only agents of Alexander IV, even after the death of the child-king in 310, but when the news of Demetrius' victory reached Antigonus' army in Syria, his soldiers acclaimed Demetrius and Antigonus as kings, thereby publicly admitting the end of the Argead dynasty. (See Plates XVIa and XVIb.)

Like Homer's heroes, Macedonian kings were military leaders, and it was the glory of Demetrius' victory at Salamis that justified the acclamation of his father

Figure 12.4. Model of the acropolis at Pergamum.

and himself as king. Within a year Cassander, Lysimachus, Ptolemy, and Seleucus also assumed the title "king," thus affirming their independence. The struggle for control of Alexander's legacy that had been interrupted by the Peace of 311 had begun again. The end came in 301, when Lysimachus and Seleucus defeated Antigonus and Demetrius at Ipsus in central Phrygia. Antigonus was dead, trampled by Seleucus' elephants, and Demetrius was in headlong flight, their dreams of empire in ruins.

Birth Pangs of the New Order (301–276 BC)

Antigonus' enemies divided the late ruler's territories in Asia. Lysimachus received Anatolia north of the Taurus Mountains, while Seleucus added to Babylonia and Iran the coastal regions of southern Anatolia, Syria, and Mesopotamia. The division of western Asia into two huge kingdoms should have created tension along their mutual borders, and so it would have except for an unforeseen development. In 301 Ptolemy had occupied Judaea, Phoenicia, and southern Syria. To protect himself, he formed an alliance with Lysimachus that was sealed by the marriage of Lysimachus to Ptolemy's daughter Arsinoë (the future queen **Arsinoë II** of Egypt), and of Ptolemy's younger son, the future **Ptolemy II**, to Lysimachus' daughter. Seleucus responded by allying with Demetrius, the son of Antigonus the One-Eyed, who now ruled a "sea empire" comprising his father's fleet and a handful of ports in the Aegean. The renewal of war seemed imminent, but it was delayed for over a decade.

Figure 12.5. The Hellenistic world.

ais

COLCHIS

Hypanis R.

Phasis •

• Trapezus

ARMENIA

Araxes R.

Lake Van

Lake Urmia

CASPIAN SEA

CHORASMIA

HYRCANIA

PARTHIA

ARAL SEA

osata

•Nisibis

arrhae

Gaugamela •

•Arbela

MEDIA

MESOPOTAMIA

Seleucids

Dura-Europus •

Tigris R.

Ecbatana •

Euphrates R.

•Antiochea

Seleucia

Cunaxa •

Babylon •

Susa •

Pasargadae •

Persepolis •

PERSIAN GULF

Building New Kingdoms and Cities

The prolonged conflict with Antigonus had forced his rivals to put off their plans for the development of their own kingdoms. Freed from this concern by his death, they devoted themselves to local affairs during the 290s. Thus Lysimachus struggled with limited success to secure his northern frontier against the Getae, who lived across the Danube, while simultaneously founding or reorganizing several major cities in western Anatolia. The most important of these cities was Ephesus, which he moved to a new site closer to the sea and renamed Arsinoea after his new wife or, perhaps, his daughter of the same name. As we shall see, Ptolemy also built on a large scale in this period, transforming Alexandria into a worthy capital for his kingdom. The greatest builder of the period, however, was Seleucus, who founded numerous cities and military settlements in Syria, including his new capital of Antioch, which he built on the site of Antigonus the One-Eyed's name city of Antigoneia near the mouth of the Orontes River.

As thousands of Greeks emigrated to Egypt and the Near and Middle East, the new cities grew and prospered. Ultimately, Alexandria and Antioch supported populations numbering in the hundreds of thousands, boasting splendid public buildings and amenities unknown to the cities of old Greece. Little is known of Hellenistic Antioch and Alexandria, although the recent discovery of extensive archaeological remains under the waters of Alexandria harbor, including portions of the Pharos lighthouse and the palace of Cleopatra VII, is finally beginning to reveal the glory of ancient Alexandria. (See Plates XVIIIa and XVIIIb.) In the meantime, an idea of the splendor and prosperity of these cities can be gained from Pergamon, the capital of the Attalid kingdom, whose architects brilliantly transformed its acropolis into an image of ordered political power. At the other end of the Greek world, at the site of Ai Khanoum, probably Alexandria on the Oxus, in northern Afghanistan, French archaeologists have discovered a large city with broad streets, elegant mansions, an agora, and all the public buildings essential to a Greek polis: monumental temples, a gymnasium, and a theater. The preoccupation with domestic affairs that occupied much of the decade after the death of Antigonus was ended, however, by the actions of his son Demetrius.

The Final Struggle

Demetrius Poliorcetes possessed a "kingdom" without a territorial base. In 294, he remedied that deficiency, seizing Macedon from the feuding sons of Cassander. His success, however, was brief. For Demetrius, Macedon was only a stepping-stone to Asia, but before his invasion was ready, his rivals struck. Lysimachus and Pyrrhus, the king of Epirus, invaded Macedon and forced Demetrius into prematurely launching his Asian campaign in 286. The result was inevitable. Outnumbered and ill, Demetrius surrendered to Seleucus and lived out the last few years of his life under house arrest near Antioch.

Demetrius' conquerors did not long survive him. Taking advantage of a bitter succession crisis in Thrace, Seleucus invaded Lysimachus' kingdom. The forces of the two aging monarchs—both were over eighty—met in early 281 at Corupedium (the Field of Plenty), in Phrygia. At the end of the battle, Lysimachus lay dead on the field and Seleucus, it seemed, finally had achieved the dream that had haunted Perdiccas and Antigonus the One-Eyed and his son: the reunion of Alexander's empire. Seleucus did not long enjoy his triumph, being assassinated by an exiled son of Ptolemy, Ptolemy Ceraunus (the Thunderbolt). The Thunderbolt's moment of glory also passed quickly. In 279, he fell in battle defending Macedon against Gauls, whose migration from western Europe had begun in the early fourth century.

The Gallic threat was brief, but it had significant consequences. The Gauls soon transferred their terror to Anatolia, but only after being defeated at Delphi and Lysimacheia by the **Aetolian League** (the organization of the city-states of northwest Greece) and Antigonus Gonatas ("Knock-knees"), the son of Demetrius Poliorcetes. Their victories over the Gauls transformed the position of both the Aetolians and Antigonus, legitimizing the emergence of the former as the preeminent power in central Greece and the protector of Delphi and the latter as king of Macedon. The final pieces of the new political system that had so gradually and painfully emerged from the wreckage of Alexander's empire had fallen into place.

The Place of the Polis in the Cosmopolis

Although the emergence of the new Macedonian kingdoms changed the character and shape of the world the Greeks knew, one aspect of Greek life remained largely unchanged: the polis continued to form the basic framework for the life of most Greeks. Old poleis such as Athens, Syracuse, and Ephesus grew and prospered. At the same time, while wars between poleis continued, cities increasingly attempted to peacefully settle international disputes by arbitration and to insulate themselves against attack by gaining recognition for themselves as *asylos* (inviolate) from their other Greek cities and kings.

Even the notorious particularism of the classical polis was partially overcome by the creation of strong federal states by the Aetolians and Achaeans. The Aetolian and Achaean leagues were alliances of cities governed by councils of city representatives, assemblies of league citizens, and elected league officials. In the Hellenistic period, both leagues shed their ethnic character by expanding their membership to include cities outside their traditional homes in central Greece and the northern Peloponnesus. By the late third century BC, the **Achaean League** included most of the Peloponnesus except Sparta, while the Aetolian League and its allies reached all the way to the borders of Attica. Not surprisingly, the two leagues were able to deal with Macedon and the other Macedonian kingdoms on a roughly equal basis for much of the third century BC.

The growing influence of Rome in Greece ended the heyday of Greek federalism. Although common enmity toward Macedon induced both leagues to become Roman allies, Rome's support of polis autonomy under the guise of "Greek freedom" drove them apart. By 189 BC, Rome had decisively defeated the Aetolian League. The Achaean League met a similar fate two generations

Figure 12.6. This Roman bronze statuette reflects the lost colossal statue of the Tyche (Fortune) of the city of Antioch in Syria, the capital of the Seleucid kingdom. The statue was created by Eutychides (c. 300 BC) and shows Tyche, the city's protective goddess, personified as a goddess wearing a crown representing the city wall seated on a swimming boy representing the Orontes River. New York, Metropolitan Museum of Art.

later, in 146 BC, when Rome crushed a revolt led by the League and established direct rule in Greece. Unlike the polarizing Athenian and Spartan leagues of the Classical era, the federal leagues of the Hellenistic Age were remembered despite their ultimate failure. Eighteenth-century students of federalism, such as the French political theorist Montesquieu and James Madison and other intellectuals of revolutionary America, even studied them as possible models for new federal states.

At the same time, political trends that had appeared already in the fourth century BC intensified in the centuries following the death of Alexander. While nominal democracy became the norm in Greek cities, democracy itself lost much of its meaning, coming to signify little more than the absence of tyranny. In reality, the role of average citizens in government steadily dwindled, and aristocratic oligarchies managed affairs from behind the scenes. Although numerous inscriptions documenting their generosity and public service attest to the patriotism of these new leaders, such core institutions of polis life as popular assemblies and elected councils inevitably declined, as poleis came to rely more and more on the assistance of such men to rescue them from recurrent financial and diplomatic crises.

Athens and Sparta

As usual, Athens and Sparta were exceptions to the prevailing political trends. Although its democracy was never fully restored, Athens prospered and continued to be the cultural center of Greece. The tone of Hellenistic Athenian culture differed greatly from that of the fifth- and fourth-century city. The change is most obvious in drama, the principal Athenian literary form. The grand tragedies and biting political comedies of the Classical era were replaced by a lighter genre known as New Comedy. The gentle, amiable plays of **Menander** (344–c. 292 BC), which reflect the new political order and the interests of its upper-class audience, are our chief surviving representatives of this literary genre.

Menander had been a pupil of Theophrastus, head of the Lyceum after the death of Aristotle. He was also a friend of Demetrius of Phalerum, another pupil of Theophrastus, whom Cassander appointed as governor of Athens in 317. Historians are disposed to believe that Menander's plays provide reliable historical evidence: a scholar in Alexandria wrote, "O Menander and O life, which one of you has imitated the other?" All Menander's plays are contemporary and depict a Greek world populated by swaggering mercenaries in search of plunder and romance, impoverished citizens who live next door to extremely wealthy people, courtesans and pimps, spendthrift youths, and respectable young women whose only appropriate destiny is marriage. Menander's characters are completely wrapped up in their private worlds, as though weary of war and political upheaval.

Slaves are ubiquitous in New Comedy, and in fact when Demetrius conducted a census in Athens there were 21,000 citizens, 10,000 metics, and 400,000 slaves (including those who worked in the mines). Even if the figures for slaves are exaggerated, still the ratio of slaves to free is likely to have been unusually high. The quarter-century of campaigns had certainly reduced many people to slavery. Entrepreneurial slave dealers also took advantage of the habit of exposing unwanted newborns. The abandonment of infants, especially females, was an acceptable means of coping with the insecurity of life in the Hellenistic period. Infant exposure forms the theme of several of Menander's plots (though literature ascribed to abandoned babies happier destinies than those that awaited them in real life). Significantly, the chief divinity in New Comedy is **Tyche** (Fortune), a fitting emblem of this chaotic era. Not surpisingly, many Hellenistic documents begin with an invocation "to Good Fortune" (*agathēi tychēi*).

The altered temper of the times was evident also in new developments in the realm of philosophy. Though they had much to say to ordinary men and women, and continue to be studied today with interest by people of varied social and economic backgrounds, Classical philosophers like Plato and Aristotle directed their teachings to affluent men of leisure who were interested in improving their political activities in the autonomous poleis. Hellenistic philosophies, on the other hand, were designed to help people cope with a world over which they had little control.

Like the establishments of Plato and Aristotle, two of the most important schools of Hellenistic thought flowered in Athens. These were **Stoicism** and **Epicureanism**.

Born in Citium in Cyprus, **Zeno** (335–263 BC), the founder of Stoicism, was a friend of Antigonus Gonatas and spent many years in Athens, where he lectured in the covered portico known as the Stoa Poikile (Painted Portico). For this reason his followers received the name of Stoics (i.e., "Porchers").

Zeno's philosophy reflected the realities of the new political order. According to Zeno, the earth stood at the center of the universe with Zeus its prime mover. Just as cosmic motions never changed and Zeus remained king of the gods, so monarchy was the divinely ordered system of government. Revolution, consequently, violated the natural organization of the world, whereas patriotism and public service harmonized with the cosmic order. Serenity, the Stoics believed, was impossible without the confidence that one had fulfilled one's duties to others, and Stoicism entailed a large dose of humanitarianism.

Zeno urged his followers to attain an inner tranquillity that was proof not only against agonizing pain—hence our word "stoical"—but against excessive pleasure as well. He did not, however, advocate withdrawal from the social and political realm, as did some of his contemporaries. Instead, he encouraged Stoics to uphold justice—but not to engage in any serious attempts at reform. Thus, while in principle Stoics considered slaves just as free as their owners, they made no attempt to abolish slavery. It was considered enough for slaves to be made aware that, deep inside, they enjoyed no more or less freedom than their masters and mistresses, who might be themselves "slaves" to greed or lust. Because they rejected excessive pleasure, moreover, Stoics embraced sex only for purposes of procreation. Their acceptance of a hierarchical sociopolitical order and their rejection of sexual pleasure are two important areas in which Stoicism anticipated the teachings of early Christianity.

In keeping with their belief in an orderly universe, Stoics believed that life was rational and could be planned. A very different position was taken by **Epicurus** (341–270 BC), an Athenian settler who left Samos after Alexander's death and returned to Athens, where in 306 he established in his home a school called the Garden. Epicurus even included women among his students. Adopting the atomic theory first put forward by Leucippus and Democritus, he rejected the determinism of the early atomists. Though he agreed that atoms fell in straight lines from the sky, he added a new element. Epicurus argued that the multiplicity of substances in the universe arose from periodic swerves in the atoms' paths, causing them to collide at a variety of angles. Like the domains continually carved out and altered by Alexander's successors, the entire universe combined by chance, and would perish and regenerate by chance as well.

This construction left little room for the gods, and in fact Epicurus contended that though the gods must exist, since people saw their images in dreams, they had no interest in humans. In the Epicurean system, the gods lived serene, untroubled lives, indifferent to such staples of Greek religious and social life as prayers, offerings, and rituals. (The good news was that the horrific punishments associated with the underworld were fictions; the bad news was that nobody on Olympus was interested in listening to complaints, offering solace, or avenging injustices.) After death, the atoms that had comprised the soul and body of each person merely dissolved.

Figure 12.7. Bronze statuette of a philosopher, possibly Hermarchus of Mytilene, the successor of Epicurus as head of the Epicurean school. Roman copy of a Hellenistic original of the third century BC. New York, Metropolitan Museum of Art.

In the absence of eternal rewards and punishments, Epicurus viewed happiness on earth as the purpose of life, thus winning for himself the name of history's first humanist philosopher. He defined happiness as the attainment of *ataraxia*, an untroubled state free from excessive pleasure and pain, much like the serenity advocated by Zeno. Unlike Zeno, however, Epicurus advocated withdrawal from a wide variety of activities that might bring pain, both the risky quest for love or money (which the Stoics would also see as problematic) and participation in politics (which the Stoics praised). For Epicureans, anything that might threaten ataraxia was to be avoided. Though in modern parlance the label "epicurean" connotes indulgence in pleasure, particularly in the pleasures of fine dining, Epicurus actually counseled moderation in food and drink to avoid indigestion and hangovers. Unlike the Stoics, Epicureans approved of sex as long as it did not entail falling in love, with all the attendant pitfalls.

Despite their substantial differences over sex and politics, Stoics and Epicureans shared a common goal: attaining tranquility in a turbulent world. A similar aim characterized two other schools of thought that evolved around the same time, **Cynicism** and Skepticism. The principal theorist of the Cynic movement was Diogenes of Sinope (c. 400–325 BC), who identified himself as a "citizen of the world" (*kosmopolitēs*). He encouraged his followers to become self-sufficient by shedding the trappings of civilization for the naturalness of animals. Denying that humans had needs different from those of other mammals, Diogenes scandalized contemporaries and earned himself the name of the Cynic (dog: *kuōn* in Greek) by brazenly maintaining that people should follow instincts just as animals do—urinating or masturbating in public, for example. The heirs to the Cynics' rejection of civilized norms were the Skeptics, who also shared the Epicureans' disillusionment with public life. Skepticism, associated with the name of Pyrrhon of Elis (c. 365–275 BC), became popular around 200 BC. Stressing the impossibility of certain knowledge, Skeptics urged people to withdraw from the world around them. The quest for truth, after all, was hopeless, as was the quest for power. Today, the words "skeptical" and "cynical" are linked when we talk about people who are not easily persuaded. In this respect the philosophies we associate with the Hellenistic world (though Cynicism began in the fourth century) contrast sharply with those of Plato and Aristotle, who really believed that knowledge was possible and could be gained through education.

While Athens continued to serve as a magnet for intellectuals, it is significant that the center of philosophical speculation in the Hellenistic era shifted not only away from Athens but also away from mainland Greece in general. The best-known Stoic thinkers, for example, came from places like Cyprus and Syria, while Tarsus, Alexandria, and Rhodes became the most famous Stoic university towns. In time Stoicism took root firmly in the Roman Empire, where it anchored the minds and souls of many men and women seeking to cope with the decadence and autocracy of the imperial government.

Almost as remarkable was the fate of Sparta. After a century-long decline that saw the number of Spartan citizens dwindle to fewer than a thousand and tensions between rich and poor become acute, two reformer kings, Agis IV (262–241 BC) and Cleomenes III (260–219 BC), revitalized Sparta's "Lycurgan" institutions. Debts were canceled, land was redistributed, and the traditional Spartan educational system, the agoge, was reestablished. For a brief while, Sparta became the Stoic model state. The Stoic notion that individual suffering is part of some great natural scheme and should be borne without lamentation struck a responsive chord in Spartans, and the idea that austerity was preferable to self-indulgence reverberated with Spartan ideals as well. For a few years Spartan arms were invincible, and the city seemed on the verge of dominating the Peloponnesus again. Greek intellectuals trumpeted once more the virtues of the Lycurgan system. Their dreams of Greek renewal were shattered when the joint forces of Macedon and the Achaean League crushed the Spartans at the Battle of Sellasia in 222 BC, forcing Cleomenes into exile. As the fate of Sparta revealed, not even the strongest polis could resist indefinitely the power of the Macedonian kingdoms that strove either to subdue them or to use them as pawns in their own diplomatic and military struggles.

THE MACEDONIAN KINGDOMS

Greek literature, with its polis bias, contains little information about the organization and day-to-day operation of the Macedonian kingdoms that dominated the Hellenistic political world. Fortunately, the discovery by archaeologists of extensive nonliterary evidence—inscriptions, cuneiform tablets, and especially papyri—has enabled historians to remedy this deficiency. More than a century of intensive study of these new sources has demonstrated that, while Macedon continued to be ruled in accordance with its ancestral traditions as described in Chapter 10, the Seleucid and Ptolemaic kingdoms were conquest states whose organization was based on two fundamental principles: first, that as spear-won land, the kingdom and its population belonged to the king, and second, that the conduct of the king's business and the performance of the king's work took precedence over all other considerations. These two principles were common to both kingdoms, but how they were implemented depended on local conditions.

The kingdom of Seleucus I and his successors extended from the Mediterranean to the borders of India, embracing the bulk of the old Persian empire. Not surprisingly, they retained much of the governmental structure created by the Persians that they found already in place. The members of the royal court were overwhelmingly Greek and Macedonian, and it was from them that the king drew his principal advisors and officials, including the satraps who governed the various regions of the empire. The subjects of the Seleucid's huge multiethnic empire, however, lived in many different forms of societies, including city-states, temple estates, petty kingdoms, and autonomous tribal confederations. Like the Persians before them, therefore, the Seleucids found that the most effective way to govern their diverse kingdom was to follow a policy of toleration, respecting local institutions and customs and not attempting to impose Greek culture on their subjects. Cuneiform tablets, for example, reveal Seleucid kings claiming to be King of Babylon and fulfilling the Babylonian king's traditional role of protector and supporter of the temples. Similarly, Seleucid royal decrees grant the Jews the right to live according to their ancestral laws. Although the sparseness of the sources allows historians to reconstruct the main features of the Seleucid state only in outline, the case of Ptolemaic Egypt is different, since the rich papyrological evidence provides scholars with a detailed picture of the actual operation of the government and society of Hellenistic Egypt.

The Case of Ptolemaic Egypt

The basis of Egypt's wealth was its agricultural land. Like the Pharaohs before them, the Ptolemies claimed ownership of all Egypt. Nevertheless, for practical purposes the Ptolemaic government divided Egyptian land into two broad categories:

Figure 12.8. This gold octodrachm showing the deified Ptolemy II and Arsinoë II was minted by Ptolemy III (246–221 BC). Arsinoë's appearance on the obverse (front) of the coin indicates her political power. New York, American Numismatic Society.

royal land for basic agricultural production and "released land." The latter category was further divided into four subcategories: cleruchic land, used to provide land grants to soldiers; gift land, used to reward government officials; temple land, used to provide economic support for Egypt's numerous temples; and private land, used for individual house and garden plots. The nonagricultural sectors of the economy were also tightly organized. Major economic activities such as textile, papyrus, and oil production were state monopolies, intended to generate the maximum revenue for the king from fees and taxes. Foreign competition for the profits of Egyptian commerce was minimized by strict currency controls and limitations on imports. An extensive administration headquartered in Alexandria supervised the entire system. Its agents—Greek at the upper levels and Egyptian at the lower ones—could be found in even the most remote village. To ensure that the king's work was done, that taxes were paid, and that the all-important irrigation system functioned properly, every adult from peasant to immigrant soldier was registered according to place of residence and economic function. Finally, the king—and eventually also the queen—presided over the whole system with all the powers of autocrats whose every word was law. The supremacy of the royal family over all levels of society was symbolized by the institution of Greek and Egyptian cults of the living ruler and his ancestors.

DOCUMENT 12.2

Athenian Hymn to Demetrius Poliorcetes (291 BC)

The psychology that made the cult of kings possible is illustrated by this hymn sung by an Athenian chorus during a visit by Demetrius Poliorcetes in 291 bc. In the hymn, Athens honors Demetrius as a living god because of his godlike power to save the city from Aetolian raids.

The greatest of the gods and (those) dearest to the city are present; the occasion has brought Demeter and Demetrius together here.

She has come to perform the holy mysteries of the Maiden, and he, gracious, as a god ought to be, and handsome and laughing, is present. Something majestic has appeared, all his friends in a circle

> and he in their midst, his friends just like stars and he the sun. O son of the most powerful god, Poseidon, and of Aphrodite, greeting.
>
>   For the other gods either are far away or they have no ears or they are not or they do not heed us, not even one, but we see you present, not wood, not stone but real;
>
>   so we pray to you. First, make peace, dearest one, for you are master....
>   Athenaeus, *Deipnosophists* 6.253d–f; Burstein 1985, pp. 8–9, adapted

Monarchs encouraged belief in their own divinity as a way of legitimizing their use of absolute power, while subjects enjoyed participating in **ruler cults** as a means of demonstrating patriotism, loyalty, and gratitude. In recognition of their belief in monotheism and of their support of the regime, only the Jews were formally excused from these observances.

Ptolemy II used both sculpture and coinage to announce the apotheoses of members of his family. In ruler cults, kings generally represented themselves as Dionysus or Heracles, while queens were portrayed as Aphrodite. Through syncretism, however, they were often equated with Osiris and Isis and considered to be actual incarnations of the divinities. The coexistence of Greek and Egyptian cultures is evident in the portraits of the deified Ptolemies. Depending on which elements of the population were more likely to view the representation, kings and queens might be depicted in purely Egyptian style, in purely Greek style, or in some combination of the two. (See Plate XIX.)

The apparent rationality of Hellenistic state organization greatly impressed late-nineteenth- and early-twentieth-century historians, leading them to view the Hellenistic kingdoms as essentially Greek institutions with few ties to their Persian and Egyptian predecessors. Closer scrutiny of Egyptian and cuneiform texts and the Greek sources, however, has revealed greater continuity with Egyptian and ancient Near Eastern political traditions in the administration of the Macedonian kingdoms than earlier historians had realized. As already mentioned, these regions maintained many of their traditional administrative structures, together with many of their key institutions. The administrative organization of Ptolemaic Egypt and Seleucid Asia, for example, remained divided into traditional subdivisions, such as nomes (provinces) and satrapies, just as they had been under the Macedonians' Persian predecessors. Not surprisingly, the Greek terminology of many of our sources often proves upon analysis to be a facade, hiding traditional institutions and practices.

In Hellenistic Egypt and Asia, the temples still played major roles in the social and economic lives of their peoples. In Egypt, the priests used the names of the Greek gods, equated the months of the Macedonian and Egyptian calendars, and translated the royal titulary into Greek to give a Hellenic cast to the millennia-old traditions of Egyptian religion and kingship. This continuity with the past is not surprising, since, like Alexander, the Ptolemies and the Seleucids were simultaneously both Macedonian kings and pharaohs and kings of Babylon, whose responsibilities included support of traditional institutions.

In addition to continuities between the Egyptian and Near Eastern past and the organization of the later Hellenistic kingdoms, scholars have also observed "irrationalities" and inefficiencies in their everyday operations. Ptolemaic Egypt and Seleucid Asia were personal autocracies. Official documents describe their governments as consisting of "the king, his friends" [the king's personal entourage], "and the army." The only effective limit on the kings' exercise of their power was fear of losing the support of their armies and generals, who alone had the power to unseat a king if provoked too far. Government officials were political appointees with often multiple and sometimes even overlapping responsibilities, who fulfilled whatever position the king posted them to, irrespective of their previous service.

Instead of the smoothly functioning bureaucratic machines envisioned by their late-nineteenth- and early-twentieth-century predecessors, therefore, the sources

Figure 12.9. Limestone statuette of Arsinoë II. A hieroglyphic inscription on the back pillar of Arsinoë's portrait indicates that it was dedicated not long after her death and deification in 270 BC. The stiff pose, with one foot forward, the dress that clings to her body, and the features of her face, including high arched brows, large, wide-open eyes, and full, curved lips, are depicted in Egyptian style, but the queen carries a double cornucopia, an attribute of Greek goddesses like Demeter that symbolizes their powers of fertility. Her corn curls were painted black, and her face as well as the exposed flesh of other parts of her body were originally gilded and painted. New York, Metropolitan Museum of Art.

reveal that the Hellenistic governments were inefficient and often arbitrary instruments, primarily designed to extract the maximum revenue from their rulers' subjects. Documents such as Ptolemy II's (282–246 BC) order for a complete economic survey of Egypt, and his letter forbidding lawyers from assisting individuals in disputes concerning taxes, bear witness not to rational central planning but to the Hellenistic kings' insatiable need for money to support their ambitious foreign policies and domestic projects. Similarly, evidence of the inherent inefficiency and corruption of these systems in actual practice is seen in the numerous royal orders forbidding government officials from exploiting the king's subjects for personal gain and the frequent recourse to blanket amnesties for unfulfilled obligations owed the government and for charges of wrongdoing by government officials.

HELLENISTIC SOCIETY

While the emergence of new Macedonian monarchies in the early third century BC posed a significant threat to the independence of the cities of Aegean Greece, the trend also created unprecedented opportunities for individual Greeks from those same cities. Whatever Alexander's plans for the governance of his empire may have been, his successors clearly judged that he had made a serious mistake in appointing Persians to important posts. In staffing the upper levels of their governments, therefore, they relied on Greek immigrants instead.

New Opportunities in a Colonial World

The resulting opportunities were greatest for the male members of the Greek elite, who quickly formed a powerful class of expatriate civilian and military officials. Inscriptions and papyri amply document the wealth and influence of members of this new governing class—men such as Apollonius, the chief financial officer of Ptolemy II, and Zenon, the Carian immigrant who managed the royal official's estate and whose financial accounts and letters written on papyri constitute an important primary source for the period. Less glamorous, but equally real and far more numerous, were the opportunities created by the kings' incessant need for Greeks to serve in their armies and to fill the multitude of minor, but potentially lucrative, administrative jobs required to govern their kingdoms. For ambitious men of this sort, the court poet **Theocritus** spoke the literal truth when he described Egypt as a land of opportunity for immigrants and characterized Ptolemy II as a "good paymaster."

DOCUMENT 12.3

Letter of King Ptolemy II to Apollonius Concerning the Revenues of Egypt (259 BC)

King Ptolemy to Apollonius, greeting. Since some of the advocates listed below are intervening in fiscal cases to the detriment of the revenues, issue

> instructions that those advocates shall pay to the crown twice the additional
> tenth and that they shall no longer be allowed to serve as advocates in any
> matter. And if any of those who have harmed the revenues be discovered to
> have served as advocate in some matter, have him sent to us under guard
> and have his property assigned to the crown.
>
> *Amherst Papyrus* 33; Burstein 1985, pp. 121–122

Opportunities were not limited to men, however; they expanded also for women, although not to the same extent. As in the case of men, they were greatest for women of wealth. Queens like Arsinoë II and Cleopatra VII of Egypt stand out in the written and artistic sources, but some Greek cities allowed women to hold minor public offices in return for their willingness to use their wealth for civic purposes. Education, which became common for upper-class women in the Hellenistic period, also created the possibility of careers in the liberal arts and in medicine for individual women, such as the Cynic philosopher Hipparchia and the professional musician Polygnota of Thebes, whose career is documented in a series of inscriptions from Delphi. More women, however, probably benefited from the modest but significant changes in their rights that occurred in the colonial society of the Macedonian kingdoms, where marriage contracts and other legal documents preserved on papyrus reveal women capable of conducting their own business and seeking legal redress for their husbands' misconduct. Not surprisingly, the explosion of new opportunities made the Hellenistic period one of the great creative ages of Greek civilization for women and men.

ALEXANDRIA AND HELLENISTIC CULTURE

Alexandria was the most famous and enduring of Alexander's foundations, and the site of his tomb. Responsibility for embellishing the city, however, lay with the first three Ptolemies, who transformed it into the foremost city of the Hellenistic world. A liberal immigration policy created a multiethnic population including Macedonians, Greeks, Egyptians, and a vibrant Jewish community occupying one-fifth of the city's area. Discoveries in Alexandria harbor have revealed that in addition to Greek statuary and architecture the Ptolemies adorned their capital with Egyptian monuments—statues, sphinxes, and obelisks—collected from all over Egypt, but particularly from the ruins of Heliopolis, the sacred city of the sun god Re, near Memphis. (See Plate XVIIIa and XVIIIb.) Perhaps the clearest symbol of the dynamism and originality of early Hellenistic Alexandria was its signature monument, the **Pharos**. Built by the architect Sostratus of Cnidus for Ptolemy II, the Pharos was the first skyscraper, a 300-foot-high polygonal tower topped by a statue of Zeus Soter ("Savior") whose beacon fire, reflected far out to sea by giant mirrors, guided ships to Alexandria. The Pharos was considered one of the Seven Wonders of the Ancient World, as were the Colossus of Rhodes and the temple of Artemis at Ephesus. It is no accident that three of the seven creations that wound up on this list dated from the Hellenistic period, for this was a time when rulers

Figure 12.10. Tetradrachm of the Roman emperor Commodus (180–192) struck at Alexandria, showing ship(s?) passing the Pharos. London, The British Museum.

were particularly eager to advertise their cities' wealth and prestige. In scale and style, these were all appropriate monuments to an age of competition and larger-than-life historical figures.

DOCUMENT 12.4

Marriage Contract of Heraclides and Demetria (311 BC)

The improved legal position of married women in the Hellenistic period is clear in this marriage contract from Egypt. The diverse origin of Greek immigrants to Egypt is evident in the variety of ethnics among the witnesses to the marriage contract between Heraclides and Demetria.

Seventh year of the reign of Alexander, the son of Alexander, fourteenth year of the satrapy of Ptolemy, month of Dius. Marriage contract of Heraclides and Demetria. Heraclides, a freeborn man, takes as his lawful wife Demetria, a freeborn woman from Cos, from her father Leptines, from Cos, and from her mother Philotis. Demetria will bring with her clothing and ornaments worth 1,000 drachmas. Heraclides will furnish to Demetria everything that is appropriate for a freewoman. We shall live together in whatever place seems best in the common opinion of Leptines and Heraclides.

If Demetria shall be detected devising something evil for the purpose of humiliating her husband Heraclides, she shall be deprived of everything she brought to the marriage. Heraclides shall declare whatever charge he may make against Demetria before three men whom both approve. Heraclides may not introduce another woman into their home to insult Demetria, nor have children from another woman, nor devise any evil toward Demetria for any reason. If Heraclides shall be detected doing any of these things and Demetria declares this before three men whom both approve, Heraclides shall return to Demetria the dowry of 1,000 drachmas which she brought, and he shall pay to her in addition 1,000 silver Alexandrian drachmas. Demetria, and those with Demetria, shall be able to exact payment, just as though there were a legal judgment from Heraclides himself, and from all of Heraclides' property on both land and sea.

This contract shall be wholly valid in every way wherever Heraclides produces it against Demetria, or Demetria and those with Demetria produce it against Heraclides, in order to exact payment. Heraclides and Demetria each have the right to preserve their contracts and to produce the contracts against each other. Witnesses: Cleon of Gela, Anticrates of Temnos, Lysis of Temnos, Dionysius of Temnos, Aristomachus of Cyrene, Aristodicus of Cos.

Elephantine Papyrus 1

The Ptolemies also strove to make Alexandria the cultural center of the Greek world. Like Alexander, whose entourage had included artists and intellectuals such as Aristotle's nephew, Callisthenes, the court historian, Ptolemy I and his immediate successors encouraged prominent Greek scholars, scientists, and poets to come to Egypt. With the enormous wealth of Egypt at their disposal, the Ptolemies could afford to subsidize intellectuals, encouraging artistic and scientific work by establishing cultural institutions of a new type.

Their principal cultural foundation was the research center known as the **Museum** because of its dedication to the nine Muses, patron goddesses of the arts. There distinguished scholars, supported by government stipends, could pursue their studies in congenial surroundings including dormitories, dining facilities, and pleasant gardens. To assist the Museum's scholars, Ptolemy I established (with the aid of Demetrius of Phalerum) a library intended to contain copies of every book written in Greek. The library's collection is said to have ultimately reached seven hundred thousand papyrus rolls.

The Ptolemies' passion for expanding the **royal library**'s collections was legendary. The Greek translation of the Jewish Bible, the *Septuagint*, was supposed to have been produced on order of Ptolemy II, and the official Athenian copy of the works of the three canonical tragedians was allegedly stolen by Ptolemy III, using the ruse that he was only borrowing it to make copies for the library. Even the books of visitors to Egypt were scrutinized and seized if they were not in the library, the owners being compensated with cheap copies. However its books were acquired, the library offered unprecedented resources for scholarly research in every field of intellectual endeavor, although an envious rival might sneer at the successful occupants of Ptolemy's "bird coop" with some justification, since subsidized intellectuals were expected to earn their keep. Doctors and writers receiving government stipends served as physicians and tutors to members of the royal family, and celebrated its achievements. The scholar and poet Callimachus created a monumental catalog of 120 books of the library that laid the foundation for the history of Greek literature. In his poem "The Lock of Berenice," Callimachus also celebrated the transformation into a comet of a lock of hair dedicated by Berenice II in 246 BC to commemorate the beginning of the Third Syrian War. In a similar vein, Theocritus' seventeenth idyll extravagantly praised the first decade of Ptolemy II's reign. The establishment of the library was instrumental in the preservation of Greek literature.

New Directions in Literature

The work of Alexandrian intellectuals was not limited, however, to satisfying the whims of their royal patrons. Alexandrian writers made important innovations in Greek literature. In his idylls, brief dialogues or monologues set in an idealized countryside, Theocritus used the pastoral mode, which his contemporary, the poetess Anyte of Tegea in Arcadia had introduced to western literature. Similarly, poets such as Posidippus of Pella transformed the epigram, originally a short commemorative poem inscribed on stone, into a flexible literary form that could be used equally for trivial subjects such as the death of a pet bird and for serious topics such as celebrating the achievements of the Ptolemies. A good example is this recently discovered elegant poem by Posidippus in which he celebrates a victory in a chariot race by Ptolemy III's wife, Berenice II, as the most recent example of such victories in Panhellenic games by the Ptolemies.

> Speak, poets all, of my renown, [if ever you enjoy]
>   saying what's known: my glory's [not of yesterday],
> My grandfather [Ptolemy (I) won] in the chariot,
>   driving his steeds over the courses at Pisa,
> And Berenice [I], mother of my father [Ptolemy II], and my father
>   again in the chariot, triumphed, king after king,
> Ptolemy after Ptolemy; and Arsinoë [II] won all three
>   harness victories at a single [competition].
> [. . .] sacred line [. . .] of women
>   [. . .] maiden [. . .]
> Olympia witnessed [all these exploits] of a single house,
>   the children and *their* children winning in the chariot.
> Sing then, O women of Macedon, of the garland taken by royal
>   Berenice in the chariot drawn by full-grown horses!
>   (*The New Posidippus* 78; Nisetich)

A contemporary of Theocritus and Posidippus, Callimachus inaugurated the tradition of "learned" poetry in works such as his *Hymns* and the *Aetia* ("Causes"), in which he retold in elegant verse obscure myths and the origins of strange customs and festivals collected from all over the Greek world. Although Callimachus famously denounced narrative poetry in the manner of Homer, asserting that "a big book was a big evil," his younger contemporary and rival Apollonius of Rhodes successfully reinvigorated the old epic genre after almost three centuries of neglect with his vivid retelling of the story of Jason and the Argonauts, the *Argonautica*.

The *Argonautica* reflected the remarkable progress in literary scholarship made possible by the Alexandrian library. Drawing on an encyclopedic knowledge of Greek myth and antiquarian lore, Apollonius not only retold the ancient legend of Jason's search for the Golden Fleece but expanded the legendary history of Greece to include the Black Sea, much of Europe, and North Africa. Moreover, his acute psychological portrait of the tragic love story of Jason and Medea humanized the forbidding heroes of Homeric epic, as in this passage describing Medea's reaction to first meeting Jason:

> yet his coming started the ill-starred miseries of passion.
> The heart dropped out of her breast, of their own accord
> her eyes misted over, a warm blush mantled her cheeks.
> Her knees she lacked strength to shift, forward or backward,
> while her feet were nailed to the ground
> (*Argonautica* 3.960–965; Green)

Apollonius' innovative portrayal of a young girl in love served as a model for the Roman poet Virgil's portrayal in the *Aeneid* of the similarly tragic love of Aeneas and Dido, the legendary founders of Rome and Carthage. Finally, another contemporary of Callimachus, Euhemerus, an ambassador of Cassander to Ptolemy I, put forward a radical and important theory about the origins of mythology: he invented the utopian travel romance in order to propound in his *Sacred Tale* the theory that the gods had once been great rulers and benefactors, who were deified and worshipped after their deaths for their gifts to humanity. Euhemerus' ideas later became a staple of the Christian critique of Greco-Roman polytheism.

The Visual Arts

The visual arts reflect the combination of old and new that is a distinctive feature of the Hellenistic Age. In the Classical period, artists had devoted themselves to the perfection of a limited number of artistic genres or types. For example, the epitome of fifth-century sculpture was the idealized figure of an unemotional youthful nude male. This type of figure continued to be sculpted as a heroic representation of Hellenistic kings. Though Hellenistic art evolved from Classical, it is characterized by variety and experimentation. Sculptors perfected an idealized figure of the youthful female nude and also produced realistic renderings of a cross section of the population of the cosmopolis displaying a variety of human emotions. Sculptures, both large and small, are additional testimony to the new focus on the individual as special and unique, rather than as an equal member of a democratic polis.

The production of small terra-cotta figures began in the fourth century and continued to flourish in the Hellenistic period. These figurines were made in molds in multiple copies and were relatively inexpensive. Like the people they represented, they were widespread in the Greek world. The figurines are our best evidence for the visual arts as a reflection of reality. As mentioned in our discussion of Menander's plays, art could be considered a mirror of life. The figurines portray people of all ages, every social status, and a range of ethnicities, including chubby children; stooped, stout, and wrinkled elderly people; elegant and graceful society women; and members of the lower classes. Small bronze sculptures, though more expensive, also depict a broad variety of people. (See Plate XIV.)

Figure 12.11. Miniature Hellenistic sculptures. (a) Terra-cotta figurine of old nurse and child. Late fourth century BC. New York, Metropolitan Museum of Art. (b) Terra-cotta figurine of schoolgirl reading a papyrus roll. Hamburg, Hamburger Museum für Kunst und Gewerbe. (c) Bronze statuette of black youth in craftsman's garb. Third to second century BC. New York, Metropolitan Museum of Art.

The development of portraiture on coins and in sculpture was fostered by interest in the individual and in the personality; such things were particularly important for people whose lives were subject to the whims of monarchs. As the portrayals of Alexander and his successors in this chapter and Chapter 11 indicate, a portrait was not only an attempt to portray the actual features of the subject, but also an attempt to influence the viewer's perception of the character. Coins may be small, but because they are numerous and circulate widely they are very influential. In larger works as well, art not only reflects the world but attempts to shape it. The Ptolemies, for example, were adept at the use of visual imagery as propaganda to gain support for their reign. Like Alexander, who encouraged belief in his own divinity and was worshipped as a god after his death, the Hellenistic rulers manipulated religion in their own interests. The monarchs' definition of themselves as divine was not mere immodesty; it also served

Figure 12.12. Nike (Victory) of Samothrace. This colossal marble statue depicting a winged goddess of victory alighting on the prow of a warship may commemorate a Rhodian naval victory of c. 200 BC. Preserved height, 8 feet, 1 inch. Paris, The Louvre.

to legitimize their use of absolute power. Members of the ruling dynasties were commonly portrayed on coins and in sculpture with the attributes and epithets of gods and heroes. The value of sculpture as a political tool is obvious in the image of Alexander in the company of Egyptian divinities (Chapter 11, Figure 11.5) and in the sculpture of Arsinoë II (this chapter, Figure 12.9) that portrays the queen as an Egyptian goddess. Even an illiterate viewer would immediately understand the message: Alexander and his successors are not mere mortals but incarnations of divinities. Furthermore, they are rightful heirs to the throne of the pharaohs as well as monarchs who rule over the Greek world.

Larger-than-life monarchs strutted proudly on the huge stage of Egypt and the eastern Mediterranean. Many of the monuments they commissioned are now fragmentary or have completely disappeared, but like the Pharos they are known through images on coins, copies made by the Romans, and written descriptions. They convey a vivid impression of the wealth and power of the monarchs and proud cities that constructed them. Artists were available to travel when such patrons beckoned. Bravura characterizes many major Hellenistic sculptures like one of the best known, the Victory (Nike) of Samothrace. This huge work was

Figure 12.13. Sculpted marble relief of the apotheosis of Homer by Archelaus of Priene, found in Bovillae, Italy. Height 3.75 feet. Late third to late second century BC. The deified poet Homer, seated at the lower left holding a scroll and scepter, is crowned by Oecumene (the World) and Chronus (Time). The other figures include Zeus and Mnemosyne (Memory) and their daughters, the Muses. A Hellenistic poet may have dedi-cated this relief to the Muses. London, The British Museum.

dedicated by the people of Rhodes to commemorate their victories over Antiochus III of Syria (222–187 BC). It was erected at Samothrace, an international religious center, where it would be seen by travelers. Victory alights on the prow of a ship. Her wet and windblown dress reveals the contours of her body, while the cloth flaring out behind the goddess symbolizes the agitation, restlessness, and continuous change characteristic not only of the art but also of life in the Hellenistic period. Her raised wings also suggest that her presence is not necessarily permanent, but

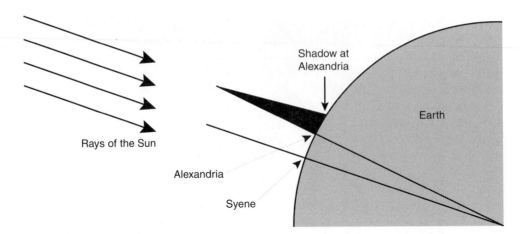

Figure 12.14. Eratosthenes' calculation of the circumference of the earth. Eratosthenes measured at Alexandria the shadow cast by a pointer at noon of the summer solstice when the sun was directly overhead at Aswan. By applying two simple geometric theorems—the angles of similar triangles are equal, and equal angles sweep out equal arcs—he concluded that the 5,000-stade distance between Alexandria and Aswan represented 1/50 of a sphere with a circumference of approximately 250,000 stades, a little over 31,000 miles (assuming eight stades to the mile).

linked to the donor's fortune. Like the goddess Tyche (Fortune), Victory can be fickle.

The visual arts also reveal nostalgia for the past, which must have seemed a safer, more secure time. Portraits of philosophers, poets, and other historical figures decorated public areas and private enclosed spaces such as libraries (cf. Demosthenes, Chapter 10, Figure 10.4). Some authors and other intellectuals were worshipped as divine. They had become as immortal as their words and thoughts. For example, portrait busts of Homer (about whose appearance nothing was known), were common, no doubt because the *Iliad* was the mostly widely read book in the Greek world, used as a text in primary school. Nevertheless, despite the reverence for the past, the evidence of the visual arts leaves no doubt that the world had changed drastically since the days of Achilles and the bards who first recited his exploits in regular lines of verse.

Scholarship and Science

The greatest achievements of Hellenistic intellectuals, however, were in the areas of literary scholarship and applied science, where their works remained unmatched during the rest of antiquity. Callimachus, together with other scholars such as the philologists Zenodotus and Aristarchus, founded the critical study of Greek language and literature; the standard texts of Homer and the other poets

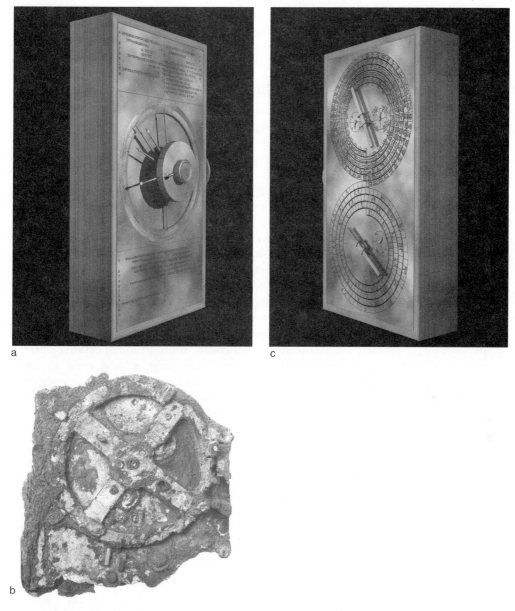

Figure 12.15. Antikythera Mechanism. (a) Reconstruction of front with dial representing motions of sun, moon, and planets. Photo: Dr. T. Freeth. (b) Main gear. Athens, National Archaeological Museum. (c) Reconstruction of rear with calendrical dials. Photo: Dr. T. Freeth.

they prepared are the ancestors of those we use today. Textbooks ultimately based on the *Elements* of the mathematician Euclid are still used to introduce students to geometry. The mathematician and geographer **Eratosthenes**, who became librarian at Alexandria in 246, established the principles of scientific cartography; he produced a strikingly accurate estimate of the circumference of the earth on the basis of evidence collected by Hellenistic explorers. The physicist Ctesibius pioneered the study of ballistics and the use of compressed air as a source of power, while other scientists experimented with the use of steam to operate simple machines. New discoveries such as the so-called Antikythera Mechanism make it clear, however, that the literary sources provide only an incomplete picture of the full range of the achievements of Hellenistic mathematics and technology. Long after the object was discovered by sponge divers in 1901 in the wreckage of a ship that was probably taking Greek art treasures to Rome, scientific analysis—using X-rays and digital photography—revealed that the Antikythera Mechanism was an astronomical calculator that allowed a person to simultaneously represent the motion through the zodiac of the sun and the moon, calculate leap years, determine the dates of the principal Greek athletic festivals, and even predict eclipses by turning a crank that was connected to a system of gears that is unparalleled for its complexity before the fourteenth century AD.

There was also important progress in the understanding of human anatomy and in medicine. The physicians Herophilus and Erasistratus made fundamental discoveries concerning the anatomy and functions of the human nervous, optical, reproductive, and digestive systems by dissecting corpses, and even vivisecting criminals, provided by the government for the advancement of science. The Hippocratic oath, which in many parts of the western world is administered to graduates from medical school, dates to the Hellenistic period. In the oath, the physicians promise to respect the physicians who taught them and to hand on their knowledge only to their teachers' sons and to paying apprentices. They swear to abstain from using their craft to harm or wrong any person and to refrain from practicing abortion and euthanasia and from divulging what patients tell them in confidence. Since there was no licensing of physicians in antiquity, and there were many conflicting medical doctrines and views of the physician's ethical role, the oath was by no means universally adhered to by Greek physicians, as is obvious from other medical texts that do discuss abortion, and from the use of vivisection on condemned prisoners.

SOCIAL RELATIONS IN THE HELLENISTIC WORLD

That Greeks were a minority in the Hellenistic world everywhere outside the Aegean tends to be obscured by the importance of their cultural achievements. This is true even of cities like Alexandria and Antioch, which were themselves only islands of Greek domination and culture in a predominantly non-Greek world. Not surprisingly, therefore, the relationship between immigrant Greeks and native populations is one of the central issues of Hellenistic historiography.

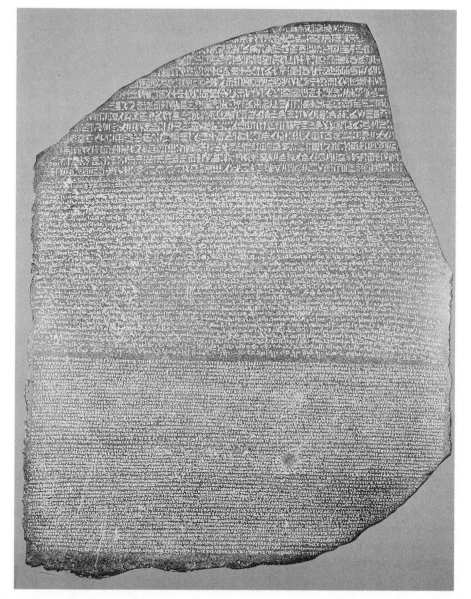

Figure 12.16. The Rosetta Stone, March 27, 196 BC. Fragment of a black granite stele found at the Rosetta mouth of the Nile containing a trilingual—Hieroglyphic (Middle Egyptian), Demotic (vernacular late Egyptian), and Greek—inscription recording a decree passed by a synod of the priests of Egypt commemorating the coronation of Ptolemy V (204–180 BC) as king of Egypt. In the nineteenth century, using their knowledge of Greek and Coptic, scholars were able to decipher the hieroglyphics on the Rosetta Stone, and thus began the science of Egyptology. London, The British Museum.

The Hellenistic historians who wrote early in the twentieth century were heartened by the results of the encounter between Greeks and non-Greeks in the Hellenistic period. They viewed the Hellenistic cities as "melting pots" in which Greek and non-Greek cultures and peoples blended into a new cosmopolitan civilization. A much harsher interpretation of Hellenistic social relations has become popular recently, reminiscent of Isocrates' dream of a conquered Asia in which natives worked just as hard to support the new Greek colonists and their Macedonian masters as they had for their Persian overlords. Supporters of this new interpretation view the Macedonian kingdoms as segregated societies in which social status and privilege were primarily determined by ethnicity. Needless to say, in this interpretation the ethnicities that counted were Macedonian and Greek.

A considerable degree of social and cultural segregation was inherent in the demography of the Hellenistic kingdoms. Since Greek settlement was predominantly urban, the countryside inevitably was largely cut off from Greek influence. Studies of Egyptian villages have revealed an almost total absence of either Greek residents or Greek influence on daily life.

Ethnic separation was not limited, however, to the countryside. Non-Greeks were denied citizenship and lived in separate residential quarters in the cities of the Hellenistic East. In Egypt distinct legal systems were even maintained for Greeks, Egyptians, and Jews. Ethnic prejudices and tensions are also well documented in the sources. Theocritus characterizes petty street crime as "an Egyptian game," and an agricultural worker complains that his supervisors hold him in contempt and refuse to pay him "because I am a barbarian," while the personal papers of a Greek recluse at Memphis are filled with references to incidents of personal harassment by his Egyptian neighbors. Finally, longing for the end of Macedonian rule is a common theme in both Hellenistic Egyptian and Jewish literature, and the history of Ptolemaic Egypt and Seleucid Asia is replete with examples of rebellions intended to achieve that goal. The Rosetta Stone alludes to such a rebellion in the first years of the reign of Ptolemy V. Some Egyptians even dreamed of the miraculous return of Nectanebo II, the last pharaoh of a free Egypt, who had fled to Nubia when the Persians reconquered Egypt in the 340s BC.

The Place of Non-Greeks

Nevertheless, the picture of the Hellenistic kingdoms as divided into two almost totally isolated societies—one Greek and the other non-Greek—distorts ancient social reality almost as much as the earlier ideal of a harmoniously mixed Hellenistic civilization. The existence of Greek versions of the Nectanebo story, such as "The Dream of Nectanebos," proves that at least some Greeks were interested in contemporary Egyptian culture. More important, serious social divisions and conflicts within the native populations of the Hellenistic kingdoms themselves precluded any unified native resistance to Macedonian rule.

In the theocratic monarchies of Egypt and the ancient Near East, the security of the state relied on the support of the gods and their priesthoods, and that remained true during the Hellenistic period. The Ptolemies subjected the temples of Egypt to greater supervision than their pharaonic predecessors, but they also maintained and even expanded the scale of state subsidy of religion, as can be seen from the vast extent of temple building that occurred during the Hellenistic period. Study of the extensive Egyptian evidence for Hellenistic Egypt is only in its infancy. But already it has revealed that under the Ptolemaic regime priestly families prospered, accumulating large estates and actively engaging in business transactions of all kinds, while expending large sums on the traditional Egyptian indicators of personal success: dedications to the gods and lavish tomb furnishings. Their prosperity also provided the basis for a vigorous revival of Egyptian culture, resulting in a variety of new and interesting literary and artistic works that are only now being studied and appreciated. It is not surprising, therefore, that in the Rosetta Stone Ptolemy V is congratulated for his brutal suppression of a native rebellion at Lycopolis in Lower Egypt that threatened the welfare of the Egyptian priesthood just as much as it did their Macedonian overlord.

Opportunity was not limited to the religious elite. Analysis of the personal archives of village officials—individuals dismissed by early Hellenistic historians as lowly and insignificant figures—has shown that such people could grow rich by exploiting their role as essential intermediaries between the Greek-speaking central government and its Egyptian subjects. Priests and local officials were loyal supporters of the Ptolemaic regime, and both were singled out for reprisal during native uprisings in the late third and second centuries BC. Similar patterns of royal patronage for the temples and priestly prosperity characterize Seleucid Asia, where the Seleucid monarchs generously supported both Babylonian temples and the temple of Yahweh at Jerusalem, receiving in return the loyal support of their respective priesthoods.

There were, moreover, social and cultural factors that tended to moderate the strong impulse toward social segregation in Ptolemaic Egypt and elsewhere in the Hellenistic world. The most important of these factors was demography. At the beginning of the Hellenistic period, intermarriage between Greeks and non-Greeks may have been relatively common, since the majority of Greek immigrants were soldiers and therefore predominantly male. Moreover, although the Ptolemies and their rivals actively encouraged Greek immigration with generous rewards, the actual number of immigrants was relatively small, and the majority of those came in the early years of Macedonian rule. The number of ethnic Greeks in Ptolemaic Egypt and elsewhere in the Hellenistic east was, therefore, probably small. Furthermore, Greeks who lived in the countryside, where the tendency toward intermarriage was greatest, assimilated somewhat to the social and cultural mores of their non-Greek neighbors. This was particularly true in the area of religion, since Greeks, like other polytheists, were already predisposed to honor the gods of countries in which they lived.

Hellenistic Religion

Greek religion underwent important changes during the Hellenistic period. Paganism and polytheism were flexible, nondogmatic religious systems, amenable to the introduction of new divinities and to the reshaping of old ones as conditions changed. So, in the Greek homeland, while the traditional cults and festivals in honor of the Olympian gods flourished, the cults of the healing god Asclepius at Epidaurus and Cos particularly prospered as public testimonials advertised the god's miraculous cures, relieving even women allegedly burdened with pregnancies lasting as long as five years! New festivals were founded. Some honored familiar gods such as Artemis at Magnesia on the Meander in Ionia, while others commemorated historical events such as the Soteria ("Deliverance"), which celebrated Apollo's miraculous rescue of Delphi from the attack of the Gauls in 279 BC. New gods also entered the pantheon. Some were introduced by immigrants, such as the Greco-Egyptian god **Sarapis**, and others by the cities themselves, who founded cults in honor of various kings and even Roman politicians such as T. Quinctius Flamininus, who had aided them in times of crisis.

More far-reaching changes occurred in the new kingdoms of the Hellenistic east, where the old polis gods came to appear anachronistic or irrelevant to their multiethnic populations. Sometimes, the powers of the old Olympian gods were redefined, since plainly their mission could no longer be conceived as defending Greek interests against those of non-Greeks. On other occasions, local gods were given Greek identities to make them palatable to the new settlers. Thus, Russian archaeologists have discovered that at Takht-i Sangin in modern Tajikistan in Central Asia, the god of the Oxus River was reinterpreted as a satyr. Likewise, in Judea a similar effort to identify the Hebrew god Yahweh with Zeus provoked a fierce revolt against Seleucid rule, whose success Jews celebrate today in the festival of Chanukah. The phenomenon is most clearly documented in Egypt, however, where a Hellenized form of Egyptian religion developed.

The most striking product of this Hellenization of Egyptian religion was to be found in Alexandria, where Ptolemy I called on the Egyptian priest Manetho and the Athenian ritual expert Timotheus to create a new god to serve as the patron deity of Ptolemy's capital and his dynasty. The new god, Sarapis, was a synthesis of Egyptian and Greek elements, fusing aspects of Hades, Osiris, Dionysus, Asclepius, and Zeus. Sarapis' combination of Osiris' role as ruler of the underworld with the accessibility and concern for human welfare that characterized Dionysus and especially Asclepius attracted Greek worshippers, who rapidly spread his cult throughout the Hellenistic world. (See Plate XVIIIa.)

Greeks living outside Alexandria worshiped traditional Egyptian gods such as **Isis** and Osiris. Acceptance of these strange deities was aided by the centuries-old Greek practice of identifying their own gods with those of other peoples (syncretism), but the process of identification itself entailed losses as well as gains. Native Egyptian practices that too obviously conflicted with Greek religious traditions, such as animal worship or mummification, were purged from the new Hellenized cults, while the Egyptian gods took on the identities of the Greek gods with whom they were identified. The result is evident in the case of Isis. Originally the devoted wife of Osiris and mother of Horus in the charter myth of the Egyptian monarchy, Isis, through her identification with Greek goddesses like Aphrodite, Demeter, and Athena, assumed a character that was unprecedented in Egyptian tradition: queen of the universe, benefactress of all people, and creator of civilization. When accommodation between Greek and non-Greek culture occurred, therefore, it occurred in such a way that the result did not challenge the dominance of Greek culture and values.

DOCUMENT 12.5

The Praises of Isis (first century BC or first century AD)

The Hellenization of Egyptian religion is evident in this inscription from the city of Cyme in northwest Anatolia with its universalization of Isis' power and identifications of Greek and Egyptian gods (Hephaestus = Ptah, the creator god of Memphis; Hermes = Thoth, god of wisdom and inventor of writing; and Cronus = Geb, god of the earth and father of the royal gods of Egypt).

Demetrius, the son of Artemidorus, who is also called Thraseas, a Magnesian from Magnesia on the Maeander, an offering in fulfillment of a vow to Isis. He transcribed the following from the stele in Memphis which stands by the temple of Hephaestus.

I am Isis, the tyrant of every land; and I was educated by Hermes, and together with Hermes I invented letters, both the hieroglyphic and the demotic, in order that the same script should not be used to write everything. I imposed laws on people, and the laws which I laid down no one may change.

I am the eldest daughter of Cronus. I am the wife and sister of King Osiris. I am she who discovered the cultivation of grain for people. I am she who is called goddess by women. By me the city of Bubastis was built. I separated earth from sky. I designated the paths of the stars. The sun and the moon's course I laid out. I invented navigation.

I caused the just to be strong. Woman and man I brought together. For woman I determined that in the tenth month she shall deliver a baby into the light. I ordained that parents be cherished by their children. For parents who are cruelly treated I imposed retribution. Together with my brother Osiris I stopped cannibalism.

I revealed initiations to people. I taught people to honor the images of the gods. I established precincts for the gods. The governments of tyrants I suppressed. I stopped murders. I compelled women to be loved by men. I caused the just to be stronger than gold and silver. I ordained that the true be considered beautiful. I invented marriage contracts. Languages I assigned to Greeks and barbarians. I caused the honorable and the shameful to be distinguished by Nature. I caused nothing to be more fearful than an oath. Anyone who unjustly plotted against others I gave into the hands of his victim. On those who commit unjust acts I imposed retribution. I ordained that suppliants be pitied. I honor those who justly defend themselves. With me the just prevails.

I am mistress of rivers and winds and the sea. No one becomes famous without my knowledge. I am the mistress of war. I am the mistress of the thunderbolt. I calm and stir up the sea. I am in the rays of the sun. I sit beside the course of the sun. Whatever I decide, this also is accomplished. For me everything is right. I free those who are in bonds. I am the mistress of sailing. The navigable I make unnavigable whenever I choose. I established the boundaries of cities.

I am she who is called Thesmophorus. The island from the depths I brought up into the light. I conquer Fate. Fate heeds me. Hail Egypt who reared me.

Inscriptiones Graecae 12.14; Burstein 1985, p. 147

These considerations have important implications for understanding the course of relations between Greeks and non-Greeks throughout the Hellenistic world. Since apartheid was never characteristic of Greek society, the combination of a relatively small number of ethnic Greeks and the Hellenistic kings' constant need for a Greek elite to provide a reliable base of support for their rule could have only one result. As time passed, many individuals referred to as "Greeks" in Hellenistic sources were persons not so much of Greek birth as of Greek culture—people, that is, who had received a Greek education, adopted a Greek lifestyle (and frequently a Greek name), and worshipped their old gods under Greek names.

Likewise, many "Greek cities" in the Near East were more and more often simply renamed local settlements whose citizen-bodies were composed largely of such acculturated non-Greeks. Some Jews sought to transform Jerusalem into a Greek polis in the early second century BC, but other Jews, under the leadership of the family of the Maccabees, opposed these efforts to Hellenize the community. (See Plate XVII.) The conflict escalated when Antiochus IV was drawn into it, forbade the Jews to carry on their traditional religious practices, and in 167 BC rededicated the temple of Yahweh at Jerusalem to Olympian Zeus. The history of this conflict is recorded in Maccabees I and II, two books preserved only in the *Septuagint*, that provide a unique picture of the Hellenistic world from the viewpoint of a subject people. They also clearly reveal the chief limitation of the process of Hellenization, its inability to affect significantly the lives of the mass of the population of the Hellenistic kingdoms.

Although Macedonian rule in Egypt and western Asia lasted for almost three centuries, assessments of the significance of this period of foreign rule vary widely. Some scholars emphasize the positive effects of the spread of Greek culture in the region, while others view it as a transitory period of colonial rule in which Greek culture was little more than a veneer, beneath which traditional social and cultural traditions survived and even flourished. Not surprisingly, the truth is more complex than is suggested by either extreme. Hellenization did occur, but its effects were little felt outside the major urban centers of the region. Likewise, native traditions did survive and were even, as has been noted earlier in this chapter, encouraged by the Ptolemies and the Seleucids. Still, their vigor was short-lived and had largely spent itself by the late first century BC. Education, culture, and elite status had always been closely connected in the region. Persian rule had not threatened that connection because the Persians themselves recognized the primacy of Mesopotamian culture in their empire. The privileged position enjoyed by Greek culture, however, severed the link between culture and status, thus providing a strong incentive for ambitious members of the local elites gradually to abandon their traditional cultures and Hellenize. Without anyone intending it, therefore, the establishment of the Macedonian kingdoms marked the beginning of the end of the ancient civilizations of Egypt and the ancient Near East.

KEY TERMS

Achaean League

Aetolian League

Antikythera Mechanism

Antigonus the One-Eyed

Arsinoë II

Callimachus

Cleopatra VII

Cynicism

Demetrius

Epicureanism

Epicurus

Eratosthenes

Greek freedom

Hellenistic period

Isis

Lysimachus

Menander

Museum

papyri

Perdiccas

Pharos

Ptolemy I

Ptolemy II

royal library [of Alexandria]

ruler cult

Sarapis

Seleucus

Stoicism

Theocritus

Tyche

Zeno

SUGGESTED READINGS

Bagnall, Roger S. 1995. *Reading Papyri, Writing Ancient History*. London and New York: Routledge. Masterly introduction to papyrology and its historical significance.

Bickerman, Elias J. 1988. *The Jews in the Greek Age*. Cambridge, MA: Harvard University Press. Brilliant analysis of the relations between Jewish and Greek culture in the Hellenistic Period.

Cartledge, Paul, and Antony Spawforth. 1989. *Hellenistic and Roman Sparta*. London: Routledge. Lucid political and institutional history of Hellenistic and Roman Sparta.

Cribiore, Raffaella. 2001. *Gymnastics of the Mind: Greek Education in Hellenistic and Roman Egypt*. Princeton, NJ: Princeton University Press. Detailed account of Hellenistic education based on intensive study of the papyrological evidence.

Empereur, Jean-Yves. 1998. *Alexandria Rediscovered*. New York: George Braziller, Inc. Lavishly illustrated account of archaeological discoveries in Alexandria, Egypt.

Erskine, Andrew, ed. 2003. *A Companion to the Hellenistic World*. Oxford: Blackwell. Valuable collection of articles on all aspects of Hellenistic history.

Green, Peter. 1990. *Alexander to Actium: The Historical Evolution of the Hellenistic Age.* Berkeley and Los Angeles: University of California Press. Brilliantly written comprehensive history of the Hellenistic period.

Habicht, Christian. 1997. *Athens from Alexander to Antony.* Translated by Deborah Lucas Schneider. Cambridge, MA: Harvard University Press. Perceptive history of Hellenistic Athens based primarily on inscriptions.

Lewis, Naphtali. 1986. *Greeks in Ptolemaic Egypt.* Oxford: Clarendon Press. Readable account of life in Ptolemaic Egypt as reflected in the careers of eight Greeks and Egyptians.

Manning, J. G. 2010. *The Last Pharaohs: Egypt Under the Ptolemies, 305–30 BC.* Princeton: Princeton University Press. Perceptive analysis of Ptolemaic Egypt based on both Greek and Egyptian sources.

Momigliano, Arnaldo. 1975. *Alien Wisdom: The Limits of Hellenization.* Cambridge: Cambridge University Press. Pioneering study of the nature of cultural interaction in the Hellenistic period.

Pollitt, J. J. 1986. *Art in the Hellenistic Age.* Cambridge: Cambridge University Press. Standard treatment of Hellenistic art.

Pomeroy, Sarah B. 1989. *Women in Hellenistic Egypt: From Alexander to Cleopatra.* With a new foreword and addenda. Detroit: Wayne State University Press. Wide-ranging survey of the social, economic, and legal status of women of all classes in Ptolemaic Egypt.

Rowlandson, Jane (ed.). 1998. *Women & Society in Greek & Roman Egypt: A Sourcebook.* Cambridge: Cambridge University. Extensive collection of translated documents dealing with the lives of women in Greco-Roman Egypt.

Sherwin-White, Susan and Amelie Kuhrt. 1993. *From Samarkand to Sardis: A New Approach to the Seleucid Empire.* London: Duckworth. Important revisionist history of the Seleucid empire drawing on both Greek and Near Eastern sources.

Thompson, Dorothy J. 1988. *Memphis Under the Ptolemies.* Princeton, NJ: Princeton University Press. Interesting history focusing on the lives of mummy makers; treats Egyptian religion, and the dreams and psyche of one inhabitant.

Waterfield, Robin. 2011. *Dividing the Spoils: The War for Alexander the Great's Empire.* Oxford: Oxford University Press. Vivid account of the wars of Alexander's successors.

Epilogue

In many ways, the early third century BC was the climax of ancient Greek history. For a brief period Macedonian power and Greek culture reigned supreme in the Near and Middle East. New Greek cities were founded at strategic points throughout this enormous region. A person could travel from Egypt to the borders of India speaking only Greek. The heyday of the Hellenistic kingdoms, however, was brief. Internal and external threats called their survival itself into question within a generation of their foundation.

The Seleucids' kingdom proved the most vulnerable. From their capital at Antioch, the Seleucids struggled with limited success to maintain control of the Asian territories of Alexander's empire. Already before the end of the fourth century BC, Seleucus I (311–281 BC) had ceded his dynasty's claims to Alexander's conquests in India to Chandra Gupta (c. 324–300 BC), who had conquered northern India and founded the Maurya dynasty. Further territorial losses followed in the third century BC. The catalyst was Ptolemy I's seizure of Coele Syria—southern Syria, Lebanon, and Palestine—in 301 BC. Although Seleucus I forbore contesting Ptolemy's coup, his successors did not, fighting five so-called Syrian wars between the 270s and the end of the century before Antiochus III finally reestablished Seleucid control of the region in 198 BC. Unremitting warfare against the Ptolemies, however, undermined dynastic unity. The critical event, the Third Syrian War (245–241 BC), had originated in a bitter dispute between the families of Antiochus II's two wives over the succession to the throne. The conflict opened a civil war between the sons of Antiochus that lasted more than a decade and enabled enemies of the Seleucids to take advantage of the confusion to attack the western and eastern frontiers of the Seleucid kingdom. In the west, the Attalids of Pergamum and other local dynasts in northern and central Asia Minor seized much of Seleucid territory in Anatolia. Meanwhile, in the east, the Parthians (nomadic invaders from central Asia) and rebellious Greek settlers carved out kingdoms for themselves in eastern Iran and Bactria.

The Ptolemies were more secure in their Egyptian fortress than their Seleucid rivals. For over a century and a half, no enemy succeeded in breaching Egypt's defenses. Ptolemy II (282–246 BC) and Ptolemy III (246–222 BC) extended Egyptian power around the fringes of the Seleucid kingdom, occupying Crete, Cyprus, most of the Aegean islands, and the Greek cities of southern and western Anatolia. For almost three-quarters of a century, Ptolemaic Egypt was the preeminent naval power in the eastern Mediterranean. Nevertheless, at the same time that the Ptolemies created a formidable overseas empire, Ptolemaic authority in Egypt weakened significantly. The demands of incessant war with the Seleucids encouraged Egyptian resistance to Macedonian rule, climaxing in the reestablishment of native rule in southern Egypt in the last decades of the century, while succession crises sapped the dynasty's strength. By 200 BC, the Ptolemies ruled only Lower and Middle Egypt.

With the total collapse of the Hellenistic state system virtually in sight, Antiochus III (223–187 BC) and Ptolemy V (204–180 BC) launched vigorous counteroffensives that seemingly restored the authority of their respective dynasties over most of their former territory. Antiochus III repeated Alexander's march to the very borders of India and even achieved his dynasty's goal of regaining Coele Syria from the Ptolemies, while Ptolemy V crushed the native rebellion and reestablished Ptolemaic rule over the whole of Egypt. But before the Seleucids and Ptolemies could fully consolidate their hold on their kingdoms, disaster struck in the form of the Romans. Roman expansion into the eastern Mediterranean was so dramatic and unexpected that the historian Polybius could justifiably begin his great history with the deceptively simple question: How could anyone not be interested in knowing how the Romans overthrew the world created by Alexander in less than half a century?

Although Roman relations with the Hellenistic kingdoms dated to the 270s BC, Rome first intervened significantly in the political life of the eastern Mediterranean in the beginning of the second century BC, inflicting severe defeats on Philip V of Macedon and Antiochus III. The Romans did not annex any territory after decisively defeating the two kings, preferring instead to pose as the defender of Greek freedom. The Roman Senate's refusal to brook potential rivals to Roman preeminence in the region, however, effectively undermined all the major Hellenistic kingdoms. By the mid-second century, the kingdom of Macedon had disappeared. Defeated in the Third Macedonian War (171–168 BC), Macedon became a Roman province. It was the Achaean League's turn next. In 146 BC, the League was dissolved, and the ancient city of Corinth was sacked and its citizens sold into slavery. A generation later, Roman power expanded across the Aegean when Attalus III, recognizing the inevitability of Roman rule, willed the kingdom of Pergamum to Rome in 133 BC, in the hope of preserving a privileged status

Figure E.1 Silver denarius of Cleopatra VII and Marc Antony, 32 BC. This coin has two obverses (fronts) indicating the equality of these two rulers. The Greek inscription above the portrait of Cleopatra reads: "Queen Cleopatra, the Newer Goddess." The Greek inscription surrounding Marc Antony's portrait reads: "Antonius, Imperator and Triumvir"—an allusion to the offices he held in Rome. The portraits of both show the "Roman nose." (For an Egyptianizing sculpture of Cleopatra, see Plate XIX.) London. The British Museum.

for the Greek cities of his realm. Only one final obstacle stood in the way of total Roman domination of the eastern Mediterranean: Mithridates VI (120–63 BC), the king of Pontus in northern Anatolia, who claimed descent from the Achaemenid kings of Persia and Alexander the Great and ruled an empire encompassing the entire Black Sea basin. In three great wars between 89 and 63 BC, he sought to rally the peoples of Anatolia and Greece against Rome, only to be finally defeated by the Roman general Pompey, who pursued him to the Crimea, where he committed suicide.

With the death of Rome's last great enemy, Roman power in the east was unchallenged. The Seleucids, weakened by dynastic rivalry and internal subversion, were locked in a losing struggle with the Parthians, which gradually reduced the once mighty Seleucid kingdom to a few cities in Syria that Pompey seized for Rome in 63 BC. Pompey also occupied the kingdom of Judaea the same year. Of the successor states of Alexander's empire, only Egypt remained independent. The Ptolemies were, in fact, to survive their Seleucid rivals by a generation, but only because the Roman Senate could not agree on which senator would take credit for the annexation of Egypt. That debate ended in 31 BC, when Octavian, the grand-nephew of Julius Caesar and the future emperor Augustus, defeated Antony and Cleopatra VII at Actium in northwest Greece. With the lovers' suicides in 30 BC, the three-century-long history of Alexander's successors ended.

Rome and Parthia turned out to be the ultimate heirs of Alexander's legacy, having extinguished the kingdoms of his successors. The demise of the Hellenistic state system did not mark the end of Greek civilization in the lands conquered by Alexander, but it did change its character and role. In the eastern portions of Alexander's empire, Greek civilization gradually lost its appeal to the elites of Mesopotamia and Iran. Macedonian and Greek rulers were responsible for the flowering of Greek culture in the Hellenistic east, and their patronage ended with the disappearance of their kingdoms in the late second and first centuries BC. Deprived of a political base, Greek culture withered as the new Parthian rulers of the Middle East sought to rally support for their regime from the non-Greek elites of their territory by favoring local traditions. In the western part of the Hellenistic world, Greek culture did not merely survive: thanks to Roman interest, it flourished.

That Rome was the savior of Greek culture in the Near East is one of the paradoxes of history. A brutality that belied the promise of "freedom" the Romans had made to the Greeks in 196 BC after the defeat of Philip V marked the Roman conquest of the eastern Mediterranean. Incidents such as the enslavement of 150,000 people from Epirus by Aemilius Paulus in 168 BC, the destruction of Corinth in 146 BC, and Sulla's devastation of Attica in 86 BC made clear to the Greeks that the Romans had come to the East as masters, not liberators. Nevertheless, while the disruption of Greek life during the almost two centuries during which Rome consolidated its rule over the eastern Mediterranean was enormous, it was not the whole story.

Like their Macedonian predecessors, the Romans were no strangers to Greek culture. Greek influence on Rome dated from the beginning of the city's history and had become an integral part of Roman culture by the time Rome intervened in the affairs of the Hellenistic east. That influence continued long after Greece had ceased to be a political and military power and had become a minor province of the Roman Empire. Not surprisingly, Greek literature and art were familiar to many upper-class Romans. Some senators, like Fabius Pictor (c. 220 BC), the father of Roman history, were fluent enough to write books in Greek. By the first century BC, Roman aristocrats routinely acquired a Greek education. Rome's gods and myths were recast in terms of Greek mythology. Latin writers constantly echoed their Greek predecessors, so that a work like Virgil's *Aeneid*, Rome's national epic, has to be read against the background of the *Iliad* and the *Odyssey* for its artistry to be fully appreciated. In the first century BC, the Roman poet Horace was only recognizing reality when he wrote that "Greece, though a captive, captured her fierce conqueror, and brought the arts to rustic Latium" (*Epistles* 2.1).

One important result of the Hellenization of the Roman upper class was the Senate's adoption of the concept of Greek freedom as the framework for the exercise of Roman supremacy in the eastern Mediterranean. In spite of the suffering they inflicted on the cities and kingdoms of the Greek east, therefore, the Romans made the support of Greeks and Greek culture the linchpin of their rule of the region. Greeks enjoyed privileged status, and Greek cities provided the structure for Roman provincial administration, which was conducted in the Greek language in the Eastern Empire. The result was a remarkable renaissance in the cultural life of the Greek cities of old Greece and the Near East during the first two centuries of the Common Era. Evidence of this revival is visible in the ruins of the splendid public buildings that everywhere in the eastern Mediterranean dominate the remains of Greek cities, and in the innumerable honorary statues that crowd our museums.

Greek writers, such as the historian Appian and the orator Aelius Aristides, had good reason to celebrate the benefits of the *Pax Romana* ("Roman peace"), although conscientious Roman governors like Pliny the Younger complained about the costs of the ambitious building projects undertaken by the Greek cities in their efforts to outdo each other in public splendor and distinction. The renaissance was not limited to architecture and the visual arts. The second and third centuries AD also saw a remarkable upsurge of Greek literary activity that historians of Greek literature call the Second Sophistic. The Second Sophistic is named after the great public orators such as Aelius Aristides who dominated the public culture of the period, but new works appeared in almost every genre of Greek literature. Many of these works, such as the biographies and essays of the biographer and moralist Plutarch and the histories of Arrian, were of considerable distinction and exercised significant influence on the development of later western thought.

Science and philosophy also flourished. Galen and Ptolemy compiled syntheses of Greek medicine, astronomy, and geography that remained authoritative for more than a millennium. Indeed, medical students were still studying the works of Galen in the early nineteenth century AD. The Egyptian-born Neo-Platonist Plotinus created the last great philosophical system of antiquity, a philosophical mysticism based loosely on the works of Plato that was Christianity's most formidable intellectual rival. Only in one area of Greek life was there no renaissance: the civic and political activities of the Greek cities themselves. Instead, during these same two centuries, the polis tradition of self-government gradually diminished.

Officially, the Romans treated the Greek cities of the eastern Mediterranean as self-governing entities. Epigraphic records of their governments' activities are numerous, but the spirit was gone. City assemblies no longer met, and city councils were controlled by narrow aristocratic oligarchies. Even the freedom of action of these oligarchic regimes was increasingly limited by the Roman government's practice of employing officials such as Pliny the Younger to monitor their conduct of affairs. Though some Greeks, like Plutarch, attained Roman citizenship, Plutarch candidly assessed the situation in an essay written in response to a young friend's request for advice about a possible political career. "Nowadays," he wrote, "when the affairs of the cities no longer include leadership in wars, nor the overthrowing of tyrannies, nor acts of alliances, what opening for a conspicuous and brilliant public career could a young man find?" Plutarch answered his own question by pointing out that "there remain the public lawsuits, and embassies to the Emperor" (*Precepts of Statecraft* 805a–b; translated by H. N. Fowler). Greek patriots such as Plutarch, who considered holding the traditional magistracies in his home city of Chaeronea a sacred obligation, found the contrast with the freedom of fifth- and fourth-century BC Greece painful. Later, other Greeks were more pragmatic. Men such as Arrian, who was governor of Cappadocia under the emperor Hadrian (117–138) and a historian of Alexander, and Dio Cassius, a historian of Rome who held the offices of consul and praetorian prefect during the early third century, abandoned their poleis and found rewarding careers in the service of Rome.

While Greeks and Greek culture prospered under Roman rule, the same was not true of the non-Greek cultures of Egypt and the Near East. The Roman emperors' patronage of the Greek cities of the eastern Mediterranean heightened the value of Greek culture and Roman citizenship. The former was the key to social and cultural prestige and the latter to a political career and its rewards. Non-Greek cultural traditions and institutions were not repressed, but they were devalued. In the second century AD, the Syrian writer Lucian expressed the cultural priorities of the new regime in his autobiographical essay *The Dream*, pointing out that without a Greek education, a man could only be an "artisan and commoner, always envying the prominent and fawning on the man who was able to speak," while the educated man was "honored and praised, in good repute among the best people, well regarded by those who are preeminent in wealth and breeding . . . and considered worthy of public office and precedence" (9–11). Lucian's calculation was correct. His Greek education and literary skill brought him fame and a lucrative post on the staff of the prefect of Egypt.

Not all peoples yielded to the assimilatory pressures of Roman imperial society. The Jews, in particular, resisted fiercely. This was a dramatic change from the generally good relations that they had enjoyed with the Hellenistic kingdoms. Indeed, except for a brief period of persecution by the Seleucid king Antiochus IV, the Jews had prospered during the Hellenistic period. Cities like Alexandria and Antioch had large and wealthy Jewish populations, and Jewish writers created an extensive literature in Greek, of which the principal surviving monuments are the Greek translation of the Bible and the numerous works of the early-first-century AD Alexandrian philosopher Philo, who interpreted the *Torah* in the light of Greek philosophy. By contrast, despite efforts on both sides to avert a crisis, tension between Rome and the Jews steadily escalated until it culminated in three massive revolts in the late first and the early second centuries AD, resulting in the destruction of the Temple at Jerusalem, the decimation of the Jewish population of Judaea, and the alienation of Jewish intellectuals from Greek thought for almost a millennium. Other peoples found in the new Christian church opportunities for the satisfaction of the ambitions of their elites. Not surprisingly, however, over time increasing numbers of non-Greeks followed Lucian's example and sought to acquire the advantages of Greek status, especially after 212, when the emperor Caracalla erased the legal barriers between Greeks and non-Greeks by conferring Roman citizenship on virtually all inhabitants of the empire.

The process of assimilation was not always free of friction. Complaints of Greek prejudice and cultural chauvinism are frequent in the writings of Hellenized non-Greeks, such as the Syrian rhetorician Tatian, who urged Greeks not to despise non-Greeks and their ideas because most Greek practices "took their origin from barbarian ways" (*Address to the Greeks* 1.1). Nevertheless, by late antiquity a significant portion of the social and intellectual elite of the eastern provinces of the Roman Empire consisted of Hellenized non-Greeks. The local languages of the region did not disappear. They survived in the vernacular speech of the urban lower classes and the countryside, even finding new written expression in the literatures of Syriac and Coptic Christianity. But the traditional cultures of Egypt and the Near East died, as the native elites that had patronized them for millennia gradually deserted them. Harassed from the fourth century on by the government of the Christian Roman emperors, they survived only in the esoteric knowledge of the priests of a few remote and impoverished temples before finally disappearing completely in late antiquity. Meanwhile, the dominant strand in the intellectual life of the eastern Mediterranean basin became what scholars call Hellenism, essentially a cosmopolitan form of Greek culture loosely based on the canon of Classical Greek literature. This literature formed the basis of both pagan and Christian education and thought, although the civic culture of the Greek city-states that had given birth to it almost a millennium earlier had disappeared. In this form, Greek culture continued to flourish in the lands conquered by Alexander the Great and influenced the medieval civilizations of Byzantium and Islam and, through them, the culture of Europe and the Americas.

Suggested Readings

Burstein, Stanley M. 2007. *The Reign of Cleopatra*. Norman: University of Oklahoma Press. A brief but comprehensive survey including a biography of Cleopatra VII and a study of Egypt and its multiethnic population during her reign.

Bowersock, G. W. 1990. *Hellenism in Late Antiquity*. Ann Arbor: University of Michigan Press. Innovative study of Greek culture and paganism in late antiquity.

Gruen, Erich S. 1992. *Culture and National Identity in Republican Rome*. Ithaca: Cornell University Press. Brilliant analysis of the role of Greek culture in the development of Roman identity in the Republic.

Thomas, Carol G. (ed.). 1988. *Paths from Ancient Greece*. Leiden: Brill. Essays by leading historians tracing the history of the Greek tradition in European and Islamic culture from antiquity to the present.

Wardman, Alan. 2002. *Rome's Debt to Greece*. London: Bristol Classical Press. Lucid analysis of the influence of Greek thought on Roman literature.

Zacharia, Katerina (ed.). 2008. *Hellenisms: Culture, Identity, and Ethnicity from Antiquity to Modernity*. Aldershot: Ashgate Publishing Limited. Important collection of essays surveying interpretations of Greek identity from Antiquity to the present.

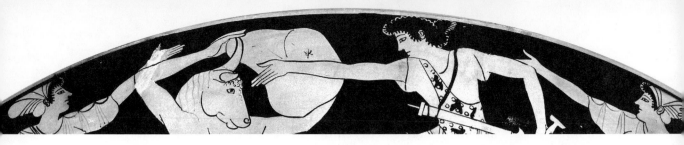

GLOSSARY

ACADEMY The school founded by Plato at Athens during the 380s BC in the groves sacred to the hero Academus. Its most famous pupil was Aristotle. The Academy continued to function until the Christian emperor Justinian ordered it closed, along with other pagan schools, in AD 529.

ACROPOLIS Literally, the upper city, the citadel of a city or town. Many citadel hills had been the sites of Mycenaean palaces and remained as special places in *polis* life. The most famous is the Acropolis of Athens, the religious center of the city, which was magnificently adorned with temples in the fifth century.

AGOGE The state sponsored educational system at Sparta which all Spartan males had to complete in order to qualify for full Spartan citizenship.

AGORA In Homer, the term for the place of gathering, the assembly of the people. In the city-state period it denoted the public space of a city or town, being both the marketplace and civic center. Lingering in the agora was the best way to inform oneself about public affairs, make business contacts, and collect gossip.

AMPHICTYONIC COUNCIL The governing body of an ancient league of Delphi's neighbors, the Delphic Amphictyony, which administered the oracle. The Amphictyony also conducted the Pythian games and dealt with transgressions against the oracle and its territory. The members were *ethnē*, of which the most important were the Thessalians, Phocians, Boeotians, Dorians, and Ionians. Votes were unequally divided among the members, so that Philip II's acquisition of the twelve Thessalian and two Phocian votes gave him a majority of the council's twenty-two votes and control of the Amphictyony.

ARCHAIC PERIOD The period of Greek history extending from the end of the Dark Age c. 700 BC to the beginning of the Classical Period c. 480 BC.

ARCHON A common title (meaning leader) for the highest-ranking magistrate in the early city-states. During the Classical period, even when the *stratēgoi* had become the most important officials in Athens, nine archons continued to be chosen (by lot) to serve judicial and administrative functions. The archontate was used in larger contexts as well: for example, as the title of the civil and military head of the Thessalian League. This archon was elected by the League assembly and served for life.

ARISTOCRACY The term *aristokratia* (power in the hands of the best men) was coined, probably in the fifth century, as the word the elite used to describe their hold on power, in preference to the less noble-sounding *oligarchia*. (Plato defines aristocracy as the good form of oligarchy.) Aristocratic power and exclusiveness were strongest in the early Archaic period and gradually weakened as strong democratic sentiments emerged in the city-states.

ASSEMBLY Along with the "council" (*boulē, gerousia*), one of the two primary elements of Greek governance. From the Dark Age on it was made up of the adult males of the community. In the Dark Age, the assembly (called *agora* in Homer) had limited power vis-à-vis the chiefs, although its concurrence was crucial. Despite attempts by the oligarchical rulers of the Archaic period to curtail further the authority of the assembly, it eventually became the deciding body of state policy. In Athens, the assembly, or *ecclēsia*, met in the open air on the hill called the Pnyx about forty times a year.

BARBAROS The term used by the ancient Greeks for all people who were not Greek in language and culture. The contrast did not necessarily imply uncivilized crudity and savagery (the highly civilized and generally admired Egyptians and Persians were *barbaroi* to the Greeks), although increasingly from the fifth century on *barbaroi* came to be stigmatized as the inferior "others," lacking the mental and moral capabilities that belonged naturally to Hellenes.

BASILEUS The term for the legitimate single ruler, the "king." In Mycenaean society, the title *qasireu* denoted an official who had charge of a village or district; with the breakup of the Mycenaean kingdoms

it became (in the form *basileus*) the title of the warrior-chiefs who ruled the villages and districts in the Dark Age. The hierarchy of *basileis* was replaced in the Archaic Age by landed aristocrats who ruled as an oligarchy.

BOULE The commonest term for the "council," which, along with the assembly, was one of the two primary governing institutions of the Greeks. Composed of the chiefs and other influential men in the Dark Age, it became the major organ of aristocratic power in the Archaic Age. In the democratizing city-states, the council became increasingly an organ of popular will. In Classical Athens, the *boulē* consisted of five hundred men chosen by lot; it prepared business for the assembly. It could also try certain court cases.

BRONZE AGE The period of Greek history extending from the appearance of bronze technology in the Aegean basin c. 3000 BC to the fall of the Mycenaean kingdoms c. 1200 BC.

CADMEA The acropolis of Thebes. Its seizure by Sparta in 382 BC provoked a major diplomatic crisis in Greece.

CELLA The inner shrine of a temple. A gold and ivory statue of Athena, over 40 feet high and now lost, stood in the cella of the Parthenon.

CITY-STATE See polis.

CLERUCHY A form of Greek colony in which colonists retained the citizenship of the founding city. In the fifth century BC Athens established cleruchies in the territory of rebellious or unreliable allies as self-supporting garrisons.

Colony The Greek term for a colony was *apoikia* (home away [from home]). Unlike Roman or modern colonies, Greek colonies normally were independent *poleis*, maintaining primarily ties of religion and kinship with their founding cities. See metropolis.

Common Peace The term used to describe a number of fourth-century treaties beginning with the King's Peace in 387 BC and ending with that sponsored by Philip II after the Battle of Chaeronea in 338 BC. The characteristic feature of these treaties was that they guaranteed the autonomy of all subscribing states.

Corinthian League The term used by modern scholars to designate the alliance organized to implement the Common Peace established by Philip II in 338 BC. The League included the principal cities and *ethnē* of Greece except Sparta and guaranteed its members freedom, autonomy, collective action against states who broke the peace, and protection against proposals to cancel debts and liberate slaves. The Corinthian League provided the framework for Macedonian domination of Greece until it was dissolved by Antipater in 322 BC.

Currency, Athenian Units of Athenian currency included the obol, the drachma, the mina, and the talent. Six obols made a drachma; one hundred drachmas made a mina; and sixty minas (i.e., 6000 drachmas) added up to a talent. A man who had a talent was rich. In fifth-century Athens, a silver drachma coin was considered good pay for a day's labor by an unskilled worker and probably represented a living wage for a small family. A drachma was the standard pay for a rower in the fleet. Maintaining a trireme cost a talent a month.

Dark Age. The period of Greek history extending from the end of the Bronze Age c. 1200 BC to the beginning of the Archaic period c. 700 BC.

Decarchies ("ten-man rules") Narrow oligarchies composed of Spartan sympathizers, supported by Spartan garrisons, that were established by Lysander after the Peloponnesian War in a number of cities of the former Athenian Empire. The decarchies had absolute authority in their cities and were responsible for maintaining their cities' loyalty to Sparta during the last years of the fifth century BC and the early 390s BC.

Delian League The modern name for the confederacy organized under Athenian leadership after the end of the Persian wars. Founded in 477 BC, the League was slowly converted into an Athenian empire as Athens began forcing unwilling states to remain in the organization, or to join it if they were not already members.

Delphic Amphictyony See Amphictyonic Council.

Demagogos Literally, a "leader of the people." This was the term some Athenians used to categorize the politicians who arose in Athens after Pericles' death. Usually it had negative connotations and suggested a man interested only in his own well-being, unlike a true statesman, who cared for the welfare of the state. Unlike the word "demagogue" today, however, it was occasionally used in a neutral way.

Democracy A form of government in Classical Greece that permitted all free men some degree of participation in politics, regardless of wealth or family background. Ideologies of equality were preached, though economic inequalities prevailed and generally brought political inequalities with them. Athens encouraged democratic governments in its allies. Like other forms of Greek government, democracies denied voting rights to women and assumed the appropriateness of slavery.

DEMOS A territory and the people who live in it; thus, "the land" and "the people." The concept occurs in the Linear B tablets in the form *damo*, meaning, apparently, a village community and its free inhabitants. Originally a neutral term, it came to be used by aristocrats (probably in the seventh century) to designate the "commoners," or the "masses," exclusively, although technically (as in legal inscriptions) it retained its inclusive meaning as "the (whole) people."

DEMOTIC The "popular" script, an extremely simplified cursive form of the hieroglyphic script used in the Hellenistic period to write Egyptian. Demotic was the principal Egyptian script in Ptolemaic Egypt and was used for writing both literary and nonliterary texts.

DICASTERIES (*dikastēria*) The people's courts at Athens. As Athens was notoriously litigious, these courts tried an enormous number of cases. A dicasterion was composed of hundreds of adult male citizens who were chosen by lottery at the last minute from those who had presented themselves for membership in the pool of jurors known as the heliaia. Both the last-minute element of the choice and the large size of the juries discouraged bribery, especially since Athenian court cases had to be decided in a single day. Since the large jury was considered to be acting in the stead of the people, there could by definition be no appeal from its decisions. Beginning around the middle of the fifth century, jurors received a small amount of pay for their services. See heliaia.

DOKIMASIA The scrutiny Athenian citizens had to undergo before assuming a position in the government. Political enemies often used this procedure as a means of keeping a man out of public office.

DRACHMA See currency, Athenian.

ECCLESIA See assembly. The Athenian assembly (*ecclēsia*) met about thirty to forty times a year on the hill known as the Pnyx. In its meetings it voted on business prepared by the *boulē*.

EPHEBE Originally an ephebe was a boy who had reached the age of puberty. Beginning in the late fourth century BC all Athenian boys who were in their eighteenth year had to undergo two years of military training called the Ephebia. The boys spent the first year in Athens under the guidance of state-employed military instructors and the second year as part of the garrisons of several frontier forts. In the Hellenistic period, the Ephebia changed, ceasing to be mandatory at Athens and elsewhere and increasingly focusing on providing boys with a cultural education centered on the gymnasium.

EPHOR (*ephoros*) Overseer. An office found in Sparta and in other Dorian states. In Sparta a board of five ephors was elected annually by the assembly; the senior ephor gave his name to the year. The ephors had great power in the Spartan state, including general control over the conduct of kings.

EPIKLEROS A brotherless Athenian girl who was compelled to marry her nearest male relative able to procreate so that her son, who was slated to inherit her father's property, would be descended from his grandfather through the male line. The word is often translated "heiress," but in fact the epikleros could herself inherit nothing, which was the whole point of her forced marriage.

Erastes ("lover") The term for the active partner in a homosexual relationship. Ideally the *erastēs* was supposed to be not only the sexual partner but also the social mentor of his partner, tutoring him in the customs of male society and introducing him into it. See eromenos.

Eromenos ("beloved") The term for the passive partner in a homosexual relationship. Ideally, the *eromenos* was an adolescent male, whose secondary sexual characteristics had not yet appeared. See erastēs.

Ethnos The term used to describe a large group of people who shared a common identity and territory but were not politically united, preferring local self-government. The story of the Greek *ethnē* is their growing ability from the sixth century BC on to act as unified states by forming federations of local and regional segments of the *ethnos*. By the fourth century, ethnic confederacies and leagues were playing a prominent, and even a dominant, role in the geopolitics of Greece.

Eunomia ("lawfulness") An ideal of good government, sometimes identified with the government of one's own state: Spartans boasted of the *eunomia* of their system, while Athenians considered *eunomia* to be democracy.

Freedom of the Greeks Propaganda slogan used by various Hellenistic kings and the Romans to attract the support of Greek cities. Although proclamations of "freedom" included guarantees that cities would be free, autonomous, and ungarrisoned, in practice kings did not hesitate to interfere in city affairs to achieve their goals.

Genos Clan. A social group composed of families who claimed descent from a single male ancestor. A *genos* was led by its most prominent family and played a prominent part as a political group in the Archaic Age. The power and influence of the aristocratic *genē* (plural) waned in the Classical period but continued to confer social prestige on the member families.

Geometric Style The Geometric style dominated vase painting from around 900 to 700 BC. A wider variety of motifs is evident than in the preceding Protogeometric period, and linear and angular patterns appear. Toward the end of the period, animal, and then human, figures appear.

Gerousia The council of elders (from *gerōn* = old man). This was the term used at Sparta and in other *poleis* for the aristocratic council. The Spartan *gerousia* consisted of the two kings plus twenty-eight men over age 60 who served for life.

Graphe Paranomon The procedure the Athenians began to use in the late fifth century BC to indict a man for making an illegal proposal in the assembly. Since the Athenians had no real constitution, it was very difficult to tell what laws might be illegal, and the procedure was usually used as a form of political attack. Those convicted were generally fined; three convictions barred a citizen from making further proposals.

Great King The Greek term for the king of Persia.

Greek Freedom See freedom of the Greeks.

Guest-Friendship (*xenia*) A form of ritual friendship whereby a "stranger" (*xenos*) entered into a relationship of mutual friendship with a man from another *dēmos*, each being obliged to offer hospitality and aid when visiting the other's community. The bond was perpetuated down through generations of the two families. A prominent feature of Homeric society, *xenia* continued throughout antiquity, evolving in the city-states into the more formal diplomatic relationship of proxeny. See proxeny.

Harmost A Spartan military governor or commander. Harmosts are first attested in the Peloponnesian War and are found after the end of the war, often stationed in cities that had previously been members of the Athenian Empire.

Hegemon A state or individual who headed an organization of states. Athens, for example, was the hegemon of the Delian League, Sparta of the Peloponnesian League. A hegemon was said to exercise hegemony; hence the period of Theban ascendancy in the 360s BC is known as the Theban hegemony. Hegemon was also the title of the leader of the Corinthian League. This hegemon was officially elected by the League council and was its chief executive and commander-in-chief of its military forces with full authority to conduct the League's military and diplomatic activities.

Hektemoroi A term used in Solonian Athens meaning "sixth-parters," referring, presumably, to poor farmers who had fallen into debt to wealthy landowners and had to hand over to them a sixth of their produce under penalty of enslavement.

Heliaia The body of prospective jurors from which *dikastēria* were selected. Any adult male citizen might present himself for participation. See dicasteries.

Hellenes The name the Greeks called themselves (and still do). They had a myth of an eponymous ancestor, Hellen, who was the son of Deucalion, the Greek Noah, and the father of the eponymous ancestors of the Dorians, Ionians, and Aeolians. There is reason to believe that the common name (and the supporting myth) arose relatively late, perhaps in the eighth century BC.

Hellenistic Period The period of Greek history extending from the death of Alexander the Great in 323 BC to the death of Cleopatra VII of Egypt in 30 BC.

Hellenization The process by which non-Greeks acquire Greek identity. In the Hellenistic Period, Hellenization usually involved learning the Greek language, obtaining a Greek education and citizenship in a Greek polis, and for males, going to gymnasia and taking part in athletics.

Helots The term used to describe groups of conquered people in Greece who were forced by their conquerors to work as serfs on their former lands. The word is most commonly associated with Sparta, where helots probably outnumbered citizens by a ratio of seven to one. The Spartan way of life both depended on and was formed by the state's ownership of the labor of thousands of helots in Laconia and Messenia. Fear of helot uprisings often discouraged the Spartans from becoming engaged in campaigns far from home.

Hetaira Meaning literally female companion, this term was normally used for courtesans in Classical Athens. *Hetairai* usually came from the metic class. They were generally more cultivated than citizen women; they were trained (usually by older hetairai) to be entertaining and interesting rather than to be thrifty managers of households. Since Pericles' citizenship laws of 451–450 made it impossible for a man to marry a metic woman and still have his children enjoy citizenship rights, many Athenian men chose to have long-term associations with hetairai simultaneously with their legal marriages to Athenian women. Some hetairai functioned as entrenched mistresses or even common-law wives, but others less fortunate were essentially prostitutes.

Hetaireiai The military systems of some cities such as those in Crete grouped men in *hetaireiai* (bands of companions), but the word is most commonly associated with Athens. There young men of the upper class frequently belonged to hetaireiai, or social clubs with political overtones, often of an antidemocratic nature. The mutilation of the herms in 415 was rumored to be the work of such a hetaireia, and the subversive activity of hetaireiai probably played a part in the oligarchic revolutions of 411 and 404.

Hetairos Companion or comrade. In the Dark Age, follower-bands of *hetairoi* formed the military and political support of the chiefs who recruited and rewarded them. Associations of hetairoi for political purposes continued to function in the city-states (see *hetaireiai*). In Macedonia, the hetairoi were an elite band of warriors and advisers who formed the retinue and personal bodyguard of the kings.

Hippeis In the Solonic system, these were "horsemen" (since they could afford to keep a horse for the cavalry), whose income

was more than 299 measures of grain, oil, and wine, but less than 500..

Hoi Agathoi ("good men") In Archaic Greek social and political discourse *hoi agathoi* referred to aristocratic males, who were believed to be superior and entitled to a privileged place in polis life by virtue of their noble birth, while "*hoi kakoi*" ("bad men") referred to all nonaristocrats.

Hoi Kakoi See hoi agathoi.

Homoioi ("similars" or "peers") The Spartan term for full Spartan citizens, referring to their common experience in the *agōgē* and the Spartan army.

Hoplite The heavily armored infantryman, named from his distinctive shield (*hoplon*). Hoplites were the dominant military arm from the seventh century on, gradually undergoing changes in weaponry and tactics. Because Greek governments did not always issue arms to their soldiers, hoplites tended to come from the middle class, men able to afford armor and swords, unlike the rowers in the fleets, who were likely to be *thētes*. See thetes.

Indo-European Languages A family of languages spoken from India in the east to Europe in the west and including, in addition to Greek, such languages as Sanskrit, Latin, and the Iranian, Slavic, Celtic, and Germanic languages. Despite its European location, Greek belongs to the eastern branch of the Indo-European language family, its closest relative being Armenian.

Ionian Migration The process by which the islands of the central Aegean Sea and the central portion of the west coast of Turkey were settled by speakers of the Ionic dialect of Greek during the Dark Ages. According to Greek legend the Ionians were refugees from Achaea who took refuge in Athens and then colonized the Aegean Islands and western Turkey under Athenian leadership.

King's Peace The agreement that ended the Corinthian War in 387 BC. A key role was played by Artaxerxes II of Persia, and Greeks were chagrined by the wording of the peace, which began, "I, King Artaxerxes, regard the following arrangements as just. . . ."

Kleros (*klēroi*). An allotment of farmland sufficient to support a citizen-family; it was passed on in perpetuity in the male line. In oligarchic states, full citizenship was frequently tied to the possession of a certain amount of land.

Kore A term meaning "maiden," used to describe the life-size or larger marble Archaic statues of clothed females, made as cult offerings or grave markers. The term *kouros* ("youth") is used of the corresponding nude male statues.

Krypteia ("the secret thing") A part of the Spartan agoge in which selected young men in their late teens wandered the countryside at night, empowered to kill at will helots who seemed less submissive than was expected. See agoge.

League of Corinth See Corinthian League.

Liturgies An indirect system of taxation whereby the rich were required to spend their own money in the service of the state. Liturgies included financing the training of a chorus for dramatic performances or financing a delegation to a religious festival in another state. The most expensive liturgy was the trierarchy, which required a man to maintain a trireme for a year and to pay for the training of its crew.

Lyceum The school founded by Aristotle in Athens in 335 BC. It became a major center for scientific study, and Aristotle's pupils also collected the constitutions of 158 states.

Mediterranean Climate Climate characterized by hot dry summers and cool, wet winters. Because of the moderating effect of bodies of water such as the Mediterranean Sea, the difference between summer high temperature and winter low temperature tends to be moderate. Such a climate is typical of central and southern Greece.

Mediterranean Triad Grains (primarily wheat and barley), grapes, and olives, the three crops that formed the basis of Greek agriculture.

Megaron A large rectangular building that served as the focal point of Mycenaean palaces. Its function as the "great hall" of the ruler continued in the reign of the Dark Age chiefs. In the city-states the ancient megaron achieved immortality as the basic plan of the Greek temple.

Metics Resident aliens in a Greek state. There were probably metics throughout Greece, but we know only about metics in Athens. Although they lacked citizenship, metics mingled comfortably in Athenian society and were often called on for help in wartime. The women known as *hetairai* were generally metics, though most metic women were probably housewives.

Metropolis Mother-city. Describing a polis that sent out a colony under its aegis. The relationship between the mother-city and the new polis was normally very close, though colonies were politically independent.

Mina See currency, Athenian.

Mothakes (singular **Mothax**) The *mothakes* were a new class that arose in Sparta during the Peloponnesian War. Some were the offspring of Spartan fathers and helot mothers, others the sons of impoverished Spartans who were no longer able to maintain their status in the corps of "equals" by contributing to the common meals.

Mousike ("verbal and musical skill") Greek education that was grounded in poetry and music and identified a cultured person.

Myth All cultures possess myths, traditional tales that treat aspects of life that are important to the collective group (e.g., marriage, initiation, food, cultural institutions, human–divine relations). The Greeks had an immensely rich storehouse of such orally transmitted stories going back to the second millennium BC, and continually infused by additions from the mythologies of the Near East. The Greek historians depended on ancient myths to reconstruct the preliterate past. Modern researchers attempt to glean from them historical or psychological realities.

Nomos (*nomoi*) Custom or law. Sometimes it corresponds to the English word "mores," connoting a way of doing things that is deeply embedded in a value system. It can also be used, however, in a legal context; thus, for example, the rules laid down by Solon were called his *nomoi*.

Nomothetai Athenian officials set up after the restoration of the democracy in 403 BC. The *nomothetai* reviewed and ratified the laws of Athens.

Obol See currency, Athenian.

Oikist The *oikistēs* (note the root of *oikos*) was the founder and the leader of a colony sent out by a mother-city (*mētropolis*). As the founder, he had great authority in the new settlement and was usually highly honored after his death.

Oikos Household. The fundamental social and economic unit in Greek society, comprehending the family group, its house, land, animals, and property, including slaves.

Oligarchy *Oligarchia* (rule by a few men) was the standard form of government in the early city-states, having replaced the system of ranked chieftains. Opposition from below the narrow ruling circle caused most oligarchies to broaden inclusion in state affairs, while other states adopted democratic governments. Democratic *poleis* were subject to oligarchic revolutions, as in Athens in 411 and again in 404 BC. Throughout the fifth and fourth centuries, tension between oligarchs and democrats—which often added up to tension between rich and poor, especially in the difficult economic times of the decades after the Peloponnesian War—was a constant factor in Greek political life and sometimes resulted in bloodshed.

Oral Composition Oral composition refers to the technique by which Dark Age poets were able to compose extended poems, both epic and lyric, without the use of writing.

Ostracism A political device introduced by Cleisthenes as part of his reforms. A person receiving at least a plurality of 6000 votes was required to go into exile for a period of ten years. The process received its name from the pieces of broken pottery (ostraca) on which Athenians wrote the names of the persons they wished to exile. Although any Athenian could in theory be ostracized, in practice the individuals who actually were ostracized were primarily major political leaders. Known examples of ostracism extend from 486 BC to 417 BC.

Panhellenism The idea that what was common to all Greeks was more important than what divided them, and that Greece was at its peak during the Persian Wars when Greeks united to defeat the Persians. In the fourth century BC intellectuals such as Isocrates argued that the solution to the problems of Greek society was for Greeks to unite in war against the Persians just as they had done in 480/79 BC. Philip II and Alexander the Great used this idea to justify their plans for invading the Persian Empire.

Paramount An anthropological term referring to the highest-ranking leader of a community or group. The major warrior-heroes of the Homeric epics, who ruled over other leaders as "first among equals," are reflections of the paramount chiefs who ruled during the tenth to eighth centuries BC.

Pediment The elongated triangular space that sat on top of the columns on the front and back of a Greek temple. They were frequently adorned with elaborate relief sculpture.

Peloponnesian League The modern name for an organization led by Sparta and dated to some time in the sixth century BC. Scholars have joked that it was neither Peloponnesian nor a league. It consisted of Sparta and less powerful allied states whose leaders swore to have the same friends and enemies as the Spartans. Thus the states were tied to Sparta but not really to each other, and some important members of the League, such as Thebes, were outside the Peloponnesus. The most important member after Sparta was Corinth, which provided naval power. After its victory over Athens in the Peloponnesian War (431–404 BC), Sparta increasingly interfered in domestic affairs in allied states, causing substantial friction. The League finally dissolved in the 360s.

Peltasts Lightly armed Greek soldiers who carried light throwing spears and small, round shields. They functioned as skirmishers and could be deployed either alone or in concert with hoplites. Although they were utilized during the Peloponnesian War, they increased dramatically in importance in the fourth century. The Athenian commander Iphicrates owed his successes to his well-trained peltasts.

Pentakosiomedimnoi In the Solonic system, these were members of the highest class, "500-measure men," since they had an estate that produced at least 500 medimnoi (bushels) of grain, oil, and wine.

Perioeci "Dwellers round about," the term used to describe neighboring peoples who were in a subordinate relationship to a dominating *polis*. The most prominent example is Sparta, which treated the people of the perioecic communities of Laconia and Messenia as half-citizens, granting them local autonomy but obligating them to military service and allowing them no say in the conduct of policy.

Phalanx The tactical formation of a hoplite army, consisting in the Archaic and Classical periods of ranks of heavy infantry, usually eight men deep. The phalanx underwent change and experiment in the fifth and fourth centuries. The highly successful form of phalanx introduced by Philip II of Macedon consisted of six brigades of fifteen hundred men each, recruited on a regional basis. Macedonian "phalangites" were armed with a short sword, a small round shield, and a long pike (*sarissa*) up to 18 feet long; they fought in rectangular formations sixteen men deep.

Phratry A subdivision of the tribe (*phylē*) and, at least theoretically, a kin grouping. In Classical times phratries were well-defined social groups concerned with defining descent and therefore citizenship. Every citizen family in Athens belonged to a phratry.

Phylai The term for the large, ancient descent groups into which a *dēmos* was divided. Ionian communities had four such "tribes," as moderns call them, Dorian communities three. The tribes functioned as organizational units in the city-states. In his reform of the Athenian government, Cleisthenes bypassed the four traditional tribes and divided Attica politically and militarily into ten new *phylai*.

Physis ("nature") Physis identified what was natural as opposed to culturally determined. The opposition of *physis* to *nomos* prefigured the modern nature/nurture conflict.

Polemarch The office of *polemarchos* (war leader) was common to many early city-states. As army commander for a specified term, usually a year, and subject to the policy of the aristocratic council, the polemarch was limited in his power. In 500 BC at Athens the polemarch was eclipsed by the board of ten *stratēgoi*, military commanders elected from the ten new *phylai*. After 487 BC, when the polemarch became appointed by lot, his functions became mainly legal and ceremonial.

Polis City, town. Beginning in the eighth century, *polis* came to designate a political community, composed of a principal city or town and its surrounding countryside, which together formed a self-governing entity, the city-state. The small polis was the principal form of Greek community throughout antiquity, numbering in the high hundreds by the fifth century BC. Except in Sparta, *poleis* generally had some sort of republican government, whether oligarchic or democratic.

Probouleutic Describing the function of the council (*boulē*) of preparing state business for consideration in the assembly.

Probouloi In Athens, a committee of ten older men that was set up to direct the government in 413 BC. The establishment of the *probouloi* resulted from the shock engendered by the disaster in Sicily.

Proskynesis Greek name for the Persian ritual greeting that social inferiors offered to their superiors and all Persians offered to the Persian king. In its simplest form, *proskynēsis* involved merely blowing a kiss. Proskynesis to the Persian king, however, required full prostration before the ruler. Although Persians did not believe that their king was divine, Greeks and Macedonians considered the performance of proskynesis to be appropriate only to deities and resented attempts to make them perform it.

PROTOGEOMETRIC STYLE A kind of pottery that developed around 1000 BC, when a faster wheel and the use of rulers and multiple brushes on a single arm, along with a shinier glaze produced by firing at a higher temperature, enabled potters to develop a wider variety of shapes. In this phase vases became better proportioned than before.

PROXENY The term used for a diplomatic arrangement whereby citizens in one state, called *proxenoi*, looked after the interests of other states in their communities. The *proxenos* was highly honored by the foreign state he represented. The system of proxeny (*proxenia*) developed from an earlier system of *xenia* or private "guest-friendship".

PRYTANIS One of the titles for the presiding magistrate (or a college of magistrates) in a city-state. In the reorganization of the Athenian *boulē* (508 BC), ten boards of fifty *prytaneis* each, chosen by lot from the ten new "tribes" (*phylai*), took turns as the officials in charge of the daily business of the *boulē* and *ecclēsia* for a tenth of the year. Each group of fifty men comprised a prytany.

REDISTRIBUTIVE SYSTEM The term for the kind of economic and political arrangements found in the Bronze Age kingdoms of the Near East and Greece: most of the agricultural and manufactured production of a region was controlled from the center (the king and his palace), which redistributed the resources as it saw fit. In the Greek city-states, by contrast, the government exercised only limited control over production and distribution. See liturgies.

REFORMS OF EPHIALTES An important series of measures proposed by the Athenian politician Ephialtes in 462 BC. The details of the reforms are unknown but the tendency was to reduce the political influence of the Areopagus council by limiting its function to that of the primary court for the trial of homicide.

RHETORES The men who chose to involve themselves intensively in Athenian politics during the fourth century, proposing decrees and making speeches in the assembly. It is often translated "politicians."

ROYAL PAGES A body of young men recruited, probably while still in their teens, from the Macedonian aristocracy. The pages lived at the royal court and were the king's personal attendants, guarding him while he slept, accompanying him on hunting expeditions, and performing whatever other tasks he might require of them. The institution was established by Philip II and served as the first step in the career of Macedonian aristocrats.

SACRED BAND Elite Theban infantry formed about 378 BC. The Sacred Band consisted of 150 pairs of lovers. It played a major role in the Spartan defeat at Leuctra in 371 and later Theban military campaigns until it was totally destroyed at the Battle of Chaeronea in 338 BC.

SARISSA The standard weapon of the Macedonian phalanx. Introduced by Philip II, the sarissa was a pike approximately 18 feet in length composed of two pieces of cornel wood—one tipped with a long leaf-shaped point and the other with a spike—held together by a metal sleeve.

SATRAP Title of the governors of the principal territorial subdivisions of the Persian empire, then of Alexander III's empire, and later of the Seleucid kingdom. During the Peloponnesian War, the coastal satraps

Tissaphernes and Pharnabazus enjoyed considerable independence from the king and entered freely into negotiations with the warring states.

Satrapy Originally a province of the Persian empire. Alexander III retained the satrapal system of the Persian empire as the administrative framework of his empire. After the division of Antigonus the One-Eyed's empire in 301 BC, the term was used to designate the largest territorial subdivisions of the Seleucid kingdom.

Second Athenian Confederacy A voluntary organization led by Athens, which many Greek states joined, some at the inception in 377 and others later. Though member states sent delegates to a common deliberative body known as the *synedrion* and hence had far greater say in policy decisions than the helpless allies of the Delian League, disaffection nonetheless developed and the alliance began to disintegrate in the late 370s. It suffered substantial defections in the 350s and was finally dissolved when the Corinthian League was established in 338 BC.

Shaft Graves Deep rectangular burial pits used to bury the rulers of Mycenae from the late seventeenth century BC to the end of the sixteenth century BC.

Sophists The itinerant intellectuals who taught and gave speeches during the latter part of the fifth century BC. Some were primarily teachers of oratory, while others engaged in thoughtful speculation about society that challenged entrenched conventions. Sophists were drawn to the climate of Athens, where response to them was mixed. Plato made the discrediting of the sophists an important part of his dialogues, accusing them of substituting showy rhetorical displays for real wisdom such as Socrates possessed.

Stasis The term first for a group of men who take the same "stand" in a political dispute (a faction) and then by extension the act itself of taking sides. In the city-states, *stasis* (civil strife) occurred between oligarchical factions and between the rich and the poor. At its worst stasis entailed bloodshed; thus containing it within nonviolent bounds was a principal objective of the city-states.

Stele A stone slab inscribed with a text, a decoration, or both. Stelae could be used to indicate graves, military victories, or property boundaries. Important texts such as legal decrees and treaties might also be inscribed on them.

Strategos The common term for a military leader. In the city-states, this office was usually political as well as military. In Athens, after 487, the ten *stratēgoi* and treasurers were the only elected high officials (the others being selected by lot); thus most of the powerful politicians of the fifth century were strategoi. In the Hellenistic era, during the reign of Alexander III and the regencies of his sons, Philip III and Alexander IV, *stratēgos* (general) was the title of the highest-ranking Macedonian military commander in Europe and Asia. The four attested strategoi of this period were Antipater, Polyperchon, and Cassander in Europe and Antigonus the One-Eyed in Asia.

Symposium In Archaic and later periods the after-dinner "drinking party," made up of fourteen to thirty men, was a frequent event in adult male social life, primarily among the elite. The *symposium* was an important bonding ritual among young aristocrats and (like the hetaireiai) was often the occasion of factional plotting. Meaning "drinking together," the Greek term is the origin of the English word symposium.

SYNEDRION A representative council such as that of the Second Athenian Confederacy or the Corinthian League. The *synedrion* of the Second Athenian Confederacy was composed of a single representative from each member state and ruled the confederacy jointly with the Athenian assembly; policy decisions had to be ratified by both bodies. The synedrion of the Corinthian League consisted of representatives of the member cities and *ethnē* of the league. The latter synedrion was responsible for upholding the Common Peace that established the Corinthian League and was empowered to arbitrate disputes among its members and to try individuals accused of betraying its goals.

SYNOECISM (*synoikismos*) The term used for the process whereby several separate communities were formed into a single political union. Synoecism also referred to the actual movement of people from several communities into a brand new composite settlement.

SYSSITION ("common meal") At Sparta all boys at the end of their *agōgē* had to be admitted to membership in a *syssition*, a group of fifteen men who regularly ate and socialized together. Membership required the boy to obtain the unanimous vote of the existing members of the syssition and to contribute a set amount of food each month to the communal meal. A boy who failed to join a syssition or to maintain his monthly food contribution ceased to be a full Spartan citizen.

TALENT See currency, Athenian.

TEMENOS In Mycenaean times and in the Dark Age, a *temenos* was a parcel of choice land given as a due to the preeminent families. *Temenos* was also the term for a sacred precinct of land given to a god or hero, containing an altar, and often other buildings, for cult and ritual. This became the prevalent meaning in the Archaic and later periods, as the custom of giving land to the leaders waned (though it did not completely vanish) with the shortage of good land.

THEORIC FUND A special fund established at Athens, probably in the 350s BC, by Eubulus. In peacetime it received the fiscal surplus remaining after all annual expenditures mandated by law had been made. The purpose of the fund was to enable poor Athenians to attend public festivals, but it was also used for various other purposes including work on the dockyards and the public arsenal. In wartime, use of the surplus for military purposes was possible by vote of the Athenian assembly, but such use was unpopular.

THETES Free men who were forced by poverty to hire out as laborers for wages. In Athens, according to the economic divisions attributed to Solon (c. 600 BC), the *thētes* formed the lowest class of citizens. A *thes* was always poor and sometimes owned no land at all.

THIRTY TYRANTS The pro-Spartan puppet government installed in Athens by Lysander in 404. The Thirty, who murdered over a thousand citizens, as well as metics whose property they coveted, were overthrown in 403.

THOLOS (*tholoi*) A type of monumental aboveground stone tomb (shaped like a beehive) favored by the elites of the Late

Bronze Age. In the Classical period, circular structures, also called *tholoi*, served as temples and public buildings.

TIMĒ ("honor, respect") The high regard in which Greeks wished to be held by their peers. Quarrels, lawsuits, and wars could break out over matters of *timē*.

TRIREME The modern term for the standard form of Greek warship (*triērēs*) in the Classical period. Propelled by three banks of oars and attaining speeds of 9 knots, the trireme used its bronze ram to disable enemy ships. Athenian oarsmen were the best at this maneuver, and Athenian fleets dominated naval warfare during the fifth century. A trireme was manned by 180 rowers and 20 soldiers.

TYCHE Fortune in both its good and bad senses. Personified as a goddess, Tyche was a source of good and evil for human beings. Cults of Tyche proliferated in the Hellenistic Period, particularly in the Near East where Tyche often appeared as a city goddess, portrayed as a woman wearing a turreted crown.

TYRANNY (*tyrannis*) The illegal seizure and control of governmental power in a *polis* by a single strongman, the "tyrant" (*tyrannos*). Tyranny occurred as a phase in many city-states during the seventh and sixth centuries and is often seen as an intermediate stage between narrow oligarchy and more democratic forms of polity. In the late fifth and the fourth century, a new kind of tyrant, the military dictator, arose, especially in Sicily.

WANAX Lord, master. The title of the monarchical ruler of a Mycenaean kingdom. The form *anax* appears as the title of gods and high-ranking chiefs in Homer.

XENIA See guest-friendship.

ZEUGITAI In the Solonic system, these were "yokemen," who could afford to own a team of oxen and whose production of grain, oil, and wine was between 200 and 299 measures.

ART AND ILLUSTRATION
CREDITS

Title page and chapter-opening art: Detail of Attic red-figure cup by Epiktetos. London, The British Museum. Photo: Museum, courtesy of the Trustees.

I.1   Attic jug depicting Odysseus and the Sirens. Photo: Erich Lessing/Art Resource, NY.

1.1a   Heinrich Schliemann. Photo: Library of Congress.

1.1b   Gold mask from shaft graves, Mycenae. Athens, National Archaeological Museum. Photo: Erich Lessing/Art Resource, NY.

1.2   Franchthi Cave. Photo: Indiana University Archives.

1.3   Neolithic marble figurine of a nude woman. Athens, National Archaeological Museum, Inv. no. 3928. Photo: Museum.

1.4   Cycladic marble figurine of flute player. Athens, National Archaeological Museum. Photo: Nimitallah/Art Resource NY.

1.5   Drawing adapted from Joseph W. Shaw, "The Early Helladic II Corridor House: Development and Form," *American Journal of Archaeology* 91 (1987), 59–79 at p. 62 figure 3a and b. Used with permission of Joseph W. Shaw.

1.6a   Plan of the Minoan palace at Knossus. After Raimond Higgins, *The Archaeology of Minoan Crete* (London: The Bodley Head, 1973), p. 41.

1.6b   Plan of the Mycenaean palace at Pylos. From Donald Presziosi and Louise A. Hitchcock, *Aegean Art and Architecture* (New York: Oxford University Press, 2000), p. 139, fig. 87. Reprinted with permission of the publisher.

1.6c   Ruins of the Minoan palace at Knossus, Crete. Photo: © Yann Arthus-Bertrand/Corbis.

1.7a   Gold ring from Knossus. Herakleion, Crete, Archaeological Museum. Photo: Hirmer Fotoarchiv, Munich.

1.7b   Bull Leaper Fresco, Cnossus. Herakleion, Archaeological Museum. Photo: Marie Mauzy/Art Resource, NY.

1.8   Rhyton in the form of a bull's head. Herakleion, Crete, Archaeological Museum. Photo: Nimatallah/Art Resource, NY.

1.9a   Plan and cross section of the Kato Phournos tholos tomb, Mycenae. Photo: British School, Athens.

1.9b   Interior vault of a tholos tomb, Mycenae. Photo: Hirmir Fotoarchiv, Munich.

1.9c   Inlaid dagger. Athens, National Archaeological Museum. Photo: Hirmir Fotoarchiv, Munich.

1.10b   The megaron hall at Pylos. Photo: American School of Classical Studies at Athens: Agora Excavations.

1.10c   "The Lion Gate." Photo: bpk, Berlin.

1.11a   Linear B Tablet from Mycenaean Knossos. From J. Chadwick, *The Mycenaean World* (Cambridge: Cambridge University Press, 1976), p. 16. Reprinted with permission of the publisher.

1.11b   A chariot tablet from Mycenaean Knossos. From J. Chadwick, *The Mycenaean World* (Cambridge: Cambridge University Press, 1976), p. 108. Reprinted with permission of the publisher.

1.12a   Bronze plate armor and boar's tusk helmet. Nauplion Museum. Photo: German Archaeological Institute, Germany.

1.12b   Vase showing line of soldiers on the march, Mycenae. National Archaeological Museum, Athens. Photo: Hellenistic Ministry of Culture/Archaeological Receipts Fund.

2.1   Late Protogeometric vase. Athens, Kerameikos Museum K576. Photo: German Archaeological Institute, Athens.

2.2a   "Village chieftain's house" at Nichoria. From William A. McDonald et al., *Excavations at Nichoria in Southwest Greece: Vol. III, Dark Age and Byzantine Occupations* (Minneapolis: University of Minnesota Press, 1983), pp. 36–37, Fig 2-22. Reprinted by permission of publisher.

2.2b   "Village chieftain's house" at Nichoria. From William A. McDonald et al., *Excavations at Nichoria in Southwest Greece: Vol. III, Dark Age and Byzantine Occupations* (Minneapolis: University of Minnesota Press, 1983), pp. 36–37, Fig 2-23. Reprinted by permission of publisher.

2.2d   Reconstruction of chief's house at Lefkandi. Hugh Sackett, The British School at Athens. Photo: British School at Athens.

2.2e   From *Lefkandi II: The Protogeometric Building at Toumba* (Athens: The British School of Archaeology at Athens 1993), edited by M. R. Popham, P. G. Calligas, and L. H. Sackett. Horses are plate 22; humans are plate 13.

2.3   Gold jewelry from the tomb of a rich Athenian Woman. Athens, Agora Museum. Photo: American School of Classical Studies at Athens: Agora Excavations.

2.4   Blind Homer. Boston, Museum of Fine Arts. Photo: Museum.

2.5   Bronze statuette of lyre-player. Herakleion, Crete, Archaeological Museum. Photo: Erich Lessing/Art Resource, NY.

2.6   Drawing of a Late Geometric krater showing a shipwreck. After Carratelli, *The Western Greeks*. (Thames & Hudson, 1996), p. 135.

2.7a   Graffiti on eighth-century vases. Transcriptions: L. H. Jeffrey, LSAG in J. N. Coldstream, *Geometric Greece* (Huntingdon, England: A&C Black Publishers Ltd., 1977), p. 298. Reprinted by permission of the publisher.

2.7b   Late Geometric vase from the Dipylon cemetery. Athens, National Archaeological Museum NM192. Photo: German Archaeological Institute.

2.8   Geographic krater from Athens. Paris, Louvre. Photo: Réunion des Musées Nationaux/Art Resource NY.

2.9   Large Late Geometric grave amphora from the Dipylon cemetery. Athens, National Archaeological Museum 804. Photo: German Archaeological Institute.

2.10   Clay model of a house or temple from Argos. Athens, National Archaeological Museum. Photo: The Art Archive/National Archaeological Museum Athens/Dagli Orti.

3.2   Limestone gorgon pediment from the temple of Artemis on Corcyra. Photo: Archaeological Museum, Corfu, Greece/Art Resource NY.

3.3   Detail of Chigli Vase. Tome, National Etruscan Museum of the Villa Giulia. Photo: The Art Archive/Museo di Villa Giulia Rome/Dagli Orti.

3.4   Bronze votive offering. Museum of Fine Arts, Boston. Fracs Bartlett Donation of 1900, 03.997.

3.5   Gold libation bowl dedicated by the Cypselids. Boston, The Museum of Fine Arts. Photo: Museum.

3.6a   Attic bilingual amphora showing the heroes Achilles and Ajax. Boston, The Museum of Fine Arts. Photo: © 2006 Museum.

3.6b   Attic bilingual amphora showing the heroes Achilles and Ajax. Boston, The Museum of Fine Arts. Photo: © 2006 Museum.

3.7   Statue of an Egyptian nobleman. Boston, The Museum of Fine Arts 07.494. James Fund Purchase and Contribution, August 8, 1907. Photo: Museum.

3.8   Marble *kouros*. New York, The Metropolitan Museum of Art 32.11.1 Fletcher Fund, 1932. Photo: Museum.

3.9   Marble *kouros*. Athens, National Archaeological Museum NM3938. Photo: Museum.

3.10   Late Archaic *korē* from the Acropolis. Athens, Acropolis Museum. German Archaeological Institute, Athens.

3.11   The *agroa* in the Archaic period, c. 500 B.C. After J. Travlos 1974. Used with permission of the American School of Classical Studies at Athens, Agora Excavations.

3.12   Sanctuary of Apollo at Delphi. Photo: The Art Archive/Dagli Orti.

3.13   The stadium in the Sanctuary of Zeus at Olympia. Photo: age fotostock/SuperStock.

3.14   Electrum coin from East Greece. Athens, Numismatic Collection. Photo: Hirmir Fotoarchiv, Munich.

4.1   View over Sparta to Mount Taygetus. Photo: © Peter Eastland/Alamy.

4.3   Laconian cup depicting rider on horseback. London, The British Museum. Photo: Museum, courtesy of the Trustees.

4.4   Spartan hoplite. Photo: Vanni/Art Resource, NY.

4.5   Bronze statuette of a running girl. London, The British Museum. Photo: Museum, courtesy of the Trustees.

4.6   Laconian bronze mirror. New York, The Metropolitan Museum of Art. Photo: Museum.

4.7   Laconian cup. Paris, The Louvre. Photo: Réunion des Musées Nationaux/Art Resource NY.

4.8   Hillare Germain Edgar Dégas' "Young Spartans." London, The National Gallery. Photo: Museum, courtesy of the Trustees.

5.1   Detail of Attic red-figure cup by Epiktetos. London, The British Museum. Photo: Museum, courtesy of the Trustees.

5.2   Water jar from Athens depicting women at a fountain hour (hydria) by the Priam Painter. The Toledo Museum of Art 1961.23. Photo: Museum.

5.3   *Tetradrachm*, Athens. New York, American Numismatic Society 1957.172.1033. Photo: Society.

5.4   Attic red-figure *psykter*. New York, The Metropolitan Museum of Art 1989.281.69. Gift of Norbert Shimmel Trust, 1989. Photo: Museum.

5.5   Statues of the tyrannicides of Harmodius and Aristogiton. Naples, National Museum. Photo: Hirmir Fotoarchiv, Munich.

5.7   Delegations bringing tribute to Persepolis. Photo: bpk, Berlin.

5.9   Herm of Themistocles. Ostia, Archaeological Museum. Photo: bpk, Berlin.

5.10a   Greek bronze helmet. Olympia Archaeological Museum. Photo: Museum.

5.10b   Assyrian bronze helmet. Olympia Archaeological Museum. Photo: Museum.

5.11   The tumulus for the Athenian dead at Marathon. Photo: Vanni/Art Resource NY.

5.12   *Ostraka* discovered in the Athenian agora. Agora excavations. Photo: American School of Classical Studies at Athens: Agora Excavations.

5.13   Reconstruction of the Athenian trireme of the Classical period. Photo: Trireme Trust.

6.1   Serpent Column, Constantinople. Photo: The Art Archive/Dagli Orti.

6.2   Section of Athenian Tribute List inscription. Athens, Epigraphic Museum. Photo: Museum.

6.4   The hill of the Pnyx, Athens. Photo: Larry Tritle.

6.5   Statue of a warrior. Reggio, Regional Museum. Photo: The Art Archive/Museo Nazionale Reggio Calabria/Gianni Dagli Orti.

6.6   Roman copy of diskobolos. Rome, National Museum. Photo: Hirmir Fotoarchiv, Munich.

6.7a   Reconstructions of the pediment of the temple of Zeus at Olympia. From Bernard Ashmole, *Architect and Sculptor in Classical Greece* (London: Phaidon Press, 1972), p. 25.

8.6   Fragmentary fifth-century herm, Athens Acropolis. Photo: The American School of Classical Studies at Athens: Agora Excavation.

8.7   Unfinished temple. Photo: Stephen Saks Photography/Alamy.

8.8   Diagram of Syracuse and Epipolae. Reprinted from Donald Kagan, *The Peace of Nicias and the Sicilian Expedition*. Copyright © 1981 by Cornell University Press. Used by permission of the publisher.

8.9   Head of a Greek statue of Socrates, Roman copy. Paris, The Louvre. Photo: Giraudon/Art Resource, NY.

9.1a   Monument commemorating the death of Dexileos in the Corinthian War. Athens, Ceramicus, Oberlaender Museum. Photo: The Art Archive/Kerameikos Museum, Athens/Dagli Orti.

9.1b   The Street of Tombs in the Ceramicus cemetery. Photo: The Art Archive/Dagli Orti.

9.2   Remains of the walls built by the Athenians after the Battle of Cnidus, Piraeus. Photo: Larry Tritle.

9.3   Decree of Aristoteles. Athens, Epigraphic Museum. Photo: Museum.

9.4   Reconstruction of the Mausoleum. Photo: Art Resource.

9.5   Fragment of the *kleoterion*. Athens, Agora Museum. Photo: The American School of Classical Studies at Athens: Agora Excavation.

9.6   *Klepsydra* ("water clock"). Athena, Agora Museum. Photo: The American School of Classical Studies at Athens: Agora Excavation.

9.7   Head of Plato, Roman copy. Paris, The Louvre. Photo Erich Lessing/Art Resource, NY.

9.8   Head of Aristotle, Roman copy. Vienna, Kunsthistorisches Museum. Photo: Erich Lessing/Art Resource, NY.

10.2   Silver *tetradrachm* of Phillip II. (Obverse: Zeus; Reverse: jockey commemorating victory of Phillip's horse at Olympia). Oxford, The Asmolean Museum, Plate 28, No. 513. Photo: Museum, Heberden Coin Room.

10.3   The Macedonian phalanx. From Arthut Ferrill, *The Origins of War: From the Stone Age to Alexander the Great* (New York: Thames and Hudson, 1985), p. 177. Reprinted by permission of the publisher.

10.4   Portrait of Demosthenes. Braccio Nuovo, Vatican Museums. Photo: Scala/Art Resource, NY.

10.5   Burial monument at Chaeronea. Photo: SEF/Art Resource, NY.

10.6   Theater at Aegae in Macedonia, modern Vergina. Photo: Vergina Museum.

11.1   Portrait of Alexander as hero-king. Paris, Louvre. Photo: Giraudon/Art Resource, NY.

11.3   The great tumulus at Vergina. Gordon W. Gahan/National Geographic Images.

11.4   Plan of the Battle of Issus. From Arthur Ferrill, *The Origins of War: From the Stone Age to Alexander the Great* (New York: Thames and Hudson, 1985), p. 201. Reprinted by permission of the publisher.

11.5   Alexander Sarcophagus. Istanbul, Archaeological Museum. Photo: Erich Lessing/Art Resource NY.

11.6   Alexander as Pharaoh. Chicago, The Oriental Institute of the University of Chicago P.38387/N.43812/CHFN 9246. Photo: Museum.

11.7   Plan of the Battle of Gaugamela. From Arthur Ferrill, *The Origins of War: From the Stone Age to Alexander the Great* (New York: Thames and Hudson, 1985), p. 201. Reprinted by permission of the publisher.

11.8   Palaces of Persepolis. Photo: Lloyd Cluff/CORBIS.

11.9   The Greek view of the inhabited world. From N.G.L. Hammond, *A History of Greece to 322 BC* 3rd ed. (Oxford: Oxford University Press, 1986), p. 622. Reprinted by permission of the publisher.

11.10   Silver five-shekel coin from Babylonia. London, The British Museum. Photo: Museum, courtesy of the Trustees.

11.11   Silver *tetradrachm* minted by Ptolemy I. (Obverse: Head of Alexander the Great; Reverse: seated Zeus with eagle) London, The British Museum. Photo: Museum, courtesy of the Trustees.

12.1   Statue of old market woman. New York, The Metropolitan Museum of Art 09.39. Rogers Fund, 1909. Photo: Museum.

12.2   Grant exemption by Cleopatra VII. Bildarchiv Preussischer Kulturbesitz/Art Resource, NY.

12.3   Bronze statuette, perhaps a portrait of Demetrius Poliorcetes from Herculaneum. Naples, National Archaeological Museum. Photo: Museum.

12.4   Model of Acropolis at Pergamon. Photo: Bildarchiv Preuissischer Kulturbesitz/Art Resource NY.

12.6   Roman bronze statue of the Tyche of Antioch by Eutychides. New York, The Metropolitan Museum of Art 13.227.8. Rogers Fund, 1913. Photo: Museum.

12.7   Bronze statuette of a philosopher. New York, Metropolitan Museum of Art. Photo: Museum.

12.8   Gold octodrachm showing Ptolemy II and Arsinoë II. New York: American Numismatic Society 1977.158.112. Photo: Museum.

12.9   Limestone statue of Arsinoë. New York, Metropolitan Museum of Art 20.2.21, Rogers Fund, 1920. Photo: Museum.

12.10   Tetradrachm of Commodus. London, The British Museum. Photo: Museum, courtesy of the Trustees.

12.11   Miniature sculpture of old nurse with child. New York: Metropolitan Museum of Art 20.2.1. Rogers Fund, 1910. Photo: Museum.

12.12   Nike of Samothrace. Paris, The Louvre. Photo: Réunion des Musées Nationaux/Art Resource NY.

12.13   Sculpted relief of the Apotheosis of Homer. London, The British Museum. Photo: Werner Forman Archives/The Art Resource, New York.

12.15a Antikythera Mechanism. Photo: © 2008 Tony Freeth, Images First Ltd.

12.15b Antikythera Mechanism. National Archaeological Museum, Athens Copyright © Hellenic Ministry of Culture and Tourism/Archaeological Receipts Fund. Photo: © 2005 National Archaeological Museum in Athens/Antikythera Mechanism Research Project.

12.15c Antikythera Mechanism. Photo: © 2008 Tony Freeth, Images First Ltd.

12.16   The Rosetta Stone. London, The British Museum. Photo: © bpk Berlin.

E.1   Silver denarius of Cleopatra VII and Marc Antony. Photo: © The Trustees of The British Museum/Art Resource, NY.

Plates

Plate Ia   Excavations at Uluburun. Photo: Institute of Nautical Archaeology.

Plate Ib   Excavations at Uluburun. Photo: Institute of Nautical Archaeology.

Plate IIa   Sophie Schliemann adorned by the "Treasure of Priam." Photo: akg-images/ullstein bild

Plate IIb   Golden diadem from the "Treasure of Priam." Photo: akg-images/ullstein bild

Plate IIIa   Terra-cotta chest, surmounted by a lid with five model granaries. Athens, Agora Museum. Photo: American School of Classical Studies at Athens: Agora Excavations.

Plate IIIb   Amphora from Eleusis attributed to the Polyphemus Painter. Eleusis Archaeological Museum. Photo: Museum.

Plate IV   Laconian cup attributed to the Arcesilas Painter. Paris, Bibliothèque Nationale de France. Photo: Library.

Plate V   Archaic poetry on Hellenistic papyrus. Photograph courtesy of the Egypt Exploration Society and the Imaging Papyri Project, University of Oxford.

Plate VIa   François Vase. C. M. Dixon/Ancient Art & Architecture Collection Ltd.

Plate VIb	François Vase detail depicting Thetis. C. M. Dixon/Ancient Art & Architecture Collection Ltd.
Plate VIIa	*Leonidas at Thermopylae*, Jacques-Louis David, 1814. Réunion des Musées Nationaux/Art Resource, NY.
Plate VIIb	Procession of life-size guards from the palace of Darius the Great, Susa, Iran. Erich Lessing/Art Resource, NY.
Plate VIIIa	Peplos kore. Athens, The Acropolis Museum. Photo: The Art Archive/Acropolis Museum Athens/Gianni Dagli Orti.
Plate VIIIb	Painted reconstruction of the Peplos kore. Museum of Classical Archaeology, Cambridge. Photo: Museum.
Plate IX	Temple of Apollo at Delphi. Amon Carter Museum, Fort Worth, Texas, Bequest of Eliot Porter.
Plate X	Bronze charioteer. Delphi Museum. Photo: Erich Lessing/Art Resource, NY.
Plate XI	Lucanian calyx crater attributed to the Policoro painter. Leonard C. Hanna, Jr. Fund
Plate XII	Aphrodite of Cnidus. Photo: Scala/Art Resource, NY.
Plate XIIIa	Green-yellow glass cup. Photo: RMN/Art Resource, NY.
Plate XIIIb	Glass pyxis. Photo: Réunion des Musées Nationaux/Art Resource, NY.
Plate XIIIc	Small glass cup with widening border and convex bottom. Photo: Réunion des Musées Nationaux/Art Resource, NY.
Plate XIV	Hellenistic bronze statuette of an African. Image copyright © The Metropolitan Museum of Art/Art Resource, NY.
Plate XVa	Wall painting of the myth of the Rape of Persephone. Copyright © The Bridgeman Art Library.
Plate XVb	The Alexander Mosaic from Pompeii. Photo: Vanni/Art Resource.
Plate XVIa	Royal tomb at Aegae, modern Vergina. Photo: Vergina Museum.
Plate XVIb	Silver *hydria* discovered in the Macedonian tomb in Plate XVIa. Photo: Vergina Museum.
Plate XVII	Tomb of the Hellenizing High Priest Jason. Photo: © www.BibleLandPictures.com/Alamy.
Plate XVIIIa	Head of a greater-than-life-size statue of the Greco-Egyptian god Sarapis. Franck Goddio/Hilti Foundation. Photo: Christoph Gerigk.
Plate XVIIIb	Sphinx found on the now submerged Antirhodos Island in Alexandria harbor. © Franck Goddio/Hilti Foundation.
Plate XIX	Basalt statue of Cleopatra VII. Photo: © State Hermitage Museum, St Petersburg.

INDEX

Bold page numbers indicate material in figures.